The Cultic Milieu

Oppositional Subcultures in an Age of Globalization

EDITED BY JEFFREY KAPLAN AND HELÉNE LÖÖW

ALTAMIRA
PRESS

A Division of
ROWMAN & LITTLEFIELD PUBLISHERS, INC.
Walnut Creek • Lanham • New York • Oxford

ALTAMIRA PRESS
A Division of Rowman & Littlefield Publishers, Inc.
1630 North Main Street, #367
Walnut Creek, CA 94596
www.altamirapress.com

Rowman & Littlefield Publishers, Inc.
A Member of the Rowman & Littlefield Publishing Group
4720 Boston Way
Lanham, MD 20706

12 Hid's Copse Road
Cumnor Hill, Oxford OX2 9JJ, England

Copyright © 2002 by AltaMira Press

British Library Cataloguing in Publication Information Available

Library of Congress Cataloging-in-Publication Data
The cultic milieu : oppositional subcultures in an age of globalization / edited by Jeffrey
Kaplan and Heléne Lööw.
     p. cm.
Includes bibliographical references and index.
   ISBN 0-7591-0203-1 (alk. paper) — ISBN 0-7591-0204-X (pbk. : alk. paper)
   1. Parapsychology. 2. Cults. I. Kaplan, Jeffrey, 1954– II. Lööw, Heléne.
BP603 .C835 2002
306'.1—dc21   2002001962

Printed in the United States of America

Contents

Introduction

Jeffrey Kaplan and Heléne Lööw

When the British sociologist Colin Campbell first published his theory of the cultic milieu, which is reprinted in its entirety in this volume,[1] the phenomenon he described so well was hardly new. That there exists within every society a small but dedicated underground of true seekers of esoteric and, very often, forbidden knowledge, is well known. The Middle Ages had its heretics, magicians and alchemists whose quests were not unlike those of the seekers described so well by Campbell as inhabiting the cultic milieu. With the explosion of literacy which took place in the Renaissance and Reformation eras, this underground of seekers grew apace; by the seventeenth and eighteenth centuries, this underground, or cultic, milieu, assuming ever more international dimensions, had taken a form very much in keeping with the description offered in Campbell's theory.[2]

Today, the academic literature and the popular press have focused on the ongoing process of globalization—a process facilitated by the end of the Cold War and the revolution in computer-based technology.[3] Globalization is creating interdependent economies as national boundaries become ever more theoretical. Transnational corporations now control greater resources than most states.[4] The European Union has adopted a common currency, while its member states have increasingly ceded sovereignty to the European parliament in Brussels and Strasbourg and to an emerging new aristocracy of bureaucrats (or Eurocrats, to use the more common terminology). All this would have been undreamed of by Colin Campbell in 1972.

What would come as no surprise, however, was that globalization would have impacted the cultic milieu of its day, and that from these esoteric reaches, an oppositional counterculture would emerge to challenge the forces of globalization in the dominant culture. 1972 we should recall, was a time of considerable oppositional ferment. The antiwar movement in the United States and Europe had reached new heights of militancy, helping to force American withdrawal following the January 1973 Cease Fire accords. The first Earth Day occurred in 1970,[5] bringing to the surface an ecology movement which heretofore had been confined to the underground of the 1960s. Indeed, a myriad of ideas—political, religious, ecological, or merely oppositional—were communicated to a receptive global youth audience in the 1960s and 1970s through a myriad of media; underground newspapers, 'zines, pop records, poster art and much, much more.[6] This was the golden age for underground mail-order companies and street corner activists.

The antiglobalization movement of the early years of the twenty-first century, like its 1960s and 1970s era antecedents, is built of a bricolage[7] of ideas and interests which converge during large-scale demonstrations that form during meetings of targeted and much-demonized institutions such as the World Bank and International Monetary Fund, which are most associated with the globalization process. There were, however, great differences between the antiglobalization protests and the movements of the 1960s and the 1970s.[8] Although, perhaps, less true of the 1970s than the 1960s, the oppositional forces whose passionate protests helped to doom an unpopular war and end American military conscription formed a mass movement of disaffected young people in the Western world whose passion was devoted to a few key issues: the antiwar movement, radical ecology, sexual liberation, or simply moving back to the land to form communal societies hoping to create ecological utopias. These endeavors were products of the dreams of large numbers of young people in North America and Western Europe, where the political, economic, technological and cultural structures converged to facilitate the emergence of these forms of large-scale protest.

No mass movement existed, and none was on the horizon, in late 1999 when the World Trade Organization (WTO) met in Seattle. Seattle was a large but laid-back, touristy town on the American West Coast heretofore known primarily for its cappuccino and for grunge music—a sound typified by the late Kurt Cobain and his band, Nirvana. The sound spawned a host of imitators, many of whom remain—when their various problems with heroin and alcohol allow—very much at the top of the pop charts. The town was completely unprepared for the appearance of a large crowd of antiglobalization protestors representing a bewildering variety of seemingly unrelated causes—anarchists of various hues,[9] environmentalists representing a wide spectrum of views, small groups representing such causes as forgiving Third World debt or the Mexican Zapitista guerilla movement, trade unions, representatives of charitable institutions, adherents of various religious communities and many, many more.[10] Thanks largely to a core of violent anarchists known as the Black Bloc and, allegedly, splinter sects from the animal rights and radical environmental subcultures, the protests were marked by violence, featuring widespread destruction of property and running battles with the police.[11]

Seattle brought this bewildering coalition—or more accurately—convergence of oppositional belief systems—to widespread public notice for the first time.[12] Over the course of the next year, in such disparate locales as Sweden, the Czech Republic and, most violently, Italy in September 2001, protests would grow in size, and violent confrontations would escalate in intensity with each meeting of world leaders or of institutions associated with the globalization process.[13]

What most surprised world leaders and those whose duty it was to provide security at these gatherings was not so much the presence of angry, occasionally violent, antiglobalization demonstrators. Rather, it was the often incongruous, at other times simply bizarre, collection of actors and activists who would seem—even to their own organizations—to have little in common with putative allies in the battle against globalization. In Gothenburg, Sweden, for example, the Attack movement found itself side by side with everyone from the Black Bloc to esoteric anti-Semites. Moreover, a couple of weeks before this clash, the far left Anti-fascist Action, the far right National Socialist Front and other radical right groups found themselves running into each other on the street corners of Gothenburg. All sides were handing out leaflets protesting globalization, albeit from different perspectives, as well as broadsides against the so-called Bilderberger groups meeting in Stenungsund outside Gothenburg. A somewhat bemused Canadian Security Service puts this bluntly:

> 7. Protest objectives extend beyond the claimed corporate impropriety, however. Multinational economic institutions, such as the World Trade Organization (WTO), the World Bank (WB), and the International Monetary Fund (IMF), are seen as establishing, monitoring, and rendering judgements on global trade practices, and are viewed as the spearheads of economic globalization. These institutions, considered to be the servants of corporate interests, exercising more power than elected governments and interested only in the profit motive, have increasingly become principal demonstration targets. Underlying the antiglobalization theme is criticism of the capitalist philosophy, a stance promoted once again by left-of-centre activists and militant anarchists.

> 8. The global parameters have encouraged disparate groups and individuals to participate in the demonstrations. In Seattle and Washington, for example, the wide variety of parading malcontents evoked the eclectic ambience of a "protest county fair." Circumstances also have promoted the involvement of fringe extremists who espouse violence, largely represented by *Black Bloc* anarchists and factions of militant animal-rights and environmental activists. *The melding of various elements and establishing of strange-bedfellow ties at individual demonstrations have contributed both to the impact and the unique character of the events.*[14] [emphasis ours]

Students of Campbell's cultic milieu theory, however, would have recognized an instant kinship between the diverse number of ideas and actors in the antiglobalization struggle and the denizens of the cultic milieu described by Campbell more than a quarter century ago. Much the same could be said of the way in which ideas were exchanged, analyzed, accepted all or in part, or rejected, even when causes or beliefs in violence vs. nonviolence, or other incompatibilities, would not allow people from differing belief systems to cooperate too closely.

The cultic milieu is oppositional by nature. The cultic milieu is a zone in which proscribed and/or forbidden knowledge is the coin of the realm, a place in which ideas, theories and speculations are to be found, exchanged, modified and, eventually, adopted or rejected by adherents of countless, primarily ephemeral groups whose leaders come and go and whose membership constitute a permanent class of seekers whose adherence to any particular leader or organization tends to be fleeting at best.[15] The ideas generated within the cultic milieu may eventually become mainstream, but long before they come to the attention of the dominant culture, they will have been thoroughly vetted, debated, reformulated, and ultimately, adopted or rejected within the cultic milieu itself. The sole thread that unites the denizens of the cultic milieu—true seekers all—is a shared rejection of the paradigms, the orthodoxies, of their societies. Beyond this element of seekership, the cultic milieu is a strikingly diverse and remarkably tolerant ethos. Ideas unacceptable to the social, cultural and political mainstream flourish. This is not to say that they find acceptance. Most, indeed, are heard and rejected, many are criticized, most are ignored. But they are heard and exchanged and passed on from belief system to belief system, from leader to leader, and from seeker to seeker.

Campbell's original essay dealt with the profusion of cultic religious groups that rose and dissolved, only to rise again in different forms that stemmed from the remarkable religious creativity of the 1960s and early 1970s.[16] Campbell noted that the adherents of these new religions had a remarkable awareness of the many, many choices on offer in the religious and spiritual marketplace of the time.[17] But as this introduction has noted, the cultic milieu is not a product of the 1960s. Rather, it is a permanent feature of society—not just this society, but of every society for which we have historical records. Campbell put this best:

> cults must exist within a milieu which, if not conducive to the maintenance of individual cults, is clearly highly conducive to the spawning of cults in general. Such a generally supportive cultic milieu is continually giving birth to new cults, absorbing the debris of the dead ones and creating new generations of cult-prone individuals to maintain the high level of membership turnover. Thus, whereas cults are by definition a transitory phenomenon, the cultic milieu is, by contrast, a permanent feature of society.[18]

This cultic milieu—oppositional by definition, seekers after ultimate truth by nature—may be seen by the dominant culture, in the words of the Canadian Security Service, as a "wide variety of parading malcontents [who] evoked the eclectic ambience of a 'protest county fair.'"

Cultic milieu theory suggests one key to understanding the linkages between the wide variety of parading malcontents. In the cultic milieu, ideas are fungible. Adherents of these ideas, however, are not so easily diffused between belief systems. Bron Taylor, in his contribution to this anthology, provides a good example of this process. Discussing the incompatibility of racist movements and militant environmentalists, Taylor notes:

> To my knowledge there is *no* overlap in the kinds of journals, novels, and even spiritual literature participants in these different subculture clusters read (although I concede there may be some overlap in the area of pagan spirituality, but again, the specific pagan literature radical environmentalists read generally tends to have a politically progressive edge.) Put more carefully, I have never encountered neo-Nazi or other overtly racist literature within radical

environmental subcultures. Moreover, despite their defacto anti-censorship consensus, Earth First!ers stridently criticize any article that is even remotely "politically incorrect" with regard to race and gender bias, as well as the editors who would be so unfortunate to publish it.

That racist and radical environmental subcultures do not overlap is due to firm border defenses. For example, after the editors of *Earth First!* ran an advertisement for a book entitled *Anglo-American Biocentric Tribalism* by Thorz Hammer (circa 1992), they discovered to their dismay that it was "nothing but entry-level neo-Nazi racist propaganda." The journal editors denounced the book as "trash" and published an apology for running the advertisement, promising to change their advertising policy, insisting on viewing sample copies before publishing book advertisements.[19]

Radical environmental subcultures are the most militantly egalitarian, antihierarchial and feminist I have ever encountered (at least their rhetoric is, most acknowledge there remain various "hidden hierarchies" within these groups) . . . their general orientation has been to express solidarity with colonized peoples (who, not coincidentally, usually have dark skin). Taken together, these dynamics strongly militate against any cross-fertilization between radical environmentalists and even the green-racist-right. Earth First! simply does not provide suitable habitat for racist (or sexist) ideologies. This is in no small measure because many of its participants cut their activist teeth in civil rights, antinuclear, and social justice campaigns. I should add one ironic qualification: If there are radical environmentalists whose worldviews are racist, they are far more likely to be biased against persons with European ancestry for presumed imperialist predispositions.[20]

Yet as Heléne Lööw notes in her contribution to this volume, racist subcultures are ardent and quite radical environmentalists. They are acutely aware of the literature, ideas and activities of the strongly antiracist subcultures of which Taylor writes.[21] And indeed, it would be fair to say that one of the first books that espoused animal rights in its modern, most radical formulation came from Savitri Devi, a passionate National Socialist of the World War II era; the group's activities would continue until her death in 1982.[22] Ideas are indeed fungible.

Adherents, however, are not so easily diffused through the cultic milieu. Racists and neo-Nazis do not easily mix with adherents of the radical environmental subculture, although the same could be said for Black Bloc anarchists and members of mainstream labor unions or adherents of the Catholic Church. Yet these latter have marched side by side in opposition to globalization—all the while denouncing the excesses or the moderation of the other, as the case may be.

This observation—and the contributions to this volume—point to a more complex picture than Campbell had envisioned in his 1972 essay. As those of us who have studied the more esoteric reaches of the cultic milieu would attest, the milieu is vast and it is indeed a permanent aspect of every society. But it is not undifferentiated. The cultic milieu in this sense may be seen as a vast, imaginary urban landscape inhabited by many neighborhoods.[23] Ideas flowed easily between neighborhoods in 1972, and with the explosion of Internet communications in the present day, ideas move with unimaginable speed to an ever increasing audience of consumers. Seekers, however, may not be as fungible. Seekers may, for example, sample many cultic religious groups or drift through the various enclaves of the racist or environmental subcultures, but they probably would not join utterly incompatible groups. An Earth First!er in this conception would be aware of ideas emanating from neo-Nazi circles, and certainly the neo-Nazis would be well aware of Earth First! ideas, but to actually cross into that space inhabited by "the other" would be almost unthinkable. Yet, because the ideas move so easily within the vast cultic milieu, it is not only conceivable, but likely, that vastly incompatible groups, belief systems, and individual adherents could (and do) materialize together, as if from the very ether itself, for events on which interests converge. At antiglobalization demonstrations, for example, a "wide variety of parading malcontents" may converge, despite the fact that politically, ideologically or religiously, they would seem to have little enough in common.

Such a convergence in 1972 would have been unlikely indeed. That was a time before mass movements had fragmented into uncountable causes and microconstituencies and before computer technology freed the dissemination of information and ideas from their dependence on the availability of mimeograph machines and the purchase of postal stamps. But in the first years of the twenty-first century, this model of convergence is the norm.

These changes had not been fully assimilated by scholars when the Swedish National Council for Crime Prevention (BRÅ) and the Centre for Migration Studies (CEIFO) at Stockholm University sponsored the conference "Rejected and Suppressed Knowledge: The Racist Right and the Cultic Milieu," in Stockholm, Sweden, from 13-17 February, 1997. Although some of these papers in this volume have been updated by participants since that conference took place, others are as they were presented in Stockholm in 1997. Their discussion of cultic milieu theory from a wide variety of academic perspectives remains vital some four years after the event.

Bron Taylor's "Diggers, Wolves, Ents, Elves and Expanding Universes: Bricolage, Religion, and Violence from Earth First! and the Earth Liberation Front to the Antiglobalization Resistance," which was extensively rewritten in 2001, provides an unparalleled look at the world of radical environmentalism. Its discussion, the ideological, spiritual and organizational roots of the militant environmental movement Earth First! is deeply informed by the author's extensive fieldwork. Taylor's essay examines in great detail the interactions—and divisions—which exist between the "neigborhoods" inhabited by radical environmental subculture and the subcultures of the far right, the far left, and indeed, of the isolated world of the Manson family as well. This latter connection provides the opportunity to consider the question of violence in even so avowedly a nonviolent movement as Earth First!

Timothy Miller offers a historical essay dealing with communal groups whose roots are of greater vintage: nineteenth and early twentieth century America. "The Historical Communal Roots of Ultraconservative Groups: Earlier American Communes That Have Helped Shaped Today's Far Right," looks at a number of communal groups. Some groups, such the Branch Davidians, the Church Universal and Triumphant (CUT), and various LDS (Latter-day Saints, or Mormons), are quite well known. Others, such as the Black Bear Ranch hippie commune, are known to few beyond their own numbers. But all interact in the cultic milieu with an array of other, often diametrically opposed groups. For example, the laid-back Black Bear Ranch became an inspiration for Jost Turner's right-wing communal experiment, the National Socialist Kindred.

László Kürti and Massimo Introvigne write of precisely the sort of movements Campbell had in mind when he penned his cultic milieu theory. Kürti offers a panoramic view of postcommunist Hungary's wildly inventive cultic milieu in his essay, "Neo-Shamanism, Psychic Phenomena and Media Trickery: Cultic Differences in Hungary." Here, a Hungarian New Age subculture is detailed, replete with ties to both the ruling political establishment and to a variety of foreign religio-political movements. Introvigne's contribution, "The Gothic Milieu," is a somewhat darker affair that nonetheless sheds considerable light on the little-known Gothic subculture—especially in its European form. Gothic music, explicit Satanism, the cult of the vampire, and role-playing games all fall within the purview of this essay.

The contribution by Mattias Gardell, "Black and White Unite in Fight?: On the Inter-Action Between Black and White Radical Racialists," is remarkably illustrative of the efficacy of cultic milieu theory. Where but in the underground in which the search for hidden and suppressed knowledge is undertaken would one find so seemingly incompatible a set of bedfellows as the stridently racialist American White supremacists and African American nationalists? Gardell's essay focuses on high-profile leaders such as the Nation of Islam's Louis Farrakhan and the White Aryan Resistance's (WAR) Tom Metzger, as well as such lesser lights as Klansman John Baumgardner and Chief Osiris of Pan-African International as they come together over the issue of racial separation. Surprisingly, in the case of the latter two, a genuine friendship seems to have developed.

Heléne Lööw broadens the context of the chapters dealing with the radical right in her contribution, "The Idea of Purity: The Swedish Racist Counterculture, Animal Rights and Environmental Protection." Lööw concentrates on the little noticed, but remarkably powerful, currents of radical environmentalism in the Swedish radical right wing. While outside observers have often dismissed this facet of right wing ideology as tangential at best, insincere at worst, Lööw demonstrates that the quest for ecological balance and animal rights has been central to the belief system throughout the post-World War II era. This quest is traced to this milieu's obsession with purity in all of its forms, be it in terms of race or in the form of the natural environment. Additionally, the essay, like that of Bron Taylor, considers the possibilities of linkages between such wildly disparate subcultures as the largely leftist and anarchist radical environmentalists and the racialist right.

From the American scene, Frederick J. Simonelli offers a fine historical examination of the revival of the Euro-American National Socialist movement in "Thriving in a Cultic Milieu: The World Union of National Socialists, 1962-1992." In his examination of George Lincoln Rockwell's efforts to build the World Union of National Socialists (WUNS) into an effective organization, Simonelli invokes Eric Hoffer's seminal ideas regarding the nature of the "true believer"[24] as he takes the reader through the idiosyncratic world of post-war National Socialism. Simonelli's chapter also offers an insight into the ideology and tactics of the early post-war generation of National Socialists—an era that in many ways represents the "lost generation" of the movement but which nevertheless laid the groundwork for the last decade's white power counterculture. In terms of cultic milieu theory, Simonelli concludes:

> Increasingly, as Rockwell concentrated his attention and effort on his struggle for dominance within the global racist right more than on any meaningful pursuit of political power, he drew a tighter and tighter circle around himself and demanded the exclusive allegiance of his followers, which increased their isolation while elevating their sense of chosenness. Rockwell's world, the world of demons and fantasy, of intrigue and conspiracy, that was the neo-Nazi culture of the 1960s, was the very "oppositional milieu" that nurtured manifestations of cult-like behavior that marked the ANP [American Nazi Party] and, to an increasing degree, WUNS [World Union of National Socialists].[25] This "supportive cultic milieu" encouraged Rockwell's deviance from the more conventional right.[26]

Jeffrey Kaplan carries on the discussion of the post-war National Socialist scene begun by Fredrick Simonelli in his "The Postwar Paths of Occult National Socialism: From Rockwell and Madole to Manson." Kaplan's chapter concentrates on the interactions of the denizens of the National Socialist subculture with an array of other oppositional—although not necessarily racialist—milieus. Thus, through these pages march such seemingly disparate communities as explicit Satanism, Odinism and other neo-pagan traditions; radical environmentalists; and the followers of Charles Manson. The interactions of these and many more, as well as the millennial religiosity of contemporary National Socialism, are at the heart of Kaplan's study.

Finally, two conference participants address in very different ways the role of the watchdog movements. Gordon Melton in his essay, "The Modern Anti-Cult Movement in Historical Perspective," considers the evolution of the anti-cult movement from its 1970s and early 1980s peak to its current nadir in the wake of the successful law suit which brought down the Cult Awareness Network (CAN). In his powerful argument for religious pluralism unfettered by the machination of the watchdog groups, Melton concludes: "Though anti-cult organizations and 'cult' experts will persist into the foreseeable future, their ability to oppose the spread and activities of the new religions in North America seems destined to fade."

Laird Wilcox is less sanguine in his powerful examination of the political watchdog groups such as the Anti-Defamation League of the B'nai B'rith (ADL) and the many smaller groups and individuals who, like the ADL, have undertaken the self-appointed mission of monitoring the doings of the far right wing. In "Who Watches the Watchman? Another Side to the Watchdog Groups," Wilcox traces in considerable detail the actions of the political watchdogs. These activities often appear to violate the basic tenets of fairness (not to mention, of strict legality) in the service of ideologies which, the author argues, are often no less extreme than those of the movements they seek to monitor. In this clash of cult and counter-cult, of the far left in the guise of concerned watchdogs and the far right as increasingly demonized outsiders, there is much of the complexity of Campbell's view of a cultic milieu, which is vitally alive to its initiates but largely opaque to the outside world.

While we believe that these essays are valuable additions to the social science literature in and of themselves, we also hope that they will help to stimulate scholarly discussion of Colin Campbell's prescient, but too long overlooked, cultic milieu theory. We believe that Campbell's insights have much to offer scholars working in a variety of disciplines, and it is our hope that this volume will be seen as a contribution to reopening this conversation.

Notes

[1] Colin Campbell, "The Cult, the Cultic Milieu and Secularization," in *A Sociological Yearbook of Religion in Britain* 5, (1972), 119-36.

[2] For a representative selection of texts, see for the medieval period: Norman Cohn, *The Pursuit of the Millennium*, revised and expanded edition, (New York: Oxford University Press, 1970); Bernard McGinn, *Visions of the End* (New York: Columbia University Press, 1998); *idem., Apocalyptic Spirituality* (New York: Paulist Press, 1979); and Jeffrey Burton Russell, *Dissent and Reform in the Early Middle Ages* (Los Angeles and Berkeley: University of California Press, 1965). On the magical beliefs of the Middle Ages, no better source can be found than the Pennsylvania State University Press series, "Magic in History." See for example, Claire Fanger, ed., *Conjuring Spirits: Texts and Traditions of Medieval Ritual Magic* (University Park, PA: Pennsylvania State University Press, 1998) and Richard Kiekeffer, *Forbidden Rites: A Necromancer's Manual of the Fifteenth Century* (University Park, PA: Pennsylvania State University Press, 1997), which are highly recommended. For the seventeenth and eighteenth century periods, still unsurpassed is James H. Billington, *Fire in the Minds of Men: Origins of the Revolutionary Faith* (New York: Basic Books, 1980). For the cultic milieu in fully modern form from the nineteenth century, see James Webb, *The Occult Underground* (LaSalle, IL: Open Court Publishing, 1975); and *idem., The Occult Establishment* (LaSalle, IL: Open Court Publishing, 1976).

[3] To illustrate the extent of this literature, a multilingual library search of the academic literature alone turned up no less than 11,000+ entries under the heading "globalization," most of them dated 2000 or later. Useful texts for the uninitiated would include: Jan Aart Scholte, *Globalization: A Critical Introduction* (New York: St. Martin's Press, 2000); Anthony Giddens, *Runaway World: How Globalization Is Reshaping Our Lives* (New

York: Routledge, 2000); Stephen Kenneth McBride and John Richard Wiseman, *Globalization and Its Discontents* (New York: St. Martin's Press, 2000); Edward M. Graham, *Fighting the Wrong Enemy : Antiglobal Activities and Multinational Enterprises* (Washington, D.C.: Institute for International Economics, 2000); Will Hutton and Anthony. Giddens. *Global Capitalism* (New York: New Press: Distributed by W.W. Norton, 2000); John D. Donahue and Joseph S. Nye, *Governance in a Globalizing World* (Cambridge, MA: Visions of Governance for the 21st Century; Washington, D.C.: Brookings Institution Press, 2000); and Paul Streeten, *Globalisation: Threat or Opportunity?* (Copenhagen; Herndon, VA: Copenhagen Business School Press, 2001).

[4] Of the top 100 economies in the world, 51 are multinationals and only 49 are nation states. *Anti-Globalization—A Spreading Phenomenon*. Canadian Security Intelligence Service publication Report # 2000/08. Available at: *http://www.csis-scrs.gc.ca/eng/miscdocs/200008_e.html*. The report cites as its source a report in the *Ottawa Citizen*, 20 April 2000. Interestingly, this situation is reminiscent of the colonial era, when trading companies commanded greater resources than states.

[5] For reflections on the first Earth Day by the sponsor of the legislation making the occasion an American national holiday, see Sen. Gaylord Nelson, "Earth Day," in Bron Taylor and Jeffrey Kaplan, *Encyclopedia of Religion and Nature* (London: Continuum, forthcoming 2003).

[6] Colin Campbell, "The Cult, the Cultic Milieu and Secularization," 123.

[7] The term was coined by the French anthropologist Claude Gustave Lévi-Strauss to describe the process by which a number of disparate ideas are combined to form an ideology.

[8] For a broad and shallow overview, see Neil A. Hamilton, *The ABC-CLIO Companion to the 1960s Counterculture in America* (Santa Barbara, CA: ABC-CLIO, 1997). For more focused and incisive works, see: Timothy Miller, *The 60s Communes: Hippies and Beyond* (Syracuse, NY: Syracuse University Press, 1999). David Mark Chalmers, *And the Crooked Places Made Straight: The Struggle for Social Change in the 1960s* (Baltimore: Johns Hopkins University Press, 1996); Umberto Eco and Robert Lumley, *Apocalypse Postponed* (Bloomington: Indiana University Press; London: British Film Institute, 1994); Gini Holland, *The 1960s. A Cultural History of the United States Through the Decades* (San Diego, CA: Lucent Books, 1999); and Alexander Bloom and Winifred Breines, *"Takin' It to the Streets": A Sixties Reader* (New York: Oxford University Press, 1995). For a comprehensive reader of 1970s era protest movements, see Harrison E. Salisbury, ed., *The Eloquence of Protest: Voices of the 70s* (Boston: Houghton Mifflin, 1972).

[9] For a sampling of these factions, see Ulrike Heider, *Anarchism: Left, Right and Green* (San Francisco: City Light Books, 1994).

[10] "Globalization Unifies Its Many-Striped Foes," *New York Times*, 15 April 2000; "From Cell, Coalition Looked Like a Movement," *New York Times*, 17 April 2000; or "USA: Seattle WTO Protests Mark New Activist Age," *Associated Press*, 25 November 2000

[11] Anti-Globalization—A Spreading Phenomenon.

[12] It was not the first appearance of antiglobalization protesters, however. Some 2,000 people appeared to protest at the G8 economic summit in London on 18 June 1999. Seattle, however, had at least ten times that number of protestors, and subsequent antiglobalization protests would grow in size and intensity with each event. *Anti-Globalization—A Spreading Phenomenon*.

[13] In September 2001, meetings of World Bank and the International Monetary Fund scheduled for Washington, D.C., on 29-30 September 2001 were cancelled in the after-

math of the terrorist attacks on Washington and New York which occurred on 11 September 2001. The Transatlantic Business Dialog meeting in Stockholm in October 2001 was cancelled for the same reason. The next G8 summit meeting scheduled after the violence-marred summit in Genoa, Italy, in September 2001, was hastily arranged at a remote mountain location in the Canadian Rockies in an effort by world leaders to avoid antiglobalization protests that marked—or on occasion as in Seattle—shut down their meetings.

[14] *Anti-Globalization—A Spreading Phenomenon.*

[15] Colin Campbell, "The Cult, the Cultic Milieu and Secularization," 120-24.

[16] Peter Jenkins, *Mystics and Messiahs: Cults and New Religions in American History* (New York: OUP, 2000).

[17] Robert S. Ellwood, *The Sixties Spiritual Awakening: American Religion Moving From Modern to Postmodern* (Rutgers, NJ: Rutgers University Press, 1994).

[18] Colin Campbell, "The Cult, the Cultic Milieu and Secularization," 121-22.

[19] "Now white boys can be tribal too!" *in Earth First* 13:2, 32, and the letter and apology ran in *Earth First* 13:3 (2 February 1993).

[20] Bron Taylor, "Diggers, Wolves, Ents, Elves and Expanding Universes: Bricolage, Religion, and Violence from Earth First! and the Earth Liberation Front to the Antiglobalization Resistance," this volume.

[21] Heléne Lööw, "The Idea of Purity: The Swedish Racist Counterculture, Animal Rights and Environmental Protection," this volume.

[22] See the recently reprinted Savitri Devi, *Impeachment of Man* (Costa Mesa, CA: Noontide Press, 1991). Cf. Nicholas Goodrick-Clark, *Hitler's Priestess: Savitri Devi, the Hindu-Aryan Myth, and Occult Neo-Nazism* (New York: New York University Press, 1998); Jeffrey Kaplan, "Savitri Devi and the National Socialist Religion of Nature," *Pomogranite* 7 (February 1999); and "Savitri Devi," in *idem.*, *Encyclopedia of White Power: A Sourcebook on the Radical Racist Right* (Walnut Creek, CA: AltaMira Press, 2000), 91-95.

[23] Perhaps the most useful real world referent would be the mosaic which is the Islamic city. To cross from one neighborhood to another is to cross into a different cultural, linguistic and cultural world, although no visible border or physical demarcation may separate one enclave from another. See Albert Hourani and Samuel Miklos Stern, *The Islamic City: a Colloquium* (Oxford, Cassirer; [Philadelphia] University of Pennsylvania Press, 1970).

[24] Eric Hoffer, *The True Believer* (New York: Harper & Brothers, 1951).

[25] The phrase "oppositional milieu" is from Jeffrey Kaplan, "Right Wing Violence in North America," *Terrorism and Political Violence* 7(Spring 1995), 44-95.

[26] Colin Campbell, "The Cult, the Cultic Milieu and Secularization," 121.

The Cult, the Cultic Milieu and Secularization

Colin Campbell

Introduction

Cult has long been the Cinderella in the family of terms that constitutes the taxonomy of religious collectivities. Consistently overlooked in favor of her "big sisters"—sect, church, and denomination—she has been relegated to a minor place within the sociology of religion's "household" and entrusted with merely menial tasks.[1] Recently, however, there have been signs of a change of heart. Sociologists have begun to show more interest in cults and cultic phenomena either as examples of cultural deviancy or as empirical evidence with which to deny the hypothesis of secularization.[2] In addition, there has been at least one serious attempt to reformulate the concept of cult and to develop an adequate typology.[3] This re-awakening of interest in the cult can be seen as a somewhat belated response by sociologists to the changes that have occurred and are still occurring in the popular cultural scene in contemporary society. Stimulated by the increasing influence of non-Christian religious ideas and the weakened position of the churches as agencies of cultural control, cultic beliefs like astrology and witchcraft have "hitched a ride" on the developing counterculture and spread themselves more widely throughout society. The cultic has therefore become a far more visible component of the total cultural system and the lack of a genuine sociological theory of the cult has become a very obvious lacuna in the sociology of religion.

The concept of cult derives from Troeltsch's triparite division of religious phenomena into church religion, sect religion, and mysticism.[4] The latter, in its pure form, is not represented by organizations at all, but to the extent that these arise, they approximate to the cult in their structure. Troeltsch's original formulation has been employed and modified by Becker, Mann, Marty, Martin, Yinger, Jackson, and Jobling and Nelson.[5] At the same time, there has been a discernable tendency to move away from Troeltsch's emphasis upon the close association of mysticism and the cult and to use that term to refer simply to any religious or quasi-religious collectivity which is loosely organized, ephemeral, and espouses a deviant system of belief and practice.[6] As a result two contrasting conceptions of the nature of cults now exist. The first view, which is closer to Troeltsch's original position, regards the distinctive characteristics of cults as being found in association with and deriving from the nature of mystical religion. The second view, as contained in the writings of Lofland, Stark, and Taylor Buckner, presents the special character of cultic groups as stemming from their deviant or heterodox position in relation to the dominant societal culture.[7] Although some writers appear to include both views in their accounts of cults and there has been at least one attempt to fuse them together into a single "synthesized" conception, they clearly remain analytically discrete perspectives implying contrasting hypotheses. [8]

That they are so frequently associated is probably due to the historical accident that has caused mysticism to approximate to a deviant religious tradition in the majority of western societies. If indeed this is the case, then we would expect to be able to find mystically based cultic groups which do not occupy a deviant status in relation to the orthodox culture of the larger society as well as deviant cults which do not espouse mysticism. Examples of the former phenomena would appear to abound in India and in the Buddhist societies of southeast Asia even if it is more difficult to find examples closer to home, while those groups which espouse a deviant scientific belief system, such as the flying saucer groups, appear to fit the latter category. Given that the Troeltschian interpretation of cults as the organizational response associated with the mystical religion may well suffer from the limitations which arise from a consideration of specifically Christian movements of the sixteenth and seventeenth centuries, it would appear as if the view of cultic phenomena as primarily deviant is to be preferred. At the same time, it should not be forgotten that mystical cults may well constitute an important element of the deviant culture in such societies as Britain and America.

Sociological accounts of the cult tend to describe it as individualistic and loosely structured, in contrast to the communal and cohesive organization of the sect. Also unlike the sect, the cult makes few demands on its members, is tolerant of other organizations and faiths and is not exclusivist. Members do not act in common as a group so much as share "a parallelism of spontaneous religious personalities."[9] Membership of such groups changes rapidly and the groups themselves are often transient. Studies of individual cults have born out this general description and reinforced the picture of these groups as precariously balanced in relation to the containing society.[10] Cults, it is argued, tend to succeed very quickly and take over the characteristics of sects or else fade away in the face of societal opposition or the absence of a charismatic leader.[11] Faced with these conclusions, it is perhaps understandable that the study of cults has tended in some cases to be absorbed into the analysis of sectarianism.[12]

However, it is by no means obvious that the correct strategy for the development of a genuine theory of cultic phenomena is to follow the example set by the development of the theories of sectarianism. That is, to accumulate case studies prior to the establishment of suitable typologies and the generation of hypotheses concerning origin, maintenance, and extinction of the various types. The contrast between sects and cults is sufficiently great to suggest that the alternative strategies may be more appropriate. For while sects are usually clearly circumscribed entities with specifically formulated belief systems and organizational structures which have a tendency to persist over time, cults, by contrast, tend to have undefined boundaries, fluctuating belief systems, rudimentary organizational structures, and are frequently highly ephemeral. They therefore present a sharp contrast with sects as convenient and suitable subjects for sociological research. There is, however, an alternative method of approaching the study of cultic phenomena.

Given that cultic groups have a tendency to be ephemeral and highly unstable, it is a fact that new ones are being born just as fast as the old ones die. There is a continual process of cult formation and collapse which parallels the high turnover of membership at the individual level. Clearly, therefore, cults must exist within a milieu which, if not conducive to the maintenance of individual cults, is clearly highly conducive to the spawning of cults in general. Such a generally supportive cultic milieu is continually giving birth to new cults, absorbing the debris of the dead ones and creating new generations of cult-prone individuals to maintain the high levels of membership turnover. Thus, whereas cults are by definition a largely transitory phenomenon, the cultic milieu is, by contrast, a constant feature of society. It could therefore prove more viable and illuminating to take the cultic milieu and not the individual cult as the focus of sociological concern.

The Cultic Milieu

The cultic milieu can be regarded as the cultural underground of society. Much broader, deeper and historically based than the contemporary movement known as *the* underground, it includes all deviant belief systems and their associated practices. Unorthodox science, alien and heretical religion, deviant medicine, all comprise elements of such an underground. In addition, it includes the collectivities, institutions, individuals, and media of communication associated with these beliefs. Substantively, it includes the worlds of the occult and the magical, of spiritualism and psychic phenomena, of mysticism and new thought, of alien intelligences and lost civilizations, of faith healing and nature cure. This heterogeneous assortment of cultural items can be regarded despite its apparent diversity as constituting a single entity—the entity of the cultic milieu. There are several sources of this unity.

At the basis of the unifying tendencies is the fact that all these worlds share a common position as heterodox or deviant items in relation to the dominant cultural orthodoxies. This fact gives rise to a common consciousness of deviance and the need to justify their own views in the light of the expressed ridicule or hostility of the larger society. The spokesmen for the various cultic movements thus have a common cause in attacking orthodoxy and in defending individual liberty of belief and practice. Arising from this there is a prevailing orientation of mutual sympathy and support, such that the various cultic movements rarely engage in criticism of each other. On the contrary, they display a marked tolerance and receptivity toward each other's beliefs which, although partly stemming from this common concern with liberty of belief and resistance to any suggestion of dogmatism, also receives a great stimulus from the presence of the mystical tradition. Since this tradition emphasizes that the single ideal of unity with the divine can be attained by a diversity of paths, it tends to be ecumenical, super-ecclesiastic, syncretistic and tolerant in outlook.[13] These tend, in fact, to be characteristics of the cultic milieu in general whether or not the belief content is mystical in the sense of pursuing the goal of ecstatic experience. As a result, the fragmentary tendencies present in the milieu because of the enormous diversity of cultural items are more than counteracted by the continuing pressure to syncretization.

Syncretization is then further facilitated and reinforced by the overlapping communication structures which prevail within the milieu. More than anything else, the cultic world is kept alive by the magazines, periodicals, books, pamphlets, lectures, demonstrations and informal meetings through which its beliefs and practices are discussed and disseminated. However, unlike the sectarian situation, these communication media are not bounded by the framework of the beliefs of a particular collectivity but are generally open. Thus not only does syncretization mean that cultic teachings are frequently mutually supportive (i.e., visitors from outer space prove to be psychic and mediums confirm that there is life on other planets), but the literature of particular groups and movements includes reviews of one another's literature and advertises one another's meetings. As a direct consequence of this, individuals who "enter" the cultic milieu at any one point frequently travel rapidly through a wide variety of movements and beliefs and by so doing constitute yet another unifying force within the milieu.

Lastly, the cultic milieu is manifestly united by a common ideology of seekership which both arises from and in turn reinforces the consciousness of deviant status, the receptive and syncretistic orientation and the interpenetrative communication structure. The concept of seekership has been employed by Dohrman, Taylor, Buckner and Lofland and Stark, and the latter in particular have developed it to apply to persons who have adopted a problem-solving perspective while defining conventional religious institutions and beliefs as inadequate.[14] Such persons are defined as "searching for some satisfactory system of religious meaning to interpret and resolve their discontents."[15] If this conception is widened beyond the restriction to a religious frame of reference, then it can be seen that this notion of seekership prevails throughout the cultic milieu. Once again mysticism supports this ideology; for the belief in the multiplicity and diversity of paths to spiritual enlightenment supplants the distinction between believer and unbeliever with the conception of degrees of "seekership." However, the basic seekership belief that truth (or enlightenment) is an esoteric commodity only to be attained after suitable preparation and a "quest" exists outside the purely mystical religious tradition. It can apply equally well to the search for interpretation and explanations of non-religious phenomena and in situations where there is no expectation of "revelatory experiences" and even in the context of the pursuit of worldly success, health or consolation.

The Culture of the Cultic World

Given that the ideology of seekership provides a common and unifying style and that the processes of syncretization are continually mutating whatever new cultural items enter, it is still necessary to describe the culture of the cultic world in a substantive fashion. This is clearly a difficult task, and until such time as a detailed cultural map is drawn up, it can only be attempted in a very general fashion. Basically cultic culture can be described as falling in the property space bounded by a religion-science axis and an instrumental-expressive orientation axis, taking for granted the prior criteria of societal deviancy. Thus there are items which are primarily deviant science, those which are deviant religion, and there are both instrumental and expressive concerns in relation to each category. There are in addition cultic movements and belief systems which represent blends of science and religion and display combinations of instrumental and expressive orientations. Attempts to classify cultic beliefs on the basis of these two axes will therefore only result in a very rough approximation to reality, especially as it is likely that it is just those systems of meaning which are able to blend cultural traditions and both orientations which will be the most successful.

As has already been indicated, the most prominent part of the deviant religious component of the cultic world is mysticism. This is the religious response which Troeltsch identified as concentrating solely on the individual's relationship with the divine and through an emphasis on first-hand experience, tending to neglect the historical, ecclesiastical and ritual concerns of religion. It has no need for dogmas, sacraments, ministry or indeed any formal organization, and as such it appears excessively individualistic. Although it is separated from the mainstream of religion by its rejection of the importance of the fellowship of believers, it does in fact include a belief in a spiritual fellowship but one mediated by the divine. These characteristics cause it to be ecumenical, super-ecclesiastical, syncretistic, and tolerant in outlook. In all these characteristics, mysticism represents almost the complete antithesis of the religion of the sects.

The basic beliefs comprising the mystical position are that the religious ideal is a state of unity with the divine; this ideal is potentially attainable by all; there is an underlying unity of all consciousness and life, and that no matter how diverse or how many versions of truth there are, all can lead to the same all-encompassing truth. Such a position leads not only to a depreciation of history, ritual and organization but also to a general indifference to all secular affairs except the most personal. Social, economic, and political problems can only be resolved when a spiritual reformation has occurred at the individual level, and this requires that the spiritualization of personal life should be the principal aim. This in turn can cause the mystical to be closely associated with the erotic and the sexual while opposing materialism. Almost all these assumptions are contrary to the primary premises of Judeo-Christian religion and have been rejected by that tradition as heresies. It is not surprising, therefore, that we should find they flourish in the cultural underground of an officially Christian society. Other world religions like Buddhism and Hinduism have mysticism as their central ingredient, and these religions and their teachings are widely disseminated throughout the cultic milieu comprising one of the principal components of that culture. In fact, certain teachings of Buddhism and Hinduism which are notably absent from the Christian tradition, like reincarnation and the prohibition on the taking of animal life, are almost hallmarks by which the cultic religious groups identify themselves. Although mysticism may be the dominant religious component in the cultic milieu, it is not the only one. The other forms of "deviant religion" which are well-represented are the pre-Christian pagan traditions of magic, witchcraft, sun worship and the like. Rarely, however, do any of these teachings appear in their pure form, but the rampant syncretism of the cultic milieu means that mysticism and magic, meditation and mediumship, astrology and ahimsa, all are likely to appear in association with one another.

They are also likely to appear in conjunction with "non-religious" beliefs and practices, for the other important ingredient of cultic culture is "deviant science and technology." Orthodox science is now at least as important as orthodox religion in defining what is truth as what is error in contemporary culture, if not more so. Scientific "heresies" abound in the cultic fringe. Of course mystic religion itself could be regarded as scientifically unsupportable, but the true heresies are not so much religious beliefs of this kind but beliefs held to be "purely" scientific which are repudiated by the spokesmen of scientific orthodoxy: the flat-earthers, or the flying saucerians who hold that extra-terrestial vehicles actually exist. Fully fledged scientific theories may also abound, notably concerning "ethers," "emanations," "fifth senses," and astral planes, together with the many and varied interpretations of the nature of time and space.

Lastly there exists the underground technology which has been built on this deviant science, primarily medical and psychiatric, but there are also technologies of communication, transportation, and divination.

The Institutions of the Cultic Milieu

The institutions of the cultic milieu can be viewed, like its culture, as encompassed by the religion-science and instrumental-expressive axes with the conception of seekership once again acting as a unifying factor. A variety of organizational forms can be seen within this framework and it is by no means obvious that the traditional conception of the cult is the dominant type. Fundamentally it is the case that the formal character of the cultic institutions derives from the nature of the cultural tradition of which they represent deviant forms. Thus, if it is heterodox science, then like para-psychology, there will tend to be "colleges" and "institutes" like the College of Psychic Science and the Institute for Occult Sciences offering quasi-educational courses, lectures, demonstrations and facilities for research. If it is heterodox religion, then one finds "orders," "lodges," "fellowships," and "brotherhoods" like the White Eagle Lodge, the Order of the Cross and the Rosicrucians. Whatever the nomenclature, however, the majority of these organizations share the same characteristics; they are organizations for "seekers," offering aid, support, facilities and a form of fellowship to those in search of truth. The exceptions to this are the revelatory cults which have adherents rather than seekers and promulgate *the* truth as it has already been revealed, together with the social institutions associated with the practice of deviant science and technology. The former, like the Aetherius Society, have many of the characteristics of a sect since belief in a revealed truth leads to a believer-nonbeliever distinction, rather than the notion of degrees of seekership prevailing in the cultic milieu in general. The latter are merely institutions for the practice of a deviant technology like faith healing, chiropractic, naturopathy, or mediumship and the appropriate individual categories are those of the practitioner and client. Numbered here would be the numerous practices of the mediums, astrologers, graphologists, diviners and healers of all sorts, together with the many clinics, nature cure resorts and other establishments offering these services on a residential basis. It is probably at this point that the cultic milieu comes most directly into contact with the larger society as a consequence of a general demand for the unorthodox services which it offers. Apart from these personal service institutions, it would appear as if the organizational form most typical of the cultic milieu is not the cult, but the "society of seekers." Indeed the cult, in the form of a group offering a particularized and detailed revealed truth, represents something of an aberration from the basic principle of tolerance and ecclesticism which is prevalent in the milieu in general, and this could possibly be one reason why it tends to have such a short lifespan.

The nature and problems of cultic organizations derive primarily from the fact that they attract and recruit seekers. Seekership is probably the one characteristic that all members of cultic groups have in common, and while this facilitates the formation of groups, it poses special problems for their maintenance. Seekers do not necessarily cease seeking when a revealed truth is offered to them, nor do they necessarily stop looking in other directions when one path is indicated as *the* path to the truth. They may in fact have lost sight of their original aim, and through the "displacement of goals" have come to accept seeking itself as the primary end. Because of this, groups face continuing pressure to widen their concerns and explore new cultic regions. Thus a group of seekers may join together out of a common concern with flying saucers, but then expand their interests to encompass all kinds of occult phenomena. Such a "strain toward variety" may cause the group to lose its focus of concern altogether and finally disappear back into the general milieu from which it arose.[16] Alternatively, if the group manages to resist these pressures and maintain its specific original focus of concern, it has the increasingly difficult task of finding something new to discuss. It is in this context that there exists the greatest possibility of an individual laying claim to some special truth and presenting himself as a revelatory "channel."

Another response to this dilemma is to institutionalize seekership within the organization. By creating several categories of membership corresponding to different degrees of initiation into the new areas of knowledge, it is possible to control the seekers' exploration of the new "mysteries" and so create within one organization the life-history that frequently occurs within the milieu in general. Skillful control of this process can convince the seeker that all he will ever need to know will eventually be made clear to him, and he can be induced to develop an even greater commitment to the organization in terms of personal identity and (not least) money. Such a response clearly requires a secretive or semi-secretive aura, and this in turn leads to the need to demonstrate that the organization's claims are genuine. There is, therefore, frequently a heavy emphasis upon the instrumental benefits of such an organization.

In line with the distinction between the cult proper and the society of seekers, there is an associated difference between the adherent of a particular brand of cultic culture and a seeker actively committed to a quest within the culture but uncommitted to a specific version of "the truth." It is the former whose particularized loyalty helps to bring the cult into being out of the general milieu, but it is the latter who supports the milieu itself by attending lectures and demonstrations and answering advertisements. There is, however, a third category of person whose support helps to maintain the cultic milieu in existence, and this is the passive consumer of the "products" of the culture. Unlike the seeker, such a person does not possess the intensity of the commitment to the quest to actively invest a considerable amount of time, emotion and money in exploring the milieu. Instead his interest in the mysterious and the bizarre is merely a general one which he satisfies through subscriptions to magazines which are principally commercial rather than ideological in orientation. (*Witchcraft* and *Man, Myth and Magic* are only the most recent and most publicized of a long line of such magazines.) Or his involvement is that of the ad hoc concern typical of a client seeking the services of a professional practitioner. Magazines like *Fate*, *Prediction* and *Zodiac Monthly*, for example, which are totally commercial in their production style and bear little resemblance to the highly committed cultic house journals *Psychic News* or *Occult Gazette*, carry several pages of advertisements on behalf of many psychic consultants and healers, including pyromancists, palmists, trance mediums, tarot experts, graphologists and absent healers as well as the more conventional clairvoyants and astrologers. It is this substantial commercial substructure which is one of the principal reasons why the cultic milieu continues to survive.

Secularization and the Cultic Milieu

Some of the most interesting questions one can ask about this milieu concern not its internal anatomy but its relationship with the containing society and its orthodox culture. How does it manage to survive in face of the continuing disapproval and even outright hostility of the organizations representing cultural orthodoxy? Through what channels are new cultural items introduced into the milieu? What are the circumstances which facilitate the transformation of deviant cultural items into variant or even dominant ones? What general functions, in fact, does the milieu fulfill? Although one can speculate on any one or more of these themes, it is clear that at present we lack the information to answer such questions. That we should seek to answer such questions would seem to follow from any commitment to explore the dynamics of socio-cultural systems. Among the hypotheses that suggest themselves concerning the cultic milieu, one might pick out the following:

1. That it is a major agency of cultural "diffusion" facilitating the accomodation of "alien" cultural items into a host culture.
2. That it is a major agency of cultural "innovation," new items arising as a result of the processes of syncretization and "revelation."
3. That it functions as a cultural "gene pool" for society, enhancing society's potential for cultural adaptation by transmitting and creating numerous cultural "mutations."
4. That it functions as a "negative reference group" for spokesmen of cultural orthodoxy, facilitating adherence to dominant scientific paradigms by practicing scientists and associated practitioners.
5. That the cultic milieu flourishes in relation to (a) the amount of "alien" culture contact and (b) the disintegration of dominant indigenous culture.
6. That the cultic milieu acts as a source of renewal for ailing orthodox belief systems.
7. That cultic movements represent a general response to "psychic deprivation."

There is a general question underlying specific hypotheses such as these concerning the nature and the extent of a societal cultural underground. If one starts with the premise that all societies will possess variant and deviant cultures in addition to a dominant one, then the assumption of the universality of an underground cultic milieu appears, a priori, justifiable. But the nature and extent of such a milieu and the precise form of its relationship with the dominant orthodoxy are by contrast subject to much variation. The content of the counterculture is clearly in part a product of the form of orthodoxy itself, just as the extent of such a culture is limited by the repressiveness of the agencies of the agencies of orthodoxy. A consideration of the functions of the cultic milieu is therefore dependent in the first instance on analysis of the total cultural system of which the milieu is a part. Clearly this is a tall order indeed, but if one were to attempt this for British society, then, at the very least, it would be necessary to relate both orthodox science and orthodox religion, firstly to each other and secondly to their unorthodox forms. The only concept that seems at all capable of fulfilling such a role is secularization, and despite the notorious uncertainties and ambiguities surrounding the usage (and abusage) of this term, it does seem worth speculating on how the postulated processes of secularization might relate to the position of the cultic milieu in contemporary society.

Primarily it would seem that the structural changes associated with secularization have been to the advantage of cultic culture. The decline in the power and influence of the Christian churches has inevitably weakened their role as custodians of "truth" and reduced the extent to which they can draw upon society for forays against indigenous "pagans" and "heretics." Thus although the churches still condemn such un-Christian systems of thought as astrology and witchcraft, these condemnations remain unsupported by secular sanctions and unnoticed by the public in general. Thus the principal bulwark against heresy and superstition has greatly diminished and the many pre-Christian and non-Christian varieties of religious belief are free, for the first time in many centuries, to spread throughout society. In addition, the relativism and tolerance of cultural pluralism which, it is claimed, are concomitants of secularization have greatly assisted the increased acceptability of these "heretical" beliefs. Increased acquaintance with other world religions as a result both of the importation of ideas and the immigration of adherents has helped to raise the average tolerance of deviant religious views while robbing Christianity of its position as the automatic yardstick of what is normal in matters of religious belief and practice. The natural consequence has been that cultic beliefs of all kinds are now closer in cultural distance to the prevailing orthodoxies of society than they were at the turn of the century. What has been traditionally treated as categorically deviant and subject to secular sanctions as well as ecclesiastical wrath is gradually becoming merely variant. Although various occult phenomena fall into this category, witchcraft is the best illustrative example, and it is interesting to speculate on whether the British pattern of institutionalized dissent can actually stretch so far as to accommodate the total rehabilitation of witchcraft.[17]

There is, however, another strand of secularization theory, which would appear to argue against the increased accessibility of cultic culture. This is the identification of secularization as a cultural process (or processes) of rationalization stimulated and supported by the social institution of science and those that derive from it. From this standpoint, it could be argued that it is misleading to view the accessibility of cultic beliefs from the perspective of their relationship to religious orthodoxy since the religious worldview, orthodox and unorthodox, is itself being steadily displaced by a rational scientific weltanschauung. Scientific orthodoxy and not religious orthodoxy is thus the proper yardstick for the identification of cultural deviance, and judged by this standard such systems of belief and practice as the occult must be regarded as just as deviant as before, if not actually more so. Support for this argument is found in the fact that sectarian and cultic movements find themselves sanctioned by the secular authorities if they attempt to implement deviant scientific theories even though their "religious" deviance goes unpunished.[18] If, therefore, scientific orthodoxy has replaced religious orthodoxy as the dominant cultural tradition in society, one would expect the cultic to be no more "accessible" now than in former decades.

This aspect of secularization theory has the implicit assumption that as the scientific worldview has significantly displaced the orthodox religious perspective on man and the universe, it will have no difficulty in overcoming the heterodox versions prevailing in the cultic milieu. The decline in the power and influence of the churches is thus counter-balanced by the rise of the power and influence of the scientific community. However, as soon as this assumption is made explicit, it is possible to observe the many difficulties which it presents. The basic incompatibility of science and religion is the central tenet underlying this assumption, and although such an incompatibility can be demonstrated at a philosophical level, it is by no means clear that the scientific and religious outlooks are behaviorally incongruous.[19] It is even less obvious that religion in all its forms should necessarily be in conflict with the scientific perspective. The potential for conflict would, in fact, appear to be greater for religions which emphasize a personal, and transcendent conception of God than those which hold to an impersonal, non-intervening and immanent notion of the divine. Even then some transcendental theologies are potentially more likely to come into conflict with science than others. It would indeed be unwarranted to assume that the conflict between evangelical Christianity and science which occurred in the nineteenth century was in any way the type-case of relationships between religion and science. If we accept that science's potential conflict with religion varies according to the nature of the religion concerned then it could well be the case that science is less likely to come into conflict with some of the religious systems prevailing in the cultic milieu than with the prevailing religious orthodoxy. The non-historical character of mystical religion, for example, means that a conflict similar to that which existed between Christianity and science over evolution is unlikely to occur. However, even if one were to assume that rationalization was occurring and the religious worldview was steadily being replaced by a "scientific worldview," it is still by no means obvious that this same view is that which prevails within the scientific community. The changeover from a religiously based to scientifically based culture does not remove the problem of maintaining a dominant orthodoxy in the face of the continuing threat of heterodoxy. In this respect the central question becomes, how effective is science as an agency of cultural control? Clearly effectiveness in this sense refers both to the problem of maintaining adherence to the dominant paradigms within each scientific discipline as well as, more importantly, maintaining adherence to the canons of scientific procedure, the premises of scientific enquiry and the ethos of science in general. There is, however, the additional problem of enforcing these norms on those outside the scientific community, and it is here that the contrast with the church is most noticeable. For it is to be doubted whether science as a body can compare with the churches in either their desire or their ability to repress heterodox views in the society at large. In part one could argue that the fundamentally democratic ethos of science means that the authoritarian measures employed in the past by the churches are not available to them. In addition, unlike the church, they lack a thoroughgoing mandate for concerning themselves with the beliefs of non-scientists. Thus, although they may have measures for enforcing orthodoxy upon the scientific community, for example by effectively ostracizing the "heretic," even this conformity may be achieved at the price of exacerbating the problem of heresy in society at large. It is only in fact the realm of applied science and particularly with regard to the practice of medicine that one finds a situation which in any way resembles the traditional manner in which the churches attempted to control the spread of heresies such as witchcraft. But even here secular sanctions against those who practice a "false" art or science of healing are not very severe or all-embracing and the trend is, if anything, toward greater tolerance of such heterodox systems as homeopathy, chiropractic and acupuncture. In sum, it does not appear as if science will necessarily be able to enforce any more cultural conformity upon society than the churches were able to do; indeed they could well be less effective.

There remains the question of whether it is reasonable to assume that the scientific viewpoint will spread through society even without any determined efforts being made to suppress heresies. Might not the enormous influence and prestige of science together with expanding institutions of education result in the gradual acceptance of the orthodox scientific outlook as "demonstrably superior" to any other? Once again the argument is more complex than it might at first seem. The demonstrable superiority of science is in many cases just not demonstrable or in other cases only demonstrable to other scientists. Even more important, the inferiority of alternative systems may only be clearly demonstrable to other scientists. Even where a system is seen to be inferior to orthodox science in its explanatory power, it may be preferred because it is more easily understood, more accessible, or more comprehensive. The principal difficulty with this hypothesis, however, is that there is no guarantee that even those people who are impressed by the demonstrable superiority of science and as a consequence desire to hold a scientific outlook will in fact be in a position to distinguish between what are orthodox and what are heterodox scientific views. They may, as a consequence, end up believing in flying saucers and ESP because of the convincing scientific "evidence." Thus there are good grounds for doubting whether an increase in prestige of science will automatically lead to a consolidation of its position as a widely accepted belief system.

Summary and Conclusion

An adequate conceptualization of the cult and some formulation of hypotheses concerning cultic phenomena is becoming an increasingly necessary task as traditionally cultic beliefs become both more visible and more accessible within society. The established approach to the study of cults, which takes the highly successful study of sects as its model, appears to promise less than an approach which concentrates on the cultic milieu in general. Such a milieu is defined as the sum of unorthodox and deviant belief systems together with their practices, institutions and personnel and constitutes a unity by virtue of a common consciousness of deviant status, a receptive and syncretistic orientation and an interpenetrative communication structure. In addition, the cultic milieu is united and identified by the existence of an ideology of seekership and by seekership institutions. Both the culture and the organizational structure of this milieu represent deviant forms of the prevailing religious and scientific orthodoxies in combination with both instrumental and expressive orientations. Two important elements within the milieu are the religious tradition of mysticism and the personal service practices of healing and divination.

A consideration of the relationship of this milieu to orthodox culture suggests that the imputed processes of secularization may be creating circumstances favorable to the growth of the milieu and the further expansion of cultic beliefs throughout society. The changeover from a dominant religious orthodoxy to a dominant scientific orthodoxy does not seem to correspond to any greater control of heterodox societal beliefs, for while the decline in power of organized

ethical religion appears to have removed the most effective control over heretical religious beliefs, a growth in the prestige of science results in the absence of
control of the beliefs of non-scientists and in an increase in quasi-scientific beliefs. Ironically enough, therefore, it could be that the very processes of secularization which have been responsible for the "cutting back" of the established
form of religion have actually allowed the "hardier varieties" to flourish, or possibly created the circumstances for the emergence, not of a secular scientific
society, but of a society centered on a blend of mysticism, magic and pseudo-
science.

Notes

[1] See H. Becker's remark that cult is a "less useful" as well as a less used concept in
sociology (T.F. O'Dea in the *International Encyclopedia of the Social Sciences*).

[2] John Lofland, *Doomsday Cult*, Prentice Hall, Englewood Cliffs, NJ, 1966; David Martin, *A Sociology of English Religion*, Heinemann and SCM Press, 1967.

[3] G.K. Nelson, "The Spiritualist Movement and the Need for a Redefinition of Cult,"
Journal for the Scientific Study of Religion, vol. 8, no. 1, spring 1969; "The Concept of
Cult," *Sociological Review*, New Series, vol. 16, no. 3, November 1968.

[4] E. Troeltsch, *The Social Teachings of the Christian Church*, Macmillan 1931

[5] L. Von Wiese and Howard Becker, *Systematic Sociology*, NY, 1932; W.E. Mann, *Sect,
Cult and Church in Alberta*, University of Toronto Press, 1955; Martin E. Marty, "Sects
and Cults," *The Annals of the American Academy of Political and Social Science,*
CCCXXXII, November 1960, pp. 125-34; David Martin, *Pacifism: An Historical and
Sociological Study*, Routledge & Kegan Paul, 1965; J. Milton Yinger, *Religion, Society
and the Individual*, Macmillan, New York, 1957; J.A. Jackson and R. Jobling, "Toward
an Analysis of Contemporary Cults," in *A Sociological Yearbook of Religion in Britain*,
ed., David Martin, SCM Press 1968; G.K. Nelson, *op. cit.*

[6] Lofland, *op. cit.* Lofland and R. Stark "Becoming a World-Saver: A Theory of Conversion to a Deviant Perspective," *American Sociological Review*, vol. 30 (6), December
1965, pp. 862-75.

[7] Lofland, *op. cit.* Lofland and Stark, *art. cit.* H. Taylor Buckner, "The Flying Saucerians:
An Open Door Cult" in *Sociology and Everyday Life*, ed. S.M. Truzzi, Prentice-Hall,
Englewood Cliffs, NJ, 1968, pp. 223-30.

[8] G.K. Nelson *art. cit.*(1969).

[9] E. Troeltsch, *op. cit.*, p. 744.

[10] Leon Festinger, Henry Riecken and Stanley Schacter, *When Prophecy Fails*, University
of Minnesota Press, Minneapolis, 1956; Lofland, *op. cit.*, Taylor Buckner, *art. cit.*

[11] Charles Y. Glock and Rodney Stark, *Religion and Society in Tension*, Rand, McNally
& Co., Chicago, 1965, p. 257; Martin E. Marty, *op. cit.*

[12] This appears to be the general trend of Bryan Wilson's work; see "A Typology of
Sects," *Acts de la X Conference Internationale* (1969), Rome, *CISR* (1969), pp. 29-56.

[13] See Troeltsch, *op. cit.* p. 745.

[14] H.T. Dohrman, *California Cult*, Beacon Press, Boston, 1958; Taylor Bucker *art. cit.*;
Lofland and Stark, *art. cit.*

[15] Lofland and Stark, *art. cit.*, p. 868.

[16] Taylor Buckner, *art. cit.*, p. 229.

[17] Can we, for example, envisage a time when covens will be registered as religious bodies for tax purposes?

[18] The treatment of scientology in Australia and Britain is an interesting example of this.

[19] See, for example, this discussion in Glock and Stark, *op. cit.*, pp. 262-88.

CHAPTER
3

Diggers, Wolves, Ents, Elves and Expanding Universes

Bricolage, Religion, and Violence from Earth First! and the Earth Liberation Front to the Antiglobalization Resistance

Bron Taylor

> *Monkeywrenching or "ecotage" is a form of worship toward the earth. It's really a very spiritual thing to go out and do. You are doing sacred work and you should have to live up to that responsibility, to that sacredness. . . . Keep a pure heart and mind . . . You are a religious warrior for the Earth.*
> —Dave Foreman, co-founder of the Radical Environmental group "Earth First!" discussing the spirituality of direct action resistance.

> *ATWA—Air, Trees, Water, Animals. ATWA is your survival on earth. It's a revolution against pollution. ATWA is ATWAR with pollution—a holy war. You are either working for ATWA—life—or you're working for death. Fix it and live or run from it and die.*
> —Charles Manson, from the ATWA Internet site

> *Anyone who will read the anarchist and radical environmentalist journals will see that opposition to the industrial-technological system is widespread and growing.*
> —Ted Kaczynski (also known as the Unabomber) in his manifesto, "Industrial Society and Its Future"

Global Bricolage and Interpretive Issues in the Cultic Milieu

As environmental degradation intensifies, so do environment-related conflicts fueled by competing economic interests and divergent religious worldviews. The preceding epigraphs pose more questions than they answer but illustrate the potential for violence in contemporary environmental disputes.

What are we to make of such diverse rhetoric: justifying by Christian principle and religious vision the bombing of a "pro-choice" political activist who had been defending ancient forests; viewing earth as a sacred being and sabotage as a venerating act; urging widespread arson and other attacks to bring down Western industrial civilization; labeling the war against pollution as a holy war. What are we to make of the similar martial, revolutionary, and misanthropic rhetoric expressed by self-identified radical environmentalists, on the one hand, and racist visionaries like Charles Manson, on the other? Are these kindred movements?

Charles Manson apparently thinks so. When asked, "Are you familiar with, or in contact with the more radical environmental groups [such as] Earth First!, Sea Shepherds, ALF [the Animal Liberation Front], etc.?" he answered in his usual cryptic manner, "We started the root thoughts for most or a lot."[1] Perhaps, if Manson is right, we should expect a proliferation of "Helter-Skelter" like terror in proportion to growth of such movements. Apart from the link claimed by Manson, many others are fanning such fears. Charles Cushman, for example, of the pro-development Multiple Use Land Alliance, thinks that forest defenders, by promoting "a new pagan religion, worshiping trees and animals and sacrificing people" have initiated "a holy war between fundamentally different religions."[2]

Such fears are lent credence by scholars who warn that radical environmentalism promotes an atavistic primitivism reminiscent of Nazi preoccupations with blood and soil,[3] or who criticize the irrationality they believe characterizes radical environmental spirituality.[4] Even Michael Zimmerman, an early and prominent proponent of "deep ecology" (a philosophy developed by the Norwegian Arne Naess positing that nature has value apart from its usefulness to humans), who had been drawing on the anti-modernist and anti-technological writings of Martin Heidegger for his constructive efforts, dramatically reversed field, embracing enlightenment liberalism when confronted with Heidegger's Nazi past.[5]

Such concerns first confronted me when attending a workshop exploring deep ecology at a wilderness gathering of Earth First! activists in southeastern Oregon in 1991. The workshop was led by Bill Devall, who co-authored the book *Deep Ecology* (1985), an early and influential book that helped promote, popularize, and build the Earth First! movement in North America. During this small workshop with about a dozen participants, his protégée Kevin Browning, commenting on articles by Earth First! activists that had been denounced by other movement activists as racist, stated that he would take "even the KKK into the movement if they put earth first." No one challenged this statement, after which Devall denounced the "political correctness" of those placing a priority on cultural pluralism. During a later workshop on "ecotopia"—a popular movement term for the hopes of an ecological utopia coined by Ernest Callenbach with his 1975 novel *Ecotopia*—Devall's position became more clear when he got into a brief debate with other Earth First!ers who felt that movement people should promote and defend simultaneously both cultural and ecological diversity. Devall stressed that the movement's first priority must be the creation of a "bioregional community" whose identity is rooted in a place.

Perhaps Browning's statement was mere hyperbole—but its poignancy was underscored when I read a call on the Manson Internet site for all lovers of ATWA to rally to the defense of the Headwaters Redwood Forest in Northern California—thereby enlisting in a campaign initiated and led by Earth First! activists. Is there fertile ground for an alliance between the racist right and radical environmentalists in the battle to save the planet?

Colin Campbell's discussion of the cultic milieu could be used to suggest the likelihood of such a possibility. He argues that a cultic milieu exists as a "constant feature of society" representing "the cultural underground of society" including "all deviant belief systems and their associated practices [including] unorthodox science, alien and heretical religion [and] deviant medicine."[6] He suggests that cultic groups "rarely engage in criticism of each other [and] display a marked tolerance and receptivity toward each others' beliefs"—especially because they share a "mystical tradition emphasiz[ing] that . . . unity with the divine can be attained by a diversity of paths."[7] Campbell also asserts that mysticism is "the most prominent part of the deviant religious component of the cultic world,"[8] and believes that consequently, cults tend "to be ecumenical . . . syncretistic, and tolerant in outlook," and moreover, that the fragmentation of ideas and groups that characterizes the cultic milieu is *"more than counteracted by the continuing pressure to syncretization"*[9] (my emphasis).

Since nature mysticism does permeate radical environmental subcultures,[10] and sometimes the racist right,[11] it does make sense to inquire about possible linkages and to wonder whether the cultural "tent" of the cultic milieu is pitched so broadly that radical environmentalists, and those from the racist right, might cross paths underneath it. Do they, or might they, reciprocally influence one another, even fusing syncretistically into new and more violent forms?

To address this question, we certainly must attend to countercultural processes of syncretism and bricolage within the cultic milieu. Bricolage (amalgamations of many bits and pieces of diverse cultural systems) is a better term than syncretism (the blending of elements of two traditions) to label the cultural processes analyzed by Campbell. Whatever the name for such processes, an analysis of "the cultural process of stealing back and forth sacred symbols"[12] is crucial for understanding both the religious and the political dimensions of the cultic milieu. Not only is it illuminating to examine the process of bricolage with regard to the production of religion and the related processes in which religion and its production is contested and negotiated,[13] an analysis of bricolage can be equally illuminating when analyzing the explicitly political dimensions of the diverse ideological streams floating within countercultures of resistance.

I emphasize the importance of political bricolage because Campbell asserted that cultic milieu mysticism led "to a depreciation of [and] a general indifference to all secular affairs except the most personal."[14] That may have been true when Campbell wrote it, but when exploring ethnographically the subcultures of radical environmentalism I have found that the mystical is political because the mundane (namely the Earth) is sacred.[15] Consequently, within these contemporary "subcultures of resistance," the bits and pieces thrown into the cultic melting pot include a wide range of deviant political ideas and ideologies, from well-known leftist ones, to forms of green anarchism, and most importantly, to an anti-modernist (and sometimes anti-humanist) ideology, amalgamated from many streams of religious and political thought, fundamentally hostile to and challenging of all industrial societies, whether organized along capitalist or socialist lines.

These subcultural enclaves and worldviews were largely unknown before mass antiglobalization protests erupted in the United States and Europe.

Stirring in diverse political bits with the eclectic religious pieces leads to a very interesting and sometimes confusing subcultural stew. Certainly radical environmental subcultures include "unorthodox science, alien and heretical religion, [and] deviant medicine."[16] The subcultures of radical environmentalism also include at least as hefty a dose of orthodox science (indeed, radical environmentalists claim that their views of science cohere better with contemporary scientific understandings than the more prevalent, theistic views dominant in Western societies). The participants in these subcultures also appropriate from and express solidarity with almost every resistance or revolutionary movement believed to have an ecological dimension.[17]

It is important to emphasize at the outset the global flavor of this radical environmental, countercultural stew. Its ingredients—religious and political beliefs, strategies and tactics; theories and perceptions; myths and heroes; rituals and mysticism—are cultivated and gathered from many places and peoples, increasingly spread via the Internet. Certainly the global bricolage that characterizes radical environmentalism today demands a careful empirical analysis, untainted by the views of anti-cult groups or law enforcement adversaries.[18] The best way to approach the questions posed by the emergence and proliferation of radical environmental subcultures is to fuse textual and archival research with the kind of experience and intuitive knowledge that can only come from extended and extensive qualitative field work. This is the kind of research I have conducted since 1990 and am drawing upon in these pages.

Radical Environmentalism from Earth First! to the Earth Liberation Front

Wolves, Roadshows, and *The Monkey Wrench Gang*

Earth First!, with its slogan "no compromise in defense of mother earth," was founded in 1980. According to Dave Foreman, the most charismatic leader among its co-founders, a strategic rationale undergirded this decision to create a *radical* environmental movement: (1) to introduce and promote sabotage as well as civil disobedience as a means of environmental struggle; (2) to shame mainstream environmentalists into taking stronger stands through brutal criticism of them; and (3) by taking on the mantle of "environmental extremism," mainstream groups might appear more reasonable by comparison, thereby gaining influence and effectiveness (the "good-cop—bad-cop" strategy). As importantly, Foreman wanted to attack anthropocentric attitudes and argue instead that the natural world has value in itself, not only when useful to humans. He felt he was not allowed to speak passionately for such values while working for mainstream environmental organizations.

In the United States, Earth First! rapidly become known for its dramatic civil disobedience campaigns, and the occasional use of sabotage, in its efforts to thwart commercial incursions into the planet's few remaining

roadless areas.[19] Many if not most Earth First! activists ground this conviction in mystical experiences in the natural world. I have previously labeled
Earth First!'s religious orientation "primal spirituality" because many within
this subculture venerate and seek to learn from and emulate the world's remaining indigenous cultures, especially those cultures unassimilated into the
global market economy. They generally consider such cultures to be spiritually and ecologically wise, and wish to be in solidarity with them against
what they perceive to be the voracious appetite of industrial civilization.

Throughout the 1980s, the entree to Earth First! for many was
one or more of its many touring "roadshows," where typically, through music, photographs, and speeches, activists promoted eco-defense actions. I
attended perhaps the movement's archetypal rally when Dave Foreman himself gave an April 1990 presentation in Wisconsin. The crowd that evening
was large, no doubt swelled by Foreman's growing infamy as a leader of an
"outlaw" organization, fueled further by his arrest the previous year for allegedly funding efforts to sabotage power lines associated with a nuclear
power plant in Arizona, a crime for which he eventually pled guilty.

Foreman gave a spellbinding, Mark Twain-style rave. He began
by spinning a yarn about an encounter on the Colorado River with Interior
Department Secretary James Watt, the Reagan-era demon of environmental
calamity. In theatrical style, he recalled regaling and threatening Watt, only
to suffer an equally vituperative attack. Foreman then quietly offered the
story's lesson, that "rhetoric is not enough"; rather, in this very moment,
characterized by the greatest anthropogenic (human-caused) extinction crisis
in evolutionary history, it is time to act.

Throughout his performance, Foreman worked the crowd, weaving loud cascades of rhetoric with quieter moments, evoking reflection. After recounting several recent extinctions and reviewing dynamics threatening many more, he urged moral introspection, identifying the roots of
environmental degradation in the anthropocentric (human-centered) idea
that the land and its inhabitants are mere commodities for human consump-
tion. He urged instead that we appropriate John Muir's[20] perception that
everything in the universe is connected, and articulated what I would call an
ethics of *evolutionary kinship*, a perspective increasingly articulated by environmentalists and eco-philosophers alike: Since all species have evolved
through the same evolutionary process, they are kin and deserve treatment
that respects their own evolution-derived lifeways.[21]

It is such a perspective that led Foreman, with other radical environmental activists and many contemporary environmental philosophers,[22]
to conclude that *all life has value, apart from its usefulness to human beings, and thus, all life ought be allowed to continue its evolutionary unfolding.*[23] Despite disagreements about many things, this simple proposition
captures the central, moral claim of participants in radical environmental
and deep ecology subcultures.[24]   In the parlance of contemporary environmental philosophy, this is biocentric (life-centered) ethics, and its ubiquity
within deep ecology and radical environmental subcultures expresses a
common-denominator value that allows us to refer accurately to all of them
as "movement" and "emerging tradition"—even while recognizing great
diversity within these subcultures in the ways their adherents conceive of,
arrive at, and act upon such values.[25]

Toward the end of his rabble-rousing speech, Foreman gave the crowd various examples of environmental action to consider, both legal and illegal. He then built to his finale, referring to Aldo Leopold's book, *A Sand County Almanac,* calling it "the most beautiful and important book written in this [the twentieth] century." In this posthumously published volume, Leopold articulated a novel, biocentric "Land Ethic": An action "is right when it tends to preserve the integrity, stability, and beauty of the biotic community . . . [which includes] soils, waters, plants, and animals, or collectively: the land. . . . It is wrong when it tends otherwise." This perspective, Leopold wrote, "changes the role of *Homo sapiens* from conqueror of the land-community to plain member and citizen of it."[26]   Foreman recounted how this ethic was born in a wilderness epiphany Leopold had as a young man working for the newly formed U.S. Forest Service. While conducting a timber inventory, Leopold and his co-workers thoughtlessly killed a wolf. Decades later, Leopold wrote of this incident in words reminiscent of the Apostle Paul's conversion on the Damascus road. Foreman recounted Leopold's words from memory,

> We reached the old wolf in time to watch a fierce green fire dying in her eyes. I realized then, and I've realized ever since, there was something new to me in those eyes, something known only to the wolf and to the mountain. I was young then and full of trigger itch. Because fewer wolves meant more deer, I believed no wolves would mean hunter's paradise, but after watching the green fire die I realized that neither wolf nor mountain agreed with such a view.[27]

For Foreman, Leopold's story provides more than a land ethic. It also offers redemption: "What we need to do is remember how to think like a mountain. We need the green fire in the wolf's eyes. We need the green fire in our own eyes. . . . We need the cry of the wolf, the spirit of joy . . . defiance . . . and love that it can bring." Foreman was exhorting the assembly members to rediscover their own wild animal selves, believing that were they to do so, they would defend wildlands with passion and commitment.

To celebrate and symbolize this passion for the wild in the world—to connect with it and with the green fire encrusted within all humans—Foreman apparently borrowed a scene right out of *The Monkey Wrench Gang.*[28] This Edward Abbey novel celebrated the exploits of a band of ecoteurs intent on dynamiting the Glen Canyon Dam—which activists decry for desecrating Glen Canyon and enslaving the Colorado. It would be difficult to underestimate the importance of this "fictional" narrative on the radical environmental movement. Inspired by an already existing guerilla movement emerging in the southwestern United States, *The Monkey Wrench Gang* struck a chord, contributing to the proliferation of various monkey-wrench gangs after 1980, and as importantly for the present purposes, this book became a primary source for appropriation by movement activists. That night, Foreman borrowed from a grizzled character in the novel, George Washington Hayduke, who at one point let out a "long and prolonged, deep and dangerous, wild archaic howl" from the edge of a desert canyon.[29] In Hayduke's footsteps, Foreman exhorted the assembly:

Howl with me tonight! Howl with defiance! Robots don't howl. Computers don't howl. But animals do. And free women and men who love the earth howl. Don't ever let them take that from you! Howl with me tonight! Howl!

Two-thirds of the congregants did, rising in a standing ovation. The rest looked furtively askance at the wilder ones in their midst.[30]

This event suggested to me that Foreman and the movement he was promoting were engaged in new religious production, developing powerful myths and ritual forms, and prescribing ethical actions in defense of a nature considered sacred. In the subsequent years, as I studied intensively this movement, its religious dimensions and the ways it precipitated environment-related social conflict would become all the more clear.

The most common perception animating the movement can accurately be labeled "pagan," namely, a spirituality involving one or more of two perceptions: (1) the Earth itself is alive and sacred, a perception that for many could properly be labeled Pantheism (a word derived by conflating the Greek word *pan* meaning "all" and *theos* meaning "god," or "all is god."); and (2) that the world is filled with non-human intelligences—often thought to be capable of communicating and communing with humans—who are worthy of reverence. These perceptions, often labeled "animism" (from the Latin for "soul"), describe the belief that various entities in nature have souls or spirits.[31]

And the most common way the movement has precipitated environment-related social conflict is through "direct action," movement parlance for everything from traditional civil disobedience (conscientious lawbreaking and passive submittal to arrest in an effort to arose the conscience of the community and foster social change thereby, often related to boycotting of companies or industries engaged in destructive practices) to more aggressive efforts to physically stop such practices, for example, through sophisticated blockades and deconstruction of logging roads, as well as by clandestine sabotage and arson.[32]

Elvish Mischief and Wilderness 'Rendezvous'

The spirituality and politics of Earth First! are developed and contested at wilderness rendezvous, where activists gather in remote places to conduct workshops, bond, and engage in revelry and ritual.

At the first such gathering I attended, held in a northern Wisconsin forest during the summer of 1990, the workshop discussions began as people recalled their paths to Earth First!. During a subsequent strategy session, the discussion turned to monkeywrenching (movement parlance for ecological sabotage, or "ecotage"). This was unsurprising, since Earth First! was founded in part to provide a forum for such discussions and because ecotage, especially the forms that might risk harm to humans, had always been controversial.

The discussion began as two individuals expressed support for civil disobedience but discomfort with monkeywrenching, specifically mentioning tree spiking, the most widely known and controversial form of ecotage. (Tree spiking involves inserting metal, ceramic, or stone spikes into trees in an effort to prevent logging.) *Ecodefense* recommended against putting spikes "in the lower three feet of the tree, where they can cause chainsaw kickback and a remote but real possibility of injury to the feller." The primer continued, "We're in it to save trees, not hurt people . . . the object . . . is to destroy the blades in the sawmill . . . [creating a] long-term deterrent effect," namely, the scuttling of logging plans.[33]

That warm summer day a shaggy young man from northern Wisconsin volunteered that, with 100 dollars and two days, one could spike 100 wooded acres. He added that ecotage is a good antidote to depression. A few years later in the spring of 1993 his therapy was suspended when, for the first time in U.S. history, he and two others were arrested and thereafter convicted for a 1989 tree spiking incident in Idaho's Clearwater National Forest.[34]

After he expressed enthusiasm for tree spiking, however, others expressed reservations. One woman worried about the resulting bad publicity and that "it might not hurt the right person." She was unaware, apparently, that the tactic was not designed to hurt anybody. Another woman agonized about how their tactics sometimes made her feel like a religious fundamentalist. A young man in a tie-dyed shirt said he opposed monkeywrenching "both spiritually and practically—I don't think it will work, especially if it endangers someone."

In the ensuing discussion, one long-term activist stressed that ecotage need not endanger anyone; another urged that it be broadly construed to include "paper" monkeywrenching, namely lawsuits and writing.[35] "Violence has always been central to social change," countered another voice, suggesting that it has its time and place.

Another long-term activist tried to bridge the apparent gap, arguing that both civil disobedience and monkeywrenching were needed to promote the desired changes and that monkeywrenching is the only way some activists can make a difference because they are poor and could not afford to get arrested or file lawsuits. He then repeated the "economic warfare" justification for the tactic, arguing that Chris Manes in *Green Rage* proved that direct action can bankrupt the perpetrators of destruction, or buy time other activists need to file and win lawsuits.

Dave Foreman in *Ecodefense*, repeatedly described precautions to ensure "nobody gets hurt." The volume is periodically naive in this regard, however, and not only about tree spiking. It discusses various ways to flatten tires, for example, acknowledging that injuries to a "vehicle operator" might result. One might expect, consequently, a prescription to flatten the tires only of parked vehicles or those certain to be moving slowly. But soon afterward the book suggests that "perhaps the best use of caltrops [sharpened metal spikes fashioned like a child's jacks] is for security in the event you are being chased, a use well-illustrated in *The Monkey Wrench Gang*."[36] It is hard to imagine a more dangerous scenario than one where caltrops are dropped in front of pursuing vehicles, yet safety precautions about flattening tires were reserved for other situations.[37] A later article in *Earth First!* (Anonymous 2 February 1988) explicitly acknowledged a risk of injury from using road spikes, urging caution about their placement. Yet Bill Wood in *American Motorcyclist* asserted that a motorcyclist was injured when he swerved to avoid 200 caltrops placed in a high-speed area of the Barstow to

Las Vegas desert race. Ironically adopting rhetoric of the sacred to make his case, Wood concluded, "The other amazing thing about this act of terrorism is that it desecrated the very desert that the members of Earth First! pretend to be protecting."[38]

Whatever the facts of the case that Wood describes (which I could not independently verify), the discussions of tree spiking and tire flattening in *Ecodefense* illustrate the danger that when consequences are unforeseen violence can occur despite nonviolent intentions. (The issue of road spiking precipitated an early watershed in Earth First! history, when Pete Dustrud, the editor of *Earth First!*, was forced out of this position due to his discomfort with discussion of tactics that came to "border on outright violence," including a discussion of spiking roads with metal stakes.)[39]

It is not uncommon to hear naïve and romanticized exhortations regarding monkeywrenching at Earth First! gatherings. During my first wilderness rendezvous in Wisconsin, for example, while discussing the U.S. Forest Service's deforestation agenda, someone suggested "a national coordinated effort to firebomb, at the same time, all forest service offices." Another voice cautioned, "We're supposed to be nonviolent. Do it when there is nobody there." Arson has been increasingly deployed as a tactic, especially since the late 1990s by activists operating under the monikers Earth Liberation Front and Animal Liberation Front, and it continues to be described and defended as a nonviolent tactic.

For his part, despite his insistence that "Monkeywrenchers—although non-violent—are warriors,"[40] and despite the many safety precautions he urged activists to scrupulously apply, Foreman periodically engaged in inflammatory rhetoric that defended, at least, defensive violence. In 1982 he wrote, "We've been nice for too long. . . . I don't know about you, but I don't plan to fight with one hand tied behind my back. I might even have a shiv or some brass nucks in my boot."[41] He also likened the rape of the earth to attacks on one's family, "If you come home and find a bunch of Hell's Angels raping your wife, old mother, and eleven-year-old daughter, you don't sit down and talk balance with them and suggest compromise. You get your twelve-gauge shotgun and blow them to hell." Although he admires nonviolent approaches such as "advocated by Gandhi and Martin Luther King," he concluded, "unfortunately, I am still an animal. . . . I can not turn the other cheek."[42] He claimed in this article that "EARTH FIRST! does not advocate violence or monkeywrenching. That is an individual choice," but concluded that he would, nevertheless, discuss such tactics in the journal.

Unsurprisingly, this editorial engendered some strong disagreement, including from two prominent Buddhists, Robert Aitken and Gary Snyder.[43] Foreman responded to Aitken in a way similar to what I have heard other Earth First!ers say on several occasions since then, "Any creature, no matter how seemingly meek, will fight back when threatened." He then asserted, "Eastern [religious] ideas of stepping out of the violent cycle are presumptuous and anthropocentric (by setting human beings apart from the semi-violent natural world)" and concluded, "I am entirely pragmatic about violence/nonviolence. We should use whichever we feel comfortable with and whichever is most appropriate to a particular situation . . . . There are many paths one can take to defend our Earth Mother. Including that of the warrior."[44]

Foreman's statements about violence have often been ambiguous or inconsistent.[45] In "Strategic Monkeywrenching,"[46] and in *Confessions of an Ecowarrior*[47] under the heading "Monkeywrenching Is Not Revolutionary," Foreman wrote in a way that seemed to allow some room for tactics certain to be painted as violent: "Explosives, firearms and other dangerous tools are *usually* avoided [My emphasis]. They invite greater scrutiny from law enforcement agencies, repression and loss of public support."[48] Such ambivalence and ambiguity is easy to find in individual Earth First!ers and in the movement itself.

Moreover, many activists scoff at Foreman's claim that ecotage is not revolutionary, including Earth First! co-founder Mike Roselle:

> What we want is nothing short of a revolution. Fuck that crap you read in *Wild Earth* or *Confessions of an Eco-Warrior*. Monkeywrenching is more than just sabotage, and your (sic) goddamn right it's revolutionary! This is jihad, pal. There are no innocent bystanders, because in these desperate hours, bystanders are not innocent. We'll broaden our theater of conflict. What happens in Bangkok, Ho Chi Minh City, Rio de Janeiro, in the frozen and radioactive waters of Siberia does matter—even if it's not in our wilderness proposal. Everything, every assumption, every institution needs to be challenged. Now![49]

Another example of an overtly revolutionary understanding of ecotage can be found in a "Black Cat Sabotage Manual,"[50] which was advertised in *Earth First!* and quietly circulated in the mid 1990s. It was compiled as a supplement to *Ecodefense* and designed to be untethered to nonviolence principles it considered anthropocentric. It included firearms instruction reprinted from anarchist tabloids, and in one article, although demurring from offering instructions about making explosives, nevertheless passed on the availability of such recipes on the Internet's rec.arts.pyrotechnics Website. The manual also cited a 1985 arson attack to demonstrate the value of ecotage as a tactic of economic warfare: "Ecoteurs firebombed a $250,000 wood chipper in Hawaii which was grinding rainforest into fuel for sugar mills (without a permit and in violation of a court order). The company then went bankrupt."[51]

The possibility that movement activists might resort to life-threatening acts of arson was underscored when in the early morning hours of 31 October 1996, the Oakridge Ranger Station, located about 40 miles southeast of Eugene, Oregon—a U.S. Forest Service office at the epicenter of long and contentious battles over logging—was burned to the ground, causing an estimated 9 million dollars worth of damage. On the roof of the Detroit Ranger Station seventy miles to the north, another incendiary device had failed to ignite. Graffiti left by the arsonists suggested involvement by the Earth Liberation Front (known by the acronym ELF), an anarchistic offshoot from England's Earth First! that formed in 1992.[52] "Tara the Sea Elf" accounced in *Earth First!* that the elves had created twenty clandestine cells in England by 1993, subsequently coordinating numerous attacks (including arson) on corporations in Europe and North America.[53]

In the United States, many of the most radical of Earth First! and green anarchist activists quickly adopted the ELF moniker, seeming emboldened by it. By mid 1999, arson and ecotage conducted by those operating mostly under the ELF or Animal Liberation Front (ALF) monikers was estimated at over 40 million dollars in 11 western states alone, nearly 30 million of which occured since the Sea Elf's 1996 announcement.[54] Targets included automobile dealers selling gas-guzzling sport-utility vehicles, "trophy homes" being constructed in or near wildlands, and research facilities believed engaged in genetic engineering. In the most expensive single incident, with a loss estimated at 12 million dollars, a mountaintop lodge at the Vail, Colorado, ski resort was burned in an act of resistance to its plans to expand into a forest designated by some biologists as "critical habitat" for the endangered lynx.

The ELF also provided a tent under which the increasingly plural bricolage of radical environmentalism could continue to evolve, one in which diverse revolutionary ideologies would cross-fertilize with various understandings of deep ecology and animal liberation. The ELF moniker caught on rapidly partly because it provided a rubric for putting a positive spin on the most radical of actions (elves are viewed positively in western literature as playfully mischievous, not malicious), and partly because the idea of elves in the woods cohered with the pagan spiritualities of many of these activists. Indeed, the ELF "perpetuates the legends of the 'Little People,' which in most European countries have a history of causing trouble, being mischievously always heard, but never seen. These 'mythical creatures' lived close to the earth in most legends," according to Sea Elf Tara.[55] These elves function as fairies do for other radical environmental activists— they are appropriated as symbolic earth warriors—conjuring images that resonate with the pagan spirituality animating many activists. All such groups, Tara concluded, both radical environmental ones and groups like the militant American Indian Movement "reflect the philosophy of many First Nations [indigenous peoples] across the world, that you have to show your enemy how serious you are in defending what you regard as sacred."[56] Nevertheless, Elves and their sympathizers usually emphasize nonviolence but do not consider property damage violent: "As always, ELF calls for no injury to life, only to profit and property."[57] Given the revolutionary rhetoric, this may seem an odd injunction, but most radical environmentalists believe that they cannot directly confront industrial nation states by force of arms. The apparent contradiction suggests that it is difficult for radical environmentalists to resolve their feelings about violence or achieve consensus about it.

After the Oakridge arson, for example, I heard several Earth First!ers express anger and dismay, acknowledging that one of the more anarchistic Earth First! brethren could well be responsible. I also heard several voices privately expressing approval of the action, or less strongly, stating they were not going to lose any sleep over it. Meanwhile, others wondered privately, and suggested to the media, that movement enemies could be responsible, trying to discredit the nonviolent resistance.[58]

Over the years I have heard many different voices on strategy and tactics, occasionally including the kind of martial rhetoric sometimes voiced by the elves. Yet in such cases, like that first weekend in Wisconsin when one activist blurted out, "We are at war—we can't refrain from anything," moderating voices often respond. On that occasion, one of the long-term Earth First! activists cautioned, "We need to distinguish monkeywrenching from war. In war or terrorism you kill a person. With monkeywrenching, you try to stop the unconscionable activity. We don't want to kill the logger [or] capitalist."

The preceding analysis suggests that in movement debates and history, there are many differences regarding strategic priorities and tactics. Yet there are significant agreements too, which make it possible to speak about radical environmentalism in the singular tense, as *a* movement with *a* worldview—despite its diverse factions, power struggles, and contested issues. In radical environmental subcultures, a process of global bricolage is at work—the borrowing and amalgamation (combined with creative invention) of bits and pieces of largely deviant (or alternative) religious and political ideas and practices. I will now examine in more detail first the religious and then the political dimensions of this global bricolage process, and how these shape tactical decisions.

The Bricolage of Radical Environmental Religion

Put briefly, religion is the human cultural process by which people orient themselves to that which they consider sacred.[59] To understand the religious dimensions of radical environmentalism we must understand what its participants consider sacred, and examine ways its myths, symbols, rites and ethics are being invented and prescribed, borrowed and creatively amalgamated. This reveals that, with sufficient creativity, almost anything is ripe for appropriation into the amalgamated and fluid religion of radical environmentalism. By examining the wild process of bricolage within radical environmentalism, I will illuminate further its *worldview*.

Myths, of course, provide narratives about how the world came to be (a cosmogony), what it is like (a cosmology), what people are like and capable or incapable of achieving (a moral anthropology), and what the future holds (an eschatology). Ethical norms are deduced from these narrative elements or presented forthrightly in them. It is important also to remember that religious traditions are plural, they are neither monolithic nor static, they are characterized by ongoing controversies over who owns, interprets and performs the myths, rituals, and rites.[60] This characteristic makes it possible—even given great internal plurality, for certain core beliefs, behaviors, and values to sufficiently unify a disparate group so as to make it possible to speak of its members as participating in a tradition.[61]

Such unifying themes can be found in Earth First!,[62] but a question arises whether this holds true as green anarchists increased their representation in the movement, beginning in the mid 1980s, and even more since then, to where by the summer of 2001, it was widely noticed that the anarchist contingent seemed on the verge of constituting a new majority within the movement. This transpired as their influence increased as a result of long and wrenching power struggles, which I cannot detail here, but that had the effect of driving many non-anarchists out of Earth First! and creating the conditions for more anarchists to immigrate to Earth First!, finding it an increasingly hospitable habitat for their activism.

The earliest such power struggles precipitated the 1990 resignations of the entire staff of the *Earth First!* journal and the withdrawal of Dave Foreman from the movement he, more than any other individual, helped to instigate. Foreman and John Davis (who he had installed as editor of the journal several years before these resignations) went on to found *Wild Earth,* drawing most movement intellectuals with them. Foreman, Reed Noss, Rod Mondt, David Johns, and others soon created the Wildlands Project, a long-term endeavor to create connected wilderness areas large enough to sustain viable populations of all native species.

There were various dimensions to the 1990 schism,[63] the most important of which was the influx of anarchists who harshly criticized Edward Abbey, Dave Foreman, and others whom they perceived to be insensitive to social justice issues. Some of the disputes were grounded on differing perceptions about the United States and Western civilization, both of which the anarchists wished to dismantle. Dave Foreman, however, despite sometimes expressing rhetoric that seemed to share such a view, and despite being (ironically) responsible for drawing anarchists to Earth First!, never demonized the government or Western civilization in as comprehensive a fashion as did the anarchists.

He recently stated, for example, "Western civilization (imperialism) and the United States of America deserve plenty of criticism. . . . But the United States is not wholly evil. No other nation can come close to the United States on protection of civil liberties. The Bill of Rights is recognized as the United States' great gift to the world. And we have given the world an even greater gift: the idea of National Parks and Wilderness Areas."[64]

Most green anarchists would scoff at such statements and one indicator of this is their pejorative label for his new journal, "mild earth." Many of these anarchist Earth First!ers disavow Dave Foreman, as he does them: "The group calling itself Earth First! today is not the group Howie Wolke and I started. Earth First! ended in the late 80s. The name and some of the assets were appropriated by people with an entirely different perspective and approach."[65]

What both parties to this dispute tend to downplay is their fundamental agreement about the intrinsic (or inherent) value of the non-human world and the need to defend it aggressively. Foreman and his allies often feel that those who are engaged in various social justice campaigns are not *really* biocentric. Often this is true of newcomers and those anarchists who have not jettisoned the anthropocentrism that until recently has characterized most anarchist thought. On the other hand, many green anarchists consistently advocate a world transformed by biocentric values, believing species can only be saved by comprehensively reordering human society along egalitarian lines. If there is a marker identifying a place where biocentric anarchists and deep ecologists agree, it may be in their nature-related epistemology, their view of how one comes to know spiritual truth and the ultimate value of life on Earth.

Natural Epistemology and Listening to the Land

We can again start with Dave Foreman's views, which express this epistemological premise. Basing his views in part on influential historians who trace anti-wilderness attitudes to Christianity,[66] Foreman once argued:

> Our problem is a spiritual crisis. The Puritans brought with them
> a theology that saw the wilderness of North America as a haunt
> of Satan, with savages as his disciples and wild animals as his

demons—all of which had to be cleared, defeated, tamed, or killed. Opening up the dark forests became a spiritual mission: to flush evil out of hiding. If we are going to survive in North America, we have to go back, metaphorically, to that pilgrim shore again. Let's seek to learn from the land this time.[67]

Foreman believes that if we are to reharmonize our lifeways within nature we must "learn from the land" herself. This epistemological premise signals an animistic or pantheistic spiritual perception.

The key to the puzzle of people like Foreman who regularly express religious views while not feeling particularly religious *may* be found in beliefs like Foreman's: that cultivating a proper spiritual perception requires "personal relationship to the natural world" which in turn requires time spent outdoors.[68] This does not seem to fit what many people would label "religion," yet there is a near-consensus about this within radical environmental subcultures. Dolores LaChapelle, for example, who was influential early in the evolution of deep ecology, includes in her books instructions about "how to set up structures so that nature herself . . . can once again begin to teach you."[69] Many other books, such as *Deep Ecology*,[70] *Green Rage*,[71] and *The Spell of the Sensuous*[72] similarly urge people to learn to listen to the land itself. It is hard to miss the paganism in such "listen to the land" epistemologies.

If time spent in wild places is the most powerful means of connecting to a sacred, natural world, this poses a problem for the movement: How can citified humans break through to such perceptions? This is an important *strategic* question for movement activists. One partial answer is that people have within their own bodies sufficient evidence of wildness and its value: so for some, promoting wildness among urban people "by all possible means," from anarchist rebellion to the radical sex community—might contribute to the arousal of the wild, ecological self.

Roadshows, the Arts, and Green Fire

A more prevalent and typical answer, however, is that many types of music and drama, poetry and prose, and visual art can reach people on an emotional and spiritual level when rational argument cannot. Like wilderness itself, such art can evoke in receptive humans the affective, intuitively available knowledge of the true, wild self that is deeply rooted in the sacred natural world in all her diverse forms. Such a moral anthropology undergirds the evangelical strategy of much deep ecological activism, including the roadshows.

We earlier saw the importance of Leopold's story of the wolf's dying green fire in Dave Foreman's roadshow performance. This narrative urges us to "think like a mountain," another way of exhorting, "listen to the land." Such a message I have seen on movement bumper stickers, and it was consistently conveyed by various performers in roadshows across America since 1981. When viewing these roadshows through the lenses of the study of religion, such performances appear as ritual.

Ritual focuses attention on the sacred and corresponding moral duties—and roadshows are an important form of movement ritualizing. They attempt, for example, to address the movement's epistemological presuppositions by bringing an experience of the wild right to urban humans, both through photographic-transparency presentations of pristine wilderness and through music. The implicit belief is that, even through these photographic proxies, the land itself can speak to us—receptive humans recognize the value of pristine places when we see them. Sometimes these photographs are juxtaposed with photographs of landscapes devastated by logging. Many activists believe that even damaged landscapes can speak to the heart, that people intuitively know, when they see it, that clearcut logging is wrong.[73] Receptive humans immediately and intuitively recognize destroyed wildlands as desecrated places.

Perhaps the central mythic narrative at these roadshows is Leopold's epiphany with the wolf. The wolf's "green fire" was appropriated not only by Dave Foreman, but in various ways in each of a series of Earth First! performers throughout the 1980s and 1990s. Some of these were even called "green fire" roadshows, including a tour in 1989 and 1990 performed by Roger Featherstone and Earth First! balladeer "Dakota" Sid Clifford. Clifford's own "green fire" ballad provided the musical climax for these roadshows, which he later labeled "ecovangelism."[74] Featherstone enlisted green fire in an effort to ameliorate mounting internal tensions that had accompanied the growth and growing diversity of Earth First! Such growth is fine as long as it is of passionate wildness and green fire, Featherstone admonished. In a cheerleading-like cadence, he then asked rhetorically, "WHAT MAKES THE EARTH FIRST! MOVEMENT? Green Fire! WHAT SETS US APART? Green Fire! WHAT IS OUR GREATEST STRENGTH? Green Fire! WHAT IS OUR MESSAGE? Green Fire!" Then addressing criticisms the male-dominated "old guard" of the movement had been facing, he continued, "What would the movement be without our 'drunk and ignorant' image, our 'fuck the human race' chanters, our misanthropy?" Nowhere, he replied, because "we need our wild side as surely as we need our brains." So, "Viva the revolution" and "burn those dozers."[75]

To summarize, although a central component of Earth First! roadshows has been to impart the central cognitive claims of the movement regarding the ecological crisis and the political and economic obstacles preventing effective responses to it, there is an abiding epistemological assumption undergirding all of them. Roadshows will fail unless they evoke our affective and spiritual connections to wild nature and thereby arouse to action the wild human believed to reside in each of us. Perhaps for this reason, all the roadshows I have witnessed appropriate Leopold's story. The wolf and its "green fire" has become a totemic symbol of life in the wild, about what life can and should be like, and this view is now deeply embedded in the ritual life of this emerging tradition. Moreover, by encouraging "thinking like a mountain" (at least metaphorically), this narrative represents an affinity with animistic and pantheistic beliefs: The wolf and other creatures, as well as the mountain itself, have their own points of view, which receptive humans can apprehend. It may be that the green fire narrative, adopted from a man who may be judged by history to be the twentieth century's most influential ecologist, is in the process of becoming the radical environmental movement's central mythic narrative, an animistic one expressing kinship among, and the possibility of communication among, humans and other natural entities.

Primal Spirituality and Shamanism

Of course, animal-human communication is a common concern of primal religions, and animal-human and human-animal transmogrification and communion are a part of shamanism. Many Earth First!ers report having had shamanistic experiences, which they generally believe to be available among a wide variety of primal peoples.

Some Earth First!ers have gained such experiences from various spiritual practitioners within the cultic milieu that is the New Age. Afterward, some of these Earth First!ers then have imported such practices into radical environmental venues. Moreover, since the New Age movement is involved in a widespread appropriation from Native American and other indigenous cultures, this movement is sometimes the vehicle by which bits of Native American ceremonies are brought into radical environmental subcultures. Despite this influence (about which many ordinary activists are probably unaware), many radical environmentalists express contempt for New Age religion. Nevertheless, this contempt inheres more to the political complacency and "flaky" otherworldliness of many New Agers, and to an utter contempt for any optimistic, golden "Age of Aquarius" eschatology, than to the affinity some New Agers have for primal cultures and religion.[76]

Michael Lewis provides a representative expression of the view that shamanism is an ecologically appropriate form of spirituality.

> Primitive humans knew that the world of dreams, myths, religion and imagination was as real as the "hard" world around them. It was important to be able to enlist the aid of the creatures of the mythic world in dealing with the everyday problems of the physical world. . . . The shaman travels to the other world, enlists the aid of the appropriate spirit and returns by the same path to bring the spirit to help the patient cure himself. . . . The shaman acts as a bridge between the two worlds, enlisting the aid of the spirit world to help solve problems in the physical, and carrying the expressions of appreciation from the physical to the spiritual. . . . Through shamanic journeys, vision quests, sweats, drumming and dancing, the shaman becomes as familiar with the spirit world as we are with our own . . . the important lesson in the shamanic approach to life is the view of the universe as an integrated, living whole. . . . If Mother Earth is indeed a living, breathing body of this Being, then we can communicate and cooperate with the Great Mother and with each part of the Mother Corpus. As we dream, hallucinate and create visions, so does Gaia, and these visions are . . . our means of communication with the Earth Mother and with her other co-inhabitants.[77]

Lewis concluded this article by encouraging people to seek shamanic experiences, such as those available from "several organized 'schools' of shamanism, such as the Sun Bear Tribe."[78]

The recommended shamanism schools fit well, for analytic purposes, under the New Age umbrella. And interestingly, several prominent activists who lead various types of spiritual workshops or movement ritualizing have been participants in the groups led by Native Americans, such as Sun Bear and Wallace Black Elk, who provide ritual experiences such as Sweat Lodge ceremonies and vision quests to non-Indians.[79]

A number of others have attended the workshops led by anthropologist turned neo-shamanist Michael Harner, who wrote the influential *Way of the Shaman* and created a Foundation for Shamanic Studies to promote shamanic journeying and healing. Still others have participated in various "breathwork" workshops, which are supposed to induce altered states of consciousness and promote "shamanic journeying" into spirit worlds and the acquisition of "power animals" and "spirit allies" in a quest to enhance the ability of participants to live properly on earth. A small number of radical environmental activists have, after participation in such workshops, taken it as their primary calling *and* ecological strategy to deepen their shamanic experience and promote widely this kind of experience among activists and non-activists alike.[80]   Indeed, some radical environmentalists believe that the environmental crisis is so grave that the only chance to arrest the presently unfolding environmental catastrophe is by fostering a massive change in human consciousness through such spiritual practice.

John Seed, a prominent international Earth First! activist from Australia who has been active in Earth First! since the early 1980s, participating in many roadshows in Australia and the United States since that time, has helped construct and disseminate widely in the United States, Australia, and Europe the ritual process known as the "Council of All Beings."[81] No other ritual process invented since the emergence of the radical environmental and deep ecology movements has been more important than the Council of All Beings.

Reputedly most effective when conducted over an entire weekend, the Council is an eclectic "ritual of inclusion" designed to connect participants in a loving way with earth and all her species as well as to bond participants together and motivate them to engage in environmental defense. The ritual is also a perfect example of an eclectic global bricolage, appropriating elements from Native American spirituality (a brief, animistic vision quest, among other things); science-based scientific narratives about the unfolding universe and biological evolution of life on earth; and pagan songs including several celebrating Gaia or otherwise venerating earth itself. Perhaps because the process was developed primarily by Joanna Macy and John Seed, two practicing Buddhists, the majority of exercises were borrowed and adapted from Buddhism.

In one of the most amusing bits of movement bricolage, a song written by Monty Python humorist Erik Idle, "Expanding Universe," was stolen for the ritual (it is also sung on other movement occasions). Seed, however, did not like the nihilistic and disempowering ending: "So remember when you're feeling very small and insecure / How amazingly unlikely is your birth"—so he wrote four new stanzas—"So sink your roots deep into the galaxy / Dance your life, Planet Earth / Sink your roots deep into reality / Dance your life *for* Planet Earth." Thereby, Seed transformed the song into a celebration of the miracle of a life mystically embedded in this earthly spot in the universe—and lived out in defense of her. Certainly, here is creative myth-making, a fascinating adaptation of scientific narrative for religious purpose.[82]

"Ecopsychology" provides another ritual resource for radical environmentalism, and much of this can be viewed as another form of neo-shamanism growing under the New Age tent. An influential branch has been pioneered by the psychiatrist Stanislov Grof, whose "holotropic breathwork workshops," induce altered states of consciousness "journeys" by combining a ritualized breathing practice influenced by and reminiscent of various Eastern meditative traditions, and blending this with the playing of sacred music from diverse cultures around the world. As the music is changed from that originating from primal cultures, to Bach and Mozart, to Gregorian chant, to the theme song from *The Mission* (a film depicting a tragic resistance by indigenous rainforest dwellers to Euroamerican conquistadors in what is now southern Brazil), these workshops and such music represent global bricolage. By likening these workshop processes to the shamanic practices of primal cultures, these workshops have drawn interest from some radical environmentalists.

Grof himself was one of the early experimenters with LSD and other hallucinogenic plants.[83] Interest in shamanism, "ethno-botany," and hallucinogens—as vehicles for altering consciousness and fostering proper and beneficent understandings of the human place on earth—is strong among some radical environmentalists and prevalent within the "ecopsychology" movement. Ecopsychology is an outgrowth of the spiritual streams of the human potential movement in the 1960s and 1970s and seems to be rapidly growing in the United States, largely within the spiritual-therapeutic sectors of the New Age movement.[84] A striking recent development is the growing cross-fertilization between deep ecology, even its politically radical streams, and this generally quiescent, middle-class subculture. Archetypal psychologist James Hillman, and a variety of ecopsychology-oriented institutes such as the Elmwood Institute, now express affinity with deep ecology. Of course, much of the ecopsychology movement has deep roots in the archetypal psychology of Carl Jung— providing thus another intriguing European piece to the bricolage process.

Despite all this, it should also be stressed that many Earth First! activists look down at organized workshops and overt ritualizing as unnecessary (and/or, contrived), again because all one must do is spend extended time in nature to encounter the sacred and its denizens. And many activists do report experiences and perceptions of interspecies communication independent of any orchestrated ritualizing, simply from spending time, attentively, in the wild; or while performing acts of civil disobedience, sitting on platforms in trees, or buried in logging roads for prolonged periods of time in efforts to prevent logging.[85]

Given their respect for and interest in primal cultures, however, there is a strong impulse for radical environmental activists to be drawn to Native American spiritualities. One such activist, Lou Gold, a former university professor who dropped out of mainstream society and eventually became a prominent member of Ancient Forest in Oregon, explained

> I don't consider myself a follower of Native American religion. . . . my spirituality is soup, it is stew . . . but when it's time to find the right metaphors, I find [Native American] metaphors come easily to me [and have become] a source of genuine religious experience. [And Native American cosmologies] give me an ability to access what I'm calling ecological consciousness . . . feeling the relationship to all this magnificent stuff we call the creation.[86]

Most activists interested in Native American spirituality, like Gold, do not claim to systematically practice Native American religion. They do, however, engage in processes and practices *inspired by and borrowed from* Native American traditions, generally in a piecemeal and unsystematic way, combining them freely with practices borrowed from neo-paganism, traditional religions (especially Buddhism, Taoism, and Hinduism), and even self-help groups and the human potential movement.

Among the practices borrowed (explicitly or implicitly) from Native American cultures are the sweat lodge, the burning of purifying sage, the passing of a talking stick during community meetings, ritual processes such as the Council of All Beings (which involve a solitary seeking of nature spirits in a way that resembles vision quests), the taking (or discovery) of "earth names," group and solitary wilderness experiences undertaken under the influence of peyote or hallucinogenic mushrooms, "tribal unity" and war dances characterized by ecstatic dancing and prolonged drumming (which bear no resemblance, as far as I can discern, to Native American dancing), neo-pagan ritualizing that sometimes borrows elements from Native American religion such as prayers to the Great Spirit in the four directions, a variety of rhetoric such as "ho" to express agreement during "tribal" meetings, and "hoka-hey," an exclamation sometimes spoken to register approval of expressions of militant defiance against the oppressors of nature, and even a willingness to die for the cause.[87] A small number of these activists live in tepees and do not cut their hair, expressing a conviction held by some Native Americans that their strength would be dissipated were they to cut it.

Yet Euro-American attraction to and borrowing from Native American and primal cultures is highly controversial, criticized as theft and even genocide both internally and by some Native Americans, and this has fostered ambivalence in the movement toward such borrowing. Such criticisms have complicated the process of bricolage and innovation, especially for radical environmentalists who strive to act in solidarity with Indians (especially traditional ones). Such criticisms have forced negotiations over the character and direction of religious production and innovation, dramatically illustrating that bricolage is often a contested process.[88]

Thus far I have focused on two major tributaries to radical environmentalism's religious bricolage: the green fire narrative and primal religion, represented by neo-shamanism and by the bits of Native American ceremony to which they have access. Yet this only has scratched the surface. It may be that with sufficient time I could find *somebody* importing into the movement *something* from each and every religion on the planet—even those extant only in the documentary record! The only prerequisite seems to be that the appropriated traditions—or the deviant (and usually mystical) streams within some broader tradition—be interpreted as earth-revering or potentially so.

The purportedly nature-sympathetic religious traditions appropriated or practiced by movement activists include Judaism, Taoism, Buddhism, Hinduism, Christianity, witchcraft, goddess and Gaia worship, Paganism, and even in a couple of cases, a flirtation with Satanism. (According to these activists, Satanism is attractive because it recognizes the dark side of nature, which like Shiva, the Hindu god of destruction, plays an important, creative role.) From within each of these traditions, any number of sub-traditions, sects, or ideas might be tapped. I have met serious and not-so-serious students of Tibettan, Zen, and Tantric Budhism; practitioners of several different schools of yoga, meditation, massage, and the healing arts originating in India (as well as several New Age offshoots from these traditions), some of which are explicitly derived from Hinduism.

The movement has a number of martial artists (some of whom seem unusually willing to contemplate the possible necessity of violence) drawing from various traditions originating in India, Japan, and China. One activist and martial arts instructor, for example, drawing on the martial arts philosophy of the Shaolin monks for his strategic thinking and views about violence, fuses such a worldview with movement apocalypticism: "There is an old proverb from the Shaolin Temple of China: *Avoid, rather than check, Check rather than hurt, Hurt rather than Maim, Maim rather than kill, For all life is precious, and none can ever be replaced.*" He then suggested that Earth First!ers learn the art of appropriate escalation from the Shaolin monks: First, start with conversation, then use the courts and legislature, then obstruct your opponents peaceably, defending yourself if necessary, "and if they seek only your ill-being then, and only then, shall you inflict upon them the annihilation that they willingly embraced."[89]

The movement also has dancers practicing Tamil, Belly- and May-pole styles—each of whom sees dance as an earth-bonding practice. To these are added Christian anarchists and pacifists in the tradition of Tolstoy and Ellul, and even an evangelical Christian influenced by the traditional "peace" churches, for whom monkeywrenching is "turning the swords of those committing violence against nature into plowshares for them."[90] Meanwhile, a number of activists have been engaged in reinterpreting their own traditions in a more nature-friendly way than traditionally has been the case.[91]

Stirring Goddesses, Ents and Fairies into Cauldron of Pagan, Nature Religion

Despite such diversity, an increasingly common solution to the quest for an authentic but unproblematic earthen spirituality, especially for radical environmentalists with European roots, is to seek it in the pre-Christian folk religions of their ancestors. Trudy Frisk well explained the rationale for this turn in the pages of *Earth First!,*

> The resurgence of pagan spirituality, especially widespread reclamation of the Goddess in all her guises, is a glimmer of hope in our unprecedented planetary ecological crisis. Paganism restores women to positions of power. . . . It also allays our envy of Native spirituality; we are all descended from people who revered the earth. [92]

And for Frisk, the Goddess provides many reinforcements, for

> She is not one but many: beneficent Demeter, sensual Aphroditi, learned Sophia, loving Freya, wild huntress Artemis, benevolent Ameratsu, dark Kali, compassionate Tara of Tibet, feline Bast, Cerridwen, keeper of the cauldron of change. She is ancient: Danu, Mother of Celts, Isis, Sovereign of the Elements, Yemaya,

Holy Mother of the West African Sea, Pacamamma of the Andes
who pre-dates the Incas, triune Hecate, Spider Woman weaving
the threads of Native American fate. She is Gaia. [93]

But radical environmental pagans are not all ecofeminist goddess
worshippers. Some prefer more macho, Norse gods. Controversial Earth
First! author Christopher Manes, for example, who studied in Iceland on a
Fullbright fellowship, promoted the pagan and shamanic "indigenous religion of Northern Europe, Asatru." In this religion, which he wrote is still
practiced in Iceland, "the cosmos was held together by a great ash tree.
[This] world tree is a shamanistic symbol. It was called Yggdrasill." According to this myth, Manes summarized, "at the cost of great suffering
[impalement on the tree] the shaman god Odin acquires [secret] knowledge .
. . and bestows [it] on the inhabitants of Middle Earth in the form of runes.
Thus the world tree establishes order and makes it comprehensible to humanity." Manes asserts that "these motifs [show that] trees do partake in the
sky, Middle Earth and the underground; they do hold together the network
of life as we know it." Logging, therefore, is "totalitarian," severing us from
the world tree, from our connection to Earth, and logging companies "are
not just cutting down trees; they're cutting us off from a meaningful
[world]."[94] In an *Earth First!* column devoted to ecotage entitled "Even
Thor Monkeywrenches," Manes writing under the pseudonym "Ned Ludd,"
insisted that the Norse god is active in the world; for example, he sent a
lightning strike that burnt a trailer that had been desecrating a sacred mountain in Arizona.[95]

Wiccan forms of paganism have been more common in America's Earth First! movement, however, and there are a number of women
witches involved in Earth First!. More often than men, they participate in
constructing and leading rituals at Earth First! wilderness gatherings and
demonstrations. (At least, women play a more prevalent role in ritual that is
so recognized; men tend to dominate the evening musical jams and song
fests, which also appear to an anthropologically informed observer to be a
form of ritualizing). Oftentimes the ritualizing draws on the lifework of
Starhawk, a contemporary witch, who through her many writings and long-
term activist career has played an important role in creating a radical environmental branch of contemporary Wicca. A number of Earth First! activists
have become ordained priestesses. One grew up in an intentional pagan
community, for example, in northern California's Church of All Worlds, and
with a number of the members from that community, became deeply involved in the radical environmental campaign to halt the logging of ancient
redwoods in northern California during the 1990s.

Buck Young is a pagan Earth First!er who believes that modern
people cannot experience the world as enchanted because they have paved
over wilderness—thereby muting the earth's sacred voices. During a 1991
interview, he told me that Earth First!ers are among the few who can still
perceive the earth's sacredness, and he credits experiences with hallucinogens (especially psychedelic mushrooms) with opening the faerie-world to
him and setting him on his radical environmental path. He also explained
that the enchanted other-world of J. R. R. Tolkien's *Lord of the
Rings* trilogy also resonated within him and facilitated his spiritual growth.
Writing under a pseudonym because of his leading role in an effective envi-

ronmental organization that uses litigation to fight deforestation, and fearing that being out of the "broom closet" would be counterproductive, Young wrote a fascinating and innovative account of the emergence of radical environmental activism, blurring the lines between the Earth of our everyday experience, the Middle Earth, and the Spirit World, while integrating characters from Tolkien novels, European faerie-tales, and contemporary Earth First! characters:

> Gnomes and elves, fauns and faeries, goblins and ogres, trolls and bogies . . . [must infiltrate our world to] effect change from the inside . . . [These nature-spirits are] running around in human bodies . . . working in co-ops . . . talking to themselves in the streets . . . spiking trees and blowing up tractors . . . starting revolutions . . . [and] making up religions. [96]

One thing that is particularly interesting about this statement, apart from the apparent appropriation of a revolutionary ideology from fairies and fairy friends before the creation of ELF, is Young's self-consciousness that he and his comrades are inventing religion. He is not alone in this awareness. A number of Earth First!ers are quietly aware of and unapologetic about their role as spiritual leaders, and they think carefully about the best ways to blend and invent a ritual life for their emerging tradition (although some of them think they are resurrecting old ways rather than inventing new ones). In Earth First!, however, leaders of any ilk are reluctant to acknowledge such a role publicly for fear of arousing the anti-leadership passions of the anarchists in their midst.

Such an awareness of the need to invent as well as borrow and pass on religious tradition is prevalent in the pagan community—and given the intersection between these subcultures within the cultic milieu—it is unsurprising that such an understanding would also be found among pagan Earth First!ers.[97] Some, like Young, have been involved in the creative appropriation of the elves, ents, wizards, dwarfs, men and hobbits of Middle Earth, again as something like radical environmental spirit-guides.

Indeed, shortly after Earth First! was founded, the movement received and published a letter purportedly from Aragorn, the leader of a mysterious group of noblemen deeply involved in a desperate and brutal defense of another sacred land—Tolkien's Middle Earth.[98] The letter expressed solidarity with the fledgling Earth First! movement, and interestingly, claimed some credit for its emergence. "Count on the cooperation and agitation of the Striders, obviously a progenitor of Earth First!" the letter entreated, and showing that borrowing and innovation can work in many strange ways and directions, the letter injected into Tolkien's narrative its own, neo-Luddite spin: "A Strider slogan is 'not blind opposition, but bare-fanged attack on progress.'" Aragorn signed his epistle after mentioning that the Striders had already been present at Earth First! gatherings![99]

Several other Earth First! activists have told me that the Tolkien novels have had a strong influence on their spiritual and activist paths. One Earth First! newsletter even borrowed its title, *Entmoot,* from the fabled Council of the Ents, explaining:

The Ents are the ancient race of tree guardians whose physical bodies and nature are close to that of trees. They were taught the languages of "the speakers" by the Elves, who called them the Onodrim. Like the Elves, Ents flourished during the Elder Days of the Middle Earth but are still roaming the wild hills . . . . Ents like trees are not hasty, but when danger arises can rally their power to defend their forests. The ENTMOOT! is a ritual assembly of the Onodrim that occurs in time of great need.

Now is such a time. Forests are falling across our lovely planet and the magic, strength, and power of Ents are needed in their defense.[100]

After an exhortation to involvement in forest defense, this newsletter introduction offered encouragement based on an animistic faith: "if you listen closely you will hear the trees speaking to you"—they will tell you what to do. The missive ended with the entish equivalent of Foreman's wolf howl/call to action: "HOOM! FROOM!"

Whatever radical environmentalists are moved by, borrow from, modify, or invent in their religious journeys, it is worth noting that few of them become radical environmentalists due to what sociologists of knowledge would call "primary socialization," or through a dramatic conversion to these traditions. My interviews, to the contrary, suggest that the "ecological consciousness" uniting most radical environmentalists usually begins early in life—in experiences I cannot here typify—long before exposure to nature-based-and-sympathetic religious traditions.[101] It is usually as young adults or later that many of the activists discover religious traditions sharing affinity with their religious sentiments. In other words, most Earth First!ers are first "generic" nature mystics. This helps account, of course, for the basic epistemological premise and exhortation to spend time in the wild. Although radical environmentalists appreciate all nature-grounded and sympathetic spiritual traditions, often borrowing freely from them, few if any individuals identify fully or dogmatically with any particular religious tradition.

The preceding discussion of traditions and tradition-bits appropriated and practiced could be misleading, however, were we to deduce from it that all traditions are of equal importance within the radical environmental cultic stew. Few radical environmental Christians and Jews, for example, find elements (or minority steams) within their traditions to draw on to reinforce their worldviews and inspire them to action. Most radical environmentalists of monotheist heritage end up concluding that such traditions are inherently anthropocentric, hierarchical, patriarchal, and perhaps as importantly, anti-erotic. Few Earth First!ers consider themselves Hindu, for example, even though many participate in one act or another of Hinduism-derived ritualizing. If I had to venture an opinion in this regard, I would probably say that, apart from time spent in wild nature, the most important resources for radical environmentalists these days are paganism (including pantheism, animism, and Wicca), Shamanism and Native American spiritualities, Taoism, and Buddhism. This must be qualified, however, with the recognition consistent with cultic milieu theory, that the borders between all of these diverse phenomena, including the New Age, remain fluid and permeable.

Apocalypticism

Apocalypticism is a critically important element of the radical environmental worldview. Radical environmentalists of all stripes, and even bioregionalists, their close cousins who tend to focus on developing environmentally sustainable lifestyles rather than on political and direct action resistance to environmental decline,[102] all share an overwhelmingly pessimistic and apocalyptic worldview. This apocalypticism fuels the sense of dire necessity and thus justifies lawbreaking. It also fosters solidarity among movement participants with the unique force that accompanies an expectation of the end of the world, and is expressed and reinforced in movement music and ritualizing. The critical thing to note in any examination of movement apocalypticism is that, here again, bricolage is at work; this time modern earth science is stirred into the worldview stew, for their belief in the end of the world as we have known it is grounded in credible scientific evidence. And this is an especially noteworthy innovation, for this may be the first time in the history of religion that modern scientific understandings of environmental degradation have become a pillar of an apocalyptic religious worldview.

I will not, however, discuss green apocalypticism in detail here, for I have done so previously,[103] except to note that some observers have mistaken the hope that some activists retain for a green future and a peaceful transition to it, with an optimistic millennialism.[104] Few if any radical environmentalists, however, believe humans will re-harmonize their lives with the earth's living systems without first experiencing the collapse of industrial civilization, which will result either from its own unsustainable weight or through a radical environmental revolution. In either case, great suffering for the humans and other species is a clear and ubiquitous expectation. There is little hope to be found within these movements, except for after the collapse of industrial civilization, and the general expectation is that this world will be a greatly wounded one, with millions of its sacred voices silenced.

Thus far we have focused on the ecological, literary, spiritual, experiential, and overtly religious bits that make up the worldview of radical environmentalism, but we have only obliquely mentioned how diverse political ideas, ideologies, and causes are also stirred into the pot. Political attitudes and beliefs are critical, however, and call for more detailed analysis.

The Bricolage of Rebellion and Revolution

The central political beliefs typically shared by radical greens and the most militant members of the word's antiglobalization resistance include the following: a common perception of their predicament (environmental deterioration is threatening many species as well as human survival), a common understanding of the causes (local and international elites first stole the land and established significant political hegemony, and today, a cabal of elite corporate figures dominate nation-states and social life, pushing global capitalism into every corner of the planet, to the detriment of ordinary people and the environment), and *a common prescription* (the land and political power must be taken from the abusers and managed according to traditional wisdom, supplemented judiciously by modern knowledge, while vigilance is maintained against those who would again usurp the commons for private gain.)[105]

There are many social critics and movements from which such convictions are derived. I mentioned in the introduction that radical environmentalists have a penchant to borrow from, express affinity with, and support, all sorts of rebellious groups whom they consider to be kindred movements. These include the American Indian Movement, the MOVE organization in Philadelphia, Mexico's indigenous Zapatista rebellion, the International Workers of the World, and pagan and anarchist activists resisting England's ongoing road-building projects. To illuminate how specific, far-flung movements and causes get drawn into the increasingly globalized radical environmental worldview, I will now discuss the Luddites and Diggers, Militant Autonomous Zones, and Native American sacred land conflicts.

Luddites, Diggers and Defending the Commons

Two short-lived resistance movements in England have been posthumously adopted by radical environmental subcultures. The Luddites, skilled weavers in the process of losing their livelihoods to mechanization early in the nineteenth century, symbolize felt hatred (or at least dislike and distrust) among movement activists for technology and its effects. The Diggers were seventeenth century pacifists influenced by the radical reformation in Switzerland and Germany who resisted the enclosure process in England (where lands previously had been held in common, with the resources shared by all and regulated by customs and mores, but through the process of enclosure, became the private property of an elite few). The Diggers were violently crushed, and evoke in radical greens outrage, for their suppression symbolizes the imperialism of modernizing and expansionist market societies which displace native peoples and destroy the land.

The Luddites are better known and far more revered among radical environmentalists. Edward Abbey dedicated *The Monkey Wrench Gang* to Ned Ludd (the boy who purportedly inspired the campaign to smash the machines threatening traditional pre-modern lifeways), and quoted Byron in an epigraph, "Down with all kings but King Ludd." Ned Ludd thus symbolized the early form of libertarian anarchism so prevalent in the movement. Dave Foreman created "Ned Ludd Books" to self-publish *Ecodefense* and other movement books, and created "Dear Ned Ludd" as a forum in *Earth First!* for the discussion of monkeywrenching as a tactic. Of course, these rebels have also been celebrated in movement music, poetry, and art.[106] Even if the most common interpretations of the Luddite rebellions are inaccurate, and the Luddites actually were engaged in class warfare or "collective bargaining by riot," in a colorful phrase coined by the famous British historian E. P. Thompson,[107] the rebellion will remain a popular one for adoption by the subcultures of radical environmentalism.

Although less well known, the Diggers are often memorialized in song at Earth First! rendezvous—and for good reason. Their story provides a powerful narrative that captures the political analysis common in much radical environmentalism and some antiglobalization resistance, a critique tracing social and environmental decline to the unceasing, voracious appetite of industrial-market capitalism for the land, everywhere, regardless of the human or ecological costs. The "World Turned Upside Down," speaks for itself:

In 1649, to St. George's Hill
A ragged band they called the Diggers
Came to show the people's will
They defied the landlords
They defied the laws
They were the dispossessed
Reclaiming what was theirs

"We come in peace" they said
"To dig and sow
We come to work the land in common
And to make the waste land grow
This earth divided
We will make whole
So it can be a common treasury for all

"The sin of property, we do disdain
No one has any right to buy and sell
The earth for private gain
By theft and murder
They took the land
Now everywhere the walls
Rise up at their command

"They make the laws
To chain us well
The clergy dazzle us with heaven
Or they damn us into hell
We will not worship
The God they serve
The God of greed who feeds the rich
While poor men starve

"We work, we eat together
We need no swords
We will not bow to masters
Or pay rent to the lords
We are free men
Though we are poor"
You Diggers all stand up for glory
Stand up now

From the men of property
The orders came
They sent the hired men and troopers
To wipe out the Diggers' claim
Tear down their cottages
Destroy their corn

They were dispersed—
Only the vision lingers on

"You poor take courage
You rich take care
The earth was made a common treasury
For everyone to share
All things in common
All people one
We come in peace"—
The order came to cut them down.[108]

This song coheres with many movement ideas and contributes well to its bricolage of rebellion.

Live Wild or Die—in Militant Autonomous Zones

Since at least 1987, there have been "anarchist workshops" at most national Earth First! rendezvous—this sections describes a workshop at the 1995 National Round River Rendezvous in California focusing on Militant Autonomous Zones—a concept and strategy pioneered by European anarchists. Militant Autonomous Zones (MAZ) are usually in urban areas where anarchist squatters establish themselves and attempt to keep out what they consider to be the repressive authority of the nation state, employing sometimes elaborate and perhaps violent defensive measures. Green MAZ activists seek to establish nonhierarchal and environmentally sustainable ways of life within them.

This particular workshop leader explained that such anarchism need not be violent nor is it hostile to pacifism. But he also noted that, although he dislikes violence, sometimes MAZ defenders must hold their ground, and he suggested activists learn martial arts or consider arming themselves. He said that MAZ activists should be ready to flee on short notice, "except when working with indigenous cultures, which we also consider to be MAZ." In such cases, where indigenous cultures consider their places sacred, leaving is not an option. He mentioned as examples the Zapatista-held areas in Chiapas, and Mohawk Indian lands in northeastern America.

After this introduction, Mike Jakubal spoke. Jakubal, an important Earth First! activist, took an Australian tactic of tree climbing to thwart loggers and, with Ron Huber, turned it into long-term tree sitting. This became an important and successful way for activists to publicize their causes in the United States.[109] He is also an anarchist who had at several movement junctures became a polarizing figure, advocating tactics that led some pacifists and Christians to leave Earth First! to form a group committed to nonviolence called the Cathedral Forest Action Group.[110]

Jakubal was also largely responsible for the creation of the occasional green-black journal *Live Wild or Die,* which was first published in February 1989 and that, on anti-technology principles, continues to be produced without computers.[111] Its purpose was to provide a forum for voices left out of *Earth First!,* to celebrate wildness in all its forms, and to systematically subvert the system. The cover of its premier issue depicted a feral human climbing a power line tower while carrying a stick of dynamite. This cover would remind the knowing reader of the Arizona power line caper and of other cases where power lines had been toppled by movement activists. In Santa Cruz, for example, power lines were toppled in an April 1990 "Earth Night" action, and *Live Wild or Die* has reported on efforts to explode such towers in Vermont as part of the campaign against Hydro-Quebec's incursions into indigenous land for their dam projects.[112]

Live Wild or Die also included discussion of tactics largely verboten in *Earth First!*, such as the construction and use of incendiary devices, until this taboo was broken in the fall of 1999. The back cover of its initial issue depicted a factory over the inscription, "Factories Don't Burn Down by Themselves. . . . They Need Help From You."[113] These graphics illustrate that *Live Wild or Die* conveys an attitude far more inflammatory, subversive, and violence-sympathetic than *Earth First!* did, at least until the turn of the centrury or so. Consequently, the anonymously edited "Black Cat" sabotage reader entitled *Beware! Sabotage!*, quietly distributed within radical environmental subcultures in the mid 1990s, drew a substantial proportion of its articles and graphics from it.[114]

Various articles in the "Black Cat" collection argued that violence is more powerful than non-violence and that violent strategies have "cycled several times before in American history [including] anarchist bombthrowers around the turn of the century [and] the Weathermen of the 1960s [but] in each case, America overwhelmingly rejected minority efforts to force change through violence."[115] Revisiting the 1982 Earth First! dispute about tactics crossing the line into violence discussed previously, sounding like Gary Snyder and Robert Aitken did then, this article insisted, "The violence professionals in the police and armed forces of the U.S. will prevail over a few Earth First! violence amateurs. You will never stop the machine by force, you will only justify it and strengthen it." This kind of caution, however, appears to be an increasingly marginal view within radical environmental subcultures.

During the MAZ workshop, Jakubal, obviously familiar with the concept, provided a rationale for the militant and even violent defense of autonomous zones. He argued that in such zones, "defending yourselves is an act of love" for what had been created. He warned that the authorities "will saturate bomb you"—so "you might as well take a few with you." They will kill you, at least until you have developed a mass movement, he concluded.

Another activist familiar with such zones asserted that "militant" means a strong resistance, not necessarily an armed one. A discussion ensued with the usual diversity of opinions, including ones drawing on Gandhi urging nonviolence as the most powerful strategy of all, even for defending such zones, while another activist mentioned the hundreth monkey idea, suggesting that a critical mass must be built for such zones to have a chance.[116]

Despite occasional disclaimers, however, pacifist ideas are often ridiculed by green-anarchists. Many such activists view pacifism as unnatural—since wild animals defend themselves when attacked, so ought humans. *Live Wild or Die* republished an article by American Indian Activist Ward Churchill under the heading "Pacifism as Pathology."[117] Pacifism is a luxury only First World activists take seriously, many radical environmental activists believe, one that inappropriately ties the hands of activists around the world who are engaged in life-and-death struggles.

The MAZ workshop also included expressions of support for the radical African-American group MOVE and for Mumia Abu-Jamal, whose execution was scheduled that summer. One activist promised, "If Mumia is executed, many places will be burning."

The wrap-up to the workshop returned to theme of love and resistance: "Our hope is to build a society based on nonviolence and cooperation." Followed by "Our hope is in mass refusal against the government, like in the Philippines and the Soviet Union." The workshop leader summed up, "Anarchy is centered on love—but this has been lost. Its about mutual aid and cooperation and self-defense, but not necessarily by arms," while another concluded, "All we were told in school about anarchism was Bakunin and bomb throwing; this is totally bull shit! We need to de-program people."

American Indians and Defending Sacred Ground

> My Heroes Have Always Killed Cowboys
> —Earth First! t-shirt, bumper sticker, and graphic, depicting a group of American Indians with rifles.[118]

Efforts within radical environmental subcultures to express solidarity and build alliances with Native Americans did not begin with the arrival of green-anarchists. In April 1981, in their first official act, Earth First!ers musingly erected a historical "monument" to Victorio, an Apache chief who, their inscription explained, "strove to protect these mountains from mining and other destructive activities of the white race."[119] This incident again illustrates the affinity of movement activists for Native Americans and other primal cultures, and shows how such affinity bleeds over into ideology and activism.

As Zakin well demonstrates, both before and after the formation of Earth First!, "longhairs" and other participants in the counterculture, and even a number of western rednecks, became involved in political struggles in solidarity with various Native American groups.[120] These early alliances resisted incursions by the dominant society into areas where Native peoples still retained access—places traditional Indians considered sacred and essential to their ceremonial life, and even to the preservation of the world.

In the American southwest, for example, beginning in the late 1960s, connections were begun between certain groups and individuals within the Hopi and Navajo nations as well as with the American Indian Movement and a growing number of environmentalists and countercultural types. Edward Abbey would later use several of the Euro-Americans who were involved as templates for characters in his novels. Much of this collaborative energy went into saving the Black Mesa in Arizona, which Zakin accurately notes was of great "mystical significance" to its defenders, including the Navajo, but especially "traditional Hopis [who] believed that Black Mesa was the final refuge on earth [and that] its destruction would signal the coming environmental Armageddon."[121] Such apocalypticism fit well with the mood of many within the emerging radical environmental subcultures. This helped fuel a substantial amount of monkeywrenching against Peabody Coal's mining plans.[122]

Since Earth First!'s founding, many of its campaigns have been centered around saving places considered sacred by Native Americans. Indeed, anyplace considered sacred by Indians is certain to be considered sacred by Earth First!ers, for who could better identify sacred land than those still closely tied to it and struggling against Euro-American civilization to practice and defend their earth-based religions?

Defending the Sacred and the Potential for Violence

Of course, violence has sometimes been used to defend or reclaim places considered sacred and therefore it is reasonable to wonder if this is a dynamic likely to emerge from radical environmentalism. I argued recently in *Terrorism and Political Violence* that there are a number of factors, both internal and external, to radical environmentalism that make it unlikely that its activists will try to kill or maim as they pursue their objectives.[123] Although I will not repeat that analysis here, I will describe incidents relevant to it. The readers may use this information to draw their own inferences, perhaps in the light of my previous argument.

During one incident of direct-action resistance against logging on Arizona's Mt. Graham—which is considered sacred by many southwestern Indians, and also by Earth First!ers for harboring the endangered red squirrel—wrestling and fistfights broke out between loggers and police on the one side, and university students who had come to support two activists perched overhead in trees. As described in *Earth First!* by Erik Ryberg, the chaos occurred because, as trees began to fall, the students simply could not bear it, so they emerged from the trees, screaming, running from one tree to another, grabbing them to prevent the loggers from cutting them. When pulled to the ground, one student "proceeded to attack the logger" and the other students joined in, fighting with loggers and police in an effort to "unarrest" their comrades, and otherwise "doing everything in their power to stop this logging." Ryberg commented,

> I have never been so proud to be a part of this movement as I was on that day. Those students, apparently prepared to die, showed me a dignity and courage and respect for this planet that does not occur outside Earth First! They turned the top of Mt. Graham not into a protest site but a battlefield, and although they were outnumbered forty to one they could not find inside themselves the will to sit and watch a species go extinct, evaporate off this planet forever.[124]

Ryberg is a long-term Earth First! activist who periodically has "pushed the envelope" on the question of violence by asking whether the time has come for the movement to abandon its commitment to nonviolence. He was "disgusted" by the hippies and layabouts he witnessed during the Redwood Summer campaign and with the focus on civil disobedience (CD), later arguing in *Earth First!* that "CD is a tool." Later, an even more controversial article entitled, "Bombthrowing: A Brief Treatise" (writing as "Pajama" 1993), which was republished in the mid 1990s in the Black Cat Sabotage manual, Ryberg wondered, "When will it be time to throw bombs?"[125] The discussion implied that, because of the imminent peril facing many species, that time might well be at hand.

In describing the melee at Mt. Graham, Ryberg had been responding to an accusation by Sea Shephard Captain Paul Watson that Earth First! had become a group of "lily livered wimps"—Greenpeace-like "bannerhangers."[126] After describing the Mt. Graham battle, Ryberg mentioned that the campaign defending Cove Mallard had developed a similar atmosphere. He then rejoindered, "If we hang a banner once in awhile, it should be considered a warning: one day soon, there might be war in those woods."[127]

When Ryberg was arrested in 1993 while attempting to lock down under a law enforcement vehicle during a raid at a movement camp, another melee erupted. Some activists threw rocks until one of the "freddies" (disparaging movement parlance for Forest Service employees, meaning "forest rape eagerly done and done in endless succession") ratcheted a shell into the chamber of his shotgun and leveled it at the activists. "I really think they'll shoot us if we get strong enough to actually stop them," Ryberg told me later, "but this doesn't mean we shouldn't try."

Try they did—perhaps especially during the summer of 1993 at Cove Mallard—where the battle for the woods became a low-intensity conflict.[128] Earth First! fielded several small groups of environmental guerrillas who were, in turn, supported by several back country camps, well equipped including full-time cooks. One small affinity group calling itself "the grundles" was particularly aggressive, experimenting with ways to ambush the "Freddies" and damage their vehicles. Sometimes they would build barricades in roads and when the Freddies got out of their trucks to remove debris, these masked and camouflaged activists would leap out and slash their tires. On another occasion, they threw a smoke bomb under a Freddie truck, and when the Freddies "ran like hell," the grundles sprang forward and "trashed" the vehicles with pulaskis (a firefighting tool with an axe at one end and pick on the other). Their objective was not merely to slow down their adversaries but to make them fight for "every single inch" of the planned logging road. The strategy was devised by activists who "understood guerilla warfare" and it included a plan to "hit the Freddies anywhere within a 30 mile radius around Cove Mallard." They wanted the Freddies to know that any truck or bulldozer that they put in the field would be at risk.

These tactics proved controversial and a few activists left the campaign as a result. Jake Krielick and others who had been organizing a civil disobedience campaign publicly distanced themselves and withdrew support for the backcountry camps, arguing that monkeywrenching and civil disobedience campaigns should not be mixed.[129] The grundles and their sympathizers, however, criticized Krielick and the other civil disobedience campaigners for misleading activists that they had invited to Cove Mallard by downplaying the dangers involved, pointing to incidents when activists were beaten or threatened with violence.

The next two logging seasons were less intense at Cove Mallard—there were fewer activists in the field, and logging had been slowed, partly by lawsuits. In 1996, however, borrowing the anti-road-building tactics being pioneered in England in the early 1990s and imported the previous year at Warner Creek in Oregon, the Cove Mallard activists, reinforced by the Earth First! forces gathered there for their national rendezvous, captured and energetically dismantled and blockaded a logging road under construction leading into the next set of logging sites.[130] (There is a transoceanic shuttling, especially between Australia-United States-United Kingdom, of radical environmental activists who study each other's movements and tactics, and radical environmental journals report on the global evolution of tactics.)

Despite all these efforts, these blockades were easily dismantled by heavy equipment during a two-day period in 1996, and for a time, the logging continued. This would not be the last word, however, for the outgoing Clinton administration established in late 2000 a new policy protecting approximately 60 million acres of America's remaining "roadless" public lands. This put at least a temporary halt to further logging at Cove Mallard. (Only time will tell whether subsequent administrations overturn the Clinton roadless policy.)

Until the increase in arson attacks by the Earth Liberation Front in the late 1990s, the Cove Mallard resistance represented the most aggressive environmental campaign in North America. It provides important, on-the-ground data for grappling with the prospect for violence emerging from radical environmental subcultures. Although I have heard of one melee occurring during this multi-year campaign, I have also witnessed activists carefully diffusing tense situations when threatened by angry (and sometimes inebriated) loggers. The reality on the ground is complex, just as are the more theoretical debates about strategies and tactics in movement literature.

It is critical to remember that disputes over monkeywrenching and violence—indeed, over whether certain tactics even *are* violent and over whether even discussing such tactics violates the predominant nonviolence principles of the movement—have occurred regularly since the formation of Earth First! An early editor resigned over the introduction of the "Ned Ludd" column in the journal and the elder poet of the movement, Gary Snyder, wrote to criticize monkeywrenching, arguing that it provided bad and counterproductive political theater. Moreover, every time over the years that Earth First! has published articles or letters to the editor suggesting that nonviolence was an inadequate strategy, a flurry of rejoinders, as well as supportive comments, generally followed. Radical environmentalists love to argue.

After the 1990 schism temporarily resolved one power struggle, another produced equally wrenching discord, consuming enormous energy over several years; it was substantially over the issue of violence. More precisely and importantly, the dispute centered on whether to establish an *Earth First!* editorial policy against publishing materials promoting (or considering) violence, or if such a policy constituted inappropriate and authoritarian censorship and the imposition of a dreaded "party line." Advocates of the policy argued that having such a policy was simply a prudent and strategic movement-building decision that well reflected the majority's strong commitment to nonviolence. Opponents argued that there was no such consensus about violence and the journal ought to reflect that diversity, and moreover, a central purpose of the journal was to provide a space where there could be no-holds-barred debates about what could and should be done to save the planet.

This debate over editorial policy regarding violence was reminiscent of the one that precipitated Pete Dustrud's departure from the journal a decade earlier, and it began when the journal published a Robert Martin article entitled "A Hunting We Will Go"[131] that some activists read as advocating murder. Actually, it explained firearms safety and ballistics, described how to enter wildlands as a hunter, suggested shooting *near* wild animals to condition them to fear humans, and detailed how to safely damage all-terrain vehicles and "muscle" trucks. The article also explained how to shoot domestic livestock without causing the animals needless pain. (Such animals, and of course, the humans who "manage" them, are blamed for causing serious environmental damage by overgrazing. A number of Earth First!ers advocate shooting domestic animals to reduce such damage, and there are now many incidents where they have apparently done so).[132] What most likely led to the charge that the article actually advocated shooting humans was the author's insertion of the lyrics of a typically sarcastic Tom Lehrer song, the chorus of which celebrates shooting "Two game wardens, seven hunters, and a cow." Martin concluded his article, "and for heavens sake, don't shoot any game wardens or hunters!" The sick humor, however, was lost on many activists (including the animal rights activists), some of whom misread the article and claimed it advocated shooting people, others who, in the wake of the bombing of Judi Bari, thought any such language, even if intended as humor, could be used against movement activists to brand them as terrorists.

In the next issue, however, two editorials further inflamed the debate. In one, Allison Slater viewed opposition to discussion of violence as inappropriately anthropocentric and discounting of human "wildness." An activist writing under the name "Sprout" asserted that "Support within our movement for shooting humans is nothing new. I doubt there is any opposition to anti-poaching patrols in Africa shooting poachers to protect non-human animals." The article ended accusing Martin's critics of "specieism."[133]

The debate raged on as well in many letters to the editors, but a third incident especially inflamed passions. Jim Flynn, an editor in the "collective" publishing *Earth First!,* ignoring a decision by his co-workers not to publish it, at the last minute inserted a cartoon depicting a hanging with the caption, "Trees Are for Hanging: Kill a Developer."[134] In the next issue, with the exception of Flynn, the collective apologized for printing it.[135] In the minds of some, this was too late, the damage had been done—such graphics could be used to portray the movement as terrorist.

The long battle over the journal's editorial policy eventuated in no official policy. One was briefly established at an activist conference in 1992, but it was quickly sabotaged, disappearing within two journal issues because certain anarchists involved in the dispute simply refused to honor any policy arrived at through consensus, viewing any "governing" body and any imposed point of view as illegitimate. This is one of many examples of the difficulty of establishing and honoring an editorial policy within such anarchistic subcultures, a tendency that led Orin Langelle, a long-term anarchist Earth First!er to complain in *Earth First!* that anarchists who sabotage consensus agreements do not understand anarchism, and to argue that when one belongs to an "autonomous collective," one must honor its decisions, even if one is absent when the consensus is reached.[136]

What the proponents of an editorial nonviolence code may not have realized at the time is that there had already been arguments in *Earth First!* suggesting that murder could be an acceptable tactic. In 1986, for example, Tom Stoddard, one of the most controversial early contributors to *Earth First!*, argued that to stop the endangered species trade, activists must

> poach the poacher [and] eliminate . . . traffickers [and] distributors . . . by whatever means it takes. . . . We must consider endangerment and extinction of our fellow species as serious as killing of a human and expect roughly the same from the guilty: death. . . . Declaring guerrilla war on the thieves of our wildlife heritage is the only method of stopping them. I do not expect a bloodbath either, because a few summary executions will frighten cowardly poachers toward honest work.[137]

Beliefs that the resistance may or must eventually become violent are not uncommon, although they are seldom published. In 1991 I received an anonymous letter from an environmental saboteur who described precautions taken to reduce the risk of injuries to loggers when spiking trees. Also included, however, was another Tom Stoddard article that apparently had fewer activists advocating an even more aggressive form of ecodefense.

> Some environmentalists say Earth First!ers are saboteurs, destroyers and even terrorists. . . . They want to save the Earth provided it is no more difficult and dangerous than walking to the corner for their newspaper. [But] The humans trying to destroy Earth have passionate determination . . . motivated by that magic elixir, greed, and its first cousin, power. Using the destroyers' gauge, Earth First!ers look as pastoral as a mountain meadow. How far should Earth First!ers go to save this battered orb? . . .
>
> Certainly as far as [timber companies] destroying our old growth forests. But probably not as far as the Catholic and fundamentalist crazies bombing Planned Parenthood Centers. . . . Assuredly as far as dedicated litterers desecrating every stream and seaside. . . . Certainly as far as the . . . fanatics wanting to waste Earth's resources keeping every misbegotten human alive at any cost. Undoubtedly as far as the Vicar of Christ and other religious ostriches who encourage every human to breed us into SRO (sic) population crises causing deforestation, drought, and desertification. . . .
>
> Defenders have too long been too tepid and too slow. Maybe that is why we are losing the race to save our planet. If we resolve to go as far as the destroyers, it would leave damn little we can't do. If we want to save Earth we had better quit taking our marching orders from our friends and start taking them from our enemies. That is how far we should go![138]

Two years after Stoddard penned those words, at the 1990 Earth First! rendezvous, Richard Bowers announced a workshop on "political assassinations." After an outcry including accusations that Bowers must himself be an infiltrator or "wing nut" (a common term used to label as crazy those advocating violence or otherwise being disruptive), he agreed to change the workshop title to "How much violence might be needed to save

Gaia?" Commenting afterward that even this concession was insufficient for the "declawed pussyfooters" who dominated the gathering, he argued that no compromise in defense of Mother Earth "might well mean more than blockades without violence."[139]

There are also some who, more intellectually, and in trusted circles, suggest that they can imagine situations in which assassinations might be morally permissible and politically necessary. In 1995, for example, after hearing one activist state he could not imagine how anyone could think a bombing campaign would promote the desired transformations, another offered a historical rejoinder. He pointed out how assassinations sometimes do alter history, musing "What would have happened if somebody took out Hitler in 1939?" He then mentioned a famed ornithologist in Brazil who was murdered, destroying a wealth of biological knowledge essential to the preservation of (literally) untold species, commenting, if assassinations can hurt *us* so badly, can you at least imagine the possibility of such violence having an important positive impact?

This was a casual theoretical discussion on a warm, pleasant day, as activists were sitting in a northern California creek in a remote wilderness area. From what I know of the activist expressing it, I doubt he would himself employ such a tactic, for he has been quite effective using legal tactics in his own region. Moreover, despite the occasional pro-assassination rhetoric expressed within radical environmental subcultures, I know of no pro-environment assassination or attempted murder. Yet such ruminations, including the rare but extreme rhetoric deployed by Stoddard and a few others, does raise the possibility that individuals, or even a small group, might one day conclude that the time for such violence has come.

A 1992 letter from an anonymous green-anarchist announcing the spiking of old-growth trees in Oregon's ancient forests and complaining about wimpy Earth First!ers who had renounced this tactic could be used as evidence that some have reached this conclusion:

> The struggle for all that is wild must . . . attack the root cause of the problem—to capitalist society itself. . . . By all and any means necessary!! THIS IS A REVOLUTION. . . THERE IS NO MIDDLE GROUND OF THIS STRUGGLE! FOR ALL THAT IS WILD WE BEG YOU TO PUT DOWN YOUR PENS AND PICK UP YOUR WRENCHES!! Look where the legal system has gotten the ancient forest: near extinction! WAKE UP! FUCK 'EM UP, HIT THEM HARD. FIGHT BACK!!!!!

By the end of the decade, articles appeared in the journal applauding arson as a tactic, and describing how to create incendiary devices; after an intense internal debate, even a short interview with Ted Kaczynski, the infamous "Unabomber," was published, a figure who some Earth First!ers consider a folk hero. [140] Shortly thereafter, in 2001, an issue entitled "What Would Geronimo Do" was published, with Geronimo's angry image, armed with a rifle, adorning the cover.[141] It included several articles promoting anarchism and superimposed an anarchist "A" over its editorial and contacts page.[142] This issue seems to symbolize the increasingly anarchist identity of the current Earth First! movement, which has also been obvious to all at recent Earth First! wilderness gatherings.

Despite these developments and the sometimes martial and violent rhetoric expressed by radical environmentalists, nobody (with the possible exception of Theodore Kaczynski, depending on whether one includes him under the radical environmental umbrella) has been convicted of crimes that have intended to kill or maim anyone. Nor, to my knowledge, have there been serious, inadvertent injuries. Nevertheless, the media and law enforcement authorities routinely label radical environmentalists "terrorists," linguistically likening their direct action campaigns and sabotage by arson with the explosive tactics of the Weathermen, Red Brigades, and figures like Timothy McVeigh. Movement activists, however, generally deny the "terrorist" appellation and some find it laughable. One anarchistic hobo, who participated in some of the earliest campaigns (in the mid 1980s) to sabotage the hunting of threatened species, and who was once arrested and convicted for an assault during an effort to prevent officials from killing American bison (although he caused no injuries), once told me, "It is a laugh to me when they call us violent or terrorists. I say, if we were, don't you think we'd have killed people by now?"[143]   In my view, his point is well taken, if we conclude from it that before evaluating whether a group is violent or terrorist, or likely to be, we should consider as our best evidence that which has occurred already.

Manson, Militia— and Radical Environmentalists?

Finally, I return to the question raised at the beginning of this exploration of radical environmentalism: whether there is a cultic milieu such activists share with participants in the racist right that might facilitate a syncretistic alliance between them, and in that way, lead to a violence-prone faction that would mimic the tactics of the far right.

Given the statements by Manson and his followers, some of which could be inserted within the *Earth First!* journal without raising eyebrows (if done without attribution!), it is reasonable to wonder if there is or could be another way terrorist violence might emerge from radical environmental subcultures. Perhaps radical environmentalists and members of the racist right (perhaps especially the ones appropriating Nordic narratives and cultural bits to construct their identities and movements) could cross paths in the cultic milieu, cross-fertilizing green and racist ideologies. Perhaps this will occur by first working in common cause on specific nature protection campaigns. Perhaps Manson cultists following the exhortation on his Internet site to defend Headwaters forest will meet the young Earth First!er who declared he would work with anyone willing to put the earth first. Perhaps the Unabomber was influenced by the racist right, or the "Environmental Rangers," a small Montana group that warned it would take up arms if necessary to prevent a proposed mine threatening the Blackfoot River, represent such a development.

Such questions are raised, and in a way answered as well, by Colin Campbell's assertion that within the cultic milieu,

> Syncretization is . . . further facilitated and re-enforced by the over-lapping communication structures which prevail within the milieu. More than anything else, the cultic world is kept alive by the magazines, periodicals, books, pamphlets, lectures, demon-

strations and informal meetings through which its beliefs and
practices are discussed and disseminated.[144]

This insight suggests that we might well wonder whether, how, and
to what extent radical environmental subcultures, and those of the racist
right, might come to influence each other. If they share, to any significant
extent, the same cultic milieu, it might become possible, or even likely, for a
process of bricolage, back and forth, between them. Perhaps they would
swap pagan narratives, unify around the desire to keep nature and nature-
people pure,[145] adopting initially a common cause in an anti-immigrant
campaign that is not obviously racist.

As interesting as such a possibility might be, based on my fieldwork, I think it unlikely. I can see almost no place on the subcultural maps
within America where individuals from these two clusters of subcultures
cross paths and communicate; if placed in proximity, fistfights would be
more likely than tabloid trading.

To my knowledge there is *no* overlap in the kinds of journals,
novels, and even spiritual literature participants in these different subculture
clusters read (although I concede there may be some overlap in the area of
pagan spirituality, but again, the specific pagan literature radical environmentalists read generally tends to have a politically progressive edge). Put
more carefully, I have never encountered neo-Nazi or other overtly racist
literature within radical environmental subcultures. Moreover, despite their
defacto anti-censorship consensus, Earth First!ers stridently criticize any
article that is even remotely "politically incorrect" with regard to race and
gender bias, as well as the editors who would be so unfortunate as to publish
it.

That racist and radical environmental subcultures do not overlap
is due to firm border defenses. For example, after the editors of *Earth First!*
ran an advertisement for a book entitled *Anglo-American Biocentric Tribalism* by Thorz Hammer (circa 1992), they discovered to their dismay that it
was "nothing but entry-level neo-Nazi racist propaganda." The journal editors denounced the book as "trash" and published an apology for running the
advertisement, promising to change their advertising policy, insisting on
viewing sample copies before publishing book advertisements.[146]

Radical environmental subcultures are the most militantly egalitarian, anti-hierarchial and feminist I have ever encountered (at least their
rhetoric is, most acknowledge there remain various "hidden hierarchies"
within these groups). As these pages have shown, moreover, their general
orientation has been to express solidarity with colonized peoples (who, not
coincidentally, usually have dark skin). Taken together, these dynamics
strongly militate against any cross-fertilization between radical environmentalists and even the green-racist-right. Earth First! simply does not provide suitable habitat for racist (or sexist) ideologies. This is in no small
measure because many of its participants cut their activist teeth in civil
rights, anti-nuclear, and social justice campaigns. I should add one ironic
qualification: If there are radical environmentalists whose worldviews are
racist, they are far more likely to be biased against persons with European
ancestry for presumed imperialist predispositions.

Whither the Cultic Milieu of Radical Environmentalism

I have tried in these pages to illuminate the central characteristics of radical environmentalism and related branches of antiglobalization resistance, focusing especially on their religious and political dimensions, and showing various ways that Colin Campbell's theory of the cultic milieu has explanatory power with regard to radical environmentalism. I have shown that diverse new and alternative religious ideas, rites, values, and actions, newly invented or borrowed from diverse traditions, places, and times, cross-fertilize with modern ecological understandings and a host of anti-establishment causes and ideologies. The result is a melting pot of green radicalism. Although the recipe for the stew is contested and strenuous disagreements abound, and each ladle spooned from it has some unique ingredients and flavors, it is a pot to which increasing numbers of activists are drawn. As it boils over the edge of the cauldron and onto the streets of our increasingly homogenous world in acts of resistance, its aroma both repels and attracts. Only time will tell what the next ingredients will be—will the resistance turn to targeting people, not property?—and how far will the nation states and law enforcement authorities go to overturn the pot and put an end to what is cooking?

Notes

[1] From the now defunct ATWA Internet home page <http://www.atwa.com/atwa. htm>, which was pointed out to me by Jeffery Kaplan.

[2] M. Satchell, "Any Color But Green: A New Political Alliance Is Battling the Environmental Movement," *U.S. News and World Report* 111:17, (1991), 76.

[3] Luc Ferry, *The New Ecological Order*, (Paris: 1992; repr. Chicago & London: University of Chicago Press, 1995). In various works animal rights theorist Tom Regan has leveled a related attack on the environmental fascism of all "holistic" environmental ethics. See John Clark's telling critique of Ferry's work which, he claims, provides "absolutely no support to his thesis that authoritarianism is implicit in the ecology movement." Ferry's central failure, Clark says, was failing to observe that the Nazi view of nature was thoroughly anthropocentric and instrumental, never suggesting that nature and non-human creatures have interests or rights deserving respect. (John Clark, "The French Take on Environmentalism" *Terra Nova* 1:1 (1996), 112-19.)

[4] Martin W. Lewis, *Green Delusions: An Environmentalist Critique of Radical Environmentalism* (Durham: Duke University Press, 1992); George Bradford, *How Deep Is Deep Ecology? With an Essay-Review on Women's Freedom* (Ojai, California: Times Change Press, 1989); Jerry Stark, "Postmodern Environmentalism: A Critique of Deep Ecology," in Bron Taylor, ed., *Ecological Resistance Movements: The Global Emergence of Radical and Popular Environmentalism*, (Albany, New York: State University of New York Press, 1995), 259-81.

[5] Michael E. Zimmerman, *Contesting Earth's Future: Radical Ecology and Postmodernity* (Berkeley: University of California Press, 1994); Michael E. Zimmerman, "Ecofascism: Threat to American Environmentalism?," in Roger Gottlieb, ed., *The Ecological Community*, (New York & London: Routledge, 1996), 229-54.

[6] Colin Campbell, "The Cult, the Cultic Milieu and Secularization," *A Sociological Yearbook of Religion in Britain*, 5 (1972), 122.

[7] *Ibid.*, 122-23.

[8] *Ibid.*, 124.

[9] *Ibid.*, 122-23.

[10] Bron Taylor, "The Religion and Politics of Earth First!," *The Ecologist*, 21:6 ([November/December] 1991), 258-66; *idem*, "Earth First!'s Religious Radicalism," in *Ecological Prospects: Scientific, Religious, and Aesthetic Perspectives*, Christopher Key Chapple, ed., (Albany, New York: State University of New York Press, 1994), 185-209; *idem., ed., Ecological Resistance Movements: The Global Emergence of Radical and Popular Environmentalism* (Albany, New York: State University of New York Press, 1995); *idem.*, "Resacralizing Earth: Pagan Environmentalism and the Restoration of Turtle Island," in *American Sacred Space*, David Chidester and Edward T. Linenthal, eds., (Bloomington: Indiana University Press, 1995), 97-151; *idem.*, Bioregionalism: An Ethics of Loyalty to Place," *Landscape Journal*, 19:1&2 (2000), 50-72; *idem.*, "Deep Ecology and Its Social Philosophy: A Critique," in *Beneath the Surface: Critical Essays on Deep Ecology*, Eric Katz, Andrew Light and David Rothenberg, eds., (Cambridge, Massachusetts: MIT Press, 2000), 269-299; *idem.*, "Earth and Nature-Based Spirituality (Part I): From Deep Ecology to Radical Environmentalism," *Religion*, 31:2 (2001), 175-93; and *idem.*, "Earth and Nature-Based Spirituality (Part II): From Deep Ecology to Scientific Paganism," *Religion*, 30:3 (2001), 225-45.

[11] Jeffrey Kaplan, "The Anti-Cult Movement in America: A History of Culture Perspective," *Syzygy: Journal of Alternative Religion and Culture*, 2:3-4 (1993), 267-96.

[12] David Chidester, "Stealing the Sacred Symbols: Biblical Interpretation in the People's Temple and the Unification Church," *Religion*, 18 (1988), 157. Chidester uses the word "stealing" as a "shorthand designation for complex negotiations over the ownership of symbols."

[13] *Ibid.*; Sidney M. Greenfield and Andre Droogers, eds., *Reinventing Religions: Syncretism and Transformation in Africa and the Americas* (Lanham, Maryland: Rowman & Littlefield, 2001).

[14] Colin Campbell, "The Cult, the Cultic Milieu and Secularization," 125.

[15] Bron Taylor, "Resacralizing Earth: Pagan Environmentalism and the Restoration of Turtle Island."

[16] Colin Campbell, "The Cult, the Cultic Milieu and Secularization," 122.

[17] Bron Taylor, ed., *Ecological Resistance Movements: The Global Emergence of Radical and Popular Environmentalism*, 18-25.

[18] Jeffrey Kaplan, "The Anti-Cult Movement in America: A History of Culture Perspective," *Syzygy: Journal of Alternative Religion and Culture*, 2:3-4 (1993), 267-96.

[19] Although originating in North America, Earth First! is now international. Bron Taylor, ed., *Ecological Resistance Movements: The Global Emergence of Radical and Popular Environmentalism*.

[20] Muir (1838-1914) was a pioneer of the American conservation movement whose preservationist philosophy shaped the mission of the National Parks System in the United States. Although the term deep ecology was not coined until 1973, Muir is considered by deep ecologists as one of their central "elders."

[21] E.g., Earth First! writer Chrisopher Manes argues that "Evolutionary theory denies the existence of a hierarchy of beings, declaring that there is only genealogy, similarities and differences arising out of a three-and-a-half-billion-year saga of organic inheritance." Christopher Manes, *Green Rage: Radical Environmentalism and the Unmaking of Civilization* (Boston: Little, Brown and Company, 1990), 142.

[22] For recent efforts to develop environmental ethics based on genetic-kinship, see Michael Soulé, "The Social Siege of Nature," in M. Soulé and G. Lease, eds., *Reinventing Nature? Responses to Postmodern Deconstruction*, (San Francisco: Island Press, 1995), 137-70; J. Baird Callicott, "A Critique and an Alternative to the Wilderness Idea," *Wild Earth*, 4:4 (1994), 54-59; Stephen R. Kellert and E.O. Wilson, eds., *The Biophilia Hypothesis* (Washington, D.C.: Island Press, 1993).

[23] In response to a letter expressing confusion about deep ecology (after the letter writer read an article about it by Bill Devall), Dave Foreman (21 December 1986) replied, "The central idea of Deep Ecology is that all things—animals, plants, rocks, rivers, clouds, etc.—have a right to exist for their own sake, without needing to justify their existence by some real or imagined value to human beings. This is the concept of 'intrinsic value.' In other words, a Grizzly Bear or a Snail Darter has traveled the same three and a half billion years of evolution we have and has just as much right to be here as we do. We have no right to consider them or anything else on Earth as mere resources for our use or abuse." This simple formulation is an excellent example of the popular definition of deep ecology that Foreman promoted and that gained widespread acceptance within the movement.

[24] This formulation has been synthesized from dozens of similar articulations heard within radical environmental subcultures, showing that it has broken out of the philosophic literature, becoming deeply rooted within such subcultures.

[25] For example, some within these movements prefer the term "ecocentrism" or "ecocentric ethics" to biocentrism, based on a concern for entire ecosystems, many parts of which are not "alive." I will generally use biocentrism as shorthand for the key moral premise just stated, for it is a term that most of those involved in radical environmental and deep ecology movements know and would endorse. For a second example, although many radical environmentalists would resonate with the "core value" as I have synthesized it, they would not all agree about whether an absolute moral "species egalitarianism" is implied by it. In other words, there remains disagreement about whether all species have *equal* moral worth, and whether a notion of *equal* moral worth applies to each individual member of every species.

[26] These quotes are amalgamated from Aldo Leopold, *The Sand County Almanac with Essays From Round River* (Oxford: 1949; repr. New York: Sierra Club and Balentine Books, 1971), 239, 240, 262.

[27] For the complete story, see *Ibid.*, 137-39.

[28] Edward Abbey, *The Monkey Wrench Gang* (New York: Avon, 1975), 24.

[29] Since Abbey helped Foreman develop his oration, its howling end was clearly borrowed from him and the style of the rave was self-consciously borrowed from the great American writer Samuel Clemens, best known as Mark Twain. Susan Zakin, *Coyotes and Town Dogs: Earth First! and the Environmental Movement* (New York: Viking, 1993), 195.

[30] For detailed descriptions of the talk see *Ibid.*, 195-99 and 292-94; Charles Bowden, *Blue Desert* (Tucson: University of Arizona Press, 1986), 95-97, describes the speech in 1983, showing that its basic outline remained the same for nearly ten years. Although Zakin perceived the influence of Foreman's Church of Christ background on his presentation style, she makes no comment on the ethical and metaphysical implications of his stump speech. She recognized that with the Watt story, Foreman was myth making, yet she missed how this myth, and *much* more importantly, the ritual repetition of the Leopold story by Foreman and many others in movement poetry and song, represented a fundamentally religious appeal. Perhaps this was because of her desire to ridicule the overtly "spiritual" among the Earth First! activists, including Cecelia Ostrow, for speaking with trees. See Susan Zakin, *Coyotes and Town Dogs: Earth First! and the Environmental Movement*, 237; cf. 322-24, 326, 328.

[31] Some scholars now eschew the term animism due to its origins as a pejorative devised to contrast "primitive" tribal religions with "higher" monotheistic ones. E. B. Tylor, *Primitive Culture: Researches Into the Development of Mythology, Philosophy, Religion, Art and Custom* (London: J. Murray, 1871). But this term has been adopted by many radical environmentalists, as well as by many involved in new and emergent religious movements, to describe their own spiritual perceptions. Severed from the pejorative implications, I will employ the term as shorthand for the percep-

tion that the world is inspirited and that interspecies communication may be possible.
[32] Bron Taylor, "Earth First! Fights Back," *Terra Nova*, 2:2 ([Spring] 1997), 29-43.
[33] Dave Foreman and Bill Haywood, eds., *Ecodefense: A Field Guide to Monkey-wrenching*, trans. by Haywood is pseudonym, 2 edn (Ned Ludd: 1985; repr. Tucson, Arizona: Ned Ludd, 1987). Logger Tom Hirons explained in an interview that a "stumping" regulation requires that trees be cut within 12 inches of the ground, which explains why spiking above the three feet level would not involve risks to the tree feller. He said no one had yet been injured by tree spiking, but that there had been close calls. Hirons complained bitterly, however, that saw blades that hit spikes in a mill shatter and ricochet and that when Earth First!ers dump silicone in a crank-case, the engine can explode, concluding "I consider Earth First! nothing more than a terrorist group." Hirons also confirmed that the prevalence of monkeywrenching was costing him dearly for security ($1,000 a month), and that even hiring watchmen does not guarantee the protection of one's equipment (3 March 1992, Portland, Oregon).
[34] They were arrested because the ex-partner of one of those arrested gave information to the authorities, fearing for her safety if he were released from jail, as he awaited trial for previously attacking her (Anonymous 1 May 1993).
[35] During a similar strategy session a year later at the national rendezvous in Vermont, a veteran Earth First!er gently said, after listening to people fret about whether their actions might hurt somebody, "I sense a lot of people are still tethered to humanism." We shouldn't focus only on the suffering of a single individual, "it's more important to look out for the next Seven Generations, and earth herself."
[36] Dave Foreman and Bill Haywood, eds., *Ecodefense: A Field Guide to Monkey-wrenching*, 101.
[37] *Ibid.*, 102, 106.
[38] Bill Wood, "Terrorizing the Desert," *American Motorcyclist* (April 1989), 46.
[39] See Pete Dustrud, "Dear Readers, You Now Have a New Editor," *Earth First!*, 1 August 1982, 2. for his resignation statement and Hank Fonda, "Road Spiking," *Earth First!*, 2:8 (21 September 1982), 6, for the article about road spiking in the next issue, which includes no expressed concern or caution about the safety of those in the vehicles that are to be damaged.
[40] Dave Foreman and Bill Haywood, eds., *Ecodefense: A Field Guide to Monkey-wrenching*, 17.
[41] Dave Foreman, "An Environmental Strategy for the 80s," *Earth First!*, 2:8 (21 September 1982), 7.
[42] Dave Foreman, "Violence and Earth First!," *Earth First!* (20 March 1982) 4.
[43] Robert Aitken, "Dear Earth First!," *Earth First!*, 2:5 (1 May 1982), 2; Gary Snyder, "Dear Dave," *Earth First!*, 2:7 (1 August 1982), 2-3.
[44] Dave Foreman, "Foreman Replies (to Robert Aitken)," *Earth First!*, 2:5 (1 May 1982), 2.
[45] Foreman recognizes his own inconsistencies, quoting Ralph Waldo Emerson, "a foolish consistency is the hobgoblin of little minds," to justify them. Dave Foreman, *Confessions of an Eco-Warrior* (New York: Harmony Books, 1991), vii; Dave Foreman, "Earth First! and Non-Violence," *Earth First!*, 3:7 (1 August 1983), 11.
[46] Dave Foreman, "Strategic Monkeywrenching," *Earth First!*, 5:6 (21 June 1985), 22-23; Dave Foreman and Bill Haywood, eds., *Ecodefense: A Field Guide to Monkeywrenching*, 10-17.
[47] Dave Foreman, *Confessions of an Eco-Warrior*, 161-66.
[48] Dave Foreman and Bill Haywood, eds., *Ecodefense: A Field Guide to Monkey-wrenching*, 16. See Anonymous graphic (1993) illustrating movement desires to burn bulldozers.
[49] Mike Roselle, "Forest Grump," *Earth First!*, 15:2 (21 December 1994), 23.
[50] Graybill, ed., *Beware! Sabotage!*, second edn (Eugene, Oregon: Unknown, 1996).

[51] *Ibid.*, 81.

[52] ELF (Earth Liberation Front), "Earth Liberation Front Ignites Britain," *Earth First!*, 13:8 (1993), 34.

[53] Tara the Sea Elf, "The Earth Liberation Front," *Earth First!*, 16:7 (September-October 1996), 18.

[54] *The Oregonian* conducted the most comprehensive publicly available study in 1999, conservatively estimating that at least "100 major acts of such destruction . . . occurred since 1980, causing $42.8 million in damages . . . in 11 contiguous Western states [and] in the last four years alone, the West has been rocked by 33 substantial incidents, with damages reaching $28.8 million." Bryan Denson and James Long, "Can Sabotage Have a Place in a Democratic Community?," *Oregonian*, 29 September 1999, Online. For the series see also *idem.*, "Eco-Terrorism Sweeps the American West," *Oregonian*, 26 September; *idem.*, "Ideologues Drive the Violence," *Oregonian*, 27 September 1999; and *idem.*, "Terrorist Acts Provoke Change in Research, Business, Society," *Oregonian*, 28 September 1999, or *http://www.oregonlive.com/news/99/09/st092620.html* (accessed August 2001). Although empirical data are currently unavailable, the rate of such crimes appears to be undiminished since this four-part report.

[55] Tara the Sea Elf, "The Earth Liberation Front."

[56] *Ibid.*

[57] *Ibid.*

[58] People in radical subcultures commonly suspect industry or governmental agent provocateurs are responsible for promoting or precipitating violence from within the ranks of the resistance, as well as conflict within it; a rational fear given the record of law enforcement infiltration and misconduct toward radical political movements, see Judi Bari, *Timber Wars* (Monroe, Maine: Common Courage, 1994). For general background Brian Glick's *The War at Home* and Ward Churchill's 1988 *Agents of Repression.* The FBI's three million dollar infiltration and arrests of Earth First! in the southwestern United States, leading to convictions against the Arizona Five, is well known and fuels such fears.

[59] My understanding of religion has been influenced by many scholars, but none more than David Chidester, who holds that "a descriptive approach to the study of religion *requires* a circular definition of the sacred: Whatever someone holds to be sacred is sacred. Our task [in studying religion] is to describe and interpret the sacred norms that are actually held by individuals, communities, and historical traditions." David Chidester, *Patterns of Action: Religion and Ethics in a Comparative Perspective* (Belmont, California: Wadsworth, 1987), 4. Chidester helpfully adds that, "what people hold to be sacred tends to have two important characteristics: ultimate meaning and transcendent power. . . . Religion is not simply a concern with the meaning of human life, but it is also an engagement with the transcendent powers, forces, and processes that human beings have perceived to impinge on their lives." *Ibid.* Such an understanding of religion is adequate even if problematic. For a study of nature-based religion that wrestles with various scholarly definitions of religion in the context of an examination of diverse forms of nature-based spirituality, see Bron Taylor, "Earth and Nature-Based Spirituality (Part I): From Deep Ecology to Radical Environmentalism," *Religion*, 31:2 (2001), 175-93; and Bron Taylor, "Earth and Nature-Based Spirituality (Part II): From Deep Ecology to Scientific Paganism," *Religion*, 30:3 (2001), 225-45.

[60] David Chidester, *Shots in the Streets: Violence and Religion in South Africa* (Boson: Beacon, 1991).

[61] Such an understanding is especially helpful when thinking about emergent religions, namely, those within the cultic milieu which are the sites of religious creative invention and innovation, of new religious production—usually through eclectic borrowing and amalgamation, or bricolage. Individuals in such groups are free to

innovate because they have in one way or another become unshackled from the authorities of church or sect who would normally control religious production.

[62] Bron Taylor, "The Religion and Politics of Earth First!"; Bron Taylor, "Earth First!'s Religious Radicalism," in Christopher Key Chapple, ed., *Ecological Prospects: Scientific, Religious, and Aesthetic Perspectives*, (Albany, New York: State University of New York Press, 1994), 185-209.

[63] Bron Taylor, "The Religion and Politics of Earth First!"; Rik Scarce, *Ecowarriors: Understanding the Radical Environmental Movement* (Chicago: Noble, 1990); and Martha F. Lee, *Earth First!: Environmental Apocalypse* (Syracuse, New York: Syracuse University Press, 1995).

[64] David Clarke Burks, ed., *Place of the Wild: A Wildlands Anthology* (Washington D.C.: Island Press, 1994), 229.

[65] E-mail correspondence, January 1996. After I suggested to him, in response, that this perspective unduly downplayed continuities between the pre- and post-schism Earth First! (he does not even mention the involvement of co-founder Mike Roselle who had been involved from the beginning but with whom he had severed relations) Foreman replied, "While the group calling itself Earth First! today has some good people and does some good work, it is an entirely different organization than the Earth First! I was involved in. And the newspaper calling itself *The Earth First! Journal* has absolutely nothing to do with the newspaper I edited" (Email, January 1996).

[66] Roderick Frazier Nash, *Wilderness and the American Mind*, 2nd edn, (1967; repr. New Haven: Yale University Press, 1973); Lynn White, "The Historic Roots of Our Ecologic Crisis," *Science*, 155 (1967), 1203-7.

[67] Harpers Forum, "Only Man's Presence Can Save Nature," *Harpers Magazine*, April 1990, 37-48.

[68] Foreman introduces his 1994 book catalogue, "I've often argued that real understanding is out there—in the Big Outside, in the great loneliness; that wisdom is more likely to be encountered listening to goose music or watching the flow of a river than in books or libraries. I believe that individuals have a direct and personal relationship to the natural world, to Aldo Leopold's 'wild things and sunsets,' and need no intermediaries." He also tends to suggest that those with whom he disagrees about things are spending inadequate time cultivating that relationship with the wild earth. For example, in his Fall/Winter 1992-93 book catalogue, puzzled by what he saw as Leopold scholar Baird Callicott's attack on the idea of wilderness, he suggested that "his interest in Leopold and the land ethic is an abstract, academic one [i.e., not grounded in experience in wilderness and] he lacks green fire in his eyes." See the debate on the wilderness idea between Callicott, Noss, and Foreman in J. Baird Callicott, "A Critique and an Alternative to the Wilderness Idea," *Wild Earth*, 4:4 (1994), 54-9; Reed F. Noss, "Wilderness—Now More Than Ever: A Response to Callicott," *Wild Earth*, 4 (4 1994), 60-63; Dave Foreman, "Where Man Is a Visitor," in David Clarke Burks, ed., *Place of the Wild* (Washington, D.C.: Island Press, 1994), 225-35; and *idem.*, Dave Foreman, "Wilderness Areas Are Vital," *Wild Earth*, 4:4 (1994), 64-68.

[69] Dolores LaChapelle, *Sacred Land, Sacred Sex: Rapture of the Deep* (Silverton, Colorado: Finn Hill Arts, 1988), 18.

[70] Bill Devall and George Sessions, *Deep Ecology: Living As If Nature Mattered* (Salt Lake City, Utah: Peregrine Smith, 1985).

[71] Christopher Manes, *Green Rage: Radical Environmentalism and the Unmaking of Civilization* (Boston: Little, Brown and Company, 1990). Manes traces the appeal of Deep Ecology "to the profound spiritual attachment people have to nature" (1990:149), and discussions on the deep ecology Internet group are often preoccupied with how to reconnect "civilized" humans to nature.

[72] David Abram, *Spell of the Sensuous: Perception and Language in a More-Than-*

Human World (New York: Pantheon, 1996).

[73] In various interviews, Judi Bari and others have described their shock when they first saw the devastation of clearcut logging. Commenting afterward, they often express the conviction that it was just so obviously wrong.

[74] Interview with Sid Clifford, Nevada City, California, November 1992. Clifford was active in Earth First! from about 1986 until the bombing of Judi Bari in 1990.

[75] The greenfire myth is represented in umpteen ways—not only through such songs, but also in movement poetry, articles, and "greenfire"-named newsletters, bookstores and video-production companies. Robert Streeter, "Wolves and Green Fire," *Earth First!*, 5:7 (1985), 19; *idem.*, Robert Streeter, "Thinking Like a Mountain," *Earth First!*, 8:1 (1 November 1987); and Dave Foreman and Bill Haywood, eds., *Ecodefense: A Field Guide to Monkeywrenching*.

[76] For a brief overview of primal religion contrasted with other types of religion, see David Chidester, *Patterns of Action: Religion and Ethics in a Comparative Perspective* (Belmont, California: Wadsworth, 1987), 7-11.

[77] Martin W. Lewis, *Green Delusions: An Environmentalist Critique of Radical Environmentalism* (Durham: Duke University Press, 1992).

[78] Lewis and other Earth First!ers endorse and practice other types of ritualizing as well, believing that eco-defense actions can themselves be ritual ceremonies bounding people to the earth.

[79] A wrenching controversy has emerged in recent years about the appropriation of Native American spirituality by New Agers and environmentalists; for a detailed case study of such a conflict within Earth First!, see Bron Taylor, "Earthen Spirituality or Cultural Genocide: Radical Environmentalism's Appropriation of Native American Spirituality," *Religion*, 17:2 (1997), 183-215. Part of what follows draws from this research.

[80] One group of such individuals founded "Earthlands," an intentional community in Maryland that regularly offers workshops fusing neo-shamanism with radical environmental activism.

[81] John Seed, and others, *Thinking Like a Mountain: Towards a Council of All Beings* (Philadelphia, Pennsylvania: New Society, 1988).

[82] For more analysis of the Council of All Beings and its function within Earth First!, see Bron Taylor, "Earth First!'s Religious Radicalism," 190-192.

[83] Stanislav Grof with the assistance of Marjorie Livingston Valier, *Human Survival and Consciousness Evolution* (Albany State University of New York Press,1988). Stanislav Grof with Hal Zina Bennett, *The Holotropic Mind: The Three Levels Of Human Consciousness And How They Shape Our Lives* (San Francisco, California : HarperSanFrancisco, 1992).

[84] For a recent work promoting such neo-animism, see Theodore Roszak, *The Voice of the Earth: An Exploration of Ecopsychology* (New York: Touchstone, 1992), and Theodore Roszak, Mary E. Gomes and Allen D. Kanner, eds., *Ecopsychology: Restoring the Earth, Healing the Mind* (San Francisco: Sierra Club, 1995); and for a fascinating intellectual defense of animistic and pantheistic perception by a person who attended Earth First! gatherings in the late 1980s, see David Abram, *Spell of the Sensuous*.

[85] One Earth First!er, for example, described "a slow dawning of awareness of a hitherto unknown connection—Earth bonding" that occurred when he was buried up to his neck blockading a logging road. John Seed and others, *Thinking Like a Mountain*, 91-92. Others have described to me direct experiences of communion with the trees they have perched in for long periods to prevent their felling.

[86] Lou Gold, "Interview with Lou Gold," *Madison, Wisconsin*, (26 April 1992).

[87] This latter expression is, according to Earth First! and animal rights activist Rod Coronado (1992), taken from Crazy Horse, the icon of Native American resistance to Anglo-European imperialism. Coronado is of Native American heritage. Rod

Coronado, "Letter to Friends," *Earth First!*, 12:8 (22 September 1992), 17, 25. The expression also appears in Edward Abbey, *The Monkey Wrench Gang*, 166.

[88] For in-depth case studies of such complications emerging from a recent effort to forge an alliance among Earth First!ers, traditional Indians, and militant American Indian Movement activists, see Bron Taylor, "Earth First! Fights Back," and Bron Taylor, "Resacralizing Earth: Pagan Environmentalism and the Restoration of Turtle Island."

[89] Anonymous 21 June 1992. He concluded, arguing: "History shows that no government ever reforms quietly or peacefully. It has always taken either a natural calamity, a total economic collapse, a revolution or a war to make a government ripe for change and social reform. Nobody wants that, but we should be aware how resilient and oppressive a threatened regime can be, and I have no doubt that the U.S. government would turn its guns on its own citizenry. Have a care, and remember, Earth First! Live Wild or Die!"

[90] Two evangelical Christians I have interviewed who once belonged to Earth First! say they no longer attend gatherings or actions officially organized by Earth First! because its members refuse to renounce tactics risking injury to humans, and because of the prevalence of anti-theistic attitudes among its members. Nevertheless, they approve of civil disobedience and some forms of monkeywrenching deployed in anti-logging campaigns.

[91] For a fascinating fusion of Judaism with animist epistemology, see David Abram's *Spell of the Sensuous.*

[92] Trudy Frisk, "The Goddess Awakens," *Earth First!*, 13:3 (2 February 1993), 21.

[93] *Ibid.*

[94] Manes later explicitly linked deep ecology and paganism (23 September 1987), describing a sun-welcoming ritual from "Othinism or Asatru" and suggesting that activists consider enacting it. He argued that "as the thinking of Deep Ecology has grown and matured, its relationship with pagan tradition has become more evident. The affinity between the two invites us to give serious thought to the pagan world view. But if paganism. . . is to [help us] reestablish the natural life . . . then . . . it must be practiced." Manes then inaugurated a short-lived philosophy insert in *Earth First!*, which he called Nerthus, "the name under which the indigenous, pagan tribes of Central and Northern Europe worshiped Mother Earth." See Christopher Manes, "Paganism As Resistance," *Earth First!*, 8:5 (1 May 1988), 21-22. He also mentions that Ron Huber named a tree in which he perched to prevent its logging, "Yggdrasil [after] the Old Norse name for the mythical tree that held up the world." *Idem., Green Rage*, 101.

[95] Ned Ludd, "Even Thor Monkeywrenches," *Earth First!*, 9:1 (1 November 1988), 32.

[96] Buck Young is a pseudonym designed to protect the safety of this activist who has received a number of death threats.

[97] Although pagan Earth First!ers have learned much from their experience with the pagan community, the lack of environmental activism emerging from the "mainstream" pagan community is a source of great frustration to them—and has resulted in some largely unsuccessful missionary efforts to radicalize the wider pagan subculture.

Most of the pagan subculture is not remotely radical, let alone revolutionary. One radical environmental pagan and male witch who is quite aware of this has accused the pagan community of "desecrating and misusing the divine energies" through a political apathy that allows "wilderness desecration [and] species extinction." He demanded pagan support for radical environmental actions including road blockading and tree spiking. This militant expression was followed immediately with an editorial statement that these views do not necessarily reflect the views of the neopagan journal which published it.

Although neo-pagan environmental radicals exist (see Margo Adler, *Drawing Down the Moon: Witches, Druids, Goddess-Worshipers, and Other Pagans in America Today*, Revised ed., [Boston: 1979; repr. Boston: Beacon, 1986], 149, 152, 238-50), the overwhelming majority of the neo-Pagan community is not environmentally militant (*ibid.*, 102, 392, 395, 399-405, 412). My own experience at a 1991 "Pagan Spirit Festival" in Wisconsin confirms Adler's impressions. At a "warrior path" workshop, no one among the 25 participants spoke about defending the Earth. (For the entire two-hour period, discussion was focused on defending the pagan community from external threats.) Assuming an Earth First! persona, I expressed frustration as to why nature mystics at such a workshop were not dealing with the militant defense of the planet. I received a chilly response, with a few individuals suggesting that they wanted nothing to do with "terrorism." Only afterward did two or three individuals seek me out to express appreciation and support for the sentiments.

[98] Aragorn, "Letter to Editor," *Earth First!*, 1:4 (20 March 1981), 5-6.

[99] Susan Zakin, *Coyotes and Town Dogs*, 91, notes that "Dave Foreman fantasized about resurrecting the Striders" a group she said was "whimsically named after [Tolkien's] woodland scouts." A real group by this name, "organized by Bill Mounsey, a Denver-based outdoor guide. . . crashed a few hearings in the mid-seventies, making outlandish [wilderness] proposals." Zakin apparently did not apprehend that in pagan subcultures one person's whimsy might well become another person's spirituality. William Bird Mounsey, "Ent Lovers Arise!," *Earth First!*, 6:5 (1 May 1986), 7, would later urge "Ent Lovers Unite!" in the pages of *Earth First!*. See also K. Peterson, "Pause for Ent (Poem)," *Wild Rockies Review*, 6:1 (1993), 19, for an Ent-inspired poem.

[100] Washington Earth First!, 1994

[101] In her study of neo-paganism, Margo Adler found similarly that pagans rarely get "converted." Rather, they feel they simply "found" or "came home" to paganism (1986:14).

[102] Bron Taylor, "Bioregionalism: An Ethics of Loyalty to Place," *Landscape Journal*, 19:1&2 (2000), 50-72; Bron Taylor, "Deep Ecology and Its Social Philosophy: A Critique," in Eric Katz, Andrew Light and David Rothenberg, eds., *Beneath the Surface: Critical Essays on Deep Ecology* (Cambridge, Massachusetts: MIT Press, 2000), 269-99.

[103] Bron Taylor, "Religion, Violence, and Radical Environmentalism: From Earth First! to the Unabomber to the Earth Liberation Front," *Terrorism and Political Violence*, 10:4 (Winter 1998), 10-42.

[104] Martha F. Lee, *Earth First!*

[105] Bron Taylor, ed., *Ecological Resistance Movements*, 342-43.

[106] Two songs praise Luddism in *The Earth First!. . . Songbook*. See Johnny Sagebrush, *The Earth First! Li'l Green Songbook* (Tucson, Arizona: Ned Ludd Books, 1986), 31, 99. The second song weaves Robin Hood into the rebellious lyrics.

[107] Robert Rossney, "The New Old Luddites: What's So Funny About Staying Alive," *Whole Earth Review*, 82 (Spring 1994), 9.

[108] "World Turned Upside Down," written by Leon Rosselson, has been recorded by a number of artists including Dick Gaughan on *Handful of Earth* (Green Linnet Records).

[109] Susan Zakin, *Coyotes and Town Dogs*, 260-61.

[110] Based on anonymous interviews.

[111] Martha F. Lee, *Earth First!*, 123, incorrectly states that *Live Wild or Die* "disappeared" after a "brief existence." The latest issue, labeled "Grow Food or Die," appeared in the summer of 1996. *Live Wild or Die* was never intended to be published regularly.

[112] This article reports on a bomb that exploded at a Hydro-Quebec transmission

tower and that dynamite that had failed to detonate was removed by authorities from two other towers (Anonymous 1995:21).

[113] Republished in Graybill, ed., *Beware! Sabotage!*, 102.

[114] This manual begins: "Corporations and consumer culture are waging an all out war against everything that lives on this planet. . . . This book is about economic sabotage [and] fighting back by throwing a wrench into the greedy gears of the corporate mega-machine. Many of the techniques of sabotage have already been published in *Ecodefense*. This book [is] broader and more militant in approach. But . . . I feel it is not radical enough. How can anything be too radical when everything you love—absolutely everything—is being threatened with extermination." *Ibid*, 2.

The manual seems protective of other radical groups, asserting that it "does not represent the views of any established group or movement." Specifically mentioning Earth First! and the Animal Liberation Front, its editor claims these groups "have a strict nonviolence code which abhors the taking of any life even humans." This manual promises, in contrast, to "take the reader past such anthropocentric taboos." The manual also stresses that, although instructions for firebombs are provided, "no bomb-making instructions are included" explaining for the weak of heart the relevant difference, "incendiaries start fires, explosives blow things apart."

For the editor of this manual, however, such scruples apparently are compatible with the publication of firearms education, see "A firearms primer for anarchists and punks." Felix Von Havoc, "Turn Up the Heat: A Firearms Primer for Anarchists and Punks," in Graybill, ed., *Beware! Sabotage* (Eugene, Oregon: Unknown, 1996). Such scruples also coexist with romantic discussions of bombs and dynamite, including a column describing dynamite as a tool of the downtrodden and how it is better to use it against people than masonry (p. 99), and with a photograph of a woman thinking, "if you can bake a cake, you can make a bomb" (p. 101). Not publishing bomb-making instructions is apparently compatible as well with the reprinting of an article implying that it is time to start throwing bombs (Ryberg as Pajama 1993, 1996) and with another reprinted article criticizing efforts to impose a Gandhian nonviolence code as incompatible with an appropriately "out of control" movement animated by "wild spirit[s] unchained." (Lone Wolf Circles 1990 & reprinted in Graybill, ed., *Beware! Sabotage!*, 21).

[115] Graybill, ed., *Beware! Sabotage!*, 20.

[116] See Jeff Juel, "Building Bridges," *Wild Rockies Review*, 5:1 (1992), 2,6, for an article by a highly respected Earth First! activist from the Northern Rockies criticizing the misanthropy he sees in the movement and stressing a love ethic.

[117] Anonymous Graphic 1994, republished in Graybill, ed., *Beware! Sabotage!*, 61; and for a similar argument, see Bats in the Rafters Affinity Group, "Nonviolent Direct Action Training: Our Tactic Vs. Their Interiority of Pacifism," *Earth First!*, 9:7 (1 August 1989), 29. The view of nonviolence as unnatural is very close to the views about violence expressed by Dave Foreman, discussed previously.

[118] Anonymous graphic 1994; see also "Children of the Earth, are you listening?" from the sabotage manual (Anonymous graphic 1996).

[119] Susan Zakin, *Coyotes and Town Dogs*, 146.

[120] *Ibid.*, 62.

[121] *Ibid.*, 54.

[122] *Ibid.*, 56-57.

[123] Bron Taylor, "Religion, Violence, and Radical Environmentalism."

[124] Erik Ryberg, "Are We Mere Banner-Hangers?," *Earth First!*, 13:3 (2 February 1993), 3.

[125] Pajama, "Bombthrowing: A Brief Treatise," *Wild Rockies Review*, 6:1 (1993), 9. Republished in Graybill, ed., *Beware! Sabotage!*.

[126] Paul Watson, "Letter From a Friend," *Earth First!*, 13:2 (21 December 1992), 3. Contrasting his impressions of the current Earth First! with his Sea Shepherd crew,

Watson continued, "Thank Gaia that I still have a crew of passionate and ass-kicking eco-buccaneers who ain't afraid to ram and sink ocean raping pirates" and who don't worry about "some politically correct agenda that defines radical environmentalism by socialist or anarchist criteria." He added, "This planet is under siege. . . . This ain't fun and games, this war [of] survival against a violent, greedy, hell-bent-on-collective-suicide enemy. Did Washington hang banners at Valley Forge to stop the British?" (Watson was arrested 2 April 1997 and slated for extradition by authorities in the Netherlands acting on behalf of Norway. Norway cited his conviction in absentia for anti-whaling efforts and an intention to try him on additional charges, possibly including those related to the scuttling of a whaling ship in a Lofoten Island port in 1992.) For updates see <http://www.seashepherd.org/>.

[127] Erik Ryberg, "Are We Mere Banner-Hangers?" Republished in Graybill, ed., *Beware! Sabotage!*

[128] The following descriptions are based on an anonymous interview.

[129] Based on interviews with Jake Krielick in Oshkosh, Wisconsin, various dates.

[130] In 1996 Earth First! demonstrated new capabilities both to mount massive civil disobedience campaigns, for example, in defense of the Headwaters Redwoods in northern California, where over 1,200 were arrested in the fall; and to blockade and monkeywrench logging roads for extended periods of time. For a more detailed discussion, see Bron Taylor, "Earth First! Fights Back."

[131] Robert Marten, "A Hunting We Will Go" *Earth First!:* 12:1 (1 Nov. 1991)

[132] Barry Clausen and DanaRae Pomeroy, *Walking on the Edge: How I Infiltrated Earth First!* (Olympia, Washington: Washington Contract Loggers Association, 1994).

[133] Sprout, "Earth First?" Earth First! 12:2 (1991), 2

[134] Anonymous graphic, 2 February 1992, 12:3, 34.

[135] *Earth First!*, 21 March 1992, 12:4, 14.

[136] Orin Langelle, "The Autonomous Collective Process," *Native Forest News International* 5 (1995), 11-12. Langelle's analysis of the power struggle over the *Earth First!*, journal's editorial policy significantly parallels my own.

[137] Tom Stoddard, "Wilderness and Wildlife (Part II)," *Earth First!*, 4:3 (2 February 1984), 4. Stoddard's rationale sounds similar to the most extreme written expression from an animal liberation perspective contained in a book entitled *A Declaration of War: Killing People to Save Animals and the Environment.* I have been unable to obtain a copy, but according to Barry Clausen and DanaRae Pomeroy, *Walking on the Edge*, 270-72, the book (Screaming Wolf 1991) was published by self-described animal rights advocates who, although uncomfortable with its advocacy of violence, thought the public should be aware of such views. Clausen says the book was purportedly written by a splinter faction of the Animal Liberation Front activists that decided their effectiveness depended on making animal oppressors fear violent reprisal. It is possible that such thinking inspired "militant vegans" in Sweden who apparently stabbed a fur-wearing woman (Heléne Lööw, personal communication, February 1997).

[138] Tom Stoddard, "How Far Should We Go?," *Earth First!*, 9:2 (21 December 1988), 27.

[139] Richard Bowers, "To Readers of Our EF! Journal," *Earth First!*, 11:1 (1 November 1990), 3-4.

[140] For an extended discussion of the Unabomber and his putative relationship to radical environmentalism, see Bron Taylor, "Religion, Violence, and Radical Environmentalism: From Earth First! to the Unabomber to the Earth Liberation Front."

[141] *Earth First!*, 21:7, (1 August 2001).

[142] For a good example of them, see David Orton, "Deep Ecology, Earth First! and Anarchism," *Earth First!*, 21:7 (1 August 2001), 18, 44-45; and Michael Lewis, "Following the Heart of the Ecowarrior," *Earth First!*, 21:7 (1 August 2001), 15-41.

[143] July 4 1997 interview with Lee Dessaux, Nicolet National Forest (Wisconsin).

[144] Colin Campbell, "The Cult, the Cultic Milieu and Secularization," 123.

[145] John Clark, in a scathing review of Ferry's 1995 claims about fascist tendencies and antecedents in environmentalism writes, "Although the Nazis appealed to such feelings as love of nature and nostalgia for a lost 'primitive' freedom, this was allied with the glorification of the state, technology, and human power over nature." John Clark, "The French Take on Environmentalism," *Terra Nova*, 1:1 (1996), 116. Such characteristics are obviously anathema to radical environmentalism. Geographer Dr. Jonathan Olsen, on the other hand, presented a paper during a panel on bioregionalism at Dumbarton Oaks in April 1997 that suggested greater affinities between Nazi ideology and environmental thought than Clark believes.

[146] The 1992 advertisement ran under the heading "Now white boys can be tribal too!" in *Earth First!* 13:2, 32, and the letter and apology ran in *Earth First!*, 13:3 (2 February 1993).

The Historical Communal Roots of Ultraconservative Groups

Earlier American Communes That Have Helped Shape Today's Far Right

Timothy Miller

A fundamental premise of historical and social scientific scholarship is that no social phenomenon emerges from a vacuum. While movements and organizations can and do have lives of their own and may well have distinctive and original features about them, they are rooted to a substantial degree in certain social and historical milieus. Several scholars have already addressed the social milieu from which far right groups and movements emerge; this chapter addresses the historical roots of such groups. Like other human social movements, the ultraconservative groups of the late twentieth century have origins in predecessor movements, origins that are often fairly easy to detect but infrequently examined in any detail.

Ignorance of the historical and cultural roots of nonmainstream religious and social groups can lead to disaster. Such ignorance led directly to the Branch Davidian catastrophe in Waco, in which U. S. government agencies presumed that they were dealing with hostage-taking terrorists and developed their strategy from that presumption, whereas some knowledge of the social and historical context from which the Branch Davidians had arisen would have helped them understand the group much more fully than they did. Fuller understanding might very well have averted the terrible tragedy that constituted the climax of the episode. More recently, scholars who wanted to avoid another Waco-style disaster intervened aggressively in the Freemen standoff in Montana in 1996, providing government agents with the social and historical perspective that had been so absent from the government's analysis of the Waco situation, and I believe that the fact that the Montana standoff ended nonviolently was due in large part to the stream of scholarly information that reached those conducting the siege.[1] In future confrontations such information may similarly have great and direct value in helping government and law enforcement officials avoid disaster.

This essay examines the communal groups of the past that constitute one of the strands of the background fabric that has given us the ultraconservative groups of today. As Jeffrey Kaplan and Leonard Weinberg have observed, "The annals of the far right wing are filled with utopian attempts at building remnant communities,"[2] and those communities have arisen from the matrix of communal movements of the past as well as from the milieu of contemporary far right ideology and culture. Here we will survey especially the various and diverse communal groups of Latter-day Saints, which together constitute a well from which current ultraconservative groups have drawn repeatedly. More briefly we will also examine other historical communal groups that have played a role in pointing the way toward the ultraconservative communal present.

I will begin my survey with a note on the Branch Davidians and the larger Davidian movement. The Davidians were not terribly important to the shaping of contemporary ultraconservative groups, but since the disastrous federal siege and fire of 1993, the Branch Davidians have become the darlings of the ultraright and one might presume, not very accurately, that before the fire they were a key rightist group. The Branch Davidians *did* have some affinities with the communal far right; they stockpiled food and other survivalist supplies to prepare for the unimaginably hard times that would accompany the end-of-the-world events they believed were imminent, and they amassed an arsenal—both as a part of their overall survivalist program and as a component of a gun-dealing business operated by some of the members. Their manual for the near future was the biblical book of Revelation, and they believed that to survive that book's predicted calamitous events they needed to be a tight communal group—one that to most outside observers resembled similar assemblages on the far right. Because the Branch Davidian/right wing connection has mushroomed since the fire, and because of general interest in the disaster at Waco, I have here included a bit of basic background on the communal Davidian movement.

Davidian Seventh-day Adventists

The term "Davidian" broke spectacularly into American public consciousness in 1993, when the federal Bureau of Alcohol, Tobacco, and Firearms (BATF) engaged in a brief gun battle with so-called Branch Davidians outside Waco, Texas, and then, failing to secure the group's surrender, mounted a seven-week standoff that culminated with a final siege and fire that swept through the main Davidian communal building, killing 74 persons (six more members, as well as four federal agents, had been killed during the initial raid). Recriminations—were the Davidians really dangerous? Should the government have mounted its attack in the way it did?—have colored the national political atmosphere ever since.

Had the raid not occurred, the group at Waco led by David Koresh in 1993 would have been only one part of the larger Davidian story. The Davidian movement was and is a splinter group of Seventh-Day Adventists founded by Victor Houteff in 1934. Houteff, a Bulgarian who immigrated to the United States in 1907, joined the Adventists in Los Angeles in 1918 and soon became active in a local church there. By 1929, however, he was publicly deviating from the official line on certain theological points, and after several quarrels with church leaders he and his followers went their own way, founding what was originally called Shepherd's Rod, and after 1942 the Davidian Seventh-Day Adventists, reflecting his conviction that the Kingdom of David would soon be restored in Palestine. His theology remained heavily Adventist, but he believed that the denomination had lost its fervor and was in dire need of renewal before the return of Christ.

Houteff believed that his followers should live communally in preparation for the millennial events on the horizon, and do so in the center of the country to facilitate missionary work throughout the land. A search committee located a place to settle consisting of 189 acres (soon expanded to 377) just west of Waco, Texas. A dozen members initially went to Waco, with more following over the next few months. Buildings were constructed, and by 1940 a substantial community with 64 residents was fully functional at the site they called Mt. Carmel. The Davidians raised much of their own food, developed their own scrip money system, operated their own school, and held daily worship services and religious education classes. Life was short on creature comforts, and the community to a fair degree succeeded in cutting itself off from the decadent outside world. As much energy as possible was to be devoted to printing literature and sending missionaries out to convert the 144,000 members who would be needed in order to make the millennial scheme of things progress.

Houteff had expected the colony to last less than a year, since powerful millennial events were expected imminently, but conviction remained high as the community continued its dedicated life for years, and then decades. Then the aging and ailing Houteff, who had been expected personally to be on hand for the ushering in of the Kingdom, died. His wife, Florence Houteff, assumed the leadership, but various splinter groups also emerged, among them one led by George and Lois Roden. The main body of Davidians sold their property, which was becoming surrounded by the city of Waco, and bought a new Mt. Carmel site east of Waco, farther out, where, using the proceeds from the sale of their valuable former headquarters, they built many homes and other buildings on 941 acres.

In 1955 Florence Houteff stepped boldly into an arena from which her husband had shied away, predicting a specific date for the establishment of the Kingdom in Palestine—April 22, 1959. Some 900 persons arrived at the new colony to join in the dramatic millennial events that were about to take place. When nothing happened, hundreds left, and a year later only about 50 faithful members remained at Mt. Carmel.[3]

The failure of Florence Houteff's prophecy caused more factional strife between her loyal remnant and the Roden-led splinter group, occasionally referred to as the Branch.[4] After exhausting court battles (and the departure of Mrs. Houteff from the area) the Rodens took control of Mt. Carmel. Things went well throughout the 1970s; Lois Roden became an effective leader who kept the believers together following her husband's death in 1978. Into this situation came Vernon Howell in 1981, a committed Adventist and guitar player who immediately became close to Lois Roden and soon became her heir apparent, to the disgruntlement of her son George, who regarded himself as his father's proper successor as leader. After a series of conflicts Howell took control of Mt.

Carmel in 1988. By then he had taken the name David Koresh, David for the monarchy Davidian theology expected to be established in Palestine and Koresh, Hebrew for "Cyrus," the messianic biblical Persian king.[5]

The controversies that preceded the raid on Mt. Carmel focused on sex and guns. Koresh took several wives (some of them girls not of legal age, although apparently with the consent of their parents) as patriarch of Mt. Carmel and had children by at least seven of them, and a few members of the group possessed a substantial arsenal—in part, at least, because they were licensed gun dealers, and bought and sold weapons to produce income for the group.[6] (It is useful to recall here that Texans are so enamored of firearms that there are reportedly more guns than persons in the state.) Allegations of the arsenal led the BATF to launch the disastrous February 28, 1993, raid. Why Koresh was not detained on one of his regular trips outside Mt. Carmel has never been adequately explained, but he and his followers acted like the typical Texans they were when attacked by gun-wielding agents—they fought back. Moreover, Koresh had taught what is for most premillennialists a fairly standard doctrine—that when the catastrophic events of the end of the world arrive, some of the soldiers of the army of Satan will turn out to be existing civil authorities. As the party of God, the Branch Davidians saw the end of all things at hand, and dug in for a long siege. After fifty-one days, on April 19, the Federal Bureau of Investigation, which had assumed command of the operation from the BATF, decided to force the defenders out by injecting gas into the buildings. Somehow a fire broke out, and most of those on the premises were incinerated.[7]

Some Davidians survive today. About fifty Branch Davidians survived the siege and fire, although so far they have not regrouped into a structured organization. Other wings of the movement that had broken off earlier continue to operate in low profile. The largest group, apparently, is the Davidian Seventh-day Adventist Association, which operates a communal headquarters outside Exeter, Missouri, and engages in extensive missionary activity. Another group, the General Association of Davidian Seventh-day Adventists, is headquartered at Salem, South Carolina.[8]

As I noted earlier, since the siege and fire, Waco has joined Ruby Ridge as a rallying point and organizing focus for ultraconservative activism. Although Americans representing a variety of sociopolitical outlooks have come to view the actions of the federal agencies at Waco as ill-informed and unjustifiable, it has been hard rightists who have most vocally pointed out the fatal injustice administered to the Waco communitarians. In the eyes of the far right, the Branch Davidians were just so many more innocent conservative Americans who were mainly cherishing and exercising their uniquely American right to keep and bear arms. From that perception stems the right's elevation of the Branch Davidians as heroes and tragic victims, as evidenced by the rightist-dominated crowds that attend the annual commemorations of the siege and fire held annually at the Mt. Carmel site. The Branch Davidians themselves were a somewhat diverse lot; some of the survivors have embraced their new friends on the right, and some have gone on to other life endeavors. It is as a symbol and focal point more than as a historical source that the Branch Davidian movement has helped shaped subsequent ultraconservative activity.

Latter-day Saints Communitarianism

The Church of Jesus Christ of Latter-day Saints (LDS) and its various offshoots have long had a tradition of communitarianism, and LDS roots can readily be spotted in many of today's ultrarightist groups, communal and otherwise. The far right, for example, has had several groups headed by leaders who claim special revelatory powers, a fairly distinctive LDS characteristic. Some groups have practiced polygamy. The survivalist theme integral to far-right communitarianism has strong roots in a Mormon church that encourages members to keep a year's supply of food on hand. And it is not entirely a coincidence that a leading geographical stronghold of ultrarightism in the United States is Idaho, a state historically second only to the adjacent Utah in LDS influence and population.

The LDS churches are also of importance to the study of the milieu of the far right because of Mormondom's long and strong ties with political movements ranging from conservative Republicanism to the farthest right. Utah and other Mormon-dominated political jurisdictions routinely elect conservatives to public office, and the Mormon church has long made conservative social pronouncements. What is perhaps less generally known is that the church also has had important connections with far-right groups and leaders. Former President Ezra Taft Benson, for example, reportedly supported the John Birch Society and distributed its literature, and the far-right Freemen Institute for years had more or less open connections to the church.[9]

Mormons today consider themselves Christians, but their theology and many of their practices are well outside what most would consider the Christian mainstream. Latter-day Saints accept the Protestant version of the Christian Bible, but they have produced a substantial body of new material they also consider scriptural—the Book of Mormon, the purported chronicles of pre-Columbian civilizations in the Americas said to be descended from early biblical peoples; the Doctrine and Covenants, a compilation of purported LDS revelations; and the Pearl of Great Price, a short compendium of several alleged revelations, translations, and stories to and by Joseph Smith, Jr. (1805-1844), the faith's founder.

The Book of Mormon is especially intriguing for the story of its miraculous origin. Young Joseph Smith began having visionary experiences as a teenager and as early as 1823, he said, he was shown a set of extraordinary plates of gold with strange characters on them. The plates were finally trusted to his personal possession in 1827, he claimed, and by miraculous means he was able to translate the odd writing into English. Thus appeared a novel account of the early history of North and South America in which refugees from the holy land came to America in two great migrations, both before the time of Christ. The first group, called Jaredites, devolved into wickedness and were divinely destroyed; the second eventually divided into two warring camps known as

Nephites and Lamanites, and the latter wiped out the former about 1,600 years ago. No generally accepted archaeological or linguistic evidence supports this fanciful history, and several anachronisms undercut its credibility (a character makes use of a steel sword, for example, centuries before steel had been invented); the golden plates, if they ever existed, are long gone. Nevertheless, most Mormons believe in their special version of history devoutly and literally, just as they believe that with the founding of their church in 1830, true Christianity was restored to humanity many centuries after it had been destroyed by bogus ecclesiastical institutions.

Several innovative ideas distinguish Mormon theology from mainstream Christian teachings. The president of the LDS church is considered "prophet, seer, and revelator," through whom the Almighty can and occasionally does communicate with humans. Although Mormons usually refer to God in the single, the theology is actually polytheistic: human beings ultimately can become Gods and have their own universes over which to preside, just as the present God was once a human being and retains a physical body. God also has a consort, a female counterpart affirmed in Mormon theology but little discussed in practice. Those who did not hear, or accept, the Mormon message in their lifetimes will get a second chance; baptisms for the dead, rituals that enable the deceased to choose Mormonism in the afterlife, are conducted in huge numbers in Mormon temples, teaching and ritual facilities that are closed to Gentiles (non-Mormons) and even Mormons not properly certified as qualified.

Many of the distinctive Mormon doctrines were ridiculed from the church's early days. Early converts were often vilified and in several cases were the victims of mob violence. Widespread rumors had it that the Mormons were little more than an organized criminal family—horse thieves and fraudulent financiers, for example—and after word of early experiments in polygamy began to leak out, the saints were decried as morally wicked as well. Self-defense against vehement criticism undoubtedly played a role in making the new religious community band closely and communally together. In due course certain new revelations among the many that Smith kept announcing further commanded the saints to move toward intentional community and hold their goods in common.

From such beginnings the LDS movement developed the strongest communal tradition of any large American, and as far as I know, world, religious organization today. Virtually the entire church was situated in a single locality (albeit a moving one, from upstate New York to Kirtland, Ohio, to northwestern Missouri to Nauvoo, Illinois) in the movement's early years. The Law of Consecration and Stewardship, first promulgated in 1831, less than a year after the founding of the church, was implemented to some degree in the Ohio settlement, and again in Missouri.[10] But these early efforts to establish the United Order of Enoch, as the Latter-day Saints called their theocratic communitarianism, amounted to little more than directing the better-off Mormons to provide assistance to the poorer ones within the flock.[11]

It was not until well after they had moved to Utah in the late 1840s that the Mormons adopted a more comprehensive communitarianism, and then only a minority of members participated in the venture. The early years in Utah were marked by cooperation in agriculture, notably in essential irrigation projects and in retail trade. Then in the early 1870s church leaders, including the president, Brigham Young, began to talk about implementing the United Order more fully than had been done in the past. Early in 1874 the first local United Order was developed at St. George in southern Utah, and other local units emerged not long thereafter. The various experiments differed somewhat in their details, because the church never set forth an explicit operational scheme, but in several cases living the United Order, especially in rural and small-town areas, meant communal living including pooling of money and real estate. The Order was less completely developed in the cities, where it resembled the modern Mormon welfare system that provides assistance to church members in need.

The textbook case of a fully developed United Order community with a highly communal lifestyle, and the longest-lived of them, emerged at the appropriately named Orderville in southern Utah. Settlement at the chosen site began in March, 1875, and the roughly 100 members immediately set to work growing crops and building a communal village. They agreed that no private property would be held by anyone, although a person was given a "stewardship" over his or her clothing and other purely personal items. Through hard work the group, while never becoming rich, achieved a high level of self-sufficiency and was regarded as a model of what the United Order could be. It fine-tuned its system from time to time, and in all developed a healthy society that might have continued for some time had not outside events intervened. As it happened, in the 1880s the federal government launched an all-out attack on Mormon polygamy, and devout polygamists in many cases had to go into hiding. Since most of the Orderville leadership was polygamous, the community lost its helmsmen, and soon the Order was dissolved. Orderville became just another rural farming community and remains that today.[12]

The death of Brigham Young, the champion of the United Order, in 1877 as well as the federal pressure on the Mormons to become more like other Americans brought an end to the most fully communal United Order experiments. John Taylor, Young's successor as president, formed Zion's Central Board of Trade as a central planning agency for economic affairs, but that agency fell by the wayside as conflicts with Washington dominated Utah's energies; Taylor, a polygamist, spent most of his term of office in hiding. In the twentieth century the church would again try to implement its old cooperative ideals with the establishment in 1936 of the church welfare program, which provided for the amassing of commodities and their distribution to those in need. Mormons are still driven by a strong sense of common purpose, and willingly sacrifice financially for the common good, many of them tithing a full ten percent of gross income to the church. They also tend to make strong time commitments to their church, most notably through the missionary program in which many young Mormons dedicate two years of their lives to unpaid work in the field. Although the LDS church is a strongly hierarchical, top-down organization, the sense among Mormons that they are supporting a community of fellow believers (rather than some remote group of rulers) is palpable.[13]

The retreat of the main LDS church from full-scale communal living has been one of several ongoing bones of contention between the church leadership and dissident members. After all, the dissidents ask, how can the law of God be repealed simply because the federal government doesn't like it? Especially in the wake of the official disavowal of polygamy in the manifestoes of 1890 and 1904, the hardest-line dissenters, who became known as fundamentalists, chafed at the new order of church life. Eventually some were excommunicated, and others withdrew from the church voluntarily, thereupon starting their own separate LDS churches, many of which embraced both polygamy and communal living.

The fundamentalists represented the latest in a long line of LDS dissenters who split off from the central organization to found churches of their own. Others go back to the aftermath of the death of Joseph Smith in 1844, when several claimants to the mantle of the founder instituted communal living in the new churches they founded. Here, following LDS historiographic convention, they are identified by the names of their founding leaders. Names of the individual organizations are often confusing, since many· of them are some close variant of "Church of Christ." In the interest of drawing some boundaries around the topic, we will confine this account to movements that clearly have stood in the larger LDS tradition, and will not delve into various Christian Identity Movement and other communal groups that have been influenced only slightly by the communal dissident LDS churches.

James J. Strang

One of the earliest splinter groups gathered in Voree (now Burlington), Wisconsin, under the leadership of James J. Strang, who claimed that Joseph Smith had personally (but privately) named him the founder's chosen successor—a claim rejected by most of the other leaders, although accepted by a number of the Mormon faithful. The Strangite church grew quickly, perhaps counting as many as 2,000 members at its peak. In 1847 Strang, seeking greater isolation, moved his group to Beaver Island in northern Lake Michigan. There a fairly prosperous commune flourished, with hundreds of persons living mainly in log houses and making a decent living from such industries as cutting firewood for Lake Michigan steamers. In 1849 Strang, who had once opposed polygamy, took a second wife; by 1855 he had five. In the meantime he had crowned himself King of Beaver Island in 1850; two years later he decided to run for the Michigan legislature, and with the help of a bloc vote from Beaver Island was elected. The community continued to do well until Strang's assassination at the hand of an apostate in 1856, after which it dissipated. The few remaining Strangites do not live communally.[14]

Alpheus Cutler

Other Mormon splinters, however, continued to keep the communal tradition of the Latter-day Saints alive much longer than the Strangites did. Alpheus Cutler and his family converted to Mormonism in 1833, and at Nauvoo, Illinois, in the 1840s he became a member of Joseph Smith's inner circle. After

Smith's death he supported the dominant Brigham Young faction, but soon thereafter undertook a mission to the Oneida and Delaware Indians in Kansas territory and decided not to move to Utah. Instead, Cutler, like other early Mormon leaders a polygamist, led a group of about 200 into community at a village they called Manti, Iowa, in 1853. There they stayed for a decade. Then, after Cutler's death in 1864, the faithful moved to Clitherall, Minnesota, where an inwardly focused commune operated for many years. Later some of the Cutlerites moved to the LDS Mecca of Independence, Missouri (the place where, all LDS factions agree, the saints will ultimately gather for the Second Coming of Christ), and there the very few members of the church continue their work, although communal living was abandoned some years ago.[15]

Smaller Early LDS Groups

The Strangite and Cutlerite groups were two of the more influential early LDS strands that adopted communal living. They were not alone, however, in their chosen lifestyle. Several other communal LDS groups, all of them short-lived, were active as well in the middle and latter parts of the nineteenth century, but many, perhaps most, did not survive into the twentieth. One successful early faction, under the leadership of Lyman Wight, operated a colony near Fredericksburg, Texas, in the 1840s and 1850s whose financial underpinning was a grist mill.[16] In the early 1850s another colony, known as Preparation, was opened in Monona County, Iowa, under the leadership of Charles B. Thompson, but it collapsed in 1858 primarily due to Thompson's venality.[17] Joseph Morris organized a communal settlement of schismatic Mormons on the bank of the Weber River thirty miles from Salt Lake City in 1861; it was crushed by a Mormon posse following an armed battle in June, 1862.[18] Other nineteenth-century schismatic Mormon communal experiments included various ones under the leadership of Sidney Rigdon, who ended up in New York state, and Colonia, headed by James C. Brewster, in Texas.[19]

Such was the nineteenth-century prelude to further United Order activity in the twentieth century, all of which was located outside the formal borders of the main Mormon church. For all that activity in the nineteenth century, no LDS communal experiments seem to have been operating as the new century dawned.

The eclipse of LDS communalism proved transitory, however, as the main church began to get serious about requiring its members to abandon polygamy in the early years of the twentieth century. The fundamentalists noted that church leaders never claimed that any divine revelation had caused them to repeal the revealed law of polygamy, and they became resolute in their own view that they were simply remaining faithful to the will of God in maintaining plurality of wives. In that spirit several polygamous United Order communes were founded outside the confines of the now-monogamous main church, typically by charismatic leaders who, in classic LDS fashion, claimed special revelation directing them to found intentional communities as well as to practice polygamy.

As the twentieth century progressed, dissident LDS communitarianism, both polygamous and monogamous, thrived. Herewith a brief historical rundown on the more prominent communities on a group-by-group basis:

Ephraim Peterson

The first communal LDS splinter group to emerge in the twentieth century, and one of the minority that did not embrace polygamy, developed in the first years of the new century in Independence, Missouri, the traditional LDS bastion. Ephraim Peterson and associates, wanting to get on with building Zion at Independence, published a plan for an ideal city and over several years, from perhaps 1905 until 1912 or so, urged others to join in their effort.[20] But the movement, known as the United Order of Equality, seems to have attracted few adherents, and it soon vanished.[21]

William Bickerton

At about the same time Peterson was establishing his small group in Independence, another venerable LDS faction instituted a colony in nearby Kansas. In 1845 William Bickerton had joined one of the many LDS groups existing in the turmoil in which the Mormon movement found itself after the assassination of its president in 1844. Eventually he concluded that the factions with which he was familiar, including the largest, by now headquartered in Utah, were all in error and felt called to establish his own branch denomination. Formally organized in 1862, the Bickertonite church, officially called the Church of Jesus Christ, survives today. At some point in its early history the church established a colony at St. John, Kansas, where Bickerton himself lived for a time. Just how long that colony endured is unclear. In any event, another colony using the name of the Church of Jesus Christ was established in Comanche County, about 75 miles south of St. John, in 1909. Whether the colony was an official outpost of the Bickertonite church or a separate splinter group is unclear, but it is known that under the leadership of Charles Tickhill and later A. B. Cadman, the church purchased 1,920 acres of ranchland near the Kansas-Oklahoma border in the hope of providing missions to American Indians in the Oklahoma territory. Building at least two buildings, the settlers grew grain and raised livestock to support their missionary work. Over 80 persons are said to have participated in the colony at one time or another. Details of colony life are largely missing, but it apparently endured for nearly two decades, closing amid disagreements and misfortunes in 1928.[22]

John Zahnd

The family of Joseph Smith, Jr., the prophet and founder of the LDS movement, did not join the dominant Utah faction but rather stayed in the Midwest, eventually settling in Independence, Missouri, and assuming the leadership of the Reorganized Church of Jesus Christ of Latter-day Saints (RLDS). Like the other branches of the larger LDS movement, the Reorganized Church has experienced schism and division, and one of them came with the withdrawal of one John Zahnd, who among other things objected to certain features of the organizational structure of the RLDS church and in addition believed the LDS movement should return to its tradition of communitarianism. In 1918 Zahnd organized the movement that he called the Church of Christ, the Order of Zion, in Kansas City. What happened thereafter, however, is mysterious. The fragmentary surviving publications of the group indicate a membership sufficient to carry on a small communal experiment, but do not tell what happened after 1918. One surviving article written by Zahnd in 1928 suggests that the group was by then no longer active.[23]

Moses Gudmundsen

At about the time John Zahnd was forming his new church in Missouri, Moses Gudmundsen started a United Order community that at first was a part of the main Utah church but eventually became a separate organization. Gudmundsen, who taught music at Brigham Young University, began to develop his movement in 1918, when he and his brother, Octavius, took out homestead claims at West Tintic, Utah. Since more homestead land was available, Gudmundsen encouraged others to join them and take more claims; before long some 60 residents were living and farming communally. Over time, however, the teachings of Gudmundsen, who headed the local Mormon congregation, began to deviate from the official stance of the LDS church, and Gudmundsen, failing to heed requests that he resign from his leadership position, began, in the familiar LDS manner, to claim that he had special revelations of his own. In the fall of 1920 he introduced his most controversial teaching, that of "wife sacrifice," in which a man could abandon his wife in favor of a new, "true," spouse. Soon thereafter, in 1921, the colony was disbanded and Gudmundsen left Utah.[24]

Lorin C. Woolley

Lorin C. Woolley was one of the most important figures in Latter-day Saint communitarianism in the twentieth century. He founded his organization, formally known as the United Effort Plan, in 1929, joining six other polygamists to form a new priesthood council in Salt Lake City. Woolley claimed to have received direction to undertake his work from John Taylor, the third president of the main Mormon church in the late nineteenth century. Woolley spent the remaining years of his life (he died in 1934) gathering followers and organizing his church. His fundamentalist movement spread quietly in various parts of Utah and nearby parts of other states.

Seeking places inaccessible to public officials out to arrest them and eradicate their movement, fundamentalists developed several isolated residential enclaves. None would prove more popular than Short Creek, Arizona, where a substantial community developed. Short Creek (usually pronounced "Crick") was marvelously isolated, cut off by the Grand Canyon from Arizona public authorities. It was also located on the Utah border, which afforded a chance for a person being sought by law enforcement agents from either state to make a quick change of jurisdiction. Polygamists began to arrive in Short Creek in

1928, many of them excommunicated from the main church for their refusal to abandon plural marriage.

The settlers at Short Creek tried not to attract the attention of public officials, but their practices were always fairly widely known and eventually several raids were conducted against them. In August, 1935, Mohave County Attorney E. Elmo Bollinger, with the encouragement of the main Mormon church, arrested six leading fundamentalists of Short Creek and charged them with cohabitation. Two of them landed in prison and became within their community great martyrs of the faith. Another assault on Short Creek came in March, 1944, when U. S. Attorney John S. Boyden decided to strike a knockout blow against polygamy by conducting simultaneous raids on United Order communities in Utah, Arizona, and Idaho. Some of those arrested were charged with federal crimes of mailing obscene literature (i.e., periodicals supporting polygamy), kidnapping, and violation of the White Slave Trade Act, which forbade the taking of women across state lines for "immoral purposes." Dozens of them were convicted, and several went to prison, although the U. S. Supreme Court eventually overturned the law on grounds of vagueness and the prisoners were released.

The last and most devastating raid took place on July 26, 1953. Arizona Governor Howard Pyle orchestrated an expedition by dozens of police officers that wound its way through the desert to Short Creek, arriving at 4 a.m. The fundamentalists, warned of the raid despite the government's attempts to keep it secret, offered no resistance, and thirty-six men and eight women (those without minor children) were arrested. The mothers and children were taken by bus to Phoenix and dispersed to foster homes, where they were forced to stay for as long as over two years. But in the end the raid ultimately backfired, as the government came under widespread criticism for its police-state tactics and the enormous financial costs of the raid and the maintenance of the hundreds of persons in custody at great public expense. Various legal procedures droned on for years, and in the end no one came out a winner.

The Short Creekers, as they are known in Mormondom, offered no resistance to law enforcement officers, and as a matter of church policy they had no weapons. The raid did not deter anyone from practicing polygamy, and the real loser was the state of Arizona, whose victory in its crackdown on Short Creek was pyrrhic. No important public interest was advanced by the raid or its aftermath—a fact that should have been, but apparently was not, the basis for some reflection by later government raiding parties. Historical memory here could have averted disaster at Waco and elsewhere.

Since the 1953 raid Short Creek, since renamed Colorado City (the portion of the town on the Utah side of the state line is called Hildale), has been left largely in peace. With changing mores concerning private cohabitation and sexual activity, public officials have been less inclined than they once were to enforce laws against adultery and polygamy generally. In this spirit of toleration, or at least peaceful coexistence, Colorado City has thrived. In the late 1990s it had between 4,000 and 5,000 residents, making it by far the largest polygamous enclave in the country and probably the largest intentional community as well.[25]

A satellite community of 500 to 600 operated at Lister, British Columbia, and other scattered pockets of the faithful brought the total United Effort population to an estimated 7,600 in the early 1990s.[26]

The LDS tradition has always been marked by schismatic dissent, and the Short Creek movement has experienced at least two splits. In 1952 the group's governing Priesthood Council divided over the appointment of Rulon C. Allred to a leadership position. Allred, a physician who was raised in a polygamous family, ended up leading his own organization that has become nearly as large as the Colorado City-based movement, although only about 500 adults live at the movement's commune at Pinesdale, Montana, the rest dwelling as families in the Salt Lake City area and in other scattered locations. The movement has survived despite the murder of Allred by followers of Ervil LeBaron, the leader of yet another fundamentalist communal church (see below), in 1977.[27] In the late 1980s another faction, originally led by Marion Hammond and Alma Timpson and now several hundred strong, withdrew over disputes with the United Effort Plan leadership and has been involved in legal battles over property rights and other matters ever since; members continue to live at Colorado City.[28] According to one recent report, twenty-one men were involved in a lawsuit against the United Effort Plan leadership which they claim has tried to evict them from their homes—which happen to be located on communal (UEP-controlled) land.[29] How the community will survive this latest challenge remains to be seen.

Alma Dayer LeBaron

Alma Dayer LeBaron was a member of the main LDS Church of sterling pedigree: his grandfather, Benjamin F. Johnson, had been a personal confidante of Mormon founder Joseph Smith, Jr., and was one of the first to be told, privately, of Smith's new revelation authorizing polygamy. LeBaron, instructed and blessed by his grandfather, became close to John W. Taylor, son of the devoutly polygamous late Church president, in Salt Lake City and soon became involved with Mormon fundamentalism, which led to a second marriage and excommunication from the Church. In 1924, he took his two wives and eight children to Mexico, where they settled at Colonia Juárez, an enclave founded in Chihuahua in the 1880s by American Mormons—with the blessing of Porfirio Diaz, the president of Mexico—seeking a haven for their unconventional marriage practices. LeBaron had a large family, and eventually no fewer than six of his sons—Joel, Ross Wesley, and Ervil, most successfully—announced that they were divinely appointed prophets and founded competing polygamous churches. Eventually the LeBaron clan started its own intentional community, Colonia LeBaron, on family ranch land not far from Colonia Juárez.

The LeBaronites came most prominently to public attention with the criminal activities of Ervil. As a member of Joel's Church of the First Born of the Fullness of Times (founded in 1955) he became engaged in a disagreement with his brother that led to his excommunication in 1971. He thereupon founded his own Church of the Lamb of God, declaring himself the embodiment of all earthly power, wielding even the power of life and death over all others. Those who opposed him were criminals and therefore, under the law of God, sentenced to death. In 1972, soon after the family schism, brother Joel became the first victim of Ervil's righteous wrath, being murdered by some of Ervil's followers.

Things thereafter only got worse. In 1974 Ervil's avenging angels attacked Los Molinos, an intentional community Joel had founded in Baja, California. Homes were shot up and burned; fifteen persons were wounded and two killed. As one recounting of the scene had it, "In the quiet of Christmas night their log cabins suddenly burst into flames from Molotov cocktails exploding all around. As the stunned, sleepy people stumbled from their blazing homes, they were picked off by staccato cracks of rifle fire."[30] Later, trial witnesses who showed up in Ensenada to testify against Ervil were shot at outside the courtroom. Other separate murders ensued as well, and those who considered themselves likely targets went into hiding. Verlan LeBaron, Joel and Ervil's brother and Joel's successor as leader of the Church of the First Born, spent years dodging his homicidal brother after Joel's death, never staying more than a few days in one place. Then in 1977 Dr. Rulon C. Allred, leader of another polygamous faction, was murdered by Ervil's agents while treating patients at his medical office, as has been noted above. Ervil LeBaron is believed to have committed or ordered perhaps twenty killings in all and to have threatened many more. He was convicted of orchestrating the murder of Allred and entered prison in 1980, dying there the following year.

Some members have carried on Ervil's work, including the murders; the church apparently continues to have a small presence, mainly in Mexico. At least two other LeBaronite churches continue to operate in relative obscurity as well.[31]

Maurice Glendenning

Maurice Glendenning, a chiropractor who claimed that he had begun receiving divine revelations soon after joining the Mormon church in the 1930s, eventually broke with the main body of LDS believers and founded his Aaronic Order, whose members are called Levites, in 1942. The initial faithful, who numbered about 20, followed Glendenning to remote western Utah in 1949 and, after experimenting with forms of communal living in several temporary settings, in 1956 established a settlement called EskDale, which is alive and well with a population of around 100 at this writing. The remote EskDale, located deep in the desert, is largely agricultural in character, with various crops under cultivation as well as a dairy operation. So successful has the movement been under Glendenning's successor, Robert J. Conrad, that small satellite colonies have been initiated, and other converts now live, noncommunally, in various places around the American West as well. After 40 years of communal life the Order of Aaron appears to be thriving.[32]

Marl V. Kilgore

Marl V. Kilgore had been a member of Maurice Glendenning's Levites for about a year when he announced that he had begun receiving divine revelations himself. In 1951 he formed his own religious movement called Zion's Order, and soon thereafter with his followers purchased land near Mansfield, Missouri, where an intentional community was created for his followers on land that eventually totalled 1,175 acres. Life was austere in the early years there, and the group has never achieved worldly prosperity, but over time basic amenities have been provided. Since the 1960s the group has conducted extensive missionary work among the Navajo Indians, and Kilgore himself resigned the presidency of his movement (in favor of one of his sons) in order to work in the mission fields. The community seems to have experienced some decline in numbers in recent years; in 1967 membership at the colony was reported to be 90, including children, but by 1993 the total had dropped to 32.[33] As with the Levites, the families in Zion's Order are not polygamous.[34]

Alexander Joseph

Meanwhile, new colonies of polygamists seem to crop up regularly. A recent prominent one was founded as the Church of Jesus Christ in Solemn Assembly by Alexander Joseph at Big Water, Utah, in 1974. Joseph, a convert to Mormonism, was briefly involved with other Utah fundamentalists before disagreements over policies and lifestyles led him to found his own church.[35] In about 1977 his movement was reorganized as the Confederate Nations of Israel, a confederation of polygamous "patriarchs" whose families embrace an estimated 400 members, many of them entirely outside the Mormon tradition. Joseph at last report had nine wives and, as mayor of Big Water, had temporal as well as spiritual power over his community in a manner reminiscent of the leadership of Joseph Smith, Jr., at Nauvoo, Illinois.[36]

Ronald Livingston

Perhaps the newest communal group derived from the larger LDS tradition began when a group of seekers led by Ronald Livingston left the Reorganized LDS Church in the 1980s. The group, reportedly about 60 strong in the early 1990s, moved to land near Lamoni, Iowa, an RLDS stronghold, and began to construct homes and develop self-sufficient subsistence agriculture on two tracts of land about a mile apart in 1988.[37] Millennial expectations were integral to the group's outlook; members interviewed in 1990 foresaw an imminent cataclysm, generated by a secret Soviet weapon or perhaps from another source, and believed that their settlement, uniquely, would survive it.[38]

In lifestyle the Livingston group resembles the Amish in its rejection of modern technology; in its early days it even rejected the use of draft animals for farming, but found the challenge of purely manual agricultural too great to overcome and finally began to use horses in the fields. The theological and scriptural heart of the community is found in the Dead Sea Scrolls. Community members call themselves Essenes, and see themselves as recreating the life of that ancient religious order. In their austere lifestyle, separation from the outside world and following a leader considered a teacher of righteousness, they do bear some resemblance to the Essenes of two millennia ago.[39] The group has also been influenced by Native American traditions; homes in the communal villages, for example, are often multi-sided, inspired by the octagonal Navajo hogan, and each member of the group, upon achieving full participatory status, receives a personal sacred bundle and prayer pipe.[40] A hint of pantheism that could have American Indian sources can be detected in the group's belief that a divine essence is present in nature.[41] The LDS scriptures, especially the Book of Mormon, help provide spiritual direction as well.

How many more?

One may conjecture that many more LDS-derived communities exist but have managed to escape much public notice. Intentional communities often exist in adverse legal circumstances and have a vested interest in keeping low profiles. Many communities are in violation of zoning laws, for example, and for their own survival try to avoid the spotlight. With a few exceptions the polygamists have shunned publicity assiduously. Gay Mormon groups, some of which have been communal, generally do not advertise themselves publicly.[42] The roster of LDS-oriented communes is undoubtedly much longer than any one person knows.

Borderline Cases

Categorization of intentional communities can be difficult, and the fringes of the Latter-day Saint communal world illustrate the problem. Is a commune properly considered among the LDS-oriented ones if its founder was interested in Mormon ideas but never actually joined any LDS church—or did join one but later quit and went down some other life path before founding an intentional community? If a commune happens to have some features in its life or thought that resemble ones often found in the LDS communities, does that suggest that the commune in question belongs in the LDS category? Two communities (one of them actually a related pair of communities) influenced to some degree by the Mormons make good examples of the many that hover along the LDS communal margins.

WKFL Fountain of the World

The Book of Mormon and other Latter-day Saint literature had an early impact on Francis H. Pencovic, who took the name Krishna Venta and founded the WKFL Fountain of the World. An admirer of Joseph Smith, Venta had numerous sexual encounters with his female followers, depicting them as polygamous marital liaisons, and the organization of his movement was inspired by that of the Mormon church, featuring a prophetic president and a council of twelve apostles. His other teachings, however, do not seem to derive from the LDS tradition.

Krishna Venta turned up in Los Angeles in the late 1940s, claiming to have originally been from the Himalayas and to have been miraculously transported to the United States in 1932. He was, he claimed, one in a long line of saviors who had attempted to rescue humanity from its errors but had never heretofore succeeded. Giving the process another try, Krishna Venta called on his followers to live communally, giving up all their possessions to the group in the interest of total unity. They were to practice the virtues of wisdom, knowledge, faith, and love, whence came the movement's titular acronym. The group survived mainly by seeking donations—of money, food, clothing, building materials, and other necessities—from the public.[43] Krishna Venta was said to be a spellbinding lecturer, often captivating a crowd for many hours.

For some years the group lived quietly in Box Canyon off the San Fernando Valley in southern California, and in the mid-1950s even spawned a satellite center at Homer, Alaska, where adherents are still remembered as the "Barefooters" for their practice of going barefooted most of the time. The California believers were probably best known to the general public as firefighters who, in the biblical robes that were their standard attire, turned up to help construct firebreaks and provide other assistance at conflagrations in their vicinity. Occasional publicity stunts also brought attention to Venta and his followers, as when, in 1955, he had his followers raise him on a large cross in a mock crucifixion ceremony on a hilltop. He eventually claimed that he had many thousands of followers in California and Alaska, although a count in the low hundreds seems more judicious.[44]

Krishna Venta's spectacular and tragic end came in December, 1958, when two disaffected male members bombed him, seven followers, and the central colony building into oblivion. They charged that Venta had been having sex systematically with female members of the movement, including their wives and various underage girls. His death did not put an end to the movement, however; his wife Ruth managed to keep many of the faithful together, and they quietly survived into the 1980s, ever loyal to the teachings of their departed prophet.[45]

Almost Heaven and Shenandoah

The rugged and remote state of Idaho has become perhaps the leading American geographical magnet for ultrarightists who seek communal seclusion, and two related communities currently under development there have Mormon ties, although only fairly loose ones. James "Bo" Gritz, a flamboyant rightist who served as a Green Beret in Vietnam and is said to be the model for the movie action character Rambo, achieved some public recognition (although not a great many votes) as an independent candidate for president in 1992. Following that campaign he purchased 200 acres near Kamiah, Idaho, which he dubbed "Almost Heaven" and divided into 30 lots that soon sold out to fellow believers who wanted to live in his new enclave. Following up on his new-found success in selling real estate, Gritz purchased another tract of 400 acres, "Shenandoah," and similarly began to sell lots there. Although the lots and homes are privately owned, both Almost Heaven and Shenandoah are focused communities of ultraconservatives. Gritz is well known on the right for his SPIKE (Specially Prepared Individuals for Key Events) training seminars that cover guerilla warfare and weapons training as well as survivalism, and his speeches routinely vilify the government, homosexuals, and international bankers—the latter generally a coded rightist term for Jews.

Many of Gritz's followers are, or have been, LDS church members, and Gritz himself at one point converted to Mormonism. His stay in the church was brief, however; the leadership in Salt Lake City, during one of its periodic campaigns to expel its potentially embarrassing ultraright adherents, began to excommunicate some of Gritz's followers, and Gritz himself resigned before his turn arrived. Thus while the two communities have no official affiliation with any LDS organization, Mormonism has had some influence on them.[46]

However one categorizes the Krishna Venta and Gritz groups, the tradition of communitarianism among the Latter-day Saints in many of their branches is alive and well, even though the main body of Mormons has deemphasized communal living for over a century. When ultraconservatives found communes, especially survivalist communes, the many and varied LDS-based communes provide good models for a new generation to study.

Non-LDS Communities

The Latter-day Saints intentional communities have received the lion's share of attention in this chapter because of their importance for understanding recent ultrarightist groups, but they are only a handful of the thousands of communal experiments in American history. A few non-LDS communal groups are also components of the milieu that is the subject at hand, and we will conclude this survey with a brief look at a few other communal encampments that prefigured or helped shape the ultraconservative communes that would follow them.

A great many American communes had varying levels and types of similarities to at least some of the ultraconservative movements—harboring an apocalyptic vision of future horrors destined to beset the world, for example, or having leaders who had more than one sexual partner each. Listing even a goodly sample of them would be much more than this chapter can undertake, but to illustrate the breadth of the phenomenon we are surveying here, I will conclude by sketching the stories of just a few of the groups that have embraced separatist communitarianism in ways that have some bearing on the understanding of today's rightist movements.

Lopez Island

Communal ultrarightist groups today typically locate themselves in remote areas and often end up in conflicts with the government, conflicts that sometimes bring the commune to an end. In those tendencies they had an illustrative forerunner in the Lopez Island colony of Pentecostal preacher Thomas Gourley in a remote part of Washington state. Gourley in his earlier life had done police work and carpentry in Kansas City, but by 1908 he had opened a Pentecostal mission in Seattle and was dreaming of a community of the faithful. The little congregation was full of energy, speaking in tongues and praying loudly—so loudly that neighbors began to complain that the lengthy meetings were keeping them awake at night.

Gourley was a "come-outer," as religious terminology of the day had it; he believed that the Bible commanded the faithful to "divorce from the world and commune with God among the elect, certain that God would always meet [their] needs," as Charles P. LeWarne has written.[47] Thus by 1911 he had moved the group to a waterfront enclave on the northwestern outskirts of the city where members built forty-two houses, a floating tabernacle, a schoolhouse, a common dining hall, and, as was the case with most intentional communities of that era, a print shop for the production of the colony publications. But the outside world still imposed itself on community life; local officials found the group to be out of compliance with sanitation laws, and at one point a vigilante group of parents arrived to "rescue" their adult children who had joined the group. Clearly the community of the saved had not sufficiently removed itself from the corruptions and persecutions of the secular world, so Gourley was driven to remove his colony as far as possible from "civilization." In 1911 he and more than 150 of his followers boarded a variety of boats and sailed to Lopez Island in the San Juans. There, after a false start on a piece of land that proved unworkable, Gourley obtained permission from an absentee landlord family to settle on a few acres on Hunter Bay.

The colonists immediately began constructing homes and other structures, including a communal dining room, a school, a laundry, and bathrooms. Life was never luxurious; the food was characterized as plain and monotonous, and Gourley's teaching against killing meant that even the harvesting of the abundant seafood was impermissible. Repeated epidemics—typhoid, tuberculosis—took a substantial toll in lives. Some members left, unable to abide the austerity of it all, but the majority stayed on. Although the colony did not actively seek new members, some did join, attracted by Gourley's powerful preaching and the colony's willingness to take in the destitute. Faith was dominant in colony life; two worship services were held each Sunday, and the daily schedule always included a good dose of Bible study and prayer.

World War I helped bring the colony to a close. Gourley counseled his followers to refuse military service, a position not welcomed by the colony's neighbors in the islands. In September 1918, he was charged with violating the Espionage Act. Although the charge was eventually dismissed, dissatisfaction arose within the colony, abetted by the ongoing hardships of daily life and rumors of Gourley's mishandling of colony funds and business affairs. Gourley finally apparently left the disorderly situation for good at the end of 1920. He would go on to further preaching and an untimely death in a train wreck in 1923. Most of the remaining colonists divided the scant resources left to them and reentered "the world." A few may have lingered on Lopez Island,[48] but the colony was finished.[49]

Holy City

The post-civil-rights movement era did not see the beginnings of communal racism, to say the least. Historically a number of groups whose members have withdrawn from the larger society have been concerned with issues of purity of bloodline and race, and no communal leader put race more prominently on the front burner than William E. Riker, who founded Holy City in 1918 to complement another organization, the Perfect Christian Divine Way (PCDW), he had established to promulgate his theories nine years earlier. While Riker preached a somewhat convoluted version of Christianity, what earned him the greatest notice was his espousal of outright racism. Riker was the peer of the Ku Klux Klan in his preaching of white supremacy and the necessity of avoiding, at all costs, the mixing of races. Many of his early diatribes sound distinctly anti-Semitic, although later in life he apparently came to believe that Jews and gentiles, as separate, unmixed racial groups, would together rule the perfect world.

Riker's writings were as convoluted as they were abundant. He provided a sample of his racial thinking in one of his pamphlets, *The Emancipator*:

> The White Man can take care of any and all kinds of business in our own, White Man's California State Home, and no longer will the White Man tolerate your undermining and polluting tactics. Farmers, Business Men and the Workers say: Orientals get out and stay out of our business. Our new Government will see that you get a job. Your polluting, undermining system of business must eternally stop in Our California And besides this, keep your polluting hands off our White Race Women; they also belong only to the White Race Man. This is the true law of our Original White Man's CONSTITUTION, these statements explain the real and true spirit of California.[50]

Riker's racism led him easily into admiration for Adolf Hitler, whom he called "a second Martin Luther," and his pronouncements let to his indictment on charges of sedition in 1942. A jury acquitted him; Riker blamed the whole episode on Father Divine, the African American communal separatist who, across the continent, had a decidedly different outlook on race than Riker did.

But Riker was more than just a racist: he had solutions for all of the problems of the human race. His Perfect Christian Divine Way was comprehensive, providing an ideal system of government, a way of funding welfare and retirement benefits for those in need, the elimination of all money worries, perfect eradication of crime, and generally peace and prosperity for all—or at least for all of the world's gentile whites, who soon would be speaking "one common language made up from the easiest spoken words from all the different Gentile White Race Peoples national languages."[51] In his effort to promulgate his program throughout California Riker ran, unsuccessfully, for governor of the state four times. As he wrote in one piece of his voluminous literature,

> California has a disgraceful, criminal, cesspool system of Government. With a man at the head of it who is not a native of California and without any true solution for this cesspool condition and what is more, it is getting worse every minute and for sure will cause the State to crack up, unless the people of California harken to William E. Riker

who has the true solutions for all of our problems and can
make the State of California Paradise to live in. [52]

On the basis of such a philosophy Riker and an initial band of about
thirty followers built their colony in the Santa Cruz mountains near the California coast in a location that provided a convenient rest stop for motorists traveling between San Jose and Santa Cruz; residents eventually numbered in the
hundreds. The "Headquarters for the World's Perfect Government" featured
gaudy, ornate architecture, a raft of tourist attractions ranging from a soda pop
factory to a zoo, and innumerable large signs advertising Riker's theories, which
included strange Depression-era economic schemes as well as the more familiar
white superiority line. The steady stream of gasoline customers and curiosity-
seekers provided income that topped $100,000 per year at its peak—money
mainly for Riker, since the primarily male and celibate followers worked for
room and board alone.

The decline of Holy City can be traced to the World War II years. The
economic basis of Holy City was always tourist trade from cars driving between
Santa Cruz and San Jose; wartime brought gasoline rationing that curtailed Holy
City's income severely. Riker's support of Hitler and advocacy of ending the
war were odious to most Californians. Gradually things went downhill. Internal
disputes broke out within Riker's following, and two major fires, both probably
the result of arson, in 1959 took a heavy toll on the elaborate facilities. A few
unsuccessful attempts to revive Holy City were made until the late 1960s; Riker,
rather surprisingly, converted to Catholicism at the age of 94 in 1966, three
years before his death.[53]

Heaven City

William Riker promised a good life for whites, but he was hardly alone
in preaching that communal living could help usher in an age of plenty and comfort. Albert J. Moore of Chicago told his followers that grand material abundance was just around the corner for those who would join him. Disaster
loomed, he told all who would hear in the early 1920s; 1923 would see a huge
financial panic, 1924 would see crippling labor strikes everywhere, 1925 would
see a reactionary worldwide revolution, and in 1926 a world war would wipe out
three-quarters of the world's population. Those who wanted to see the "new
dawn" thereafter had best get on board sooner rather than later; in return they
would live in bliss, with everything in life available free.

Moore, a Welshman, first attracted notice in the early 1920s, when he
founded what he called the Life Institute, which quickly spawned detractors as
well as adherents for its promises of faith healing and resurrections from the
dead; Moore was convicted of fraud in 1922, but the conviction was overturned
on appeal and Moore and 28 followers went on to establish Heaven City. This
paradise was founded in 1923 near Harvard, Illinois, on 130 acres. Private property was forbidden, and strict behavioral rules, including a ban on wearing jewelry, were imposed. Members operated a farm and a private school system and
lived in family quarters, although they did most daily chores—cooking, laundry—in common.[54] Most of the community's cash income came from seven

members who worked in Chicago as visiting nurses. Membership peaked at about 75 in the mid-1930s.

In the 1930s the group moved heaven from Illinois to Mukwonago, Wisconsin, where they continued to observe strict community of goods, ran their own school, and enjoyed what have been characterized as fairly liberal sexual relationships—not surprisingly for a movement headed by a man who seemed to have a special way with women and was once quoted as calling the "sex instinct" the "creative force of the world."[55] For many years members ran a motel with bar and restaurant as their main business. A slow decline in the community was accelerated by Moore's death in 1963 at age 82; the motel eventually was transferred to private ownership and was reported still in operation in the 1990s. The faithful of Heaven City seem not to have achieved the vast abundance their founder predicted, but for all that lived fulfilling and comfortable lives.[56]

Children of Light

Many intentional communities with millennial expectations live in out-of-the-way places, keeping themselves apart from the worldly masses who will surely be doomed when the final trumpets sound. Many of the communities surveyed above live in such isolation; one other that does not fit readily into any specific category employed above needs to be noted as well. This small enclave of believers waiting for the apocalypse has existed quietly in the Arizona desert since 1963, when a previously mobile community stopped and took root there. The Children of Light had their beginnings in British Columbia in 1949 when Grace Agnes Carlson, who took the spiritual name Elect Gold, had a Pentecostal visionary experience that predicted the imminent coming of the Kingdom of God. With the end of the world at hand, she proclaimed, God called on believers to repent and required the faithful to separate themselves from the hopeless rest of the world. The dozen or two persons who became persuaded of the validity of her vision soon agreed to live their dedication fully, pooling their possessions and living sinless, celibate lives. Initially they sequestered themselves in a farmhouse, causing a sensation in their small town of Keremeos, British Columbia. Then, nineteen strong, they left Keremeos and for twelve years traveled as a group throughout North America waiting for God to direct them to a place of safety in which to survive the coming catastrophe and picking up an occasional new member. In 1963 Elect Gold announced that God had directed them to settle at Agua Caliente, Arizona. Eventually they purchased 80 forlorn acres on which they built various buildings and began to grow trees and vegetables. There, having made the desert bloom, they remain, living simply and quietly waiting for the end of the world. Their faith remains powerful; when local officials tried to evacuate them in the face of a flood on the Gila River in 1993 they refused to leave, relying on divine protection—and survived.[57] In 1995 Elect Gold was bedridden and nearing 100 years of age; aging and death were taking a toll on the group. But the seven survivors were still living out their commitment to their unusual faith.[58]

Theosophical Communities and the Church Universal and Triumphant

One cluster of intentional communities that has some significance for ultraconservative movements emerged from the Theosophical Society and its offshoots beginning in the late nineteenth century. Theosophy, founded under the visionary guiding leadership of Helena P. Blavatsky in 1875, blended ideas taken from spiritualism, various ancient wisdom traditions, and several Asian religions, especially Hinduism, into an imaginative new religious and philosophical school of thought. Among other things, Theosophists believe that certain Ascended Masters, beings who constitute a sort of intermediate spiritual hierarchy between the human and the divine, communicated to humans the divine wisdom that became the theological basis of the Theosophical movement and (for some Theosophical groups) continue to communicate vital information today. Theosophy splintered amid leadership disputes following Blavatsky's death in 1891, and several of the resulting factions ended up founding intentional communities. The best known and most elaborate of them was Point Loma, begun near San Diego by Katherine Tingley in 1897. Point Loma was especially prominent because of its striking architecture with domes, ornamental globes, elaborate tracery, and violet glass in abundance.

Many Theosophical groups have had a millennial side to them. Some have seen catastrophic events on the horizon; others have seen a progressive, peaceful millennium at hand.[59] In several cases this concern for profound changes in the imminent future meshed well with the Theosophical penchant for community-building. In 1946, for example, one M. Doreal founded a communal home called Shamballa Ashrama for his Temple of the White Brotherhood outside Sedalia, Colorado, in a deep canyon whose thick rock walls were believed to be high in lead content and would thus protect settlers from a coming atomic holocaust. Doreal died in 1963, but the movement and the village continue, disseminating the founder's courses he said were rooted in the teachings of Tibetan masters.[60]

In terms of its significance for the contemporary far right, the most important Theosophically based intentional community was established by the Church Universal and Triumphant (CUT) in Montana just outside Yellowstone National Park in 1981. The CUT is descended from a wing of the larger Theosophical movement known as the "I AM" Religious Activity, which developed in the 1930s on the basis of the claim that its founder, Guy Ballard, had met the Ascended Master Saint Germain and through him had come into contact with the Great White Brotherhood, a council of highly evolved spiritual beings who directed all worldly activity. The torrent of messages to the human race allegedly communicated by the Brotherhood through Ballard was published in a lengthy series of books and magazines.[61] The "I AM" theology affirmed the existence of one God along with the lesser hierarchy of Ascended Masters that radiated spiritual light to humans who would receive it. The Master Jesus and the Master Saint Germain were of special importance, and pictures of them were prominent in "I AM" worship centers.

Ballard died in 1939, and a period of turmoil in the movement followed. Former members filed lawsuits accusing Ballard (and his surviving wife,

Edna, and son Donald, his successors in the leadership) of being frauds, of teaching unbelievable doctrines to fleece unwary and ignorant victim-followers, and public officials weighed in by filing criminal charges of mail fraud. The various suits culminated with a Supreme Court ruling that the objective truth or falsehood of any religion was beyond the power of any court to determine, and that as long as the Ballards sincerely believed what they taught they could not be prosecuted for fraud. That ruling, in United States v. Ballard (322 U.S. 78) has been widely cited as a benchmark in the interpretation of First Amendment free exercise of religion ever since.[62]

Although the Ballards won their pivotal legal cases, the "I AM" Activity soon had other problems to face, notably as new messages from Ascended Masters began to be issued through other persons than the surviving Ballards. One of the new generation of purported recipients of messages from the Masters was a young man named Mark L. Prophet, who by the early 1960s was teaching through a new organization he called the Summit Lighthouse. He soon met and married Elizabeth Clare Wulf, who also began receiving messages. Gradually the couple expanded their circle of adherents, establishing a headquarters in Colorado Springs in 1966. In 1973 the still-young Mark Prophet died suddenly, and leadership passed to Elizabeth, who soon declared that Mark had himself become an Ascended Master known as Lanello. Under Elizabeth Prophet the headquarters was moved to a former college campus renamed "Camelot" near Malibu, California, and in 1981 the movement, known since the mid-1970s as the Church Universal and Triumphant, began acquiring land in Montana. There church officials purchased the 12,000-acre Malcolm Forbes ranch (later expanded), and in 1986 the headquarters was moved to the new site from the Malibu campus.[63]

Elizabeth Prophet considers her movement a Christian church, and has emphasized elements of esoteric and Gnostic Christianity, including "lost" teachings of Jesus, in her teaching. She has also remained the most active of spiritual communicators in the Theosophical vein, regularly claiming to receive messages from a variety of spiritual guides. Among other things, since the early 1970s Prophet's invisible mentors have warned of impending events that, if they are not averted by the righteous faithful, will bring catastrophes that only the best-prepared will be able to survive. As a church publication warned members in 1973,

> Be prepared for cataclysm, but do not expect it lest by your very attention you cause it to come to pass. Be prepared for foreign invasion and foreign takeover. . . . Be prepared for economic collapse, for famine and pestilence. . . . It is better to have a life preserver and to never use it than to need one that you do not have.[64]

On the basis of such prognostications the CUT has developed what may be the most thorough and extensive survivalist program in the world today. Among other things, the church has constructed large, well-supplied bomb shelters in a mountain on its ranch. It has also been accused of amassing an arsenal in classic survivalist fashion, especially after the church's security chief was arrested on weapons charges in 1989 following his purchase of $120,000 worth of weapons, ammunition, and survival equipment under an assumed name, a venture in which church vice president Ed Francis, then Elizabeth Prophet's husband, also turned out to be involved. The group has struggled in ensuing years to assure the outside world of its peaceful intentions, and claims that any weapons now on the property consist mainly of privately owned hunting rifles. In any event, sensational press accounts—some of them exaggerated, some probably not—fanned nationwide fear of the activities in Montana both when the group began its projects in the late 1980s and then after the siege and fire at Waco in 1993.[65]

Like many rightist groups the CUT long focused its apocalyptic fears on the former Soviet Union, which was expected to attack the United States in a cataclysmic nuclear war. With the decline of the Soviet threat Prophet has suggested that catastrophe may arise elsewhere in the world, but that the ensuing times of trial, if not averted, will be no less grim than otherwise predicted. The CUT has also in some cases aligned itself with the anti-environmentalist conservatives who oppose all restrictions on their use of their property, working against "takings," zoning or other governmental restrictions that interfere with full freedom to use one's land as one sees fit.[66] Environmentalists have been watching CUT actions carefully since the group moved to the property, fearing that untouched wilderness—most of the church's property is in such status—will fall to development. Environmentalists' fears were especially aroused in 1990, when over 30,000 gallons of diesel fuel and gasoline were spilled from storage tanks for the main bomb shelter, although the church mounted an aggressive cleanup.[67]

For all of that, the CUT is not populated entirely by conservatives, and much of its theology and practice would be quite distasteful to the Christian right. In some situations its stance has been more environmentalist than not, and more liberal than conservative. Nevertheless, it stands as an important link between the American communal past and the ultraright of today.[68]

The 1960s Communes: Black Bear Ranch

At first glance, one would probably not see the great wave of hippie communes of the 1960s era as having much to do with the ultraconservative movement of the 1990s. However, the 1960s-era communes did focus the attention of the nation on separatist communal living as a viable lifestyle, and some of them pioneered the nurturing of political activism in remote communal locations. During the intense domestic controversy over the Vietnam war, several communes were founded just south of the Canadian border in Washington and Vermont as waystations for draft resisters seeking sanctuary in Canada. Others saw themselves as crucibles of the revolution they believed was just over the horizon. Radical politics was a theme found at many of the 1960s communes, and the theme worked itself out in a variety of ways. Given the massive scale of the communal tidal wave of that era—many thousands, probably tens of thousands, of communes, with hundreds of thousands, possibly over a million, participants—it is inevitably the case that some who became involved in later ultraconservative activities got their basic education in the communes of the 1960s.

Kaplan and Weinberg cite one such case, that of Jost Turner, who despite his white-supremacist outlook felt drawn to the leftist hippie communards he encountered in the wilds of northern California. "I especially liked their idea of destroying the system by non-participation," he wrote, and he admired their "staggering amount of research" and great practical progress in self-sufficient homesteading, developing such arts and sciences as midwifery, natural medicine, organic gardening, and alternative education.[69]

An excellent example of a radical 1960s-era political commune, and one of the specific ones that inspired Turner, was Black Bear Ranch, established in an extremely remote area near the tiny settlement of Forks of Salmon, California, in 1968. The founders of Black Bear had been active in radical politics in the San Francisco Bay area, and sought to establish a remote training ground for radicals and revolutionaries. They raised a down payment to purchase an old mining claim with several existing buildings in the mountains of north central California. Remoteness was imperative, because the ranch was to be a refuge for radical political fugitives and because one of the activities to be carried on there was weapons training, and no commune surpassed Black Bear in being far from civilization: it was not only located several hours' drive from any major city over miles of poor roads, but also surrounded by national forest land and thus ten miles from the nearest neighbors. As one of the principal founders put it years later,

> The original group weren't thinking of commune; they were thinking of a mountain fortress in the spirit of Che Guevara, where city activists would be able to come up, hide out, practice riflery and pistol shooting, have hand grenade practice, whatever. My plan was to have half a dozen people come up, spend that first winter, prepare the place, get it ready for the revolutionary activists to come up, but what actually happened was that about a hundred people came up from Haight Street all at once, and just occupied everything. I remember saying, I can either just turn around and leave, or I can give in and stay, just go with it, and I stayed.[70]

The 80-acre Black Bear property was a mining ghost town that had once boasted the richest gold mine in the area. In the 1860s hundreds of miners, many of them Chinese, had worked the lode, and the boomtown of Black Bear had dozens of buildings and even a post office. When the mine played out, however, the population disappeared, and by 1968 the property was for sale for $22,500. Several members of the informal collective behind the purchase raised a good chunk of the price in a variety of ways. One group went to Hollywood and collected some $15,000 from various entertainment-industry supporters, although high "expenses" caused them to return with far less than that. Other money came in in various ways—through one large unexpected angelic gift and the proceeds from a major LSD deal, among other things. In 1987 the individual in whose name the land had been held signed it over to the Black Bear Family Trust, an act that should ensure that the Ranch is community land for a long time to come.

Initially facilities were tight; as many as 60 persons slept on wall-to-wall mattresses in the not-gigantic main house. Personal habits and sexual activities were soon known to all. Gradually those who planned on staying built their own cabins, but the main house remained an active community center and the site of most meals. One historical account records some of the social experiments that were conducted, such as the (temporary) total abolition of private property, in which even all clothing was shared. The program enacted when parents feared for the safety of their children in this land of bears, cougars, and lynx involved setting timers so that "once every hour, the coffee-klatching and the bitching was suspended and people poured outside to run around the house, screaming at the tops of their lungs to drive away potential predators."[71] A social experiment with a decided 1960s flair was the adoption of a rule that no one could sleep with the same person for more than two consecutive nights to avert "coupling." Coupling was indeed thwarted; when a venereal disease turned up and the members decided they had to chart sexual contacts to see who might be infected, one who was there recalled,

> We made up a chart with who slept with who, just go down and put a little "X" on it, and it turned out that I think we had to treat everybody. But the funny thing was, people would look at the chart and say "Joe, you bastard, you cheated on me with that bitch?" And I remember coming up and going, "Look at that son of a bitch Michael, he screwed everybody! And look at me, I got no marks next to my name!"[72]

Given Black Bear's isolation, its residents were more self-reliant than most. The community could be snowed in for a month or two at a time in the winter, so preparedness was essential. The residents gathered prodigious amounts of firewood, made a major food run for bulk staples every fall, slaughtered animals for food, and built a small hydroelectric system. The Ranch kept a goodly stock of medical supplies on hand and managed to treat illnesses ranging from hepatitis and staph infections to gonorrhea as well as to deliver a good many babies and do its own veterinary medical work. The members ran their own sawmill, maintained their own chainsaws and vehicles, and schooled their own children. At least one member built his own cabin—beginning by felling trees and ripping them into lumber by hand. Black Bear disdained welfare, partly because the members didn't want social workers or anyone else snooping around, and for two or three years managed to support themselves on whatever odd bits of income came their way. One of the biggest cash expenses was the $25 monthly mortgage payment, which in the early years was sometimes paid by sympathetic dope dealers in the Bay area. By the third year residents hit upon a fitting part-time employment opportunity: they fought forest fires. That seasonal work produced enough cash to meet basic needs, including the big annual food run.[73]

The isolation and common political outlook of the residents meant that a strong sense of community prevailed for years. Many daily tasks were undertaken collectively, and peyote rituals and sweat baths became treasured communal events. One of the more unusual communal rituals was the eating of the placenta following each childbirth on the Ranch. On the other hand, members loathed rigid rules and a good dollop of anarchy was always present. One member recalled years later that only two rules, both rather mundane, were ever enacted; in the wake of a hepatitis epidemic a new sanitation rule outlawed sitting on the kitchen counter, and another rule stipulated that, as the former member put it, "you couldn't turn the handle on the cream separator, because it used to drive people crazy when people would sit in the kitchen and play with the handle on the cream separator. Those were the two rules. We decided we had to compromise and allow some rules to happen."[74] Actually, there was also another rule that made sense for a commune of radicals: no individuals could hold stashes of illegal drugs; the community would have one dope custodian who would keep a single horde well hidden. That rule worked well. When the inevitable raid occurred, the six carloads of police officers, looking for a marihuana-growing operation, uprooted some newly planted seedlings—that turned out to be tomatoes.

Sometimes hard decisions had to be made. Like many other communes, Black Bear had a dog problem, and solved it and the problem of getting winter food (when the commune was snowed in) with a single blow. As one visitor observed,

> Lots of people decided to stay in the winter, and of course everybody had brought their fucking dog! They got part way into the winter and were going out to the world to get supplies and pack them back in, and they were bringing in hundreds of pounds of dog food, okay? It dawned on them that this was not productive, it didn't make a lot of sense. And so the dogs became food. They had a long, long meeting, and if you wanted your dog to live, you could leave. So they ate all the dogs.[75]

A radical leftist political outlook prevailed at Black Bear, but mundane realities and chores dominated daily life. In the absence of rules about work, some used persuasion to get common tasks completed. At one point one of the founders realized that the commune was in bad need of firewood, and

> we had a whole bunch of dependent people there, helpless, half of them reading comic books all day, waiting for someone to light the fire, who would rouse themselves when they smelled something cooking. So we founded the Black Bear Get-With-It Party, and we wrote a credo and went and nailed it up like Martin Luther on the door of the main house. It said, "We came up here to take over the world, to take over our own lives, and as a first step, we're announcing that we're going to take over Black Bear Ranch." It caused great consternation. Our tactic was to get up at the first light, have a bowl of porridge, and get to work and work all day—unheard of, right? Never mind smoking dope, you know—get to work.

Gradually more and more of the slackers started showing up for the work projects, and "it turned the whole experience around. It uplifted the whole tenor of life at the Ranch that winter."[76]

Traditional communal and family duties were undertaken as well, as when the mother of one member moved in to live out her final days; the story of her dying as related in the commune's book *January Thaw* is a touching tribute to the larger spirit of community.[77]

Black Bear Ranch was remarkable among the 1960s communes for its forthright self-sufficient lifestyle as well as for its longevity. Most of the founders have long since departed, but a second generation is thriving at this writing and appears likely to keep the tradition alive for years to come. Thus does a piece of the radical spirit of the 1960s live on in remote northern California.

Conclusion

We end where we began: no social phenomenon emerges from a vacuum. While movements and organizations can and do have lives of their own and may well have distinctive and original features about them, they are rooted to a substantial degree in certain social and historical milieus.

This chapter has explored only one (or one set) of those many milieus, that of historic intentional communities. Such enclaves have a venerable American history, having been on the scene continuously for over 300 years. Never in those years has there not been a time in which some persons have felt called to leave the dominant individualistic American cultural setting and throw their lots in with others, committing themselves radically to a certain vision and an unconventional lifestyle.

All (or most) intentional communities have some characteristics that place them in social and historical relationships with today's far right. As a matter of definition of the genre, intentional communities involve some degree of disavowal of the larger society, a sense that somehow the larger culture is off course. Some respond to that perception by seeking to change society, to drag it back on the right track; others respond by fleeing, perceiving the larger society to be not only hopelessly misguided but too massively entrenched to change. In either case a commune can be attractive: in the first case it can be an organizing base, a place from which the needed changes can proceed; in the second it can serve as a refuge in which one can find right living and do one's best to ignore the disastrous problems afflicting those not similarly withdrawn into righteous enclaves.

Communities generally also have some sense of self-sufficiency. Real self-sufficiency is hard to achieve in modern life, and most communes limit their aspirations in that regard, but a common thread in contemporary and historic communal life has been the attempt to meet many human needs by the use of group resources and effort. A great many communes, and virtually all of them in rural areas, have tried to grow at least some of their own food. Some have eschewed internal combustion engines that are invariably dependent on outside resources. More than a few build their own buildings, do their own maintenance work, and sew at least part of their own clothing. Self-reliance is inherently gratifying, and should truly hard times arrive for the nation and the world, as many communards fear, those who have already moved far down the path of self-sufficiency will be better poised to survive than the majority who have not.

Intentional communities, again as a matter of definition, have some kind of vision to which they are dedicated. A group of people living together without any kind of unifying concept or philosophy are roommates or neighbors, not communards. Sometimes communities have elaborate, specific precepts that form the moral core of the enterprise, as in the case of a particularistic religious community based on the teachings of a charismatic leader or planted in a specific historical tradition. In other cases the common principle might be nothing more than a conviction that communal living is environmentally sound and socially constructive and that the whole human race would be far better off organized into sharing communities. The nature of the vision can vary widely, but some kind of integrating purpose must be there for a commune to exist.

Those kinds of elements characterize all communities. Thus to survey the larger topic at hand one would need to undertake nothing less than a comprehensive survey history of American communal living--something that has never really been done, and probably never can be, although good samplings of the American communal tradition have been published many times.[78]

The goals of this chapter have been more modest than that. Here we have sought to identify a relatively few American communes that have specific affinities with the contemporary far right. As we have seen, what has gone before has had some real impact on the contemporary scene. The communes of Mormon fundamentalists, Theosophists, and even 1960s-era radicals were not simply historical anomalies that bloomed briefly and then vanished; in fact the communal world has been a fabric, one that has had a continuous, if not exactly seamless, existence. The milieu that they created were breeding grounds for ideas and practices that have spread in diverse directions over decades and centuries.

Notes

[1] On the Freemen standoff from a religious studies perspective, see Catherine Wessinger, "The Montana Freemen," in idem., *How the Millennium Comes Violently* (Syracuse, NY: Syracuse University Press, forthcoming); and Jean Rosenfeld, "The Importance of the Analysis of Religion in Avoiding Violent Outcomes: The Justus Freemen Crisis," *Nova Religio* 1:1 (Fall 1997).

[2] Jeffrey Kaplan and Leonard Weinberg, *The Emergence of a Euro-American Radical Right* (Rutgers, NJ: Rutgers University Press, 1998), 145.

[3] For a survey of Davidian history through the Florence Houteff era, published before the siege and fire at Mt. Carmel in 1993, see Bill Pitts, "The Mount Carmel Davidians: Adventist Reformers, 1935-1959," *Syzygy: Journal of Alternative Religion and Culture* 2 (1993), 39-54. For a brief post-siege historical synopsis see Pitts, "The Davidian Tradition," *From the*

Ashes: Making Sense of Waco, ed. James R. Lewis (Lanham, Maryland: Rowman & Little-field, 1994), 33-39; for a longer version, see William L. Pitts, "Davidians and Branch Da-vidians: 1929-1987," *Armageddon in Waco: Critical Perspectives on the Branch Davidian Conflict*, ed. Stuart A. Wright (Chicago: University of Chicago Press, 1995), 20-42.

[4] Generally the group did not use the term "Branch Davidian." Members whom I inter-viewed a few months after the fire expressed bewilderment when that became the accepted name for the movement in press accounts; they said that their association had no formal name, but that informally they called themselves "students of the Seven Seals."

[5] Much of this post-1959 Davidian history is based on James D. Tabor and Eugene V. Galla-gher, *Why Waco? Cults and the Battle for Religious Freedom in America* (Berkeley: Univer-sity of California Press, 1995).

[6] Tabor and Gallagher, *Why Waco?*, 64-67.

[7] For a critical but comprehensive account of the raid, siege, and fire, see Albert K. Bates, "What Really Happened at Waco? 'Cult' or Set-up?" *Communities: Journal of Cooperative Living* no. 88 (Fall, 1995), 50-60.

[8] J. Gordon Melton, *Encyclopedia of American Religions* (Detroit: Gale Research, fourth edition, 1993), 754-55.

[9] On the Mormon-far right connection, see James A. Aho, *The Politics of Righteousness: Idaho Christian Patriotism* (Seattle: University of Washington Press, 1990), chapter six.

[10] On these early and limited attempts at communitarianism see Mario S. DePillis, "The De-velopment of Mormon Communitarianism, 1826-1846," Ph.D. dissertation, Yale University, 1960; Lyndon W. Cook, *Joseph Smith and the Law of Consecration* (Provo, UT: Grandin Book Co., 1985).

[11] The Latter-day Saints conducted various experiments in cooperation and community from their early days in Kirtland, Ohio, onward. Some communal sharing is mandated by passages in Mormon special scriptures (see, for example, Mosiah, chapter 4, in the Book of Mormon, and sections 42 and 82 of the Doctrine and Covenants). Several histories of LDS communi-tarianism have been written; the most comprehensive is Leonard J. Arrington, Feramorz Y. Fox, and Dean L. May, *Building the City of God: Community and Cooperation Among the Mormons* (Salt Lake City: Deseret Book Co., 1976).

[12] Several useful historical surveys of Orderville have been published. See, for example, Andrew Jenson, "Orderville: An Experiment in a Communistic System, Called the 'United Order,'" *Utah Genealogical and Historical Magazine* (July, 1916), 128-41; Mark A. Pendleton, "Orderville United Order of Zion," *Utah Historical Quarterly* 7 (October, 1939), 141-59; Emma Carroll Seegmiller, "Personal Memories of the United Order," *Utah Histori-cal Quarterly* 7 (October, 1939), 159-200.

[13] On the United Order in Utah and the cooperative economic arrangements that have been created since its time, see Arrington et al., *Building the City of God, passim.*

[14] On Strang and his movement, see Milo M. Quaife, *The Kingdom of St. James: A Narrative of the Mormons* (New Haven: Yale University Press, 1930); Roger Van Noord, *King of Bea-ver Island: The Life and Assassination of James Jesse Strang* (Urbana: University of Illinois Press, 1988).

[15] On the Cutlerite movement, see Daisy Whiting Fletcher, *Alpheus Cutler and the Church of Jesus Christ* (Independence, MO: author, 1970); Biloine W. Young, "Minnesota Mormons: The Cutlerites," *Courage* (Lamoni, IA) 3; reprinted in *Restoration* 2 (July, 1983), 1, 5-12.

[16] Ernest G. Fischer, "Mills of the Mormons," *Marxists and Utopias in Texas* (Burnet, TX: Eakin Press, 1980), 89-121.

[17.] Constant R. Marks, "Monona County, Iowa, Mormons," *Annals of Iowa*, series 3, v. 7 (April, 1906), 321-46.

[18] C. LeRoy Anderson, *For Christ Will Come Tomorrow: The Saga of the Morrisites* (Logan: Utah State University Press, 1981).

[19] On the post-Mormon phase of Rigdon's movement, see Thomas J. Gregory, "Sidney Rigdon: Post Nauvoo," *Brigham Young University Studies* 21 (Winter, 1981), 51-67. For Peterson, see Steven L. Shields, "United Order of Equality," *The Latter Day Saint Churches: An Annotated Bibliography* (New York: Garland, 1987), 140-41. For Brewster's movement, see Shields, "Church of Christ (James Colin Brewster)," *Divergent Paths of the Restoration: A History of the Latter Day Saint Movement* (Bountiful, UT: author, third edition, 1982), 55-56. Additional references to each of these movements can be found in my *American Communes, 1860-1960: A Bibliography* (New York: Garland, 1990), 364-420.

[20] Ephraim Peterson, *An Ideal City for Ideal People* (Independence, MO: author, 1905).

[21] Shields, "United Order of Equality," *The Latter Day Saint Churches*, 140-41.

[22] "Religious Colonies," *Comanche County History* (Coldwater, KS: Comanche County Historical Society, 1981), 164.

[23] Shields, *Divergent Paths of the Restoration*, 118-20.

[24] A brief sketch of the colony can be found in Shields, *Divergent Paths of the Restoration*, 117-18; for a more complete account, see Carlton Culmsee, *A Modern Moses at West Tintic* (Logan: Utah State University Press, 1967).

[25] The standard work on the Short Creek fundamentalists is Martha Sonntag Bradley, *Kidnapped from That Land: The Government Raids on the Short Creek Polygamists* (Salt Lake City: University of Utah Press, 1993).

[26] D. Michael Quinn, "Plural Marriage and Mormon Fundamentalism," *Fundamentalisms and Society: Reclaiming the Sciences, the Family, and Education*, ed. Martin E. Marty and R. Scott Appleby (Chicago: University of Chicago Press, 1993; vol. 2 of The Fundamentalism Project), 246.

[27] For a memoir of life in Allred's personal polygamous family, see Dorothy Allred Solomon, *In My Father's House* (New York: Franklin Watts, 1984).

[28] Quinn, "Plural Marriage and Mormon Fundamentalism," 246-47.

[29] Maureen Zent, "Polygamy War: Polygamists Battle Each Other Over Real Estate in Southern Utah," *Private Eye Weekly* (Salt Lake City), January 9, 1997, 8-10.

[30] Solomon, *In My Father's House*, 247.

[31] A basic source for tracking the divergent United Order groups is Shields, *Divergent Paths of the Restoration*. Information on various LeBaronite churches is found on 142-43, 159-63, and 189-90. The most complete account, with detailed biographical information on the various members of the family, is an insider work: Verlan M. LeBaron, *The LeBaron Story* (Lubbock, TX: Keels and Co., 1981).

[32] The major monograph on the Aaronic Order/Levites is Hans A. Baer, *Recreating Utopia in the Desert: A Sectarian Challenge to Modern Mormonism* (Albany: State University of New York Press, 1988). For brief historical notes from the movement itself, see Robert J. Conrad, "Eskdale Community: A Contemporary Commune Intentionally Sited in a Remote, Desert Area," *CALL: "Communes at Large" Letter* no. 6 (Summer 1994), 26-27 and no. 7 (Winter 1995/6), 23.

[33] The report of 90 members is provided in William A. Hilles, "Of Razor Blades and Beards," *Modern Utopian* 2 (September-October, 1967), 2. The count of 32 members in 1993 is given in a listing in the *Communities Directory: A Guide to Cooperative Living* (Langley, WA: Fellowship for Intentional Community, 1995), 208.

[34] Material on Zion's Order is located in Shields, *Divergent Paths of the Restoration*, 155-58, as well as in the two articles cited just above.

[35] For opinions about Joseph among members of the Rulon Allred family, see Solomon, *In My Father's House*, 236-37, where Joseph is called "Ronald Ellison."

[36] J. Gordon Melton, *Encyclopedic Handbook of Cults in America* (New York: Garland Publishing, 1992), 52-53; Quinn, "Plural Marriage and Mormon Fundamentalism," 250-51.

[37] Livingston at some point after the founding of the rural community decided to quit using any human name and was thereafter informally known only as "Grandpa" to group members. I continue to use "Livingston" here as a matter of convenience and clarity.

[38] Paul Wenski, "Iowa Group Waits for Armageddon," *Kansas City Star*, April 9, 1990, A1, A6.

[39] The Essenes have shunned publicity. One of the few outside articles on the group was an Associated Press feature that ran in several newspapers in late 1992 and early 1993 and that emphasized the community's interest in the earlier Essenes. See David Briggs, "Are They Serving God, or a Sect; Opinions Differ in Iowa," *Wichita Eagle*, January 23, 1993, 10C.

[40] Leland Mark Searles, "Returning to Babylon: Processes of Social Change and the Characteristics of Former Participants in a New Religious Movement," M. A. thesis, Iowa State University, 1993, 43, 52. This thesis appears to be the most substantial scholarly study of the movement.

[41] Wenske, "Iowa Group Waits for Armageddon."

[42] One gay Mormon commune was the United Order Family of Christ, founded in 1966 in Denver. It subscribed to strict community of goods and apparently survived into the 1970s, but little beyond that is known. See Steven L. Shields, *Divergent Paths of the Restoration*, 175-76.

[43] Asaiah Bates, former WKFL member, interviewed for the 60s Communes Project, September 12, 1996.

[44] Ibid. Bates estimated that the membership reached a peak of perhaps 140.

[45] Several sources provide an overview of the history of Krishna Venta and his movement. The more substantial ones, perhaps not surprisingly, tend toward sensationalism. See, for example, Richard Mathison, *Faiths, Cults, and Sects of America* (Indianapolis: Bobbs-Merrill, 1960), 212-19; Maurice Beam, *Cults of America* (New York: Macfadden, 1964), 76-90. The survival of the movement until the 1980s is affirmed by Melton, *Encyclopedia of American Religions*, fourth edition, 654.

[46] On Gritz and his connections to the ultraright, see Michael Barkun, *Religion and the Racist Right* (Chapel Hill: University of North Carolina Press, 1994), 211. Almost Heaven and Shenandoah are discussed in Patricia Kind, "Bo Gritz Builds His 'Heaven,'" *Newsweek*, September 5, 1994, 37.

[47] Charles P. LeWarne, *Utopias on Puget Sound, 1885-1915* (Seattle: University of Washington Press, 1975), 227.

[48] One former colonist was still there in 1944. See Margaret Marshall, "Solitary Settler at Hunter's Bay: 'Grandpa' Wilson Is Last Remaining Resident of Lopez Island Religious Colony," *Seattle Times*, December 4, 1944, magazine section, 11.

[49] The foremost historian of Lopez Island, as of other intentional communities in the Pacific Northwest, is Charles P. LeWarne. The most complete of his several recountings of the colony's history is "'And Be Ye Separate': The Lopez Island Colony of Thomas Gourley," *Communal Societies* 1 (1981), 19-35.

[50] Quoted in Betty Lewis, *Holy City: Riker's Roadside Attraction in the Santa Cruz Mountains* (Santa Cruz: Otter B Books, 1992), 57.

[51] William E. Riker, *Heart and Blood Government* (Holy City: author, n.d.), 8.

[52] Quoted in Lewis, *Holy City*, 57.

[53] For an illustrated history of Holy City, see Lewis, *Holy City*. See also Paul Kagan, *New World Utopias: A Photographic History of the Search for Community* (New York: Penguin, 1975), 102-17.

[54] The principal early source on Heaven City is Ernest S. Wooster, "Heaven Everywhere," *Communities of the Past and Present* (Newllano, LA: Llano Colonist, 1924), 143.

[55] Michael Zahn, "Heaven City: Time Locks 'Love' Religion into Past," *Milwaukee Journal*, August 13, 1979, part 2, 1, 5.

[56] Much of this information comes from Zahn, "Heaven City," and a sequel article by Zahn, "Heaven City Dies with Founder," *Milwaukee Journal*, August 14, 1979, part 2; 1, 3. For a brief account based in large part on these articles, see J. Gordon Melton, "Heaven City," *Encyclopedia of American Religions* 4th edition supplement (Detroit: Gale Research, 1994), 59.

[57] Tony Perry, "Members of 'Children of Light' Say God Will Provide for Them," *Los Angeles Times*, February 28, 1993.

[58] Most information about the Children of Light seems to have appeared only in the popular press. At this writing the most recent article was Michelle Boorstein, "'Children of Light's' Aging Survivors Keep the Faith," *Los Angeles Times*, December 10, 1995, A49.

[59] See Catherine Lowman Wessinger, Annie Besant and Progressive Messianism (1846-1933) (Lewiston, New York: Edwin Mellen, 1988). See also Wessinger's later work on varieties of millennialism, including *How the Millennium Comes Violently* (forthcoming).

[60] Pasquale Marranzino, "Denver Mystic Is Constructing Atomic Armageddon Refuge," *Rocky Mountain News* (Denver), August 30, 1946, 22; Michael Mehle, "Mountain Village Fights Cult Image, Mysterious Past," *Rocky Mountain News*, October 14, 1990, 13.

[61] Many of Ballard's books were published under the pseudonym "Godfré Ray King." See, for example, Godfré Ray King, *Unveiled Mysteries* (Chicago: Saint Germain Press, 1934); King, *The "I AM" Discourses* (Chicago: Saint Germain Press, 1935). The movement's principal periodical was *The Voice of the I AM*.

[62] For the text of the Supreme Court opinions in the case, see "United States v. Ballard," *Toward Benevolent Neutrality: Church, State, and the Supreme Court*, by Robert T. Miller and Ronald B. Flowers (Waco, TX: Baylor University Press, 1977), 49-55.

[63] For a survey history of the Church Universal and Triumphant that traces its roots in Theosophy and the "I AM" Activity, see J. Gordon Melton, "The Church Universal and Triumphant: Its Heritage and Thoughtworld," *Church Universal and Triumphant in Scholarly Perspective*, ed. James R. Lewis and J. Gordon Melton (Stanford, CA: Center for Academic Publication, 1994), 1-20.

[64] Quoted in Jocelyn H. DeHaas, "The Mediation of Ideology and Public Image in the Church Universal and Triumphant," *Church Universal and Triumphant in Scholarly Perspective*, 27.

[65] See, for example, Richard Lacayo, "Heading for the Hills," *Time*, March 26, 1990, 20.

[66] The CUT's relations with neighbors have often been marked by conflict. For the church's view of the situation, see "Meet the Neighbors of Church Universal and Triumphant," *Royal Teton Ranch News* 8:2 (Spring/Summer, 1996), 1, 3-5, 10.

[67] For a more complete account of local controversies over CUT activities, see DeHaas, "The Mediation of Ideology and Public Image," 21-37.

[68] Robert S. Ellwood, "Theosophy," *America's Alternative Religions*, ed. Timothy Miller (Albany: State University of New York Press, 1995), 322; J. Gordon Melton, "Church

Universal and Triumphant," *Encyclopedia of American Religions*, fourth edition, 800; George A. Mather and Larry A. Nichols, *Dictionary of Cults, Sects, Religions and the Occult* (Grand Rapids, MI: Zondervan, 1993), 125-28.

[69] Jeffrey Kaplan and Leonard Weinberg, *The Emergence of a Euro-American Radical Right*, 155.

[70] From the 60s Communes Project interviews, University of Kansas.

[71] Peter Coyote, *Sleeping Where I Fall: A Chronicle* (Washington, D.C.: Counterpoint, 1998), 152.

[72] From the 60s Communes Project interviews, University of Kansas.

[73] *January Thaw: People at Blue Mt. Ranch Write About Living Together in the Mountains* (New York: Times Change Press, 1974), 21.

[74] From the 60s Communes Project interviews, University of Kansas.

[75] From the 60s Communes Project interviews, University of Kansas.

[76] From the 60s Communes Project interviews, University of Kansas.

[77] *January Thaw*, 86-90.

[78] At this writing the latest survey of American intentional communities, one that will endure as a standard work for some time to come, is *America's Communal Utopias*, ed. Donald E. Pitzer (Chapel Hill: University of North Carolina Press, 1997).

CHAPTER
5

Neo-Shamanism, Psychic Phenomena and Media Trickery

Cultic Differences in Hungary

László Kürti

What best signals the close of the twentieth century and the dawn of the twenty-first in Hungary may be described as an era of cultic ambivalence, societal fragmentation and chthonic ferment. At the threshold of the third millennium, one is obliged to acknowledge the many-faceted new religious, political and cultural developments the country and its people have experienced since the collapse of communism. On the one hand, one could argue that this is the era of "transition"; the leaving behind the state socialist system and entering into what may loosely be characterized as a market economy and parliamentary democracy. Together with such a fundamental economic and political transformation, changes in the cultural and religious spheres are bound to happen. Yet, stressing the overwhelming nature of a transitory age and its coeval societal side effects will not necessarily provide adequate answers to many of the questions concerning the rise of new alternative political, cultural and religious phenomena signaling the beginning of a new millennium. Rather, and this is what I would like to emphasize here, we will have to search for meaningful explanation and analyses of the kinds of developments which grew out of the societal milieu of the last decade of state socialist rule and its aftermath. The millenarian atmosphere is certainly felt in the alternative milieu which has emerged during the past decade. In fact, the notion of "milieu" is what I see as a useful term to apply here. But not just any kind of milieu: a milieu which could include such diverse concepts as social space, habits, culture and many of their postmodern and post-communist critical descendants.

Instead of reinventing this as a new term, I resort to the phrase of the British sociologist Colin Campbell, who introduced the notion of the cultic milieu more than two decades ago.[1] Campbell's phrase is intriguing for many reasons. For one, it is perhaps the first theoretical analysis by a sociologist calling attention to the fact that cults exist, but they do so only when there is a social context which allows their flourishing and reproduction. Another reason is that Campbell's study started a whole new way of thinking about cults and cultic phenomena in the early 1970s; whole collections followed.[2] Yet, strangely enough, most sociologists, Campbell among them, who used the notion of the cult and the cultic extensively, did not take notice of the anthropologist Anthony Wallace who in his classic study

Religion: An Anthropological View utilizes the same notion, but with different meanings to incorporate religious phenomena in an evolutionary scale.[3] There is no sense in trying to search for reasons why Campbell did not use any anthropological insights; nobody really utilized Campbell's model either! The reason why Campbell is interesting to us after more than two decades of silence is the fact that there are similar "occult milieu" phenomena occurring throughout the world in the 1990s. This is true as much for North America as for the recently liberated eastern part of Europe where new and alternative religious phenomena have become the accepted staple of life. We only have to be reminded of the extreme suicidal cults (Solar Temple, Heaven's Gate) in the West; or the re-emergence of non-state religions and communal cults all over the former Soviet bloc. Campbell's early 1970s thesis seems to be a projection into the late 1990s as we can see it from the widespread semi-political religious revivalism the world over.

Looking at the changes and the new developments in Hungary, I want to recall Ernest Gellner's[4] earlier point concerning our own society—that modernity may be best understood as an ironic culture, one in which most of us take the rational canons and science as the only way of thinking and relegating everything else freely to the informal sphere of leisure activities.[5] At the close of the 1990s, with the postmodern and post-communist world coalescing, irony seems to be focusing on connecting science to other forms of reasoning. In this sphere everything could, and with Murphy's Law (!) will happen; the mystical, the occult, the psychic, and the pseudo-scientific are all allowed to thrive largely because they do not matter and do not pose serious challenges to the real scholarly—empirical, observed, tested, and rationalized—enterprise. As Tanya Luhrmann, who studied English witches and magical practitioners, puts it: "The larger cultural order probably tolerates magical practice because it seems unthreatening—foolish perhaps, but not genuinely heretical."[6] Neither do they, I might add, seem to pose any threat to state ideology either. Although there are some real differences in the proportion of people accepting and participating in the alternative religions, most Hungarians, similar to citizens of neighboring states, only shake their heads in disbelief when they see Buddhists, Hare Krishna followers, psychics, and urban neo-shamans of all kinds. Yet, more and more of them do not turn away, but engage in these activities as their friends are drawn into them and, consequently, invite them to join as well.

Thus, it is high time to ask the question: what makes East-Central Europeans in general, and Hungarians in particular, turn away from state religions and accept alternative world views and religious practices? Most surveys of the 1970s and 1980s revealed that only a small fraction of Hungarians were practicing Catholics and Protestants, and the state has managed to maintain its secularized profile. Although long gone were the days of Stalinist forced atheism, even during the 1980s, when more people admitted their religious adherence than before, most young people were indifferent to church affairs. The only place where a frenetic religious activity took place was a small Bosnian town, Medjugorje, where the apparition of the Virgin Mary converted hundreds, and later, tens of thousands of followers to a revived sense of Roman Catholicism.[7]   However, since 1990, a reinvigorated religious fervor has been in the air, and for many young Hungarians Western-style youth culture seems to provide salvation. This is true not only with regard to mainstream and alternative religions, but to popular culture and its deleterious side effects as well. Recent estimates, for instance, stress that the number of drug users may be as high as 53,000 with an additional hundred thousand people also involved with drugs on an occasional basis.[8] The drug phenomenon is, of course, a world phenomenon and the globalization of culture also means globalization of drug trafficking. Yet, drugs are only one aspect of the fundamental changes which came to Hungary after the fall of communism.

Clearly, something has happened since the late 1980s, when the state socialist, Moscow-directed system collapsed to transform Hungarian society so fundamentally that tons of heroin and hashish are confiscated by border guards, arsenals are discovered and multi-millionaires are sentenced for bribery while, at the same time, thousands find new values and gods to celebrate the coming of the New Millennium. My task in this chapter is simple, for alternative groups and circles are given more and more prominence in Hungarian cultural life as society is experiencing the multifarious side effects of post-communism and globalization. In fact, with 1989-1990, we are at the heart of the cultic milieu for many alternative semi-political and religious groups—from the Maharashi to the Bio-Shield Positive Thinkers—claim that the demise of the communist system was not by chance: they argue that mystic and cosmic forces facilitated its easy collapse. Thus for the alternative thinkers this collapse was by no accident. Many claim that they too, or the powers that may be had a lot to do with it. As we will see, many of these circles operate in semi-legality, others quite openly, but both claim knowledge of the truth and answers to long-debated scientific facts while relying on the "best" available explanation of supernatural phenomena. We see now televangelists speaking out not in hide-away shelters but in public squares and theaters; Billy Graham, for instance, filled the largest stadium in Budapest when he visited Hungary the first time in the early 1990s. In June 1997, Jehova's Witnesses organized the largest weekend in a Budapest sport arena, with tens of thousands of converts celebrating the church's reawakening in Hungary. Pope John Pope II also had visited Hungary twice, with millions listening to his sermons, but Catholicism is a state religion (as it has been for the past 1,100 years) and so does not concern us here.[9]

In the shadow of the twenty-first century, Hungarian governmental policy seems to be a wholehearted acceptance of mainstream religions, a fact supported by the signing of agreements between Hungary and the Vatican on June 20, 1997.[10] Even religious fundamentalism, while relegated to the spheres of church matters before, now is out in the open and taking more and more of a leading role in political, economic and international relations. But there is something odd, or rather extraordinary to say the least, when hundreds and thousands of people from all walks of life find outlets in sects and cults which were imported to Hungarian soil only a few years ago. Some of these are well known in the West, others are a mixture of home-grown surprises and an imaginative blend of mysticism and nationalism.

What characterizes the social tapestry of Hungary at the beginning of the new millennium and during much of the 1990s is the appearance of the new cults, alternative medicinal practices, and the mushrooming of various belief systems or folk religions. After 1990, even the magic circles in wheat fields, known for many years all over the world, have appeared in Hungary, a sign signaling for many the arrival of the Age of Aquarius. Many of the alternative religious and quasi-religious political groups, long familiar to Westerners, have been entering Eastern Europe in an astonishing frenzy after 1990.[11] Among them, the Hare Krishna, or the Society of Krishna Consciousness, is one of the largest groups which has become the most visible phenomenon of the 1990s. While their religious practices are relegated to far-away country retreats, during the winter of 1996-1997 the Krishna Society offered warm soup for the homeless in Budapest, an act which certainly helped to legitimize the group in the eyes of the authorities as well as the general public. More and more one can see the shaved, orange-robed groups marching in the cities; it is easy to establish that youth in their twenties and early thirties are the largest percentage of faithful devotees. Their religious commune opened in the spring of 1997, with thousands of followers and interested bystanders watching as the gathered Krishna believers consecrated their newly finished temple and its compound of communal living spaces.

However, while the Krishna groups are common sights all over Europe these days, another quite influential religious group which suddenly emerged in Hungary is the Buddhists. In fact they are the hundreds of followers of the Dalai Lama, a world-renowned figure of human and minority rights. The success of this group is more clearly understandable once we realize that the Dalai Lama already visited Hungary twice, the last time in 1996. Because of his stature on the international scene, the Dalai Lama was received by statesmen, ranging from the mayor of Budapest, ministers, the prime minister and even the president of the country. Having such an "instantly political famous" person behind them, the Hungarian followers were extremely successful in collecting large amounts of money—the origin of some of it is not well ascertained, but some claim that international donations make up a fair chunk of it. As a result they were able to build an impressive *stupa* in Zalaszentgrót, a small village in the southwestern part of Hungary.

But alternative lifestyles and information networks may be detected in other areas of contemporary life as well. New ethnic-based parties and policy organizations are now accepted as regular players in the post-1989 Hungarian political life. Nobody now questions the legitimacy of dozens of Gypsy civil rights and cultural organizations, not to mention the scores of political factions. And no one looks suspiciously at other political circles such as the Knights of Malta, the Lions and the Free Masons, groups which now can boast an exquisite membership, among them being illustrious figures of the artistic and cultural life as well as members of the political elite.

To a certain degree it is to be expected that following the collapse of the strict state control on religious and cultural life, communal cults and religions of all sorts are now in vogue among old and young alike. The Jewish community in Hungary is experiencing a religious revival with its Dohány street synagogue restored to its earlier pre-war glory and the Jewish theological school admitting more and more students from East-Central Europe. While before only a few individuals dared to speak out against the official religions—the Roman Catholic priest, Father Bulányi, and his movement the "Circle of Bushes" [*Bokor Kör*] was one of them—after 1989 all churches in general have developed an openly confrontational stance with state authority.[12] Now one can see religious fervor in more traditional churches as well, not only within the borders of the Hungarian nation-state, but in the neighboring countries as well. In particular, one can observe a full-scale radicalization of both the Hungarian Catholic and the Hungarian Protestant faiths in Slovakia and Romania, respectively.

Fundamentalist Christian religions are the most numerous in Hungary. They range from small evangelist schools, such as the Mahanaim Association, to middle- and upper-class denominations, such as the Association of the Faith, an exclusivist group with important political connections. The Mahanaim Association only gained notoriety since the early 1990s, though the group was registered already in 1989, when it started its evangelic mission in the open.[13] However, one of the newest home-grown fundamentalist Christian groups is the Association of Faith [*Hit Gyülekezete*]. This group appeared in the mid-1990s in the media, but achieved instant fame in the beginning of 1997 when several of its leaders decided to speak openly about their membership in the church.[14] Included among them are major politicians, professionals, artists and prominent members of Hungary's noveau riche.[15] Organized somewhat similarly to the Church of Scientology, membership is voluntary, but all novices must make a serious commitment to the organization: for instance, in addition to their silence about their involvement in the organization and upholding its fundamental Christian tenets, ten percent of the members' income must be offered to the Association on a yearly basis. Such a solid economic base allows the group to purchase expensive real estate and businesses, a fact which elevates the Association of Faith above the rest of new religions.

Another recently founded religious movement is even more cultic (in the classic sense of the concept as being more mystical, marginal and connected to the transcendental sphere) than the Association of Faith. This is New Babylon [*Új Babylon*], a religious cult operating from an apartment in the Óbuda district of the nation's capital. Created first as a foundation, New Babylon is a Christian fundamentalist movement—of the sort of Christian Identity in the United States— playing as it is on extreme nationalistic ideology as its base. The cult followers believe that Hungary was the location where the stories of the Bible took place, and even Jesus Christ was Hungarian.[16] The sect's slogan is "With God for Earth and People," a sentence which combines, in addition to its religious fervour, historical, nationalistic and ecological concerns. They also advertise themselves as "free of all religion and politics," an interesting twist on words and ideas from such a fundamentalist religious body.

According to the cult's doctrine, the original Bible was written in Hungarian and there are now two Messiahs walking in Hungary among us. Their identities, however, are only revealed to a select few. Already the cult lists fifty organizations nationwide, a figure roughly corresponding to about five hundred practicing followers. During their religious meetings, members sit around a large table with twelve chairs, utilizing the symbols of the national tricolor and the triple cross—representing the founding of the Hungarian state. They often recite poetry from Hungarian poets and utilize embroidery to create religious iconography. According to the leader, Heaven will be achieved in this earth but must be created by willing participants; it will, naturally, be a Hungarian-speaking Earthly Paradise. Another significant aspect of the New Babylon community is that they also gain their ideological strength from Hungarian prehistory: they are working to reunite the ancient twelve Hungarian tribes.[17] There is one cautionary note, however: among its mystic followers there is one person who gives cause for worry; his name is Albert Szabó, Hungary's self-proclaimed Nazi leader.[18]

This said, it must be mentioned, that even the so-called historical religions—referring to the Roman Catholic, Protestant, Greek Orthodox, and Jewish churches—are now in much better shape than before as the result of the socialist-liberal government's attempt to settle sensitive state-church issues. For example, Gyula Horn, Hungary's socialist prime minister since 1994, agreed with the Vatican to return all church property to the Hungarian Catholic Church, which was nationalized after the communist takeover in 1948.[19] In such a mild political climate, and with the "historical churches" tamed, radical anti-state stances and programs are only to be expected from religious groups which are outside this religious state contract. As more and more of these historic churches receive support from the state, alternative religions seem to thrive on their own as well. This interesting pattern may be explained by the fact that with more radicalism and openness, more people seem to question the fundamental tenets of the Bible and the teachings of both Roman Catholicism and Protestantism.

Religious life is not, however, the only sphere for the thriving cultic milieu. It is felt throughout even the state-supported media: the film industry, television, theater and the publishing world. Most of film and television, I must stress, is a cheap imitation of Western, specifically American, shows. As an accepted facet of the current popular cultural scene all over Eastern Europe, instant new stars and programs have been created; with the new stars—former actors and actresses, rock artists and media personages—a new cult also develops. Among Hungarian teenagers, the "Xenia Fever" (a playful UFO-like, semi-educational and semi-competitive, but in any case, a manipulated program) is gaining more and more faithful followers.

In comparison, in the Czech Republic, one of the most watched programs is Fero Fenic's "Sunday Night Show"; it is a compilation of documentary and America-style comedy shows, all congested into the Czech reality.[20] In Bucharest, Romania, the independent PRO TV provides all the up-to-date and hip programs for Romanian audiences, accustomed as they were to heavily censored state programs.

In the Hungarian popular media scene, one individual in particular deserves to be mentioned here: Sándor Friderikusz, whose name epitomizes best the world of media wackiness and the new success story of media wizardry of the mid-nineties in Hungary. Friderikusz, an agile man with journalism training, has been part of the rising independent media scene in Hungary for the past two decades.[21] However, his meteoric rise to fame began in 1992 when he was given a chance to start his own talk show on national television. Styled after the American Oprah Winfrey, Conan O'Brian, or Jay Leno, the Friderikusz show became the show to watch for the Hungarian populace. In fact the showman claims that while other major productions are watched by 2 million people at the most, his shows manage the highest viewers' rating with four million Hungarian converts watching.[22] Since Friderikusz now produces four different programs for Hungarian television, his success is not only an enigma, but a reflection of the sudden emergence of media leaders in a way which may be best described as cultic.

On Thursday nights, Friderikusz's almost two hours of vignette-style programming has been the legitimate place for Hungarians to see and hear for the first time homosexual couples, AIDS victims, high-style call girls, Western movie stars (singing Hungarian songs), maffiosos, parental killers and fallen politicians. By May 1997, the show had lost some of its popularity, its viewers' index still shows that it held a steady fifth place among the ten most watched television shows in Hungary.[23] To apply to this show Campbell's notion of the cultic milieu and its connection to the religion-science axis, it must be stressed that the Friderikusz program is not only a production of television producers and show writers; on the contrary, Friderikusz himself proclaimed openly that he managed to gather a group of well-known Hungarian sociologists and writers to provide his managing team with new ideas and a "scholarly" input as to the shows' content and packaging.[24]

After the 1994 political change, the new regime wanted to cut certain television programs and decided to rearrange programming by replacing a large segment of television leadership. Some programs and department heads were replaced quietly. However, when the new president of the (still) state-controlled television announced the cancellation of the Friderikusz show, there was immediate backlash. It turned out that Friderikusz had a devilish yet a stylish plan of his own. This new self-styled media mogul claimed that he had a multi-million dollar law suit against the TV company to counter his lost investments in television programs. While the arguments ensued for months, the Hungarian population made the final decision: Friderikusz was put back on the air and, thus, every Thursday night millions may watch all the oddities of contemporary life in an almost ritualistic programming. One of Friderikusz's earlier guests was Lui Padre, the Magician; today, this mystic operates out of his office, offering special services for and against black magic and love magic.

The media and everyday politics provide enough gossip on corruption and horror stories, so the smaller occurences rarely make heads turn anymore. There are crimes committed in Hungary in the past five years which were unheard of before: bombing of major buildings, kidnapping, serial killers on the loose, the collapse of major banks, and con artists swindling hundreds of millions of forints of tax payers' money. One could go on with this endless list of horror, gore and Hollywood-type hyper-textual realities played out on the streets of Hungary. But the media is not an innocent bystander: for it not only reproduces society and reality, it also creates it. Books, magazines and video tapes are being produced in amazing quantities to feed the hungry minds of the populace. Books long familiar to Westerners are being translated into Hungarian and sold in legitimate bookstores. Wictor Charon's *Akashic Records* and Abd-Ru-Shin's (Oskar Ernst Dernhardt [1875-1941]) book *The Message of Gral*, are present rediscoveries of the popular prophecies of the Nostradamus kind. The mind-control techniques of "the Silva method" started in Hungary as soon as the Iron Curtain was taken down. But out-of-body experiences, UFO abductions, lost continents, mediums and psychics are just as popular now as books and tapes on Hungarian superstitions, witchcraft, and reincarnation.[25]

There are now the witch-crazed believers on television whose middle-aged managerial leadership is going berserk declaring that they have nothing to do with Satanists, another group of loosely organized cult followers. One leader, in fact, claimed that the early 1997 San Diego Heaven's Gate cult suicide was nothing but Satanism out of control, a possibility because of the inadequate and amateur Satanists around the world.[26]   Both the witches' society and the Satanist groups now operate in Budapest and large regional cities, and both enjoy the support of middle-class and middle-age populations; the society of witches do not kill cats but strongly believe in their black power.[27]   All over Hungary, one can buy witch dolls, a fad with strong sexual overtones, for many of the dolls represent old hags with bare behinds. Hungarian Satanist are also a strange brew of people, just as they are elsewhere in Europe. They do not advertise themselves—as the witches do with their Witches Boutique in Budapest—but try to manage to foster a self-image of distinction and exclusivity by operating in semi-secrecy. The Church of Esoteric Teachings is even more cultic. Founded in the early 1990s, this church makes no secret of its mission and function. In 1997, it advertised the beginning of a special "Esoteric and Parapsychological University," a two-year program with an entrance examination and a diploma at the end for those successfully completing the courses ranging from bioenergetics, radiestesia, distance-healing, anthroposophy, astrology, chiropractice, herbal healing and other oddities.

It is interesting to see the interconnectedness between the cultic media programs and mainstream popular culture and science. With the continual rising of drug prices and medical care, Hungarians find a good rationalization for turning to faith healing and alternative medicinal practices, all of which now utilize both printed and electronic media to boost sales and create a popular demand. While until 1986, all homeopathic medicine was illegal in Hungary, since 1990 all sorts of medical practices are allowed to thrive. Today, Russian herbal doctors and massage therapists, some even working with precious and semi-precious stones, are especially welcomed among the elderly, the sick and the desperate. In the regional city of Kecskemét, a certain Chinese miracle doctor, by the name of Dr. Li Yue Geang, openly advertises his practice of acupuncture and massage for all kinds of illnesses. Some of these alternative healers rent small storefronts, others advertise in local newspapers, and still others gain more and more followers through word of mouth. However, there are drug makers who are quite professional and operate their large-scale enterprises with the blessing of the medical authorities.

The name of the Béres drops may not ring familiar to Western ears, but to most Hungarians it conjures up the images of the miracle drug, a potent mixture of herbs and (secret) ingredients that successfully fight cancer. Which kind of cancer? All kinds of cancer! The Béres family, operating several major pharmaceutical companies throughout Hungary, is an illustrative example of the making of the new post-communist entrepreneurs. The family, by all counts one of the richest family clans in Hungary, started in the 1980s by manufacturing small bottles of tinctures claiming that it was a natural blocker to the growth of cancerous cells. Under the last years of state socialism, most people only laughed at it—while the desperately ill were already hooked on it. The family tried in vain to obtain scientific credibility as well as a permit to operate legally. But, and this is where we can see the cultic milieu's influence on daily politics and the society at large, as soon as the tight control of food, drugs and the medical system started to crack, the Béres family found more and more supporters. They came not only from among the elderly and the desperately ill, who sought a cure and were in need of pain killers, but even people who had no illnesses began to take the Béres drops—which were becoming a hot commodity on the black market—claiming their beneficial side effects. As one young enthusiast claimed: "If it doesn't hurt, why not take it?"   So clearly, the task of any scholar who is bent on understanding the "culture of the cultic milieu," to use Colin Campbell's expression, is to connect those elements which may define, broadly speaking, the religion-science axis.[28]   The story of the Béres drops is a clear indication of how this axis operates in the current more lenient and free socio-economic and political climate of Hungary.

After 1990, the Béres family's acceptance is easily discerned in the availability of the drops in legitimate drug stores, by their many drug manufacturing factories in Hungary, and, this is no small feat, by having the spokesman of the family openly claiming medical successes in the fight of cancer. (Just in passing, it must be mentioned that nobody in the family is a doctor or even a certified pharmacist). Now the family proudly boasts that in some African countries and even in places of the former Soviet Union, there are hospitals and clinics administering the famous cancer-fighting miracle drug. By 1992, the Béres firm is the largest (and perhaps the most respected) herbal-homeopathic drug-producing family in Hungary. Even when people who are regular users of the Béres drops were surveyed as to the exact effectiveness of the medication, they declared openly that they did not know why but they felt healthier and more energetic when using it. It should be added, however, that by now there are "legitimate" doctors working for the firm involved with "scientific" testing of the Béres drops.

In order to further legitimize themselves, the Béres family embarked upon a philanthropic and social mission by offering their products to hospitals, the homeless and the needy. In addition, the family offers humanitarian benefits by appearing as a promoter and organizer of various artistic activity throughout the country. At this point there are no more debates and scientific arguments against the Béres drops, most people take it for granted that it is on the store shelves, and if it is sold—so goes the folk wisdom—it must be useful for something!

Following in the footsteps of the successful Béres drops, there is another recently "discovered" miracle drug on the market now. It is called Somadrin and is for, among other things, curing asthma. Its discoverer is István Somogyi, a loner and a painter by profession who lives in a small apartment in Budapest and has no knowledge of medicine and pharmacy whatsoever. According to a personal story, he has spent his life's fortunes on making and perfecting this drug. To administer it, the drug must be put into water and, in no time, a chemical reaction takes place, replicating the special air of a cave. The claim is that, similar to underground caves, this mixture exudes vapors which, when inhaled, are supposed to work on the sick person's throat and air passages. Following Somogyi's elevation into national fame with the help of radio and television, there are several of these "in-house caves" in Hungary where asthmatic patients can go for the miracle cure. There is, to be sure, a strange inversion with miracle drugs: the more people know about them, the more successfully they will fight many diseases. By now Somadrin is used against the flu, allergies, and other kinds of breathing disorders.[29]

Other commonly known Western herbal and mystery drugs are also flooding both the Hungarian and Eastern European markets. The food and liquor industries, not surprisingly, are also involved with the cultic phenomenon in Hungary. The famous Tokaj wine is perhaps one of the best-known marketable commodities the country has to offer. A recently created company named Geoproduct now bottles and sells this famous wine together with the healing rocks gathered on the Tokaj mountains. The small bottle—with rocks and small stones actually in the bottle with the wine—is advertised as "healing the mind and the body." The label also advises buyers to use a small glass every morning and evening for "the healthy heart and soul" to thus achieve "a healthy 120 years of life." Not only wine, but miracle water may be also bought in alternative stores and health-food shops. Water enriched with bio-energy—also referred to as the "water of life" or simply as "π -water," replicating Japanese "scientific" research, is being marketed together with small water-purifying appliances. Those who cannot afford these machines may simply go to these stores and buy only the water. Among other miracle drugs on the alternative market are the all-health-reinforcing "energy stimulating" foot support named Piokal; the Life Crystal tincture (advertised with the name of a certain American Dr. George Merkl, with the Zodiac sign as his emblem); the Kapsipap creme against rheumatism; the disease preventive Q10; and the Tethys primal sea salt, a miracle drug manufactured by the Society for the Healing Miracles Minerals.

There are more glaring examples of the acceptance of the cultic milieu, or to follow Campbell's notion, how society supports it. Holistic or alternative medicine has become not only the accepted but the supported and demanded medicine by many in Hungary. Now we may attend holistic or herbal medicine workshops in major towns all over the country. The Maharishi Transcendental Meditation workshops are already popular among young Hungarians willing to participate in the special sessions. Alternative medicine meetings are numerous. Some of the sessions advertised in 1997 were: reiki workshops, radioestesia, aura diagnostics, bioenergetic healing, transbreathing and regression techniques, folk healing and traditional Thai massage, bone setting, psycho-kibernetics, and chakra-based meditations.[30] There are now several seers and self-proclaimed psychics in Hungary who achieved nation-wide notoriety because of their skills in the magic arts. The psychic Rózsa Müller is a successful spirit medium; her male colleague, Antal Bujka, is well known for transversing with the dead as well as being knowledgeable in the art of love magic (he advertises himself all over the various media by giving his mobile telephone number). Another well-known practitioner is Emma Ilona Veres, a middle-aged woman who travels continents in her dreams; she received her extrasensory knowledge during her various (both real and imagined) trips to the Egyptian and Mexican pyramids and the lamaist monasteries in Tibet.[31]

They are not as famous, however, as the well-known celebrity with extrasensory and mystical knowledge by the name of Ferenc Dombi. A parish priest, he was born into a poor family with twelve children. Dombi became a Catholic priest, ordained in 1954, but developed a conflict with state authorities in 1960, from which time he was forbidden to practice. Working in semi-legality, the priest developed an interest in the occult sciences, including mysticism, zodiac and Indian beliefs; in the late 1980s, he spent two months in Medjugorje, a city in Yugoslavia where miracles happened as the result of the apparition of the Virgin Mary. Father Dombi claimed that in Medjugorje, he received miraculous cures and as a result has begun to hear "the Voice." In 1991, after a long and arduous fight with the authorities (both church and lay), he received permission to practice as an assistant to the chaplain in his home village, Inárcs. His conversations with "the Voice" (the Virgin Mary and other "Heavenly Creatures") have been published since 1993, a series which by now consists of twenty-four "the Voice" books![32] These small books faithfully capture the messages from the Voice concerning diverse topics on love, politics, karma, local affairs, personal traumas, and other quasi-religious matters.

While Father Dombi clearly exists on the margins of accepted and tolerated religious world views, there are others with supernatural powers whose status among locals are both accepted and questioned and thus, feared. In Lajosmizse, the small town where I was born and to where I returned to live, about sixty-eight kilometers south of Budapest, there is a woman known simply as Aunt Éva, although many simply refer to her with the obnoxious term "old hag." Born in 1930 and living in this settlement for thirty-seven years, she is a lonely woman with extreme Roman Catholic belief mixed with a good dosage of mysticism and occultism. A mother of five girls, she advertises herself as a seer, palm-reader, fortune-teller and a faith healer, an advertisement which is now becoming more sophisticated since the local cable television started its operation. While earlier she was simply dismissed as a "crazy spinster" —also called "Eve, the Hitchhiker" by many—by the early-1990s, she was an accepted religious and cultic figure among both locals and visitors outside the vicinity of Lajosmizse.

Aunt Éva started her arduous professional career in the late 1980s when Hungarian media and society experienced more and more freedom from state repression. She was featured in 1986 on the talk show of a small-time media host by the name of Sándor Friderikusz (!). As more and more people consulted her, slowly she turned into a minor local celebrity; she is now admitted into the mayor's circle of friends and holds regular sessions for regional politicians, local officials and even the police. During the regular local summer festivals, Aunt Éva has a special tent set up for those wishing to hear the future, find their lost ones or try their luck. Now, with the help of a translator, she even tells fortunes, sees the dead, and gives advice for love magic and sicknesses to foreigners traveling through the town. She is making a real alternative career by claiming supernatural powers as a necromancer.

When three years ago a double homicide took place, leaving policemen gasping for air, the police chief turned to Aunt Éva to hear what she "saw" in the zodiac and the Chinese calendar. She was, indeed, not very far from the truth: the killer was a relative of the old couple murdered! More recently, she was also featured in various regional newspapers for foretelling the location of a dead man's body.[33] Building upon successes of a similar kind, she is now featured regularly in the local and regional papers offering her wisdom concerning the constellations of the stars, astrological signs, health and even fundamental Christian ethics. She is also a regular on the regional radio station and is featured with other alternative religious and cultural personages.[34]

I do not know what kind of license she was able to obtain—probably none besides her ownership license for the small storefront grocery store she runs, a shop which is advertised as "the place of truth"; accordingly, she promotes herself as "Eve, the Truthsayer." In the shop, she sells alcohol, cigarettes, stationery and even condoms. Half of her store is curtained off: this is her sacral corner, her altar. On the walls there are plenty of reproductions of Catholic iconography, with letters written to her by her admirers. In addition, she sells her book, a small but nicely crafted volume with her yearly forecasts.[35] Actually if one dares to ask her for a book, she does a personal reading for free. Already in its third printing, Aunt Éva's books and daily, monthly and yearly personalized forecasts are making the rounds far beyond the confines of her town, making her into a mystic media celebrity.

But she is not alone. In the past year, two more people also appeared on the scene in my town alone: one is a self-titled graphologist and the other opened a store selling health food, medicine and herbs for all kinds of problems. Other faith-healers, holistic curers and bonesetters are also making their rounds all over the country. The profession of bonesetting—the Hungarian equivalent of chiropractors—started on a massive scale in Hungary after 1990 when the American chiropractor Steven Anderson introduced his own special techniques. Following this, several international sessions and workshops—to which Russian, German and American specialists were invited—were held.[36] Today, together with the Hungarian Medical Acupuncture Association, chiropractors form one of the largest alternative medical societies in Hungary.

We may also find other forms of faith healing and miracle work. For example, Imre Oláh, living in the western town of Győr, is a well-known distance healer. There is a special healing coin, charged with cosmic energy, which one can purchase from the paraphenomen L. Harasztosi. Another nationally known "energy-healer" is József Gyurcsok—the healer of Visegrád, as he is known—operating from the northern town of Nagybörzsöny and possessing five different mobile phone numbers to provide telepathic, or "distance healing," for various health and mental problems.[37] His choice of this small settlement is telling of his art and extraterrestrial knowledge: he claims that the settlement's energy is given by UFOs who have been using this point as a meeting and landing site for centuries. He, as well as his select apprentices, are also in constant contact with them. He already developed a serious group of followers and is open to all kinds of sick people and children, the latter being treated free of charge. Gyurcsok is not only a successful UFO-abductee and astro-healer, but a seer of Nostradamus's caliber. In fact, he foretold a great cosmic natural disaster—an unavoidable cosmic dust storm—causing havoc on earth in 1998.[38]

Health, beauty and youth are the three most important areas which are interconnected in the alternative and mainstream health professions. It seems that long gone are the days when women only worried about their make-up and men about their growing waistlines. In major newspapers one can read advertisements similar to this one:

> Become beautiful! Become rejuvenated! With us you become slim and attractive! You may know your future and yourself. Our address is 5th. Dist. Hercegprímás street, No. 13. We offer: horoscopes, tarot, soul-seeking, graphology, medical pedicure and manicure, reflexology, hairdressing, make-up, solarium, Vacu-press celluloid treatment, slimming, firm breast creation, wrinkles-less face, body-wrapping. Call us! [39]

The fact that advertisements of this type may appear in legitimate and not alternative newspapers is itself a proof that such ideas and services are not only accepted but also sought after by Hungarians. We can see the seriousness of the cultic phenomenon in question by the large number of individuals involved in both providing such services and utilizing their impact on their bodies as well as souls.

Many of the practitioners of alternative thinking and religious beliefs are women, a fact that leads to this question: is there a gender issue here with regard to the cultic milieu's popular acceptance?   The next personality profile will answer this.

From the material I gathered, it seems convincing that the prime movers behind the cultic phenomena are both men and women, young and old. One such celebrity with a long history of alternative thinking is Gábor Papp, an art historian in his late fifties. His eccentric views helped him to gain national recognition among Hungary's university students and middle-age intellectuals. Papp, whose name incidentally means priest in Hungarian, emerged in the 1980s as a free and uncompromising alternative thinker.[40] His lectures and public seminars are filled with interpretations of ancient and contemporary phenomena: he has analyzed, among others, the building of the pyramids (both Mayan and Egyptian), Scythian art, the chakras of India, Celtic mythology, Arabic medicine, lost continents, medieval alchemy, the music of Zoltán Kodály, and Hungarian peasant art. He can be also credited with discovering a Hungarian eccentric who wrote several manuscripts, posthumously titled *Arvisuras*, a combination of Eastern philosophical and Hungarian prehistoric writings. Several of Papp's followers have become professionals themselves, disseminating the views straddling the religion-science axis. An important figure is Marcell Jankovics, a filmmaker of national repute. Jankovics achieved acceptance as a filmmaker when he devised, quite nicely I must add, a whole series of animated new interpretations of Hungarian folk tales. However, Jankovics did not stop there. He became a self-titled scholar: now he has several books to his credit on subjects ranging from the symbolism of the sun to the meaning of trees.

I was able to witness the influence of Papp and his art on the widespread development of neo-shamanism in Hungary in the summer of 1995 when Papp led a mission to Siberia to find some of the "ancient locations" where "important" events described in the *Arvisura* took place. Accidentally, I ended up with his group, although my research concerned the political-cultural changes among hunting and fishing tribes as the result of the collapsed state-controlled economy and politics in Russia. The group's original premise was surprisingly scholarly and close to applied anthropology at first. By improvising several rituals, Papp and his followers utilized drumming, songs, incantations and offerings to bring back the "force." By revitalizing the spiritual life among Hanties and Mansies, small tribal hunters of the Siberian north, they were hoping to reverse the "evil energies" caused by modernization and Sovietization. Since all of the wooden idols were destroyed, burned or taken to museums by the Soviet government,[41] one of the functions of these rituals was to reinstall tribal spiritual presence in these lands. In one of its rituals, the group offered a wooden idol to Hanty elders who then, with all seriousness, put the effigy in its proper sacred and secret tribal shelter. To indicate that this group is not made up of uneducated individuals, I should mention that members included a film director, a theater director, and a female ethnographer. In addition, one woman "seer," or psychic, also followed the group; her presence was overwhelming since before every major step the group wanted to make, she was consulted.

With the help of a translator, she also read the cards for many people, one of whom was the governor of the region. After the seance was over, the governor expressed his awe, arguing that many of the seer's statements were in fact in his last night's dream! During the trip, a frail woman in her mid-thirties was consulted several time by the group's female seer and male neo-shaman. Once the two found out that she was willing to share her dreams and personal stories, including the ones of a childhood filled with mystical stories and folkloric events, she was given instructions that she should "find the lost energy within her." Obviously disturbed by the family's poverty, her husband's alcoholism, job insecurities and perhaps even physical abuse, the woman was urged to "step out of her depressed state" and take up shamanism, for one of her ancestors was a truly great shaman.

Shamanism was not mentioned by mistake, for shamanistic or neo-shamanistic practice is in vogue among Hungarian intellectuals and alternative religious thinkers. The small group had its own shaman (in real life, he is a theater director), who brought his drum and offered seances three times during the trip. His initiation into shamanism is also an interesting aspect of the Hungarian cultic milieu. He received his "knowledge" and "power" from the American anthropologist-turned-shaman Michael Harner, who visited Hungary several times. Harner's shamanistic seances, while novelties at first, were crucial in initiating several Hungarian young men.[42] Now they initiate others and practice shamanism as the true folk religion of the Hungarians. I should mention that shamanism is also rising in Russia, and the notion of a practicing urban shaman will not turn any heads now. In fact, the American anthropologist Marjorie Balzer makes an apt point with regard to the similarities of Siberian urban shamans and New Age shamanism in Europe and America: "The two have in common a straining to get at some inner core of human affect, to break the bonds of received distinctions between reality and unreality, and to touch people spiritually and aesthetically."[43] The similarities, for example, between Hungarian neo-shamanist believers and those of Siberian urban shamans are revealing. As Balzer notes with regard to Siberian native Sakha (Yakut) practitioners:

> Some Sakha healers are turning to Slavic-style "new age" seminars for "extrasense" training in Moscow and Kiev, whether or not purist ethnographers approve. They find it feasible to add theories about energy transference, auras, and Indian chakras to their shamanistic heritage. Some call them charlatans, and indeed their curing abilities vary widely. But one patient's charlatan can be another's curer.[44]

In Hungary, books are now being published on shamanism with renewed vigor. Shamanistic seances and trancing or drumming parties are rather frequent occurrences among the country's middle-aged elite. The basic differences between classical shamanism and neo-shamanism as it is practiced in Hungary are that the latter is not tribal, it concerns present-day affairs, and it is kept alive in an urban environment among intellectuals who see no conflict between basic Christian tenets, folkloric magic and various shamanistic world views. Neo-shamans and alternative religious enthusiasts, for example, organized several international events in 1997, actions which reveal the seriousness with which these followers view their art and knowledge. In April, the Fifth Esoteric Spiritual Forum was held for two days; in August 1997, an International Shaman Expo went on for almost one month, with various activities including initiations, teaching sessions, trance seances and talk shows. This event was advertised as follows: "Mystical Encounters. Old Sciences—Today. Supernatural phenomena, extraterrestials, UFOs, witches, shamans, magicians and herbal doctors will meet at the International Shaman Expo. Shamans live among us!" Also in August in the same year, an alternative esoteric music and poetry festival was organized by enthusiasts in Kecskemét.

There is a fundamental connection between the scholarly world and popular neo-shamanism, for the latter find enjoyment in reinterpretations of classical studies on shamanism. For example, one of my colleagues—an ethnographer by training and with a regular job at the Academy of Sciences— makes his living as a researcher of shamanism; in fact, many of his publications serve as food for thought for today's neo- and urban-practicing shamans. This person one day admitted to me that he found out by chance that he has an extra bone in his body: the only explanation is that he is now a true shaman as well![45] This age, as Gellner once said, is truly an ironic age.

What is even more fascinating with regard to neo-shamanistic rejuvenation is the fact that the meteoric rise of some of these young devotees may just signal the beginning of the twenty-first century. In the eastern town of Nyíregyháza, a young man opened his private shaman school (*Táltos Iskola*), a place where one can gain first-hand knowledge of the supernatural phenomena. It should be remembered that while there were some individuals in the mid 1980s who claimed "extrasensory" powers and toyed with the idea of the supernatural—

painters, musicians, dancers and others of the same artistic bent—it was the beginning of the 1990s when all this became accepted as it grew outside the confines of secret clubs and closely knit urban communities.

Interestingly, groups within the cultic milieu do not only look at the past but, similarly to Western cultic phenomena followers, also look at science fiction and the extraterrestrial UFO world, which is to them not the unknown but the reverse, the well-known universe. There are now circles calling themselves UFO Research Groups, the one, for example, in Szeged is well known for its outspokenness for UFO rights, and this organization finds parallels in many other towns in Hungary. They openly declare the existence of extraterrestrial life and the real story behind UFO abductions, and they rely on the constant communication with UFOs, an act which is only available to a few and carefully chosen individuals. The American sci-fi series "The X Files" and the magazine with the same title inadvertently support the belief system of such groups and the growing camp of UFO believers. Other journals started immediately after 1990, such as the *UFO Magazine*; their subscribers organized the "2nd Meeting of the Encountered Ones." There are even some who have analyzed the mystical inscriptions found on the UFO crash at Rosswell in 1947. According to András Oláh, Hungary's foremost UFO-abductee and UFO mystic, the runiform writings can only be deciphered as an archaic Hungarian message,[46] a point of view which puts him in opposition to the American Michael Hesemann, who proposed the Phoenician origin of the Roswell inscriptions. Another amazing development in the current Hungarian search for extraterrestrial life is the way in which present psychics and historical figures are connected in this milieu. One such group is the Báthory Philosophical Society, whose leader Gizella Bartha—a philosopher by training, she claims—takes pride in declaring that she is able to converse regularly with Anna Báthory, a sixteenth-century Transylvanian princess whose name the society now bears.[47]

John Fiske makes an apt point with regard to popular culture, that it must be disseminated in order to achieve its hegemonic aim:

> Popular culture circulates in a number of ways . . . always encompassing a wide variety of social formations. Popular culture is made when these cultural resources meet the everyday lives of the people. It may consist only of this dialogic relationship between the reader and the industrial text, it may exist only in the interior fantasy, but it will remain at this level in all cases: the interior fantasy will typically demand some form of social circulation.[48]

Surely enough, this is what seems to happen with the cultic culture in contemporary Hungary and elsewhere in Eastern Europe. There are now special journals for uniting all these types of mystics, religious fundamentalists and alternative consciousness groups. One of them, titled *Open World* [*Nyitott Világ*], is a real treasure for anthropologists and cultural studies specialists. It is published in the regional city of Kecskemét by a group called "Association of the Bio-Shield Positive Thinkers" [*Biopajzs Pozitív Gondolkodók Egyesülete*]. What is interesting about this group is its unrelenting belief that the Hungarian nation is the chosen nation with a long prehistory originating in the lost continents of Mu and Atlantis.[49] This association, together with the New Babylonians, is very close in its mystical beliefs to other recently founded occult groups such as the one operating the magazine *Other World* [*Túlvilág*], a journal already in its third year.[50] While some of the chosen individuals see the other world and claim to possess powers to communicate with the dead, others offer horoscope readings for politicians and political parties. In the first instance we find popular Hungarian actors and celebrities talking about their other-worldly experiences.[51] In the latter case, readers and astrologers offer their opinions concerning Hungarian political parties and major politicians; in fact Hungarians have discovered the utility of political horoscopes.[52]

There are important connections between these Hungarian developments and what is already well known in the West. Some of the leaders of these groups— similar to neo-shamans—are not only fans of their Western counterparts, but they take an active role in Western seminars, retreats and workshops. One such alternative school visited by Hungarians is the Royal Titan Ranch in Montana, a retreat where they can learn everything from specialists from the United States and elsewhere. Participants' experiences are then given publicity in *Open World*. In this journal one may find a reinterpretation of biblical stories, faith healing successes, dream interpretation, interpretation of medieval history, UFO encounters, and current reincarnation stories. This interesting journal has a sentence from Goethe as its motto: "Whether we are true or not, as living creatures we have the responsibility to help the living and prepare the future." This statement makes it clear that for this group, the past and future are all one, and going back into the past and meeting historical figures, or traveling into the future and meeting UFOs is just as easy as a sneeze. At the same time, there is something of the utopian and millenarian kind in it too. For instance, one article published in *Open World* titled the "Chosen Nation"[53] discusses the notion of why Hungarians must fight together against the current wave of privatization, capitalism, and Western cultural influences. In the words of the author:

> Western financial institutions give us money knowing well that some of it will end up, where? Among other places in Cuba. We sold our country to the west. For what? So we can pay back the loans they gave us. Today money rules our life.[54]

From this type of declaration it is easy to unravel that such cultural groups operate in a frame of mind utilizing chiliastic and nationalistic themes ad libidem. For them, the current evils—breakdown of social values, unbridled capitalism, consumerist drives, threat of Westernization—must be fought with the spiritual strength which is outside the accepted and mainstream culture. Thus, nothing serves this better than alternative values, lifestyles and religious practices which provide, in their minds, both explanations for the past problems and solutions for the present ills of the world.

Rock musicians have long been associated with the cultic world (one thinks immediately of the early David Bowie and the American film *Repo Man*). One of Hungary's established alternative rock bands, the Galloping Morticians

[*Vágtázó Halottkémek*] continues to pride itself as being the speaker for eccentric mysticism and supernatural shamanistic knowledge. Despite the lack of state funding and sponsorship, this group has been extremely skillful in managing, during the past two decades, to be one of the most original inventors of the alternative musical scene in Hungary.[55] The group's vision, while quite chaotic at times, plays off neo-shamanism with its transcendental themes, rage and violent sounds, and mystic blend of the fantastic. The group's leader, Attila Grandpierre, has admitted often to experiencing, while on stage, an elevated state bordering on the altered states of consciousness of shamanistic performances.[56] Whether such neo-shamanic performances are any indication of the seriousness of this alternative musical sound is one thing, yet we cannot disclaim that the group's long success and faithful followers have allowed this unique band to exist for such a long time. The leader's involvement, however, is ample proof of the serious connection between Hungary's educated elite and the new religious phenomena sweeping through the country.[57]

Another former rock star, Péter Müller, the lead singer and founder of the once-famous Siami-Siami punk-rock band, is now lecturing on the usefulness of alternative lifestyles and religious beliefs, a curious mixture of fundamentalist Christian teachings, Far Eastern mysticism of all kinds, and nationalistic slogans.[58] His book, *The Cross and the Snake*, has been a big hit on the Hungarian book market.

No other institution, however, provided more grounds for national reawakening and for the elevation of peasant folkloric themes into the urban popular culture than the dance-house movement. This example is perhaps one of the most well-known alternative recreational activities not only in Hungary, but outside of it.[59] It is also an important and most specifically a Hungarian national/cultural movement. Starting as a genuine youth subculture in the mid-1970s, by the late 1980s it became an accepted and state-sponsored activity. In fact, this is one of the most amazing success stories in the cultic milieu in Hungary. This movement, a largely folkloric recreational activity mostly by urban youth, was able to transform itself from subculture into the mainstream popular culture of the day. Now followers of the dance-house movement may go and imitate folk dances, sing folk songs and enjoy the ambiance of urban "folk cafes" and restaurants.

Television, radio and stage productions now offer dance-house music, an art form which loosely follows traditional peasant musical styles. While this itself would not really be classified as part of the cultic milieu, we must realize that there is a whole new way of using ideological explanations to save traditional peasant culture by transmitting various folkloric aspects to today's youth. There is a tendency within the revivalist folkloric music genre to try to produce an archaic sound, a sound which, as claimed by the performers themselves, faithfully captures the archaic and even shamanistic elements in Hungarian folklore. One group is in fact named "Táltos," a historic name of Turkic origin describing the figure of the Hungarian shaman.[60] For example, there are theater groups and dance ensembles—Tranz Danz and Shaman Theater—which are also toying with this historicizing idea. Other performers are even more daring than this. Levente Szörényi, songwriter and musical director of the popular folk rock musical,

"Stephen, the King," even fashioned a instrument which, to his mind, is closer to the authentic historic sound he was trying to create than any musical instruments in use today. Such a sound aside, "Stephen, the King," was a smash hit among Hungarians, a success which set the stage for many similar productions to come.

Historic themes of the Hungarian past received an incentive from the state as Hungary celebrated its 1,100th anniversary of settlement in the Carpathian Basin in 1996. There were in fact several horseback riding tours imitating the wanderings of the Hungarian tribes in the tenth century AD. The first—lasting over six months—was in 1995, and the adventurous group trekked over five thousand kilometers from southern Russia to Hungary.[61] Although largely symbolic, some of these events reaffirmed that, deep down into the national psyche, there are many elements of this past which have survived into the twentieth century. Nothing proves this better than the hit film of 1996, *The Conquest* [*Honfoglalás*]. Directed by Gábor Koltay, the film is a cinematographic testimony of the myths and histories of how the Carpathian region was settled by the Hungarian tribes in the ninth and tenth centuries AD. While the film—whose lead star is the Italian actor Franco Nero—is not an exceptional achievement, its soundtrack is already a platinum album. Its music, of course, was written and edited in the long tradition which is the hallmark of Koltay, a director of "Stephen, the King." That popular culture has tried to capitalize upon historical themes is not novel: regional identity politics has also been undergoing a historicization process itself. For instance, since 1990, four Hungarian counties changed their names back into their pre-war antecedents, a pattern continuing at the moment when local councilmen are debating whether the southeastern county of Békés should change its name to the historic designation of Zaránd.[62]

The folkloric revitalization movement, an important anti-state activity in the 1970s and 1980s, has also gained an important legitimizing momentum in 1996. At the 1996 Summer Folk Dance festival in the southern town of Szeged, the theme was heavily accented, the stress being on shamanism. One group invited to the festival was a revival dance and performing ensemble from the city of Yakuts, from the southern Siberian state of Yakutia in Russia. Its neo-shamanistic performance set the stage for the whole evening. At the end of the show, Hungarian folk dancers from various regions of Hungary and elsewhere in East-Central Europe filled the stage, performing contemporary folk dance choreographies. The evening had one clear message: this is where we came from, and this is where we are now, with the shamanistic Siberian herdsmen tradition being firmly cemented in the European-style peasant culture and tradition.

Such public performances certainly underline what John Fiske referred to above as the social circulation of popular cultural elements in everyday life. Increasingly, as Hungary's alternative cultural brokers seem to be celebrating the country's Europeanness, they seem to be relying on the ancient, on the distant, and on the non-European differences. For this to happen, the practitioners of popular culture find support in mainstream scholarly practice, reaffirming the fundamental interconnectedness of the cultic with the scientific. There are established folklorists and ethnographers who support this movement whether they wish or not.[63] Through their publications, lectures and public presentations, practitioners find what they are looking for in their quest to identify the "real Hungarian," "the real ancient," the "real traditional," and what is solely a "Hungarian" element. Even if scholars speak of the opposite, in their mystical beliefs the cultic followers only read and listen to what they want to hear. Their knowledge in even the most minute aspect of the long-gone peasant culture, while certainly impressive, is utilized sometimes to excesses by cultic followers. But more and more, one can see individuals whose knowledge of past traditions is cursory and inadequate, yet they seem to be existing as gurus of this revitalization movement.

This kind of activity is not novel to Hungary, of course, and we may witness such folkloric revivals all over Europe and elsewhere. The Korean state, for example, can be credited with inventing the concept of "national treasure," a phrase referring to those folk art specialists who are recognized for their skills and given special status as well as privileges by the state. (Even UNESCO has initiated a whole series of programs to identify "national treasures" in various countries.) While in itself such support of artists is not cultic, at least not in the sense of Campbell's usage of the term, yet the involvement of the state and supporting organizations in their feverish search in finding such "treasures" may border on the cultic. In Hungary, outstanding performers of peasant traditions—even though most of them have nothing to do with the peasantry anymore—receive the state's official title of "Master of Folk Art"; their young disciple was named the "Young Master of Folk Art." Such a prize may be interpreted as an innocent and naïve cultural recognition of singers, musicians, dancers, storytellers, carvers, weavers, and tailors. However, the way in which this culture relates to other aspects of cultural life certainly arouses the suspicion that this is just as much a part of the cultic milieu as the growing number of witch doctors, alternative religious communes, and the celebrated media clowns.

The real celebrity of the dance-house movement—for this too has its own charismatic person with whom the followers identify—is not a person from Hungary, but, as many characterize him, a scholar from "historic Hungary." Here the label is important for he is none other than the folklorist Zoltán Kallós, a Hungarian from Transylvania, Romania. Kallós is not just a folklorist, however. Originally a teacher by profession, he had the worst experiences of a Hungarian living in Ceausescu's Romania. Charged with treason, jailed on charges of homosexuality, placed at odd jobs in different parts of the country, his house searched many times, his friends and family members intimidated by the secret police, Kallós had his share of trying to live like a Hungarian in the Romanian majority region of Transylvania. Nonetheless, his determination paid off; being in different, often distant, locations he sought out the oldest and best local singers, performers, balladeers, and weavers the region had to offer. Meticulously he collected tales, ballads, and songs; filmed dances and rituals; and obtained old peasant utensils, clothes and objects of local flavor. Now he has dozens of books to his credits, claimed by many in the dance-house movements as the best Hungarian folklore ever collected from Hungarians living in Transylvania. He is a regular presence in Hungary, visiting dance clubs, reciting his favored songs, or selling his latest books or cassettes of folk songs. In 1996, he received the prestigious Kossuth prize, an honor bestowed by the president of Hungary and only given to the selected few in recognition of their work for the country. He also started his own foundation and recording label in his home village. On the family property he demanded back from the state, he built a large campground, and every summer hundreds of willing participants from all over the world now can learn how to sing Hungarian folk songs, play the country fiddle, or learn a few dance steps. At nights, village bands from the region provide authentic music and all can dance until the wee hours.

A movement which had the flavor of an anti-state subculture in the 1970s and 1980s has achieved the well-nigh impossible: teaching Hungarian youth about Hungarian folklore outside the channels of formal educational system. This sanitized view of Hungarian village life closely parallels Gellner's warnings about nationalistic movements.[64] However, this is not quite what Gellner had in mind at first: the dance-house generation is a lively but small subculture which will never win over the hundreds of thousands of Hungarian youths from disco, rap, and techno pop. It will always remain within the confines of the folk dance clubs, summer camps, and in the imagination of a few charismatic figures, figures like the native-scholar Kallós himself, who often said that the world would be a better place if people would learn each others' dances and songs. What is wrong with that? In the present cultic milieu, there is nothing wrong with that at all.

Conclusions

Clearly what Colin Campbell had in mind when he argued that the culture of the cultic milieu falls "in the property space bounded by the religion-science axis and an instrumental-expressive orientation axis,"[65] was to call attention to the fact that these axes, as he put it, "only result in a very rough approximation to reality." Sure enough, when looking at the cases presented above, it can be easily ascertained that in the post-communist world of emerging democratic traditions and Western values, religion and science, magic and fantasy are all intertwined in the thinking of the followers making up a certain portion of their realities. More than that, some of the prime practitioners are even playing with the possibility of wish-fulfillment. The quest seekers and the mystics are all bounded up in a strange time-travel relationship: on the one hand, they are both approximating and negating the past-present-future time axis; and on the other hand, they know (many, of course, only sense) that the present day realities are harsher than ever before and that paradise on earth will only be made in a constructed magical world of their own. Yes, in fact, this would be not unlike a miniature and a folksy version of the "magic world" of Disneyland transplanted and nationalized to Hungarian soil. This may indeed be called an ironic age—resorting again to Campbell—an age where the mainstream and scientific are blended with the marginal and half-beliefs.[66] In short, we are in an age which can be best described as the cultic age. This is a period in which modernity and Europeanness is emphasized together with the ancient and Asiatic; in which more and more people remove themselves to find consolation and salvation not in the mainstream political and cultural phenomena but, on the contrary, in the marginal, the alternative and the semi-secretive world of the cultic.

There remain many questions which must be answered: one of the most intriguing is, how can such a new cultic milieu thrive not only in Hungary, but all over the former communist bloc? One simple answer may just be that such movements extend into the formerly isolated communist world, an area now viewed as the primal land for new missionary territory. Turning away from the communist past brings a host of New Age mysticism and alternative churches such as neo-shamanistic societies in Russia and the Council of All Being in Poland. Another explanation is that such movements are not novel to the post-communist world. In Bulgaria, the Bogumils, in Russia various sects of Old Believers and mystic societies were well known in the past. Since the turn of the nineteenth and twentieth century, Baptists, Church of the Nazarenes, populists, peasant and mystic seers, Neo-Gnostics, and Jehovah's Witnesses were already on Hungarian soil. As one observer aptly noted:

> This phenomenon signaled that people on the margins of society have given up on the hope of progress and positive development of their plight, thus abandoning all hopes for changing the current state of affairs. People joining these sects waited for a miracle, the coming of the new Christ, and trusting the Messiah to change the hellish country into the world of God. Instead of acting to their benefit, they opted for withdrawal and escape; the withdrawal from the everyday situation— both intellectual and political—and the acceptance of a dream world in which truth and justice will rule.[67]

It is true that East-Central Europe was not outside the orbit of European religious and political developments. Not only alternative religious groups but the inter-war extreme right and the Nazi parties also prove this point. Home-grown Nazi and religious-right movements developed everywhere in East-Central Europe following the general trend in Western Europe.[68]

Despite some of these legacies, it is clear, however, that after the fall of the strong central control of cultural, religious and leisurely life, all sorts of religious and political activities are allowed to thrive. These include, of course, formerly rejected and persecuted groups which now celebrate openly their existence and flourishing. What may be a slightly different interpretation from Campbell's is the problem centering around the process of increasing secularization.[69] For in Hungary, just as elsewhere in the former Soviet Bloc, secularization goes hand in hand with increasing radicalization of religious life. It just may be that we can refine Campbell's notion and argue that the growth of the cultic milieu will also be rapid in spite of or in opposition to religious orthodoxy. Also, it must be realized that there is, as Campbell aptly suggests, a wide array of substantial "commercial substructure," which allows such complexes to survive.[70] More and more magazines, advertisements, television programs, cable channels, and retreats are being publicized in the open, which legitimizes such cults for the population at large. In addition, one must not forget that there are important figures of national (some even international) stature who are now the spokespersons for the cultic phenomena. Every country has its own Shirley MacLaines and Jim Joneses (or, to remain with the events of 1997, its Applewhites), hopefully the former and not the latter. They are the high priestesses and priests of the alternative religious world-views and prominent life-seekers who, in a strange but by no means unusual twist, return to the fundamental Christian tenet of man as the *Homo viator*. When actors and media stars declare on national television that they gather in Budapest at a cave chapel every Sunday for fundamentalist services, it takes no time for some of the young to imitate them.

Finally, I must mention that there has been a fundamental connection since 1990 between local leaders and psychics and those operating in Western Europe and North America. Now there is no need to import chief shamans or chiropractors from the West, for there are plenty to go around in Hungary alone. Those few who are invited occasionally only come to reinforce the movement and/or recharge "the psychic and mental energies," as one of the participants of an urban housing complex vision-quest noted.

And this last point may just also be the good news: for if we are able to pinpoint that one of the reasons for the increasing popularity of cults and the cultic milieu is the media sensationalism as projected to the fans by celebrities, politicians and mainstream scholars, then it should follow naturally that the disappearance, or at least their confinement within a minute part of the populace, will also be the result of stars giving up, changing their minds, or simply withering away with their ideas. As fads and fashions seem to pop up unexpectedly from time to time, so too do the cults come and go, with every new generation discovering its own (neo)shamans, psychic healers and media tricksters. In fact, discovering the truth, or rejecting the basic tenets of science, is the raison d'être for every generation that feels most satisfied with and happy with its own creation of cultic milieu. Whether such milieus are able to maintain themselves for the time being or not is only a matter of a presence of a charismatic leader or an elite group's desire to lead them on. Nothing summarizes this better than the statement of a pop shaman who, when asked about reincarnation, answered: "Yes, I do believe it. And I hope that in my next life I will be a politician, so I can change the world into a much better place than it is now."

Notes

[1] Colin Campbell, "The Cult, the Cultic Milieu and Secularization," in *A Sociological Yearbook of Religion in Britain* 5 (1972).

[2] See for example, E. Tiryakian, ed., *On the Margin of the Visible: Sociology, Esoteric, and the Occult* (Englewood Cliffs, NJ: Prentice Hall, 1974); and I. Zaretsky and P. Leone eds., *Religious Movements in Contemporary America* (Princeton, NJ: Princeton University Press, 1974).

[3] Anthony Wallace, *Religion: An Anthropological View* (New York: Random House, 1966).

[4] Ernest Gellner, *Legitimation of Belief* (Cambridge: Cambridge University Press, 1974).

[5] Ernest Gellner, *Nations and Nationalism* (Ithaca, NY: Cornell University Press, 1983).

[6] Tanya Luhrmann, *Persuasions of the Witch's Craft* (Cambridge, MA: Harvard University Press, 1991), 343.

[7] M. Bax, "Marian Apparition in Medjugorje: Rivaling Religious Regimes and State-

'ormation in Yugoslavia," in E. Wolf, ed., *Religious Regimes and State Formations* (Albany: tate University of New York Press, 1991), 29-54; Laszlo Kürti, "A Mennyek Asszonya" The Lady of Heaven], (forthcoming).

Although there are no reliable estimates as to how many young people are drug abusers, 10st scholars would agree that it is on the rise since the early 1990s; see, *Népszabadság*, 19 une 1997, 1.

State and church relations are by no means unproblematic, even in this post-communist 10ment; for a clear analysis, see the chapters on Hungary in J. Pungur, ed., *An Eastern* uropean Liberation Theology (Calgary: Angelus Publishers, 1994).

) See, *Népszabadság*, June 21, 1997, 1. The agreement, however, did not go smoothly. Both 1e governing Liberal Social Democratic Party and opposition parties objected to the overnment's preferential treatment of the Roman Catholic church. This conflict was resolved /hen the government took the immediate action of inviting all historic church leaders for a oundtable discussion to work out cooperative agreements between the state and the churches. 'his treaty concerns the nationalized church properties during the communist take over, eligious education, and state subsidies to churches and religious orders.

In Romania for instance, the Minister of Cults sent a circular letter to all mayors in ℟omania with a list of the 15 recognized religions which are authorized to build places of /orship. Not included are: Buddhist, Hindu, Anglican, Lutheran, Methodist, Presbyterian, alvation Army, and Bahai's. This prompted the Helsinki Committee and the Human Rights Vithout Frontiers (Brussels) to condemn the "biased decision" of the Romanian government; ee press release, Human Rights Without Frontiers, 9 May 1997.

² Joseph Pungur's short but informative analysis on the Bulányi movement will be helpful for on-Hungarian readers. See Pungur, ed., *An Eastern European Liberation Theology.*

³ The group's full name is the Complete Evangelic Christian Community of the Mahanaim ⅄ssociation [*Teljes Evangéliumi Keresztény Közösség Mahanaim Gyülekezete].* It is a 'rotestant fundamentalist school upholding the primacy of Jesus Christ and the evangelistic eachings of the New Testament by trying to convert non-believers to Christianity. In 1997, he association already claimed six groups in Budapest and operated Bible classes in 180 chools throughout the city. In addition, it produces its own religious tapes and operates a 3ible book store. For information, see "A Mahanaim Gyülekezet," [The Mahanaim Associa-ion], *Magyar Nemzet*, 28 June 1997, 12.

⁴ See the interview with the leading minister, Sándor Németh, "A Hit Gyülekezete nem akar olitikai hatalmat, [The Association of the Faith does not want political ower]."*Népszabadság*, 7 March 1997, 9.

⁵ Ibid. The membership is recruited largely from Hungary's professionals, prominent usiness people and politicians; its party base is strongest among the second governing party n Hungary, the Free Democrats [SZDSZ]. The two most prominent members of the associa-ion are Sándor Németh, who is the religious leader of the group, and Péter Hack, leader of the ⅃ZDSZ party.

⁶ For an interview was printed in Hungary's number one daily with the female leader of the ult; see Viktor Kiss, "Új Babylon: magyar egyház születik Óbudán?" [New Babylon: A ⅃ungarian Church Is Born in Óbuda?] *Népszabadság* 17 June 1997, 9.

⁷ *Ibid*, 9.

⁸ I have analyzed the scene of the Hungarian neo-Nazis in my chapter; see László Kürti, 'Skinheads, Neo-Nazis and Racist Youth: The Emergence of Right-Wing Extremism in ⅃astern Europe," In Jeffrey Kaplan and Tore Bjørgo eds., *Nation and Race: The Developing* ⅃uro-American Racist Subculture (Boston, MA: Northeastern University Press, 1998).

⁹ This is, of course, no small amount: around $100 million US. It will not be, however,

monetary repayment, for most of this will be through reinstated property rights to forme church land and real estate holding. I should mention that before World War II Hungary' Catholic Church was one of the largest landholders in Hungary .

[20] See the interview with Fero Fenic in "A dokumentátor" [The Documentator]," *Népszabadság*, 7 May 1997, 14.

[21] That Friderikusz has been a national institution is proven easily by the fact that Hungary' monthly cultural magazine, *Mozgó Világ*, published a special issue to deal with the Frideri kusz phenomenon; see vol. 23, 6, June, 1997, 3-50. In this, several media critics and person alities discuss Friderikusz and his television programs, most from a positive perspective.

[22] Friderikusz claimed this figure in a recent interview; see Zoltán Farkas, "Interjú Friderikus Sándorral," *Mozgó Világ*, vol. 23/6, June, 1997, 7.

[23] It will be instructive to see the top five shows on Hungarian television in May 1997 number one was the Hungarian sitcom "Neighbors" [Szomszédok], "Dallas" was second, th third an American series, fourth a Hungarian-style talk show, and fifth was Friderikusz; lis published in *Népszabadság*, 19 June 1997, 9.

[24] The names are mentioned in the same interview; *Ibid*, 6.

[25] In fact a whole series of videos being produced now with the title "The Nether World." I the first, we may watch spirit mediums performing, table dancing, conversing with dea relatives and other curiosities. The film's producer and director, Károly Sirkó, admits that h is in contact with the spiritual world and the undead himself. See the advertisement i *Túlvilág*, July, 1997, 29.

[26] For a slightly amusing but insightful understanding of the Heaven's Gate, see the shor collage in *The New Yorker*, 17 April 1997, 31-33. I would like to thank Marjorie Balzer fo providing me with this article. To be fair, Hungarian UFO believers also looked at th Heaven's Gate with criticism and trepidation; see "Intelligens erő [Intelligent power]," *UFC Magazine*, Julius, 1997 (8/7), 38-39.

[27] Earlier I presented my findings among Hungarian villagers in the Transylvanian region o Romania. In 1990, animals were returned to individual families as the result of the disassem bling of former state farms. With the cattle returned to the homes, witchcraft beliefs an accusation were also revitalized among young and old alike (Kürti 1995).

[28] Colin Campbell, "The Cult, the Cultic Milieu and Secularization," 124.

[29] See K.A., "Az asztmások csodaszere: a Somadrin [Somadrin, the miracle drug fo asthma]," *Nyitott világ* 2/4 (1996), 14.

[30] In fact, every single one of these was held in the first half of 1997 throughout Hungary. Th sessions were led by one of Hungary's famous healers, by the name of László Faragó, wh lives and operates in the regional city of Kecskemét. See his printed brochure: "Holisztiku természetgyógyász tanfolyamsorozatok, jan. 18.-júl 1, 1997." Although single sessions cos between USD 30-50 (between 3,200-7,200 Hungarian forints, or roughly an average weel salary), the healer advertises his workshops even for those who have no money: "Even if yo cannot pay the fees, come and meet me, let the rest be taken care of by the Universe."

[31] An interview with her was published recently in the occult journal *Open World*: "Vigyázz A vágyad beteljesül! [Watch out! Your desires will come true!]," *Nyitott Világ* 3/2, 1997, 10.

[32] For these volumes see the series of publications all titled the same and numbered consecu tively; Ferenc Dombi, *A hang: Egy katolikus pap párbeszéde égi lényekkel* [The Voice Conversations of a Catholic Priest with Heavenly Creatures] (Inárcs: Author's Publications).

[33] Articles of this were printed about her in both national and local papers, see: "Lajosmizse Halottlátó" [The Necromancer of Lajosmizse], *Mai Nap*, 5 July 1997, 24; and "Aki meg mondta, hogy hol a halott" [She told where the dead was], *Petőfi Népe*, 8 July 1997, 6.

[34] This feature article—with a glossy picture of her—was titled: "Mrs. Eve on the sound-waves'

Éva néni az éteren]," *Hölgyválasz*, 3/5, May 1997, 17. She was hosted on the Kecskemét radio talkshow, a call-in program during which she told the future by asking people's birth dates and relating them to the various signs of the Chinese zodiac.

[5] F. Horváth, *Az Igazmondó Éva Asszony. Bübáj koktél* [The Truthsayer Mrs. Eve. Magic cocktail], Kecskemét: Petöfi Nyomda [1995].

[6] K. Borics, and G. Kürti, *Csodatévö csontkovácsok* [Miraculous chiropractors] (Budapest: MILU, 1990).

[7] J. Gyurcsok, "Elmélkedés egy hipotézisröl. Gigantikus katasztrófa [Thinking about a hypothesis: A gigantic catastrophe?], *UFO Magazin* 8:7 (1997), 27.

[8] *Ibid.*

[9] In fact, this advertisement was placed in the largest circulation program weekly, *Pesti Müsor,* December 12-18, 1996, 46.

[10] For an interview with him, see "Beszélgetés Pap Gábor müvészettörténésszel" [Conversations with the art historian Gábor Pap]," *Zöldövezet* 2 (1993), 29-43.

[11] That indeed this was not the fancy of the neo-shamanistic group, but a historical fact which is easily proven by the ethnohistorical records; for a discussion on how the Soviet government eradicate "pagan" and shamanistic religious views, see Marjorie Balzer, "Flights of the Sacred: Symbolism and the Theory in Siberian Shamanism," *American Anthropologist* 98:2: (1996) 305-18; J. Forsyth, *A History of the Peoples of Siberia* (Cambridge: Cambridge University Press, 1992); and Y. Slezkine, *Arctic Mirrors: Russia and the Small Peoples of the North* (Ithaca: Cornell University Press, 1994).

[12] It is, in fact, the book of Michael Harner, *The Way of the Shaman* (1982), that has become the bible of these young neo-shamanic enthusiasts.

[13] Balzer, "Flights of the Sacred," 312.

[14] *Ibid.*, 313.

[15] For the kind of scholarship I am discussing, see M. Hoppál, "Nö-hegy-fa" [Women-mountain-tree], *Zöldövezet* 2 (1993), 69-79.

[16] A. Oláh, "Rosswelli feliratok [The inscriptions of Rosswell]," *UFO Magazin* 8:7 (1997), 34-35.

[17] See *Nyitott Világ*, 2/4 (1996), 2.

[18] John Fiske, *Understanding Popular Culture* (Boston: Unwin Hyman, 1989), 174.

[19] A. Kovács, and S. Molnár, *Tanítás: Az Isten által megdicsöitett Világ üzen a jelen és a jövö kor emberének* [Teaching: The blessed- by-God-World sends a message to the man of the present and future] (Kecskemét: Pro Humanitate, 1996), 5; and A. Oláh, "Rosswelli feliratok [The inscriptions of Rosswell]," 34. An earlier alternative thinking associated ancient Hungarians with the Sumerians; such publications prompted Géza Komoróczy, one of Hungary's foremost Near Eastern specialists, to write a book against this Sumerian hypothesis. The current mystic world-view, however, offers an even more far-fetched understanding of Hungarian ancient history. MU, the lost continent, being the original homeland; Zeus being the Founder; Pallas Athene the Hungarian "Father-Mother" God; Buddha the Hungarian princes Buda and so on, ad nauseam.

[50] The magazine *Túlvilág* [*Other World*, or *Nether World*] is published in Budapest by a group of individuals committed to the psychic and the supernatural world and mainly concerns itself with other-worldliness; articles and interviews are printed about near-death experiences, time travel, reincarnation, and other occult subjects.

[51] The retired opera diva Ibolya Duba, for example, discovered the Enokh cult and can be credited with bringing the American mystic J. Hurtak—whose book *The Key of Enokh* has just been translated into Hungarian—to Hungary several times; see "Az emberiség célja nem lehe t más mint ISTENEMBERRÉ válni" [The purpose of man is to become GODMAN], *Túlvilág,*

July 1997, 18.

[52] For example, Margit Bojta and István Báró are well known for the political horoscope printed in the pages of the alternative magazine *Túlvilág*. In volume 3/2, 1997, the horoscope concern all major political parties.

[53] In fact, every time I read this journal [*Open World*], or had to translate it into English, always remembered another, rather similar expression: that of the philosopher Karl Popper's "open society." One is left to one's intellect to make sense of the spiritual and philosophical dimensions (connection?) between the two.

[54] See J. Szabó, "A választott nemzet [The Chosen Nation]," *Nyitott Világ* 2/4 (1996), 6.

[55] Laszlo Kürti, "How Can I Be a Human Being?: Culture, Youth, and Musical Opposition in Hungary," In Sabrina Ramet, ed., *Rocking the State: Rock Music and Politics in Eastern Europe and Russia* (Boulder: Westview, 1994), 73-102.

[56] Grandpierre is not only an astronomer and a musician, he is also an avid poet. To give a taste of his neo-shamanism, I will cite an excerpt from his poem "World talk" [*Világbeszéd*]: Dance calls. / Drum. / Numbness. / Covered face. / A child's face. / Looking at you knowing that you look back. / Music nears. / Eyes are sparkling. / Swallowing you (Grandpierre 1990:44).

[57] Grandpierre also offered an interview on cosmic phenomenon in which he was characterized as the "shaman-scholar," "A Vágtázó Halottkémek Nap-útja" [the Solar voyage of the Galloping Morticians], *Nyitott Világ*, 3/2, 1997, 3.

[58] See "A Miatyánk' spirituális értelme [The meaning of 'Our Father']," *Nyitott Világ* 2/4 (1996), 8-9.

[59] In my earlier article on Hungarian popular music, I discussed this and argued that in the early 1980s folkloric elements in rock music served, albeit in rudimentary forms, an anti-state stance on the part of youth—Laszlo Kürti, "How Can I Be a Human Being?" 94. Yet, it is quite obvious that certain aspects of this folkloric movement closely relate to what Gellner calls simply nationalism. He argues: "Nationalism is not what it seems, and above all it is not what it seems to itself. The cultures it claims to defend and revive are often its own inventions, or are modified out of all recognition." Ernest Gellner, *Nations and Nationalism* (Ithaca, NY: Cornell University Press, 1983), 56. Searching for pristine peasant men and women, who can sing, dance, weave and carve, and identifying them with one's past may result in a distortion of facts, histories and what we call tradition. Just like culture heroes in epic sagas, national treasures in an industrial—in fact in many cases, post-industrial—society are somewhat of an enigma bordering the "ironic age" dilemma espoused also by Ernest Gellner.

[60] I have described this connection elsewhere in detail in Laszlo Kürti, "Language, Symbol and Dance: An Analysis of Historicity in Movement and Meaning," *Shaman* 2:1 (1994), 3-60.

[61] See "Kimerült Honfoglalókkal a Kárpátokban." [Tired home-settlers in the Carpatian Mountains]," *Népszabadság*, 16 September 1995, 18.

[62] Name changes of streets, squares, cities and counties were the phenomena of the transition period from communism to capitalism following the collapse of the state socialist system in 1989. The four Hungarian counties which underwent name changes since 1990 are: Komárom-Esztergom, Jász-Nagykun-Szolnok, Györ-Moson-Sopron, and Szabolcs-Szatmár-Bereg. See, *Népszabadság*, 19 June 1997, 1.

[63] There have been some ethnographers who have been marginalized by mainstream ethnographic scholarship but whose influence has been enormous among Hungary's alternative thinkers. Such a figure, no doubt, is Gábor Lükö, who has been writing about Hungarian peasant art in an eloquent but quite individual perspective. For Lükö's more recent work, see his analyses on peasant art (1983) and the more esoteric words on religion (1993). G. Lükö, *Kiskunság régi müvészete I* [Old art of the Kiskunság region] (Kecskemét: Bács-Kiskun Megyei

Iüvelödési Központ, 1983); idem., "Az ige, a magyar ige," [The Word, the Hungarian Word],"
öldövezet 2 (1993), 48-49.

Ernest Gellner, *Nations and Nationalism.*

Colin Campbell, "The Cult, the Cultic Milieu and Secularization," 124.

Colin Campbell, "Half-Belief and the Paradox of Ritual Instrumental Activism: A Theory
)f Modern Superstition," *British Journal of Sociology* 47:1 (1996), 151-66.

Gy. Borbándi, *A magyar népi mozgalom* [The Hungarian Populist Movement] (New York:
üski, 1983), 69.

T. I. Berend, "Jobbra át [Right Face]. Right Wing Trends in Post-Communist Hungary," in
Held, ed., *Democracy and Right-Wing Politics in Eastern Europe in the 1990s* (Boulder:
.ast European Monographs, 1993), 105-34.

Colin Campbell, "The Cult, the Cultic Milieu and Secularization," 135.

Ibid., 129.

The Gothic Milieu

Black Metal, Satanism and Vampires

Massimo Introvigne

The New Satanism

In Italy Marco Dimitri, the young leader of the Italian Satanist group, the Luciferian Children of Satan (Bambini di Satana Luciferiani), was arrested twice in the same year on charges of rape. In France graves were desecrated in Toulon (and subsequently in other towns in southern France): four members of a small Satanist band were arrested. Similar incidents took place in Romania, Russia and other countries. The media were taken by surprise, considering that by 1996, the Satanism scares of the 1980s and early 1990s had largely subsided.

Modern Satanism appeared in the seventeenth century. Satanism should not be confused with witchcraft. While witchcraft is a popular and normally unorganized phenomenon, modern Satanism is the worship of the Devil within the frame of organized movements and elaborate ritual. Modern Satanists—unlike participants in earlier witchcraft—are largely members of the middle and upper classes. Similarly, Satanism scares are different from witch hunts. Unlike the latter, the former credit Satanists not only with bloody crimes and relationships with the Devil but, more specifically, with the power to secretly influence —if not direct—the life of whole nations and the course of human history. Organized Satanism and Satanism scares manifest themselves in the history of the West in a cyclical way.[1] Groups of Satanists (normally quite small) are detected and their activities are magnified by this modern invention, the press (in later cycles, TV). As a reaction, a Satanism scare arises, where anti-Satanists usually grossly exaggerate both the number and the power of the Satanists, insisting that they are behind contemporary social movements they perceive as disturbing. In a third phase, anti-Satanism is disqualified by its own exaggerations, becomes disreputable and opens the way for new open activities of Satanists, thus for a new cycle.

The first important cycle started with the activities of a group of Satanists at the court of the French King Louis XIV between 1662-1679. When the main Satanists were tried for a number of crimes, press coverage and pamphlets guaranteed an international notoriety to the case. Between the end of the seventeenth century and the beginning of the eighteenth century, a Satanism scare followed, where anti-Satanists suspected Satanists (actually a few dozen people in the French incident) of conspiring in the dark to promote Enlightenment skepticism and anti-Christian culture and politics. Ultimately anti-Satanist literature became so extreme as to be easily discredited. This paved the way for the occult revival of the years of the French Revolution.

The French Revolution, however (and the visibility of occult and magical groups in the same years), prompted another Satanism scare which lasted through the 1850s and was revived in the 1890s. The Revolution, Christian anti-Satanists argued, was so incredible that it could not be a mere political phenomenon, and a whole religious literature attributed it to the conspiracy of secret societies such as the notorious Illuminati or, more directly, to Satanists directed by the Devil in person. Apparently, small groups of Satanists were in fact active in France, Belgium and possibly other countries in the 1850s. Their activities caused the usual anti-Satanist overreaction. The Satanism scare (which tried to explain also the surprising success of Spiritualism through Satanic conspiracy theories) had a first scholarly phase where Catholic intellectuals discussed theories on Satanism and Satan's influence. In a second phase—after the success of Joris Karl Huysmans' novel *Là-bas* (1891) had familiarized the public with Satanism and Black Masses—scholars were replaced by journalists. At least two of the latter—the notorious Léo Taxil (1854-1907) and his co-conspirator, Charles Hacks—were clever frauds who, having spread incredible tales about Satanists, later admitted to have exploited the gullibility of certain Catholic conservative readers for a variety of purposes. The game could not go on indefinitely, and Taxil had to admit the fraud in 1897. His confession discredited the Satanism scares for decades, and only after sixty years did a truly international scare manifest itself again. A large sociological literature exists on the Satanism scares of the 1970s-1990s; it was an overreaction to the visibility of contemporary Satanist organizations dating from the foundation of California's Church of Satan in 1966 and a manifestation of larger hostility to "cults."

By the early 1990s, the theory that underground "generational" Satanic cults were widespread and preyed on day-care toddlers had been largely debunked by social scientists and law enforcement agencies throughout the United States and Europe.[2] Memories "recovered" in therapy of past "satanic" ritual abuses are increasingly rejected as court evidence in both United States and Europe. Only small pockets of Christian counter-cult activists and fringe therapists still believe in the factual reality of "satanic" ritual abuses recovered during memory therapy.

Although the 1996 incidents have been greeted by these groups with a "we-told-you-so" attitude, the scenario was in fact quite different. The Satanism discovered by Italian and French law enforcement agencies in 1996 is not the same Satanism exposed in the core books of the anti-Satanist movement in the 1980s. It is also different from "classic" Satanism of organizations like Anton LaVey's Church of Satan or Michael Aquino's Temple of Set. The scenario introduced in the Satanism scares of the 1980s postulated that Satanists are very difficult to recognize. They are lawyers, doctors, corporate executives. In fact, their activities are so clandestine that they could be discovered only in therapy by inducing their victims to recover post-traumatic memories. The 1996 Satanists are, if anything, too evident. Marco Dimitri and his followers dress all in black, wear a plethora of Satanic symbols, and have appeared as spokespersons for Satan in popular Italian TV talk shows. While not as famous as Dimitri, members of the Toulon gang also dressed like a Satanist is supposed to dress.

Classic Satanism was born in California in the 1960s. The Church of Satan was established in San Francisco by Anton Szandor LaVey (1930-1997) in 1966 as a development of an organization called the Magic Circle that he co-founded in 1960 with Hollywood underground filmmaker Kenneth Anger. In 1975 most of the leadership of the Church of Satan left LaVey's organization and followed Michael Aquino into the splinter group Temple of Set. The Church of Satan became mostly a mail-order organization during the 1980s, but experienced a comeback of a sort in the 1990s through new leaders, the publication of the newsletter *The Black Flame,* and the appearance of some dozens of sister organizations throughout the world. Although LaVey believed that Satan is only the metaphor for a higher (and more selfish) human potential while Aquino maintains that Satan (or, rather, Set) is a personal being, both are heavily indebted for their worldviews and ceremonies to British magus Aleister Crowley (1875-1947). While Crowley did not believe in the personal existence of Satan and despised Satanists, his rituals have been adapted—with the appropriate changes—by almost all modern Satanist groups.

At least before the mid-1980s members of classic Satanist groups were typically middle-class urbanites in their forties and fifties. Except for ceremonies, they would wear a jacket and a tie rather than black leather "Satanic" clothing. This is certainly true for European offshoots of classic Satanism such as the two Churches of Satan based in Turin, Italy. Additionally, their leadership needed to be rather cultivated, since the magical works of authors such as Crowley are not easy to grasp and require a solid background in Western esotericism. The situation somewhat changed in the late 1980s, when the Temple of Set and some of the smaller groups inspired by the Church of Satan realized that a sizeable youth subculture potentially interested in Satanism existed and tried, with mixed results, to get in touch with it. The original Californian Church of Satan and the Italian Churches of Satan, however, still largely maintain the original character. By contrast the new Satanist groups—such as those "discovered" by the police in Italy and France in 1996—are typically led by youths in their thirties and have as members mostly teenagers, and it is extremely rare that their leaders are well educated in traditional Western occult lore. They are much more interested in music.

The Gothic Milieu from the 1970s to the 1990s

The Gothic milieu (occasionally called the Dark Wave, as a submilieu of the 1970s New Wave) has largely been created by rock music, although fiction, comics, movies role-playing games and later the Internet also had a relevant influence. Although the term Gothic was created by outsiders, it was quickly accepted by the movement, notwithstanding the fact that the latter largely ignored eighteenth and nineteenth century Gothic literature (with the possible exception of *Dracula*, whose inclusion in the Gothic genre is disputed by contemporary critics). Gothic music should not be confused with heavy metal. Metal plays on the power of extreme human emotions and feelings. Gothic concentrates on human reactions to particular emotions associated with death, corpses, blood, the macabre, and vampires. Although the Devil is often mentioned, he is not always a key player in the Gothic scene. Besides, Satan is mentioned in many brands of rock music that are not Gothic (and so are vampires, who make frequent guest appearances in heavy metal music).

The origins of Gothic come from many different sources. Gothic themes emerged around 1970 in England and the United States with artists and groups like Alice Cooper and Black Sabbath. Although these musicians were not purely Gothic, fans of Alice Cooper were largely responsible for introducing the Gothic outlook, with its black-leather clothing and silver earrings for males. In 1976 David Letts founded The Damned in England, a band that was originally a punk group, but later focused mostly on Gothic. Letts changed his name into David Vanian (from "Transylvanian") and focused on the vampire theme (although Nazi symbols were also occasionally introduced). In the same year, Bernard Sumner, Peter Hook, Ian Curtis (1957-1980) and Terry Mason (later replaced by Stephen Morris) decided to start a band in Manchester. Originally called Warsaw, they changed their name to Joy Division in 1978 so as not to be confused with a pre-existing London punk group, Warsaw Pakt. The name came from the line of huts where young deported women were forced to prostitute themselves to German officers in Nazi concentration camps. Notwithstanding the name, Joy Division denied any Nazi sympathies and in fact appeared at the Manchester Rock Against Racism benefit concert in 1978. Although Joy Division occasionally used Nazi paraphernalia on stage, its portrait of Nazism was, if anything, sad, as evidenced from the following lines of its hit "They Walked in Line," which begins:

> All dressed in uniforms so fine,
> they drank and killed to pass the time.
> Wearing the shame of all their crimes
> with measured steps they walked in line.

And continues:

> They walked in line.
> They carried pictures of their wives,
> and number tags to prove their lies.
> And made it through the whole machine,
> with dirty hearts and hands washed clean.
> They walked in line.

Joy Division eluded classification, but its haunted and ghostly atmospheres had a deep influence on later Gothic. On May 18, 1980, just before Joy Division was to leave England for its first U.S. tour, Ian Curtis hung himself in his kitchen. Without its talented singer and lyricist, who was replaced by Bernard Sumner, the group continued as New Order and remained influential on the alternative (but much less on the Gothic) music scene. In the years when Joy Division was becoming popular, a more cultivated version of Gothic was introduced in England by singer Suzie Sioux, "Siouxsie." Sioux came from punk and was inspired by groups like the Sex Pistols. She was also a friend of Genesis P-Orridge, an Aleister Crowley enthusiast and the founder of the Temple of Psychick Youth (TOPY). P-Orridge's music—the first wave of industrial, or "industrial culture" —was as far from Gothic as possible, but his contacts with Sioux did much to introduce Crowley in the Gothic milieu. Later, P-Orridge would become an inspiration for the birth of the "second wave" or industrial music, much closer to the Gothic and was, in fact, occasionally labeled "industrial Gothic." This further subgenre would emerge in the late 1980s around the Wax Trax circle in Chicago, which would become well known with the Nine Inch Nails of Trent Reznor and its influential album *Pretty Hate Machine* (1989), and would eventually triumph with Marilyn Manson. In the late 1970s Sioux founded Siouxsie and the Banshees. Robert Smith, the leader of a much more famous band, the Cure, worked with Siouxsie and the Banshees in 1983-1984 following four influential Cure albums.

Largely responsible for defining Gothic as a genre was Bauhaus, whose leader Peter Murphy continued as a popular Gothic musician after the dissolution of the group in 1983. By 1983—the year when another early Gothic group, the Misfits, also separated—Gothic music was experiencing a boom. New groups emerged, including the Sisters of Mercy and later, in 1988, Dark Theater whose leader, Vlad, wears portable fangs and claims to actually drink blood (originally only from his wife, Lynda, who later divorced him and now proclaims herself a "lesbian Goth"). Blood-drinkers are, at any rate, a small distinct subculture within the Gothic milieu, perhaps closer to sadomasochism than to teenage Gothic.[3]

While classic punk was experiencing a crisis, Gothic groups, including the 45 Grave, inherited some of its features and its fans.[4] By 1990 the Gothic scene was truly international, with bands in countries such as Japan, Sweden, Finland, New Zealand, Poland, and Italy, in addition to Germany, the United Kingdom, and the United States. By 1990, the Gothic subculture was well established with specialized magazines, including *Propaganda* (established in New York by Fred H. Berger and perhaps the most important voice for the Gothic) and *Ghastly*.[5]

Non-Gothic groups such as Iron Maiden and Kiss felt compelled to issue at least one album with Gothic themes. But readers of *Propaganda* and other members of the Gothic subculture typically skipped the most famous groups as being too commercial. They rather regarded themselves as part of an elite subculture, lionized less well-known groups and remained apart from the larger world of rock fans. Being part of the Gothic milieu for many was not a Saturday evening concert affair, but a permanent lifestyle. Goths dress in black every day of the week, wear peculiar jewelry and use their own jargon. Rather macabre allusions and jokes—whose meanings are often lost to outsiders—are a trademark feature of their style.

Around 1990 the Gothic milieu, born from music, started to be increasingly defined by its literary preferences as well. Two Gothic role-playing games focusing on vampires—*Ravenloft*, which emerged in 1990 from the fantasy game *Dungeons & Dragons*, and *Vampire: The Masquerade*, introduced by White Wolf in 1991— had an important influence on the milieu. Considering the Gothic milieu's love affair with horror literature (including frequent allusions in its music to such classics as *Dracula*), it is surprising that references to Stephen King are virtually nonexistent. King is probably just too popular for a subculture glorying in its minority status. He also insists that his novels do not promote any kind of worldview. By contrast, Anne Rice—who occasionally *does* claim that she is introducing a worldview, with increasingly apparent Gnostic and Kabbalistic references—is immensely popular in the Gothic milieu. Classics of Gothic and horror literature, from "Monk" Lewis to Lovecraft, are largely ignored, with the occasional exception of *Dracula*. Gothic events, including the 1989 Theatre of the Vampires held in Long Beach, California; musicians such as Tony Lestat (a main participant in the 1989 event and singer of Wreckage);[6] shows such as Tony Sokol's *La Commedia Del Sangue: Dances From A Shallow Grave—The Vampyr Theatre*,[7] Gothic bands such as Lestat and the Italian Theatre des Vampires; fanzines such as *Savage Garden* (published in English in Milan and now renamed *Wistaria*) all borrow their names (and much more) from Anne Rice. Later, in 1992, another New Orleans female horror writer, Poppy Z. Brite, wrote a cult novel for the Gothic milieu, *Lost Souls*, featuring the encounter of real undead vampires with the Gothic subculture of a small American town.

As of the mid-1990s the very success of the Gothic threatens its existence as a separate genre in rock music. Contemporary rock is eclectic, and it is often difficult to tell what genre a group is all about. Such labels as post-punk, dark metal, doom metal, garage rock and trash are difficult to define and often include Gothic themes. If anything, some of the new labels mean to convey a passion for the outrageous and the extreme, and regard the Gothic bands of the 1980s as moderate. The most extreme subgenre which emerged in the 1980s is black metal, mixing heavy metal and Gothic. Black metal is both musically and culturally less sophisticated than Gothic, but fans may switch from one to another and still remain part of the same Gothic subcultural milieu.

Generally credited with starting black metal is a British band, Venom. Formed in 1978 and originally named Oberon, Venom assumed its name in 1980 and introduced Satanism and the cult of death as a main heavy metal theme. Their song "Black Metal" (1982) defined the subgenre and became an anthem for the movement, which opens with:

> Black is the night, metal we fight
> Power amps set to explode.
> Energy screams, magic and dreams
> Satan records the first note.

And concludes:

> We chime the bell, chaos and hell
> Metal for maniacs pure.
> Fast melting steel, fortune on wheels
> Brain Hemorrhage is the Cure (Venom—*Welcome to Hell*, 1997).

Proclaiming themselves the "Sons of Satan," Venom called to:

> Live like an angel, die like a devil,
> Got a place in hell reserved for me,
> Live like an angel, die like a devil,
> Gonna burn in Hell, that's where I'm gonna be
> ["Live Like An Angel (Die Like a Devil)," 1981, in Venom—*Welcome to Hell* 1997].

Another of Venom's most famous—and both Satanic and vampiric—hits, "In League With Satan" (1981), boasts:

> I'm in league with Satan
> I was raised in Hell
> I walk the streets of Salem
> Amongst the living dead

And ends with the declaration:

> I need no one to tell me
> What's wrong or right
> I drink the blood of children
> Stalk my prey at night (Venom—*Welcome to Hell* 1997).

Specialists of metal discuss whether after Venom there is a difference between black metal and death metal, the latter being more brutal, more interested in drugs and sex, and more faithful to Venom's original inspiration. One problem is that some of the most famous bands have evolved through the years. Bathory, started in Sweden in 1983, was originally very much influenced by Venom but by 1987, with *Under the Sign of the Black Mark*, started evolving toward a new style, later called "modern" or "Northern" black metal. In 1990, with *Hammerheart*, an element of Viking romanticism started playing a key role. The Swiss group Hellhammer between 1982-1984 was one of the bands defining black metal; renamed Celtic Frost in 1984 they quickly evolved out of black metal and continued until 1993, insisting that they were not part at all of the black metal scene. The early albums of the German band Sodom, established in 1983, were black metal, while their later productions could rather be classified as speed metal, a different subgenre. By contrast, Florida bands such as Death (established in 1985), Obituary, Deicide and Morbid Angel (who came to Florida from North Carolina) are usually classified as death (rather than black) metal. Contemporary doom metal may be regarded as a later development of death metal.

Black metal has become popular in segments of the Gothic milieu in a number of countries, including Greece, Brazil, France, Poland, Norway and Sweden. A frequent feature of black metal, particularly in its "modern" or "Northern" form, is extreme hostility to Jesus Christ and Christianity. The anti-Christian theme keeps together different worldviews. Some black metal groups are pagan; others are Satanist. Some are not interested in politics, while others are overtly neo-Nazi or promote a nationalism rooted in pre-Christian Northern Europe. In Norway—and subsequently in other countries—the anti-Christian activities of some black metal groups took the illegal form of "esoterrorism," or esoteric terrorism. Two black metal groups—Emperor and Burzum—were involved in burning Christian churches, including historical monuments, and in desecrating Christian cemeteries. Emperor one-time member Bård Eithun killed a gay man who approached him at night in a Lillehammer street in 1992. Vandalizing graveyards seems to be a popular activity in segments of the black metal milieu in a number of countries, including Italy and France. Varg Vikernes ("Count Grishnackh," or "The Count"), the leader of Burzum—who somewhat converted from Satanism to "a National Socialist form of racialist Odinism"[8] —not only was involved in the burning of at least ten churches, but was later sentenced to 21 years of prison after killing in 1993 fellow black metal musician Oystein Aarseth Euronymous. Although the press liberally described the homicide as "Satanic" and "ritual" —and Varg himself claimed that the unfortunate Euronymous was a "false Satanist" and a "communist"[9] —in fact the main reason for the crime was a quarrel over money and the management of the musical label Deathlike Silence. Varg remains a popular character in the black metal milieu, and continues to write music and articles for the specialized fanzines from jail. In 1997 he published his "sacred text," *Vargsmål*, and announced that he had discovered a forerunner and (alleged) pioneer racialist Odinist in Vidkun Quisling (1887-1945), whose very name is synonymous with collaboration with the Nazis, not only in Norway. From a musical point of view, Mayhem—Euronymous' band, started in 1984 and coming back in 1994 after Euronymous' death—remains the most influential model of "modern" Black Metal. In 1990 they recorded *Live in Leipzig* which included one of their most famous songs, "Carnage":

> Witchcraft, blood and Satan
> Meet the face of Death
> Blood
> Fire
> Torture
> Pain
> KILL

Culminating with:

> Winds of war, winds of hate
> Armageddon, tales from Hell

The wage of mayhem, the wage of sin
Come and hear, Lucifer's sings (Mayhem, "Live in Leipzig,"1990).

The earlier "Deathcrush" (1987) was not more reassuring:

Demonic laughter your cremation
Your lungs gasp for air but are filled with blood
A sudden crack as I crushed your skull.

And, as if that were not enough:

Death, nicely crucified
Death, heads on stakes.
The barbecue has just begun.
Deathcrush—Deathcrush—Deathcrush
(Mayhem, "Deathcrush" 1997).

As the fate of Euronymous sadly confirmed, violence in the Norwegian black metal scene was not purely a matter of lyrics. Without burning churches, groups such as Bekhira and Osculum Infame in France, or Marduk in Sweden are not less anti-Christian. A 1995 CD of Marduk (evolving from a 1991 demo) is called *Fuck Me Jesus*, and its cover shows a young girl masturbating with a crucifix. A look at the catalogue of the French musical distributor Osmose Productions (specializing in black metal) shows bands with names such as Impaled Nazarene (from Finland), Rotting Christ (from Greece), Diabolos Rising (with musicians from Greece and Finland), and Fallen Christ (with a number of references to Aleister Crowley). In France some industrial rock bands, including Dissonant Elephants and Non, have jumped onto the anti-Christian bandwagon, although with a different musical style. In 1996 Dissonant Elephants released a CD, *Our Eyes Like Daggers*, with liberal quotes from the ubiquitous Aleister Crowley and a cover featuring Jesus Christ on the cross with a clown-like red nose. The activities of these groups are among the reasons for the establishment of a Catholic Anti-Defamation League in France in 1997.

On the other hand, it is important to note that black metal is not really representative of the Gothic milieu in general. It is a small segment, a subculture within a subculture. There is a larger number of musical and other groups inspired by Anne Rice, whose worldview is not anti-Christian but rather a brand of gnostic Christianity (as suggested in Rice's novel *Memnoch the Devil*, 1995). Black metal is also anti-Jewish, with frequent references in its fanzines to the infamous *Protocols of the Elders of Zion*, while Rice's 1996 novel *Servant of the Bones* is a tribute to Jewish esoteric culture. Black metal also emphasizes Satanic and pagan symbols and has no colours but black, while the mainstream Gothic subculture, influenced by the glam rock music of Kiss, and by Tom Cruise's movie portrait of Anne Rice's vampire Lestat, increasingly includes elaborate and baroque ways of dressing, quite far away from the old black leather jackets.

The Gothic Milieu as a Metanetwork and the Emergence of Gothic Movements

The Gothic milieu is loosely organized. Its main organizing agents are magazines such as *Propaganda*, but more obscure fanzines with limited circulation also have an important influence. It could be described as a network or—more accurately—as a metanetwork, where participants in different networks convene. There is, for instance, a recognizable network of Anne Rice fans, and thousands attend the yearly Gatherings of the Coven organized in New Orleans by the Anne Rice's Vampire Lestat Fan Club (established in 1988) and by the Louisiana writer herself. Most of these fans dress like the vampire Lestat only once a year, and have no contacts with the larger Gothic milieu. Some, however, do adopt a Gothic lifestyle. For them the network of Anne Rice fans is the door to enter the larger metanetwork of the Gothic subculture. Similar comments are in order for the many fans of Gothic role-playing games such as *Ravenloft* or *Vampire: The Masquerade*. (There are also darker role-playing games for the black metal milieu, but their following is not very large.) Hundreds of thousands of them certainly do not dress in black, and are not even interested in Gothic music. But again, active involvement in these role-playing communities (and their lively exchange over the Internet) may become a door to access the Gothic metanetwork. This does not mean that every fan of role-playing games is on his or her way to becoming a Satanist. This view is promoted by professional anti-Satanists such as Pat Pulling who, after the suicide of her son Bink in 1982, founded BADD (Bothered About *Dungeons and Dragons*), claiming that role-playing games were literally "stalking our children for Satan."[10] Groups like BADD are part of a larger Evangelical counter-cult (and anti-Satanist) scene and seems to have become less influential in recent years. At any rate, it is when fans of Gothic music also become interested in Anne Rice, and when *Ravenloft* players start attending Gothic clubs and dressing in black that the metanetwork really takes shape. As mentioned earlier, participation in one of the Gothic networks does not necessarily mean that one takes the next step and becomes a participant in the metanetwork or part of the Gothic milieu.

Further, being part of the Gothic milieu does not mean that one joins a particular movement. Dressing mostly in black, wearing silver jewelry with macabre themes, and focusing musical preferences on Gothic groups not well known in rock's mainline market are the trademarks of the Gothic milieu. In Stark and Bainbridge terms,[11] many or most participants in the Gothic milieu only participate in audience or client cults, not in cult movements. Occasionally, however, movements emerge, but they only involve a minority of those who participate in the milieu.

It seems appropriate to distinguish between pre-existing movements recruiting in the Gothic milieu, and movements born from the milieu itself. Among the first are some "old" Satanist and neo-pagan groups. As mentioned earlier, some classic Satanist groups have realized that the Gothic milieu may be an interesting ground for recruiting new members. The Temple of Set has designed its Web page in order to attract the Gothic subculture, and on February 1,

1997 Don Webb, High Priest of the Temple of Set, introduced his movement at the Hellhouse of Hollywood, a (now defunct) California bookstore typically catering to Gothic clients. Classic Satanist groups are quite small, and even the addition of a few new members could be significant in order to preserve their very existence. Their success in recruiting in the Gothic milieu is not, however, spectacular.

Most Gothic bands are not particularly interested in Satan or Satanism. Some black metal fringes certainly are, but they typically scorn organizations like the Church of Satan or the Temple of Set as "moderate" or "liberal" Satanism. Uww, the founder of French black metal fanzine *Deo Occidi* (published in English), contrasts "liberal Satanism" and "fascist Satanism" and embraces the latter. The "liberal Satanism" of classic American movements is regarded as extreme individualism and as a shameless apology for capitalism. Uww also mentions that Anton LaVey is a "moderate Jew." Additionally, classic Satanism is accused of dealing only in words. Black metal prefers actions and events, and clearly admires Scandinavian esoterrorism. It is also against capitalism, liberalism, democracy, and Judaism according to classic European Nazi models.[12] Small Satanist groups catering to the black metal Satanist fringe include the Black Order, the Order of the Nine Angles, the Ordo Sinistra Vivendi (formerly the Order of the Left Hand Path), and the Order of the Jarls of Balder. None of them has more than fifty members and all belong to a network called the Infernal Alliance. Although this wing of Satanism had its most important centers in the United States and New Zealand, combining fringes of classic Satanism and black metal, it is now present in European countries such as the United Kingdom and France. Most of these groups are openly Nazi. In the version of the Black Mass of the Order of the Nine Angles, participants affirm their belief that "Adolf Hitler was sent by the Gods to lead us into greatness." In bad but not difficult to understand Latin, they worship Hitler together with Lucifer. The priest gives the cup to the priestess with the words: "Suscipe, Lucifer, munus quod tibi offerimus memoriam recolentes, Adolphus." All reply: "Hail Hitler."[13]

Some neo-pagan groups have also attracted individual members of the Gothic milieu. This is particularly true for continental European and Scandinavian Odinist movements (who have in turn attracted portions of the black metal fringe), while the British and American Wicca is largely remote from the Gothic style. English-speaking neo-paganism and Wicca have matured beyond their early anti-Christian phase, while it is precisely the anti-Christian theme of continental neo-paganism that may occasionally attract black metal fans.

An interesting, if controversial, movement is the Temple of the Vampire based in Lacey, Washington, not to be confused with the Order of the Vampyres within the Temple of Set. The Temple appears to have been created outside the Gothic milieu but with the specific purpose of attracting members of it. Its founder, Lucas Martel, is a former member of the Church of Satan, and like LaVey's, his is largely a mail-order organization. It claims to continue an ancient religion called Hekal Tiamat and to keep its sacred book, the *Shurpu Kishpu*. The Temple is not Satanist; it mostly teaches how to contact the Vampire Gods through a ritual in seven steps. The crucial step is the fourth, where the celebrant offers to the Vampire Gods his or her own life force and the life force he or she has captured from other weaker human beings. Signs such as "ringing in ears" or "unusual pulling sensations at the solar plexus" confirm that the Vampire Gods have accepted the offering.[14] The Temple's worldview is also apocalyptic, since "we are now approaching the Final Harvest," when "the human stock shall be drained in a carnage of energy release unlike anything seen before." The energy released by killed humans would allow the Vampire Gods to descend and rule on Earth with their faithful followers, the initiates. "The humans shall . . . continue to serve as slave and food" when "the Great Undead Gods shall return to their mighty thrones of Power."[15] Given the popularity of the vampire theme, many in the Gothic milieu check out the Temple of the Vampire. Few stay, fearing that the mail-order scheme may simply be a money-making business, or disagreeing with the brutal worldview. After all, in contemporary literature, "postmodern" vampires are often depicted as not entirely evil, but caring for humans (Chelsea Quinn Yarbro's Saint-Germain) or at least psychologically ambiguous (Anne Rice's Lestat).

Finally, a number of movements have really and entirely originated from portions of the Gothic milieu. While some of these movements are pagan and anti-Christian but not technically Satanist—including the Sacred Order of Emerald in France—most claim to be Satanist. One of them, however, the French Confrérie spirituelle sataniste les Croisades de la Nouvelle Babylone, declares to promote the "unification" of "Satanists, Luciferians, pagans and neo-pagans."[16] The larger Satanist group emerging from the Gothic milieu has been, before its disruption by the Italian police in 1996, Marco Dimitri's Luciferian Children of Satan (Bambini di Satana Luciferiani—BSL). BSL grew in the 1980s from Dimitri's precocious interest in Aleister Crowley and classic Satanism. But it proclaimed that classic Satanism was a thing of the past, and that a new, bolder Satanism was required. The history of BSL is a paradoxical tribute to the power of the media. BSL was originally a small, local group. It was only when, from 1989, it was targeted by the Catholic milieu of Bologna (Dimitri's city and home to the largest Italian Catholic counter-cult group, GRIS) and later by secular anti-cultists that BSL attracted the interest of the national press. This led to Dimitri's participation in some of the most popular Italian TV talk shows as a spokesperson for Satan.

While classic Satanists in Italy have wisely avoided the media (and criticized Dimitri for not following their example), Dimitri was only too eager to oblige talk show hosts desperately in need of someone "from the other side" to animate prime time shows on Satanism, which would be boring if limited to anti-cultists and theologians. The "success" of some talk show appearances was astonishing. True, Dimitri was generally ridiculed by hosts and fellow guests alike. But—among millions of viewers—he never failed to attract a dozen or more teenagers who later contacted him at his not-too-confidential Bologna address. The Italian black metal milieu somewhat adopted Dimitri as a fellow traveler, despite reservations by some. By 1996 BSL had grown to some 200 members over north and central Italy. In 1992 Dimitri was arrested for obscenity, but this was not a serious matter. Much more serious was the prosecution started against him and fellow members in 1996, citing rape of a female follower un-willing to fully comply with her sexual duties as priestess and the participation of children in rituals. On 20 June 1997, a jury of the court of Bologna found all defendants in the Children of Satan case not guilty of rape and child abuse. The leader, Marco Dimitri, was, however, found guilty of a minor tax offense. The prosecutor, herself an active participant in Bologna's anti-cult milieu, appealed the decision, but lost again in 2000. It is certainly true that the BSL book *Van-gelo Infernale* (Infernal Gospel) —intended for private circulation only—at least symbolically suggests that sexual abuse and pedophilia may be part of an ac-ceptable Satanic lifestyle. *Vangelo Infernale* is not a particularly memorable esoteric text, and it is unlikely that it may have attracted much interest. Ulti-mately, there were the anti-Satanist campaigns of secular anti-cult and Catholic counter-cult movements that introduced the BSL to the media and made them more well known than they originally were.

On the other hand, the burning of churches in Norway and the profana-tion of cemeteries in southern France confirm that, although small, some move-ments arising from the Gothic milieu, particularly from some of its black metal fringes, are indeed dangerous and may be involved in criminal activities. Law enforcement agencies are to be commended if they keep a watch on these movements, particularly those combining Satanism and neo-Nazism. Undue media emphasis on their activities could, on the other hand, backfire and induce copycat remakes of their most spectacular deeds. It would surely be unfair to blame the activities of a small group of movements, including a few hundred members throughout the world, on all neo-pagan or occult organizations, whose activities are normally carried out within the limits of laws. It would be even more unfair to regard the most extreme Nazi or Satanic fringe of black metal as representative of the entire Gothic milieu (and indeed of the entire black metal subgenre, where many groups are neither Nazi nor Satanist). Although uncon-ventional in its way of dressing and lifestyle—designed, as with previous movements, to shock adults and express teenagers' independence—the Gothic milieu is not normally engaged in criminal activities, nor primarily interested in Satan or Adolf Hitler. The evolution of horror literature may also exert a posi-tive influence on the Gothic milieu. The heroes of this literature, in its postmod-ern versions, are no longer monsters who, like the Judeo-Christian Satan, are totally evil, but, psychologically complicated characters—epitomized by Anne Rice's Lestat—caught in the middle of eternal dilemmas about good and evil. One such character is Angel, the only vampire portrayed sympathetically in the Gothic fad of the late 1990s for teenagers, the TV series *Buffy the Vampire Slayer* (which, of course, also has a significant non-Gothic—and non-teenager—following). The other role models in the series are vampire *slayers* such as Buffy, or techno-pagan good girls such as Buffy's best friend, Willow, who combines witchcraft and high computer literacy in order to battle evil vampires and other preternatural creatures. Following the evolution of its preferred fiction, the Gothic milieu—no longer dressed only in black—may simply become, as other previous countercultural movements, a collective rite of passage introduc-ing teenagers to meaningful questions about life and death.

Notes

[1] Massimo Introvigne, *Indagine sul Satanismo. Satanisti e anti-satanisti dal Seicento ai nostri giorni* (Milan: Mondadori, 1994).

[2] Ibid.; James Richardson, Joel Best and David Bromley, (eds.), *The Satanism Scare* (Hawthorne, NY: Aldine de Gruyter, 1991).

[3] Jeff Guinn, with Andy Grieser, *Something in the Blood: The Underground World of Today's Vampires* (Arlington, TX: The Summit Publishing Group, 1996), p. 156.

[4] Brian Sheppard, "The Vampire in Music—A History," *The Vampire Information Exchange Newsletter*, 61 (February 1993), pp. 13-16.

[5] J. Gordon Melton, *The Vampire Book: The Encyclopedia of the Undead* (Detroit: Visible Ink Press, 1994).

[6] Chad Hensley, "Wrought from the Wreckage: An Interview with Tony Lestat," *Delirium 3* (1996), pp. 17-19.

[7] Sophie Diamantis, "La Commedia Del Sangue: The Vampyr Theatre," *Delirium 3* (1996), pp. 18-20.

[8] Jeffrey Kaplan, *Radical Religion in America: Millenarian Movements from the Far Right to the Children of Noah* (Syracuse, NY: Syracuse University Press, 1997), p. 160.

[9] "Uww" "Le satanisme aujourd'hui," originally published in *Morsure—La Bible noire*, reproduced in *Thelema*, new series, vol. I, n. 1-2 (1996), p. 45.

[10] Pat Pulling, with Kathy Cawthon, *The Devil's Web: Who Is Stalking Our Children for Satan?* (Lafayette, LA: Huntington House, 1989); Massimo Introvigne, *Indagine sul Satanismo*, pp. 359-60.

[11] Rodney Stark and William Sims Bainbridge, *The Future of Religion: Secularization, Revival, and Cult Formation* (Berkeley, Los Angeles and London: University of California Press, 1985), pp. 26-30.

[12] "Uww" "Le satanisme aujourd'hui," pp. 43-44.

[13] "La messe hérésiarque" ritual of the Order of the Nine Angels, published in *Thelema*, new series, vol. I, n. 1-2 (1996), pp. 47-48.

[14] *Temple of the Vampire* n.d., p. 8.

[15] Ibid., p. 25.

[16] Tract, n.d.

Black and White Unite in Fight?

On the Inter-Action Between Black and White Radical Racialists

Mattias Gardell

Introduction

Following race riots in St. Petersburg, Florida, in the fall of 1996, a coalition of Florida Klans and the black separatist group PAIN staged two joint demonstrations, and confused residents of a predominantly black neighborhood could observe white Identity Christian racialists in Klan robes embracing black racialist spokespersons in traditional African outfits. Despite the fact that the Nation of Islam, the most vociferous black nationalist organization in the United States, identifies the white man as the devil, white racists all over the country sing the praises of its present leader, Minister Louis Farrakhan. Furthermore, the Nation seems perfectly willing to invite the devil to participate in its meetings and roundtable discussions. A series of overt and covert contacts link together America's white and black racialist organizations. This fascinating phenomena is the main focus for the present chapter. Setting the stage will be a guided tour of the American conceptions of race and nation, religion and identity. Following an account of the centrality of race in the American project will be a discussion about competing ideas of "nation" involving the same population and territory. Thereafter, the Nation of Islam and white religious nationalist creeds will be briefly introduced. Space limitations make any attempt of covering all aspects of this subject impossible, and the informed reader will hopefully bear with the many oversimplifications. The two following sections will present in more detail part of the multifaceted web of interaction between contemporary black and white racialists, in the United States and abroad, followed by an interpretative conclusion.

Race and the American Project

The United States of America represents a fantastic project, ultimately aimed at establishing the abode of liberty on earth. To the shores of North America came people from all corners of Europe in pursuit of a brighter future for themselves and their heirs. The attempts of the original colonial powers to recreate the rigid social order of their homelands proved doomed to failure. The nobility and the monarchs, the state churches and the intolerant religious hierarchies, the strict class divisions and repressive code of laws seemed far away. The settlers viewed North America as a virgin land, provided to them by its Creator whose providence led them to multiply and to subdue and cultivate its vast interior. Here, every man could find success if he was willing to work hard and till the soil or exploit other avenues to earn his way. Out of the conquered land grew radical thoughts that would culminate in the American Revolution.

Inspired in part by the British seventeenth century philosopher John Locke, Thomas Jefferson wrote about the God-given rights of mankind in the Declaration of Independence: "We hold these Truths to be self-evident, that all Men are created equal, that they are endowed by their Creator with certain un-alienable Rights, that among these are Life, Liberty and the Pursuit of Happiness." Politically, Jefferson was a radical who envisioned a decentralized government by the people, in which each local community would be a self-governed populist republic cooperating voluntarily with other autonomous republics in a loose federation that would steer clear from any reestablishment of centralized state authority. The constitution agreed upon a decade later does not reflect the radical populism of Jefferson, but was nonetheless uniquely radical in its democratic orientation compared to any contemporary European standard. James Madison and his co-architects attempted to achieve a balance between centers of power, state versus federal authorities, president versus congress, and American citizens were guaranteed individual liberties and rights in a series of amendments that guaranteed the freedom of speech, the freedom of assembly, freedom of religion, and the right to bear arms. The first president, George Washington, is in American historiography described as the personification of the revolutionary ideals. He is the just, decent, moral, humble, God-fearing leader for an enlightened and liberty-loving populace.

These heroic apostles of liberty had yet one more thing in common: *they were all slave owners*. Thomas Jefferson owned hundreds of slaves. Slaves worked his Virginia plantation, slaves washed his clothes and cooked his food and, according to a persistent rumor in black America, slaves bore his children. James Madison, born and raised at the Montpelier plantation not far from Jefferson's, similarly held hundreds of slaves whose work made him an affluent man. George Washington speculated ingeniously in slaves and became one of the largest and most prosperous plantation owners.

How can this be possible? How can the very same individuals simultaneously speak so loftily about indisputable God-given human rights of freedom and liberty and be slave owners? The apparent contradiction is explained by their perception that it was *the white man who was the model of mankind*. Blacks were not fully human, but a curious mixture of beast and man, "property, not persons," defined in the constitution as "three-fifths of a man."[1]

Racism as such was not yet born. We have to wait another century before the thoughts that we all belong to the same human family but are of different races made its breakthrough. During the time under discussion, we are in the midst of the Indian Wars, where yet another dimension of the American saga is added to our story. This is a time when the America interior was colonized and the world was neatly divided between wilderness and civilization, chaos and order, untamed nature inhabited by savage man and refined culture populated by civilized man, a transition period of American history that came to contribute heavily to the American national mythos.

Race is an integral part of the foundation of Americanism, but one cannot claim that slavery was due to racism. Rather, racism is a product of slavery and colonialism and is thus connected to European expansion. Pre-imperial, Medieval European knowledge of black Africans was untainted by racist notions and we find artist and scholarly presentations hailing the accomplishments of African civilizations and African rulers.[2] Following the age of conquest was the rise of racist speculation that came to pervade all spheres of organized thought, including religion and science.

Christianity was transformed in step with the ongoing European imperial growth. Medieval Europe had its black Madonnas and artists could use darker tints when depicting Jesus, but during the imperial conquest, West Asian Joseph, Mary, Jesus and the Apostles became increasingly more European in a development that culminated in the construction of a white, blond, blue-eyed savior. The importance of the early African churches in Ethiopia and northern Africa was diminished, and the African fathers of the Church were presented as "Greeks." Troublesome facts like the existence of black saints were explained by theological rationalizations. Thus, the black St. Benedict the Moor was said to originally having been a beautiful white man who prayed to God to make him so ugly that he could resist the temptations from the opposite sex. God granted his wish and made him black.[3]

Light and dark is a basic dichotomy applied in Christianity to symbolize the distinction between the realm of God and Satan. What is good and innocent is "white" and what is evil and cunning is "black." Thus we speak of "innocence as white as a lily," an acceptable lie is a "white lie" and magic with benign intention is "white magic." But a "black cat" brings bad luck, an evil soul is "black" and if the stock market crashes, it is a "black" Monday. This kind of color symbolism acquired new meaning when it was applied to people of white and black complexions. To explain a diversity of races descending from a single created couple, morality was associated with skin color. Black skin was a divine punishment for past transgressions. Blackness as the curse invoked upon Ham and his son Caanan was sometimes said to be a mild form of leprosy with an excess of pigment as the only symptom. Alternatively, the cursed progenitor of the black race could be substituted with Cain, who was marked by God with blackness, in turn inherited by his offspring. So pervasive was the merging of moral quality with complexion that a good black man was said to have a white soul. Blacks, unlike whites, required spiritual bodies of a different hue in the resurrection. They would be cured of their deformity and rise in perfected white.[4]

In the scientific community, an intense debate raged over the issue of whether blacks could be regarded as human. Maybe whites and blacks were distinct species of different origins. Diversity of origin, polygenesis, would explain the apparent differences in intelligence, morality and civilization between the black and white man. In a much-quoted research report by Professor Louis Agassiz, we learn that "the brain of the Negro is that of the imperfect brain of a 7 month old infant in the womb of the White."[5]

Advocates of a diversity of species claimed that mulattos, like mules, were infertile, but had difficulties with proving the thesis as well as with the theological implications: if only whites were descendants of Adam and Eve, had only whites inherited the original sin? Were mulattos half-saved, half-damned? Were blacks and Indians non-sinners? Why then the missionaries? The debate did not close until the ascendance of evolutionary theory during the late nineteenth century, which asserted that we all belonged to the same human family. The differences between them and us were explained by an evolutionary process, akin to what Darwin had proposed in natural science. Mankind had gone through a series of evolutionary stages, and living proof could be found along the route of European expansion. Technological development was equated with mental evolution: the intellect of the "savage" was as primitive as his tools. The researchers projected their findings back into prehistoric times and made the contemporary African, Australian and American Indian cultures an image of the European cultural beginning. From this "primitive," "savage," or "natural" (as opposed to cultural) stage, man had gone through a mental evolution reaching ever higher stages and finally resulting in the pinnacle of cultures—the European civilization as the crown of creation.

Colonialism could thus be presented as a global project of civilization, in which the European imperialist shouldered the responsibility to spread light on "the dark continent," and to give the subdued peoples who had lived their unsaved lives in barbarous fear and superstition the blessing of a refined Christian civilization. Slavery and colonialism were depicted as the "white man's burden," as Rudyard Kipling, the poet of English imperialism, put it:

> Take up the White man's burden
> Send forth the best ye breed
> Go bind your sons to exile
> To serve your captives need.[6]

Slavery was thus in the best interest of the black man. Abolition was a heartless cruelty as it would "deprive the Negro of the guardian care of his owner," leaving him "subject of all the depression and oppression that comes with his inferior condition."[7] In response to a British diplomatic request that slavery would not be allowed in a soon annexed Texas, State Secretary John C. Calhoun cited an official study proving that abolition would be "neither human, nor wise." Free blacks "invariably sunk into vice and pauperism, accompanied by the bodily and mental afflictions incident thereto—deafness, blindness, insanity and idiocy—to a degree without example." Calhoun states that "retain[ing] the ancient [master-slave] relations" between the races, blacks have "improved greatly in every respect—in number, comfort, intelligence and morals."[8]

Race came to pervade the American project. The opposite poles of liberty and slavery became foundations in a social system logically congruent only through a gradually systematized and institutionalized racism, the repercussions of which still resound in American society.

Racial Nationalism in American Society

Although nationalists typically ascribe to "nation" a permanent existence, as if mankind always has been made up by various nations, the modern usage of the word stems from the eighteenth century. It became popularized through a political usage meant to produce sentiments of loyalty and solidarity between the inhabitants of a given territory and a state as an administrative form. Nationalism thus produces nation and not the other way around. "Nation" is an *imagined* community of people on the basis of selective criteria such as language, history, culture, religion or ethnicity, to which feelings of belonging, solidarity and loyalty are attached. The imagined character should be emphasized as any member of the community in practice will meet only an insignificant minority of those with whom he feels solidarity. Because it is an imagined product of ideology and culture, the perceived "nation" can alter in time and space, a social fact of greatest importance for our purpose. On American soil, competing ideas of "nation" have been at work throughout history and continue to be a centerpiece of communality and conflict as different ideologies involving the same people and territory clash with each other.

"Nationalism" is an ideology which gives priority to the "nation" over other imagined communities such as class or gender. A nationalist believes that a worker has more in common with an employer of the same nation than with workers of another nation, or postulates that a woman has less in common with women of other nations than with men of the same nation. Politically, a nationalist believes that national self-determination in a separate state or confederation of states is the only legitimate form of government. Explicitly exclusive and easily aligned with chauvinism, xenophobia and racism, nationalism postulates the unique and corporate character of the nation, to which a defined system of meaning is ascribed. Nationalism produces national awareness and identity through a nostalgic projection of the imagined community back into mythological or legendary times. From the perceived origin, a common history and shared destiny is envisioned, in a mental universe where members of a nation are inevitably and eternally linked with each other.

This mythical dimension is represented also in the semi-religious nationalism that produced the notion of an American nation. It differed from its European counterparts in that it could not project the communality too far in history without risking a transfer of loyalty across the Atlantic. The Revolution marked a break with history and the particular European identities immigrants were supposed to substitute with an American identity. Migrants from a wide variety of different European cultures should merge into a new nation. But what exactly was the American national identity? What was the meaning of being American? The search for answers was simultaneously ahistoric and historically productive. The early history acquired a sacred dimension. The pilgrims, the pioneer spirit, the Wild West mythos, the farmer ideal, and puritan religiosity became cultural foundations and merged with optimistic visions about eternal progress and development in a land in which utopian liberty was held as a realistic possibility.

In the construction of a new national identity an American civil religion was succesfully established, making Americanism a creed and the United States an instrument of God's work in the world. Biblical symbols are utilized in a sacralization of history. The Americans are identified with "the Chosen People" who through an "Exodus" from Europe were led to "the Promised Land" to build "the New Jerusalem." Americanism has its own prophets (Benjamin Franklin, Thomas Jefferson, George Washington), its own martyrs (Abraham Lincoln, the Kennedy brothers, all soldiers killed in war), its sacred events (the Declaration of Independence, the Boston Tea Party), its sacred text (the Constitution), its own sacred places to which pilgrimages are made (Lincoln Memorial, the Tomb of the Unknown Soldier, Gettysburg), its solemn rituals of commemoration (Thanksgiving Day, Memorial Day, Veterans Day, 4th of July) and its sacred symbols (Statue of Liberty, the Stars and Stripes, the White House).[9]

As the sacred expression of the American dream, Americanism preaches all the values, norms and ideals associated with the American Way of Life. The United States is the safeguard of freedom, democracy and moral decency against every form of totalitarianism. In this fortress of individual freedom with equal opportunities for all, every man can reach success. Countless Hollywood productions recycle the epic of the American cultural hero identified as the honest, hardworking God-fearing underdog who fights his way against all odds to become prosperous and victorious. Americanism thus pays homage to the lone individual and denies the existence of collective injustice.

But who was to be part of this new exclusive national identity? Who was to be included as an American and who was to be excluded as an alien? Centered around this question, a continuous struggle has been fought, slowly expanding the definition of "American" as new groups fought their way toward acceptance in a still ongoing process with an uncertain outcome. Sparking decades of "nativist" conflicts, "American" changed from its original "white Anglo-Saxon Protestant" definition to include Catholics in the early 1900s.[10] After the end of World War II, anti-Semitic laws were cleared to succesfully make room for Jews, after which the American project was presented as having a "Judeo-Christian" foundation. The civil rights struggle of the 1950s and 1960s gradually came to incorporate blacks in a not yet fully completed or unanimously accepted expansion. Controversy can still be said to rage over the status of Hispanics, East and Southeast Asians, and Muslims, who have yet to be fully incorporated. The importance of these post-WWII changes for the emergence of a vociferous white separatist movement will be discussed later. Now we will turn to the construction of black nationalism, and thus step back in time.

The much-discussed melting pot through which immigrants of separate native cultures were reshaped as "Americans" was long for "whites only." Slavery functioned as yet another melting pot, in which Africans of various cultures were remodeled. Herein were cast individuals of every creed and profession: teachers, farmers, warriors, scholars, jurists, philosophers, priests, hunters, artisans and artists, Christians, Muslims and adherents of "native African" religions, to become slaves, a subhuman mixture of man and chattel who were renamed Smith, Jones, Brown or whatever other name the owner might have had. Racially excluded from equal participation in the American project, an alternative racial nationalism emerged in the land in the mid-nineteenth century. Its architects were informed by the contemporary Western notion of race as an organic entity and drew heavily from the German völkish tradition. The different "races" and/or "nations" of the world were said to be corporate organisms, each one with its distinct "personality," endowed by "nature" with certain physical, intellectual, mental and spiritual features. Being different by "nature," the "natural" situation was logically then for each race to be separate and to cultivate its characteristics.

Removed from their roots, raised with notions about Africa as a dark continent and taught to be grateful for having the opportunity to live in a Christian civilized country and bask in the glow from the crown of creation, blacks in America had to struggle with a problem of identity. Caught up in the peculiar situation of being Americans, but yet not Americans, Africans, but yet not Africans, black nationalists suggested various concepts for their own national identity, none of which was met with universal acceptance. The heated debate over whether or not they should call themselves Negroes, Colored or Blacks, Negro-Saxons, Anglo-Africans, Euro-Africans, Afro-Americans, African-Americans, or, most recently, African Americans highlights the emotional significance of the dilemma.

Religious black nationalists add another question: what is the meaning of us being here? What did God have in mind when He let this happen? Generally, black religious nationalists advance the race-organism theory with a mythic and cyclic notion of history in their quest for answers. Differing in details and elaboration, a common "basic myth" of black religious nationalism projects the idea of a corporate black nation back to the Origin of Time. The blacks are envisioned as the "Chosen People," created in the likeness of the black God(s). The aboriginal black culture is held to be the cradle of civilization, where it all began. The black Original Man was elevated to a state of perfection yet unsurpassed in human history and points to a level of true bliss, i.e., a bliss to which the black man is preordained to return. For various reasons, not infrequently said to be a punishment for past transgression or a necessary degradation in order to fully master some divine knowledge, blacks lost their leading position to other races. Colonization and slavery are presented as hard but necessary parts of a greater divine plan in which the blacks are predestined to once again become the guides of mankind. Frequently a mystic blackosophic dimension, a national gnosis, is added which stipulates that the blacks must first wake up from their "sleep" or "mental death," and realize their true divine identity. Black religious nationalists have championed alternative concepts for their national identity, reflecting the perceived divine meaning of existence. In the United States, movements can be found that advocate that African Americans properly should be named Ethiopians (African Orthodox Church, Rastafarians, and others), Moors (the Moorish Science family), Jews (various black Hebrew organizations), Nubians (the Ansaaru Allah Community), Bilalians (American Muslim Mission), and Chemis (PAIN). The most successful movement of this category is the Nation of Islam, which, in identifying blacks as the Original Black Asiatic Man, is an early proponent of this tradition.[11]

A Black Nation of Islam

The Nation of Islam (NOI), often referred to as the Black Muslims, originated among southern migrants in the rapidly expanding inner-city areas of the industrial North. Founded during the Great Depression by a mysterious prophet later identified as God in Person, it was led by the Last Messenger of God, Elijah Muhammad until 1975. He was succeeded by his son Imam Warithuddin Muhammad, who initiated a rapid transformation process aimed at merging the movement with mainstream Sunni Islam. This period is known as "the Fall of the Nation" among the followers of Minister Louis Farrakhan, who heads by far the most successful of the various "resurrected" Nations that operates in black America. A former night club entertainer, Farrakhan is the epitome of black preacher artistry, who with inflammatory rhetorical skill has succeeded in making the Nation the center of radical black racialist aspirations. Under his leadership, the Nation of Islam today enjoys a popularity unsurpassed in its history, and black militant Islam has become an integral part of a contemporary black youth culture with its message rhythmically pumped out through popular hip hop stars. Though constantly controversial, Farrakhan has made a remarkable breakthrough in national politics after leading the greatest demonstration in U.S. history in the Million Man March of 1995.

Being one of the first comprehensive black theologies in the United States, the Nation interprets Islam through the perspective given by the African American experience in a way so distinct that many mainstream Muslims refuse to accept it as Islamic. This claim derives from a notion of Islam as one, eternal, unchangeable entity shared by many Islamists and Islamologists alike, but its validity may be seriously questioned. Deconstructed and studied in its multiple forms in various social contexts, we find that the meaning of "Islam" varies considerably in time and place and can at best be understood as an umbrella concept, bringing together a wide variety of *different histories*. The creed of the Nation may depart considerably from legalistic Sunni Islam, but it does share fundamental ideas with Sufism and Shi'i Islam, especially with its Ismailiyya tradition.[12] As it is impossible to do justice to its theological complexities in this limited space, a grossly simplified outline will be offered with a special emphasis on its political applications.[13]

The Nation teaches that the black man is not an inferior creature whose future is necessarily as a welfare recipient in the black urban ghettos, but the Original Man, in himself a locus of all the divine creative powers. Blacks are "gods of the universe." In the Beginning of Time, a first emanation of divine intelligence took the form of Primordial Man, who took the color from the black space out of which he emerged. The divine energy and creative powers can only manifest in man, and a succession of Man-Gods took charge in creating the world as we know it. In the original divine civilization, the black Man-God mastered all disciplines from mathematics to architecture, symbolized by the pyramids that were placed as a sign of this magnificent past, in itself containing parts of the keys to unlock the secrets of the universe. What is in the Bible described as the Fall of Adam represents an event of cosmic significance at which mankind fell into its present beastlike state. "God in His fallen state is man, and man in his exalted state is God."[14]

The black gods "died" mentally, a metaphor used to describe the black man's unawareness of his true identity. World supremacy was given over to a white race of evil, grafted through a process of gene manipulation out of the black man. In essence, the white man is the abstracted and concentrated potential for evil that was present in the first black man, as all creation is composed of the negative and the positive. Ruled by his inner negative side, manifest as the blond, blue-eyed devil, the black man was to suffer in his effort to learn how to master the Quranic imperative "enjoining what is right and forbidding what is wrong."[15] The true secrets of the universe were concealed to a closed circle of divine Gnostic sages, "the hidden imams" of Shi'i Islam, or the "four and twenty elders" of Christianity, and was not to be revealed until the cycle of confusion ends and the cycle of unveilment commences. Reconnecting with the roots implies embarking on a black path of gnosis, and as knowledge of Self equals knowledge of God, the spiritual journey ultimately guides the black man and woman back into the exalted state of divinity defined as the *reason d'être* of mankind. This is symbolized in the concept of "I.s.l.a.m.," which if one breaks it down stands for I-Self-Lord-Am-Master.[16]

The reign of the devil explains the phenomena of colonialism, slavery, racism, economic hardship and oppression that blacks have experienced in recent history. The white devil was commanded by God to subdue the world and establish his supremacy in fulfillment of Revelations 6:8: "And behold a pale horse; and his name that sat upon him was Death, and Hell followed with him." A pale horse rode into Africa, America, Asia and Australia, Farrakhan exclaimed, and "wherever you Caucasians went you brought Death to the people. Wherever you went you brought Hell to the people."[17] But, as Revelations also informs us, there will be an end to the righteous' suffering. The white devil was to rule for 6,000 years, and that era is now rushing to its end. The countdown to Armageddon started in 1555 when a white devil named John Hawkins arrived at the shores of Africa onboard the slave ship *Jesus* to capture the black tribe of Shabazz, and bring them as slaves to the "wilderness of North America." With this, God's words to Imam Shabazz (known biblically as Abraham) in Genesis 15:13-14 came true: "Thy seed shall be a stranger in a land that is not theirs, and they shall serve them; and they shall afflict them for four hundred years; and also that nation, whom they will serve, will I judge." The fulfillment is stressed by the Nation as irrefutable evidence that identifies blacks as the principal actors of the Scriptures, reducing to impostors any other nation with claims to be the Chosen People. In effect, slavery brought the original man as a Trojan horse into the fortress of evil, giving the African American a key role in the approaching apocalypse.

Close to the expiration of the 400 years, a self-fulfilled God and member of the Gnostic circle named Master Farad Muhammad came to Detroit on the 4th of July 1930. He was raised as a poorly educated son of a Georgia share cropper to become His Messenger, and then departed to the abode from which God supervises the destiny of mankind. Elijah Muhammad spread the gospel and embarked on the black path of divinity until he was elevated into a black Messiah and taken to God.[18] Elijah the Messiah entrusted Minister Farrakhan to guide the lost-found Nation of Islam through the turbulent times to come and will immanently return to judge the wicked as the sun sets over the devil's world.

Far from being an escapist movement, passively awaiting God's intervention, the Nation is a *religion of practice* that teaches blacks to use their inherent divine powers to create their own destiny. Most significant for our purpose is to outline the way Islam was used as a marker for the black nation. Sharply criticizing the black Church, which at that time had gone from its earlier activist position to become largely politically quietist and other-worldly,[19] Elijah Muhammad taught that Islam was the aboriginal religion of the black man. Christianity was said to be a slave religion, a pie-in-the-sky philosophy, that taught the blacks to turn the other cheek to oppression and set all hopes for a dead white man nailed on a cross to give them compensation beyond the grave. Islam restored black self-respect, and in its demand for social justice turned into a creed of black empowerment.[20] Inspired by black Islamic theology as preached by Elijah Muhammad and Malcolm X, black Christians in the late 1960s began developing a black theology of liberation, reasserting the activist standpoint of the early church. Today, black nationalist Christianity and Islam cooperate freely, with black as a theological concept bridging the man-made borders of different creeds.

The black-man-is-god concept can be seen on a psychological level as an extreme version of a very American *positive thinking,* destined to break the mental chains of inferiority by which the black man is said to be chained at the bottom ladder of society. The Nation urges the black man to stop whining over injustice past and present. Nothing good can be expected from the devil. The government of the United States is one of the most powerful on earth and would have solved all its domestic problems long time ago had it been genuinely interested. The United States is equated with Babylon and any demand for assimilation with the foul spirits in the city of evil at its brink of destruction is an insane suicidal policy.

Aloof from the civil rights struggle for desegregation, the Nation taught separation from evil. Blacks were not Americans, but a *separate nation* with legitimate claims of self-determination in a territory of its own. In compensation for centuries of unpaid slave labor, the Nation demanded land, in America or Africa, and reparations in equipment and cash to get the new nation started. It adopted its own flag, which is red with a white star and crescent, and composed its own national anthem. Elijah Muhammad, and later Farrakhan, regard themselves as the head of a theocratic shadow cabinet, governing a rightfully independent nation state from its headquarters, "the Black House," in Chicago. Organizationally, the Nation is modeled as a sovereign state administration, with departments for finance, education, health, defense, law, foreign relations, and so on. Its efforts to "rebuild" an economic black national infrastructure have been remarkably successful. During the time of Elijah Muhammad, the Nation evolved into the most potent economic force in black America.[21] It owned tens of thousands of acres of farm and grass lands, a modern transportation fleet including trucks and a jet plane took care of distribution, and in the cities there were restaurants, super markets, real estate, bakeries, hotels, print shops, a bank and numerous other ventures. The economic empire crumbled during the Fall, due to privatization of the companies and legal suits, but has slowly been rebuilt during the present government.

Emphasizing re-education as a key to national liberation, Muslim schools are now mushrooming throughout the country, but still fall short of meeting the national demand. The health ministry, presently headed by Minister Dr. Alim Muhammad, not only runs programs for better diet and exercise, but also operates a chain of AIDS clinics. The defense department is in charge of a black Muslim army which gained national attention when its soldiers started to intervene in downtrodden neighborhoods to clear the streets of drug dealers and prostitutes in the late 1980s. Later incorporated as NOI Security, the Islamic patrols today have contracts in at least five different states and are employed as guards at black housing projects. This could partly be seen as the Nation's first serious effort to expand its jurisdiction in black America. Its prison ministry has won great prestige for its outreach efforts, and is also responsible for what is held to be the most effective rehabilitation program for criminals and drug addicts. Internationally, the Nation engages in trade and Farrakhan is today greeted as a head of state when he travels across Africa and Asia. Charges of having working relations with dictatorial governments counted as foes to the United States are brushed aside as interventions in the affairs of a sovereign state, and besides, who is the United States to criticize other nations for friendly relations with foreign dictatorships?[22]

Long at the margins of black America, the Nation of Islam grew out of its sectarian position during the 1980s and gradually gained wider acceptance for its separatist message. For a long time, black America was largely caught up in the civil rights struggle and kept the dream of Martin Luther King, Jr. alive. A gradually diminishing gap in income, the standard of living, and health and education seemed to confirm the vision of a multiracial American nation as a realistic possibility. Affirmative action placed individual blacks in visible positions of power and blacks made an inroad into public affairs as elected representatives on county, city, state and federal levels. Reaganomics marked a dramatic reversal of this trend, and during the 1980s and early 1990s whites and blacks effectively were pushed apart—economically, socially and politically. The blacks in the United States are the only Western population whose life expectancy rate is *declining*. With 50 percent of black children raised in poverty, a dramatic school drop-out rate, high unemployment numbers, one third of black males either in prison or out on parole, and a crime rate that makes black inner city war zones deadlier than the Vietnam War, Farrakhan is considered more a realist than an extremist when he, paraphrasing the Kerner Commission, concludes that "there already exist two nations in the United States. One black and one white. Separate and unequal." Since 1995, the black-on-black crime rates have dropped dramatically. Besides all credit that might be given to the Clinton administration, the Muslim impact deserves recognition. Farrakhan's unique rapport with young blacks in concert with black Islamic rappers is a part of the picture. Touring the nation with a "stop the killing" campaign, Farrakhan in 1992 succeeded in effecting a truce between the notorious Los Angeles-based gang federations Bloods and Crips. Expanding the peace process, increasingly more gangs with a total membership of several hundred thousand signed up. The Million Man March encapsulated much of the same spirit, as more than a million black men atoned for their failure to take responsibility for their own families and communities. Renouncing the path of self-destruction, they pledged to rebuild their neighborhoods, renounce drugs and violence, get educated, and take charge of their own futures. This "spirit of the Million Man March" should be considered when trying to explain the dropping crime rates in black America.

Ideologically, the Nation of Islam can be seen as a Third Positionist organization, a black Islamic version of leftist National Socialism. It hails God, Nation and the nuclear family and preaches a morality compatible with conservative American middle-class standards. Its disciplined members are clean-living, non-drinking, hard-working and law-abiding national soldiers, kept in shape by a strictly hierarchical and undemocratic chain of command. Farrakhan is elected by God and not the black citizens, and can, according to the NOI Constitution, appoint and discharge his Ministers and other officials at will. The corporate character of the racial nation is emphasized, and though appealing to the poor masses, their problems are explained primarily by race and not class. Anti-capitalist and anti-Communist, the third way envisioned merges ideas from black nationalism with the third way of Islam and the nationalist Islamic socialism of Mu'ammar al-Qadhdhafi. At this writing (1997), the Nation of Islam is the most successful of the radical racialist movements in the United States, dwarfing its competitors in black America as well as the radical racialists of white America to whom we now will turn.

White Religious Nationalism

As indicated earlier, racism pervaded all spheres of organized thought, including American nationalism and religion. Racism was at the heart of the country, part of its very foundation. It was not disputed, other than among groups at the margins of society. White supremacy was truly a way of life, the "natural" order on which civilization rested. Scientific racism was established in learned academic circles, racism was part of the conventional Christian denominations, it was a chief principle in the judicial system, it was the upholder of decent morality and it organized the social space of society. White religious racism only emerged as a systematic *deviant* theology to form the basis of a separate nationalist quest following the gradual and painful deconstruction of institutionalized white supremacy and the subsequent inclusion of blacks as part of the American "nation." Its formative period coincided with the first attacks on racism as state-sanctioned law and the norm of society. Initially, it held a largely conservative outlook, which successively was pushed further out to the margins. During the past few decades it has become increasingly more radical and revolutionary, as a diminishing number of white radical racialists believe that there is something left to conserve. Its present resurgence and international pan-Aryan networking seems to be connected to the process of globalization, and its adherents are today interconnected in a global, though uneasy, network. While white religious nationalists still may be found in mainstream denominations—like racism it cannot be said to have been excised from everyday life—these dimensions are not of main concern for this chapter. Here we will briefly discuss three distinct families of organized white racial nationalist religious thought, Christian Identity, "race as religion," and Odinism.

   Christian Identity is an umbrella concept for numerous related theologies and ministries, the histories of which are beyond the scope of this chapter.[23] In grossly simplified terms, Christian Identity can be described as the recasting of the older British-Israelite creed on white racial nationalist, anti-Semitic, and, largely, National Socialist grounds. British-Israelism took shape in England at the latter part of the nineteenth century. Inspired in part by seventeenth century Puritan teachings and the visions of British naval officer Richard Brothers (1757-1854), who claimed to be a direct descendant of King David, British-Israelism identifies the Northern European, and by extension white American, nations with the lost tribes of Israel. It differs from Puritan beliefs in claiming not only a spiritual, but a genealogical identification with the Chosen People of God. This makes Europeans the principal actors of the Bible and thus implies an ambiguous relationship with the Jews, who would be either relatives or masquerading impostors. British-Israelism proper generally resolved this tension by identifying Jews with the House of Judah. This conclusion led British-Israelites to enthusiastically support early Zionism as it would mean a reunification of the two Kingdoms in the Holy Land, which was then a British protectorate.

   Alarmed by Zionist demands for an independent Jewish state which in effect would ruin the British-Israelite project of world salvation, a latent anti-

Semitism transpired, voicing doubts as to the Jews' true identity. This negative attitude would be greatly accentuated on American soil, where British-Israelism metamorphosed into Christian Identity. Early proponents of the new gospel in America were M. M. Eshelman, minister in the Church of Brethren and author of *The Two Sticks or the Lost Tribes of Israel Discovered* (1887), and J. H. Allen, whose *Judah's Scepter and Joseph's Birthright* (1902) became a bestseller, spreading British-Israelism in Adventist and Bible study groups, and it is still widely read in Identity circles.

Though separate congregations were established in the United States, British-Israelism mainly gained ground as a theological tendency among individual ministers and laymen of conventional denominations, who were bound together in loose networks or associations. Its theology was, of course, not all that new in a land incorporating an (analogous) "New Jerusalem" identity as part of a national creed. Mormonism had already taken this notion a step further, claiming a genealogical connection between its adherents and biblical Israel. Struggling with its relationship to the Jewish people, Mormonism, like British-Israelism, in general adopted a philo-Semitic position, although schismatic groups have developed a virulent anti-Semitism on par with Christian Identity.

The formative period of Christian Identity could roughly be said to be the three decades between 1940 and 1970. Through missionaries like Wesley Swift, Bertrand Comparet and William Potter Gale, it took on a white racialist, anti-Semitic, anti-Communist and a far-right conservative political outlook. Combined with the teachings of early disciples Richard G. Butler, Colonel Jack Mohr and James K. Warner, a distinct racist theology was gradually formed. Whites were said to be the Adamic people, created in His likeness. A notion of a pre-earthly existence is found in an important substratum, teaching that whites either had a spiritual or extraterrestrial pre-existence. Blacks were either pre-Adamic soulless creatures or represented fallen, evil spirits, but they were not the chief target of fear and hatred. This position was reserved for Jews. The latent anti-Semitism found in British-Israelism rose to prominence. Jews were, at best, reduced to mongrelized impostors, not infrequently identified with Eurasian Khazars without any legitimate claim to a closeness with God, and at worst denounced as the offspring of Satan.

While many Identity Christians interpret this relationship between Jews and Satan as a spiritual bond, many Identity theologians advocate a more literal blood-line linkage. Most renowned is the two-seed theory, according to which Eve not only gave birth to Adam's son Abel, but also to Satan's son, Cain, after having been seduced in a more down-to-earth manner.[24] The subsequent murder of Abel was thus not a fratricide, but the first attempt to exterminate God's children. Whites and Jews are thus representations of the divine and the diabolical on earth, locked in an eternal combat now approaching its predestined end. This opposition could be accentuated into philosophical dualism, like in the teachings of Robert Miles, who taught that God and Satan represented two primal forces that used earth as a battleground to which they had sent down armies of look-alike races, angelic soldiers of light versus darkness, in their quest for cosmic dominion. An accentuated apocalyptic consciousness pervaded Christian Identity, whose adherents awaited a future more uncertain than most prophecy-believing millenarian mainstream Christians.

In general, Christian Identity gave no room for the "rapture," the miraculous physical escape from the impeding world destruction common in fundamentalist Christianity. On the contrary, Identity believers understood their task in terms of the Old Testament, in which God used his people as combat soldiers. There was to be a global war, and true believers had better to be prepared for the coming onslaught in which evil would be exterminated by the army of God, led by "General Jesus."[25] Thus, a militarized white racial religion took hold in the United States.

Identifying the Teutonic-Anglo-Saxon-Celtic-Scandinavic peoples with the lost tribes of Israel strengthened the sacred dimension of the American project. This *was* the Holy Land, taken by "divine conquest," as God, as in the Old Testament, mandated His People to "go in and kill every human being and possess the land."[26] White Americans were of Mannaseh, prophesied to become a "great nation,"[27] which in effect made the American "nation" racially exclusive by divine command. Identity logically held the Articles of Confederation and the original Constitution to be biblical documents. The extent to which Mosaic law would be followed in all its pedantic details varied among Identity congregations, from the strictest observance—including circumcision of male children—to a more conventional Christian understanding, claiming that Aryan Jesus had made the ritual ordinances unnecessary. Many chose Hebrew names for their children and celebrate Sabbath, Passover, and other Jewish holidays.

The next generation of Identity ministers, notably Pete Peters, Mark Thomas, Bob Hallstrom and Michael A. Hoffman II, would continue the path of radicalization. The formative years coincided with the rise of the black civil rights movement and the subsequent transformation of American race relations. Segregation was a painful process for many white racialists, who found themselves in opposition to a federal government that at times did not hesitate to force its will against whites in a racial conflict. Black Power grew as a dynamic force, and a series of violent race-motivated upheavals struck fear in many American hearts. Affirmative action was viewed as reversed racism, and for the first time many white Americans found a racially motivated system to their disadvantage.[28] Immigration laws that had restricted the bulk of new Americans to racial kin were altered to pave the way for a huge influx of Latin American and Asian migrants. Were white Americans to become a minority in their own country? The defeat in Vietnam added to the confusion. For the first time in American history, a war did not end in a victory. Unable to explain how the largest military power in the world could be so embarrassingly beaten to the ground by a small nation, the betrayed-by-their-leaders theory took hold as a viable explanation and was recycled in an endless stream of movie productions.[29]

All these traumatic social tribulations contributed to the mental universe of the second generation Identity adherents. During the 1970s and 1980s, the far right went through a process of increasing radicalization. Where the earlier generation had been mainly conservative and reactionary, revolutionary sentiments now proliferated as the federal government gradually emerged as the enemy of the white race. During this time, Christian Identity became widely diffused in National Socialist and right wing extremist circles as a religious rationale for racialist thought. Most of the more prominent leaders were either Christian Identity ministers or passed through Christian Identity. Identity become a unifying element in the otherwise fragmented and in-fighting American radical right. Through ministries managing to stay slightly above the complex intrigues, yearly gatherings during the 1980s were held at Miles' Mountain Church in Flint, Michigan, and Pastor Butler organized Aryan world congresses at his Church of Jesus Christ, Christian at Hayden Lake, Idaho. The latter headquarters, Aryan Nations, also became a symbol for a separatist tendency that called for whites to establish a secessionist state, mostly, though not exclusively, placed in the northwestern United States. Christian Identity also pervaded other significant movements of these decades, notably the radical localist Posse Comitatus, which refused to accept any federal authority as constitutionally legitimate. The military impetus gave rise to armed compounds of Christian congregations at which were held survivalist training for Armageddon.

Militarism was also a distinct feature of the second category of white religious nationalism that rose in the 1970s and 1980s. Not all white racialists were content with the Jewish identity claimed for Aryans. Christianity was held to be both alien and superstitious, negating the "law of nature" as well as logical reasoning. Ukrainian-born Ben Klassen founded the Church of the Creator (COTC) in 1973 in an effort to develop a creed based on the concept "race as religion." Creativity sharply ridiculed Identity doctrine, questioning why any sane white man would "break [his] neck to distort history" only to pose as "a descendant to such trash" as the ancient Hebrews. Klassen states that there is no historical evidence that the Ten Tribes of Israel ever existed and got lost, and if they did—good riddance![30] With at times brilliant sarcasm and irony, Klassen confronts all "spook believing" creeds with the iconoclastic fervor of a nineteenth-century atheist. Christianity was described as a destructive force, created in an effort to reduce the warrior spirit in the nature of the white man. In *Nature's Eternal Religion* (1973), *The White Man's Bible* (1981) and *RaHoWa: This Planet Is All Ours* (1987), a kind of religious dimension was added to a mainly secular socio-Darwinism. Based on "nature's law," a vision is outlined of the white man as a realized Nietzschean superman.

These anti-Christian teachings resulted in a falling out between COTC and Identity leaders and distanced Klassen from much of the Klan. Strongly opposed to the federal government, described as composed of race traitors in the pocket of conspiring Jews, the COTC organized the White Brigades at its Otto, North Carolina, headquarters. Followers were invited for a couple of weeks at a time, learning "survival skills, martial arts and how to use [military] weapons."[31] Creativity split following its leader's suicide, but an attempt at reviving the COTC led by Pontifex Maximus Matt Hale came in 1996 from its new headquarters in Illinois.[32]

The 1990s is characterized by a further radicalization of white racialism. The removal of the Soviet bloc as a distracting enemy allowed a clearer focus on the United States' government as the force of evil. President George Bush's talk of a New World Order was interpreted as confirming the white racialists fears of a conspiracy to establish a one-world government. Irrespective of whether this was interpreted in Identity terms as the prophesied global reign of the anti-Christ, or understood in more secular terms, the conclusion that white Americans were to be subjugated was clear. Federal violence, symbolized by the 1992 killing at Ruby Ridge and the burning flames of Waco in 1993 left no doubt in believers' minds about what should be expected.[33]

The paramilitary culture merged with mistrust of the government to give birth to the militia movement. Soon, different militias of various sizes and durations mushroomed in the United States, preparing to defend the remnants of American liberties. Though far from all of them harbor explicit white racialist world-views, many of them, like, for example, the Oklahoma White Militia, do. Mistrusting media, government agencies and other channels of public information, conspiracy theories experienced new heights, informing concerned citizens about various schemes ranging from secret federal concentration camps in which freedom lovers would be rounded up, to a satanic cabal involving presidents, international bankers, and congressmen, who met in secret for cannibalistic and necrophilic rites.[34]

It seemed as if America as a white nation had irrevocably lost federal recognition. Whites appeared to be "the only people on the face of the earth that have no national state."[35] The separatist imperative was voiced by the Aryan Nations in their *Declaration of Independence,* which was "unanimously adopted" on March 12, 1996. "The United States and its 'New World Order' has as one of its foremost purposes, the eradication of the white race and its culture." Its object is to establish "absolute [global] tyranny." "Appealing to the supreme God of our folk" the representatives of the Aryan people therefore "declare that the Aryan people of America, are and of rights ought to be, a free and independent nation."[36]

In the 1990s another white nationalist religious impetus came into the limelight: Odinism. With roots in the occult and/or pagan tendency of German National Socialism, early American Odinist writers like Else Christensen and the New Age-inspired pagan revival of the 1970s and 1980s, Odinism made its breakthrough among America's white racialists. It attracted Christian Identity believers "who flirted with Identity because it was simply the only racial theology out there,"[37] as well as anti-Christian Creativity adherents who felt the slogan "our race is our religion" did not carry far enough. "There must be something more to it."[38]

Odinism, or Wotanism, is a concept used to denote a racially exclusive understanding of pre-Christian Norse religion, or Ásatrú. Ásatrú is a polytheist tribal religion, more akin to Native American traditions than to monotheistic Christianity. Whereas the omnipotent and omniscient God of Christianity is of a nature fundamentally different from His creation, no such unbridgeable gulf separates the realm of the Gods and Goddesses in Ásatrú from this world. Ásatrú is a self-experienced spiritual path whereby man can reconnect with the divine within and with the animated universe in this world and beyond. Through ritualization it is thought possible to connect with the spirits of the land, the ancestors, and the guardian forces of nature. Leaders of the rites, the male *gothi* and female *gythia,* are not priests in the Christian sense and are invested with authority by the *kindred* (congregation) only if they prove themselves worthy in terms of knowledge and spiritual growth. Rather than being obeyed and/or prayed to, the Gods and Goddesses are invoked and invited as participants in the communal rituals, *blots*, that follow the yearly cycle of nature.

Many travelers on the Nordic Path in addition practice meditation, runic yoga or rune divination techniques. The polytheist perception of divinity is reflected in the Ásatrú belief in multiple souls and multiple destinies. Though many variations exist here, generally it is said that one soul goes to the abode of the dead while another soul departs to the abode of the yet unborn to await his next reincarnation or recurrence. Many Ásatrúers believe that this follows family lines, and here we touch on an aspect that opens up to racial speculation. Although "race" is a late concept in the history of mankind and was unknown to the ancient pre-Christian Scandinavian cultures, its modern practitioners can hardly avoid its present-day reality.

The Ásatrú revival has much to do with a search for roots and identity, in a similar manner in which many black Americans search for their African roots or Native Americans want to honor their traditions. This may or may not merge with racist ideas, and it should be emphasized that modern Ásatrú encompasses a broad spectrum of adherents, and far from all of them are inclined toward racialist ideologies. In its position on race, it ranges in a continuum from the radical racialist pole of Odinism to the anti-racist pole of many kindreds organized in the Ring of Troth network. In the middle are found two of the larger networks, the Ásatrú Folk Assembly and the Ásatrú Alliance, whose spokespersons try to distance themselves from either pole. Mike Murray of the Ásatrú Alliance describes it as the ethnic religion of Northern European peoples,[39] and Stephen McNallen of the Ásatrú Folk Assembly advances the concept of *meta genetics* as an avenue for embracing an ancestral faith without falling into the trap of negative racism.[40] An analysis of the Ásatrú pagan revival in contemporary United States falls outside the scope of this chapter. Here will only be discussed the racialist Odinist tendency, which probably composes only a minority of the wider Ásatrú community.[41]

Representing more than a hundred congregations, or "kindreds," operating in the United States and abroad, the racialist Odinist tendency is propagated by groups and federations such as the Odinist Fellowship, Wotan's Folk and Rook. Dissatisfied with the multiracial reworking of the American "nation," Odinism aims at "reaching deep into the ancestral past" to reconnect with the "roots of our race" in order to redevelop a lost "folk consciousness."[42] Asserting that each race has a genetic pool of spiritual identity, Odinism believes that "all Aryans today retain an element of Wotan consciousness," a revival of which would liberate the white man.

David Lane, imprisoned member of the Bruder Schweigen[43] and leading Odinist propagandist, argues that the Aryan race is at the brink of extinction. "All the once White nations" are controlled by traitors who are in the pockets of the Zionist enemy, and Lane suggests that Christianity is a main reason for the decay of the Aryan culture and the rise of a globalist society. Christianity, Lane says, is diametrically opposed to the natural order that the Gods have created. It teaches us that we all primarily belong to a universal humanity and wants us to love the alien as much as ourselves and to turn the other cheek when we are being treated unjustly. "God is not love," Lane emphasizes. "God the Creator made lions to eat lambs, he made hawks to eat sparrows. Compassion between species is against the law of nature. Life is struggle and the absence of struggle is death." If we are to survive as a race, the otherworldly and self-denying Christianity must be abandoned in favor of Odinism, a religion based on nature's order. "A natural religion" that "preaches war, plunder and sex."[44] Viking Rock and Skinhead culture shows that the old Gods are alive and vibrant. The ancient gods rekindle the natural instinct of self-preservation in the slumbering Aryan folk soul, Lane states. Through the Hammer of Thor a unified white national state will be rebuilt, and Lane points to Hitler's Germany for evidence of the project's possibilities of realization. "Nowhere since Viking times has the direct, singular effect of Wotan consciousness been more evident than in the folkish unity of National Socialist Germany."[45]

Through white power music, radical racialism has become part of a surging white youth subculture in a pan-Aryan networking. Much broader in appeal than Christian Identity ever was, white power youth culture embraces all of the above tendencies and extends its reach to include as white people Slavs and (white) Hispanics who had often been excluded in the past. Overtly aggressive, white power music hails often bombastic warrior ideals and evokes such primal concepts as honor, blood, pride, strength, might, fight and racial solidarity. Through record companies, concerts, tapes and CDs, white power music has truly globalized its message and is a far more powerful propagator of Aryan nationalism among white youth than any other means of propaganda.

George Hawthorne, lead singer in RaHoWa (Racial Holy War), co-founder of Resistance Records and editor of *Resistance Magazine*, one of the most professional racialist papers, says that his "basic message is that you shouldn't feel guilty to be a white man, you should feel proud to be a white man. You have a [tremendous] genetic heritage that you have to live up to." The name of the band reflects Hawthorne's view that:

> the history of the world is a racial holy war. It's for the survival of one race or the other. Life is a battle ground. Everything in life is live or die, fight or die. Throughout history our people have survived through plagues, through the invasions by Genghis Khan and the Mongol hordes of Europe, through the invasion by Attila the Hun, survived through the Moorish invasion of Europe. We have destroyed and fought and conquered wherever we've went . . . . The soil, even of America, has been soaked with the white man's blood, so that their progeny could live here, and we mock the sacrifices of these men who allowed us to come and live on this land by calling them murderers because they killed

the Indians when they came here. Well, every piece of land on this planet was once owned by a different people who killed the people that used to live there. Every species on this planet will push other species out if need be to survive and prosper. We are the strongest, we are the smartest, we are the bravest and the boldest. We have been. This is what our ancestors were, and just like the wolf should not be embarrassed or should not be guilty or ashamed for having to kill the deer, so should we not be embarrassed for being strong. We should be proud of being mighty! This is how our ancestors, our people have been and this is who we are. [46]

Racial pride and militancy are two parallels between white and black nationalist music that boomed in the 1980s and 1990s. Not only are these two cultures aware of each other, but to a certain extent, they share key elements of their world-views. We now turn to a discussion of this interaction.

The Inter-Action Between Black and White Radical Racialism

When looked at from a cursory perspective, the unholy connection between black and white racialists seems utterly bizarre. Why are organizations that preach doctrines as incompatible as black and white supremacy, and that, like Christian Identity and the Nation of Islam, both reserve for themselves the racially exclusive claim of being God's Chosen Nation, able to forge links of co-operation and mutually respectful understanding? Unlikely as it might seem, this kind of linkage goes back in American history to the cooperation between white slave owners and black separatist freemen in the early days of the repatriation efforts that laid the ground for the establishment of the republic of Liberia.

The common ground was later laid forth by Marcus Garvey, the father of populist black nationalism, who said that he "believed in a pure black race, just as all self-respecting whites believe in a pure white race." Garvey argued that all whites shared the perspective of white supremacy, but differed in the methods used to make its hegemony permanent. White liberals, unionists or communists pretended to be friends of the black man to divert his attention from the race struggle to "the impossible dream of equality that shall never materialize." The greatest enemy of the African American are those whites who "hypocritically profess love" for the black man while "in reality they despise and hate him." Garvey regarded the Klansman as a far better friend of the black man than any pseudo-philanthropist, because "potentially, every white man is a Klansman as far as the Negro in competition with whites socially, economically, and politically is concerned, and there is no use lying about it."[47]

This line of reasoning was adopted and accentuated by the Nation of Islam in the theory of the genetic evil of all whites, reducing the difference between white racists and professed anti-racists to a distinction between the devil's strategy to get his prey: the people of color. In the NOI terminology the dual categories of devils are termed "wolves" and "foxes," and like Garvey, leading NOI spokesperson Malcolm X undoubtedly preferred the former. He stated that "white conservatives aren't the black man's friends, but at least they don't try to hide it. Like wolves they show their teeth in a snarl that keeps the black man aware of where he stands with them. White liberals are foxes who also show their teeth but pretend that they are smiling. White liberals are more dangerous . . . and as the black man runs from the growling wolf he flees into the open jaws of the smiling fox."[48]

A series of open and covert relations developed between the Nation of Islam and various leagues of wolves. NOI spokespersons like Jeremiah X participated in Klan rallies and Imperial Wizard Robert Shelton publicly praised the Nation. In 1962 American Nazi Party leader George Lincoln Rockwell was invited to address the NOI convention, and flanked by ten Stormtroopers he praised then-leader Elijah Muhammad for being to his people what Hitler was for white people. Led by Malcolm X, an NOI delegation conducted a series of secret meetings with the Klan for the purpose of developing a joint action program for racial separation.[49] The two once-leading Klans, the Invisible Empire and the Knights of the KKK, routinely informed the Nation of its public rallies so it could keep its members from participating in potential anti-demonstrations. The Nation sought and found Klan support when it bought farmland in the deep South, keeping white racist resistance to black-owned farmland to a minimum.[50]

These kinds of occasional contacts continued after the shift of NOI leadership to Louis Farrakhan. During the 1980s, an intricate web of contacts was woven between the Nation of Islam and various white radical racialist organizations and spokespersons in the United States and Europe. The white nationalist organizations that appear most wholeheartedly in favor of Minister Farrakhan seem to be of the Third Positionist camp, where the Nation quite correctly is embraced as an ideology akin to its own. The "Third Position" is in short a leftist National Socialist ideology, emphasizing both race and class. Its roots are in the left wing of early Italian fascism and the leftist National Socialism of the German brothers Greger and Otto Strasser. The Strasser brothers advocated a kind of national bolshevism, founded on class struggle, back-to-nature ideals and völkish national romanticism, and criticized Hitler for his increasingly more far-right position. Well-read Third Positionists usually condemn Hitler for betraying "true" national socialism when he purged the Strasser brothers from the German NSDAP (the German acronym for the "National German Socialist Workers Party").

Third Positionists can be found as a more or less suppressed faction among members of more conventional National Socialist groups or in separate organizations. In Rockwell's American Nazi Party (ANP), Arizona organizer Elton Hall in vain tried to move the ANP toward a more class-based white worker direction and to get it engaged in union organizing.[51] One of the most successful organizations with a Third Position orientation in the United States is the California-based White Aryan Resistance (WAR), led by Tom Metzger. Appealing to "white workers" fearing "direct competition with millions of new [non-white] arrivals" and unemployment as "the super-rich dismantle the industries and move to all areas of the non-white world," where they may "treat workers in a near slave-like" manner as they once did with "white [workers] in this country," Metzger declared the need for racial class war. Gravitating toward the far right through the John Birch Society and the tax protest movement of the 1960s and 1970s, Metzger founded Identity.

As an ordained Identity minister, Metzger worked with William Potter Gale, Bertrand Comparet and James K. Warner. Through Warner he met David Duke and became active in his Knights of the Ku Klux Klan, before establishing his own Klan organization in California after a personal falling out with Duke.[52] In 1980, Metzger won the Democratic Party's nomination for a congressional seat and, although he lost in the general election, began to receive high name recognition as a racial activist propagating "the rights of white workers." After leaving both the Klan and Identity behind, Metzger established WAR in the early 1980s, hoping in vain to recruit a majority of the tens of thousands of Californians who had voted for him.[53]

Religiously, WAR adopts the slogan "our race is our religion" and says it refuses to "let religious theories . . . interfere with Aryan survival and advancement." From the start, WAR declared that it would ally itself with "any individual or group that makes a positive contribution toward racial separatism," including black nationalists.[54] Already as a Klan leader, Metzger occasionally contacted the black Muslims when needed. These contacts were mainly to avoid confrontations, such as an incident in the 1970s when a black worker had been shot. Word in the black community blamed Metzger's Klan and, knowing that his Klan was not involved, he phoned the Muslims, who were preparing for action, asking them to call off the heat until the murder's identity was known. A more intimate relationship developed following the establishment of WAR and was to peak in 1985. In that year, Metzger was invited to an NOI rally for black economic empowerment at the Forum in Los Angeles. Donating one hundred dollars as a symbol of support, Metzger was quite impressed with what he saw. The same year, he flew to Virginia for a meeting with Alim Muhammad, Minister of the NOI Mosque in Washington, D.C., to discuss the possibilities for a closer cooperation. They agreed to meet again in Chicago and Alim indicated the possibility of Metzger addressing the NOI convention of that year.

While discussing what common ground they might work out, Metzger offered the Muslims a business deal. Metzger had a friend who was very close to ousted Liberian President Layman. Through the former president, who aspired for a comeback, there was a chance for taking over an oil-producing company, and Metzger suggested a joint WAR/NOI venture. While the American racialists worked out the details, Farrakhan was touring in West Africa when a coup attempt against the Liberian regime was exposed. Apparently, Metzger says, the former president had involved South Africans and four white American Nazis in the conspiracy. Farrakhan got cold feet, maybe suspecting that Metzger had more than oil on his agenda. The deal never materialized and Metzger says that their relationship never really got serious after this incident. More resembling the level of the 1970s, it is confined to an exchange of information and occasional supportive articles in Metzger's paper.

Metzger continues to work with other black separatist groups, such as the Black Panthers and the Pan-African Internationalist Movement. In the early 1990s, Metzger was invited as key guest speaker to address the Black Panther convention in Austin, Texas, and claims to have received a standing ovation. Asked what common ground he finds with black nationalists, Metzger says that "we're separatists and we're straight out with it, and we simply say, 'let's make a deal. There's gonna be a fight in this country and that's either gonna be a winner-takes-all situation, which is gonna be really bloody, or there may be that we could make a deal on territory.'" Metzger thus advocates a division of the country in monoracial states, but abstains from explaining how it can become a reality. In the meantime, the groups allegedly have "decided on separate spheres of influence," in the form of a treaty of non-interference in each other's communities. Allegedly, black nationalists have agreed to stay out from white working-class areas and Metzger should keep his men out of black neighborhoods. After the Los Angeles uprising of 1992, Metzger again reached out for an agreement, saying that his men will support a black uprising "as long as you wanna attack the government buildings, you wanna attack the Beverly Hills or rich areas. . . . Just don't come in to the white working-class community, because then we would have a problem." Metzger says that they made an agreement, "but the question is how much control they really have when things start."[55]

Black separatists as potential allies against multiracial universialism was a recurrent theme in the British National Front (NF) publications during the 1980s. It was mainly the result of a skillfully planned coup that brought a group of Strasserite theoreticians to power in John Tyndall's previously more conventional National Socialist organization. With the neo-Strasserites espousing anti-capitalism, anti-communism, environmentalism and class-based racialism, an interest in black nationalist and Third World ideologies followed. The two NF publications *Nationalism Today* and *National Front News* began running a series of positive articles about African revolutionaries such as Burkina Faso's Thomas Sankara, Ghana's Jerry Rawlins and Libya's Mu'ammar al-Qadhdhafi, but also flirted with Islamist movements, praising Ayatollah Khomeini. American black nationalists Marcus Garvey, Malcolm X and Elijah Muhammad got recurrent praise, and Garvey was seen as the predecessor to the new NF project, as being the first to establish a "broad front of racialists of all colors."[56]

Through its support for Jesse Jackson during the 1984 presidential primary, NF discovered Louis Farrakhan, whom it lyrically hailed as a "Godsend to all races and colors" and invited *Final Call* editor Abdul Alim Muhammad to contribute a five-page article, including a photo-essay and the NOI program. Logically, the next step was to establish direct contact with the Nation as "common cause must be turned into practical cooperation."[57] In May 1988, a senior NF official traveled to the United States and was met by American Strasserites Mat Malone and Robert Hoy, who had developed contacts with black separatist organizations. During his U.S. tour, the NF official was invited to Washington, D.C., by Minister Alim Muhammad to study the much publicized NOI drug-busting program. Back in Britain, the NF leadership began to distribute leaflets in support of the Nation of Islam and declared in its papers that "Black and White power are . . . allies. Unity in diversity is not a slogan. It is a Way of Life."

The path of closer working relationships with black nationalists was not unanimously accepted by the NF rank and file as leading in the right direction. The Manchester chapter notified the leadership that it refused to distribute issue 99 of the *National Front News* because of its front page slogan "Fight Racism" encircling a clenched black fist. Under the caption "Rantings from the bunker," the editorial board published correspondence from dissident members charging the leadership with "Bolshevik jargon." "I prefer Hitler as 'comrade' to any black power hottentot who wants to shake my hand," one letter stated, "because Hitler is of my people, my culture, and my ideological kindred," while wondering what weird kind of National Socialism the leaders had developed in calling Farrakhan a comrade. The Strasserite theoreticians continued espousing their ideas, declaring that they had "little or nothing" in common with its Nazi predecessors. They viewed "negative racism" as a product of Britain's imperial past, arguing that true racialism was an anti-racist ideology, dedicated to the preservation of all races and cultures. Mindless thoughts of white supremacy had to go, and the membership was advised to not tell racist jokes as it would cause division among allies.[58] In the end, the NF membership turned against its leaders, who found it wise to flee the country under fake identities.

The British National Front thus represents a more ideologically coherent line than Metzger, who kept racist jokes and "nigger bashing" as a key recruiting tool among working-class youth. When Metzger was asked how he on the one hand could engage in working relations with black nationalists and espouse racial hatred on the other, he admitted that it "seems strange" but said it boils down to adopting a strategy that is so aggressively militant that the authorities will be forced to listen. "We want them to know that if it takes pure hatred to gain what we want, we will use it."[59]

The British black-white racialist coalition peaked in 1989, when NF candidate Patrick Harrington, backed by black separatists, campaigned in immigrant-dense Vauxhall in South London. Receiving fewer votes than even the sectarian Revolutionary Communist Party, which is a backer of the armed Peruvian Maoist underground, Senduro Luminoso [Shining Path], was a humiliating experience for the leadership, which was soon ousted by a membership in revolt. In the United States, the Third Positionist support of black separatism was carried further in Klan/Pan-African cooperation and by the small National Democratic Front, led by Gary Gallo, an American ally of the British NF, who was invited to publish his white separatist program in the *Final Call*.

The white racialist support of black separatist organizations is not confined to the Strasserite element, but is voiced throughout the whole spectrum, from populist Willis Carto to underground activist Louis Beam to George Hawthorne. Populist Party founder Willis Carto, editor of *Spotlight*, the largest far-right weekly with more than a hundred thousand subscribers and twice as wide a circulation, had nothing but praise for Minister Farrakhan.[60] In 1990, Farrakhan granted *Spotlight* an exclusive interview in which he confirmed the white racialist position that the United States was "founded by white people for white people," and elaborated on the theme of racial separation: "You're not going to integrate with the blacks in the ghettos of Washington," Farrakhan stated. "But when we [the NOI] get finished with these people, we produce dignified, intelligent people. The American system can't produce that. We can. Give us a chance to make our people worth something."[61]

Identity-preaching Louis Beam, former Grand Dragon of David Duke's Texas realm, is mentioned as a possible successor of the aging Richard Butler of the Aryan Nations, a position he says he will abstain from in favor of being a freelancing activist. Beam's propagation for "leaderless resistance" has won wide acceptance in the movement of the 1990s as the only effective revolutionary strategy. Inspired in part by the cell-organizing principle of the far left, government infiltration will be countered by avoiding pyramidal organizations in favor of autonomous underground groups or individuals, taking whatever action is needed to further a white revolution. Beam claims to have developed covert links with black separatists in general and Farrakhan in particular, and tells of his and his associates' exchange of information with the Nation. Supporters in the intelligence communities could, for example, leak information about CIA cocaine-trading operations to Beam, who would pass it on to the Nation for public use.[62]

This marks an interesting shift in white racialist perceptions of blacks and their potential capabilities. Traditionally, blacks have been viewed as so intellectually inferior that they were functionally incapable of leading their own struggle. The civil rights and black power movements were thus considered to be Jewish-led conspiracies against the white race, orchestrated by scheming Jews who manipulated the gullible black masses for their own evil ends.[63] Today, white supremacy as the state-sanctioned norm of American culture is gone and white racists see their views discarded on the ideological junk yard as politically incorrect. And while racialist ranks are scattered and reduced to small sects engaged in constant infighting, black racial nationalism triumphantly leads the largest gathering ever in the Million Man March of 1995, led by a man who not only is obviously both capable and intelligent, but also strongly opposed by leading Jewish organizations. White racialists of today can thus pass on information to black racialists because the latter is seen as more competent and in a better position to make use of it effectively.

In the late 1990s we are observing the completion of an interesting shift in which white racialists admire the accomplishment of black radical nationalists, are visibly influenced by them and regard them as far more successful than themselves. Many white radicals I have interviewed acknowledge the influence the black power movement has had on their own thinking; white power, white pride, and the white Americans' search for their ancient European roots in legendary or mythological times are all inspired in part by their black nationalist counterparts. Most white racialist leaders I have spoken with express the need to emulate the strategy of Minister Farrakhan and the Nation of Islam: white separatists should, it is said, build their own economic empire with white-owned farmland, factories, and retail stores. They should establish their own educational institutions, adopt their own flag, declare their independence and demand a separate state of their own. And everyone dreams of the day that they are able to call a million men to manifest their unity in a mass demonstration in Washington, D.C.

George Hawthorne is representative here when underlining that what Aryan revolutionaries:

> need to do first of all, is what the Nation of Islam has done. We need to actively recruit our own people to our cause. We need to have a good number of our people believe in us. We need to be able to mobilize a million white people. When we can mobilize a million white men, like the Nation of Islam did. [Then] when we have our own companies, our own business, our own lobby groups, we could lobby the government for change. Then, our million white men could meet in Washington, D.C. with the million black men of the Nation of Islam and we could shake hands. We could say "together we will work to bring back sanity in this country. Together we will work for true racial separation, the only true dignity that can exist."[64]

The introduction of anti-Semitism in the Black Muslim world-view, a theme too complex to be dealt with here, has become another facet of the mutual understanding between white and black radical racialists. Emerging as a powerful body of organized devils, white Jews today almost rival the Masons as arch-devils in the NOI understanding of reality, and Jews have been made responsible for the slave trade in an infamous study called *The Secret Relationship Between Blacks and Jews*. While white racialists formerly could talk about blacks as "king of the soulless beasts of the field" or as the "servant race," slavery is today generally regarded as a decisive mistake. It is seen as brought about by the Jews in an effort to destroy the purity of the white race and as a chief tool for the implementation of Jewish global hegemony, or the New World Order.

The extent to which this common understanding of Jews as architects of "the peculiar institution" has developed through a racialist black-white exchange of ideas is still somewhat unclear, but it is safe to say that the black and white racialist arguments in this area have been mutually reinforcing. White anti-Semites refer repeatedly to the NOI study that can be bought at white racialist book stores or through post order companies such as the National Alliance Vanguard Books. The Nation of Islam in a similar way makes use of and sells white anti-Semitic works, books that together with other white racialist conspiracy literature often is found in many Afrocentric book stores around the country. Revisionist historian Arthur Butz was invited as guest lecturer at the 1985 NOI convention, and NOI soldiers were present as security at a public lecture by revisionist David Irving in Oakland, California, on September 10, 1996.

While mutual recognition and certain levels of covert and overt links do exist, the question of how to understand the nature of this relationship remains. The alliance theory suggested by Lisbeth Lindeborg, *Searchlight,* Stieg Larson and Anna-Lena Lodenius, that with slight variations propose that a white-black extremist coalition has been established, seems to give too much credence to the fantasies of a "New Axis," cultivated by certain small white separatist groups, and is mainly derived from a reading of British NF publications of the 1980s. A kind of coalition has been forged between a cartel of Florida Klans under the auspices of Identity believer John Baumgardner and Chief Osiris' Pan-African International, an issue-based alliance described below. The groups involved are all relatively small, however, and, at best, regional rather than national in scope.

When it comes to the larger organizations, such as Farrakhan's Nation of Islam, the links seem to be of a less permanent character. Farrakhan's remarkable breakthrough gives him a role among the major players, nationally and internationally, and he has no real need for too close a cooperation with the Aryan revolutionaries. In a 1989 interview, Farrakhan bluntly denied having any direct contact with the white organizations earlier mentioned. "I have never met with any of them or their leaders," he said. "I have never written to them, nor have I received any correspondence from them."[65] This, I believe, could literally be true, as other NOI Ministers, such as Dr. Alim Muhammad of Washington, have been delegated the responsibility for the contacts that do exist. Farrakhan sees himself as head of the exile government of a sovereign black state, and like other head of states needs deniability, but it is also a sign of the lesser status these contacts have. On the other hand, Farrakhan does acknowledge similarities between his own ideology and that of Aryan radical nationalists and says that he "respects any white man who wants to keep his race white, 'cause I certainly wanna keep mine black."

When questioned about the fact that these same organizations and groups are brutally attacking black people in the United States and Europe, Farrakhan vowed to always defend his people, but asserted that whites offending and murdering blacks should simply be seen as a behavioral manifestation of a predisposition "in the nature of white men." The increase in racial antagonism is, according to Farrakhan, only a sign of the setting sun. In the transitional period of time leading to the Final Battle, the nations are supposed to separate and polarize in an escalating racial war. As God informs mankind in the Holy Quran 30:14: "And when the Hour comes, that day they will be separated." The Ku Klux Klan, Nazi Skinhead and WAR violence is thus, Farrakhan asserts, "part of the drama, the worldwide drama the prophets foretold."[66] The black man needs to wake up to the reality of the evil nature of the white man and move out of Babylon in order for the final phase of Armageddon to begin. White aggression against black people helps to dig the white man's grave as it fulfills prophecy and hastens the dawn of the Final Showdown. White racists will be exterminated in due time, but they are temporarily useful and pedagogically suited to exemplify the NOI teaching of the white man as the devil.

Most of the white racialists who have developed links with the Nation of Islam in a similar but reversed fashion seem to have made a tactical decision based on the logic of "the enemy-of-my-enemy-is-my-friend." Farrakhan, black Muslim rhetoric, and black nationalism is applauded for its opposition to a multiracial concept of the American "nation" and can hopefully put fear in the hearts of ordinary citizens. White racialist leaders like Beam, Butler, Hawthorne or Metzger will, if necessary for "racial survival and expansion," take on the black nationalists in due time. For now, they share the common conviction that only racial separation is a viable solution to America's problems. The "alliance" is thus mostly pragmatic, based on a common recognition of enmity and partition.

A PAINful Kind of Klan Konnection

A case that might indicate support for the "alliance theory" is found in the co-operation between a cluster of Florida Klans and two groups of black separatists, the Pan-African Internationalist Movement (PAIN), led by Chief Osiris Akkebala and the Atlanta-based Lost-Found Nation of Islam, headed by Silis X Muhammad. As indicated in the introduction, joint public demonstrations between black and white radical racialists have been held in St. Petersburg following severe race riots that exploded in this west coastal town of Florida in 1996. Far from being a unique occurrence, the mutual understanding that was demonstrated is rooted in the meeting between two dedicated champions of racial separation, Chief Osiris Akkebala and John Baumgardner.

Chief Osiris Akkebala, born Jack Mitchell in 1937 in Orlando, Florida, is the founder of black religious nationalist PAIN. A former Baptist minister, Chief Osiris gravitated toward black separatism and the teachings of Marcus Garvey after years of increasingly radical activism, first in the NAACP and then in CORE.[67] Attracted by pre-Christian African religions, he left the church during the late 1960s and set out on a spiritual quest that, after a brief flirtation with black Islam, led him to "reconnect" with "the spiritual knowledge of our ancestors." In line with the earlier outlined basic myth of black religious nationalism, PAIN teaches that the primordial Man-God established the first civilization on the face of the earth at Chemi, today known as Egypt.

Through the channels of direct communication with the Divine and the ancestral pool of stored knowledge, Chief Osiris is able to take history "beyond where Western scholars start," to the Beginning of Time. Like in the NOI creed, a self-created primordial Being takes the form of man and embarks on a journey of which we now are a part. Originally populating another planet, the Man-God descended on what was then a virgin earth. The grandiose civilization he established surpassed by far any evolutionary stage the pale earthly races later were able to achieve, as is demonstrated by the fact that pyramidal architecture still contains so many unsolved riddles. Due to a gradual decline and slack morals, a separation between man and God was allowed to occur, and blacks fell into a state of collective cultural amnesia. Invaded by hordes of "evil spirits" in pale carnal hues, Africa was colonized and a significant number of blacks were reduced to subhuman chattel slavery in an alien land. To rebuild primordial Man, to resurrect divine consciousness, the Africans in America must first perform a mental liberation and cast aside all thoughts with white origins. Black liberation is primarily a spiritual struggle, and having renounced all non-original beliefs, one is ready to "click into the genetic bank of our ancestors." Readopting the ancient gods of Chemi set the stage for a physical repatriation. As in Jewish religious nationalism, a direct connection is said to exist between the Holy Land and the quest for re-ascending into divinity. A mental liberation will automatically produce a "re-established [Pan-] African nation," inhabited by a superior race able to master the destiny of mankind.[68]

John Baumgardner, born in Georgia in 1954, is not the stereotypical Klansman. A former counterculture hippie, with a past membership in Students for a Democratic Society who still keeps Che Guevara on the wall and favors reggae music, he combines full-time activism with home schooling his two children. Baumgardner joined the Invisible Empire of the Ku Klux Klan in 1984 and as Grand Dragon was instrumental in its increased Florida visibility. He was then promoted to Imperial Klaliff and shouldered the responsibility as editor of the *Klansman*, the Empire's national publication. Following the demise of the Invisible Empire, the Florida klaverns broke up in more than twenty independent Klan organizations, a number including klaverns from the remnants of the Knights of the Ku Klux Klan. Baumgardner today heads the underground Florida Black Knights and is chief architect of the Inter-Klan Kartel, a networking of most of the existing Klans in the state. A staunch Identity Christian,[69] Baumgardner retains in part the class focus of his leftist past and has a working relationship with Metzger. Baumgardner has "constantly preached revolution" to a "traditionally reactionary Klan" and is pleased by the increasing militant radicalism of a present-day Klandom finally about to realize that "the government is the enemy."

Emphasizing that the struggle mainly is "spiritual," Baumgardner deems change through conventional electoral politics utterly unrealistic. Refusing to acknowledge the system by voting "is the first revolutionary step." Fundamental change at the brink of disaster requires multiple means of resistance, including armed resistance. "We need people to be preparing for guerrilla war, we need terrorists, we need that!" he exclaimed. "Because a system that breeds violence, practices violence, only understands violence!" Baumgardner believes that we are entering the turbulent "Messianic Age," "and we are not going to be pulled off into the sky and saved from a world of destruction." God will use his Chosen as a military strike force to accomplish "apocalyptic change on this planet, the dawn of God's government."[70]

In 1987 a civil rights march though all-white Forsyth County in Georgia had been attacked by the community in a major racial clash that was played up in the media for months. Baumgardner, who of course defends the integrity of that monoracial community, then heard that (almost) all-black Etonville in central Florida was to celebrate its centennial and decided to bring the Klan there to express its support. Four hundred policemen surrounded the two robed Klansmen who stood for the whole parade and had dialogue with the people who came up to them. In Etonville, Chief Osiris had his own radio talk show and invited Baumgardner to appear. They got "into some very deep conversation about race and the system,"[71] learned that they were both racial separatists, and have "been friends ever since."[72] Their mutual friendship has since intensified and they now talk with each other several times a week. In March 1992, they agreed it was time to go public "to show that such a dynamic relationship can exist." Some 50 robed Klansmen and more than 20 PAIN members met at the old slave market in St. Augustine, Florida, for a demonstration that received quite extensive media coverage and caused controversy in both Klandom as well as in the black separatist world. Since then, they have engaged in several other joint actions. In St. Petersburg in 1996, PAIN, the Black Knights and parts of the Klan Kartel showed up in the black quarter "to offer a solution to their problems. Which is, of course, racial separation, repatriation and the payment of reparations."[73]

But how do people react to robed Klansmen and black separatists in African outfits standing together for a joint cause? Both Chief Osiris and John Baumgardner chuckle at the question, relating anecdotal glimpses before getting serious. Past Klan activities like lynching, castration and nightly terror have planted a negative image of the Klan in the mind of black folks, Osiris admits. But what they don't understand is that this is a very different breed of Klansmen. The Klan of the 1920s and 1960s was part of the southern power structure, the unofficial arm of white justice. Today, there are no powerful people left in a Klan as revolutionary and anti-system as their fellow black separatists.[74]

Baumgardner acknowledges that "traditionally, the Klan has been pretty ignorant in its public appearances," but like Osiris he emphasizes the differences between Klans of different eras. He does, however, admit that this transracial linkage has met with opposition from "the reactionary remnants" within the Klan. Initially, resentment was greater and Baumgardner named his group the Black Knights partly because they "were the black sheep of the Klan." Baumgardner points to the historical connections between the Klan and Garvey, and proves his points by the successful propaganda of the deed. Baumgardner's strategy has gradually won over most white separatists in the Kartel. Though still getting bewildered reactions from the public, Baumgardner underlines that "all of us separatists get along fine. It's the rest of these civilians who have a problem. We're beyond hate. We figured it out, you know. Be honest enough to abide by your feelings and don't seek to assimilate. We don't have a problem with each other. We get along fine."[75]

The progressive friendship between Baumgardner and Chief Osiris led to further developments, expanding the contacts between black and white racialists. Baumgardner invited David Duke to meet with Chief Osiris in the late 1980s. Their coming together resulted in PAIN's endorsement of David Duke's 1988 presidential campaign on the Populist Party ticket, and Osiris accompanied Duke to Washington, D.C., to assist him in a lawsuit to get him on the ballot in several states.[76] Chief Osiris also backed the British National Front in its unsuccessful 1989 campaign in London. Through Osiris, Baumgardner was introduced to Silis X Muhammad, Saleem Muhammad and Ida Hakim of the Lost-Found Nation of Islam (LFNOI). Though founded by Silis X half a year earlier than Farrakhan established his Nation, the LFNOI never really caught comparable attention in black America. The LFNOI has a much smaller membership, distributed among some 25-30 mosques over the country. Obsessed with being dwarfed by the Nation, the LFNOI long directed most of its energy to combating Farrakhan as "the second beast of the revelations" in a development that stopped short of an internal black Islamic civil war.[77] Following a failed truce effort, Farrakhan is today seen as the Anti-Christ. In the 1990s the LFNOI has tried to grow by concentrating on the issue of reparations, filing complaints with the United Nations and organizing coalitions to advance the issue.

In support of reparations for the purpose of repatriation, Baumgardner has published articles in Klan and Muslim press,[78] which marked a closer working relationship with Ida Hakim. The latter is a white woman, who is married to "a God," i.e., a black man, and associated with a Lost-Found Nation of Islam she can never become a member of due to her race.[79] In 1991, inspired by a suggestion of Silis Muhammad, Ida Hakim founded Caucasians United for Reparations and Emancipation (CURE) as a white lobby in support for reparations, which now embraces the Ku Klux Klan and any other white organization or individual that might support the cause.[80] Both Hakim and Baumgardner are convinced that slavery was a decisive mistake and believe that only black repatriation will save America from an impending race war that will make the ethnic cleansing in former Yugoslavia a minor incident. Together, they are now researching which families benefited from the slave trade, where that money went, and who the heirs of the old slavocracy are, for the dual purpose of writing a book and filing suits for reparations.[81] The expanding networking further includes freelance black agitator Khallid Abdul Muhammad, formerly of Farrakhan's Nation of Islam, and negotiations are presently held with pan-African socialist Black Uhuru.[82]

Through Baumgardner, Chief Osiris has been introduced to Tom Metzger, who although willing to meet with PAIN seems doubtful that anything more than talk will come of it.[83] The same might be said concerning the present negotiations held between Chief Osiris and John Trochman's Militia of Montana (MOM). Introduced by Baumgardner, Osiris has asked Trochman if his militia would be willing to train a black separatist militia, organized for three purposes. First, to deal with any situation in the black community that is not just. Second, to deal with black-on-black crime, and, last, to organize a black counterpart to the South African-based mercenary army called the Executive Outcome.[84] Negotiations began between PAIN and MOM in July 1996 and has been confirmed by John Trochman.[85] A public announcement was scheduled for January 1997,[86] but the outcome is still pending.

What we have here, then, is perhaps an embryo of an alliance between black and white racialist organizations, although neither PAIN nor the Klan Kartel is of major national significance. Moreover, it is still unclear to what extent it is dependent on the friendship between two remarkable individuals, John Baumgardner and Chief Osiris. Central in the Christian Identity and PAIN ideologies is the literal demonization of the Other. Time will tell if the intimate friendship that blossomed between an evil spirit and a soulless mud man will translate into ideological change, toward a metaphoric interpretation that will move the color symbolism from the biological to the psychological plane and thus make a broader racialist coalition somewhat more feasible.

Final Discussion

White religious nationalism has gone through several phases. Originating as an ideological product of European imperialism and an economic system based on the enslavement of people with black complexions, it became the sacral dimension of white world supremacy. The American "nation" was long understood as a white Christian nation under a God. Though many blacks in America engaged in a struggle for equal inclusion in the "nation," an important counter tendency elaborated an alternative nationalism. Inspired by the same völkish tradition that informed white racialism, black nationalists sought to create national awareness through projecting the idea of a corporate racial community back to the Beginning of Time. As in white religious thinking, the realities of slavery and inequality in a creation said to be made by a benign, omnipotent and omniscient divinity had to be accounted for. Much like its white counterparts, black religious thought associated morality with skin color, in many ways developing a mirror reflection of conventional white racialist theology. Through religion, the social and economical gap that separated the white and black nations was strengthened, giving divine impetus to black demands for self-determination.

Following the reworking of the American "nation" in a more inclusive and multiracial direction, racialist Christianity crystallized in defense of the old world-view. Unable to reverse the new development, an increasing radicalization of white nationalism followed. The Constitution, long revered as a sacred document, now began to acquire an opposite interpretation as an evil document. The United States, slavery as an institution and imperialism now took on an appearance as steps toward the completion of the New World Order. White Americans had been used to seeing themselves as the defenders of the free world in a struggle with apocalyptic overtones. Following the defeat of the "Evil Empire," many Americans woke up to a reality they did not recognize. It seemed as though world power slipped through their grasp at the moment of triumph. The process of globalization was made possible through modern science, technology, and capitalism—institutions originating in the West, and therefore believed to be Western. Now, Westerners suddenly realized that what had been disseminated were instrumental techniques, something that could be learned by people of any culture, creed or race.

Modernity proved to be plural, and booming Asian economies left the Western world behind. Giant multinational corporations dominate world economy and the quest for profit, expansion and development make racial considerations utterly irrelevant. In a few decades white world supremacy was gone and its pockets of believers were left in a state of confusion. The much feared one-world conspiracy seemingly had achieved victory. Was the crown of creation an illusion in the making of the king of fools? Globally, whites are a shrinking minority and fears of extermination added a sense of desperation in the white radical racialist world-view of the 1990s.

All these factors combined gradually led to the formation of what I term a *white racialist counterculture*. The concept is partly inspired by Colin Campbell's discussion of the "cultic milieu."[87] Observing the transitory character of Britain's New Age groups in the early 1970s, Campbell shifted focus from the individual organizations that emerged and declined, transformed and mutated, to the milieu in which they operated. Composed by heterogeneous elements, brought together by their deviance from the orthodoxies of the dominant culture, the cultic milieu gives birth to new groups, absorbs the remnants of defunct ones and facilitates creative processes of syncretistic *bricolage*. Catering to a community of seekers, dissatisfied with the truths of public society are institutions for propagation of alternative knowledge in a milieu in which individual groups often experience a high level of membership turnover.

Though Campbell's article in many other respects is somewhat outdated, this insight suggests an avenue to comprehend the racialist "cultic milieu" of the contemporary United States. Analytical tools developed to understand sects or social movements appear less relevant because there is no such thing as a white racialist movement in the United States. "Movement" implies a unified body going somewhere and this is far from reality here. Much more fruitful is to see the phenomena in terms of a white racialist counterculture, formed as a response to an increasingly more multicultural society.

Nursing values, knowledge and norms derived from an outgoing epoch of white world supremacy, the white counterculture constitutes a dissident substratum of American public culture. Within this counterculture operate many different organizations, sects, tendencies and parties that are engaged in constant infighting, in vain trying to unify and electrify the culture's participants into a revolutionary movement. With varying success and disparate ideologies, Klan groups, Identity Churches, National Socialist Fronts, Satanists, Occultists, Odinists, and other "Aryan" organizations emerge and disappear, re-emerge in new constellations to enjoy a transitory phase of fame before waning away with its members absorbed into the general counterculture or any of its organized groups. Individual participants of this culture often move freely between the competing organizations, not infrequently belonging to more than one organization or subscribing to several papers of ideologically conflicting nature.

During my field work, I often came across individuals who had "tried out" several Nazi parties, Klans, Identity Churches and Odinist kindreds, not necessarily terminating all ties as they move on. Leaders and long-time cultural participants share an awareness of each other and the subculture is preoccupied with gossip, circulating stories of this leader being an "FBI informant," that leader being a "secret Jew," another a "secret gay." Like in Campbell's cultic milieu, over-lapping communication structures facilitate syncretistic creativity. Some Identity Christianity incorporates Odin as an Israelite, Christian Klansmen may embrace Nazi occultist speculations and racialist Ásatrúers can look into the left-hand path of Satanism.

Catering to the counterculture are book stores, post order companies, electronic news agencies, Web pages, periodicals, prison outreach ministries, record companies and cultural manufactories. Countercultural expressions manifest in forms of music, novels, poetry, art and ritualized behavior that transcend the more narrow sectarian boundaries. Selective adoption of products of the outer culture turns unifying icons, like Braveheart, Conan the Barbarian, Ultimate Fighting Championship or the young Arnold Schwarzenegger. The counterculture pays homage to its own martyrs and heroes, of which Bob Mathews, famed leader of the Bruder Schweigen, occupies a most special position. His 1984 death in the flames during a shoot-out with federal authorities on Whidbey Island in Washington state is hailed as an ideal death for the Aryan Warrior, and many songs and odes are composed to his honor.

White racialism, once the highest truth of learning, was left on the ideological trash heap. With racist knowledge, once a respected science and translated into governmental policies, now discarded by public institutions and academia, it found itself in a parallel position with other alternative truth systems in the broad category Michael Barkun has termed "stigmatized knowledge."[88] The term is used to denote truths that claimants regard as empirically valid but are rejected, suppressed, ignored or otherwise unacknowledged as such by the institutions that conventionally distinguish between knowledge and falsehood (universities, research centers, scientific publications, etc.). Of special significance for our purpose is the subcategory of "suppressed knowledge."

White racialist spokespersons of the 1990s claim that racialist truths have been barred from public recognition due to a conspiracy aimed at the destruction of white civilization.[89] This conviction seems to make believers more ready to embrace or accept as possible other forms of alternative knowledge: if the government and the public institutions of learning do not recognize what is being said as true, then there must be something to it. The militia milieu is characterized by a bewildering diversity of contradictory elements with only their lack of recognition by official America as a common denominator. New Agers, fundamentalist prophecy believers, UFO abductees, anti-Semites, Christian Identity preachers, Odinists, herbalists, magick vendors and black separatists come together in a practice as tolerant as their theories are intolerant.

Conspiracy-believing Americans seem willing to listen to anyone who claims that nothing is as it appears to be. The American readiness to embrace conspiracy theories can further be explained by reference to the cultural emphasis on the individual, which paves the way for an actor-centered world-view in which abstract complex causes becomes personified in scheming cabals.[90] Exposures of actual conspiracies seem moreover to lend an aura of credibility to secrets "not yet exposed." Thus, a government capable of orchestrating the complex Oliver North/Contra/Iran scheme could well engage in any other conceivable or inconceivable plot with nothing excluded.

In a 1996 militia conference in Denver, Colorado, lectures were given on a wide range of subjects, all devoted to some form of rejected or suppressed knowledge. The audience was informed about the Satanic takeover of America; advanced government techniques for absolute mind control; United Nations schemes for subjugating the United States; the composition of the inner circle of the New World Order conspirators; concentration camps built in secret for incarcerating freedom-loving Americans as enemies in the government's attempt to enforce the abolition of the Second Amendment (the right to bear arms); and evidence proving that the prophecies of Revelations now are being fulfilled as the reason why we had better prepare for the approaching Armageddon. Among the lecturers was Joyce Riley, who talked about the cover-up of the Gulf War illness.[91] In the weeks that followed, the authorities acknowledged what for long had been denied, that American soldiers might have been exposed to chemical and biological agents during the war and that there was a medical foundation for the sometimes fatal illness many veterans claimed. When the suppressed knowledge presented by Joyce Riley at the conference proved to be at least in part confirmed, it gave a certain credence to the other information presented in the lecture series.

Black and white racialists share the same world and have to a significant extent come to recognize each other. How then should their relationship be chiefly understood? In my study of the NOI, I used the metaphor of a chess game. In chess, the white and black men exist to defeat each other, but share a mutual understanding of the nature of the game and make similar moves. Skillful players can express mutual respect, they can be inspired by, and learn successful strategies from each other. Black and white racialists share a conviction of race first! Insisting on the primacy of race, they can join ranks against any non-racialist world-view, be it postmodern deconstruction of race, religious universalism, multiracial state policies, humanitarianism and sex- and/or class-based ideologies.

Both black and white racialists agree that "race" is an organic entity, endowed with its distinct "personality," genetically engraved on its members. The organic unity of the Race is its "natural" state and any other understanding thus becomes "un-natural." Both white and black racialism represents an effort to produce an awareness of "nation" other than given by public institutions. Transcending the borders of the present-day national states, it aims at creating sentiments of loyalty in a pan-Aryan and pan-African direction respectively. The method of its achievement is, as has been demonstrated, a nostalgic projection of the imagined national unity back into legendary or mythological times. Thus the many competing religious nationalist organizations that depict the racial nation as a divine creation and the interest for ancient heroes and symbols that are expressed by otherwise more secular nationalist organizations.

Black and white radical racialism thus manifest structural and ideological similarities but should not be reduced to mirror reflections of each other. Black nationalism originated as a response to black exclusion from a white racist American society, and the contemporary white racialist counterculture came into being as a reaction against the as yet incomplete deconstruction of the same. On a certain level, both share an opposition to universalism and the process of globalization, however incorrectly perceived, which has enabled limited forms of mutual recognition as well as instances of overt and covert links. While the major players in the field to date have limited the level of contacts to tactical information and shared pools of conspiracy theories, the level of cooperation has been taken a step further by minor leaguers, here represented chiefly by the joint efforts of Klan leader Baumgardner and black separatist Chief Osiris to form links of a more enduring character. Together they have established a network called "United Separatist Front," allegedly involving "several hundred" separatist movements, "everywhere from Mexico to India." Though atypical a creation with an instrumentality yet to be seen, its very existence is an interesting phenomena as it brings together separatists across all national and racial borders. If nothing else, it represents a somewhat ironic illustration of an increasingly more global social reality in which even opponents to the global village out of necessity operate globally.

Notes

[1] The [Original] Constitution of the United States of America, Article I. For the debate about whether slaves should be considered persons or property and the winning compromise, see James Madison in Clinton Rossiter (ed.), *The Federalist Papers* (New York: Mentor Books, 1961), 336-41.

[2] Roland Sanders, *Lost Tribes and Promised Lands: The Origins of American Racism* (New York: Harper Perennial, 1992 [1978]).

[3] Roger Bastide, "Color, Racism and Christianity," *Daedalus,* 96, no. 2, 317 (1967). For the de-Africanization process of important aspects of European civilization, see Martin Bernal, *Black Athena: the Afroasiatic Roots of Classical Civilization* (London: Free Association Books, 1987).

[4] Joseph R. Washington, *Anti-Blackness in English Religion 1500-1800* (New York and Toronto: Edwin Mellen Press, 1984), 19, 470; Bastide, R., 1967:315.

[5] Quoted in William Stanton, *The Leopard's Spots* (Chicago: The University of Chicago Press, 1960), 100.

[6] Cited in Sven Lindqvist, *Utrota varenda djävel* (Stockholm: Albert Bonniers förlag, 1992), 6.

[7] State Department Secretary John C. Calhoun, August, 1844, cited in William Stanton, *The Leopard's Spots*, 62.

[8] State Department Secretary John C. Calhoun, April 1844. Cited in ibid., 61.

[9] For the ground-breaking discussion of the subject, see Robert N. Bellah, "Civil Religion in America," *Daedalus* 96, no. 1 (1967).

[10] See, for instance, David Bennet, *The Party of Fear: The American Far Right from Nativism to the Militia Movement* (New York: Vintage Books,1995).

[11] Mattias Gardell, *In the Name of Elijah Muhammad: Louis Farrakhan and the Nation of Islam* (Durham, NC: Duke University Press, 1996).

[12] Among the similarities are basic doctrines such as cosmogony, anthropogony and eschatology. Ismailiyya teaches that a self-created God in the Beginning of Time creates the universe through a series of emanations. The first divine ray, the Divine Intelligence (black intelligence in NOI terminology) takes the form of Primordial Man. Next in creation is, according to NOI doctrine, a circle of twelve greater and twelve lesser "scientists" or "gods," which recalls the doctrines of both Ismailiyya and Imamiyya, in which the Imams are creations of divine light that predates the creation of the material universe. The ideas of Imams as embodiments of the Divine are emphasized in Ismailiyya and

could be taken to extremes, as in the Druze doctrines of al-Hakim as God in Person—an idea akin to the NOI notion of Master Farad Muhammad. Ismailiyya and the NOI share ideas about cyclical time, although it is far more elaborated in the astronomical speculation among the former. Much like the NOI, Ismaili doctrine informs us that in the beatific cycle prior to the present cycle of confusion, there was a race of humans superior to ours. They lived in a time ushered in by the Universal Adam, who appeared in the first cycle's sixth millennium on the island of Sri Lanka. The true knowledge was openly preached and man lived an "angelic" life until the cycle of epiphany closed and the cycle of occultation began, in which the true Gnosis is concealed and only taught to a closed circle of earthly angelic descendants. One of them, Adam, who is not identical to the universal Adam, but a partial or episodic Adam, who manifests to initiate each cycle, is invested as the enunciator of the new law. Adam is accordingly not the first man but one of the last survivors from the previous cycle. In the Ismaili exegesis of Quran 2:30, it is the angels of the previous cycle (the Original People in NOI terminology) who abhor the introduction of the new era and question Imam Adam (NOI's Mr. Yacub) who gravely responds, "I know what ye know not." The hardship experienced by fallen man in the present cycle is a necessary phase, the completion of which leads to a perfected state, the aim of Creation. Central in both NOI and Ismaili Gnostic speculation is the divine potential a priori embedded in man as focus for man's ambitions. Ismailiyya holds the aim of mankind to be a resurrectional process in which by a knowledge of Self, man undergoes an "angelomorphosis," a doctrine, though differing in terminology, which is shared with the NOI. The NOI's division of mankind into two opposing categories, "gods" and "devils," is similar to the Ismaili classification of those who have an angelic potential, those who, on this plane in this time cycle, reflect angelic archetypes from higher planes at times past and times to come, and those who are representations or manifestations of Iblis or the diabolic (see Mattias Gardell, ibid., chapter 7. For an excellent analysis of Ismailiyya doctrines, see Henry Corbin, *Cyclical Time and Ismaili Gnosis* (London: Keagan Paul, 1987).

[13] For a fuller description and analysis of the complex NOI creed, see Mattias Gardell, *In the Name of Elijah Muhammad*, chapters 6-8.

[14] Muhammad, Jabril, "Path to God Revealed to Blacks," *Final Call*, October 3, 1988.

[15] *The Holy Quran* 3:110, translated by Yusuf Ali.

[16] The blackosophic mysticism of the Black Islamic creed is discussed extensively in Mattias Gardell, *In the Name of Elijah Muhammad*, chapters 6 and 7.

[17] Farrakhan, Louis, speech in Los Angeles, February 2, 1992.

[18] The NOI teach that Elijah Muhammad never died in 1975. He learned of a conspiracy against his life and was rescued by black extraterrestials and taken to the abode from which God supervises the destiny of man. Farrakhan claims that another man was buried in Elijah's place, which explains why his son Imam Warithuddin Muhammad removed his grave site. In the NOI head mosque in Chicago is a secluded area called the Holy of Holies in which an empty sarcophagus symbolizes the miracle of the living Messiah.

[19] For excellent studies of the multifaceted and evolving black church, see C. Eric Lincoln and Lawrence H. Mamiya, *The Black Church in the African American Experience* (Durham, NC: Duke University Press, 1990); and Gayraud S. Wilmore, *Black Religion and Black Radicalism* (New York: Orbis Press, 1986).

[20] See, for example, Elijah Muhammad, *Message to the Blackman* (Philadelphia: Hakim's Publications, 1967); *The Flag of Islam*, (Chicago, 1974).

[21] C. Eric Lincoln, *The Black Muslims in America* (1973), 97.

[22] Mattias Gardell, *In the Name of Elijah Muhammad*, chapters 3, 6 and 10.

[23] The best introduction of Christian Identity is found in Michael Barkun, *Religion and the Racist Right: The Origins of the Christian Identity Movement* (Chapel Hill: University of North Carolina Press, 1997).

[24] The different theories explaining the various races on earth are not necessarily exclusive but have proven able to be combined in multiple variations, without altering the basic theme of a cosmic combat between forces of good and evil represented on earth in human form.

[25] See, for example, "There Is Nò Pacifism in the Bible," *Correspondence Bible Course*, The American Institute of Theology (used by Butler's Aryan Nations), 1981 (1970), chapter 86.

[26] Definition given by Identity believer John Baumgardner, MacIntosh, Florida, Nov. 1, 1996.

[27] Although, as we know, representatives of other tribes also moved here. Britain was Ephraim, in Genesis 35:11 prophesied to become a "company of nations," and Mannaseh was to be a "great nation," i.e., the United States. "Saxons" were "Isaac's son," "Dan" become Dan-mark (Denmark), and so on.

[28] The practical impact of affirmative action has been marginal compared to the centrality it has in the white racialist world-view where it is used as a symbol for the alleged anti-white government policies.

[29] For an illuminating discussion of the new warrior ideal in American male culture, see James William Gibson, *Warrior Dreams: Violence and Manhood in Post-Vietnam America* (New York: Hill and Wang, 1994).

[30] Ben Klassen, *RaHoWa: This Planet Is All Ours* (Otto, NC: Church of the Creator, 1987), 124ff.

[31] Interview with Ron McVan, former White Brigade commander, St. Maries, Idaho, September 25, 1996.

[32] Matt Hale, "It's Decided!" *The Struggle: Dedicated to the Survival, Expansion and Advancement of the White Race*, XI, (May 1996).

[33] During an eleven-day siege of white separatist Randy Weaver's remote Idaho cabin, under the pretext of his arrest for a minor firearms violation, federal agents first killed his teenage son and then shot his wife to death when she went out with their baby in her arms. In Waco, Texas, a 51-day federal siege of the Branch Davidian communal settlement ended in disaster on April 19, 1993, with nearly 80 sect members consumed in flames.

[34] Conversation with conspiracy believer Eva Vail, Coeur d'Alene, September 26, 1996, information gathered at a militia conference, Denver, Colorado, November 8-10, 1996. For an account by a woman claiming to have been abused by the CIA as its mind controlled sex slave, see Cathy O'Brien and Mark Phillips *Trance Formation of America Through Mind Control* (Nashville, TN: G.T.F.I., 1995).

[35] "Platform for an Aryan State," Aryan Nations.

[36] "The Declaration of Independence," revised edition, March 12, 1996.

[37] Interview with Katja Lane, St. Maries, Idaho, May 6, 1997.

[38] Interview with Ron McVan, St. Maries, Idaho, September 25, 1996.

[39] Interview with Mike Murray, Payson, Arizona, April 28, 1997.

[40] Interview with Stephen McNallen, Grass Valley, California, December 18, 1996.

[41] Ásatrú propagandist, author and scholar Edred Thorsson (Stephen Flowers) estimated that about one third of the Ásatrú world were racialist oriented (interview in Austin, Texas, April 17, 1997), while Mike Murray thought that they composed some 40-50 percent. For an informed scholarly discussion and analysis of American Ásatrú, see Jeffrey

Kaplan, *Radical Religion in America* (Syracuse: Syracuse University Press, 1997), chapter 3.

[42] Interview with Ron McVan of Wotansfolk, St. Maries, Idaho, September 25, 1996.

[43] The Bruder Schweigen is a small closely united group of underground activists, known as the Order. Led by Robert Mathews, the Order initiated in the early 1980s an armed struggle for the liberation of the Aryan race. Following a series of armored car robberies and the 1984 assassination of Alan Berg, a liberal Jewish talk radio host in Denver, a dramatic man hunt took place which culminated in Mathews' death and the subsequent capture of the militants. David Lane was sentenced to 190 years, but says that he does not regret anything: "I was only doing my duty and obeyed the will of the higher powers, just as I do now in the greater plan the Gods seem to have for me." During the years that have passed, the Order has grown in significance and David Lane is not infrequently referred to as the Mandela of the white revolution.

[44] Interview with David Lane. November 12, 1996. Maximum Security Prison, Florence, Colorado.

[45] Lane, David. "WOTAN—Will of the Aryan Nation," *Wotan's Volk*, (St. Maries, ID: 14Word Press).

[46] Interview with George Hawthorne, Windsor, Canada, October 2, 1996.

[47] Amy J. Garvey, ed., *The Philosophy and Opinions of Marcus Garvey, Vol. 1 and 2*, (Dover, MA: Majority Press, 1989); Marcus Garvey, 1989a (1923): 37; Marcus Garvey, 1989b (1925): 70f.

[48] Malcolm X, "Gods Judgment of White America," in Benjamin Kareem, ed., *The End of White World Supremacy* (New York: Seaver Books, 1971), 137.

[49] See Mattias Gardell, *In the Name of Elijah Muhammad*, 273f.

[50] Interview with Don Black, West Palm, Florida, October 31, 1996; Interview with John Baumgardner, Ocala, Florida, November 1, 1996: Mattias Gardell, *In the Name of Elijah Muhammad*, 274.

[51] Interview with Elton Hall, Cave Creek, Arizona, December 23, 1996.

[52] Metzger claims that he broke away from Duke because Duke on several occasions had proved himself a "physical coward" and because of his many erotic adventures among women in the movement.

[53] Interview with Tom Metzger, Carlsbad, California, December 16, 1996. WAR was first known as White American Resistance, reflecting the hopes of building a mass movement. When this failed, Metzger changed the meaning to White Aryan Resistance, "more to inflame my enemies than anything else."

[54] Tom Metzger, "White Aryan Resistance Positions," *WAR Declared*.

[55] Interview with Tom Metzger, Carlsbad, California, December 16, 1996.

[56] "Garvey's Vision," *Nationalism Today* 42 [undated].

[57] Ibid.; A.W. Muhammad, "Nation of Islam," *Nationalism Today* 39; "A common Cause," editorial, *National Front News* 93.

[58] "Rantings From the Bunker," *Nationalism Today* 39; "A Common Cause," editorial, *National Front News* 93; "Race: The New Reality," *National Front News*.

[59] Interview with Tom Metzger, Carlsbad, California, December 16, 1996.

[60] Interview with Willis Carto, Escondido, California, December 22, 1996.

[61] "Islam Nation Leader Says Blacks Must Gain Equality Separately," *Spotlight*, July 23, 1990.

[62] Conversation with Louis Beam, Coeur d'Alene, Idaho, September 26, 1996.

[63] See, for example, Evelyn Rich, *Ku Klux Klan Ideology 1954-1988, Volumes I and II* (Ann Arbor, MI: UMI, 1996 [1988]), passim.

[64] Interview with George Hawthorne, Windsor, Canada, October 2, 1996.

[65] Interview with Louis Farrakhan, Chicago, Illinois, May 18, 1989.

[66] Interview with Louis Farrakhan, Chicago, Illinois, May 18, 1989.

[67] NAACP = National Association for the Advancement of Colored People; CORE = Congress of Racial Equality.

[68] Interview with Chief Osiris, Orlando, Florida, November 2, 1997.

[69] Baumgardner agreed to be called Identity Christian "for the purpose of classification" but thinks of himself as a "Christian." Theologically, Baumgardner is influenced mainly by Pastor Pete Peters and James Wickstrom. Other sources are Pastor Richard G. Butler and the first generation Identity preachers, chiefly Bertrand Comparet and Wesley Swift.

[70] Interview with John Baumgardner, MacIntosh, Florida, November 1, 1996; "Who Is that Masked Man? A Short Autobiography by John Baumgardner," *Florida InterKlan Report* (April, 1996). "Grand Dragon" is the highest Klan rank in a state, and "Imperial Klaliff" is national vice-president, second in command to Imperial Wizard.

[71] Interview with Chief Osiris, Orlando, Florida, November 2, 1997.

[72] Interview with John Baumgardner, MacIntosh, Florida, November 1, 1996.

[73] Interview with John Baumgardner, MacIntosh, Florida, November 1, 1996.

[74] Interview with Chief Osiris, Orlando, Florida, November 2, 1997.

[75] Interview with John Baumgardner, MacIntosh, Florida, November 1, 1996.

[76] Interview with John Baumgardner, MacIntosh, Florida, November 1, 1996.

[77] For a more extensive description of LFNOI, its theology, politics and relations with NOI and the outer society, see Mattias Gardell, *In the Name of Elijah Muhammad*, p. 215-25

[78] Baumgardner, John, 1996, "A Historic Meeting"; "A Case for Reparations," *InterKlan Report* (February 1995); "A Letter From Ku Klux Klan," *Muhammad Speaks*, March (?), 1995.

[79] The'blackosophy of LFNOI is akin to the NOI's, but where Farrakhan's teachings makes divinity a remote possibility but attainable (if at all) only after years of spiritual growth and dedication, the LFNOI declares a *fait accompli* for its members. A black Muslim male is thus God, and Silis is the Most High (Earthly) God, the redeeming Savior of the black race.

[80] Interview with Ida Hakim, Chicago, Illinois, May 24, 1997. CURE, Caucasians United for Reparations and Emancipation, was incorporated in 1992.

[81] Interview with Ida Hakim, Chicago, Illinois, May 24, 1997; interview with John Baumgardner, MacIntosh, Florida, November 1, 1996.

[82] Interview with John Baumgardner, MacIntosh, Florida, Nov. 1, 1996. To the author it seems highly unlikely that the talks with Black Uhuru will get any practical results, but as many other unlikely thoughts have become a reality, it should nonetheless be noted.

[83] Interview with Tom Metzger, Carlsbad, California, December 16, 1996.

[84] Interview with Chief Osiris, Orlando, Florida, November 2, 1997.

[85] John Trochman, Denver, Colorado, November 9, 1996; interview with John Trochman, Noxon, Montana, September 27, 1996.

[86] Interview with Chief Osiris, Orlando, Florida, November 2, 1997, confirmed by John Trochman, Denver, Colorado, November 9, 1996.

[87] Colin Campbell, "The Cult, the Cultic Milieu and Secularization," *Sociological Yearbook of Religion in Britain*, Vol. 5 (1972).

[88] Barkun, Michael, "Conspiracy Theories as Stigmatized Knowledge: The Basis of a New Age Racism?" in Jeffrey Kaplan and Tore Bjørgo, *Brotherhoods of Nation and Race: The Emergence of a Euro-American Racist Subculture* (Boston, MA: Northeastern

University Press, forthcoming).

[89] Interview with David Duke, Mendeville, Louisiana, March 6, 1997; Interview with Colonel Jack Mohr, Little Rock, Arkansas, March 13, 1997; Interview with Katja Lane, St. Maries, Idaho, May 6, 1997; Interview with Pastor Richard G. Butler, Hayden Lake, September 22, 1997.

[90] This point has been aptly raised by Mark Rupert.

[91] Joyce Riley, "Cover-up of the Gulf War Illness," speech, Coliseum, Denver, Colorado, November 9, 1997

The Idea of Purity

The Swedish Racist Counterculture, Animal Rights and Environmental Protection

Heléne Lööw

I myself am a misanthrope, in the respect that I feel that it would be better if all the humans disappeared, regardless of race or religion, so that the animals could live in peace and besides it doesn't work either with an ozone that breaks down and therefore I must say that it's awful, it really is, that the animals have to suffer for all the things that we are responsible for. They are innocent truly innocent. How many whites or blacks that die do not matter to me, but the animals, that they have to die because of us, that hurts me. I think humans are that disgusting that they deserve to die. (—Leif Larsson, former leader of Föreningen Sveriges Framtid (The Association for Sweden's Future), interview 12 December 1991)

The obsession of National Socialists and race ideologists with purity and *gesundheit*—ideas which are strongly connected to the perception of moral enemies—is an important, but seldom discussed, component of the racist rhetoric. The elimination of moral enemies is an important component in the anti-Semitic ZOG-discourse.[1] Moral enemies should, in this respect, be understood as advocates for free access to abortion, homosexuals, drug addicts, the pornography industry, pedophiles, rapists and so-called antisocial elements.

The questions addressed in this chapter deal with the idea of purity, the concept of moral enemies and the moral codes that in many ways govern the movement, even if for many activists they remain a model, an idealistic dream of how they want to be. The main issue addressed in this chapter is the involvement in the racist subculture of animal rights activists and demands for stronger environmental controls—areas which could lead to new unexpected single-issue alliances in the form of militant vegetarian or animal rights groups. Another reason for this chapter is that these aspects of the racist or National Socialist ideology are seldom discussed.

Homosexuals are very often hate targets in White Power magazines and songs. Homophobia is a central part of the idea of the importance of fighting "moral enemies." Homosexuals are looked upon as "inferior" and "perverted." Homosexuality is also said to be something "the Jews" have invented in order to destroy the white race. Homophobia has for decades been an important element in the ideology of the Swedish National Socialists and anti-Semites. Campaigns against homosexuals were, for example, an important part of the anti-Semitic publication *Vidi*.[2] A negative attitude toward homosexuals is not only a part of the ideology of the Swedish racist underground. In *Valkyrie*, issued by the British Patriotic Women's League, the following declaration was made: "Homosexuality and pornography will be made illegal. We must protect our children from the perverts and the sick sex industry, now a common thing in this materialistic society."[3] The anti-homosexual epithet is also part of the lyrics of White Noise music.[4] Another example of the anti-homosexual epithet is "Utan Nåd," (Without Mercy) by the former Swedish White Noise group Dirlewanger:

> The democracy gives them money and rights
> to spread their disgusting way of life
> We see them in the media and in the schools
> where they oppose the laws of nature
> Money for their benefit is taken from your salary
> To promote AIDS nests in every corner
>
> But there will come a dawn
> Yes a new era will come
> Then you will have reason to fear for your life
> Because for your evil deeds
> there is no quarter no mercy.[5]

The song was dedicated to the manager of the band, who in 1985 murdered an elderly Jewish homosexual.[6] Child molesters and other sex criminals are the objects of a virulent hatred by the movement.[7] The movement is also basically moralistic, and an important part of the idea of cleanness and *gesundheit* are the negative views about pornography held by the activists.[8]

The idea of purity is naturally a central part of the race ideology. Immigration of non-whites is seen as a disease: "An unknown substance is permeating the Swedish folk organism, that is, the alien races. As long as this substance is kept isolated it is possible to solve the problem, but if this substance mixes with the blood the consequences will be fatal: a slow but sure eternal death."[9] The idea of purity and the importance of a healthy lifestyle is also found in the recommendations to the activists of how they should live.[10] The surrounding society is considered impure. The democratic state is regarded as "impure," "perverted" and full of "decadence," "disloyalty" and "hypocrisy."[11] The idea of purity versus impurity is also found in the ideology and rhetoric of classic National Socialism.[12] Riksfronten [Reichfront], a race ideologist group, claims, for instance, that all "races" should be kept apart.[13] Its successors, Folksocialistisk Samling [Peoples' Socialist Union], claims that as the "differences between the human races were created by nature, what gives us the right to destroy them? Can we even comprehend what the consequences might be? It is our fast and steady opinion that it is negative to mix races and cultures with each other."[14] It is primarily "race mixing" that the activists look upon as a disease. Or to quote one activist: "bastards disgust me, it turns my stomach when I think about them, I feel sick just thinking about it."[15] This is, however, an old theme. In the anti-Semitic publication *Svea Rikes Nyhetstjänst* [Svea Rikes News Agency] the following statement could be found in 1935:

> It is nowadays virtually impossible to go to a restaurant without
> seeing black Jews together with white, blond Nordic girls. It's about

time to make the public aware of these conditions so that WW [i.e., the world] could react to this bad behavior. And the Jews should be reminded that we do not want our race destroyed. And the Swedish girls should remember that nowadays, that kind of company with the Jews is race treason![16]

A modern example could be found in the magazine *Sveriges Framtid* [The Future of Sweden]:

> The worst thing is that the immigrants have started to mess with our white people. It breaks my Swedish heart to see Swedish women and men walk hand in hand with some immigrant. And don't you just want to scream when you see a blond Swedish woman dragging around a carrier with a mulatto in it?[17]

"Race mixing" is also a common theme in the White Noise music, like in Somalie Kickers "Blattesvin" [Black Bastards]:

> Vad gör ni här (What are you doing here)
> era jävla blattesvin (you bloody black bastards)
> Försöker förgöra vår nordiska folkstam (Trying to destroy our Nordic race)
> jävla blattesvin (fucking black bastards)
> Och rasblandar med med våra blondiner (and race mixing with our blondes)
> jävla blattesvin (fucking black bastards)
> Men ni ska nog få smaka på kanga (but you will taste …)
> jävla blattesvin (fucking black bastards)
> Vi ska dränka er i bensin (We will drown you in petrol)
> jävla blattesvin. (fucking black bastards)[18]

The idea of purity versus impurity is also part of the ideology and the rhetoric of the classical National Socialists.[19] The groups that are defined as "non-Aryans," "racially defective," "genetically evil" and "racially inferior" are presented in metaphors and reduced to "vermin," "parasites," and in the end non-humans. They are successively undergoing a dehumanization process, which in the end deprives them of any human attributes. They have, in the eyes of the National Socialists, ceased to be humans. Humans are only those defined as "sound." The modern groups are, like their predecessors, supporters of race hygiene measures.[20] The Australian researcher Judith Bessant states, "Images of 'maggots,' 'plague' and 'disease' are deployed to generate quiet powerful emotional, moral and physical disgust. Young neo-Nazis are told how 'foreigners' smell a particular way. It is a strategy that effectively activates feelings of revulsion, anger and disgust."[21] One Swedish activist, for instance, stated that he could smell if someone was Jewish, homosexual or 'racially inferior':

> I can smell it of course, you can always tell, I don't know but maybe they just can't stand facing us Aryans, you can smell their fear of us, their envy of our purity, they envy us and fear us because we are humans they are not . . . They smell like something sick, rotting, something that has been laying in the sun for too long. . . . I hate the smell, I hate the sight of them, and I hate the fact that they dare to show themselves among true humans.[22]

The race ideological message is presented in magazines, music, and, in more brutal form, in anonymous stickers with slogans like "White Power— Black slaughter."[23]

The idea of purity is also present in the various recommendations about how to live and the importance of sound living that is constantly appearing in various types of material.[24] The demand for a sound lifestyle is nothing new among the National Socialist groups. Nordic Ungdom (Nordic Youth) had during the 1930s a long list of special rules for how to live and how not to live that the members had to follow. The underlying motive for these demands was to create a hard cadre of disciplined, dedicated and ruthless youngsters.[25] Further, in Vikings' (Wiking), the National Socialist Youth organization, the guidelines for the members state that they should be loyal, dedicated, truthful, train their bodies and minds to meet the "coming struggle," to live simply, etc.[26]

The surrounding society is basically seen as something impure. The state and the modern society is in the same way held responsible for the environmental problems. One activist explained it in the following way:

> It's also a part of the National Socialist ideology to protect the animals and the nature. . . . We are also a part of the nature . . . they miss out there the green ones and Greenpeace, they are supposed to care for the species on the brink of extermination and so on, but we take that argument to its full length and demand that the Nordic human being should be preserved as well. All this about the nature is deep down like the Danish National Socialists have written on a poster: "National Socialism is life it self."[27]

For parts of the Swedish race ideological subculture, people who they believe pollute the environment and scientists who conduct experiments on animals are also included among the moral enemies, or to quote *Werewolf*: "Even the ones who pollute our environment with effluents and torture defenseless animals under the cover of science, do best to look once or twice when they take a late walk."[28] And the Frisinnade Unionspartiet [Liberal Unions Party] wanted life in prison for people who maltreated animals.[29] Other groups such as the new Church of the Creator (COTC), have a less radical view. A member of the group stated:

> Animal protection and animal rights activism is good, as long as they keep themselves in normal limits, i. e., as long as they obey the law, and try to fight for the rights of the animals. We think it's wrong to attack multinational companies, by burning down their transport cars etc., that is doing no good. But of course it's important to protect the animals and the nature, it is because of nature we exist.[30]

They were, however, in favor of prompt actions to fight the pollution of the environment, such as banning of unnecessary packages, poisonous emissions from factories, etc.[31] Matti Sundquist, lead singer in Swastika, stated that he dreamed of a society which is free from pollution, and that a sound people should always work to improve society."[32] The animal protection motif can also be found in the lyrics of the movement, as in the battle song of NRP's RAG (Nordic Reich Party's Reich Action Groups)

The men of RAG will never abandon the promises they once gave

That all men in RAG are the same, fighting for law and right
Fighting against the torture of animals
Fighting against anarchy
Sweden shall remain ours
The banner of the Sunwheel should be raised
Flaming like a fire against the sky
The banner of the sunwheel, black, red and beautiful
Encourage us to fight. [33]

Göran, one of the members in the White Power band Vit Aggression, claimed in an interview that the environmental questions were very important to him, and he was in favor of harsh punishment for those who dumped poisonous material in the enviornment and destroyed the forests, etc.[34] Many activists are deeply engaged in environmental protection and saving the animals. One activist explained why: "Well it's the most important thing, almost, because we must have a functioning environment in order to have a functioning world. We have too, and its almost too late to save the earth, there must be some radical changes, if we are to stand a chance."[35] Another activist claimed that his dream society was a society built on "racialsocialism," and on ecological grounds.[36] The vegetarian, environmental discourse is also present among the British groups, such as Blood and Soil and Patriotic Vegetarian & Vegan society.[37]

The same ideas can more or less be found among the Swedish chapter of the Church of the Creator:

> Let me once and for all point out that what I believe in is the laws of nature, and to live in harmony with them. The laws of nature are the basis for our biological existence. During thousands of years our ancestors conquered the wilderness and enemies. The scrupulous and weak were automatically sorted out, and the generations improved as time went by. Some races vanished completely. It is this struggle we are still fighting today, weakened by Trojan horses who are trying to split us up with Jewish commandments " human rights," " we are all one in God" and a lot of other rubbish! Make this crystal clear reader; each one of you who welcomes the wave of strangers, who goes to bed with a stranger or adopts one is our enemy! I take no interest in their egoistic tales of pity, religion or looks. It is my people's biological existence I'm interested in, nothing else. Why? Because it is evident that if the white race continues with abortions and open borders there will come a day when everything that we call civilization is gone. Who is it who keeps Africa under their arms? . . . We must return you to the eternal laws of nature; and it does not only exclude race mixing, homosexuality and pollution of the environment, but also self-destruction with booze and cigarettes! [38]

Slogans like protecting the animals and fighting the torture of animals have been a long-standing part of the National Socialist propaganda. Organizations like the Nordic Reich Party has for a long time published feature articles and think pieces on these subjects.[39] As early as 1970, the NRP launched a campaign against the use of fur coats.[40] Another example is this article from 1988 about animal experiments:

> The mainstream public has little understanding of the fact that perfectly healthy animals, like apes, cats or dogs are to be sacrificed in animal experiments, just because disgusting fags, drug addicts,

whores and their customers want to be cured from the self-inflicted
AIDS disease.[41]

In the quote above a number of primary issues for the NRP such as
moralism, homophobia and animal protection are tied together. In the NRP's
party program from 1972, there is a special paragraph about the fight against the
maltreatment of animals. The party demanded, among other things, harsher
punishment for the torture of animals and the banning of painful experiments on
animals.[42] The fight against cruelty against animals is—as are most of the party
issues—sometimes linked to anti-Semitism. In the *NRP Bulletinen* before the
1985 election, the NRP claimed that "a very great percentage of all vivesec-
tionists around the world were Jews."[43] In connection with a much-noticed TV
program about vivisection in 1984, the NRP printed a leaflet about the question,
which they distributed to various animal protectors and organizations for animal
protection, like Nordiska Samfundet mot plågsamma djurförsök [The Nordic
Federation Against Painful Experiments On Animals], which were terribly upset
about the way the National Socialists supposedly tried to exploit their issues.[44]
In an ironic article under the title "But They Don't Mind The Nazis' Money,"
the party leader of the NRP, Göran Assar Oredsson, responded that even if
Nordiska Samfundet mot plågsamma djurförsök minded the leaflets, it sure
hadn't minded the donation of thousands of Swedish krones that the late party
member Tyra Persén had given the organization.[45] Tyra Persén was a very
wealthy woman, and she hit the news in the late 70s when the fight over her
money between various animal rights organizations and others began.[46] The
NRP couple had extensive contact with her—she often wrote articles in the party
press—and had also received some financial contributions from her. In a letter
to the author (Lööw), Oredsson explains his relationship with Tyra Persén:

> I never meet Tyra Persén in person. I have only talked to her on the
> phone a couple of times during the 70s, everything else was by let-
> ters. From the beginning of the 60s she sent us a monthly contribu-
> tion, it could vary between 100 to 200 krones. Maybe not all 12
> months but most of them. Apart from that she contributed to the pur-
> chase of our first eletrocopymachine. In that sense, her contributions
> went to "my Nazi propaganda" and during all these years, a lot of
> NRP articles and leaflets were printed and distributed against painful
> experiments against animals, all in harmony with our ideology. I also
> helped Tyra Persén as a thank you for her contributions with a cou-
> ple of elstenciler and prints and distributed leaflets she had written
> herself. [In]1965 during the so called Lundahl-Expressen - affair,
> when the debate was high in the media and I was wrongfully
> dragged into it, Tyra Persén helped me with money so I could buy
> some machinery and start my own business as a gardener. There is
> no doubt that Tyra Persén would have given me some money in her
> will, maybe everything, she hinted that a couple of time. But all that
> came to nothing, when at the end of the 70s that couple stepped in
> and took care of her business, money and all that was left. From that
> day my contacts with her were over. [47]

The NRP's leaders deny that the NRP has ever taken part in the
liberation of animals or attacks on the meat industry, and hold a strong opinion
toward the young militant vegans of the 90s. In a letter Oredsson states:

Our opinion is that the people who are practicing this kind of anarchy, are talking in their night hat, and the other night on the news on
TV there were pictures from a demonstration, where the speaker was
comparing today's slaughter with "the nazis extermination of the
jews." "The animal rights people," are in fact fighting for the jews,
who are practicing the cruelest slaughtering method of all, against
the regime, that forbade them this! [48]

Some activists, however, stress that the NRP's anti-cruelty against
animals propaganda is just a trick, or to quote one Göteborg activist:

I think they can ban experiments with cosmetics and stuff like that,
but the medical experiments on animals are OK, completely OK,
that's my opinion anyway, the way NRP goes on and on about these
animal experiments, well according to me it's just a way to attract
new members. [49]

That is most likely wrong. Animal rights activism has been a part of the
National Socialist ideology since the 1930s. In the party program of the Organization Solkorset [The Sun Cross], one could find paragraphs about the spiritual
and physical health of the people and about the state providing opportunities for
sport and outdoor activities and the banning of centralization, and demands that
every industrial town should have parks and areas of nature available for
everyone.[50] Environmental control is another important issue for the NRP.
Already in 1966, before the big general debate started, the party published a
long series of articles about the necessity of environmental control. In one of the
articles, Vera Oredsson argued strongly against nonreturnable packages, the use
of chemicals in agriculture, experiments on animals, poisoned lakes, and the
like.[51] And in 1975 the party demanded protection for species on the brink of
extinction, a long-term ban on cutting down trees so that the forests should have
a chance to recover, a sanctuary for wild birds, and measures to secure the
existence of the Swedish wolves, etc.[52] In 1987, the following could be found in
the party magazine *Nordisk Kamp* concerning environmental control:

What are we supposed to drink when the water is poisoned? What
are we going to eat when the seed and the animals are poisoned, and
what shall we breed when the air is full of poison? MONEY? . . . We
demand that the laws against environmental damage are sharpened,
and that people should be made aware of what it really means to
disturb the balance of nature. [53]

The environmental question has long been part of the NRP party
program.[54] These questions are sometimes linked to anti-Semitism and sometimes to immigration policy.[55] Another of the long-term organizations that has
animal protection on the agenda is Frisinnade Unionspartiet—a local National
Socialist party on the west coast of Sweden.[56]

Environmental issues and animal protection are also part of the agenda
for the young racialist activists. *Info-14*, published by Stockholm's Young
National Socialists, noted with great satisfaction that it "finally" had been issued
rules for pet keeping, such as minimum sizes for bird cages, etc.[57] The National
Socialist Front in Karlskrona demanded humanitarian animal keeping and
ecological farming in its program.[58] In the party program of Folksocialistisk

Samling (FSF), the ecological issues played an important role. The party was against nuclear energy and for a development of alternative and environmentally sound sources of energy. It wanted a radical fight against the pollution of the environment, more ride sharing and fewer cars, a fight against global pollution, a ban on poison and chemicals in the water, food, clothes and houses. The party was also in favor of ecologically sound farming, and state benefits to every farmer who stopped using chemicals in the farming process. This, the party believed, would make poison-free food a cheaper and thus more popular alternative. The party stated:

> The human being is a part of nature. She is depending on nature and nature's resources, the richness of its species and its regeneration. By protecting the life giving processes of nature, the humans will be able to sustain their own living. To be able to do this, we must increase our environmental consciousness. Our whole way of producing and consuming most be changed. Our people have over thousands of years been modeled according to our unique environment. Our physical appearance is based on the climate and the environment. If the ecological balance is changed it will have devastating and often irreparable consequences.[59]

The fondness for herbal medication and fitness have always been important parts of the National Socialist ideology, and it still is. In the party program of Folksocialistisk Samling, one can, for instance, find warnings against the over-consumption of medications or, to quote the program: "The over-consumption of medication like antibiotics must be stopped; if not, we are likely to see an explosion of diseases that are resistant against our medication, and that will lead to epidemics of catastrophic dimensions, comparable to the black death."[60] One important aspect of the fascist FSF's message was environmental protection and animal care. The environment was one of the first issues addressed in the party program.[61] Leif Larsson, the founder of the group, claims that the environmental issues were the most important ones. Larsson states:

> If you look at it in the short run, the most important thing is the environment, no doubt about it, because without a sound environment, all the races will die. If you understand what I mean, but if you look upon it in the long run, the most important thing is to protect our own race, protect it from being mixed with other races and if this goes on, we will disappear eventually and be replaced with bastards. Some people want that to happen, but I would find it hard to think [about] that for my children, whom will be 100 percent white, and their children. Well I want that to go on, I don't want a lot of niggers mixing with my kids, I want the race to be pure. I would feel sick if I was lucky enough to live to let's say 80 years, and see my grandchildren walk around with some bastard and have a bastard child—then my whole family would be lost. I would take that very, very hard. That part has nothing to do with racism, it has to do with feeling, strong, strong feelings that you have inside, that makes you mentally ill when you see all those who walk around mixing and who don't feel like you. But if you don't feel that way you can never understand how I feel either, just as I can't understand what you feel.[62]

FSF was also in favor of banning painful animal experiments.[63] Some members were also in favor of direct actions, or to quote one of them:

> Don't be surprised if you one day discover that we are in fact rescuing animals, or if you one day see a bunch of black and white racialists chained to a factory that pollutes the environment, as an act of protest—this is just as important to us as the fight against the Jews, because the Jews are behind it, they use every means to destroy us, our animals, our land—and to hurt us, they know how much the white man loves his animals—or have you seen a Jew or a nigger care for a dog like we do?[64]

And the local racialist group Smålands SA had a special section in its party program of 1996 about environmental protection.[65] The animal protection issues were also evident during the so-called White Rebel era during the late 1980s. It was among other things presented in the protests against kosher slaughter.[66] The need to protest against kosher slaughter, however, seems a bit unnecessary since it has been forbidden in Sweden since 1937. The protests against kosher slaughter, however, have been part of anti-Semitic propaganda since the 1930s.[67]

Another part of the idea of purity is the anti-drug campaigns. Most factions of the racist subculture strongly resent drugs.[68] The NRP, for instance, has since 1962 launched campaigns against smoking.[69] In 1968 the NRP launched an anti-drug campaign in the form of preprinted postcards with demands that action be taken against the use of drugs. The cards were sent to Tage Erlander, who was prime minister by that time.[70] According to Oredsson, the party managed to collect thousands of cards, but received no media attention. Oredsson also stressed that one of the tactics they used was to hand the cards out at taxi queues and walk from car to car and ask the drivers to sign the cards.[71]

In an article in *Nordisk Kamp* in 1974 the following statement was made:

> On the 26 of October . . . TV reported the alarming news that that terrible heroin drug was now available on the illegal market here in Sweden. Already thousands of drug addicts were in fact, sometimes youngsters 13-14 years old . . . Mothers and Fathers! It wasn't to this kind of a life we brought the children to this world. Surely it wasn't this kind of a disaster we foresaw, when we happily announced in the papers "we got what we wanted—a boy." Or took the first pictures of the baby, or with curiosity checked the ads of newborns in the papers. Surely it wasn't for the sake of the drug maker and the international syndicate that you carried your child during the nights when it was ill with toothache or stomach pain. You surely didn't expect your child to die in a rundown drug apartment when you walked it to school for the very first time. [72]

The NRP's anti-drug agitation was also linked to the resistance against immigrants and refugees—groups that were said to be the root of the "increasing drug problems."[73] In the 1973 election campaign, the NRP argued for a ban on the sale of beer and liquor to youngsters. They demanded stronger actions against drugs.[74] And in connection with the 1975 Party Congress, the NRP sent a protest letter to Olof Palme, who was prime minister at that time, and demanded among other things that Palme should apologize for calling Franco a "Bloody murderer." The NRP demanded that asylum on political grounds be granted refugees from Eastern Europe (the NRP has never been against all immigration, only non-white/European immigration). It also demanded that Sweden should do everything in its power to free Rudolf Hess, provide stronger protection for historical monuments, ban the use of poison in the agriculture, and stop poisoning lakes and the air. The NRP also pleaded for "adequate treatment of patients who had been maltreated by doctors or dentists!"[75]

The NRP has during its more than 40 years launched a number of campaigns against pornography, cruelty against animals, drugs, abortions, etc.[76] The campaigns have been part of a deliberate attempt by the party leadership to try and reach out with a part of the party program that is important to them but is virtually unknown outside its own circles. Oredsson comments on the outcome of the campaigns:

> We had naturally hoped that our various campaigns should get publicity and reach the public and give them a knowledge about what the NRP stands for and what our goals are and that they are far from what most people want to connect our ideology with. But it turned out to be wishful thinking. We have often been the cause of the public debate despite that, but we have never, ever been invited to participate in [that debate], nor in the radio or the TV. We have been forced to swallow that our arguments on other issues than Jews and migrants have been taken up by others, without mentioning our name, but taking every chance they can to take their hands off us [i.e., to distance themselves from us], or denying that we do have the same opinion.[77]

In the music 'zine *Nordland*, the activists were encouraged to live healthy lives—in harmony with nature, to avoid chemical products, drugs, etc., which were said to "damage the Racial material."[78] Many of the activists in the racist counterculture are vegetarians and try to live by strict rules of fitness and healthy living. For some, however, this is mostly a dream, and they have constant nightmares about not being able to live up to the standards of the movement.[79] The vegetarianism and the keep-fit ideology were also evident among National Socialists of the pre-War period. One of the most important advocates for a healthy lifestyle was Carl-Ernfrid Carlberg, who was born in 1889. He was to become one of the most prominent protectors and financiers of the Swedish National Socialist movement. Carlberg was a businessman and an athlete. He was part of the Swedish gymnastic team in the 1912 Olympics in Stockholm, and won a gold medal.[80] Carlberg was also the owner of the fitness magazine *Gymn*.

In 1930, he took the initiative to found Sveriges Antibolsjevikförbund [The Swedish Anti-Bolshevik Association]. In the beginning of the 1930s he also founded Nationella Bokhandeln [The Nationalistic Bookstore] or Svea Rikes bokhandel [The Bookstore of the Svea Reich] in Stockholm.[81] The bookstore and the publishing company tied to it had specialized in National Socialist literature.[82]

In 1932, Carlberg participated as a representative for Gymns—which was also a keep-fit organization—at the Svenska Nationalsocialistiska Partiet [Swedish National Socialist Party's] congress in Göteborg. He also met Hermann Göring during his visit in Stockholm.[83] In 1933, he started a hostel in Stockholm, with the idea of creating a meeting place with physical training facilitates for the local SA members.[84] And in January 1934, he founded a National Socialist press agency, Svea Rikes Nyhetstjänst,[85] and the educational organization Manhem, which attracted many prominent academics.[86] Its board consisted of professors, managing directors, priests, artists, writers, and nobility.[87] Carlberg also contributed financially to the academic world by financing a chair in the history of ideas at the University of Uppsala, and managed to gather parts of the Swedish upper classes around him and his various organizations.[88] He also had long-ranging international contacts with, among others, various German organizations.[89]

The lecture and debate evenings arranged by Manhem attracted a large number of people. In a police report from September 1941, the following can be found:

> Yesterday I visited Samfundet Manhems' first autumn lecture. The public has since spring undergone some change and has nowadays a strong attraction for the upper classes, apparently a result of the German-Russian war. The room was so full that a number of visitors had to sit behind the podium, behind the speaker, or stand the whole evening. [90]

Anti-Semitism was a common theme of the lecturers. Regarding a meeting in April 1944 the police reporter stated:

> The whole speech was about the destructive power of the Jews, and a Finnish man, Mark (the speaker, HL), pointed out that if Germany lost the war, the whole world would be turned Bolshevik and the Jews would accomplish their final goal to dominate not only our part of the world, but the earth itself. Even Reverend Hannertz "added to this" by pointing to the Jewish influence in the various administrations, before Mark finally tried to pinpoint what a dangerous future the Jew was. The public was approximately 75 people, who were most favorable to the message. [91]

During the first years after the war, Carlberg was involved in Hjälpkommittén för Tysklands Barn [The Help Committee for the Children of Germany]. Behind it was a number of prominent National Socialists and some of Herman Göring's Swedish relatives such as Fanny Willamowitz-Möllendorf.[92] The organization was in many ways a cover-organization for helping former National Socialists financially and in other ways to a new life.

After the war, Carlberg was involved in many projects to reorganize the National Socialist movement.[93] During the 1950s he was among other things involved in the magazine *Nation Europe*, issued by the so-called Malmö Movement, founded in 1951.[94]

In 1957, Carlberg founded the so-called Carlbergska stiftelsen [The Carlberg Foundation].[95] The primary goals for the foundation were to keep a library of nationalistic literature, fight communism and "form the young generation to a sound way of life from sports and outdoor life." Another goal for the foundation was, of course, to fight "the international Jew."[96]

In 1960, some of the members of the foundation joined Fältsport-föreningen Wiking [The Fieldsport Organization Viking], which had as its primary goal to promote male sports. Wiking received financial support from Carlberg personally and from the foundation. Closely connected to Wiking was

Idrottsföreningen Thor [The Thor Sports Association] —also founded in 1960. Thor was an association for boxing, fencing, weight lifting and gymnastics. The association had financial support from the state. When this fact became public, a heated debate began as to whether or not a National Socialist sport association really was entitled to state benefits.[97]

Carl Ernfrid Carlberg died under mysterious circumstances in a hospital in Stockholm in January 1962. He was found shot to death in his bed. At first the police suspected suicide, but his fingerprints were nowhere to be found on the gun that was found in the room, although someone else's were. That person has never been found, and the true circumstances of Carlberg's death remain a mystery.

Another figure who has functioned as a bridge between the old and the new National Socialists/race ideologists and who has had vegetarianism, environmental protection and animal rights on his agenda is Nils Erik Rydström and his magazine *Wärendsbladet*. Rydström, in common with many other activists, has a past history of membership in the NRP.[98] In 1962, he started to publish *Wärendsbladet*. *Wärendsbladet* has during the past 30 years been dominated by the following themes: sound healthy living, i.e., the teachings of the Norwegian pre-war National Socialist Arne Waernlands, agriculture, religious issues and the occult. In the 1996 issues (*Wärendsbladet* is issued at least twice a month), a number of articles about Atlantis, UFOs and Christian spiritualism can be found.[99] The magazine and its founder have a great interest in the spiritualistic teachings of one Cora Rickmonds.[100] In addition, there was a Swedish/American sect, the Church of the Soul (active in the Chicago area in the 1890s),[101] that unfortunately I have been unable to find any information about apart from the material published in *Wärendsbladet*. The magazine has also published a large number of historical articles, most with occult themes.[102]

During the 1990s, Rydström, who holds the new movements and activists in high regard, started to open his magazine to their articles, ads and publications, and they in turn started to publish and distribute his material.[103] In 1996, he started a network for the Waerlandian health philosophy and he cooperated with, among many other groups, NS-activists in Oslo who had opened a vegetarian restaurant in the spirit of Arne Waerland.[104] In the same year, Rydström also joined the Hembygdspartiet [Homeland Party].[105] The Hembygdspartiet is run by Tommy Rahowa Rydén[106]—the former leader of the Swedish chapter of the Church of the Creator (COTC)—and the environmental, health and animal protection issues are very important to the party. In the leadership, one can also find the previously mentioned Leif Larsson, and the long-time activist Leif Zeilon-Eriksson, who has played a central role in several organizations during the past 20 years. Both have a keen interest in vegetarianism, animal protection and environmental issues.

Among the new organizations, the Creators are the ones that have pressed hardest on the keep fit ideology. One former leading Swedish member of the COTC explained:

> It is a part of the Church teaching, with creativity and all. It's basically about the health circle, from drinking clean water, to sunbathing the right way, to be able to benefit from vitamins and things like that. Even in the bible [i.e., *The White Man's Bible*] we write about this.[107]

He also claimed that these ideals function as a kind of necessary barrier when it came to recruiting new members, and added:

> It's a good barrier, because those who are unable to understand how right it is, so to speak, well, we are not really interested in them because they are so impure in their way of living, so it's well to have these kind of rules, its a good selection really.[108]

The rules for the members of the COTC included among other things: only eat ecologically sound food, no involvement with chemicals, engage in physical training, do not use medicinal drugs, etc.[109] The Creators even say no to vaccination—many of them believes that the cause of the growing number of children with cancer can be found in the use of vaccines.[110] They also believe that the vaccine can cause allergies and brain damage.[111] In a circular from the Ben Klassen Academy—an organization founded by Tommy Rydén after he left the mother church in 1993—he outlined the following guidelines for how to live:

> 1. Eat only raw food, in its natural state. Predominately fruit, vegetables, seed and nuts.
> 2. Keep yourself in good physical condition. Train in a fashion that keeps the heart and lungs working, preferably jogging, swimming and other activities.
> 3. Avoid all kinds of chemicals. That includes alcohol, nicotine, caffeine, sugar, preservatives, insect poison, drugs and medication of all kinds, be they prescription or not.[112]

In a newsletter from DeVries Institute, Rydén stated that meat produced various problems and he therefore recommended parents to give their children vegetarian food from infancy and mothers to breast feed their children as long as possible.[113] The Creators also claim that all healing is self-healing and that disease, sickness, ailments and suffering are abnormal, unnatural and unnecessary and that unhealthy practices inevitably produce diseases.[114] Another group that was strongly pushing the healthy lifestyle was Folksocialistisk Samling. In its party program it wanted to increase gymnastics and health information in the schools, and educate the citizens about the benefits of exercise, good food and other measures to live a healthy life.[115]

The idea of a healthy living has also had some impact on the way of life among the activists and on their sobriety at public demonstrations, White Noise concerts, and on internal discipline. The Göteborg chapter is the one that, besides the Creators, has argued most strongly for a healthy lifestyle and sober and disciplined demonstrations. In leaflets and circulars issued before demonstrations, it pointed out that the participants had to be sober.[116] Accordingly, the number of drunk activists at public demonstrations has declined dramatically in the past years. The dead drunk skinhead dressed in a Swedish flag, screaming "Sieg Heil," is on the way out, and is slowly but surely being replaced by a disciplined, sober, black-dressed activist—who very often happens to be a vegetarian—who participates in a silent, strictly ritualized protest against a society he despises and has chosen to live outside. Not all groups are in favor of a vegetarian lifestyle. The National Socialist European Workers Party, a local group from the city of Norrköping, stated the following as a reference to the schools' adjustment to vegetarians, Muslims and Jews; "All adjustments that have been made for vegans and non-white cultures must be banned. They will have to solve their food problems by themselves."[117]

Notes

[1] ZOG=Zionist Occupation Government

[2] Nils Weijdegård, "Tidgivningen Vidi och det 'homosexuella kloakträsket'" [The Vidi Magazine and the 'Homosexual Dump'], *Lambda Nordica*, nr 1, 1995.

[3] "What Are We Fighting For," *Valkyrie: Voice Of The Patriotic Women's League* 1 (1995), 6.

[4] See for instance, "Rosa Gardiner [Pink Curtains]," by Division S, (CD); "We Play For You," No Remorse, "Thailändska småpojkar" [Little Boys From Thailand], (CD); Pluton Svea, *Stöveltramp*, [The Sound Of The Marching Boots] (CD) 1995 Sweden Calling, Ltd.; "Bögjävlar" [Fucking Fags] *Dead Future*, (CD) I *Nationens tjänst* [In The Service of the Nation], 1995, Sweden Calling Ltd. Cf. my article, "White Power Rock Roll—A Growing Industry," in Jeffrey Kaplan and Tore Bjørgo, *Nation and Race: The Developing Euro-American Racist Subculture* (Boston, MA: Northeastern University Press, 1998).

[5] "Utan nåd," (translated by the author) Dirlewanger (CD).

[6] Anna-Lena Lodenius & Per Wikström, "Nazism med vikingamask" [Nazism with a Viking Mask], *Kommunalarbetaren* 6 (1994).

[7] This topic is also part of the lyrics of the White Noise groups. See for instance, "Living Nightmare," No Remorse, (CD) *No Remorse Songbooks nr 2*; "Farbror snusk" [Dirty Old Man], *Death Future*, (CD) *I Nationens tjänst*, 1995, Sweden Calling Ltd.

[8] Föreningen Sveriges Framtid program, 5.

[9] "Läran om kroppen" [The Teachings about the Body], *Rikslarm*, (höstnr. 1992), 11.

[10] See for instance, "Vad tror kreativister på?" [What Do Creators Believe In], leaflet (1991); or "Kvinnans livsuppgift" [The Life Goal of the Women], *RAHOWA*, 3, (1991), 3-4.

[11] See for instance, "Tack demokrater" [Thank You Democrats], *Sveriges Framtid* 3/4 (1990), 6; "En introduktion till Riksfronten," [An Introduction to Reichfront] *Rikslarm sommarnr* (1992), 5; or "Bygg på sanningen" [Based on Truth], *Sveriges Framtid* (vår/sommar 1990), 4.

[12] See for instance, Richard Rubenstein, *Förintelsens lag* [The Law Of Extermination], (1980), 40,102.

[13] "En av RF:s talesmän trakasserad" [One Of The Functionaries Of RF Has Been Harassed], *DSF* 1 (1996), 4.

[14] "Folksocialistisk samling; Det enda alernativer" [The Only Alternative], *FS förlag* 1997, p 9.

[15] Interview with an anonymous activist, 3 April 1991.

[16] "Judarna på Stockholms restauranger" [Jews in Stockholm's Restaurants], *Svea Rikes Nyhetstjänst* 13 - II. (27 March 1935), 5.

[17] Jesper Johansson, "Ett vitt land, ett vitt folk, en vit framtid - Sveriges Framtid" [A White Land, A White People, A White Future—Sweden's Future], *Sveriges Framtid* 3-4 (1990), 11.

[18] "Blattesvin," Somalia Kickers; *Swedish Skins*, (CD) Last Resort Records 1995.

[19] Richard Rubenstein, *Förintelsens lag*, (1980), 40, 102.

[20] "Se t ex Rashygien - en självklarhet för varje civilisation som vill överleva" [Race Hygienics—A Necessity For Every Civilization That Wants To Survive] *Rikslarm* 4 (1994), 9f.

[21] Judith Bessant, "Political Crime and the Case of Young Neo-Nazis; A Question of

Methodology," *Terrorism & Political Violence* 7 (1995), 110.
[22] Interview with activist who wants to remain anonymous, April 1992.
[23] Vit makt—Svart slakt, anonymt klistermärke, i författarens ägo [White Power—Black slaughter] (anonymous sticker, in the authors possession).
[24] See for instance, "Vad tror kreativister på?" ["What Do Creators Believe In?"], *flygblad* (1991); "Kvinnans livsuppgift" [The Goal of the Women], *RAHOWA* 3 (1991), 3-4; "Levnadsregler" ["Life Rules"], *Stormpress* 6 (1996), 9.
[25] Lööw (1990), 131.
[26] *Vikings ernmidran, reglemente för vikingarna* [A Vikings guide , Regalia for the Vikings], (Copy in the possession if the author).
[27] Tape interview with "Gregor" 12 January 1992.
[28] "Terror skall bemötas med terror" [Terror Should Be Met With Terror], *Werwolf, Krigskomminike* 9, 14.
[29] Ellerstam etc. 1982, s 103.
[30] Interview conducted by E-mail, November 12, 1996.
[31] "Might Is Right," http://www.ariskkamp.com.wcotcswe.might.htm.
[32] MS 4/7 1994, Kl XX.
[33] RAG-sången, NRP-sånghäfte (undated in the possession of the author).
[34] "Död åt Zog" [Death to Zog], *Nordland* 5 1996, 14.
[35] MS 4 July 1994.
[36] KL 21/9 1992.
[37] "Environmental Concern," *Last Chance* 15 (1993), 20-21.
[38] "Imperium, Information från [Imperium Information from] Tommy Rydén 880728," (in the possession of the author).
[39] See for example, "Vad som hänt och händer i Sverige" [What Happened and Still Happens in Sweden], *Nordisk Kamp* 3 (1976), 3; "Finns dessa bilder ännu i verkligheten" [Where Are These Pictures In Reality?], *Nordisk Kamp* 2-3 (1977), 17; "Lögnen och dess trofasta tjänare" [The Lie And Its Faithful Servants], *Nordisk Kamp* 2 (1992), 6-8; "Om grymheterna i demokratins heliga namn ingenting att orda," *Nordisk Kamp* 2 (1985), 18; Göran A Oredsson, "men den som hejdar växtens fart och lägger jord igen begår en synd av värre art än den som dräper män," *Nordisk Kamp* 4 (1985), 2ff; "I solhjulets tecken för en ny Nord, Nordiska Rikspartiet," *Nordisk Kamp* 1 (1986), 22; "Klädbekymmer" [Clothing Problem], *Nordisk Kamp* 1 (1973), 21 , Göran Assar Oredsson, "Genmanipulation brott mot naturen och människorna, och blir bondestammens åderlåtning," *NRP Bulletin* 2 (1987), 10-11; "Kamp mot djurplågeriet Röster och idéspridare" [The Struggle Against Maltreatment Of Animals], (undated flier in author's possession) *NRP Bulletin* 3 (1976), 19; "En lien bit på baksidan," *NRP-Bulletin* 1 (1971), 14; "En sprut," *Nordisk Kamp* (okt-nov 1965), 17; "Djurplågeri vid tävlingsbanor" [Maltreatment Of Animals on the Racing Track], *Nordisk Kamp* (August-September 1965), 9; "Ditt samvete," *Nordisk Kamp* 3 (1964), 14; Tyra Persén, "När juldagsmorgon glimmar jag vill till stallet gå" [When Christmas Day Comes I Want To Go To The Stables], *Nordisk Kamp* (januari 1966), 26; Tyra Persén, "Är djurförsök nödvändiga" [Are Animal Experiments Necessary], *Nordisk Kamp* 4 (1966), 22f; "Grymhet och förnedring," *Nordisk Kamp* 3 (1967), 29-31; "har man tappat huvudet," *Nordisk Kamp* 11 (1967), 17; "Djur är ej skapade åt människors godtyckliga handlingar," *Nordisk Kamp* 1 (1969), 11-13; "Kamp mot djurplågeriet," *Nordisk Kam* 2 (1970), 11; "Demokratisk mörkläggning omkring vivisektionen," *Nordisk Kamp* 2 (1975), 23-25.
[40] "Om vi inte ville bära päls" [If We Don't Want To Carry A Fur Coat] *Nordisk Kamp* 6-7 (1970), 31.
[41] Göran A Oredsson, "När det passar nämner man Nordiska Rikspartiet, men mestadels passar det inte alls" [When It Suits Them They Mention The Nordic Reich Party, But Most Of The Time It Doesn't Suit Them At All], *Nordisk Kamp* 1-2 (1988), 3.

[42] NRP kämpar för..., 33.

[43] *NRP-Bulletin* 2 (1985), 9.

[44] NRP had got hold of the register of members and supporters of the organization, and started to distribute material to them, Göran Assar Oredsson, Letter to the author, 26 March 1997.

[45] Göran Assar Oredsson, "Vi förtydligar ur KVP-artikeln och kommenterar" [We have a Few Comments on the KVP Article], *NRP-Bulletinen* 1 (1984), 5.

[46] See for instance "Tyras pengar är slut - och till jul blir det kvarskatt" [Tyra Has Run Out Of Money and the Taxes are Due at Christmas], *Aftonbladet* 29/6 1979.

[47] Letter from Göran Assar Oredsson to the author, 26 March 1997.

[48] Ibid.

[49] GBG, 1 September 1991.

[50] "Våra Idéer" [Our Ideas], *Solkorset.*

[51] Vera Oredsson, "Nationalsocialismen och naturvården" [National Socialism and Environmentalism], *Nordisk Kamp* (January 1966), 19.

[52] "Nordiska Rikspartiet," *Nordisk Kamp* 2 (1975), 14-15.

[53] "Miljökatastrofen vid Rhen" [The Environmental Catastrophe at Rhen], *Nordisk Kamp* 1 (1987), 7.

[54] "NRP kämpar för...," 31; See for instance, "Naturvård och överlevnad" [Environmentalism and Survival], *Nordisk Kamp* 1 (1971), 7-13.

[55] "Vi lånar vårt land av våra barn" [We Are Only Borrowing This Land From Our Children], *Nordisk Kamp* 1-2 (1990), 7.

[56] "Öppet brev" [Open Letter], *Frihetsfacklan* 11-12 1991, p 1.

[57] "Framåt för djurens rättigheter" [Move Forward For The Rights Of The Animals], *Info-14* (November 1995), 3. The law will be effective from the first of April 1997.

[58] "Stadgar för NSF" [Rules For National Socialist Front], *Den Sanne Nationalsocialisten* 1 (1996), 3.

[59] Folksocialistisk Samling : Det enda alternativer" [Folk Socialist Union: The Only Alternative], *FS förlag*, 1997, 8.

[60] Ibid., 14.

[61] "Föreningen Sveriges Framtid," *Sveriges Framtid* 1 (1989-90), 8.

[62] LL 12 December 1991.

[63] *FSF program*, 10.

[64] Interview with ER 29 November 1991.

[65] *Handlingsprogram 1996*, 4.

[66] "Stoppa kosherslakten" [Stop Kosher Slaughter], *Vit Rebell* 4 (1989), 6.

[67] Lööw, "1935 motionerade NSAP/SSS t ex i Göteborgs stadsfullmäktige om ett förbud för kosherslakt" [NSAP/SSS Suggested In The Gothenburg Local Council That Kosher Slaughter Should Be Banned], (1990), 349.

[68] "Se t ex Demokratins dubbelspel" [The Democratic Double Deal], *Nordisk Kamp* 2-3 (1980), 7; *Handlingsprogram 1996*, 5; "Narkotikan—och dess syfte som vapen mot den vita rasen" [Narcotics—And Why They're Used As A Weapon Against The White Race], *Nordisk Kamp* 3 (1967), 23; "Opinionen mot knarkbödeln: Narkotikan visar ett sjukt samhälle" [Opinion Against the Drug Killers: Narcotics Are the Sign of a Sick Society], *Nordisk Kamp* 1 (1969), 1.

[69] "Djävulsdans" [The Dance of the Devil], *Nordisk Kamp* 3 (1962), 3.

[70] "Tack Erlander" [Thank Erlander], *Nordisk Kamp* 1 (1969), 10.

[71] Göran Assar Oredsson, "Brev till författaren" (Letter to the author), (August 1996).

[72] Göran Assar Oredsson, "Hur vill vi forma det Sverige som våra barn och barnbarn skall leva i?" [How Should We Create A Sweden That Our Children And Grandchildren Can Live In], *Nordisk Kamp* 6-7 (1974), 3.

[73] See for example, "Nyårsbrev från ny medlem Strängnäs" [New Year's letter from a new member], *NRP-Bulletin* 1 (1982), 7.

74 "Därför röstar vi på Nordiska Rikspartiet," [The Reason We Vote for The Nordic Reich Party] *Flygblad* (1973).

75Till, "statsminister Olof Palme och Sveriges Socialdemokratiska regering" [Prime Minister Olof Palme and the Social Democratic Party] *Nordiska Rikspartiet* 1 (1976) (bilaga).

76 För dessa kampanjer se ideologikapitlet.

77Göran Assar Oredsson letter to the author, August 1996.

78 Jesper Johannson and Peter Andersson, "Vad innebär egentligen svensk patriotism?" [What Is The True Meaning Of Swedish Patriotism], *Nordland* 3 1995, p 8.

79 This is a fact that has become evident during interviews with activists over the past 14 years.

80 "Nazifinansiären Carlberg under förmyndare fyra år" [The Nazi Financier Carlberg Put Under Observation], *Arbetaren* 23 December 1944.

81 RPS SÄK arkiv PM, akt 3P 398.

82 See for instance, *Hitler answers Roosevelt, Reichcancelor Adolf Hitler's Speech before the great German Reichstaff 28th of April 1939* (Svea Rike ltd Stockholm 1939); Adolf Hitler, *"I Believe in a Long Peace," Speech at the First Great German Reichstag on the 30th of January 1939* (Svea Rike ltd 1939); Göran Göransson, "Henry Ford and the Jews," Reverend Nils Hannerz, "The Words of the Living God, Sifia Rabe, The Women in the National Socialist State."

83 RPS SÄK arkiv PM, akt 3P 398.

84 RPS SÄK arkiv PM, akt 3P 398.

85 RPS SÄK arkiv, PM angående Svea Rikes Bokhandel, Stockholm 3 December 1935.

86 "Manhems föreläsnings institut" [Manhems Lecturing Institute], *Svea Rikes Nyhetstjänst* 23 - II (den 15 August 1935), 1.

87 "Manhems årsting" [Manhems Annual Meeting], *Svea Rikes Nyhetstjänst* 22 -II (Den 15 July 1935), 1.

88 "Samfundet Manhem utdelar 4.200 kr i Stipendier" [Manhem Gives Away 4.200 kr in Scholarships], *Svea Rikes Nyhetstjänst* 14 - II (3 April 1935), 1.

89 RPS SÄK arkiv PM, akt 3P 398.

90 RPS SÄK arkiv, PM 6.9 1941.

91 RPS SÄK arkiv, "Rapport från Samfundet Manhems möte, tisdagen" [Report from Manhems Meeting Tuesday], 18 April 1944, kl. 20-22 å Manhemssalen.

92 Carl Ernfrid Carlberg 70 år, Fria Ord nr 8 1959.

93 The group managed to establish a co-operation with members of Nils Flygs old organization and with the right wing extremist Young Swedish Club.

94 Lodenius & Larsson, 1994, 81.

95 Carl E Carlbergs Stiftelse, stiftelseurkund, Stockholm den 24 February 1957.

96 Carlsson 1993, 20-21.

97 Carlsson 1993, 25-26.

98 Lodenius & Larsson, 1994, 87.

99 See for example, "Mystiska platser" [Mysterious Places], *Wärendsbladet* 7 (1996), 1ff; Doktor A A Alexandersson, "och kristen spirutualism i seklets början" [Christian Spiritualism at the Beginning of the Century], *Wärendsbladet* 6 (1996), 1ff; "Den empiriska och duala livsprinncipens tidskrift" [The Empirical And Dualistic Lifeprinciples Magazine], *Wärendsbladet* 24 (1994), 6; and "Döden i livets tjänst" [Death in the Service of Life], *Wärendsbladet* 3 (1996), 3.

100 "Tidskrift för waerlandismen i Norden" [Magazine for Waerlandism in Scandinavia], *Wärendsbladet* 10 (1996), 4; Cora Richmonds, "Spiritualism," *Wärendsbladet* 9 (1996), 4; "Var det Cora Richmond som lade grunden till den sanna arbetarrörelen i USA 1852-1896" [Was It Cora Richmond Who Laid The Fundament To The True Working Class Movement In The USA In 1852-1896], *Wärendsbladet* 20 (1995), 3; "den tyska nationalsocialismens vård av kvinnorna och kvinnligheten" [German

National Socialists Care For Women and Femininity], *Wärendsbladetr* 23/24 (1995), 5-6; "Förtrycket av den sanna ursprungliga kvinnligheteb är nu – 1995 - värre än någonsin" [The Oppression of the True Femininity Is Now 1995—Worse Than Ever], *Wärendsbladet* 22 (1995), 3.

[101] "se t ex Korset i dagdroppen eller rosenkreutzarnas dröm" [See for instance the Cross in the Fall of the Rosecrution Dream], *Wärendsbladet* 9 (1996), 7; (Sommarkrönika juli 1994), *Wärendsbladet* 11 1994, 8; "Smålänningen Dr AA Alexandersson var en av de tolv män som" [The Smålänning Dr AA Anlexandersson Was One Of The Twelve Men Who], *Wärendsbladet* 3 (1996), 3.

[102] Se t ex "Grav - och dödsbenskulten i den västerländska kuluren" [Grave And Deathbone Cults In Western Culture], *Wärendsbladet* 24 (1994), 3.

[103] Se t ex "Annons för Svea Boklubb," [Advertisement for Svea Book Club], *Wärendsbladet* 24, (1994), 5.

[104] "Är du intresserad av hälsa och frisksport" [Are You Interested In Health And Sports?], *Wärendsbladet* 9 (1996), 1, 3.

[105] *Grindvakten* 2 (1996), 13.

[106] Tommy Rydén left the leadership of Hembygdspartiet in the spring of 1997, and the current party leader is Leif Larsson. On the history of the Hembygdspartiet in English, see Tommy Rydén, "Rydén," in Jeffrey Kaplan, *Encyclopedia of White Power* (Santa Barbara, CA: ABC-CLIO, forthcoming).

[107] D.T 20/9 1991.

[108] Ibid.

[109] "Saluubriskt leverne" [Salubrious Living], *Kreativistens Kyrka*; "En koryt introduktiomn till den vita rasens religion" [A Short Introduction To The Religion of the White Race], odaterad broschyr utgiven av KK i Säffle, s 11-12.

[110] "Adolf Hitler, Rudolf Hess och Heinrich Himmler var alla vegetarianer" [Adolf Hitler, Rudolf Hess and Heinrich Himmler Were All Vegetarians], flygblad odat (i författarens ägo).

[111] Kosten [the Food], Stridszon; ett nyhetsbrev för bidragsgivare, [Balltlezone: Newsletter for Contributors], November 1993, p 7.

[112] "Naturlig näring, nyckeln till kreativ superhälsa" [Natural Nutrition, the Key to a Creative Superhealth], January 1993.

[113] Exklusiv information från DeVries-institutet våren 1997 Exklusiv information från DeVries-institutet [Exclusive Information From the DeVries Institute 1997].

[114] "Salubrious Living Section," *White Resistance*, 5 (1993), p 6.

[115] Folksocialistisk Samling 1997, 14.

[116] "Manifestation 6 November 1992," flygblad, Anhängarbulletinen April 1992.

[117] Vad vill NSEAP, Info Europa nr 1 1997, 5.

Thriving in a Cultic Milieu

The World Union of National Socialists, 1962-1992

Frederick J. Simonelli

George Lincoln Rockwell (1918-1967), America's preeminent post-war Nazi, founder of the American Nazi Party (ANP) and of the World Union of National Socialists, was a major oppositional figure throughout the racist right of the 1960s. He was also a major catalyst in the fusing of Nazi ideology and mysticism that marked much of the post-war rightist fringe. His presence is felt in many, if not most, of the cultic milieus that made up the racist right of his day, and his legacy is strong in those circles to the present.

Contemporary adherents to diverse religious and quasi-religious fellowships, from Christian Identity to Satanism, honor Rockwell as a spiritual inspiration. He is among the pantheon of heroes, often the first among them, of virtually every contemporary right-wing, racist clique.[1]

Rockwell was a true believer. Before his conversion to Nazism, Rockwell's life was, at best, intermittent flashes of brilliance in a dark sky of failure and rejection. But in the notion of a racial community—*volksgemeinschaft*—he found the meaning and values missing from his life. His holy cause—the trinity of race, blood, and land—compensated, to a considerable degree, for the desperation and emptiness at his core. In the service of this cause Rockwell, like an earlier generation of Nazis, found purpose and peace as symbols and shibboleths rose as "metaphysical commandments" and bestowed a special sanctification upon fanaticism.[2] It is in this cultic milieu that he thrived and had his greatest impact.

This chapter examines one aspect of Rockwell's work: the building of an international coalition of neo-Nazi national parties, which he called the World Union of National Socialists (WUNS). While this study concentrates on the organizational and political aspects of WUNS, many of the comrades Rockwell attracted shared his fascination with the mystical aspect of their calling; all shared his devotion to the "holy cause" of race, blood, and land; all were, like Rockwell, classic "true believers."[3]

From its founding in 1962 to the European neo-Nazi resurgence following the fall of communism and the reunification of Germany, the World

Union of National Socialists played a key role in preserving the ideology, mythology, and rhetoric of Nazism and in transferring that belief system to subsequent generations of adherents. WUNS was the organizational bridge between
the leading neo-Nazi movement in post-war America—George Lincoln Rockwell's American Nazi Party—and the fragmented and disparate national neo-
Nazi cells in post-war Europe. To a significant degree, WUNS offered cohesion
to those attempting to sustain the unconnected remnants of National Socialist
parties in western Europe and gave national Nazi movements a vehicle for cooperation and communication. Most significantly, by organizing around the brash
and charismatic George Lincoln Rockwell, a combat-decorated pilot-officer in
the United States Navy, WUNS put the victors' uniform on Nazism for a new
era.

To observe that the Nazism of the 1960s was not the Nazism of the
1930s is merely to state the obvious. "Neo-Nazism" has entered current usage to
distinguish post-war revival movements from the dominant political party of the
German Third Reich. Yet, the essential difference between the Nazism of Hitler
and the German NSDAP (the German acronym for the "National German Socialist Workers Party") and the neo-Nazism of Rockwell and WUNS is not
merely one of time or access to power. The essential difference is that the cult-
like aspects of Hitler's regime—and there were many—are magnified as the
defining characteristics of post-war neo-Nazi movements. Those characteristics
make the neo-Nazi incarnations, like WUNS, more easily understood as cults
with quasi-religious features than as conventional political movements. It is in
this cultic milieu that WUNS thrived and helped shape the idiosyncratic nature
of subsequent manifestations of the fundamental "Nazi" impulse.

George Lincoln Rockwell organized the American Nazi Party in 1958
as a political expression of his anti-democratic, anti-Semitic and racist views.[4]
Rockwell's thirteen-year journey from distinguished military service with the
U.S. Navy in World War II to political pariah took him from conventional, albeit
extreme, right-wing politics to increasingly marginalized fringe groups. Not
incidentally, his journey also included a failed marriage, several failed businesses, and an irreparable breach with his respectable New England family.
Rockwell finally abandoned attempts to camouflage his racist and anti-Semitic
views with traditional, socially acceptable symbols and rhetoric. In 1958, he
openly embraced Adolf Hitler as his political hero and flaunted Hitler's theories
of racial purity as the bedrock creed of his new party. That party adopted the
swastika as its emblem. Rockwell's ANP Stormtroopers consciously modeled
their dress and behavior on pre-war German Nazis. Jew-baiting, crude racist
caricatures, and unsubstantiated charges of communist conspiracies within the
U.S. government marked Rockwell's speeches and writings.

Virtually at the same time that he was organizing the ANP, Rockwell
began searching for like-minded activists in Europe willing to openly organize
national units of an international movement based on the German National Socialist model. Rockwell's goal was nothing less than "the establishment of an
Aryan world order" founded on an ideology of racial purity.[5] In his increasingly
inflated—some would claim delusional—conception of his role on the world

stage, Rockwell saw himself picking up the standard that fell with Adolf Hitler in 1945 and carrying that standard to global victory.[6]

Rockwell's first effort at international organization, the World Union of Free Enterprise National Socialists (WUFENS), formed in early 1959, failed to attract much notice in the international community. Rockwell persisted. In 1960 he began sending ANP literature to National Socialist and other right-wing activists and politicians throughout western Europe. ANP literature began to circulate among the informal network of Nazis and right-wing racialists in Europe. The first significant contact Rockwell made in pursuing his worldwide organizational strategy was with Colin Jordan of Great Britain, that era's most open and visible European advocate of National Socialism and founder of the British National Socialist Movement (NSM). Jordan knew of Rockwell and had been following Rockwell's American exploits with growing interest since 1960, when he received several ANP mailings.[7] By early 1962, Rockwell and Jordan were in regular contact. The Rockwell-Jordan correspondence quickly focused on the need for an international organization designed to promote a National Socialist resurgence.

In the summer of 1962, Rockwell secretly traveled to England to attend a meeting of National Socialist leaders from seven nations—the United States, Great Britain, Germany, France, Austria, Ireland and Belgium—in the remote countryside of the Cotswold hills of Gloucestershire. In this, their first face-to-face meeting, Rockwell and Jordan formed a quick friendship that would last until Rockwell's death five years later. From that first meeting it was clear, although unspoken, that Rockwell, and not the more experienced and senior Jordan, would be the leader in their transatlantic partnership. Those assembled at Cotswold agreed on the organizing principles of a new international organization, to be called the World Union of National Socialists.[8] The signers became the organizing cadre of WUNS and the document they signed, the Cotswold Agreements, became the manifesto of neo-Nazi revival worldwide.[9] The document declared the formation of a "monolithic, combat efficient, international political apparatus to combat and utterly destroy the International Jewish Communist and Zionist apparatus of treason and subversion." WUNS pledged "an eventual world ORDER, based on RACE" and a "final settlement of the Jewish problem." As the de facto constitution of WUNS, the Cotswold Agreements defined the criteria for recognition of national affiliates, stipulating that "no organization or individual failing to acknowledge the spiritual leadership of Adolf Hitler" would be admitted to membership.[10]

Besides Colin Jordan, the most influential European founding members of WUNS were two veteran Nazis with personal ties to the Third Reich: Savitri Devi of France and Bruno Ludtke of Germany. Neither Devi nor Ludtke were active in national Nazi organizational efforts, although Devi was revered as the grande dame of French Nazism by her countrymen. They were thinkers and strategists. Rockwell was impressed by their intellectual abilities and more than a little impressed by their direct connection to the Third Reich.

Savitri Devi, born Maximiani Portas in Lyons, France, on 30 September 1905, was a chemist who moved to India in the early 1930s to study ancient

Aryan philosophy and rituals. By 1935 she was a devoted National Socialist and admirer of Adolf Hitler. During World War II she was an active Nazi collaborator and served the Nazi cause in India, for which she was imprisoned following the defeat of Germany. Devi fit Rockwell's ideal of the new Aryan woman and her influence over him was significant. Savitri Devi's prophetic visions of a Nazi resurrection helped form Rockwell's own growing mysticism and the sense of divinely directed purpose that molded WUNS's early formation.[11]

Bruno Ludtke, more than any other single individual, shaped Rockwell's thinking on National Socialism's revival as an international political movement. An invalid suffering from the progressive debility of multiple sclerosis, Ludtke nonetheless possessed an agile mind and insight into the ego-driven Rockwell. The sycophantic Ludtke manipulated Rockwell's belief in his own destiny as Hitler's cosmic heir in a voluminous personal correspondence that lasted from 1960 to Rockwell's death in 1967. Bruno Armin Ludtke was born in Harburg, Germany, on 15 November 1926. From an early age, Ludtke idolized Adolf Hitler, which brought him into frequent bitter conflict with his father, a committed anti-Nazi. In 1940, Ludtke joined the Hitler-Jugend over his father's objections, causing an irreparable breach between father and son. Ludtke attempted to join the SS in 1943 but was rejected because of his poor health. As the war deteriorated for the Germans, the Wehrmacht lowered its physical standards, allowing Ludtke to volunteer for combat in October of 1944.

At the end of the war, Ludtke studied engineering, was briefly married, and drifted from job to job while his health declined with the advance of his disease. Ludtke re-married in 1956. He and his second wife had four daughters and Ludtke worked when able, but spent most of his time writing philosophical and political tracts on the only real passion of his life: Adolf Hitler and Hitler's dream of a racially pure National Socialist world. Savitri Devi introduced Ludtke to the writings of George Lincoln Rockwell in 1960 and Ludtke immediately saw in the bold American Nazi the best and only hope for a Nazi resurgence. Ludtke's initial letter to Rockwell soon led to a regular transatlantic correspondence. Ludtke instructed Rockwell in the subtleties of National Socialism and in the history of Hitler's rise to power in Germany while carefully ingratiating himself with Rockwell by emphasizing the similarities between Hitler and Rockwell. Where none existed, Ludtke created them.[12] Because Nazi advocacy, recruitment, and agitation were illegal in post-war Germany, Ludtke suffered numerous arrests and long periods in prison. But the Rockwell-Ludtke correspondence continued during Ludtke's incarceration and Ludtke continued to advise Rockwell on organizational matters concerning WUNS.[13]

In its formative years, Rockwell's tireless proselytizing and Colin Jordan's organizational skill fostered WUNS's growth. By 1965, WUNS had operative chapters in twenty countries, twelve of them—Great Britain, the Republic of Ireland, West Germany, France, Belgium, Hungary, Switzerland, Spain, Italy, Denmark, Sweden, Iceland—in Europe, and five—the United States, Canada, Argentina, Chile, Uruguay—in the Americas. Much of Jordan's organizational work was done despite intermittent incarceration in Great Britain for subversive activities.[14] Soon WUNS had additional chapters in Africa, Australia, and Asia. Through the efforts of Rockwell and Jordan, there was soon a neo-Nazi presence, affiliated with WUNS, on every inhabited continent on the face of the earth.[15]

Rockwell's American Nazi Party constituted the U.S.-WUNS chapter and was the flagship chapter of the worldwide WUNS network. Colin Jordan governed WUNS-Europe under Rockwell's authority as International Commander. Each national WUNS chapter theoretically reported to Rockwell, with those in Europe reporting through Jordan. In practice, however, WUNS governance was not nearly so well structured. Some chapters adhered to the model's leadership structure, others did so in name only. Since the WUNS leadership did not have the funds to subsidize emerging chapters, or to assist existing chapters in times of crisis, it had little leverage to enforce its mandates. Instead, what control Rockwell did exercise emanated from the force of his personality and the intensity of his will. As the Fuehrer-apparent within an autocratic tradition, even without traditional means of coercion, Rockwell's authority over WUNS chapters was significant though uneven.

WUNS chapters on the American side of the Atlantic enjoyed varying levels of success. Rockwell's own ANP, the WUNS U.S. affiliate, never matched its inflammatory rhetoric and flamboyant public stunts with actual numbers of adherents. In Chile, Franz Pfeiffer, a former SS-colonel and the last commander of Hitler's "Leibstandarte," drew on large numbers of Nazi exiles to create an active National Socialist party, the Partido Nacionalsocialista Chileno. Pfeiffer's party thrived until late 1964 when it was banned by the Chilean government. Pfeiffer refused to curtail his activities and was arrested and jailed in February of 1965.[16]

In Argentina, Horst Eichmann, Adolf Eichmann's son, headed the Argentine National Socialist Party. Although Eichmann had a substantial following within the German expatriate community in Argentina and a recognized name worldwide, his tepid loyalty to Rockwell kept him outside the WUNS inner circle.[17]

Aggressive anti-Nazi governmental action in Canada thwarted Rockwell's early efforts there. From 1961 to 1965, Rockwell worked through Andre Bellfeuille's Canadian Nazi Party (CNP) to coordinate Canadian-American activities. Janos Pall, Bellfeuille's CNP deputy, helped Rockwell organize the World Union of Free Enterprise National Socialists, predecessor organization to WUNS, and later, WUNS itself. Bellfeuille's CNP was the first WUNS-Canada chapter.[18] By 1965, fragmentation and infighting had hopelessly split the Canadian racist right. Several competing groups—including Bellfeuille's CNP, Jacques Taylor's Canadian National Socialist Party, and Don Andrews's Western Guard Party—sought designation as the official WUNS-Canada chapter. Rockwell avoided embroiling himself in Canada's internecine wars and selected a relative newcomer, John Beattie, to head WUNS-Canada. The choice of Beattie proved fortuitous for Rockwell and WUNS as he soon consolidated power within the racist right and built one of WUNS's most active and aggressive chapters.[19]

Europe contained the largest concentration of WUNS chapters. In Scandinavia, indigenous National Socialist parties—particularly in Sweden—predated WUNS and, to varying degrees, pre-empted WUNS's incursion into that region. In Sweden, Goren Assar Oredsson's Nordic National Party (Nordiska Rikspartiet), which he founded in 1956, was actively agitating for racist and anti-Semitic causes before Rockwell's own conversion to Nazism and the formation of both the ANP and WUNS. Oredsson and his wife and partner, Vera, were unwilling to place their organization in a subordinate position to an international federation that had less strength and visibility in Sweden than their own. Although Oredsson developed a close personal friendship with Rockwell, and cooperated with Rockwell on National Socialist strategy in Scandinavia, he maintained the independence of his Nordic National Party. At the heart of Oredsson's refusal to officially affiliate with WUNS was his animosity toward the United States for its role in the destruction of the Third Reich. Several years after Rockwell's death, Oredsson explained that although he admired Rockwell and regarded him as a comrade, he could "never accept the idea that the head-quarters for a World Union of National Socialism [*sic*] should be in the USA."[20] In Denmark, Sven Salicath, leader of the Danish National Socialist Workers Party, organized WUNS-Denmark and was a devoted Rockwell disciple. Bernhard Haarde led an active WUNS chapter in Iceland, which claimed over 300 members.[21]

Outside of Scandinavia, WUNS national chapters advanced unevenly, dependent on local conditions and local leadership, far more than on anything Rockwell or WUNS did or failed to do, for their growth. Ireland's Irish National Union languished for several years until Bernard E. Horgan took command of WUNS-Ireland in 1966 and energized that chapter.[22] In Spain, a German expatriate and Third Reich veteran, Friedrich Kuhfuss, organized and led WUNS-Spain. While Kuhfuss remained the leader of WUNS-Spain in all but name, his deputy, Antonio Madrano, a native Spaniard, was the nominal leader.[23] England, France, and Belgium boasted the largest, strongest, and most active WUNS chapters in Europe. England's Colin Jordan, and his deputies, John Tyndall, Roland Kerr-Ritchie, Denis Pirie, Peter Ling, J. D. F. Knight, and Gordon Hingston, as well as his mother, Bertha Beecham Jordan, and wife, Francoise Dior-Jordan, formed one of the most active and energetic National Socialist movements in Europe, although internal divisions and power struggles tempered its effectiveness.[24]

Second only to England among WUNS chapters, and far more problematic for Rockwell, was the volatile French National Socialist movement under its unstable leader, Yves Jeanne. Even before the Cotswold conference, Bruno Ludtke identified France as the most promising site for neo-Nazi organization.[25] In 1962, Savitri Devi and the Comtesse R. H. de Caumont La Force—Colin Jordan's future wife, Francoise Dior—provided the organizational impetus, and probably the funds, to form WUNS-France. Devi represented France at the Cotswold conference. Francoise Dior, the privileged daughter of a wealthy and influential family, brought her ample checkbook and connections to the French aristocracy to the effort. Dior brought Claude Normand—pseudonym of Claude on the Eastern Front during World War II—to the movement.

on the Eastern Front during World War II—to the movement. Normand/Janne, along with his secretary and confidant, Anne Houel, and his deputy, Raymond Dubois, formed the first leadership cadre of WUNS-France in 1963.[26]

In 1964, Yves Jeanne seized control of WUNS-France from Claude Janne and almost immediately started organizing a coup against his European superior, Colin Jordan, for the leadership of WUNS-Europe. With Rockwell's timely backing of Jordan, Jeanne's coup failed. Although he remained affiliated with WUNS for several years, Jeanne's grab for European command split the movement in France, with Savitri Devi siding with Jeanne and Francoise Dior remaining loyal to Jordan (she was married to Jordan from October 1963 to October 1966).[27]

Yves Jeanne's ambition had a disruptive influence in Belgium as well. In 1965, Jeanne attempted to consolidate all French-speaking National Socialists under one command. He proposed to Rockwell and Jordan that command boundaries, which normally followed national boundaries, be altered to incorporate the French-speaking regions of Belgium under the jurisdiction of WUNS-France. Fearful of alienating the most important WUNS chapter in Europe, Rockwell acquiesced. Rockwell's capitulation to Jeanne infuriated the leadership of WUNS-Belgium, J. R. Debbaudt, Nicholas Janssens, and Henri Devos, who resigned en masse from WUNS. With the damage to WUNS-Belgium evident, Jeanne withdrew his request for consolidated French-Belgian leadership. The man Rockwell selected to lead WUNS-Belgium following the Debbaudt-Janssens-Devos resignations, Rudiger van Sande, proved totally incapable of healing the breach and rebuilding the party. WUNS-Belgium never recovered.[28]

In Germany, the spiritual Fatherland of the neo-Nazi movement, anti-Nazi laws enacted by the West German government under Allied mandate after World War II prohibited organization of an openly National Socialist or neo-Nazi political party. WUNS activities had to be underground and clandestine. In 1960 and 1961, at great peril to himself, Bruno Ludtke smuggled Rockwell's writings into Germany, translated them into German, and distributed them among his former Nazi comrades and younger sympathizers. Ludtke's devotion to the cause, and his courage on the "front line" of battle, impressed Rockwell. By early 1962, Bruno Ludtke was the de facto head of WUNS-Germany and a trusted member of Rockwell's inner circle. Ludtke maintained a secret network of Nazis throughout Germany,[29] and he worked tirelessly to enlist his former comrades in Rockwell's movement. He advised Rockwell on organizing Europe and provided him with regular, detailed reports on his efforts in Germany.[30]

The preceding summary of WUNS organizational efforts conveys one aspect of the quantitative reality of neo-Nazi resurgence in the post-war world. To understand its qualitative reality, however, one must look beyond personalities and numbers to the social and psychological motivations that gird and sustain such movements. In some very important ways, the neo-Nazi revivalist movement of the early 1960s emanated from political and cultural instincts that marked prior fascist incarnations. Rockwell and Jordan, the ANP and WUNS, embraced the essential beliefs around which a fascist system inevitably "coagulates:" a cult of tradition; the rejection of modernism as inherently corrupt; action for action's sake; the conviction that disagreement is treason; irrational fear of difference; a populist appeal to a frustrated middle class; obsession with plots and conspiracies; a sense of diminished self-esteem in the face of the wealth and power of perceived enemies; the belief that life is permanent warfare; contempt for the weak; the cult of heroic death; misogyny and homophobia as related expressions of exaggerated machismo; reverence for a leader who embodies the "Common Will" and an attendant disdain for democracy; and a devaluation of complex and critical reasoning. These essential beliefs represent the "fascist essence," the core of a system used to "unite, purify, and energize" a disaffected affinity group and to mobilize them for political and/or social action.[31]

For the neo-Nazi groups of the post-war world, and specifically for Rockwell's WUNS, these attributes were more than a belief system upon which a political program rested; they were the political program itself. Embracing of its tenets by WUNS leaders and members became the litmus test of acceptance by the group. Without access to power, and without the tempering influence that the real potential for power can bring to political discourse, WUNS leaders had no external restraint upon their dogmatic and rhetorical excesses. While never admitting how far they were from actually realizing their political ambitions, even to themselves, Rockwell and the WUNS leadership regarded unquestioning loyalty and ideological purity among WUNS members as critical to their ultimate success. Undeviating adherence to the group-creed was magnified as a test of legitimacy within the group. Marginalized politically, the neo-Nazi resurgence of WUNS exhibited behavioral characteristics more appropriate to a cult than to a comprehensive political movement.

The cult-like nature of WUNS is also evident in the increasing emphasis on Rockwell as the infallible leader. In 1962, Rockwell was the brightest star in a constellation of WUNS organizers that included Colin Jordan and Savitri Devi. But by early 1964, Rockwell held not only the official command of WUNS, but had no meaningful restraints upon how he exercised that command. Only those who unquestioningly and enthusiastically followed Rockwell's strategic and philosophical direction—Colin Jordan, Bruno Ludtke, Matt Koehl—retained positions of authority in WUNS throughout the Rockwell regime. In a political culture not known for subtlety and restraint, Rockwell's outrageous words and deeds marked WUNS as the avant-garde of the Nazi revival movement. Rockwell's excesses, evident to those outside his circle, were regarded as tactically brilliant by his followers within WUNS. As in any true cult, the charismatic leader "has a hold over his people that allows him to say things which his followers accept as truth but which strike rational people as madness." Rockwell offered a safe home for the true believer, a "haven to the dispossessed."[32]

Recent scholars—notably Michael Barkun and Jeffrey Kaplan—have explored the millenarian aspects of the racist right, within which Rockwell's ANP and WUNS clearly fall. They correctly identify the evolution of such groups in the post-World War II era from secular political movements to rigid belief systems that exhibit characteristics of apocalyptic religious sects. According to Barkun, these groups encompass "a worldview that is complex, all embracing, and culturally deviant" built around a specific set of core beliefs: Identity theology, a four-tier racial cosmology in which Aryans hold the top position and Jews the bottom, the existence of a worldwide Jewish conspiracy, Nazism as the optimal political vehicle to bring about racial purity, and a millenarian view of history.[33] While WUNS did not originally posit the millenarian or Identity theology elements of Barkun's identified core beliefs, Rockwell, under the tutelage of Bruno Ludtke, recognized the political value of a spiritual dimension to his propaganda arsenal and was in the process of incorporating his own unique theological twist into the neo-Nazi cosmology when he was murdered in 1967.[34]

Increasingly, as Rockwell concentrated his attention and effort on his struggle for dominance within the global racist right more than on any meaningful pursuit of political power, he drew a tighter and tighter circle around himself and demanded the exclusive allegiance of his followers, which increased their isolation while elevating their sense of chosenness. Rockwell's world, the world of demons and fantasy, of intrigue and conspiracy, that was the neo-Nazi culture of the 1960s, was the very "oppositional milieu" that nurtured manifestations of cult-like behavior that marked the ANP and, to an increasing degree, WUNS.[35] This "supportive cultic milieu" encouraged Rockwell's deviance from the more conventional right.[36]

By the time of Rockwell's death in August of 1967, the course he had set for WUNS was firmly established. WUNS would eventually be eclipsed within the international racist right by newer, more vigorous and more violent incarnations of the neo-Nazi impulse, but that decline was consistent with the behavior within a "cultic milieu [that] is continually giving birth to new cults, absorbing the debris of the dead ones and creating new generations of cult-prone individuals."[37] By the early 1990s, Colin Jordan, Bruno Ludtke, and Matt Koehl—Rockwell's successor as head of the ANP and as international commander of WUNS—were old men. They had lost none of their zeal, but their activities were limited to publishing racist tracts, hagiographic biographies of Rockwell and nostalgic recollections of a time they saw as their "golden age." They were incapable of controlling the passions that exploded on the racist right over the fall of communism and the reunification of Germany. A new generation of seekers and outcasts found answers within an "idealization of violence."[38] They seized upon the answers offered by neo-Nazism for their alienation and found in the camaraderie of other true believers as relief from their isolation.[39] While they regarded the old leaders as irrelevant, the new true believers soon reestablished the familiar international network, exploiting the channels first established by Rockwell and WUNS. The network reformed around new leaders— Ingo Hasselbach in Europe and Gary Rex Lauck in the United States—while retaining the essential mission to "unite, purify, and energize" those like them who crave the security of a like-minded cadre within an "oppositional milieu."

More than any other neo-Nazi leader of the early 1990s, Gary Rex Lauck (AKA Gerhard Lauck) embodied the Rockwell tradition for a new generation of neo-Nazis. Ambitious and shrewd, Lauck's NSDAP/AO (the acronym for the German "National German Socialist Workers Party/Foreign Organization") mirrored Rockwell's ANP in organizational structure, rhetoric and international ambition. In 1992, Lauck struggled with, and overthrew, the leadership of WUNS-Europe, Danish Nazi Party commander Riis-Knudsen, but it was Lauck, not Knudsen or WUNS, that was the ideological and tactical heir of George Lincoln Rockwell.[40] Even Lauck's signature "White Power" movement had its origins in Rockwell's core strategy.[41]

Lauck's future, or the future of any specific leader or group within the neo-Nazi movement, is impossible to predict. Only the instability of individuals and organizations within that continuing cultic milieu is safely predictable. Strategies and tactics have evolved, and will continue to do so. At the close of the twentieth century, neo-Nazis are fully utilizing new technology which changes the form of presentation, but the message—violent racism, anti-Semitism, illiberal politics—is unchanged.[42]

Notes

[1] Among the works that explore various aspects of the connection between Nazi ideology and mysticism as manifested in post-war neo-Nazism, and of Rockwell's role in that process, are: David H. Bennett, *The Party of Fear: From Nativist Movements to the Militia Movement in American History* (Chapel Hill, NC: University of North Carolina Press, 1988); James A. Aho, *The Politics of Righteousness: Idaho Christian Patriotism* (Seattle: University of Washington Press, 1990); Roger Griffin, *The Nature of Fascism* (New York: Routledge, 1993); Michael Barkun, *Religion and the Racist Right: The Origins of the Christian Identity Movement* (Chapel Hill, NC: University of North Carolina Press, 1994); Ingo Hasselbach with Tom Reiss, *Führer-Ex* (New York: Random House, 1996); Walter Laqueur, *Fascism: Past, Present, Future* (New York: Oxford University Press, 1996); Sara Diamond, *Roads to Dominion: Right-Wing Movements and Political Power in the United States* (New York: Guilford Press, 1997); and Frederick J. Simonelli, "Preaching Hate with the Voice of God: American Neo-Nazis and Christian Identity," *Patterns of Prejudice* 30 (April 1996), 43-54.

[2] Joachim Fest, "Enthusiasm and Confusion" in Allan Mitchell, ed., *The Nazi Revolution*, 3rd edition (Lexington, MA: D.C. Heath & Co., 1990), 112.

[3] See Eric Hoffer, *The True Believer* (New York: Harper & Brothers, 1951).

[4] See Frederick J. Simonelli, "The American Nazi Party, 1958-1967," *The Historian* 57(Spring 1995), 553-66; for a contemporary view, see Charles Krause, "George Lincoln Rockwell: A Myth or Real Threat to America's Peace," *Private Affairs* (June 1962), 52.

[5] William L. Pierce, *Lincoln Rockwell: A National Socialist Life* (Arlington, VA: NS Publications, 1969), 24.

[6] See George Lincoln Rockwell, *This Time The World*, 3rd edition (Liverpool, WV: White Power Publications, 1979).

[7] Colin Jordan to author, 7 September 1995.

[8] Also present at that initial meeting in Ireland was John Tyndall, NSM's deputy commander who later broke with Jordan and formed a rival National Socialist group in Great Britain, the British National Party. Although transatlantic organization was WUNS's primary focus, Rockwell and Jordan envisioned WUNS as a truly worldwide organization. Between the creation of WUNS in 1962 and Rockwell's death in 1967, national affiliates included chapters in Lebanon, Japan, South Africa, and Australia.

[9] See Frederick J. Simonelli, "The World Union of National Socialists and Post-War Transatlantic Nazi Revival," in Tore Bjørgo and Jeffrey Kaplan, eds., *Nation and Race: The Developing Euro-American Racist Subculture* (Northeastern University Press, 1998); author to Colin Jordan, 27 July 1995; Colin Jordan to author, 10 August 1995 and 7 September 1995; Colin Jordan telephone interview by author, 29 January 1996.

[10] "First Working Draught of the Cotswold Agreements," Folder: Followers & Supporters, Rockwell, 60-62, Box 138, Blaustein Library, American Jewish Committee.

[11] "Savitri Devi: A Souvenir," *NS [National Socialist] Bulletin #330* (Fourth Quarter, 1992), 7. Devi's main works of Aryan mysticism and National Socialist philosophy are *Gold in the Furnace* (1949), *Defiance* (1951), *Pilgrimage* (1953). Cf. Nicholas Goodrick-Clark, *Hitler's Priestess: Savitri Devi, the Hindu-Aryan Myth, and Occult Neo-Nazism* (New York: New York University Press, 1998).

[12] Bruno Ludtke to GLR, 11 January 1962; Bruno Ludtke to GLR, 7 July 1965. Private collection of James Mason.

[13] Bruno Ludtke to GLR, 29 June 1964, Ludtke defers to his precarious legal position by admonishing Rockwell that "you should never announce me to anyone as 'commander of the German unit.'" Also see, Bruno Ludtke to GLR, 19 February 1966; Bruno Ludtke to Colin Jordan, 28 June 1965; Bruno Ludtke to Matt Koehl, 16 January 1966. Private collection of James Mason.

[14] GLR to Colin Jordan, 20 January 1963; Bertha Beecham Jordan to GLR, 22 December 1962. Private collection of James Mason.

[15] Colin Jordan to GLR, 18 August 1962; GLR to Bruno Ludtke, 25 December 1963; Bruno Ludtke to GLR, 4 November 1965. Also see, Erika Himmler [aka Barbara Warren] interview, *Spiegel* 39(19 September 1966), 130. Translated by Bruno Ludtke for Rockwell, Bruno Ludtke to GLR, 23 September 1966. Private collection of James Mason. Himmler/Warren was Secretary of the ANP's Chicago Unit and the only female to hold a position of authority in the ANP.

[16] [Franz] Pfeiffer to GLR, 6 December 1962; GLR to Colin Jordan, 3 September 1962, and 29 July 1963; GLR to Bruno Ludtke, 19 September 1964; Bruno Ludtke to GLR, 20 July 1965; Bruno Ludtke to GLR, 14 September 1964; Colin Jordan to GLR, 4 February 1965; GLR to Colin Jordan, 20 February 1965. Private collection of James Mason.

[17] Bruno Ludtke to Colin Jordan, undated [ca. July, 1964] and 18 February 1967; GLR to Colin Jordan, 20 December 1964, and 1 January 1965; Bruno Ludtke to GLR, 10 March 1965, and 26 December 1966. Private collection of James Mason. Also, audio tape, GLR at the University of North Dakota, November 1965.

[18] Fine and Himmelfarb, *American Jewish Year Book 1961*, 108-9; Fine and Himmelfarb, *American Jewish Year Book 1962*, 287.

[19] Colin Jordan to GLR, 16 June 1965. Private collection of James Mason. Robert Smith to author, 28 June 1991. Smith is the National Secretary of the Nationalist Party of Canada, the re-named Western Guard Party, and chief aide to Don Andrews. Bruno Ludtke to GLR, 7 July 1965; GLR to Colin Jordan, 15 May 1966, and 26 June 1966; GLR to John Beattie, 6 May 1967. Private collection of James Mason. For internal political purposes, Beattie always played down his connection to Rockwell, but their relationship was close, friendly, mutually supportive, and cooperative. In addition to the correspondence cited above, see John Garrity, "I Spied On the Nazis," *Maclean's Magazine,* 1 October 1966, quoted and cited in Fine and Himmelfarb, *American Jewish Yearbook 1967*, 268. According to Fine and Himmelfarb, the Canadian Jewish Congress confirmed the Garrity article as to its "general accuracy." In the article, Garrity documents a meeting between Beattie and Rockwell and concluded that a strong and dependent link existed from Beat-

tie to Rockwell. To research the article, Garrity, an investigative reporter, infiltrated Beattie's organization.

[20] Helene Lööw to Jeffrey Kaplan, 3 April 1996, from translation of her interview with Goren Assar Oredsson. Professor Lööw generously provided copies of correspondence and publications relating to Goren Assar Oredsson and the Nordiska Rikspartiet for this study; "What Is the Meaning of NAZISM?" (Nordiska Rikspartiet, ca. 1975). Also, Tore Bjørgo, "Militant Neo-Nazism in Sweden," *Terrorism and Political Violence* 5(Autumn 1993), 32-33.

[21] See Colin Jordan to GLR, 26 May 1965; Friedrich Kuhfuss to Colin Jordan, 13 May 1965; Bruno Ludtke to GLR, 24 May 1965. Colin Jordan to GLR, 23 September 1962; Colin Jordan to GLR, 26 May 1965. Private collection of James Mason; Lööw to Kaplan, 3 April 1996; George Lincoln Rockwell to Vera Lindholm, Nordiska Rikspartiet, 7 September 1962; also see, *Frjals Europa*, December 1962.

[22] GLR to Colin Jordan, 20 November 1964, and 15 May 1966; Colin Jordan to GLR, 9 March 1964, 20 August 1964, and 31 October 1964; Bernard E. Horgan to GLR, 26 March 1966; GLR to Bernard E. Horgan, 20 April 1966. Private collection of James Mason.

[23] "Friedrich Kuhfuss" was the pseudonym used by an unidentified German Nazi. Colin Jordan to GLR, 29 July 1964, and 19 August [1965]; Friedrich Kuhfuss to Colin Jordan, 13 May 1965; Friedrich Kuhfuss to GLR, 30 May 1965. Private collection of James Mason.

[24] Colin Jordan to GLR, 19 November 1963. Private collection of James Mason.

[25] Bruno Ludtke to GLR, 5 May 1962. Private collection of James Mason.

[26] Bertha Beecham Jordan to GLR, 22 December 1962; Colin Jordan to GLR, 27 August 1963, 3 August 1963, 27 July 1963, 29 July 1963, and 28 October [1963]; Bruno Ludtke to Colin Jordan, undated [ca. December, 1963]; Before recruiting Normand/Jannes, Rockwell and Jordan suffered a "false start" when they tried to work with Jean-Claude Monet, editor of *Le Viking* and head of the French Organization of the Swastika. That collaboration was unsuccessful. See Colin Jordan to GLR, 25 August 1963. Private collection of James Mason.

[27] Bruno Ludtke to GLR, undated [ca. 1965]; Colin Jordan to GLR, 19 August [1965], and 26 May 1966; Colin Jordan to Yves Jeanne, 1 August 1966. Private collection of James Mason. The circumstances of Yves Jeanne's assumption of command from Claude Janne (aka Claude Normand) are unclear from extant documents. One former ANP member I interviewed believed that Yves Jeanne was just another pseudonym for Claude Janne and that the "old fighter" himself led the abortive coup. Although not to be dismissed since, in the Byzantine world of Nazi politics of this era, *anything* is possible, I found no corroboration for this theory and believe it mistaken.

[28] Colin Jordan to GLR, 20 July [1963], 3 August 1963, and undated memo [ca. August 1965]; Colin Jordan to GLR, 28 October [1963]; Colin Jordan to Rudiger van Sande, 29 July 1965; Colin Jordan to GLR, undated memo [ca. August 1965, and 16 August 1965; Colin Jordan to Rudiger van Sande, 29 July 1965; Bruno Ludtke to Colin Jordan, 29 October 1966; Bruno Ludtke to GLR, 17 April 1966. Private collection of James Mason.

[29] Bruno Ludtke to GLR, [2?] September 1961, 9 November 1961, 4 February 1962, and 18 August 1962; GLR to Bruno Ludtke, 1 October 1961. Private collection of James Mason.

[30] Among the most active disciples Ludtke enlisted were Wolfgang Kirchstein, Erich Lindner, Reinhold Ruppe, Werner Knoss, and Dietrich Schuler. GLR to Bruno Ludtke, 11 July 1964; Werner Knoss to GLR, undated [ca. March, 1964]; GLR to Werner Knoss,

5 April 1964; Bruno Ludtke to GLR, 5 May 1964, 24 May 1964, and 31 July 1965; Bruno Ludtke to Colin Jordan, 2 August 1965, and 18 February 1967; Colin Jordan to GLR, 26 May 1966; Bruno Ludtke to William L. Pierce, 10 August 1966. Private collection of James Mason. Also see, "Are Europe's Jews in Danger?" *The ADL Bulletin* 22 (September, 1965), 1-2, 6. The West German government frequently complained to the U.S. government about the flood of pro-Nazi and anti-Semitic literature entering that country from the United States. See FBI File #9-39854: George Lincoln Rockwell, Monograph, "American Nazi Party," June, 1965. Rockwell was the source and Ludtke the distributor.

[31] See Umberto Eco, "Ur-Fascism," *The New York Review* (22 June 1995), 12-15. Also, Stanley G. Payne, *A History of Fascism, 1914-1945* (New York: Oxford University Press, 1996), 48, and Robert O. Paxton, "The Uses of Fascism," *The New York Review* (28 November 1996), 48-52.

[32] Michael Scott Cain, "The Charismatic Leader," *The Humanist* 48(November/December 1988), 23.

[33] Michael Barkun, "Millenarian Aspects of 'White Supremacist' Movements," *Terrorism and Political Violence* 1(October 1989), 417-18. Also see Jeffrey Kaplan, "The Context of American Millenarian Revolutionary Theology: The Case of the 'Identity Christian' Church of Israel," *Terrorism and Political Violence* 5(Spring 1993), 30-82.

[34] See Frederick J. Simonelli, "Preaching Hate with the Voice of God: American Neo-Nazis and Christian Identity," *Patterns of Prejudice* 30(April 1996), 43-54. Also see Michael Barkun, *Religion and the Racist Right: The Origins of the Christian Identity Movement* (Chapel Hill: University of North Carolina Press, 1994), 50-56.

[35] The phrase "oppositional milieu" is from Jeffrey Kaplan, "Right Wing Violence in North America," *Terrorism and Political Violence* 7(Spring 1995), 44-95, and includes groups within the U.S. racist right that "share such primary characteristics" as "a Golden Age Myth, the perception of a 'Theft of Culture,' scripturalism, a manichaean world view, a conspiratorial view of history, a vision of the group as an 'elect' . . . and finally, an apocalyptic or chiliastic analysis of society." (46)

[36] Colin Campbell, "The Cult, the Cultic Milieu and Secularization," *Sociological Yearbook of Religion in Britain* 5(1972), 121. For a useful analysis of the phenomenon of alienation and cult formation within the racist right, see Gilbert Abcarian and Sherman M. Stanage, "Alienation and the Radical Right," *The Journal of Politics* 27(November 1965), 776-796, and Arnold M. Eisen, "The Rhetoric of Chosenness," *Society* 28(November/December 1990), 26-33. For a more general understanding of cult formation and behavior, see Jeffrey E. Pfeifer, "The Psychological Framing of Cults: Schematic Representations and Cult Evaluations," *Journal of Applied Psychology* 22(April 1992), 531-44.

[37] Campbell, 121-22; Rockwell's surviving disciples maintained allegiance to his core beliefs long after his death. See, for example, Colin Jordan, "The Way Ahead, Part 4: Folk," *Gothic Ripples* (March 1996).

[38] Jurg Dedial, "Living With Neo-Nazism? *Swiss Review of World Affairs* (January 1993), 4.

[39] See Ingo Hasselbach, *Fuehrer-Ex*; also, Jonathan Schell, "Hatred's Roots Run Deep," *Newsday*, reprinted in the *Sacramento Bee* (17 December 1992) and Tom Reiss, "Interview with Ingo Hasselbach," *At Random* (December 1995), 12-19.

[40] Erik Jensen, "International Nazi Cooperation: A Terrorist-Oriented Network," in Tore Bjørgo and Rob Witte, eds., *Racist Violence in Europe* (New York: St. Martin's Press, 1993).

[41] See George Lincoln Rockwell, *White Power* (Reedy, WV: Liberty Bell Publications, reprinted, 1983) and Frederick J. Simonelli, *American Fuehrer: George Lincoln Rockwell and the American Nazi Party* (University of Illinois Press, forthcoming 2000).

[42] See Les Back, Michael Keith, and John Solomos, "Technology, Race and Neo-Fascism in a Digital Age: The New Modalities of Racist Culture," *Patterns of Prejudice* 30(April 1996)3-27. The authors trace utilization of the Internet, electronic bulletin board systems, the World Wide Web (WWW), and e-mail by contemporary neo-Nazis. The extent of such utilization is considerable. In Sweden, for example, the authors have identified up to 20 active neo-Nazi bulletin board systems (BBS) accessible through the Internet. Also, Web Pages such as "Greater White Amerikkka" (<http://www.io.com/~wlp/aryan-page/cng/other.html>)and "Stormfront" (http://www.stormfront.wat.com/stormfront/>), in addition to racist, anti-Semitic, and neo-Nazi messages and illustrations, provide electronic links to over three dozen other racist and anti-Semitic sites. Those sites, in turn, often provide additional linkages to still other sites.

The Postwar Paths of Occult National Socialism

From Rockwell and Madole to Manson

Jeffrey Kaplan

Someone did say that prior to 1945 we were a party, since 1945 we have been a religion. —James Mason[1]

The Commander

The 1967 assassination of the American Nazi Party (ANP) leader George Lincoln Rockwell had a tremendous impact on the evolving Euro-American radical right. At a stroke, the primary candidate for trans-Atlantic movement leadership was removed from the scene, leaving not only the ANP in turmoil with no obvious successor to the "Commander," but returning the World Union of National Socialists (WUNS) to its original essence: a quarrelsome band of radical nationalists with no central focus to their interminable arguments and utopian scheming. In assessing the impact of Rockwell's loss, we need but to note the ambivalent sentiments of Swedish National Socialist leader Göran Assar Oredsson who in 1956 founded the Nordiska Rikspartiet in Malmö, Sweden:

> I can never forgive the USA's war against Europe, even if the guilt is not to be put on the U.S. National Socialists. . . But I want to stress that my friendship with Lincoln Rockwell was total, and so was our co-operation with him as a person and American NS-leader.[2]

Yet this same Oredsson was devastated upon learning of Rockwell's death:

> I was on my way down south [when] . . . I stopped to pick up the evening papers. The headlines cried out to me: "He wanted to be America's Hitler" (*Afonbladet*); "[A] Sniper killed America's Hitler" (*Kvallsposten*); "He wanted to be a new Hitler. . . . His dream ended here" (*Expressed*).
>   At that movement I wanted to believe—yes wish—that I was dreaming, that I had read wrong. BUT NO, it came clear to me that George Lincoln Rockwell, the USA's National Socialist leader, was no more among us. Again I had to face how a friend, an ideo-

logical companion and battle comrade had fallen in our united battle-field in the struggle against our united enemy.

In movements like this . . . there are no barriers and distances between the different continents. The distance to a friend and battle companion is never more far away then the distance to your own hearth. It was sometime during 1957 that I first came into contact with Rockwell. It was from letters. Rockwell's letters were many and long. My English was surely not what it should be, but with a friend's help our correspondence was the best you could ask for. Rockwell's letters revealed a brain as sharp as a knife. . . .He gave in his letters almost philosophical explanations and had the most interesting explanations . . . regarding National Socialism and its ideologists. Why he had the swastika as a symbol, why he called his party Nazi, etc. etc.

I first judged him as a deskfighter. Yes even as a fruitless theoretician. But I was soon to change my mind. It was when his papers *The Rockwell Report, National Socialist Bulletin* and *Storm-trooper* arrived. From pictures and articles, his movement proved to be the most brave and hard fighting Stormtroopers as any one could ask for. And everywhere in these pictures of the struggle, the leader Rockwell was in the front, as the leader, the speaker, the organizer and the hero, when it comes to courage and fighting spirit. [3]

Rockwell's death in fact left a vacuum from which the highly fragmented National Socialist world is yet to recover. Within that vacuum there is considerable space for the occult paths of National Socialism (NS) to take root and grow. This should come as little surprise. Occult currents were never far from the surface of the Third Reich's inner circle,[4] and even so avowedly an atheistic figure as the Commander, Rockwell himself, would confide in his closest confidants his own deeply mystical attachment to the figure of Adolf Hitler. In this, Rockwell was always of two minds. On the outside, his approach to religion had a strongly utilitarian quality to it. How better to awaken the slumbering white masses to the imminent danger he saw to the race than by means of a religious appeal? It is notable that in 1958, Rockwell did not see the Jewish conquest of the nations of the earth as yet accomplished. Such was the tenor of the radical right of the 1950s and 1960s. It was felt that if only people could be awakened, there was still time to reclaim the nations of the earth from the dread machinations of the "International Jew." But how to awaken the sleeping masses before it was too late?

The answer occurred to key Rockwell associates early on, but the Commander was reluctant until it was made clear that the religious strategy was a mere Trojan horse. Why not link National Socialism to religion—and in particular, to Christianity? For Rockwell, National Socialism was already his religion in every sense of the term, and he revered the figure of Adolf Hitler in clearly soteriological terms.[5] In his autobiography, *This Time the World!*, and even more openly in the writings of two generations of movement hagiographers, Rockwell describes his own conversion to National Socialism in explicitly religious terms.[6]

First, there was the motif of the spiritual quest—in this case in the San Diego public library in a frantic search for the truth underlying the dross of everyday events. Then there was the discovery of *Mein Kampf* on a back shelf in a musty book shop. This was a truly life-changing experience, and William Pierce's description of Rockwell's fascination with the book eerily presages the scene in his influential apocalyptic novel *The Turner Diaries,* in which the protagonist, Earl Turner, is allowed to read the Organization's Holy Book which, like Rockwell's reading of *Mein Kampf,* suddenly drew away the veil of illusion which masked the numinous realities of the world. In Pierce's accounts, neither Rockwell nor the fictional Turner would ever again see the world in the same way following this deeply mystical experience.[7] But there was more. According to intimate comrades, Rockwell confessed to having a series of extraordinarily vivid and nearly identical prophetic dreams in which, in a variety of everyday contexts, he was called aside from crowded commonplace situations to a private room where standing before him was his newfound god, Adolf Hitler.[8] It was not long before Rockwell was moved to build a literal alter to his deity, hanging a Nazi flag that covered an entire wall of his home, under which he placed a table containing a bust of Hitler, three candles and candle holders, and

> I closed the blinds and lit the candles, and stood before my new altar. For the first time since I had lost my Christian religion, I experienced the soul thrilling upsurge of emotion which is denied to our modern, sterile, atheist "intellectuals" but which literally moved the earth for countless centuries: "religious experience." I stood there in the flickering candlelight, not a sound in the house, not a soul aware of what I was doing—or caring.[9]

William Pierce, an intimate of Rockwell and the publisher of the ANP's party organs, waxes lyrical over this experience. Describing it in terms familiar to any student of mysticism, East or West, Pierce writes:

> It was a religious experience that was more than religious. As he stood there he felt an indescribably torrent of emotions surging through his being, reaching higher and higher in a crescendo with a peak of unbearable intensity. He felt the awe inspiring awareness for a few moments, or a few minutes, of being more than himself, of being in communion with that which is beyond description and beyond comprehension. Something with the cool vast feeling of eternity and of infinity—of long ages spanning the birth and death of suns, and of immense, starry vistas—filled his soul to the bursting point. One may call that Something by different names—the Great Spirit perhaps, or Destiny, or the Soul of the universe, or God—but once it has brushed the soul of a man, that man can never again be wholly what he was before. It changes him spiritually the same way a mighty earthquake or a cataclysmic eruption, the subsidence of a continent or the bursting forth of a new mountain range, changes forever the face of the earth.[10]

Having come face to face with the ineffable, little wonder that Rockwell would be dubious of linking National Socialism with any other religion. But America is a deeply religious nation,[11] and to build a mass movement in the United States, it is essential that this reality be addressed. As a competitor in the religious marketplace, National Socialism clearly had little mass appeal. While far more secular in orientation than America, Europe too evinced a spiritual void that some of Rockwell's closest domestic allies as well as influential voices within the World Union of National Socialists hoped to fill. Finding a way to graft National Socialism with Christianity was one option. The established racialist doctrine of Christian Identity suggested yet other possibilities.

The syncretic melding of National Socialism with Christianity was an obvious non-starter on both sides of the Atlantic. In America, the intensely negative association of the term "Nazi" had a certain utility to Rockwell in gaining attention for his fledgling movement, but to seek to link the much demonized figure of Hitler to Christ, even obliquely, would surely have aroused outrage greater than even Rockwell was prepared to contemplate while at the same time risking alienating his base of NS true believers.

Prospects for success in such an endeavor in Europe were little better. There, besides the predictable public outrage, there was the problem of the state churches to deal with. It was a problem that was never fully solved in Hitler's Germany, despite the terrifying power at the disposal of the state to enforce compliance with its will.[12] Thus it is the figure of Dietrich Bonhoeffer who is remembered and revered today, while those in the churches who compromised or collaborated are long forgotten. But if not the dogma of Christianity, at least its organizational structure—particularly in its Catholic form—could serve as a model for a National Socialist church structure that one day, after the "great awakening" of the European masses to the clarion call of the Führer's vision, would supplant "Jewish Christianity." And what a delicious irony it would be for the Jews (and no doubt for most Christians) to wake up one day to find that "thousands of priests and monks [would] suddenly throw off their habits and robes . . . and reveal the full glory of their National Socialist organization."[13]

The prime mover in this plan seems to have been the German WUNS leader, Bruno Ludke, although as early as 1957 Rockwell seems to have toyed with the idea of creating some sort of National Socialist Christian front group.[14] The Ludke/Rockwell discussions began in 1962 when Ludke, the German translator of *This Time the World!*, suggested that passages critical of dealing with Christianity be softened. For Ludke, the Catholic church presented a marvelous model in which Rockwell could speak with the "political authority of the Führer and the moral authority of the Pope."[15]

This unlikely aggregation was to be called the Christian Naturalist Church whose primary dogma appeared to center on stressing the similarities which they perceived between Hitler and Jesus. In this, the historic role of Christianity in persecuting the Jews made the proposition of creating a false flag form of "Christianity" to accomplish this purpose doubly attractive. Ironically, the WUNS member most skeptical of the enterprise was England's Colin Jordan, who in the 1990s would devote much of his writing in his journal *Gothic Ripples* to strongly religious themes of a decidedly Odinist flavor.[16]

Of course, the Christian Naturalist Church, like so many of Rockwell's stratagems, went nowhere. The press of events, the rush of ideas, the constant pressures of leading an organization boasting a bare handful of capable followers, and incessant street confrontations allowed Rockwell little time to see any idea through to fruition. But if the Christian Naturalist Church was not to take the movement by storm, Rockwell's flirtation with Identity Christianity had greater potential. Identity, after all, in its earlier incarnation as British Israelism, already had roots in England, while in the 1950s, modern Christian Identity was emerging in a big way on the American racist scene.[17]

Once again, Rockwell believed that Identity could serve as a cover for the emergence of a trans-Atlantic National Socialist revolution. He would not be able to see the plan to fruition as he was felled by an assassin's bullet before significant Euro-American linkages could be established in the Identity world. But unlike the fanciful Christian Naturalist Church, Christian Identity did have significant appeal beyond American shores.

Rockwell's introduction to the esoteric world of Identity Christianity took place in the early 1960s through his friendship with Richard Butler, then an engineer in California and a disciple of Wesley Swift, the father of American racialist Identity. Butler introduced Swift to Rockwell, who in any case was well acquainted with a number of Identity figures of the era.[18] Rockwell proposed some form of merger between the ANP and Swift's organization;[19] an idea which was never to come to fruition but which indicated the degree of respect the two held for each other. This did not, however, mean that Rockwell was about to fall under the charismatic Swift's spell and adopt Identity as his own.

Rather, Rockwell saw an opportunity to infiltrate the Identity movement and to turn it gradually to National Socialism. For the purpose, he tapped an ideal candidate, Ralph Forbes, a young ANP captain and the commander of the organization's western division who even then was known to possess a marked mystical streak. In 1965, Rockwell laid his scheme before Forbes, who enthusiastically accepted the assignment.[20] Rockwell would not live to see the outcome of the plan. Had he lived, however, the history of Identity Christianity may have been considerably different. As it was, Forbes' "conversion" eventually evolved from a covert operation to a true believer, and he remains to this day an Identity minister in Arkansas. Other ANP stalwarts who would leave or fall victim to Matt Koehl-era purges too drifted to Christian Identity—James Warner comes to mind in this regard.[21]

James Hartung Madole

James Hartung Madole—a contemporary of Rockwell—was an obscure East Coast National Socialist figure too idiosyncratic by far for the Commander's American Nazi Party. This alone would be no small claim to fame. However, what launched Madole to relative prominence was a 1954 investigation of

American fascism by the House Un-American Activities Committee (HUAC). The Committee, better known as being at the cutting edge of the Red Scare of the 1940s-1950s, in the interest of even-handedness occasionally opened hearings in regard to the activities of such right-wing figures as Gerald L. K. Smith.[22] By 1954 however, the HUAC, in a less sanguine mood, opened new hearings on domestic fascist groups. By then, books such as the influential tome by Ralph Lord Roy, *Apostles of Discord* (1953), had given added credence to earlier investigations of post-war fascism by authors such as the pseudonymous John Roy Carlson, which argued that American fascism, though much diminished, had survived the war.[23]

This apparent resurgence of native fascism alarmed Congress sufficiently to move the House Un-American Activities Committee in 1954 to reopen hearings specifically focused on the subject for the first time since the 1938 examination of the German American Bund. Congressional reasoning continued to equate fascism with communism; a belief which the 1954 report stated succinctly:

> Both totalitarian doctrines [fascism and communism] are basically incompatible with the principles of our Republic. Both seek to destroy our constitutional government and supplant it with a godless dictatorship in which the individual is deprived of his rights and liberties to become an abject slave of the state. Both derive strength by dividing the opposition—communism choosing to set class against class, while fascism incites racial and religious discord.
>
> Furthermore, the appearance of neo-fascist organizations and methods in the postwar period serves only to impede the intelligent, united effort necessary in the current life or death struggle with communism.[24]

With this formulation, the HUAC neatly dismissed the radical right's self-image as the "watchmen on the wall" in the nation's battle against international communism. This settled, the Committee quickly set its sights on James Hartung Madole and his National Renaissance Party (NRP) as the prime exemplar of contemporary American neo-fascism. Madole, a strong admirer of Francis Parker Yockey's *Imperium*, retained a strong interest in events in Europe, as well as the emerging Third World liberation struggles, but his true legacy to the movement was his later efforts to link National Socialist doctrine to the occult, and in particular, to the worlds of Theosophy and of explicit Satanism in the 1960s. Madole was largely an isolated figure at this stage of his life—communicating his highly eclectic message through the pages of his *National Renaissance Bulletin* until his untimely death from cancer at the age of 51.

After his death, Madole was largely forgotten by the movement to which he contributed so much. Today, however, Madole is experiencing something of a personal renaissance in the writings of movement figures on both sides of the Atlantic as a visionary whose thought was decades ahead of his time.[25] Moreover, Madole helped to plant the seeds for renewed transatlantic cooperation through his European contacts, especially in Sweden. Yet at the same time, Madole's National Renaissance Party endorsed a strongly activist platform, which contrasted sharply with the borderless racial nationalism that the NRP held equally dear. It is a schizophrenia which afflicts the movement to this day. It would therefore be valuable to consider the NRP's original nine-point platform which appears to hold two central, and utterly contradictory tenets; racial nationalism and nativist Americanism. Published in the October 1953 issue of the *National Renaissance Bulletin*, the platform's preamble affirms a dedication to the welfare of the racial collective over the interests of any individual, and states that the current political parties serve "the interests of international Jewry." The preamble reveals a constellation of beliefs which would become ubiquitous in the movement; a fear of declining white birthrates, fear of intermarriage (especially with Jews), but of greatest resonance, a preoccupation with purity and disease, both in its metaphorical and clinical senses. This said, the NRP's nine point platform reads as follows:

(1) To encourage racial nationalism among the peoples of Europe, Africa and Asia as an antidote to the spread of international communism. . . . We must also repudiate the operetta-state of Israel unless we wish to drive the entire Middle East into the open arms of Soviet Russia in order that our political windbags in Washington may appease a howling pack of New York kikes, whose sole contributions to American culture have been syphilis and usury.

(2) To enforce a strict policy of racial segregation in America in order to preserve and advance the culturally dominant White Aryan Race which brought the cultural and social benefits of Western Civilization to our shores in 1492. (By the "Aryan Race" we refer to the Nordic, Celtic, Anglo-Saxon, Latin and Slavic peoples.)

(3) To bring about a gradual deportation of those racial elements which cannot be assimilated with the culturally predominant White Race. Laws must be passed to prevent racial intermarriage. (Those racial elements which cannot be assimilated in the Aryan racial community are the Puerto Ricans, Negroes, Jews and Asiatics.)

(4) The Jewish race which constitutes the motivating financial and intellectual force behind Communism, shall be deprived of their American citizenship and hence barred from all political and professional posts. Marriage between Jews and the dominant White Race will be forbidden. (During the past 20 years the Jews have managed to obtain a tremendous hold on American politics, art, culture and commerce. No people on earth with a vestige of pride in itself and national honor will tolerate such a domination of the KEY professions by members of a completely ALIEN race. At the same time, the Jews are a determining factor in those political parties which have sought to undermine the last vestiges of racial and national pride in America. The Jew constitutes an Alien virus in our national bloodstream and as such must be purged from our cultural, economic and political life.)

(5) To bring about the withdrawal of the United States from the United Nations in order to prevent further exploitation of American resources and manpower by foreign parasites. (In regard to foreign trade, America must develop a policy of preserving the American

market for the American farmer and manufacturer. America must "Buy American" and subsidize, if necessary, American scientific ingenuity toward the end of producing chemically many of those products which are not found in here in America but upon which the nation is dependent.)

(6) The alliance of German scientific and military genius combined with American technology, mass production technique and manpower could dominate both the American and European continents. Therefore our foreign policy must have the three fold objective of realizing a German-American alliance in Europe, a Moslem-American alliance in the Middle East, and a Japanese-American alliance in Asia.

(7) The Creation of an American Corporate Economy wherein labor and management will be equally represented in an Economic Dept. of the Federal Government . . .

(8) The abolition of parliamentary government [in favor of a] national minded elite.

(9) The use of all educational facilities to imbue the American youth with an intense feeling of racial and national pride as a sure antidote to the international poison of World Communism.[26]

The NRP's 1953 program document is a remarkable encapsulation of the dilemmas facing the movement today. Save for the somewhat archaic references to the menace of "international Communism," the same themes that are endlessly rehashed in contemporary movement discourse are set forth. There are in these nine points a number of remarkable juxtapositions. Point one, the exhortation to racial nationalism, is a staple of modern movement discourse. It is written so as to embrace the Christian Identity doctrine of all creation being returned to its original place and status as based on the Identity hermeneutic of Genesis, but it as easily fits the contemporaneous pattern of the rise of the Non-Aligned Movement on the world stage, or the later convergence of interests between American black nationalists such as the Nation of Islam and the white separatist movements of the 1980s.[27] Indeed, Madole would have a number of successful conclaves with black nationalist organizations.[28] Finally, the reference to Jews having assumed control in Washington presaged the Zionist Occupation Government (ZOG) discourse just as the reference to Jews as bearers of disease linked Madole's anti-Semitism to a far older tradition of anti-Semitic discourse. Yet it is significant that the NRP's platform as an avowedly white nationalist party would be centered on world affairs first, with American concerns added almost as an afterthought. Here in 1953 are the seeds for the creation of a trans-national racial consciousness which is only today taking root in the movement.

Points three and four are standard fare for the time, and have aged not at all, dealing as they do with the forced separation of the races and the Jew as an "alien virus" in the pure bloodstream of America.

Of greater interest are points five and six. Here in stark juxtaposition lies the central contradiction of the post-war movement. Point five is a purely nativist exhortation to look inward, to "buy American" and to utilize science to produce artificially whatever resources cannot be obtained domestically. The sentiment could have been drawn from any number of Depression-era demagogues as easily as it could echo the most fanatically suspicious member of the militia movement of the 1990s. Yet how to reconcile this jingoistic ideal with the international alliance structure mandated by point six, demanding regional alliances with the Arab states and to each of the defeated Axis powers?

In this riddle lie two important observations which hold true of the radical right throughout its modern history. First, anti-Semitism and its concomitant elements of conspiritorialism, an intense quest for "purity" (be it of blood or of the natural environment), and a sense of vulnerability—of a race under siege and in imminent peril of extinction—is the movement's driving force. All else is of secondary import, and it is under the banner of anti-Semitism that any number of contradictory statements and actions can be rationalized by a milieu that is otherwise highly resistant to accepting contradictory information.[29]

Second, for all of its seeming isolation, the radical right is well aware of world events and is on the whole probably better read and more thoroughly informed on current evens than are most citizens. This stems from the ceaseless search for "hidden truths," the bits and pieces of data that are assembled from an eclectic and wide-ranging corpus of sources to assemble in jigsaw-puzzle fashion a picture of the hidden hand underlying the seemingly random course of everyday events. In the process, however, the denizens of the radical right wing come to unconsciously mirror the world they so despise. Thus point one's unconscious encapsulation of the rise of Third World nationalism that would culminate only two years later in the Bandung Conference and the formal creation of the Third Path of the Non-Aligned Movement. And so too point six's suggested alliance pattern at a time when NATO would soon be joined by a series of U.S.-led regional alliances in Asia and Latin America. In many ways, the radical right serves as a kind of caged canary—the bird which miners would take into coal mines to warn of hidden dangers long before they reach the level of consciousness. The study of this esoteric subculture can foretell national controversies yet to take place.[30]

The final points merely seek to institute the practices of the German National Socialist government in 1950s America. Point seven is little more than a lionization of the German National Socialist economic model, while point eight has much the same intent in the political sphere. Point nine completes the trilogy in the area of education.

Like all American radical right wing groups, the National Renaissance Party never amounted to much in terms of numbers, with estimates running as high as 700 or as low as 50.[31]

Madole, an inveterate street corner orator, attracted a small coterie of like-minded followers, a larger group who attended the meetings to heckle or disrupt the proceedings, and a shifting crowd of curious onlookers amused by the spectacle. Yet the group's importance transcends mere numbers. Through its ranks or in the pages of the *National Renaissance Bulletin* passed a number of key figures in the American radical right. The head of the NRP's Nazi uniformed bodyguards for the diminutive Madole, for example, was Matt Koehl, later to take his uniform into the service of George Lincoln Rockwell and the American Nazi Party—an organization he would inherit and through his inept leadership decimate on the death of the Commander.[32] Eustace Mullins, the acolyte of Ezra Pound and later an influential conspiracy theorist, found his early voice in the *National Renaissance Bulletin,* as did such intellectual fascists as Fredrick Charles Weiss and another key figure in the later American Nazi Party, Dan Burros, the author of the ANP's *Stormtrooper Manual* and sometimes Klansman and Odinist. The Jewish Burros, who once seemed headed for a career as a cantor, proved the greatest embarrassment, however, committing suicide in the home of government informant Roy Frankhauser when newspaper revelations of his Orthodox Jewish childhood effectively ended his movement career.[33]

Of interest to the genesis of a post-war transatlantic movement was the NRP's creation of a grandiosely named Overseas Office under the command of Mana Truhill, whose real name was from a movement standpoint less attractive; Emmanuel Trujillo.[34] The NRP's primary overseas contact, according to the HUAC report, was the Swedish father of Holocaust denial, Einar Åberg.[35]

James Madole and his National Renaissance Party would not enjoy the movement's accolades as did Einar Åberg, but he too leaves behind a remarkable, if remarkably different, legacy. The NRP played an important role in paving the way for the more flamboyant and charismatic Rockwell and the WUNS. But of greater import, by the 1960s, Madole's occult explorations began to open new pathways from the occult and neo-pagan revival into the world of anti-Semitism and explicit National Socialism. In truth, an examination of the *National Renaissance Bulletin* over the nearly three decades of its existence reveals little to recommend it to the movement or to historians of the period in any sense other than its mystical explorations along the path first blazed by William Dudley Pelley in the 1930s.[36] Madole's writing style was uninspired,[37] his support for the Soviet Union under the banner of world anti-Semitism was, to be charitable, naïve, and his anti-Semitic screeds and coverage of world and local events added new dimensions of tedium to the term "superficiality."

Moreover, his predictions of American economic and political collapse and the ascendance of world totalitarianism of both the left and the right, which he repeated with all the imagination of the grayest Stalinist aparatchik imaginable, read today as the stuff of farce rather than serious propaganda. But Madole's occultism was of another level altogether. Here, Madole's florid imagination both reflects the occultist currents of the cultic milieu of his day and serves as a kind of archetype of imagined history in which the white race is credited with every achievement of human civilization. Best stated in his ongoing "New Atlantis" series in the 1970s-era *National Renaissance Bulletin,* Madole outlines his conception of the past glories of the race and the chiliastic world to come. In his own words, Madole states that the series' purpose is to "impart to ARYAN MAN both his immense racial heritage stretching back over ONE MILLION YEARS into prehistoric times and his forthcoming Divine Mission to create a higher type of humanity beside which mankind of the 20th century will appear as mental and physical anachronisms."[38] Built of an idiosyncratic reading of history and such spiritualist sources as Madam Blavatsky and the Theosophists, Madole writes:

> The subhuman elements in our society, dominated by the accursed Jew, can only intimidate and govern Aryan Man while he remains in abject ignorance of his glorious racial heritage derived from the hoary archives of Lost Atlantis, Tibet and Mother India. In short, as long as Aryan man remains Christian he will inevitably remain a slave to the Jew who imposed his Semitic heresy upon the Aryan mind! [39]

This formulation was not new, and it would be a recurrent theme in the writings of Odinists, National Socialists, the Church of the Creator, and with the cosmetic change of the adjective "Jewish," in the Christian Identity polemic against "Jewish" Christianity.

Quite unlike other racialists of his generation, the occult explosion of the late 1960s did not catch James Madole unawares. Rather, he was a man ahead of his time for whom the proliferation of religious experimentation of the day was tailor made. Pushing ever further into these explorations, Madole was quickly aware of the formation of Anton LaVey's Church of Satan (COS), and maintained an active and friendly correspondence with LaVey himself. Moreover, such explicitly racialist satanic organizations as the Detroit-based Order of the Black Ram, formed by the Michigan state organizer of the National Renaissance Party, Seth Klippoth, may be traced to Madole's early influence, and maintained close contacts with him and his NRP throughout the 1970s.[40]

Interestingly, the Order of the Black Ram did not choose to make its connections to Madole or its racialist origins and intent part of its own official history, emphasizing instead only its connection to the Church of Satan.[41] The Church of Satan's internal correspondence, however, is much more enlightening on the matter. This material well illustrates both the intertwining of occult and racialist belief systems and the trans-national appeal of racialism's occult path. The material is reproduced in Michael Aquino's unpublished history of the Church of Satan, in which he got his start in the world of satanism and where, before his break with Anton LaVey, he was a member of the COS's governing Council of Nine. LaVey's attitude toward Madole is instructive:

> The N.R.P. headed by Madole is composed largely of acned, bucolic types transplanted to New York. They spend their time getting jeered at in street demonstrations. Yes, the Nazis did it too, but they had a fresh approach. Nowadays swastikas sell books and movies . . . I know Madole personally, and have been to N.R.P. headquarters. Even have a card. They would do anything for us. So would [the] Klan for that matter. I do not endorse either, but acknowledge camaraderie from any source. Madole is actually a nice chap who is doing his thing. No need to fret over Hell's Angels types. They will come in handy one day, whether they be American Nazi Party or Jewish Defense League.[42]

LaVey's genial tolerance of Madole and the NRP was typical enough of the COS and of the wider cultic milieu, but at the same time internal efforts were begun to both co-opt the NRP and to distance the Church from overt associations with National Socialism. The latter undertaking in Aquino's account involved both LaVey and Aquino. The immediate source of their concern was the activities of Seth Klippoth in Detroit. LaVey had been apprised of the news that, soon after his resignation from the COS, Klippoth and other NRP. activists brought their newly formed Order of the Black Ram to an Odinist gathering in Toronto which included representatives of Canada's Western Guard and the National Socialist White People's Party (Matt Koehl's renamed American Nazi Party). Moreover, Madole had made subsequent efforts through Klippoth and others to recruit COS members into their organizations.[43] The result was an intensive round of internal correspondence which would define the Church of Satan's, as well as the later Temple of Set's, official position on Nazism.

It is important to note that to both Aquino and LaVey, German National Socialism and the figure of Adolf Hitler are not seen in a negative light. To Aquino, *Mein Kampf*, if read with the mental resolve to eliminate its references to anti-Semitism as a mere personality quirk of the Führer, is an unrivaled political textbook whose efficacy meets the primary satanic criteria for excellence: it and the governmental doctrines that were propounded under its blueprint work, for they "are the true essence of political power."[44] It is with anti-Semitism, however, that the COS parts company with Nazis:

> Now you may understand why all avowed neo-Nazi groups are pariahs in the eyes of the Church of Satan. First, they know nothing of the true keys of power employed by Hitler. Instead, they glorify the anti-Semitism and the more ostentatious attributes of Nazi Germany which have been glamorized by Hollywood. Secondly, they openly champion Nazi Germany by name, setting themselves up publicly against the Auschwitz taboo. Thirdly, they propose 1930s solutions to 1970s problems.[45]

Aquino concludes with the accurate observation that these "Hollywood Nazis" are regarded by most Americans as "refugees from a loony bin" and that if their longed-for right-wing backlash did occur in the United States, they would be the first to be eliminated, as an American Führer would appear in a business suit rather than a swastika armband and would be touting the values of America in 1776 rather than Germany in the 1930s.[46]

LaVey himself endorses these sentiments, but reveals a more machiavellian turn of mind. Based on his own experience with the NRP and its leader, LaVey sets out the foundation for much of the later interaction between the satanic and the National Socialist worlds which would be so prominent a feature of the 1990s movement:

> The N.R.P. is enamored with the Church of Satan. Their racist ideals are also worn on their sleeves and, I believe, are as removable as their armbands . . . symbolism and symbolism alone supplied their identity. That is how it is with most outlaw groups. There are only two

ingredients necessary for their existence: a symbol and a scapegoat. The N.R.P. already has the swastika, but obviously is drawn to our sigil. They have the "Jews and Niggers," but if properly propagandized could transfer their wrath to our enemies. How? Through just such extensions of propaganda as *Occult Reich* which have emerged from *Satanic Rituals* . . . [Their belief patterns are simple and we] are dealing with intelligence levels on which ideals and imagery are easily interchangeable . . . [thus they think] All my life I've been the weakling, but with my swastika I am strong. My Satanic amulet gives me power. I'm not a misfit anymore, with pimples and a heart murmur and flat feet. What does it matter if I can't play baseball or spell too good? So what if I can't get a girl—I got my armband . . . Maybe we can get the C/S to help us defeat the kikes and niggers so America can be pure again. [47]

It is this desperate search for allies and acceptance in the face of nearly universal hostility and scorn which makes the National Socialist enthusiasts under Madole such ideal candidates for recruitment into the Satanist churches. In the event, LaVey proved prophetic, for this would be a major pattern in the milieu of the trans-national radical right of the 1990s.

This would do little enough for Madole in his lifetime. James Hartung Madole died in 1978. His mother, Grace, tried to keep the already nearly defunct National Renaissance Party alive for the last two years of her life, to little effect. Then in an irony that perfectly symbolized Madole's life's work, the last leader of the NRP died in a common street mugging and the organization's records were scattered to the winds over the blood-spattered highway.[48] Madole and the NRP soon faded from memory.

Yet it was Madole who did much to establish trans-Atlantic contacts, open new paths to National Socialist beliefs, and would through his tireless activism keep the flame of National Socialism alive in the bitterly hostile post-war years. His organizational model, not to mention the use of uniformed activists, predated Rockwell's own American Nazi Party, and it is likely that much of Rockwell's early organizational structure was borrowed in toto from the NRP through the defection of Matt Koehl among others from the NRP to the American Nazi Party.

It is true that National Socialist occultism is not for everyone, and even today it is a minority trend in the world movement. But where in the 1990s this is a vital and much traveled path, in the 1950s and early 1960s, it was virtually unheard of—especially in America. Madole was simply decades ahead of his time, and his current obscurity is very much a product of this isolation.

The Movement Today:
James Mason, Joseph Tommasi and the
National Socialist Liberation Front

Pray for victory and not an end to slaughter. —Joseph Tommasi[49]

The Allies won the war,
But Hitler won our hearts.—Varg Quisling Vikerness [50]

The most striking changes at the cutting edge of the current National Socialist movement involve the increasingly open mysticism, and indeed, religiosity, which has always been the hidden face of the radical right. Today, the occult paths are well trodden. Where Rockwell's mystical experience of unity with the Führer had to be hidden and shared with only his most trusted comrades, the occult has become a ubiquitous part of the modern race movement. With the trend toward an increasingly open racial mysticism, there has been a concomitant drift toward syncretism. That is, such seemingly incompatible ideological mixtures as Christian Identity and National Socialism or National Socialism and explicit Satanism are becoming increasingly more common.

These adherents may well be dubbed the "children of Madole," so prevalent have currents of National Socialist mysticism ranging from Satanism to Odinism become within their ranks. But while the Rockwell generation has gradually faded from the scene, a few of the movement elders remain active and influential. Colin Jordan in England continues to publish at irregular intervals his newsletter, *Gothic Ripples*. William Pierce, author of the *Turner Diaries*, has through his writings in such NS journals as *Attack!* had a considerable impact on the trans-Atlantic movement that transcends the meager number of adherents of National Socialism.[51] Nonetheless, the Rockwell generation is fast fading from the scene. Göran Assar Oredsson announced his 'retirement' from active politics and sold his archives to a Swedish academic research institution. The "old fighters" who remain on the scene are simply that—old. They are no longer fighters, although one notable exception is the ebullient Finnish expatriate activist Nils Mandel. Mandel's role is to link the movement's Eastern and Western European activists with their source of stickers and published propaganda in London. He is a fixture at the annual skinhead celebration cum riots which mark Rudolf Hess' birthday in Belgium.[52]

One of the more controversial American activists of the immediate post-Rockwell generation is James Mason, currently associated with the Universal Order. Mason, currently incarcerated in Colorado, is a survivor whose National Socialist pedigree should hold considerable allure for the younger generation of NS activists. His long history with the movement, his current international following, and the syncretic appeal of the Universal Order make Mason worthy of some further consideration.

James Mason's biography is typical of the National Socialist faithful of his generation.[53] Born in 1952 in Chillicothe, Ohio, Mason's awakening to the world of radical political activism took place with the onset of puberty. This awakening was, moreover, primarily oppositional rather than racial. Mason despised the status quo, and in those days the primary opponents of the values of the American middle class were black. The civil rights movement of the mid-1960s was in full swing, and Mason recalls being on the whole rather admiring of his black classmates.[54] A common thread running through the biographies of many current movement activists is a perception of always being oppositional, always different. In this, it is the availability of an oppositional milieu rather than the persuasiveness of a particular ideology that will often first draw the activist to the movement. Mason is no exception:

> My interests always diverged from the mainstream. I rather don't like competition, preferring to have a field more or less to myself. If necessary, I'll always invent one of my own. I've seen it that what I pick out early often has a way of catching on. Not surprising that when that happens I usually move on. When just beginning in this [National Socialism] about 1966 or 1967, I felt absolutely confident I'd make some mark, if only through sheer default.[55]

His epiphany came from a viewing of a news report of an American Nazi Party march in Chicago. Here was a movement that was both oppositional and universally despised by Americans. Better, it was led by a charismatic and fearless fighter of his own race. Here was a movement to which Mason could belong, and here too was a form of political activism which, under the swastika banner, could strike fear into the hearts of its opponents in a way that Klan robes no longer could. At the age of 14, a life-long National Socialist was born.

Determined to be a Nazi, what could a poor boy from backwater Ohio do to contact these distant urban heroes? Showing the same remarkable ingenuity that many another fledgling race activist would demonstrate in establishing his first tenuous link to the movement,[56] Mason made contact with a classmate who had a reputation of being "something of a Hitler Youth," and thus was given a book, *Extremism U.S.A.*, which contained a picture of ANP West Coast activist Allen Vincent in front of a truck emblazoned with the address of the Berkeley, California, party headquarters.[57] A letter to Vincent quickly produced the Arlington, Virginia, address of Rockwell's ANP. James Mason became a dues-paying member at the age of 14.

Soon finding himself in trouble for chronic truancy, Mason saw the opportunity to leave Chillicothe behind for the more exciting world of ANP headquarters in Arlington, Virginia. A call to ANP central resulted in a conversation with Mason's hero, William Pierce, who told him (perhaps unwisely, given his age) to hop a bus and come on down. Mason was then still a minor at 16. Pierce for his part was indeed concerned about Mason's age, thus nothing was at first kept in writing, and Pierce paid Mason's expenses out of his own pocket.[58]

Mason loved the life of the party activist. Indeed, his enthusiasm for doing "whatever needed to be done" was less than universally popular with older and less daring Nazis. It would be the first, but hardly the last, conflict

Mason would have with the movement's conservative majority. Nonetheless, when Mason reached 18, he was sworn in as a full-fledged member of the National Socialist White People's Party, Matt Koehl's successor to the martyred Rockwell's ANP. But Koehl's leadership fragmented the movement, an event which ironically brought a small portion of the National Socialist movement into a revolutionary direction.[59]

The ideological basis of this split centered on the competing theories of mass action versus the creation of a revolutionary vanguard,[60] although personality played at least as great a role in the movement's atomization. At the core of the split was the conflict between Pierce and Matt Koehl.[61] Fueling this split was, on the one hand, the generational shift between the younger activists and the older leaders. But on the other hand, more fundamentally, the roiled period of the late 1960s with the primacy of left-wing radicalism deeply affected the younger National Socialists. The key figure to arise from this group of youthful revolutionaries was Joseph Tommasi.

> Joseph Tommasi, as founder of the NSLF [National Socialist Liberation Front], was the first of a new breed. A hero and a martyr to the Cause. What he wanted most was to provide the movement with its much overdue HIT TEAM and not to set himself up as some sort of cheap, tin horn demi-god like the rest. Tommasi personified the kind of man we MUST have: those desiring to serve the movement—and do so with great facility—not pose around in gaudy uniforms as "Hollywood Nazis." [62]

Tommasi is little remembered today, but he was nonetheless a seminal figure. On the one hand, he was forthright in his faith in American exceptionalism:

> White people in America are not like those who participated in past European struggles. Americans tend to go against the "grain" on practically everything. We are not Europeans and won't respond as Europeans.[63]

Yet, on the other hand, Tommasi's thought, as is true of so many chronicled in these pages, was far ahead of its time. Joseph Tommasi emerged from the fractious California cadre of Rockwell's American Nazi Party, which in those days included such figures as Alan Vincent and James Warner. Even there, he was less than universally admired.[64] A deeply committed National Socialist, Tommasi held out for some years after the Commander's assassination before he too fell victim to Matt Koehl's ongoing purge of the party. But where so many others similarly disgusted with Koehl and company departed for other belief systems throughout the radical right, Tommasi was an NS true believer who, until his expulsion from the party, believed in Koehl to the end.[65] His analysis of the sad state of affairs of the post-Rockwell movement marked the first attempt to adapt the stereotypical Nazi subculture of the 1950s to the youth culture of the late 1960s and early 1970s. The results were intended to be revolutionary, and they were.

The National Socialist Liberation Front (NSLF) was founded in 1969, but unknown to most, the real inspiration from (well) behind the scenes was William Pierce. This was odd in that, according to James Mason's recollection, Pierce and Tommasi couldn't abide one another. Yet from the late 1960s to date, whenever talk of violence in NS circles is seriously contemplated, Pierce is usually involved, albeit always at a safe remove. Thus, Pierce conceived the NSLF as a front group to compete with the radical left on the college campuses. Tommasi, whose speech at the Second Party Congress in 1970 electrified some and appalled most with his denunciation of the conservative majority of the party, by chance coincided with Pierce's split with Koehl, and he was thus the ideal candidate to lead the NSLF.[66]

The NSLF concept did not really go anywhere until 1973, however, when Tommasi was unceremoniously booted out of the National Socialist White People's Party by Matt Koehl for his un-National Socialist behavior of smoking marijuana in Party headquarters and entertaining young women within those hallowed precincts.[67]

In 1973 or 1974, Tommasi's slogan—which remains current to this day in NS circles—became known to such East Coast Nazis as James Mason, and in that year too the NSLF held its foundational meeting. Tommasi's dictum, "THE FUTURE BELONGS TO THE FEW OF US WILLING TO GET OUR HANDS DIRTY. POLITICAL TERROR: It's the only thing they understand," appeared on a poster featuring a .38 caliber pistol and a swastika. It would not be the last time Tommasi would borrow slogans, style and eventually even dress and physical appearance from the New Left of the 1960s. Even more striking in this vein was the slogan which opened Tommasi's *Building the Revolutionary Party* pamphlet; the Maoist truism: "POLITICAL POWER STEMS FROM THE BARREL OF A GUN."[68] Indeed, even the group's name is strongly reminiscent of the Vietnamese National Liberation Front, while the name of the group's journal, *Siege!*, was borrowed from the Weather Underground.[69]

The NSLF's revolutionary ideology was based on the rejection of the "conservative" theory of mass action which Tommasi correctly believed was paralyzing the NS movement. Under the mass action doctrine, no serious anti-state actions were contemplated until the Party could build up a coalition of supporters which would in aggregate form a mass movement capable of mounting a popular revolution. By 1969, it was clear that if any mass movement was capable of building a revolutionary mass, it would be a movement of the left rather than the right. By 1974, even this hope was dashed. Clearly, to delay the revolution until the slumbering American masses could be awakened was tantamount to a vow of permanent ineffectuality. So, based on the model of the Weather Underground and other leftist guerrilla formations of the day, the NSLF would "seize the moment," regardless of how unpromising that moment might appear to the uninitiated.

Certainly, 1974 was a decidedly unpromising moment to seize. Thus, of necessity, Tommasi formulated an early version of "leaderless resistance" or lone wolf tactics that would not come into vogue in the movement until the late

1980s, when the failure of the Silent Brotherhood's ill-starred revolutionary activism moved Louis Beam to write the original "Leaderless Resistance" tract and led William Pierce to promote the concept in his fictional follow-up to the *Turner Diaries*, called *Hunter*.[70] The credo of the NSLF was violent revolutionary action, and its propaganda in the pages its original journal, *Defiance*, and the more well-known successor to that publication, *Siege!*, suggested that the NSLF had already formed armed cells and launched the "first blows against the empire."[71]

According to NSLF propaganda, the group's foundational meeting held on 2 March 1974—a full five years after Tommasi created the group—hosted "forty-three National Socialist revolutionaries" in El Monte, California.[72] It was at this meeting that the mass action strategy was officially put to rest in favor of revolution now. The NSLF was conceived as an activist, and thus violent, revolutionary organization. It was structured in a manner reminiscent of David Lane's current theories of organization, with an aboveground membership that may have numbered perhaps forty or more, and a tiny underground contingent of lone wolf revolutionaries.[73] The underground core of the NSLF never numbered more than four, including Karl Hand and David Rust:

> Yes, the N.S.L.F. of Tommasi had four persons who carried out the illegal activities. The remainder, the majority, weren't that much different from the N.S.W.P.P. [Koehl's National Socialist White People's Party] members except they were a lot more forward thinking.[74]

James Mason was a close friend and collaborator with Tommasi and the group, but he never officially joined the NSLF. However, within a year, Tommasi was dead, and it was not long thereafter that his successors David Hand and Karl Rust were imprisoned for their acts of leaderless resistance. The underground in reality died with Tommasi.[75] The legacy of the tiny movement however, is far greater than its meager victories would suggest.

The primary accomplishment of the NSLF was that it was the first NS group in the post-war period to attempt to adapt to the times. Tommasi had no qualms about taking lessons from the radical left, and he had no interest in the puritanical outlook of the post-war radical right. Nor was Tommasi a man to deceive himself that the world of explicit National Socialism would ever be able to attract a significant enough following in the United States to justify the movement's mass action theory. Clearly, mass action was synonymous with organizational impotence. If the time to seize the gun was not the chaotic year 1969, then when would it be? Thus, the credo of the NSLF was one of action, and action now!

Yet the NSLF could not escape the reality of its minuscule numbers. It was fine for Tommasi to borrow the communist belief in a cell structure, but the grim truth was that had the NSLF's combatant core formed a fighting cell, it would have had to quite literally put all its eggs in one basket! On an ideological level, however, it was not difficult to find a rationale, and a hope, for ultimate victory in the face of overwhelming odds. For one, the National Socialist faith has always been at heart religious and deeply millenarian. Ultimate victory was assured to the faithful simply by virtue of their faith and of their ultimate "rightness."

On a more immediate level, Tommasi believed with Rockwell and Evola and Hitler too that the masses were in essence female, waiting to be swept off their collective feet by a leader whose daring and charisma would guide them into the timeless racialist dream.[76] Thus the suicidal audacity of the NSLF's "operations." Thus too the ease with which the organization was smashed and surviving members jailed. David Rust, Tommasi's first successor, went down on firearms charges. Karl Hand, Tommasi's final successor, was imprisoned briefly in 1980 for firing a gun into the home of a black neighbor and then received a fifteen-year sentence for other weapons violations and attempted murder.[77]

The shell of the organization carried on, at least in name, for several years after Tommasi's 1975 murder. By then, James Mason was something of a full-fledged member by virtue of his having been sent an unsolicited membership card by Karl Hand, and a few other activists soldiered on as well. By 1978, the NSLF's mantle fell by default to Mason, with the same Allen Vincent, whose picture in *Extremism USA* had so impressed a young Mason, handling party propaganda.[78] Like many another right-wing group whose non-existent cadres are filled out by the deeds of others, the NSLF's journal, *Siege!*, which went on under the editorship of James Mason until 1986, was not reticent about either claiming as its own or simply cheering on any act of white racial violence.[79] The truth was, however, that the NSLF as a combatant group was dead, but its influence did not end there. Indeed, in an emotional farewell to Tommasi, Mason writes:

> it were now as if Tommasi never went away. He'd have admired Oklahoma City. "Pray for Victory and not an end to slaughter." [80]

Charles Manson and the Universal Order

All we wanted was peace on earth man, but you guys are the ones who made us take our shovels and turn 'em into guns. —Charles Manson[81]

All live for ATWA [Air, Trees, Water, Animals] or no one lives. All must have a one world government, money, army, all in order to bring order fast and reset all ATWA for life itself and all life support systems set in order, balance and God's will. —Charles Manson[82]

James Mason continued for some time to publish *Siege!* as a journal, and to head his own one-man band, the short lived National Socialist Movement, which by Mason's own admission soon foundered.[83] Then came Mason's discovery of the teachings of Charlie Manson. This association ended Mason's connection with his old comrades. Manson urged Mason to jettison the NSLF in favor of a new grouping, the Universal Order, and as a result, Mason and Karl Hand amicably agreed to part ways, with Mason holding *Siege!* as the organ of the Universal Order and Hand keeping *Defiance* as publication of the NSLF.[84]

Despite Masons' earlier contention that he was not among the movement's "religionists,"[85] Mason's adulation of the Manson family and his tireless efforts through his current vehicle, the Universal Order, to present Manson to the international movement as an avatar of the coming National Socialist revolution on the level of a Rockwell or a Tommasi, and perhaps even of Hitler himself, is a religious quest par excellence! From 1982 until the journal's demise, *Siege!* became the primary vehicle for the glorification of Charles Manson.

Mason himself was no stranger to the occult aspects of National Socialism, and like so many of the movement's '60s generation, he was drawn for a time to the teachings of Anton LaVey and the Church of Satan. Mason notes that in 1969, he purchased a copy of Anton LaVey's LP *The Satanic Mass* from a fellow ANP trooper, and has "cherished it ever since."[86] But while Satanism, particularly in its Church of Satan guise, was no stranger to the world of National Socialism, the figure of Charles Manson was quite something else. The selection of Charles Manson and his largely female following as NS heroes seems as unlikely on first glance as was the elevation of Horst Wessel from dissolute street fighter to the selfless martyr of the original NSDAP (the German acronym for the "National German Socialist Workers Party").

Certainly, the Universal Order's insistence on this recognition of the role and leadership of Charles Manson has not met with much success among the conservative majority of National Socialists. It has also encountered significant criticism among the fighters of the skinhead movement—young men who for the most part were not born until after the sensational capture and trial of the Manson family.[87] The reaction to this thesis by the young readers of *Resistance* magazine was so overwhelming that the editor, George Eric Hawthorne, presented in the next issue a full-fledged debate on the proposition from two of his magazine's readers. His introduction to this debate is a fair representation of the "resistance" the Universal Order has faced in its quest to promote the thought and example of Charlie Manson:

> In the last issue of *RESISTANCE* Magazine, James Mason, author of *Siege*, took a fairly unpopular platform and proceeded upon a difficult thesis: although few people in the pro-White movement realize it, Charles Manson is actually ideally suited to be "the" leader of our generation, and for us to win, we must recognize it. We were literally flooded with letters and phone calls from irate readers who firmly disagree with this concept, stating that any connection to Manson is pointless and dangerous to our credibility. One distributor even clipped out the Manson article from the issue before distributing it.
>
> But on the other side of the subject, there is a growing body of Manson supporters that see the public view of Manson as a late 20th Century icon who carries weight and influence with his name, so much so that it may be the tool we need to sway the youth of our generation.[88]

But there is more here than meets the eye, and the Universal Order's fealty to the legacy of the Manson Family deserves some attention both for what it has to teach of the state of the contemporary movement, and, of more pressing import, for the key adherents this movement has gathered in both the United States and Europe. The appeal of Manson is well summed up by one of these younger activists, Michael Moynahan, whose Storm Publications brought James Mason's early writings to a considerably wider audience through the publication of Mason's book, *Siege!:*

> Manson is extremely important, as he is one of those rare individuals capable of operating on many levels at once. This applies equally to his life, message, and actions. I am less interested in the murders he allegedly directed, and I don't think anyone will ever know exactly what really happened and what led up to them. I am much more compelled by Manson's mind and what he has to say. For whatever reasons (and it is made even more puzzling by his criminal background) he often verbalizes incredibly erudite and obscure concepts which can be traced back to much earlier native European spirituality. There is no doubt that he expresses some very deep, subconscious thoughts which very few people are aware of or even understand in the present day and age. The fact that he is able to instinctively convey these things is unique among any modern man of public renown.[89]

The question of Manson's resurgent appeal is of considerable importance. While only a small minority of the National Socialist race movement has embraced Manson, the rebirth of his celebrity among a broad spectrum of disaffected youth is undeniable. What follows is therefore a preliminary attempt to wrestle with some of these issues. We thus begin with a fascinating academic approach to the Manson personality type by art historian Stoddard Martin. Following this scholastic interlude, this chapter will consider other aspects of Manson's appeal in more specifically movement-oriented terms.

In an interesting exploration of the mystique of radical individualism—and indeed the aura of evil—as a cultural phenomenon, Stoddard Martin sees Manson as but one of a long line of figures whom he dubs the artist-manqué.[90] For Martin, the artist-manqué is a man out of time. He is an artist burning for recognition, but one who is all too well aware that he has yet to fully realize on the canvas of his own cultural reality the full implications of his vision. Unable to achieve the glory the artist-manqué feels is his due, and driven by a quest for expression that he can never fully transform from the ether of ideas to the physical world" the phenomenon of artistic frustration is likely to exacerbate tendencies to shock . . . challenge conventional morality, explore areas of decay, parade the ego, cast one's personae as messiahs, and sensationalize crime."[91]

With this conception, Martin offers a long line of contemporary artist-manqués. Two of these, Hitler and Manson, abandoned their art to become men of action. Others, Herbert Marcuse, de Sade, and Nietzsche, for example, would remain men of ideas—often with great success—but would never realize the level of recognition that they believed was their due, and would always live in an adversarial relationship with their respective societies.

Yet for all of the long history of this personality type, there was something special about the 1960s, and particularly the pivotal year of 1969. The '60s was a time of instant gratification. Manson could never display the patience or doggedness of an Adolf Hitler in achieving his ends. Moreover, 1969 was the year of the Rolling Stones' Altmont concert, the success of the Beatles' *White Album* and their subsequent break-up, and the beginning of the Manson Family's apocalyptic Helter Skelter plan for race war, which foresaw the imminent emergence of the Family to assume ultimate terrestrial power.[92] If ever a life was lived as an art statement, it was Manson's in the late 1960s. Not surprisingly, those most susceptible to the appeal of Manson's leadership today are drawn from the occult fringes of the movement. Many are artists in their own right, and the National Socialist life in the present day is nothing if not a particularly theatrical art statement.

The Universal Order thus has been able to gather only a relative handful of adherents and hangers on in the United States and in Europe. It is, in any case, a "state of mind" movement rather than an organization with a membership per se.[93] But their primary mission, to create around the aura of Charles Manson a kind of soteriological cult, has met with some success. Manson is indeed more of a ubiquitous cult figure today than ever before. From the playful "Charlie Don't Surf" T-shirts that became something of a fad in California to the recording of Manson's songs by such popular rock bands as Guns and Roses to the appearance of Manson-related World Wide Web sites, the visage of Charles Manson has become well known to a new youth generation. Indeed, a profitable cottage industry has sprung up around Manson, with CDs of Manson's music and words becoming available again, with articles about Manson proliferating throughout the underground, and with publishing houses bringing a number of Manson-related books back into print.[94]

This apparent disconnect between the lack of success of the Universal Order's championing of Charles Manson as a prototype of the successful modern National Socialist leader and Manson's current cult status throughout the international underground calls for a moment's reflection. What is it about the Manson persona which attracts James Mason and his NS comrades on the one hand, and the decidedly non-National Socialist youth culture on the other? What follows is an attempt to analyze the key elements of Manson's contemporary charismatic appeal.

In particular, the vital import of the Manson legend (as opposed to the more prosaic reality of his life and thought) will be analyzed. So too will the key component to any successful youth appeal; alienation. Elements of this alienation center in particular on radical environmentalism (the ATWA concept alluded to in the opening of this section) and Manson's increasingly open racialism and anti-Semitism, which may have been a prominent component of his teachings from the beginning. Another facet of this alienation is what might be termed a backlash against feminism by both Manson and his female followers. Conversely, this racialist message may as easily be a product of Manson's uncanny ability to act as a mirror capable of reflecting any particular belief system back to his interlocutor of the moment, making it appear that agreement exists where it in fact does not. As with the malleability of the Manson legend, herein lies a major ingredient in the return of Manson to public consciousness.

For the National Socialists and the wider youth culture alike, there is little question that it is the perennial reality of youth alienation which is at the root of Manson's cult icon status today. But alienation takes many forms, and here the malleability of the Manson legend is of key importance. In this conception, the truth of the events which took place in 1969 are of less substantive importance than the ambiguity of the legend itself. Whether one chooses to believe the official version of events, or that of Charles Manson and his original "family," or of some idiosyncratic mixture of both, the story could hardly fail to attract a following of the alienated or merely curious.

The outlines of the official version of the "Manson Family" are well known. Vincent Bugliosi's book *Helter Skelter* and the movie based on this text etched this version deeply into the public consciousness. In this scenario, Manson, the crazed leader of a largely female drug and sex cult, became frustrated at his lack of success in the music business. Enraged, Manson brooded in the California desert until the Beatles' 1969 *White Album* inspired him to invent an apocalyptic scheme, which he dubbed Helter Skelter. In this version of racial apocalypse, an imminent race war in America would be the signal for the Family to hide in a deep hole in the desert until the inevitable victory of American blacks. However, as in Manson's view, blacks are neither intellectually nor temperamentally equipped to govern, representatives of the black race would rush to the emergent Manson group and beg them to take the reigns of power. When the race war was not immediately forthcoming, the murders for which the Manson Family was charged were committed with the idea that the outrages would be blamed on blacks and thus ignite the longed-for war between the races.[95] Other sources embellished this already lurid tale with the trappings of Satanism and diabolical doings via the alleged ties between Manson and the Process Church. These titillating tidbits were contributed in the first edition of Ed Sanders' *The Family*,[96] but were deleted from subsequent printings when the Process Church filed a lawsuit in Chicago against both the book and the author. An agreement was reached out of court on 6 March 1972, which stipulated that:

> all references to the Process Church of the Final Judgment will be deleted from all subsequent editions of the book, including the proposed paperback edition. They have also agreed that this will apply to any portion of the book which may be published in any other media. The publishers have also agreed to issue a joint press release with the Church to this effect, and to place the release of all unsold copies of the book which are in the publisher's possession at this time.[97]

Lurid stuff indeed. The story according to Manson and his associates is considerably less colorful. In this version, the murders were committed for a more rational, if less colorful purpose:

> The real motive was to get a brother, Bobby Beausoliel, out of jail by committing "copycat" murders that would convince the authorities that Beausoliel could not be guilty of the murder (of Gary Hinman) for which he had been arrested on August 6, 1969. This motive is much more realistic and has much more circumstantial support than

the DA's fantastic "helter skelter" motive. It's the real motive. There's only one thing wrong with it from the prosecutorial point of view: It's not a personal motive for Charles Manson.[98]

In this version of events, Mason personally emerges all but blameless for any of the killings. Moreover, he pictures himself as the victim of a monstrous judicial frame-up in which he was denied the right to defend himself, cross examine witnesses, or in any way present the court—or subsequent parole boards—with the truth. This truth centers on the contention that ATWA, not helter skelter was the ideological core of the group of cast-offs and runaways that gathered around Manson because no one else wanted them (thus the original impetus for the self-view of garbage people as both a literal description of their food source and their view of themselves as the refuse of the American dream).[99] The incarceration of Manson is thus facilitating the destruction of the ecology and, indeed, the world. Moreover, the alleged fixation on the Beatles, the apocalyptic dreams of race war and imminent terrestrial power, the "drug and sex cult" stereotypes, ad infinitum were simply exaggerations aimed at both inflaming public opinion and, of more immediate import, allowing the prosecutor, newspapers and pulp writers to make a fast buck off the story.[100]

Today, Michael Moynahan is undoubtedly correct in his view that: "I don't think anyone will ever know exactly what really happened."[101] What is certain is that whichever version of the story one chooses to believe, there is some element with which any alienated seeker may choose to identify.

In terms of the wider youth culture, the Manson message does have a resonance. Manson's primary message of rebellion and the nation's betrayal of its young is rooted in the 1960s but resonates again all the more strongly in the rapidly changing environment of the 1990s. Consider in this regard a tale, perhaps factual, perhaps apocryphal, which Manson relates on *Manson Speaks* and which was adapted on a cut from Michael Moynahan's Blood Axis CD, *The Gospel of Inhumanity*. This CD is of considerable relevance in that it has the potential to break out of the underground genre of the Satanist and National Socialist music scene and to cross over to a wider audience.[102] In the Blood Axis cut "Herr, nun laß in Frieden," Manson intones a monologue over the funereal tones of a Bach organ cantata which relates a story told to him by his grandmother of his grandfather's experience in WWI in which, standing atop the body of an enemy soldier, he finds a Bible in the pocket of his fallen foe, and inside the Bible, a picture of the man with his wife and daughters. In a flash, the realization dawns that beneath the differences of uniform and language, both men were alike, and he wonders what kind of a government would send out a man to kill his brother over nothing.[103] Prefacing this, Manson alludes to the Vietnam experience—and perhaps both to the charges against him and the recent betrayal of the Family by Tex Watson as well, when he states:

> He lost his brotherhood . . . . He lost his swastika and he lost his brotherhood. For lying. 'Cause he thought it was a big joke to stab somebody in the back who just took a life for him. If somebody's giving their life for you and they're going into the battlefield for you,

you can't very well laugh at 'em when they come back. If a man's over there in Vietnam and he's over there in the mud and the blood and he's over there fighting and dying for you and then you spit in his face, what kind of fucking country can that be? You see what I'm saying? Does that make sense? So it's the same way all the way down the line.[104]

Here, Manson sounds many of the themes which underlie the current search for a post-nationalist community based on race and culture: the sense of betrayal by a nation which, for the profit of "others" would set racial brother to kill racial brother, the small thanks that the returning warrior can expect upon his return "home," and the swastika as the badge of honor which the race activist must strive with each new day to prove himself worthy of bearing. From a wider perspective, if one eliminates the imagery of the swastika, Manson sums up in its totality the anomie which is so well described among the Vietnam—and the post-Vietnam—generation of American men by James William Gibson in *Warrior Dreams*.[105]

This sense of alienation from, and abandonment by, the country and its government pervades Manson's teachings. Moreover, in recent years, Manson's rhetoric has become more openly racial and anti-Semitic, providing a key to the suggestion by James Mason and others that Charles Manson as the movement's only hope for victory. Racial separation has always been a facet of Manson's thought—no doubt born both of his impoverished rural roots and experience as a career prisoner. At his 1970 trial, Manson stated this in relatively clear terms (as opposed to Manson's notoriously opaque pronouncements on most subjects):

Yours is yours, and I don't care what it is. Whatever you do is up to you, and it's the same thing with anyone in my family, and anybody in my family is a white human being, because my family is of the white family.

There is the black family, a yellow family, the red family, a cow family and a mule family. There is all kinds of different families.[106]

Over the years, this racialism would become more pronounced. In the *Manson Speaks* CD, racial stereotypes are frequent. So openly was this racialism expressed that Manson regaled the 1986 parole board hearing with a statement that was hardly calculated to impress:

Black Muslims with white hats are pimps with white whores. Black women with white shoes are black whores with white tricks. Black people are sub-underworld people for long over 700 years. This will be the fifth wave of negro babies your system has been bussing up your own children's ass. Negroes eat white people. Like wolves eat dogs.[107]

Add to this the denunciation of Jews in the Hollywood recording industry and it is little wonder that there would be a natural connection to a new generation of

National Socialists. As with the question of race, Manson has become more out-spokenly anti-Semitic in recent years, blaming Jews for his lack of success in the 1960s-era music business. For example:

> I think a guy called Hitler said it: *it's a Jewish problem*. Because eve-rything we get going, they'll end up selling it to us. As soon as Hank Williams died, they bought his guitar and gave it to Bobby Dylan, then told the world that Bobby Dylan was actually Hank Williams . . . and they sold the image of Hank Williams through Zimmerman [Dy-lan's birth name]. It's the same thing they've done all the way down the line, every time one of us dies they just buy up the graveyard and sell it back to us. Every time we make a mistake, they just move on in, 'til they end up running it. They're slick motherfuckers—they're running it.
>
> When I went to Hollywood they offered me these positions and I told them "No, no." And then they want to pick who's going to play in my band, and who's gonna do this, and I told them "No, I can't." So then the Jew told me, he said, "As long as you're in this town, you'll never get no music out." In other words, they want to control the music. I'm not a racist kind of guy; I never thought one way or another what a guy is, but then I see how the Second World War has made people racists—whatever "racist" is. We're all for our-selves to start with, so that makes us racists.[108]

Moreover, the appeal of this racialist and anti-Semitic message resonates in the revolutionary fringe of the movement through an uncritical acceptance of the apocalyptic helter skelter race war scenario. In this conception, whether it was truth or prosecutorial fiction is of little import. It is taken throughout the popular culture as truth, and could not but attract like-minded adherents.

To James Mason, the Manson allure as the prototypical NS Führer goes much deeper. In the pages of *Siege!* after 1982 when the journal became in ef-fect the organ of the Universal Order, the case for Manson as a movement ar-chetype is put forth in depth. This appeal goes beyond the Manson Family's alleged chiliastic dreams of race war—a fantasy that has never lost its allure to the American movement. On a deeper level, Mason points out the painful fact that Charles Manson's following was primarily female. In a movement which manages to attract very few women, this is no small matter.[109]

Mason's view is simple and to the point:

> good as it now poses is limp prick at best and people who are still alive sense this. Hence, the fascination with "evil" which at least has some life to it. Hitler being the best example. Manson being another. Women flocked to them both.[110]

Implicit in this analysis is a critique of contemporary feminism which speaks much to the Manson mystique. Manson is unabashedly paternalistic, and the women in the Manson group do not hesitate to point this out as the key to their attraction to the man and to the Family. This anti-feminist critique is inex-tricably intertwined with the approach the Manson loyalists take to ATWA and the radical ecology movement. Sandra Good, upon her release from prison, claims to have been in contact with such radical environmental groups as Earth First!, the Sea Shepherds and the Animal Liberation Front, while Manson himself states: "started the root thoughts for most or a lot" of their ideology.[111] One of the self-described Manson women describes this view well:

> Women are especially responsible [for the environment] because woman is the earth. It's her nature and job to take care of the earth. Women have been raising and holding children with fears and insecurities to go for the paychecks, to uphold the present way of life. Women fear real change and reflect their fear upon the children, and it's her fear that holds down positive change. The USA is living in a matriarchy centered in fear and money, not earth and survival and life on earth is dying because of it. Males for the most part are reflections of their mother's and other women's fears.[112]

With this remarkable statement the connection, and obvious disconnect, with the radical environmentalists is made plain. Certainly, there are voices in movements such as Earth First! which do equate women with the earth in both body and spirit. But equally present in this rhetoric is a strong condemnation of patriarchy, which is seen as being in part responsible for the dying planet.[113] For the Manson group, it is precisely the collapse of patriarchy that is at the root of the problem. Patriarchy in this view is the natural order of things, and upsetting this natural balance can not but have the most dire consequences on the web of life of which man is but one small part. Little wonder that Sandra Good would express her disgust for the environmental groups in no uncertain terms:

> Part of my 15 year sentence was for telling all the environmental groups "Quit Faking!" We gave our lives for brother and for ATWA and after all of those years none of those groups saw or responded. They can't see our real because they are all fakes. They play all that, "It's wrong to kill or go to war to save your own life on earth." I'd say: This is a war on pollution, on the problems, a war for life.[114]

One need only compare these statements with the following assertions of ecofeminism to understand why the Manson Family would enjoy so little success with the ecology movement:

> Gender domination in humym [sic] society is a prerequisite for the domination of Gaea, Mother Earth. Deep ecology proposes to eliminate domination and deconstruct all forms of hierarchy, among humyns themselves and particularly to alleviate humyn domination of all other species with whom we share the habitat of this planet. Ecofeminism suggests that the domination of womyn and the domination of species originate in the same philosophy, that which promotes the commodification of life.[115]

Or this more radical formulation:

> The patriarchal system is not reformable. . . . This system of hierar-
> chy and dominance is inherently rotten. . . . We must . . . work to-
> gether for our liberation from patriarchal cultures. We need womyn
> loving womyn . . . to explore our lesbian spirits—she lies within all
> of us. Who says loving womyn has to be only in spirit? And coupled
> or not, it is our duty as womyn to masturbate and smash the state![116]

Charismatic male authority is thus at the root of the appeal of Manson
to his female followers, and is a prime ingredient of the movement's adherence
to the Leadership Principle as well. For what National Socialist could disagree
with the analysis of yet another of the Manson women?

> Society in general is living in a matriarchy. Manson is not in a matri-
> archy. He is a patriarch. He's a true patriarch. He has true authority
> and surety. It doesn't come from ego or a desire to manipulate. It
> comes from God. Authority can be tender. It can be fierce. It's
> knowing. There's no fake, phony, jive ego purposes behind true
> authority. [117]

Manson and his women were no mere armchair revolutionaries. Like
Tommasi before them, they seized the moment and acted. The Manson murders
are thus of little consequence to James Mason and the adherents of the Universal
Order, given the apocalyptic intent of the crimes.[118] Manson in this conception
emerges as the ultimate realist. The leader who like Hitler and Rockwell had
torn aside the veils of illusory sentiment and the blinders of "system lies" to
reach true freedom in that Nietzchean plateau which transcends mundane conceptions of good and evil. It is a detachment that Mason himself aspires to, but
even such repugnant apologias as the dismissal of the murder of Sharon Tate's
unborn baby with the contemptuous: "With regard to the eight-month-old fetus
Tate was carrying, it was, after all, a Jew"[119] ring hollow before Manson's
amoral example.

Finally, it is the apocalyptic messianism inherent in the Manson legend
which is a prime attraction to the race movement. Here once again, it matters
little what the truth of the helter skelter scenario might be. It is the legend of
race war and the emergence of a white elite to terrestrial power that is a perennial movement fantasy. From the anonymous *Franklin Letters* of the 1950s to
the contemporary *Turner Diaries*, the dream has never wavered.[120] All that is
needed is a leader, a man on a holy mission to bring an end to the suffering of
the faithful and lead them from the darkness of persecution and rejection into the
light of a new dawn. For James Mason and others, why not Charles Manson, and
why not now? For his part, Manson, while denying any claims of leadership,
had this to say on the subject at the time of his 1986 parole hearing:

> Your government invented the Watergate cover-up but never did say
> what they were really covering up [was] a Holy War invoked from
> the soul. When Manson, aka Lord Krishna, Jesus Christ, Mohammed,
> the Buddha, by the press and THE PEOPLE VS. Manson, you con-

demned yourselves. You condemned yourselves in the so-called
Manson family, putting the son of God on the prison cross again. I
broke no law, not God's nor Man's law. God knows this, the Holy
Spirit knows; and anyone in the truth knows. What you are buying
and selling in God's name, you will suffer. With your own judgments
convicting yourselves of being Satan, the anti-Christ, you stand your
world on fire. I am Abraxas, the son of God, the son of Darkness, and
I stand behind ALL the courts in the world. Until I get my rights, no
one has rights. I'm God's messenger from and in the truth, brother
and son to all men. (666 your computers will print the same read out
to your book brains) Until I get the same rights my fathers had, I will
stand in Nixon's place, convicted as the false prophet, as fire burns
and the children starve and the land dies along with the air, as the
wildlife becomes poisoned and the trees are being cut so fast that
wildlife will not survive NOT WITHOUT WORLD CHANGE.

I did say I "did" invoke a balance for life on Earth. From
behind the time locks of courtrooms and worlds of darkness, I did let
loose devils and demons with the power of scorpions to torment. I did
unseal seven seals and seven jars in accord with the judgments placed
upon me, upon my circle. All who had no forgiveness will have no
heart, and did set loose upon the earth destruction in the balance of
their own judgments. These are the people who gave their own children no chance for survival. These are the people locked in death
wishes which they project into the minds of the children. [121]

This is a powerful apocalyptic claim for leadership by a man who
steadfastly denies any wish to lead. It has thus far had little resonance with the
race movement beyond the fringes of the National Socialist and Satanist subcultures. Thus, when James Mason took his case for the consecration of Charles
Manson as movement leader to the aficionados of White Noise music in the
pages of *Resistance* magazine, it was a kinder, gentler Führer that was on offer.
Accompanied by a photograph of a smiling, bespectacled Manson who looks
uncannily like a grandfatherly version of Alan Berg, the Jewish radio talk show
host who was murdered by the Order in Denver, this Manson is presented as the
logical successor to Rockwell's mantle of leadership. After all, not only did
Manson carve the swastika into his own flesh, announcing to the world his ir-
revocable allegiance to the National Socialist dream, but the motto of the Family, ATWA (Air, Trees, Water and Animals) is offered as the encapsulation of
the movement's emphasis on ecology; itself a natural outgrowth of the movement's obsession with purity in every form. [122] Mason concludes with the exhortation:

> White man, now is the time to use your secret weapon, your *brain*,
> and see and embrace your leader. Charles Manson. Then and only
> then can you effectively use your renowned weapon, fury and skill in
> battle, without being undone by the scheming Jew and his filthy,
> ZOG system. [123]

The relative success—or lack of same—of this call for Manson's ascendancy will reveal much of the future direction of the occult paths of National Socialism.

Conclusion

This chapter's concentration on the lives and teachings of some of the leading figures in the post-war world of occult National Socialism should not obscure the fact that there are numerous other small, often inter-related, movements of a variety of ideological and theological hues that share much with the individuals and groups noted in these pages. For example, in Britain, David Myatt and his occult National Socialist organization Reichfolk interacts closely with Anton Long and Christos Beest, who are the moving forces behind the National Socialist-oriented Satanist group, the Order of the Nine Angles (ONA). Myatt, an avid and compelling writer, has published extensive treatises on various aspects of National Socialism, racial nationalism, and various occult themes. The primary dogma of Reichfolk is that National Socialism is in itself a religion, and Adolf Hitler is seen as the head of that faith in explicitly soteriological terms.[124]

The Order of the Nine Angles is closely associated with Reichfolk—so much so that many in the milieu believe that all are run by the same person using a variety of pseudonyms. While this is not true, the waters in the world of NS-oriented Satanism are exceedingly murky, with groups borrowing (or expropriating) materials, and sharing names despite having little or no connection to each other. The ONA compounds this confusion by allowing its voluminous materials to be rather freely reproduced by other groups under a variety of names. The key point here, however, is that the ONA is very much a mail order ministry whose numbers are infinitesimally small but whose goals are world changing.[125] They co-operate closely with Reichfolk—at times even sharing a post office box—based on mutual agreements in some areas and an agreement to disagree on other areas. Both, however, would like to withdraw to a rural communitarian existence to which like-minded adherents from around the world are invited to join. The problem with realizing this goal, however, is money—a problem which seems at the moment insoluble.[126]

The final NS-oriented Satanist mail order ministry to consider is by far the most confusing to document: the Black Order. All agree that the Black Order was founded by Kerry Bolton in New Zealand as a successor to his Order of the Left Hand Path.[127] The group met with some success in attracting an international following, but like many of Bolton's projects, it was eventually supplanted by fresher inspiration and the Black Order was turned over to a group in England. From there, it grew to have adherents throughout the world, with the first U.S. group founded only in 1996.[128]

All of this is clear enough, but the name Black Order has been taken up by an array of groups around the world without any formal linkages being established. Thus, Göran Gullwang's Swedish Black Order, which has become notorious in Sweden for the convictions of its leader and at least one of its members for murders committed in a ritual context,[129] was unknown to the British group until they read of Gullwang in a manuscript copy of one of my articles! Gullwang's membership application is identical to that of the Black Order, save that it has been translated into Swedish (although respondents are asked to reply in English!). In any case, the Black Order is, like the ONA, a remarkably influential purveyor of NS-oriented occultism throughout the world.

Much more could be written about these small but fascinating occult National Socialist groups. In terms of the dominant culture, they are and will remain marginal actors. However, within the cultic milieu, and in particular in the complex and often fratricidal world of National Socialism, they represent an important constituency which has, since the days of the Third Reich, staked a powerful claim for the soul of the movement.

Notes

[1] Interview with James Mason, 28 November 1996.

[2] Göran Assar Oredsson interview with Dr. Heléne Lööw, 1996. A brief history of Oredsson's NRP is provided in Göran Assar Oredsson, *News of the NRP*, undated pamphlet distributed by the NRP.

[3] *Nordisk Kamp* 10 (26 August 1967). This was a memorial issue dedicated to George Lincoln Rockwell. Translated by Dr. Helene Lööw.

[4] Nicholas Godrick-Clarke, *The Occult Roots of Nazism* (New York: New York University Press, 1985, 1992).

[5] For a convincing argument along these lines, see James M. Rhodes, *The Hitler Movement: A Modern Millenarian Revolution* (Stanford, CA.: Hoover Institution Press, 1980). For coverage of the internal debate along these lines within NS circles, see Jeffrey Kaplan, "Religiosity and the Radical Right: Toward the Creation of a New Ethnic Identity," in Jeffrey Kaplan and Tore Bjørgo, eds., *Brotherhoods of Nation and Race: The Emergence of a Euro-American Racist Subculture* (Boston, MA: Northeastern University Press, 1998).

[6] This account is primarily based on three sources: George Lincoln Rockwell, *This Time the World!* (Arlington, VA: Parliament House, 1963); William L. Pierce, *Lincoln Rockwell: A National Socialist Life* (Arlington, VA: NS Publications, 1969), and New Order, *The Religion of Lincoln Rockwell* (Milwaukee, WI: New Order, n.d.).

[7] William L. Pierce, *Lincoln Rockwell: A National Socialist Life*, 12.

[8] Ibid., 15-16. Pierce dates these dreams as occurring in 1957-1958.

[9] New Order, *The Religion of Lincoln Rockwell*, 5.

[10] William L. Pierce, *Lincoln Rockwell: A National Socialist Life*, 18.

[11] How deeply religious is revealed in the 1994 General Social Survey conducted by the National Opinion Research Center. According to this data, fully 94 percent of Americans report some belief in a higher power while only 2 percent evince no belief at all. By far the largest cluster of respondents, 64 percent state that they "believe without doubts." The next largest cluster, 16 percent, "believe with doubts." Glenn H. Utter and John W. Story, *The Religious Right* (Santa Barbara, CA: ABC-CLIO, 1995), 78.

[12] Klaus Scholder, *The Churches and the Third Reich*, 2 vols., 2nd edition, (Philadelphia, PA: Fortress Press, 1988).

[13] Letter from George Lincoln Rockwell to Bruno Ludke, 11 February 1963, in Frederick J. Simonelli, *American Führer*, 223. Much of the religiously oriented material contained

in *American Führer* is reprised in Frederick J. Simonelli, "American Nazis and Christian Identity," *Patterns of Prejudice* 30 (April 1996), 43-54.

[14] The 1957 discussions took place with Emory Burke, an anti-Semite later charged but not convicted in the 1958 bombing of an Atlanta synagogue. See Frederick J. Simonelli, "American Nazis and Christian Identity."

[15] Letter from Bruno Ludke to Rockwell, 15 May 1962, in Frederick J. Simonelli, *American Führer*, 220.

[16] Ibid., 220-225. On Jordan's more recent writings, see the ongoing "The Way Ahead" series in the 1995-1996 issues of *Gothic Ripples*. The series in fact is strongly reminiscent of many of the ideas broached by James Madole in his 1970s-era "New Atlantis" series.

[17] The definitive history of this development is Michael Barkun, *Religion and the Racist Right: The Origins of the Christian Identity Movement* (Chapel Hill, NC: University of North Carolina, 1994).

[18] Frederick J. Simonelli, *American Führer*, 217. On Swift's role, see Michael Barkun, *Religion and the Racist Right*, ch. 4; and Jeffrey Kaplan, *Radical Religion In America: Millenarian Movements from the Far Right to the Children of Noah* (Syracuse, NY: Syracuse University Press, 1996), ch. 2.

[19] Frederick J. Simonelli, *American Führer*, 226.

[20] Ibid., 226-27.

[21] Jeffrey Kaplan, "Right Wing Violence in North America," *Terrorism and Political Violence* 7:1 (Spring 1995), 56-57.

[22] House Committee on Un-American Activities, *Investigation of Un-American Propaganda Activities in the United States (Gerald L. K. Smith)*, 79th Congress, 2d sess., 1946. On the more general question of the Red Scare, see Joel Kovel, *Red Hunting in the Promised Land: Anticommunism and the Making of America* (New York: Basic Books, 1994).

[23] Ralph Lord Roy, *Apostles of Discord* (Boston: Beacon Press, 1953); John Roy Carlson, *Under Cover* (New York: Dutton, 1943); and Idem, *The Plotters* (New York: Dutton, 1946).

[24] House Committee on Un-American Activities, *Preliminary Report on Neo-Fascist and Hate Groups*, 17 December 1954, 1-2.

[25] "James Hartung Madole: Father of Post-War Fascism," *Nexus* (November 1995). Madole's utopian vision of a Völkisch National Socialist America was serialized in his *National Renaissance Bulletin* throughout the mid-1970s as "The New Atlantis: A Blueprint for the Aryan 'Garden of Eden' in North America." Cf. Rick Cooper, "A Brief History of the White Nationalist Movement." E-text distributed by Don Black's Stormfront BBS.

[26] James H. Madole, "The Program of the National Renaissance Party," *National Renaissance Bulletin*, (October 1953), 3-4. The document is reproduced in House Committee on Un-American Activities, *Preliminary Report on Neo-Fascist and Hate Groups*, Exhibit 2, 21-22.

[27] See Mattias Gardell, "Black and White Unite in Fight? On the Inter-Action Between Black and White Radical Racialists," in this anthology.

[28] "James Hartung Madole: Father of Post-War Fascism," *Nexus*, 23.

[29] For a fascinating treatise on the subject, see Joel Carmichael, *The Satanizing of the Jews: Origin and Development of Mystical Anti-Semitism* (New York: Fromm, 1992).

[30] This controversial fact has been noted by a bare handful of researchers. For an erudite exposition, see Nicholas Godrick-Clarke, *The Occult Roots of Nazism*, (NY: New York University Press, 1992), 1, who states that "fantasies can achieve a causal status once

they have been institutionalized in beliefs, values and social groups. Fantasies are also an important symptom of impending cultural changes and political action." The same observation has been made in conversation with long-time observer Laird Wilcox.

[31] The 1954 HUAC report estimates "anywhere from 200 to 700 persons," although even in this source the numbers were seen as sharply declining after 1954. House Committee on Un-American Activities, *Preliminary Report on Neo-Fascist and Hate Groups*, 10. The more realistic lower figure is from Gordon Hall, a contemporary observer of the scene. Hall is quoted in John George and Laird Wilcox, *American Extremists, Supremacists, Klansmen, Communists and Others* (Buffalo, NY: Prometheus Books, 1996), 325.

[32] Rick Cooper claims that Koehl was never a member of the NRP. Whether a member or not, Koehl was certainly very close to the NRP, and to be a leader of the uniformed guard would seem to require membership. For his contrary view, see Rick Cooper, "A Brief History of the White Nationalist Movement."

[33] On Burros, see A. M. Rosenthal and Arthur Gelb, *One More Victim: The Life and Death of a Jewish Nazi* (New York: New American Library, 1967). NRP members and associates are noted in John George and Laird Wilcox, *American Extremists*; House Committee on Un-American Activities, *Preliminary Report on Neo-Fascist and Hate Groups*; "James Hartung Madole: Father of Post-War Fascism," *Nexus*; and especially in the pages of the long-running *National Renaissance Bulletin*. On Frankhauser and his "work" for the Bureau of Alcohol, Tobacco and Firearms (ATF), see John George and Laird Wilcox, *American Extremists*, 232-37.

[34] John George and Laird Wilcox, *American Extremists*, 324-325. According to this text, many believe the highly eccentric (even by the standards of this milieu) Trujillo was an informant for, among others, the Anti-Defamation League of the B'nai B'rith.

[35] House Committee on Un-American Activities, *Preliminary Report on Neo-Fascist and Hate Groups*, 5.

[36] "America's SS—The Silver Shirts!," *New Order* 113 (November/December 1994), 3-4, 6, 12. Cf. William Dudley Pelley, *The Door to Revelation: An Intimate Biography* (Asheville, NC: Foundation Fellowship, 1935).

[37] Sharing this view is Michael Aquino, *The Church of Satan*, Third Edition, (San Francisco, CA: Michael Aquino, 1993), 272.

[38] James H. Madole, "'The New Atlantis' A Blueprint for an Aryan 'Garden of Eden' in North America! (Part VIII)," *National Renaissance Bulletin* 7 and 8 (July and August 1975), 5.

[39] James H. Madole, "'The New Atlantis' A Blueprint for an Aryan 'Garden of Eden' in North America! (Part XI)," *National Renaissance Bulletin* 3 and 4 (March and April 1976), 4.

[40] "James Hartung Madole: Father of Post-War Fascism," *Nexus*, 25-26. The events are described by Madole himself in the *National Renaissance Bulletin*, March and April 1974. A sample of Madole's early recruiting pitch to Church of Satan adherents is preserved in a letter to COS member Stuart Levine: "I am trying to find a small group of people [and] utilize their services in breaking some of our NRP officers and men into the more advanced concepts of occult philosophy." Letter from James Madole to Stuart Levine, 17 September 1974, in Michael Aquino, *The Church of Satan*, 272.

[41] "A Brief History of Satanism in Detroit," *An Introduction to the Order of the Black Ram* (Warren, MI: Order of the Black Ram, n.d.), 1-2.

[42] Letter from Anton LaVey to Michael Aquino, 24 June 1974, in Michael Aquino, *The Church of Satan*, 270.

[43] Michael Aquino, *The Church of Satan*, 269-70. On the Western Guard and other far

right wing movements in Canada, see Stanley R. Barrett, *Is God a Racist?* (Toronto: University of Toronto Press, 1987).

[44] Michael Aquino, *The Church of Satan*, 271.

[45] Ibid.

[46] Ibid.

[47] Letter from LaVey to Aquino, 5 July 1974, in Michael Aquino, *The Church of Satan*, 271-72.

[48] "James Hartung Madole: Father of Post-War Fascism," *Nexus*, 26.

[49] Joseph Tommasi, *Building the Revolutionary Party* (nd).

[50] Letter from Varg Quisling Vikerness, 10 September 1996.

[51] See for a representative selection the National Alliance's "greatest hits" volume: *The Best of Attack!: Revolutionary Voice of the National Alliance* (Hillsboro, WV: National Vanguard Books, 1984, 1992).

[52] Interview with Nils Mandel, Stockholm, 19 August 1995. In 1996, the Belgians grew tired of hosting this chaotic event and it was moved to Trollhattan, Sweden, where violent clashes took place between skinheads and anti-racist activists. The highlight of the celebration, however, was the appearance of a group of naked anarchists who painted themselves blue to illustrate "the naked truth about fascism." "Swedish Neo-Nazi March Ends in Violence," *Reuters Wire Service* 17 August 1996. The report was downloaded and made available to the movement by the ANA e-mail news service.

[53] The primary source of Mason's history is M. M. Jenkins' introduction to James Mason, *Siege* (Denver, CO: Storm Books, 1992). Storm is the publishing house of Michael Moynahan, a writer and artist whose Blood Axis CD is arguably the best musical work to date to emerge from the occult current of National Socialism. For a revealing insight into Mason's early life, see "James Mason," *No Longer a Fanzine* 5 (n.d.), 11-16. Cf. Aaron Garland's interview with Mason, "Politics Beyond the Pale," *Ohm Clock* 3 (Spring 1995), 4-11; and "W.O.T.A.N. Interviews James Mason," *W.O.T.A.N.* 2 October 1996, 2. W.O.T.A.N. is the British voice of Combat 18. For a tongue-in-cheek interview, see the mordant comments of Alan Prendergast, "Beyond the Pale," *Denver Westword* vol. 16, no. 48 (28 July-3 August, 1993). The interview was supplied to this research by Aaron Garland at the suggestion of James Mason, proving conclusively that, contrary to popular opinion, Nazis do have a sense of humor.

[54] Mason notes that his impression not only of blacks, but of Jews as well, was on the whole rather positive in his early years. "James Mason," 11-12.

[55] Interview with James Mason, 28 November 1996.

[56] As one striking example, Sweden's Tommy Rydén recalls from his own small town boyhood reading a newspaper account at the age of 13 of the American Ku Klux Klan. Putting together scraps of information from a number of sources, Rydén was able to obtain the address of American Klan leader Bill Wilkinson. Interview with Tommy Rydén, Linköping, Sweden, 28 July 1995. In a not atypical denouement to this story, Wilkinson, who was most helpful to Rydén's early endeavors, turned out to be a long-time FBI informant. On Wilkinson, see John George and Laird Wilcox, *American Extremists*, 373-374.

[57] John Carpenter, *Extremism U.S.A.* (Phoenix, AZ: Extremism USA, 1964). The photograph Mason refers to is on page 137. The book actually says remarkably little about right-wing extremists, saving greater vitriol for the left. In both cases, the text is an exercise in middle-of-the-road "Americanism" of little historical value. The classmate soon became disillusioned and dropped out of the movement. He committed suicide in 1992 or 1993. Interview with James Mason, 28 November 1996. Cf. "James Mason," 13.

58 Interview with James Mason, 28 November 1996.

59 This point is confirmed by Mason, using as an example the West Coast faction of the movement which splintered under Koehl's leadership, thus driving some of the younger and more daring adherents into the camp of Joseph Tommasi and the violent revolutionary appeal of the National Socialist Liberation Front. Letter from James Mason, 17 December 1996.

60 For a brief discussion of the mass vs. revolutionary action theory, see Jeffrey Kaplan, "Right Wing Violence in North America," 57.

61 The conflict was irreconcilable and Pierce left for the National Youth Alliance, a front group formed by Willis Carto that grew out of the 1968 George Wallace presidential campaign. The ideological point of contention centered around Pierce's charge that Koehl was a "cultist," but at a deeper level, Pierce had already begun his shift from the movement's typical conservatism to embrace revolutionary violence. Interview with James Mason, 28 November 1996.

62 James Mason, *Siege!* XI, 5 (May 1982).

63 Joseph Tommasi, "Building the Revolutionary Party," in James Mason, *Siege!*, 383.

64 One former member who left the movement at his wife's insistence in the early 1970s recalls Tommasi's derisive nickname, "Tomato Joe," given both for his Italian surname and less than Nordic complexion. This same adherent recalls that while many were privately caustic about Tommasi's appearance and ethnicity, he was nonetheless respected as "a total fanatic," although many of the West Coast group would have nothing to do with the Universal Order or Tommasi's extremism. Interview with an Odinist adherent, name withheld by request, 7 January 1997.

65 Interview with James Mason, 28 November 1996. On the fragmentation of the Koehl-era party and the expulsion of Tommasi, see Jeffrey Kaplan, "Right Wing Violence in North America," 57.

66 Interview with James Mason, 28 November 1996.

67 Given the common perception in movement circles of Koehl's homosexuality, one suspects that it was as much the girls as the illegal substances which brought the ire of the NSWPP down on Tommasi's head. Whatever the source of this rivalry, it would cost Tommasi his life. In 1975, he was assassinated by an adherent of the NSW On the movement's perception of Koehl's sexual orientation, see Rick Cooper, "Brief History of the White Nationalist Movement." Indeed, the widespread rumors of Koehl's homosexuality so disturbed Rockwell that at one point the Commander imported an attractive and devoted female party member whose mission was to seduce Koehl and thus put to rest any suspicions regarding his virility. The mission was a fiasco. See Frederick Simonelli, *American Fuehrer*, 145. On Tommasi's death, see John George and Laird Wilcox, *American Extremists*, 337. The ADL weighs in on the subject in Anti-Defamation League of the B'nai B'rith, *Extremism on the Right*, 43. James Mason recalls that a lesser known charge of financial improprieties was lodged against Tommasi by California Koehl loyalists. Interview with James Mason, 28 November 1996.

68 Joseph Tommasi, "Building the Revolutionary Party," in James Mason, *Siege!*, 381. The original NSLF poster is reproduced in idem., 19.

69 James Mason, *Siege!*, 5.

70 Beam's now ubiquitous "Leaderless Resistance" essay may now be obtained on Beam's homepage via Don Black's Stormfront Web page. It originally appeared in its final form in Beam's now defunct journal, the *Seditionist* 12 (February 1992). This was to be the last issue of that publication. The essay also appeared in the report of the meeting of Pete Peters' Scriptures for America Bible camp, which is widely (and largely errone-

ously) considered to be the genesis of the American militia movement. The meeting by chance took place during the tragic denouement of the events surrounding Randy Weaver and his family at Ruby Ridge, Idaho, and the report is a record of the attendees' reaction to the killing of Weaver's wife and young son by federal agents. See Louis Beam, "Leaderless Resistance," in *Special Report on the Meeting of Christian Men Held in Estes Park, Colorado October 23, 24, 25, 1992 Concerning the Killing of Vickie and Samuel Weaver by the United States Government* (Laporte, CO: Scriptures for America, n.d.). Cf. Andrew Macdonald, *Hunter* (Arlington, VA: National Vanguard Books, 1989).

[71] Joseph Tommasi, "Strategy for Revolution," in James Mason, *Siege!*, 378-80. "Blows Against the Empire" was the title of an early 1970s Jefferson Starship album which held a certain vogue in right as well as left wing circles of the day. E-mail conversation with former national spokesman of the Minutemen, R. N. Taylor. Tommasi and the NSLF took the same playful approach to hippie culture, for example "Big Brother and the Holding Company," *Siege!* 2 (1974), 5. The article concerns an attack on the "law and order" preoccupation of the right wing, picturing police in contemporary leftist terms as pigs paid to enforce the American status quo. Big Brother and the Holding Company was also the name of Janis Joplin's first band.

[72] Joseph Tommasi, "Strategy for Revolution," in James Mason, *Siege!*, 379.

[73] Interview with James Mason, 28 November 1996. On founding Order member David Lane's revolutionary theories, see Jeffrey Kaplan, *Radical Religion in America*. For primary source documents on Lane's "Wotan" theories, see David Lane, "Wotan Is Coming," *WAR* (April 1993).

[74] Letter from James Mason, 16 December 1996. Mason was responding to the suggestion that this core/peripheral membership was at the root of differing claims by both Tommasi and Mason of the level of NSLF support, which was variously reported as either 4 or more than 40.

[75] James Mason, *Siege!*, 104. Interview with James Mason, 28 November 1996.

[76] For a view of the truth of this axiom holding the masses to be essentially feminine, see the autobiography of Leni Riefenstahl, *Leni Riefenstahl: A Memoir* (New York: St. Martin's Press, 1992). For a theoretical view, see Julius Evola, *Revolt Against the Modern World* (Rochester, VT: Inner Traditions International, 1995), 157-66.

[77] John George and Laird Wilcox, *American Extremists*, 338.

[78] Interview with James Mason, 28 November 1996.

[79] For the ultimate example of this wish fulfillment, see Richard Kelly Hoskins, *Vigilantes of Christendom* (Lynchburg, VA: Virginia Publishing Co., 1990).

[80] Interview with James Mason, 28 November 1996.

[81] Michael Moynahan, "Charles Manson," *Seconds* 32 (n.d.), 64.

[82] Charles Manson, "Quotes from Manson," ATWA, e-text document copyrighted by Sandra Good, 5 November 1996.

[83] James Mason, *Siege!* XI, 5 (May 1982). It was in any case seen primarily as a personal vehicle for Mason's views. Mason notes that this was very much in keeping with the one-man outfits common to the NS scene. Interview with James Mason, 28 November 1996.

[84] This peaceful parting of the ways is so atypical of the fractious NS milieu that today Mason calls it: "one of the most decent and honorable things anyone has ever done within the movement." Interview with James Mason, 28 November 1996.

[85] James Mason, *Siege!*, 87. For a discussion of the religionist/anti-religionist split in NS ranks, see Jeffrey Kaplan, "Religiosity and the Radical Right: Toward the Creation of a New Ethnic Identity," in Jeffrey Kaplan and Tore Bjørgo, eds., *Brotherhoods of Nation and Race*. Mason notes that he found that religion is, after all, of key importance during

his present incarceration, and he observes that the current situation in the world matches almost precisely the scenario of the Book of Revelations. Interview with James Mason, 28 November 1996.

[86] James Mason, *Siege!*, 362. Today, Mason states that while he continues to admire Church of Satan founder Anton LaVey, he remains convinced that Satan "couldn't care less" about our doings, and if he did, he would most likely appear as "a three-piece suited, Ivy league politician" wanting your vote to move into "the Brave New World. Or the New World Order." Interview with James Mason, 28 November 1996.

[87] Mason took his case for Manson to the skinhead and White Power rock world in James Mason, "Charles Manson: Illusion vs. Reality," *Resistance* 4 (Spring 1995), 20-22.

[88] "The Manson Debate: Two of Our Readers Take their Sides," *Resistance* 5 (Fall 1995), 31-33.

[89] Interview with Michael Moynahan, 19 December 1996. Indeed, Manson's recorded musings can be hypnotic, seemingly touched at one moment by crazed genius and at another as so obscure as to be incomprehensible, or even mad. James Mason notes in this regard that he once sent a CD of Manson talking to a psychiatrist of his acquaintance who wrote back that Manson "demonstrated a lot of 'free association' commonly connected with schizophrenia. But that immediately gave way to other considerations like simply being under-socialized, no social skills, or perhaps genius." Letter from James Mason, 16 December 1996.

[90] Stoddard Martin, *Art, Messianism and Crime: A Study of Antinomianism in Modern Literature and Lives* (New York: St. Martin's Press, 1986).

[91] Ibid., 3.

[92] This by now ubiquitous view of Manson's motives for the murders for which he was charged and sentenced to death is hotly denied by Manson and the remnants of his core group. This issue will be explored more fully in the discussion below of the utility of the Manson legend.

[93] Interview with Michael Moynahan, 19 December 1996.

[94] Manson CDs are available from White Devil Records and Storm Books. The most fascinating of these is the double CD *Manson Speaks* on White Devil Records. 'Zines featuring Manson articles are too numerous to mention. Some of the more interesting Manson books to return to the market include the "lost classic," John Gilmore and Ron Kenner, *The Garbage People* (Los Angeles: Amok, 1995); Nuel Emmons, *Manson In His Own Words* (New York: Grove Press, 1986); Nikolas Schreck, *The Manson File* (Los Angeles: Amok, 1988); and of course, the old war horse has returned in book and tape versions, Vincent Bugliosi with Curt Gentry, *Helter Skelter* (New York: W. W. Norton, 1974). In addition, Manson family members and alums such as Susan Atkins and Charles "Tex" Watson have reappeared in the market. Manson for his part in *Manson Speaks* states that *Manson In His Own Words* has little to do with anything he said and even the semi-legendary *The Garbage People* is garbage, having nothing to do with Manson, despite Manson's nearly eighteen-year-long relationship with the author. *Manson In His Own Words* raises particular ire. According to Manson: "Is there no way to stop [that] book? That thing has been a curse. It's destroyed us all, [and] ATWA for over ten years." *Lies About Charles Manson*, e-text copyrighted by Sandra Good, 2 January 1997.

[95] Vincent Bugliosi with Curt Gentry, *Helter Skelter.*

[96] Ed Sanders, *The Family* (New York: E. P. Dutton & Co. Inc., 1971).

[97] Letter from Father Christian of the Boston chapter of the Process Church of the Final Judgment to William Bainbridge, 9 March 1972. The letter is in the Process section of the J. Gordon Melton archives at the University of California, Santa Barbara.

[98] *Lies About Charles Manson.*

[99] "Where does the garbage go, as we have tin cans and garbage alongside the road, and oil slicks in your water, so you have people, and I am one of your garbage people." Charles Manson, *The Testimony of Charles Manson, November 19, 1970*, e-text, copyright by Sandra Good.

[100] *Lies About Charles Manson.* Manson himself is on record with all of these sentiments in his various statements to the court and parole hearings. See for example *The Testimony of Charles Manson, November 19, 1970*; *Manson's 1986 Parole Hearing Statement*; and especially *Thought*, a text which contains several of Manson's rare letters and the complete transcript of the 1986 parole hearing. All available as e-text, copyright by Sandra Good. The profitability aspect is a particularly sore point, as Manson contends to this day in nearly all of the above documents that his music was stolen by Brian Wilson of the Beach Boys and he was cheated by Terry Melcher, a record producer in the 1960s.

[101] Interview with Michael Moynahan, 19 December 1996.

[102] The influence of the Blood Axis CD is such that Rahowa lead singer and entrepreneur of Resistance Records George Eric Hawthorne has expressed a desire to work with Moynahan based on his admiration for *The Gospel of Inhumanity*. See the interview with Hawthorne in the French 'zine *Raven Chats*: "RAHOWA Racial Holy War," *Raven Chats* 7 (nd). For Moynahan's noncommittal reply, see idem., "Blood Axis." *Raven Chats* neither dates its issues nor provides page numbers. Issue 7 is dedicated to the late Icelandic Ásatrú leader Svienbjorn Beinteinsson. On the importance of Rahowa and *Cult of the Holy War*, see Heléne Lööw, "White Power Rock'n' Roll—A Growing Industry," and for a discussion of *The Gospel of Inhumanity*, see Jeffrey Kaplan, "Religiosity and the Radical Right: Toward the Creation of a New Ethnic Identity," both in Jeffrey Kaplan and Tore Bjørgo, eds., *Brotherhoods of Nation and Race.*

[103] Blood Axis, "Herr, nun laß in Frieden," from the CD *The Gospel of Inhumanity*. It should be noted that a virtually identical scene takes place in the novel *All Quiet on the Western Front* by Erich Remarque.

[104] Blood Axis, "Herr, nun laß in Frieden," from the CD *The Gospel of Inhumanity*.

[105] James William Gibson, *Warrior Dream: Violence and Manhood in Post-Vietnam America* (New York: Hill and Wang, 1994).

[106] *The Testimony of Charles Manson, November 19, 1970.*

[107] *Thought*. This theme, more like a jazz riff than a coherent thought, is brought out to much greater effect on the *Manson Speaks* CD.

[108] Michael Moynahan, "Charles Manson," 67.

[109] James Mason, *Siege!*, 345-46. This dearth of women in a movement which sees the race as on the verge of extinction is perhaps the most vexing problem facing movement activists on both sides of the Atlantic. It is a problem to which much thought has been given, and few answers found. Milton Kleim, e-mail message, 2 October 1996. In the same message, Kleim notes that: "The Manson thing made me want to lash out in disgust." Moreover, when Kleim decided to leave the movement, the ever increasing prevalence of the occult in the world of National Socialism was a major factor: "I find completely repugnant any sort of occult/Satanic viewpoint, and found the attempt to link the 'cause' with an occult meaning to be completely unacceptable. It definitely planted seeds in my mind when I encountered this type of crap." On women in the race movement, see Katrine Fangen, "Separate or Equal? The Emergence of an All-Female Group in Norway's Rightist Underground," *Journal of Terrorism and Political Violence* 9:3 (Autumn 1997), 122-64.

[110] Interview with James Mason, 28 November 1996.

[111] *ATWA*. On the radical environmental movement itself, see Bron Taylor, *Ecological Resistance Movements: The Global Emergence of Radical and Popular Environmentalism* (Albany, NY: State University of New York Press, International Environmental Policy and Theory Series, 1995).

[112] *ATWA*.

[113] E-mail message from Bron Taylor, 21 January 1997.

[114] *ATWA*. For an interesting analysis which warns precisely of the prevalence of patriarchy in the rhetoric emanating from some radical environmentalists which centers on the feminization of the earth, see Lois Ann Lorentzen, "Phallic Millennialism and Radical Environmentalism: The Apocalyptic Vision of Earth First!," in Charles B. Strozier and Michael Flynn, eds., *Two Thousand: Essays on the End* (Albany, NY: New York University Press, 1997).

[115] A. Hodgins, and A. Petermann, 1995. "Why a Womyn's Issue," *Alarm: A Voice of Revolutionary Ecology* 12 (1995), 2-3.

[116] Ibid. Both of these quotes were supplied by Bron Taylor.

[117] *Quotes From Red and Blue*.

[118] The import of the crimes themselves appear to have only passing interest to those associated with the Universal Order or sympathetic to Manson as an NS icon. Witness, for example, Michael Moynahan noting in an interview that he was born in 1969, "the year of the fork," referring to the fork left in Leno Labianca's stomach, or Vidhar von Herske's caustic observation that Manson is being held in prison seemingly forever despite the fact that he killed no one. Interview with Michael Moynahan, 18 November 1996; letter from Vidhar von Herske, 22 August 1996.

[119] James Mason, *Siege!*, 328.

[120] Anonymous, *The John Franklin Letters* (New York: The Book Mailer Inc., 1959); Andrew Macdonald (William Pierce), *The Turner Diaries* (Arlington, VA: National Vanguard Books, 1978).

[121] *Manson's 1986 Parole Hearing Statement*.

[122] James Mason, "Charles Manson: Illusion vs. Reality," *Resistance* 4 (Spring 1995), 21.

[123] James Mason, "Charles Manson: Illusion vs. Reality," 22.

[124] See, for example, David Myatt, "Reichfolk—Toward a New Elite," unpublished but widely distributed text provided by David Myatt. This new elite is to be dubbed, according to this document, the Legion of Adolf Hitler. Other Reichfolk titles include "The Arts of Civilisation: Aryan Culture and the Importance of Honour, Curiosity and Conquest," and "National Socialism and the Occult," to name but a few. Cf. Kaplan interview with David Myatt, 29 April 1996. Myatt's texts are widely published throughout the NS world, in a number of racially oriented underground 'zines, and via the Internet.

[125] The ONA has, among its other accomplishments, succeeded in frightening a number of people. For a somewhat humorous example, see the unnerving adventures of the Reverend Kevin Logan who, having arranged for the protection and surveillance of the local constabulary, braves the dark and lonely moors of central England to conduct an interview with Christos Beest. Kevin Logan, *Satanism and the Occult: Today's Dark Revolution* (Eastbourne: Kingsway Publications, 1994), 129-37. Reverend Logan managed to survive the ordeal. Indeed, apprised of the Logan book, Beest forwarded the shaken churchman a sharply worded letter demanding evidence of some of the charges leveled against the ONA in *Satanism and the Occult*, particularly of lurid accusations of child sacrifice, sexual abuse, and cannibalism ("The sex could be with a baby, a young child . . . the fat of babies, sometimes even unborn babies, was prescribed for certain annointing

oils."). Rev. Logan did not, however, deign to reply. Letter from Christos Beest, 3 February 1997. Mr. Beest thoughtfully included a copy of his letter to Rev. Logan, dated 14 January 1997.

[126] Letter from Christos Beest, 16 September 1996. Mr. Beest also notes that another closely associated organization, the Order of Balder, is in the process of putting together its own communal experiment, the Jomsberg Community, which is seen as a cultural and community center. All three groups share a Web site.

[127] Letter from Christos Beest, 16 September 1996. Letter from Vidharr Von Herske, 22 August 1996. Typical recruiting appeals of the Bolton-era Black Order are "Black Order," and "Dualism and the Cycles of Time," all available as e-text from Kerry Bolton. Each Bolton-era Black Order essay would end with the credo: "The Black Order is an esoteric body of men and women established to present the 'dark' or 'Shadow' side of the European unconscious."

[128] The premier issue of the American Black Order's publication, the *Abyss,* appeared in the summer of 1996. Since then, the group has had a falling out with some members of the New Zealand branch of the Black Order over the latter's acceptance of homosexuals. As a result, the American branch changed its name to the White Order and has approached R. N. Taylor as a possible leader. Taylor, head of the Ásatrú Alliance kindred the Wulfing tribe, became known to the American Black Order through his connections with the Process Church in the 1960s. On this, see R. N. Taylor, "The Process: A Personal Reminiscence," in Adam Parfrey, (ed.), *Apocalypse Culture*, Second edition, (Portland, OR: Feral House, 1990), 159-71. On the Order's change of direction, e-mail messages from R. N. Taylor, 22 October 1996; 26 October 1996; and 22 January 1997.

[129] For details of the Swedish Black Order, see Jeffrey Kaplan, "Religiosity and the Radical Right: Toward the Creation of a New Ethnic Identity," in Jeffrey Kaplan and Tore Bjørgo, eds., *Brotherhoods of Nation and Race*. In 1996, the Swedish Black Order was again in the headlines with the arrest of several of its adherents for the ritual sexual abuse of young girls, which included the drinking of their blood in a vampire-inspired ceremony. E-mail message to Kaplan from Heléne Lööw, 18 November 1996.

The Modern Anti-Cult Movement in Historical Perspective

J. Gordon Melton

The rise in the 1970s of what became an important reactionary social movement in the West in the last quarter of the twentieth century can be seen as a response to the global religious diversification in the decades since World War II, but owes its origin to the peculiar circumstances accompanying the diffusion of Asian and occult religion in the United States in the early 1970s. The post-war spread of what became known as new religions followed two very different patterns in Europe and North America.

A gradual penetration of the European nations by "new" religions (i.e., Asian religions) began soon after the dust settled from not so much World War II as the Chinese revolution and the declaration of Indian independence. Migrants brought their religions into the nations of Europe through the colonial systems, especially into England, France, and Holland, and by the government-sponsored migration of needed laborers into Germany and Switzerland. At the same time, Western vagabonds began their now legendary treks into Asia in search of spiritual wisdom only to return to their homeland as initial converts to unfamiliar (to the rest of us) faiths. The change was gradual, and problems with migrants tended to focus on ethnic and racial issues rather than religion.

Much of the new religious life was and still is confined to the migrant ghettoes, but increasingly religious teachers visited and then settled in Europe. They added to the religious diversity already created by the home-grown religious dissidents who had emerged as founders of new alternative religious communities through the nineteenth and twentieth centuries. Beginning with the formation of the Swedenborgian church, numerous new religions (alternatives to traditional Christianity) emerged in Europe. Most notable were the post-Mesmerist magical (Rosicrucian, Neo-templar, and Martinist) orders that appeared in France; Spiritualism, which diffused across the continent from Great Britain and Paris; and Theosophy. Through the twentieth century, almost every country from Bulgaria (Great White Brotherhood) to Denmark (Martinus Institute) to Great Britain (New Age Movement, Wicca) contributed to the emerging pluralism as Gnosticism revived in the climate of post-Enlightenment religious freedom.

In America the pattern of diversification was quite different due to the passing of a series of laws in the first decades of this century which prevented migration from Asia. The culminating Asian Exclusion Act of 1924 was in force until the fall of 1965, when it was rescinded as a result of Presidents Kennedy and Johnson calling upon the member nations of the Southeast Asian Treaty Organization to support the war effort in Vietnam. The price of cooperation was the removal of insulting and discriminatory immigration policies against member countries by the United States. Domestically, their policy resulted in the sudden influx of hundreds of thousands of Asians into the United States and the opening of the country to the endeavors of Asian religious missionaries (usually arriving under such titles as swami, bhagwan, yogi, guru, pir, sensei, or master).

The sudden availability of Asian teachers coincided with a unique situation in American life, the coming of age of the post-war baby boom generation. That very large generation had been a problem for more than a decade as it first put pressure on the public school system, which had to find space and teachers to accommodate them, and now confronted the business community with the need for jobs, jobs which were simply unavailable. One response was the development of a new subculture, the street-people culture. The street people emerged in urban centers across the United States but were especially pronounced along the Pacific Coast, where both the climate and a socially tolerant society provided them with the greatest degree of freedom. Of additional importance, each summer the subculture swelled with college kids (especially those rich enough not to have to work all summer) who idealized the lifestyle of the street people and joined them for their annual vacation period.

Thus in America, as new religious leaders began to pour into the country at the end of the 1960s, they joined those indigenous leaders already actively working this self-selected "lost" generation living on the streets. Swami Prabhupada (Hare Krishna) began in Greenwich Village, Yogi Bhajan (Sikh Dharma) in Los Angeles, and the Unification Church in Eugene, Oregon, and Washington, D.C. They were joined by several groups founded in the United States, most prominently the Church of Scientology and the groups of the Jesus People movement, as well as the imports from Europe (Wicca, Friends of Meher Baba). Earlier Alan Watts, who became the great popularizer of Zen, had migrated from England. Each of these groups adapted itself to the young people on the streets and their love of psychedelic drugs, and took a high percentage of their initial recruits from among them.

The penetration of the street-people culture by new religions might have largely gone unnoticed were it not for the large number of summer hippies who swelled its ranks. Many of the recruits to the new religions came from these vacationers, who found membership in a new religion to be a welcome alternative to their return to college life and the prospect of a professional career which had been wished upon them by their middle- and upper-middle-class parents. While the majority of parents were quite tolerant of their sons' or daughters' new religion, some were quite upset, not so much with their children's flirting with a new faith, but with its implications for their children's future life—their dropping out of school, their turning over their income/inheritance to a strange foreign group, and/or their assuming a position in the organization as their life's career. To put it bluntly, how do secular parents tell acquaintances that their offspring has become a missionary working the streets for a low-status religion rather than a doctor, lawyer, or executive?

The actual number of young adults who joined the new religions was low, but just enough dropped earlier career plans that by the early 1970s, a few upset parents began to voice their anger publicly and quickly found that they were not alone. The first networks of what was to become a national movement began to emerge. The alarm over what was occurring was also sounded by the Jewish community. In 1972, several evangelical Christian organizations announced plans for what was to be known as "Key '73," a massive door-to-door campaign designed to present every household in America with the evangelical gospel. Among those who quickly signed on in support were the many Jewish evangelism groups, who saw an opportunity to canvas the Jewish community where they had been quietly working since the 1920s. The leaders in the Jewish communities across the country reacted quickly and denounced the effort. In the process of negotiating their concerns with the leaders of the Key '73 campaign, they became aware of a host of other missionary groups both Christian (Unification Church, Children of God, the Way International) and Eastern (primarily Zen and Hindu guru-led groups) that were accepting Jewish converts. The formation of the Jews for Jesus in the San Francisco Bay Area was especially disturbing.

A history of living as a tiny minority within a Christian-dominated society has made Jewish leaders especially sensitive to any coordinated efforts aimed at the religious conversion of Jews (even those low-key attempts of many Eastern religions). Following the discovery of the new religions, Jewish leaders initiated a debate over the number of young Jews being attracted to the groups and increased defenses against the perceived dangers of conversionist organizations. As a result, Jewish communal organizations across the country developed anti-cult task forces and became prominent supporters of the various parent-led anti-cult organizations. Efforts to alert Jews to this latest danger to the community's existence[1] led to the formation of counseling centers and the emergence of activists specializing in removing Jews from the new religions.[2] Several such activists became prominent leaders in the larger movement. James and Marcia Rudin, for example, used their position within the national Jewish-Christian interfaith movement to build anti-cult sentiment within liberal Protestant circles.[3]

By the mid 1980s, though still supportive of the anti-cult perspective, most Jewish leaders perceived that Evangelical Christianity was still their basic problem. Ignoring agreements reached with some Evangelicals as a result of the Key '73 controversy, independent missionaries persisted actively proselytizing within urban Jewish communities. Quietly, through the 1980s, those agencies charged with protecting the interests of the Jewish community re-emphasized preventative measures against Christian conversionist efforts.[4]

From FREECOG to CFF[5]

The first of the new religions to attract major controversy was a Christian evangelical group, one of the early Jesus People groups, which had emerged around a former holiness minister, David Berg, in southern California. As early as the 1970s, informal groups of parents began investigating the group which had begun among the street people enjoying the sand and surf at Huntington Beach. The loosely organized beach ministry had changed dramatically in 1969, when members heeded a prophecy by Berg on impending doom for California. After eight months of wandering across America, Berg emerged as Moses David and his followers as the Children of God.[6]

Parents concerned about their offsprings' involvement in the group formalized their anger and concern in 1972 by forming the Parents Committee to Free Our Sons and Daughters from the Children of God, later shortened to Free the Children of God (or FREECOG), the first of the anti-cult groups. Parents tried direct appeals to their offspring, and in their failure in persuading them to return to their former life, tried more coercive measures including the intervention of law enforcement agencies.[7] These efforts culminated in the actions of the attorney general of the state of New York, who in 1974 issued a report on the Children of God, accusing them of a laundry list of crimes, but he took no action, as most of the alleged crime occurred outside of his jurisdiction and most of the members, following Berg's vision of leading a worldwide missionary organization, had left the United States.

The efforts of FREECOG, including its taking out ads in newspapers in southern California, brought media coverage as well as inquiries from parents whose young adult offspring had affiliated with other new groups. Thus it was that in late 1973 the leadership of FREECOG transformed its organization into the more broadly based Volunteer Parents of America (VPA). VPA soon folded due to organizational inadequacies and was superseded by the Citizens Freedom Foundation (CFF), arguably the most successful of the 1970s anti-cult groups. Originally CFF was confined to California, but similar organizations under a variety of names sprang up around the country. They included the Citizens Organized for Public Awareness of Cults (Greensboro, North Carolina), Personal Freedom Foundation (Baltimore, Maryland), and Love Our Children, Inc. (Omaha, Nebraska). These organizations were generally built around the zeal of one or two people, were constantly limited financially, and experienced a rapid overturn of members as members (i.e., parents) resolved their personal situation in some manner and dropped out.

During the mid-1970s, several attempts were made to construct an umbrella organization which could coordinate the efforts of the many local groups and make some national impact. In 1976 the Ad Hoc Committee Engaged in Freeing Minds was able to entice Senator Robert Dole (of Kansas) to hold hearings at which parents and others could present their complaints. However, both the committee and a second national organization, the International Foundation for Individual Freedom, proved ineffective and soon passed from the scene.

The anti-cult movement of the 1970s never satisfactorily resolved its essential problem. Members actually opposed the new religion for two specific reasons. One group had religious qualms with the new religions and did not want their offspring to associate with any group other than the one in which they were raised. The larger percentage, however, was angered that its young adult offspring had rejected parental guidance and had given up on higher education and a "normal" career for membership and work within a cult. But neither concern fell into the realm of government concerns. Adults, even young ones, had a perfect right to change careers and religious affiliation, and government and law enforcement officials were largely unresponsive to parental demands for intervention. Thus that very real concern had to be recast and the parental concern groups had to change into anti-cult groups, and the leadership began a search for both an alternative program (given the inactivity of the courts and police) and an articulated ideology which shifted attention from the unacceptable choices of the youthful convert and to the organizations which they had joined.

The process of demonizing the new religions began very early. During the days of FREECOG, members had encountered the counter-cult literature which had been circulating for a generation in evangelical circles. That literature had adopted the term "cult" to designate various non-Christian and Christian-heretical groups, and FREECOG members quickly adopted the term to designate the targeted new religions. Prior to the mid-1970s, almost all material on cults had been written by Protestant Christians, and the adoption of the term by the new anti-cult groups created a rather complex pattern of interaction. The term cult was familiar to many people, and Evangelicals had already projected their concern for the new cults which had emerged since 1965. Additionally some Christian counter-cult groups had both a stable organization and a national distribution system for their literature. At the same time, the more prominent Christian writers on cults, such as Walter Martin, clearly understood that those who branded conversionist groups like the new religions as manipulative and deceitful could easily turn on Evangelical Christian groups and attack them on the same ground.[8] Only a few Evangelicals joined sociologist Ron Enroth in aligning themselves with the new anti-cultists.[9]

Although a major source, Christian counter-cult literature also presented problems for the new anti-cultists. Since they could not build a program around their true concern (disapproval of their children's choices), they had to generate a polemic against cults in general. Christian literature also broadly attacked cults, but centered the attack upon some older, more successful groups and included some large influential groups such as the Mormons and Unitarians, and even Roman Catholics. Each time the anti-cult movement gained some audience with legislators, seeking them to act against cults, its efforts were undermined by the Christian literature. Circulated around a state assembly, outspoken legislators tended quickly and tactfully to withdraw support from any legislation that would suggest disapproval of the religious affiliation of their fellow legislators.[10]

Program and Ideology

Even before finding a perspective which would provide a launching pad for a broad assault upon the new religions, anti-cultists hit upon a program. Actually, it appears that the first deprogrammings took place even prior to the founding of FREECOG. Reportedly, the process was developed by Theodore "Ted" Patrick, at the time an employee of the state of California, who had become concerned about his son's and a nephew's encounter with the Children of God. He met some COG people and allowed them to evangelize him. He would later call their conversionist activity "brainwashing," by which he meant that the group manipulated people to the extent that they were turned into robots and mental slaves. The anti-COG groups adopted the "mind control" terminology, and in its first newsletter, the Citizens Freedom Foundation defined deprogramming as

> the process of releasing victims from the control of individuals and organizations who exploit other individuals through the use of mind control techniques. Once released, the victims, rid of the fear that held them in bondage, are encouraged to again think for themselves and to take their rightful place in society, free from further threats to their peace and security.[11]

Not covered by the formal definition, deprogramming, as touted by CFF and practiced by Patrick, involved detaining the subjects (sometimes kidnapping them off the street) and forcing them to participate in an intense harangue denigrating COG (or some other group) and its leader. The victims of the deprogramming were suddenly cut off from any support supplied by other members of the groups and confronted with the emotional outpouring of parents and other family members begging them to renounce the group and straighten up their lives. The number of deprogrammings increased steadily through the decade. Patrick quit his job with the state and became a full-time professional deprogrammer in late 1971. His book describing his work appeared in 1976.[12]

While deprogrammings were by no means successful in all cases (and exact numbers are difficult to determine), enough were successful that some of those who went through the process joined the ranks of the deprogrammers and/or became prominent advocates of the anti-cult perspective. As the coercive nature of the process became better known, it became the subject of a variety of court actions. On several occasions Patrick was tried and convicted, though he usually received only a token sentence.

Drawing upon the ideas supportive of the practice of deprogramming, a mechanistic perspective of religious conversion in general (which had survived in some psychological circles), and popular hysteria over Chinese thought-control practices used against American prisoners during the Korean War, the leaders of the anti-cult movement by 1975 were freely using the term "brainwashing" to describe the process of becoming and remaining involved in a new religion. Potential members were described as psychologically vulnerable individuals who combined an intense youthful idealism with an inability to adjust to their social situation, especially in college.

According to the developing polemic, it was this naive young individual who was attacked by the cult. The first step was, through deceit, to trick the person to attend a group event. There, without revealing their true goals, the group leaders began a subtle process of manipulation which began with the staged smiles, openness, and happiness expressed by members of the group. Before the potential recruit had time to think about what was occurring, he or she would be enticed (coerced) into membership and then held in that membership by the repeated application of subtle psychological techniques. The recruit gradually lost his or her ability to think and choose another way. The understanding of this process was in fact developed from a superficial presentation of the recruitment process of one group, the Unification Church of Reverend Sun Myung Moon, who often recruited street people by first inviting them to dinner, and only after the potential recruits gained a favorable impression of the group did a discussion of group belief and practice begin. However, as a whole, new religions had a more standard approach that began with an introduction to the group. There was, in fact, no way to hide what was occurring when one first visited a Hindu temple whose members adopted Indian dress.

Early anti-cultists found substantiation for the use of brainwashing as a descriptive term from psychologist Robert Jay Lifton and his book, *Thought Reform and the Psychology of Totalism*,[13] which described the processes of thought control used in the Korean prison camps and compared them with the various practices operative in different social groups including revivalistic religious groups.

Not only was deprogramming seen as necessary to "freeing" a person psychologically trapped in a group, but some form of continued post-deprogramming counseling was also recommended. Jean Merritt, a psychiatric social worker, and one of the first psychological professionals attracted to anti-cultism, saw the treatment of ex-cult members to be a difficult but significant part of their return to normalcy. In an open letter written in 1975, she noted,

> Ex-members are so weak once they have been presented with the realities of how they have been psychologically, financially and sometimes sexually abused, that they have need of constant attention. Ironically, this causes the parents and professionals to act similarly to the cults in their close surveillance. Once there is some restoration of ego functioning, the weaning process takes place again and hopefully the person is on the way to recovery. Some that are not so fortunate have to be hospitalized because they are so dependent, suicidal, or because they have suffered complete breaks with reality. The recovery process takes almost a year, for the person to be back to where they first began in the cult.[14]

This added perspective on the problems of people who have been deprogrammed led to the formation of several rehabilitation centers, the most famous being the Freedom of Thought Foundation in Tucson, Arizona, and they continue to be an important part of the deprogramming efforts.[15]

Once the various local anti-cult groups began to associate with each other on a national level, they also began to appeal to the government to handle the "cult problem." They found a sympathetic ear in the person of Kansas senator Robert Dole, but the hearing provided parents of members of the new religions with very little beyond a media event. Dole did write letters to both the Internal Revenue Service concerning the tax status of the Unification Church and to the Justice Department, attempting to set up a meeting between the Attorney General and two scholars identified with the anti-cult movement, but neither letter led to any action.

The dead end in Washington was followed by a series of actions at the state levels. Over the next few years, a number of bills were introduced into state legislatures calling for various repressive measures against the new religions. Some bills focused upon accusations of criminal activity, but most attempted to make involvement in new religions a concern of mental health professionals. For example, the legislation in Vermont introduced in 1976 looked at such diverse alleged activities as fraudulent fund-raising activities, tax evasion, and the possible mental subjugation of citizens. A bill introduced in Texas in 1977 called for an investigation of reported mind control activity by cults. All of these bills failed to pass; and as the decade drew to a close, it appeared that the anti-cult movement was dying a slow death. Then everything changed on November 18, 1978.

Jonestown and the Revival of Anti-Cultism

On November 18, 1978, Congressman Leo J. Ryan, those who had accompanied him to Guyana to visit the communal settlement of the Peoples Temple, and some 900 followers of the Temple, including its leader, Jim Jones, died in combined acts of murder and suicide. In spite of the many books that have appeared, including several by survivors, what occurred at Jonestown is still far from clear. Some facts such as how many died by murder and how many by suicide may never be known. However, many of the facts await only the release of the mass of documents assembled by the House of Representatives committee assembled to investigate the event, especially the death of Congressman Ryan. To date those documents, including papers relative to a number of independent investigations by various national, state, and local government agencies remain locked up, immune to release under Freedom of Information requests, apparently for reasons of national security.[16]

Whatever questions remain concerning the events at Jonestown, there is a clear picture of the role that Jonestown played in the revival of the anti-cult movement. As the story of the disaster at Jonestown began to unravel in the media, the group suddenly became a "cult." It became the subject of a U.S. Senate hearing and then a congressional investigation, and over the next two years, anti-cultists worked to turn it into the symbol of everything that was bad about the new religions. The year 1979 became a bumper one for books on the issue of cults. The effort to attack new religions through the state legislatures were renewed, and finally, a more or less stable national anti-cult organization emerged.

Senator Robert Dole took the lead in responding to Jonestown. Even before the Congress had prepared for hearings on Ryan's death, Dole organized a set of hearings based upon the suggestion that Jonestown was a harbinger of tragedies about to break forth from the youth-oriented new religions such as the Unification Church. The hearing, originally set up to provide a platform for anti-cult spokespersons, turned into a sideshow as spokespersons for the new religions demanded equal time and as civil libertarians and a new group of scholars who had studied new religions through the 1970s rose to counter the accusations of anti-cultists with the data of their research. Dole's zeal and public support for the anti-cultists was considerably softened by the entrance into the hearings of a senator from Utah, who happened to be a Mormon.

The actual hearings on Ryan's death were not as spectacular as they could have been, as much of the work was done behind closed doors and the real findings of the committee never revealed. In the end, a five-volume report was released, but it was somewhat lost in the flood of journalistic productions. Not only were a dozen or more books on Jonestown released, but a host of books on new religions as cults appeared. Many of these books were accounts of former members' lives and breaks with a group, all concluding that the proper reaction would be support of anti-cult activities.[17]

In the wake of Jonestown, anti-cult bills appeared in Massachusetts, Illinois, Minnesota, Connecticut, Pennsylvania, Texas, Maryland, Oregon, and most importantly, New York. These bills varied widely in their sophistication and support. Most were defeated at the hearing stage as civil libertarians, representatives of mainline churches, and experts on new religions mobilized against the legislation. The one exception was New York, where the Unification Church, the best known and most disliked of the several new religions, had its headquarters and seminary. The Unification Church had been an issue in the state as it pursued a state charter for the seminary at Barrytown; and in 1977, one state assemblyman had sponsored one of the more frivolous anti-cult bills which would have made it a felony for anyone to found or promote a "pseudo-religion," whatever that was. The 1980 New York legislation, generally known as the Lasher bill for its author, Assemblyman Howard Lasher, would have amended the mental health codes to allow parents widespread powers of conservatorship for purposes of deprogramming their offspring, specifically adult offspring, who joined one of the new religions. The bill passed the assembly twice but was vetoed by the governor on both occasions. By the time of the second veto, it had become obvious that such legislation was not going anywhere nationally and further efforts which were taking a significant amount of anti-cult resources were abandoned.

The Jonestown tragedy revitalized the anti-cult movement and provided the motivation for its reorganization. Taking the lead in that restructuring was the old Citizens Freedom Foundation (soon to become known as the Cult Awareness Network) and the relatively new American Family Foundation (AFF). On November 18, 1979, a date appropriately chosen to coincide with the first anniversary of Jonestown, 65 people from 31 anti-cult groups met in Chicago to reorganize the ineffective International Foundation for Individual Freedom. IFIF had been too decentralized to accomplish its self-assigned task, but now there was an agreement to seize the initiative provided by Jonestown. After some debate a decision was made to reorganize around the Citizens Freedom Foundation, the strongest of the regional groups. CFF became the Citizens Freedom Foundation-Information Services, and the 1979 meeting was designated as the first of what became annual national meetings. Different tasks were assumed by regional affiliated groups in Minneapolis, Pittsburgh and southern California.

The new organization still did not provide the strength many felt was needed by the movement, and in 1983 a five-year plan was placed before CFF's leadership. It suggested that CFF needed to build a more stable organization which could gain legitimacy in the public eye as the most knowledgeable source of information on cults. Four specific goals were set: gain financial stability, develop professional management, create an efficient communications system, and publish a quality newsletter. As a first step in implementing this program, in 1984, CFF changed its name to Cult Awareness Network of the Citizens Freedom Foundation and soon became known simply as the Cult Awareness Network. A central headquarters was established in Chicago, and an executive director hired (since 1987, Cynthia Kisser). The national office was organized to respond to inquiries from the media, academia, and individuals. An aggressive public relations program was initiated to place the Cult Awareness Network before the public.

Simultaneously with the reorganization of CFF, the American Family Foundation was founded under the leadership of John Clark. Clark, a psychiatrist in practice in Weston, Massachusetts, and an adjunct professor at Harvard, had been the leading public spokesperson for the anti-cult movement through the 1970s, but had been largely silenced after receiving a formal reprimand from the Massachusetts Psychiatric Association. In contrast to the more activist approach of CFF/CAN, AFF was conceived as an organization of professionals who would focus upon research and education. It provided a place where academics, psychological professionals, and social scientists could relate to the movement and launched a program of public education and issued a set of publications centered upon *The Advisor*, its newsletter, and the *Cult Studies Journal*, modeled upon standard academic journals. A number of the publications were authored by Clark as chairman of the executive committee and psychologist Michael Langone, AFF's director of research.

The emergence of AFF and the reorganization signaled an important transition in the anti-cult movement. The many anti-cult groups which had formed around the country in the 1970s had been created and led largely by parents concerned with the membership of their sons and daughters in the more controversial of the new religions (the Unification Church, Scientology, Hare Krishna, the Children of God, the Way International, the Divine Light Mission, and several Evangelical Christian groups). These groups were relatively small, the largest being the Way International which peaked at about 12,000 members. Only a small minority of parents were ever concerned about their offsprings' association with these groups, and by the early 1980s, only a few had been able to sustain any zeal, either because their problem had been resolved or they had decided to live with the unhappy situation.

However, in the meantime, in their effort to gain the support of the courts and government agencies to their cause, the parents discovered that they needed the assistance of a variety of experts, who became their spokespersons. The most important of these were psychological professionals, some of whom were quick to identify with the plight of parents who were disturbed at the "loss" of their offspring to the religious life. The professionals became expert witnesses in court cases and addressed the legislative hearings attempting to investigate the cults.

Already in the mid-1970s some professionals who had become identified with the cause of the parent groups formed Return to Personal Choice under the leadership of psychiatric social worker Jean Merritt. The organization, headquartered in Lincoln, Massachusetts, welcomed psychological professionals, lawyers, and clergy into membership. The relatively small Return to Personal Choice was superseded by the American Family Foundation and its more expansive program, and Merritt moved to Washington, D.C., as the head of AFF's government affairs program, which has shown some substantial effect in influencing government officials with the anti-cult perspective. Meanwhile, through the early 1980s, in large part as CFF implemented the goals of its five-year plan, the professionals also assumed control of the organization. Since the renaming of the CFF in 1984, the majority of the board members and speakers at the annual conference have been professionals (a natural change given the attempts of the organization to gain legitimacy). CAN and AFF developed contemporaneously and tried to project an image as quite separate organizations. Over the decade, however, the organizations developed interlocking boards, several joint programs, and combined lobbying efforts in Washington, D. C., which had made it ever more difficult to distinguish them.[18] Basically, while AFF focused upon public education, CAN assumed a more activist role in spreading the anti-cult perspective in the media and relating directly to parents who had relatives in the various new religions.

The transition to professional control of CAN was also somewhat dictated by the intense controversy over deprogramming which hit CFF in the early 1980s. Deprogramming had been an important, if erratic, element in the anti-cult program through the 1970s. The various anti-cult organizations kept in touch with deprogrammers and served as contact points for parents who wished to avail themselves of it. By the mid-1970s, a number of professional deprogrammers were operating in both North America and Europe. Some of these were former cult members and others simply entrepreneurs. Immediately after Jonestown the number of deprogrammings (and concurrently the number of deprogrammers) rose dramatically. The Unification Church, the Hare Krishna, and the Way International were the primary targets, though other groups labeled as cults also came under attack.

The spread of deprogramming created a strong reaction. Besides its traditional critics, a number of people who had been successfully deprogrammed began to denounce the handling they had received from the deprogrammers.

Christian counter-cult spokespersons led by Walter Martin separated themselves publicly from the use of what he considered "un-Christian tactics" in the attempt to win people from membership in the new religions. Also, the new centralized CFF began to realize that it stood legally vulnerable for the activities of its members around the country, including deprogrammers. Thus in 1981 it took steps to separate itself from the actual practice of deprogramming and the possible excesses of its practitioners. In a formal public statement, CFF withdrew support, as an organization, from kidnapping or holding a person against his/her will and advocated what is usually termed "exit counseling," a form of anti-cult counseling into which the member enters voluntarily. Reacting to both the denunciation of deprogramming and the threat of criminal and civil action, many former deprogrammers increasingly limited their activity to exit counseling, though the policy statement in no way prevented individual board members or executives such as Cynthia Kisser from openly praising deprogramming and deprogrammers.[19]

In the United States, by the mid 1980s, the actual number of deprogrammings dropped significantly, though they continued to occur with the aid of the informal network built around CAN's most activist members around the country. Through the mid-1980s, the Cult Awareness Network developed as a true "network" in the contemporary use of that term. The national board and office in Chicago "networked" with a number of independent experts and activists and with the loosely affiliated local groups around the country. Its office staff and its individual leaders in the autonomous local groups also "networked" with a number of deprogrammers who might or might not have been formal members of the Network. Thus, while as an organization, CAN had "officially" distanced itself from the practice of deprogramming, it fully advocated and supported the practice by (1) its choice of speakers at its meetings, (2) providing a context (at its annual meeting) in which deprogrammers and potential clients could meet, and (3) informally referring people to deprogrammers through its network. Deprogrammers, especially those who lacked a public profile, relied upon referrals from the CAN network for a steady supply of paying clients.[20]

Internationally

Soon after the emergence of anti-cult organizations in the United States, anti-cult sentiment emerged in Europe. This sentiment was generated out of the controversy over Scientology in England in 1968,[21] the movement of the Children of God into Europe in the early 1970s, and the highly publicized tour of Rev. Moon to Europe in 1972. As early as 1973, deprogrammers from America went to Europe to seize Americans who had moved there as members of the different groups and stayed on to deprogram various European converts. French-speaking Europeans were also affected by the incident of the Trois Saints Coeurs (the Three Holy Hearts). Founder Roger Melchior had written his doctoral dissertation at the University of Louvain in the subject of "terror as a system of domination." It appears that he then founded a small religious community and put what he had learned into practice. Arrested for sexual abuse of a minor, the trial created a sensation in Belgium and France though was little noticed elsewhere.[22]

The emergence of the Unification Church and the involvement of its members in right-wing French politics served as the catalyst for the materialization of anti-cult sentiment into an organization, L'Associasion pour la Défense de la Familie (ADFI), incorporated in 1974 by Clair Champollion, whose son Yves had joined the church. It brought together several previously existing regional anti-cult groups. Early identified with the Catholic Church, ADFI was soon joined by a more secular group, the Centre de Documentation, d'Education et d'Action contre les Manipulations Mentales (CCMM), also known as Centre Roger Ikor, founded by an atheist author whose son had died from following a strict macrobiotic diet.[23] ADFI gradually moved to a nonsectarian position, and with the financial support of the government, ADFI had become possibly the most substantial anti-cult group in Europe.

In England, one of the first of the European anti-cult groups, Family Action Information and Rescue (FAIR), emerged in 1975 as a parents' group similar in purpose and program to CAN. Founded by a Member of Parliament, Paul Rose, it got off to a fast start but was immediately slowed by Rose's loss of a lawsuit brought by the Unification Church. FAIR soon found a new champion in Lord (John Francis) Rodney, who had been active in the cult controversy since the 1960s and who effectively used his position in the House of Lords on behalf of the organization. FAIR was joined two years later by Deo Gloria Trust, a Christian counter-cult organization. Across the channel in France, several small anti-cult groups were galvanized into a national organization by their reaction to the Trois Saints Coeur affair and the 1975 pronouncement of the French Roman Catholic bishops that the sects (as new religions were called in Europe) were diverting people hungry for true spirituality from the true church. Germany followed a similar course in 1977 when its smaller anti-cult organizations merged to form Aktion für geistige und psychische Freiheit, Arbeitgemeinschaft der Elterninitiativen e.V. (AGPF). Year by year similar organization were founded in neighboring European countries.[24]

Of the several European countries, Germany provided the most fertile ground for growing anti-cultism. The Lutheran Church lent its support through its Office for Sects and Ideologies, the base of operations for Pastor Friedrich-Wilhelm Haack. The author of numerous books and booklets,[25] Haack attacked what he termed the Jugendreligionen for their drawing young people away from their careers and any responsible position in society, an argument which found more favor in Europe than in North America. The Lutherans were joined by the German Roman Catholics as well as the government's Ministry for Youth, Family and Health, which provided needed financial support for AGPF concerns. As early as 1978 the government showed its support by subsidizing a conference on New Youth Religions held by the German Society for Child and Youth Psychiatry and the Federal Conference for Educational Counseling, the first of many over the years.

As in England, the issue of the Church of Scientology arose in Germany as a special case above and beyond the general anti-cult controversy. By

the end of the 1970s, Aktion Bildunginformation, an organization devoted espe-
cially to opposing the church, was warning the public to avoid Scientology.
Taking an activist stance, it filed and won a series of suits against the church for
proselytizing in public places. Its 1979 book, *The Sect of Scientology and its
Front Organization*,[26] presaged a veritable cottage industry in German anti-
Scientology publishing. In 1981, Aktion Bildunginformation founder Ingo
Heineman brought her special animus toward Scientology into her new role as
director of AGPF.

As with Americans, the Jonestown incident created a new level of concern about new religions among Europeans with several notable results. In December 1980, ADFI hosted an international conference in Paris of anti-cult representatives and other interested people. At this time, the representatives from
14 countries, including American Henrietta Crampton, one of the prominent
leaders of CFF,[27] established an international anti-cult network. While Europe
has not lacked in leadership on cult issues, with the likes of FAIR's Ian Howath
and Pastor Haack, it has continued to rely upon the theoretical perspective generated in the United States.

Through the early 1980s, the European section of the anti-cult network
expanded across Europe to include such groups as S.O.S. (the Netherlands), the
Dialogue Centre (Denmark), FRI (Association to Rescue the Individual, Sweden), Comitato per la Liberazione dei Giovani dal Settarismo (Italy), and Association Pro-Juventud (Spain).

Subsequently, through the mid-1980s, the Dialogue Centre (really a
Christian counter-cult organization rather than a secular anti-cult center) withdrew from formal cooperation with the other groups, and Comitato was superseded by ARIS. Association Pro-Juventud would host the next international conference in Barcelona in 1987, at which several of the prominent Cult Awareness
Network theoreticians would be featured speakers. By this time the international
network had spread to South America and was especially strong in Argentina. In
several countries, multiple anti-cult groups emerged as leaders but disagreed
over specific tactics and goals.

Jonestown occasioned greater government involvement in cult issues.
In Germany, for example, the Ministry for Youth, Family and Health sponsored
a major study of members of new religions, their friends and family. The Ministry charged the staff of the European Centre for Social Welfare and Research in
Vienna with this important research project, but then largely ignored its findings. Actually, the report provided some support for the Ministry's perspective,
especially in its documenting the values conflict between group members and
the larger society, but also offered a host of disconfirmations. Researchers were
unable to find any sign of mental pathology among sect members and found
little evidence that joining a new religion caused youth to withdraw from society.[28] However, the Ministry shelved the Vienna report and in 1980 issued its
own report that emphasized its charge that new religions contributed to the
"flight from reality" of the younger generation.[29] Some 25,000 copies were
printed and distributed through churches, youth groups, and the AGPF.

From England, Richard Cottrell, a Member of the European Parliament, convinced the Parliament's Committee on Youth, Culture, Education, Information, and Sport to consider the cult issue. The Committee in turn appointed Cottrell to write a report that was completed in 1983 and approved in 1984. It called for an exchange of information among European nations on new religions, the establishment of a data bank, and the implementation of measures designed to prevent the movement's abusing members and their families. The report might have had greater influence except for the opposition to specific parts of it by the Executive Committee of the British Council of Churches. As the impact of Jonestown faded, it was soon forgotten.

In France, ADFI lobbied for action by the Chamber of Deputies, who in 1979 asked its legislative commission to initiate an inquiry into sects in France. The inquiry began two years later. It was finished in 1983 and published in 1985. It reached similar conclusions to the Cottrell report, but again as the emotional jolt caused by Jonestown lessened, like the Cottrell report, it too was soon forgotten.[30]

The Rise and Fall of Brainwashing

In the mid-1970s, the primary understanding of destructive cults as centers engaged in "brainwashing" their members through what was variously termed "coercive persuasion," "mind control," and/or "thought control," was developed. Central to that development was the trial of newspaper heiress Patty Hearst in San Francisco in 1975. Hearst had been kidnapped by a radical political group, and had undergone an intensive indoctrination program that included being locked in a closet and other personal abuse. However, eventually Hearst converted to the group and participated in a bank robbery where she was photographed carrying a weapon. When finally captured, she was tried for armed robbery.

During the trial, the defense suggested that Hearst had been brainwashed and was hence not responsible for her actions. The jury rejected that argument and convicted her. However, Margaret Singer, one of the psychologists who had testified at that trial, even though for technical reasons not allowed to speak on the brainwashing issue, testified the following year as an expert in a case in which a conservatorship was sought over five members of the Unification Church. She testified that the members, all young adults, had been victimized by artful and designing people who had subjected them to a process of "coercive persuasion." As a result, the five should, she recommended, be sent for a period of reality therapy at the Freedom of Thought Foundation in Tucson.

Singer went on to found a counseling service for former members of the new religions, most of whom had been severed from the group through deprogramming. She presented the developing conclusions in several articles published in 1978, the most important being "Coming Out of the Cults" in the popular newsstand magazine *Psychology Today* (January 1979). The article was frequently reprinted in both Europe and North America. Through the early

1980s she developed her concept of brainwashing which was presented in the various legislative hearings, in testimony in trials, and in several talks given before meetings of the Cult Awareness Network. As developed by Singer, the concept of brainwashing became the keystone of the anti-cult polemic against cults. Through the early 1980s, the testimony of Singer and several colleagues who accepted and reinforced her perspective became crucial in a series of multi-million dollar judgments against a string of new religions. She became a professional witness who devoted her full time to legal consultation. Her testimony was particularly effective as she had worked with E. H. Schein, who had studied the Korean prisoners of war, though Singer had never done primary research with the prisoners.

Singer's work, though difficult to assess as she wrote only a few papers laying out her thought, became the subject of intense debate in both psychological and sociological circles. Her initial assertions were received as the proposal of a new and radical theory. Given its implicit rejection of some strong trends in psychology over patient rights, the burden of proof was placed upon Singer to provide supporting evidence of her perspective. The result of that debate was the overwhelming rejection of her approach to the new religions by her academic colleagues, though a handful of psychological professionals such as Louis J. West of University of California at Los Angeles' Psychoanalytic Institute were vocal supporters.[31] However, through the 1980s Singer's thought was accepted by the courts and strongly influenced the deliberations of juries.

At the same time, the conflict between Singer and the great majority of her academic colleagues who had been studying the new religions finally led to a series of actions that has resulted in the collapse of her work on brainwashing. Those events began in 1983 when a proposal was made to the American Psychological Association (APA) that a task force be established to examine and report on the techniques of coercive persuasion being used by various psychological and religious groups. In 1984 the "Task Force on Deceptive and Indirect Methods of Persuasion and Control" with Margaret Singer as chairperson was established. In the meantime Singer was called upon to testify in a case, *Molko vs. the Holy Spirit Association for the Unification of World Christianity*, in which two former members of the Unification Church had charged it with psychological injury due to coercive persuasion. The lower court had dismissed the suit in part because it accepted arguments that Singer's testimony (and that of a colleague, Samuel Benson) lacked scientific foundation.

The case was appealed. As the appeal process was working itself out, the APA board prepared and submitted an amicus brief critiquing Singer's stated position and supporting the exclusion of her and Dr. Benson. This brief was circulated among a number of scholars known for their work on new religions, and many additional signatures (including that of this author) were added. As the submission of the brief became known, some supporters of Singer argued that it was improper for the APA board to submit such a document while it had a standing committee working on the very subject to which the brief proposed conclusions. Thus early in 1987, the APA board withdrew its support of the document, though those who had additionally signed on kept it before the court.

Meanwhile the Task Force report was submitted for review. Both outside reviewers and two members of the Board of Social and Ethical Responsibility for Psychology concurred in the inadequacies of the report and the Board rejected it. A memorandum to Singer and the committee members dated May 11, 1987, cited the report for its lack of both "scientific rigor" and an "even-handed critical approach." It noted that, given the evaluation of the report, members of the committee could not use their work on the committee to credential themselves in the future.

The board of directors of the APA could now resubmit the brief, but the Molko case had moved on and eventually collapsed when it was discovered that some of the stated facts in the case had been incorrect. However, almost immediately a new case appeared in the horizon, *U.S. vs. Fishman.* In his defense, which concerned the relationship between Mr. Fishman and the Church of Scientology, Fishman called upon Singer and another colleague, sociologist Richard Ofshe, to testify to the deleterious effects of the Church of Scientology's manipulation of him. The key document in the case became a lengthy restatement of the position of the previous APA brief and an analysis of the writings and statements of Singer written by psychologist Dick Anthony. Anthony argued persuasively that Singer postulated a "robot" theory of brainwashing that lacked scientific support.[32] The court accepted his arguments, and as a result, Singer and Ofshe were denied the stand. Fishman's defense collapsed. As a result of the Fishman ruling, published in 1990, both Singer and Ofshe were subsequently denied the stand in several additional cases. It became evident that the Fishman case had become the precedent through which the court accepted the position of the majority of scholars on the new religions and the idea of brainwashing.

Europe in the 1990s

Sociologist James Beckford has called attention to the very different legal and social situations affecting the cult controversy in the different countries of Europe. Each country has followed a very different course relative to the new religions, both in relation to each other and to the United States. Especially, in contrast to America, most European countries possess no operative principle of separation of church and state. Public moneys flow to the support of state-approved religious bodies, and the larger religious groups often serve as government agents for the delivery of necessary social services. Belgian sociologists J. Billiet and Karel Dobbelaere have called attention to what is termed the "pillar" system used in several countries which support such services as schools, hospitals, and employment insurance through religious groups (or their secular counterparts). In those countries, membership in a sect effectively isolates individuals from necessary structures for which they pay taxes.[33] At the same time, while sects were a matter of ongoing coverage in the press and periodic court cases, the more offensive actions of the anti-cult movement in the United State—the attempt to seek conservatorships and deprogrammings—were quite rare. At the beginning of the 1990s, it appeared that Europe would make a relatively smooth transition to the new level of pluralism brought by the new religions, especially given the small percentage of the population that had actually affiliated with them. That situation changed with the suicide/murders of the Solar Temple.

The death of 53 people in Switzerland in October 1994 sent shock waves through Europe, especially French-speaking Europe. Many who had seen Jonestown and even the incident with the Branch Davidians as somehow peculiar to the American experience were deeply disturbed at the multinational group's deadly action. The threat posed by the Solar Temple was then punctuated by the gassing of the Tokyo train station by the AUM Shinrikyo in March 1995 and the subsequent suicides of Solar Temple members in December 1995. Energized, the anti-cult groups across Europe, especially in France, Belgium, Switzerland, and Germany, demanded action, and government agencies began to respond.

Among the first to act, the French National Assembly appointed a commission to study the sect phenomenon that met through the latter part of 1995. ADFI operated as a consultant and major source of information for the committee. Its report was completed in December and released in January 1996. Some 172 groups were singled out and listed as sects. Although a few specific new religions were singled out for their commission of illegal acts (from fraud to disturbing the peace), the primary accusation directed broadly against the sects was their practice of "mental manipulation" (what was being called brainwashing in the United States) that in turn led to the mental destabilization of group members through the imposition of disciplined behavior and spiritual practices such as chanting and meditation. A variety of measures were suggested to counter the influence and growth of the sects.[34]

The French report found immediate popular support, but also aroused the reaction of scholars who had studied the new religions and rejected the committee's use of brainwashing theory in the absence of any substantive charges against the overwhelming majority of the sects. Civil libertarians and leaders in the larger churches added their concern over some of the perceived dangers inherent in the committee's conclusions. The French scholars, many of whom had previously associated themselves with the Center for Studies of New Religions (CESNUR), an international association of new religions scholars, organized opposition to the report, and joined by concerned scholars from around the world, opened a Paris office and issued a lengthy response.[35] To date, only one recommendation of the report has been acted upon: Parliament has opened a national Observatory of Cults with a phone line for people to report complaints about sect activity. CESNUR France has continued its critique of the report by organizing several conferences and publishing their proceedings.

In February 1997, the Canton of Geneva (in French-speaking Switzerland) issued a report calling for new federal legislation against mind control (now under consideration by the Swiss parliament) among other measures recommended against the sects. The Canton has thrown its financial support behind local anti-cult groups. Most recently, in April 1997, a parliamentary commission on sects in Belgium issued a 600-page report whose content and recommendations were similar to that of the French, with the very important addition of its recommending that a new crime of mental manipulation be designated. It singled out 189 groups (including such prominent American groups as the YWCA, the Assemblies of God, and the Quakers) on its black list.[36] Scholars associated with CESNUR have offered opposing opinions on both reports following lines similar to those in the reaction to the French report.

As of the summer of 1997, the situation in Europe remains extremely fluid. While it is difficult to predict the future course of the current wave of anti-cult sentiment with any exactitude, the major arenas where the issue will be fought out have been designated. Following the French lead, a commission on sects has been established in Germany. While the Solar Temple and the AUM Shinrikyo occasioned the Parliament's action, the formation of the commission comes as the public debate over Scientology has reached a new fever pitch. On the one hand, the controversy is integrally related to the larger issue of new religions, but on the other hand, the animus toward Scientology also continues a long-standing confrontation independent of the other groups. Far beyond their critique of such groups as the Unification Church or the Hare Krishna movement, German anti-cult spokespersons have challenged the very nature of Scientology as a religious movement. Through the 1990s rhetoric and provocative actions on both sides have escalated, and no resolution has yet appeared on the horizon.

In addition to the German commission, the question of new religions is being debated in the European Parliament where the Commission of Public Liberties and Internal Affairs has been asked to draft a report on sects. Also, strong anti-cult resolutions (supported by several Eastern European nations and Germany) have been introduced in the Council of Europe (an advisory body including all of the European nations, not just those of the European Union) calling for a Europe-wide sect observatory and anti-cult laws in all countries. The sentiments expressed in the European Parliament and the Council of Europe indicate a continent-wide revival of efforts to reverse the spread of new religions. Standing behind these sentiments is an intense resistance to the growing religious pluralism now generally observable in all the European nations.[37] In the former Communist countries, where a tradition of religious freedom has never emerged, anti-cult sentiment is undergirded by intense anti-Americanism (symbolized by the influx of American Evangelical groups, which are currently warring with more traditional groups for religious hegemony).[38]

Integral to the contemporary European critique of the sects, however, are the American brainwashing theories (though that term is generally avoided in favor of the less offensive "mental manipulation"). As these theories have been tested and found wanting, there is every reason to believe that the present anti-cult sentiment will diminish as the weaknesses of the brainwashing theories are brought to the forefront.[39]

The Contemporary American Scene

The results of the Fishman ruling have been far reaching. Recognizing the threat, within a very short time CAN leaders began to target as "cult apologists" those scholars who had opposed them. Most directly and immediately affected by the decision, Singer and Ofshe filed suit first in federal court and then in the state of California, claiming a conspiracy by the American Psychological Association, the American Sociological Association, and a number of individual scholars to deny them their livelihood as expert witnesses. Both cases were dismissed with prejudice and in the latter case, the court accepted a motion requesting that Singer and Ofshe pay the legal fees of the defendants. The Fishman ruling and the dismissal of the two law suits cost the Cult Awareness Network and those scholars who had accepted Singer's work a significant amount of credibility.

The string of court reverses dealt the Cult Awareness Network a fatal blow. First, it meant that deprogrammers associated with CAN could no longer call the "experts" to their assistance if brought to trial following an unsuccessful deprogramming attempt. Second, it meant that the continued association of CAN's national office, however indirect, with those who conducted forceful deprogrammings left CAN vulnerable to court action.

The issue of CAN's continued association with deprogramming (as opposed to voluntary exit counseling) culminated in the 1995 trial of deprogrammer Rick Ross and two associates, who were sued by Jason Scott, a member of a congregation of the United Pentecostal Church, an older denomination not considered by most people either a cult or new religion. Through the 1990s, the Church of Scientology had been systematically gathering data on CAN's continuing involvement with deprogramming, and it lent both that data and one of Scientology's lawyers, Rick Moxin, to Scott. Moxin won the case and Ross was handed a multi-million dollar judgment. At the same time, the jury found CAN partially responsible and leveled an additional one million dollar judgment against it for having served as a necessary connecting link between Ross and Scott's mother, who had initiated the deprogramming attempt. As a result of the judgment, CAN was forced into bankruptcy. It was eventually dissolved by the court and its assets turned over to a trustee for sale. Its name was purchased by a coalition of new religions previously targeted by CAN, who now operate a Cult Awareness Network office to disseminate what they feel is a more correct perspective on new religions.

Conclusion

The demise of the Cult Awareness Network brings to an end an era in the cult wars in North America. But it is by no means the end of the controversies which have surrounded the new religions. CAN's sister organization, the American Family Foundation, continues to operate, and the leaders and spokespersons for the former CAN have been hard at work to reconstitute the organization. Margaret Singer has moved to rehabilitate her position by writing a new book-length defense of her position and creating the Singer Foundation to perpetuate her ideas on coercive persuasion, though the foundation has struggled to get off the ground.

Even if it succeeds in reorganizing, CAN will take many years to re-build the organization to the level it enjoyed prior to the negative court actions. CAN's activist stance constituted its unique role. While a renewed organization could offer some assistance to families by its promotion of exit counseling, it would remain vulnerable should any of its exit counselors such as Ross also engage in any deprogrammings.[40]

In the meantime, anti-cult spokespersons have suffered a loss of posi-tion as a legitimate voice on cult issues, as was clearly demonstrated in the re-cent cases of the Solar Temple and Heaven's Gate. In spite of attempts to re-claim their hold on the media, spokespersons quickly showed their lack of awareness of either group prior to their demise and had little to add to the infor-mation the media was gathering elsewhere. Though anti-cult organizations and cult experts will persist into the foreseeable future, their ability to oppose the spread and activities of the new religions in North America seems destined to fade.[41]

Notes

[1] For a list of the large body of Jewish anti-cult literature, see Jack N. Porter, *Jews and the Cults: Bibliography* (Fresh Meadows, NY: Biblio Press, 1981). Porter's 49-page compilation, of course, covered only the first decade and the amount of Jewish literature has continued to grow.

[2] The most controversial anti-cult activity was carried out by members of the Jewish De-fense League. Cf. Shea Hecht and Chaim Clorfene, *Confessions of a Jewish Cult Buster* (Brooklyn, NY: Tosefos Media, 1985).

[3] James A. Rudin and Marcia Rudin, *Prison or Paradise?: The New Religious Cults* (Philadelphia: Fortress Press, 1980).

[4] On the current state of Jewish counter-cult activity, check the Internet sites of such or-ganizations as Jews for Judaism or Outreach Judaism.

[5] Basic information about the first generation of the anti-cult movement can be found in Anson D. Shupe, Jr., and David G. Bromley, *A Documentary History of the Anti-Cult Movement* (Arlington, TX: Center for Social Research, University of Texas, 1985); An-son D. Shupe, Jr., and David G. Bromley, *The New Vigilantes: Deprogrammers, Anti-Cultists and the New Religions* (Beverly Hills, CA: SAGE Publications, 1980); Anson D. Shupe, Jr., David G. Bromley, and Donna L. Oliver, *The Anti-Cult Movement in Amer-ica: A Bibliography and Historical Survey* (New York: Garland Publishing, 1984); J. Gordon Melton, *Encyclopedic Handbook of Cults in America* (New York: Garland Pub-lishing, 1992); and Anson D. Shupe, Jr., and David G. Bromley, eds., *Anti-Cult Move-ments in Cross-Cultural Perspective* (New York: Garland Publications, 1994).

[6] On the Children of God (now known as the Family) see: James R. Lewis and J. Gordon Melton, eds. *Sex Slander and Salvation: Investigating the Family/Children of God* (Stan-ford, CA: Center for Academic Publication, 1994).

[7] While a decade later, the successor organization to the Children of God, the Family,

would become known for its questionable sexual practices (especially the use of sex for evangelism [flirty fishing] and in the mid-1980s face charges of sexual child abuse, at this stage of the cult controversy, the group was primarily charged with taking young adults out of a normal career trajectory.

[8] Cf. Walter R. Martin, *The New Cults* (Santa Ana, CA: Vision House, 1980). Recent events in Europe have, of course, confirmed the accuracy of Martin's predictions concerning attacks upon Evangelicals as cults.

[9] CF. Ronald Enroth, *Youth Brainwashing, and the Extremist Cults* (Grand Rapids, MI: Zondervan, 1977).

[10] The extensive Christian counter-cult movement based in the Evangelical denominations in the United States is beyond the scope of this essay. With a few prominent exceptions, its spokespersons have kept their distance from the Cult Awareness Network, refrained from participation in activist programs based either on deprogramming or government action, and continue to emphasize its doctrinal differences with all non-Trinitarian Christian belief systems.

[11] "What Is Deprogramming?" *Citizens Freedom Foundation News* 1:1 (November 1974), 1.

[12] Ted Patrick, and Tom Dulack, *Let Our Children Go!* (New York: E. P. Dutton, 1976).

[13] Robert Jay Lifton, *Thought Reform and the Psychology of Totalism* (New York: W. W. Norton & Company, 1961).

[14] Jean Merritt, August 3, 1975, quoted in Shupe and Bromley, op.cit. (1985).

[15] At present, the primary rehabilitation center for deprogrammed cult members is Wellspring Retreat & Resource Center at Athens, Ohio, headed by Christian psychologist Paul R. Martin. Martin is the author of *Cult Proofing Your Kids* (Grand Rapids, MI: Zondervan, 1993).

[16] Interestingly enough, Patricia Ryan, the daughter of Leo Ryan, and an anti-cult activist since the early 1980s, broke with the anti-cult perspective on Jonestown and charged in a suit filed against the Central Intelligence Agency that the United States government was responsible for her father's death.

[17] See for example: Christopher Edwards, *Crazy for God* (Englewood Cliffs, NJ: Prentice-Hall, 1979); Barbara Underwood and Betty Underwood, *Hostage to Heaven* (New York: Clarkson N. Potter, 1979); and Rachel Martin, *Escape* (Denver, CO: Accent Books, 1979) for typical accounts by ex-group members.

[18] It should be noted that the psychologists and other professionals who identified themselves with the anti-cult movement have a distinct problem. Almost none of them had ever studied the groups about which they were now to evaluate as experts. Their entire knowledge of the new religions came almost totally from the stories of ex-members, accounts heavily distorted by the deprogramming process. Their appraisals received constant negative critiques from the growing number of scholars who had actually studied the groups and were broadly familiar with the literature both pro and con on the different groups. The work of these scholars (which by the mid-1980s numbered in the several hundreds) would be a major irritant for the anti-cult movement and in the end lead to the destruction of the brainwashing hypothesis.

[19] The terms deprogramming and exit counseling are often used interchangeably and a distinction is made between voluntary and involuntary deprogramming. In this chapter we have retained the more common usage of deprogramming for situations in which the subject enters the process against his/her stated desire with an accompanying use or threat of use of force to coerce initial participation.

[20] CAN's continued involvement in referring people to deprogrammers was demonstrated in the Jason Scott case in 1995, and led to the sizable judgment against it. Also, in 1993, during his trial after a botched deprogramming attempt, it was revealed that contrary to its stated public policy, CAN had paid deprogrammer Galen Kelly a monthly stipend for many months during the 1990s.

[21] Their 1968 banning of foreigners from entering England for the specific purpose of studying Scientology was rescinded in 1980.

[22] Y. Lecerf, ed., *Les Marchands de deiu. Analyes Socio-Politiques de l'Affaire Melchior* (Brussels: Complexe, 1975).

[23] Cf. CCMM/Centre Roger Ikor, *Les Sectes etat d'urgence* (Paris: Albin Michel, 1995).

[24] On the first decade of the European reaction to the new religions, see James A. Beckford, *Cult Controversies: The Social Response to New Religious Movements* (London: Tavistock Publications, 1985). Beckford's analysis provided invaluable background for this chapter.

[25] Among his titles are: *Die neuen Jugendreligionen* (München: Evangelischer Presseverband für Bayern, 1976); *Jugendreligionen: Ursachen, Trends, Reaktionen* (München: Claudius Verlag, 1979); and *Europas neue Religion* (München: Claudius Verlag, 1991).

[26] *Die Scientology-Sekte und ihre Tarnorganisationen* (Stuttgart, 1979).

[27] *Cult Awareness Network of the Citizens Freedom Foundation: Who We Are. . . and. . . What We Do* (Hannacroix, NY: Citizen Freedom Foundation, 1984).

[28] H. Berger and P. Hexel, *Ursachen und Wirkungen gesellschäftlicher Verweigerung junger Menschen unter bosonder Berücksichtigung der "Jugendreligionen"* (Vienna: European Centre for Social Welfare Training and Research, mimeo, 1981).

[29] *Die Jugendreligionen in der Bundesrepublik Deutschland* (1980).

[30] Alain Vivian, *Les Sectes in France: Expressions de la liberté morale ou facteurs de manipulations?* (Paris: La Documentation Française, 1985).

[31] The details of the anti-cult position were best presented in the collection of papers in David A. Halperin, ed., *Psychodynamic Perspective in Religion, Sect, and Cult* (Boston: J. Wright, 1983). The critique can be seen in David G. Bromley and James T. Richardson, eds., *The Brainwashing/Deprogramming Controversy: Sociological, Psychological, Legal, and Historical Perspectives* (New York: Edwin Mellen Press, 1983). By 1984/85, the issue had largely been decided, and while anti-cult scholars continued to publish and circulate papers reflecting the anti-cult perspective, these were published almost exclusively by anti-cult organizations such as AFF and found little audience in the larger scholarly community.

[32] See Dick Anthony and Thomas Robbins, "Law, Social Science and the 'Brainwashing' Exception to the First Amendment," *Behavioral Sciences and the Law* 10 (1992): 5-29, for a discussion of this phase of the controversy.

[33] Cf. J. Billiet and Karel Dobbelaere, "Vers une Désinstitutionalisation du Pilier Chrétien?" in L. Voyé et al, eds., *La Belgique et Ses* (Louvain-la-Neuve: Cabay, 1985).

[34] Alan Gest and Jacques Guyard, *Les sectes en France* (Paris: Assemblée Nationale, Commission d'enquête, Rapport no 2468, 1996).

[35] Massimo Introvigne and J. Gordon Melton, eds., *Pour en finir avec les sectes. Le débat sur le rapport de la commission parlementaire* (Paris: Devry, 1996).

[36] The French and Belgian reports highlighted another important issue between American and European perspectives concerning new religions. American sociologists had drawn a distinction between sects, groups which broke from the larger, more-established denominations and were progressively moving toward denominational status, and cults, groups which had a very different religious background. In Europe, with its state-church tradi-

tion, the term sect was used to designate all of the smaller religious groups from Baptists to Buddhists, from Pentecostals to Scientologists. Thus the authors of the European reports lacked a handy term to separate older Christian sectarian groups from the newer non-conventional religions.

[37] In the two years since this chapter was originally penned, several important changes have occurred in Europe. First, the European Parliament's committee inquiring into the sect question concluded its work without issuing a report. That action effectively takes the sect off of the Parliament's agenda for the foreseeable future. The German Commission, surprisingly, issued a report finding that the sects were not a threat to the state and that it could find no evidence for "brainwashing" theories, though it continued opposition to the Church of Scientology.

The French and Belgian governments have continued their opposition to the new religions in their countries, and the French have discontinued their sect observatory in favor of a new office to make "war" on the sects. Their most important action has been the move against Jehovah's Witnesses, whose status as a religion and whose tax exemption has been called into question in an ongoing court case. That office has issued a variety of documents aimed at mobilizing the country in opposition to the sects, though in the meantime it has been embarrassed by some court rulings that have favored new religions; most importantly, a dismissal of the case against several members of the Family. Human rights advocates now see France as the major Western European country attempting to implement a government policy designed to turn back the new religious pluralism. In the wake of the French action, the government of Sweden has issued a report criticizing the French stance, the Swiss Canton of Ticino has issued a report calling for an end to what it terms "anti-cult terrorism," and the government of Spain has moved to adopt a code of religious freedom following the Italian model.

The situation in Europe remains fluid, but the outlook for religious freedom is more optimistic than seemed possible just a few years ago.

[38] Eastern European sentiments were highlighted in the spring of 1996 when the court supported an orthodox priest who had been sued for libel for writing an inflammatory booklet attacking various new religions.

[39] It is, for example, difficult to argue for the reality of mental damages due to the action of new religions. After a generation during which several million individuals have joined new religions, it is obvious that mental health professions have experienced no influx of clients damaged by their participation in such groups nor have psychologists been able to locate pockets of mental disease in their studies of contemporary members.

[40] Following the negative judgment in the Scott case, CAN supporters appealed. In separate decisions, on 8 April 1998, the appeals court upheld the one million dollar judgment against CAN, and on 30 July 1998, it ruled against the effort to recover the name that had been sold to the coalition of new religions formerly attacked by the organization. A heated court battle continues over possession of the former CAN's files. In the meantime, energized in part by anti-Scientology activists, anti-cult leaders moved to reorganize under a new name, "CULTinfo" and with a completely new leadership. The announcement of its initial meeting in February 1999 included no mention of deprogramming or exit counseling (though several exit counselors were among the speakers), and in light of the Scott decision, it remains questionable whether the new organization can again assemble a network to continue any coercive deprogramming activity.

[41] As documented in the various editions of the *Encyclopedia of American Religions* (Detroit, MI: Gale Research Company, 6th ed. 1998), the number of new religions has steadily grown in North America for more than fifty years. That pattern of growth has

continued through the years of the emergence of the anti-cult movement and shows no signs of abating due to its activity. While the two dozen or so groups upon whom the movement has focused have changed over the last two decades, and a few have suffered from internal turmoil (most notably the Church Universal and Triumphant and the Unification Church), all remain strong and continue to grow worldwide, and anti-cult activity shows no overall effect upon their progress. The possible exception to this pattern is the group built around the recently deceased Zen Master Rama. The future of this small group is very much in doubt, given his sudden demise.

CHAPTER 12

"Who Watches the Watchman?"

Another Side to the Watchdog Groups

Laird Wilcox

Introduction

In the 35 years that I've been studying extremist groups of the far-left and far-right, including acquiring material for my collection at the University of Kansas Library,[1] it has caught my attention on numerous occasions that the various "watchdog" organizations that monitor these groups often develop a strange symbiotic relationship with them. Watchdog organizations tend to identify themselves in terms of their opposition, i.e., the various individuals and organizations they call "extremists," and depend upon this opposition to justify their existence and their fund-raising activities. The observation made by an acquaintance that "when the last Ku Klux Klansman and neo-Nazi turns out the lights and locks the door, a lot of people will be out of work" is very poignant.

In addition to their preoccupation with their subjects, the watchdog organizations also tend to adopt the position that the end justifies the means. Although the watchdog organizations are ostensibly oriented toward human rights and democratic concerns, they frequently venture far afield from these in the service of their crusade. This is most notable in their intelligence-gathering activities, their propaganda campaigns and in their legal offensive against their opposition.

Another issue of concern with certain left-oriented watchdog organizations is that they have roots in extreme ideologies themselves, and in some cases go so far as to encourage potentially violent confrontations directed against their opponents. The Center For Democratic Renewal (CDR) and Political Research Associates (PRA) both have well-documented Marxist-Leninist "links and ties" as well. On the other hand, the more elite of the watchdog organizations, such as the Anti-Defamation League (ADL) and the Southern Poverty Law Center (SPLC), generally oppose physical confrontations and attempt to distance themselves from the more radical anti-racist groups. While they may give lip service to civil liberties, freedom of expression and other constitutional guarantees, watchdog groups often operate just on the edge of those protections, often advocating formal censorship or government reprisals against their ideological opponents simply because of their values, opinions and beliefs.

In the case of the Anti-Defamation League and the Southern Poverty Law Center, their practice of acquiring undue influence to advance their agenda with law enforcement agencies and their practice of using civil law to accomplish de facto criminal prosecutions without the benefit of the appropriate constitutional guarantees is simply wrong, and it would be wrong no matter who did it.

The Center for Democratic Renewal and Political Research Associates appear so thoroughly compromised by a hard-left agenda that they might reasonably be considered representatives of the opposing extreme. They are "anti-extremism" only in the sense that they oppose the extremism of the right, while opposing that of the left only in cases of sectarian ideological differences.

In certain important aspects, watchdog groups have become models of intolerance, in spite of their public pronouncements to the contrary. Although they would object to the stereotyping of those they defend, they hardly hesitate to stereotype their critics and opponents, and often in the worse possible terms. Austin Turk observes,

> At the extreme, the process of stereotyping eventuates in dehumanization: the enemy is judged to be so inhumanly evil or contemptible that anything may be done to "it" without subjectively compromising one's own humanity and sense of morality.[2]

Militant anti-racist and anti-fascist groups, like militant groups of all kinds, tend to see themselves in terms of their intentions, which they claim are selfless, noble and altruistic, and they tend to be very generous in their assessment. A much clearer picture of their activities emerges when one views them as interest groups, which like other interest groups are engaged in benefiting a particular constituency, usually to the disadvantage of others.

By claiming the so-called moral high ground, and by appearing to act "for the good of others," they often manage to elude the kind of critical examination that befalls other less fortunately situated interest groups. Hence, a distortion, hoax, fabrication, or just plain lie is easily overlooked and forgiven, and is often attributed to their over-enthusiastic zeal to "do good." This is an enviable position to be in. Moreover, because they claim to be anti-racist and anti-fascist, they can easily call into question the motives of their critics. It's as if to say, "We're anti-racist and anti-fascist, and if you oppose us or something we are doing, what does that make you?

Watchdog organizations represent a special problem for academics. Often, they are the only source for quotable information about the groups they monitor. Where does one go for information on the paramilitary militia groups or so-called hate groups? Sociologists Betty A. Dobratz and Stephanie L. Shanks-Meile observe that watchdog groups engage in claims-making in which they draw attention to certain causes in order to promote their agendas. They say,

We relied on the SPLC and ADL reports for general information, but we have noted differences between the way events were sometimes portrayed in *Klanwatch Intelligence Reports* as more militant and dangerous with higher turnouts than we observed. Also, "watchdog" groups promote "claims" that are compatible with their political agenda and neglect other ones as they attempt to wield political influence among policymakers.[3]

"Links and Ties"

If we accept the argument advanced by most of the watchdog activists such as Chip Berlet and Leonard Zeskind, that anyone who has aspired to be a neo-Nazi, or who has consorted with neo-Nazi organizations can be justifiably "linked" with and bears a burden of guilt for the atrocities of Nazism and fascist regimes, then we might consider the argument that anyone who has aspired to be a Marxist-Leninist, or who has consorted with Marxist-Leninist organizations can be justifiably "linked" with and bears a burden of guilt for the atrocities of Marxist-Leninist regimes.

The issue of "links and ties" necessarily involves the problem of guilt by association. This rhetorical device is widely used by the watchdog groups to "link" or "tie" an individual or group to an odious ideology because of some association with a tainted organization, such as attending a meeting, one's name appearing on a list, or so on. As we see in this report, it can also be applied to the watchdog group.

"Guilt by association" or links and ties have both legitimate and illegitimate uses and it largely depends on the actual strength of the link or tie as well as its context and its actual relevance to the issue at hand. If someone has been an active member of an organization for several years, or a consistent writer for a publication, or routinely and regularly associates with a particular ideological crowd while professing sympathy and solidarity with them, and this has bona fide bearing on a particular issue, then the link or tie may be significant. Otherwise it might just be another way of calling someone bad names.

Also it must be borne in mind that agreement with some issues on a group's agenda does not necessarily imply agreement with all issues. Here again, this depends on the group. Some organizations demand conformity from their membership while others do not. The more "extreme" the group, the more conformity is usually required. Marxist-Leninist groups often demand considerable compliance with doctrine. I don't think that Chicago Area Friends of Albania, for example, is going to let someone become a founding member unless that person is in substantial agreement with its ideological program.

Another issue has to do with committees to protest alleged civil liberties violations or to organize the legal defense of a particular organization or its members. Many people, including myself, have signed petitions in protest of civil liberties violations of radicals, left or right. The question is whether the object of interest is civil liberties, due process, or freedom of expression per se, or whether it's merely to defend the interests of a particular ideological organization or its members. Someone who regularly defends the rights of Marxist-Leninists or other radical leftists, for example, but never anybody in the opposing ideological camp can hardly claim to be "just a civil libertarian." Under such circumstances it might be reasonably assumed that this person is a sympathizer interested in the legal defense of groups, individuals or ideals that he or she supports.

Moreover, any link or tie, no matter how strong, should not divert attention from the truth or falsity of a particular statement by the individual. These statements have to be judged on their merits. Sometimes the links and ties of an individual may be cited in an attempt to divert attention from the more legitimate aspects of the message. Each case deserves careful consideration.

In detailing the "hidden" background of these watchdog organizations, I don't mean to imply their concerns are without merit, that they do not focus on groups and individuals that probably bear watching, or that they do not do valuable work in fostering improved interracial and intergroup relations. I have no quarrel with much of what they claim to stand for. I think it's important that we realize that we must all get along in this world. I was active in the civil rights movement of the 1960s and I've been a member of the American Civil Liberties Union since 1962. What I object to are their tactics, their often hidden agendas, and their contempt for freedom of expression and association.

Cultic Behavior

With respect to the theme of this volume, which is the cultic milieu, I think that—broadly defined—watchdog organizations, whether dealing with political extremist groups or new and unusual religions, can easily take on a "cult-like" character themselves. Part of this has to do with the "holy cause" nature of the watchdog milieu itself—often viewed in terms of a valiant battle between good and evil. Part of it has to do with their heightened sensitivity and in-group solidarity, as in Irving Janis's concept of "groupthink." Janis says,

> I use the term "groupthink" . . . to refer to a mode of thinking that people engage in when they are deeply involved in a cohesive in-group, when the members' strivings for unanimity override their motivation to realistically appraise alternative courses of action.[4]

The four groups profiled in this chapter take elaborate physical security precautions which enhance the belief that someone is out to "get" them, just as they are out to "get" someone themselves—which, after all, is what watchdog groups do. In the case of the Southern Poverty Law Center, it has constructed a special bomb-proof building as its headquarters. There's a sense that "the paranoids are after us" among these groups without admitting that they might have acquired a kind of paranoia themselves. It shows up in their heightened sensitivity to nuance and hidden meanings, i.e., the "subtle" manifestations of bigotry and prejudice. It's reminiscent of an observation by Dr. David Shapiro, a psychologist:

> [For the paranoid] a subjective world can be constructed in which facts, accurately enough perceived in themselves, are endowed with a special interpretive significance. . . . Thus, the subject matter of his interest has to do with hidden motives, underlying purposes, special meanings, and the like. He does not necessarily disagree with the normal person about the existence of any given fact; he disagrees only about its significance.[5]

Finally, all of these groups regard themselves as the "protectors" of some important value, something they believe is seriously endangered by their "enemies." This heightened sense of righteousness promotes a kind of "crusader" mentality with all of its accompanying potential for abuse. Orrin E. Klapp, in his seminal *Collective Search For Identity,* observes,

> The goal of a crusade is to defeat an evil, not merely to solve a problem. This gives it the sense of righteousness. . . . The crusader may think of himself as a hero and define his opponents as villains. Indeed, the crusade classifies as a kind of vilifying movement.[6]

These considerations, then, are what motivated me to ask the question, "who watches the watchman?"

The Watchdog Elite

The Anti-Defamation League

The Anti-Defamation League was established in Chicago, Illinois, in 1913 as a subdivision of B'nai B'rith, a Jewish fraternal order. Over the years the tax-exempt organization has grown enormously and maintains offices in 31 cities through the United States and overseas offices in selected European cities. It has an annual budget of $34 million and over four hundred employees including an extensive legal staff. The primary mission of the ADL is, and has always been, to expose and combat anti-Semitism.

In November 1991, the ADL held a two-day conference in Montreal, Canada, which produced a consensus that "Anti-Semitism, both in North America and abroad, is on the rise, and Jews have to stop keeping quiet about it." According to ADL executive director Abraham Foxman,

> we have reason to be concerned and frightened by what seems to be a rising tide of anti-Semitism here and around the world. . . . The virus has become more active. The restraints and taboos have disappeared.[7]

In addition to its community, civil rights, public relations, and lobbying activities, and reports on various organizations, the ADL is widely known for its annual audit of anti-Semitic incidents in the United States. In January 1994 for example, the ADL reported 1,867 anti-Semitic incidents involving threats, harassment, assaults, vandalism, graffiti, and other behaviors, or one incident per 139,000 Americans. These included one arson, one attempted arson and one attempted bombing.[8]

The ADL annual audit claimed 788 acts of vandalism (one per 330,000 Americans or slightly over two per day in a country of over a quarter billion people), down 8 per cent from the previous year. Of these, 325 involved graffiti on bridges, buildings and signs. Nationwide, according to the ADL, in 1993 there were only sixty arrests in these 325 cases, revealing that the vast majority of these incidents were unsolved and no identified culprit was apprehended. Vandalism is always a criminal offense and could be prosecuted if there was anyone to prosecute. The ADL lobbies hard for prosecution when the perpetrators are identified.

The ADL's Perception of Anti-Semitism

I'm sure these incidents were distressing to those who experienced them, but these figures do not support any claim of a serious and significant trend toward anti-Semitism in the United States. A critique of alarmist tactics was circulated by the Jewish Telegraphic Agency in 1993. Debra Nussbaum Cohen noted that:

> The reality, experts say, is that Jews no longer face serious discrimination in American society—not in the community, the workplace, politics or academia. . . . But American Jews are convinced more than ever that anti-Semitism remains a serious threat, although few have encountered any real bias themselves.[9-]

This dilemma, Ms. Cohen avers, is occasioned by the very organizations that promote awareness of anti-Semitism and solicit funds to combat it. With apparent reference to the ADL's annual audits, she says,

> The very lumping together of graffiti and epithets with occasional acts of violence in order to emphasize an upward trend in anti-Semitism may obscure the issue and raise undue alarm.[10]

Ms. Cohen quotes a source which she identifies as a "senior staffer" at a mainstream Jewish organization.

> By focusing on small and dramatic expressions of anti-Semitism which don't mean much, they're sending an alarmist message which is, at bottom, irresponsible.[11]

In January 1992 the American Jewish Committee released a report, based on detailed survey data, that racial and religious tolerance is increasing and anti-Semitism is declining. According to their data,

> The study found that anti-Jewish attitudes are at historic lows. . . . Jews were even perceived in the 1990 General Social Survey as leading whites in general, southern whites, Asian-Americans, Hispanic-Americans and blacks in terms of who was regarded as harder working, richer, less prone to violence, more self-supporting and more intelligent.[12]

The American Jewish Committee said that "the report should come as a relief to American Jews who fear a possible increase in anti-Semitism."

This problem of perception versus reality is not a recent phenomenon. In 1988, J. J. Goldberg, writing in *Jewish Week*, observed

> A majority of the Jewish community's professional experts insist there is no detectable jump either in the rate of anti-Semitic acts or in the level of anti-Jewish feeling among the American population at large.[13]

Goldberg's article quotes sociologist Steven M. Cohen, who believes that an increase in reporting anti-Semitic incidents fuels the claim that they are increasing. Cohen says,

> Jews are more sensitive to anti-Semitism than they've been in the past. So one of the reasons we may be seeing a rise in reports of anti-Semitism is that local people see incidents as anti-Semitic more readily. And secondly, the national media give it more prominence than in the past. . . . You have to conclude that to some degree, Jews construct anti-Semitism.[14]

Five years later, writing in *The New Republic*, Goldberg said that the very definition of "anti-Semitism" had been changed by some Jewish groups in order to support their agenda.

> Before World War II, anti-Semitism was defined as wanting to harm Jews. In the post-war era, it was broadened to include prejudice that might lead one to wish Jews harm. More recently, it's come to mean any stereotype—or disagreement—with the Jewish community. The very term has become a weapon.[15]

Goldberg commented on the hyping of anti-Semitism by Jewish organizations, noting that people give money when motivated by fear.

> In private, some Jewish agency staffers insist the alarmist tone set by a few national Jewish agencies, mainly for fundraising purposes, is a key cause of Jewish anxiety. Fingers point most often at the ADL and the Los Angeles-based Simon Wiesenthal Center,

both of which specialize in mass mailings warning of impending doom and urging donations.[16]

The issue of an obviously interested organization compiling its own statistics to justify its own agenda and to raise funds is highly questionable in itself. Moreover, it's not widely known that the ADL actually solicits reports by circulating questionnaires to its own mailing list—a group which it has carefully sensitized to the very subject of anti-Semitism. If a commercial polling firm engaged in such practices, it would be regarded as highly unethical and possibly fraudulent.

The ADL has established a reputation within and without the Jewish community as a major defender of civil rights for Jews and other minorities, a staunch opponent of bigotry in all forms, a fearless watchdog over racist and anti-Semitic groups and a major educational resource on human rights issues. Little known was its far less scrupulous espionage, disinformation and destabilization operations, not only against neo-Nazis and Ku Klux Klansmen, but against leftist and progressive groups as well.

The San Francisco ADL Spy Case

The ADL's "other side" came to light in January 1993, when a rapidly developing investigation by the San Francisco, California, police department into the activities of police intelligence officer Tom Gerard produced evidence of an extensive network of illegal ADL penetration into confidential police files in San Francisco and elsewhere. According to news reports,

> In 1991, Gerard joined other law enforcement officials on an "ADL law enforcement mission" to Israel, [ADL regional director Richard] Hirschaut said. "The law enforcement missions further ADL's mandate of monitoring and exposing extremist and anti-Semitic groups." [17]

The investigation quickly focused on Roy Bullock, a paid ADL operative and well-known figure in the San Francisco homosexual community, who had possession of an extensive ADL "enemies" list of some ten thousand individuals and 1,000 organizations. Bullock, who had worked for the ADL for fully 35 years and who was regarded as its "top spy," had developed an illegal "intelligence sharing" relationship with Gerard, who regularly stole information from police files for transmittal to the ADL and in some cases to Israeli intelligence agencies. Other information developed throughout the course of the investigation that there were Bullock and Gerard "clones" positioned in or close to police departments throughout the country.[18]

What was striking about the "enemies list" was that most of the individuals and organizations listed were of the leftist, progressive persuasion. Given the scarcity of bona-fide racist and neo-Nazi organizations, it is not surprising that few of them would be listed. Also not surprising is that many Arab human rights organizations would be. What was shocking was the range of left groups, including many civil rights organizations ordinarily counted among the

ADL's allies. Groups such as the American Civil Liberties Union, the National Conference of Black Lawyers, the Black United Front, the Center for Investigative Reporting, the Asian Law Caucus, and the San Francisco Anti-Apartheid Committee were on the list. Predictably, this produced a howl of protest from a sector of the American political spectrum that might have been expected to condone the ADL's harassment of the far right. According to news reports:

> A small group of undercover operatives throughout the nation is being paid by the Anti-Defamation League of B'nai B'rith to spy on pro-Palestinian, black nationalist and white supremacist groups, according to a San Francisco law enforcement official.
>
> The operatives rely on local police and sheriff's deputies to provide access to confidential law enforcement and motor vehicle information, in probable violation of criminal law . . .
>
> "This Gerard-Bullock thing is the tip of the iceberg—this is going on nationwide," another law enforcement official said. Capt. John Willett of the Police Department's special investigations division said officers examining evidence in the case already had discovered from up to 20 police departments and other law enforcement agencies throughout the state . . .
>
> "The ADL uses techniques to monitor hate groups that make you cringe," said Boston lawyer Harvey Silverglade, a Jew who belongs to the civil rights panels of both the ADL and the American Civil Liberties Union.
>
> Some 12,000 computerized files were seized Dec. 10 [1992] in searches of ADL offices in San Francisco and Los Angeles.[19]

Why leftist groups, particularly traditional civil rights groups? One reason might be the specter of an alliance between black and other minority civil rights movements with the Palestinian cause in Israel, which in certain respects resembles the plight of American blacks. There are few things that the ADL fears more than a popular civil rights movement on behalf of the Palestinians.[20]

Some of the best coverage of the ADL scandal appeared in the *San Francisco Examiner*, where reporters Dennis Opatrny and Scott Winocur covered the story almost daily from its inception. In an April 1, 1993 article, they quoted a (presumably police) source close to the case.

> The ADL is doing the same thing all over the country. There is evidence that the ADL had police agents in other cities. The case just gets bigger every day. The more we look, the more people we find are involved.[21]

Detailed overviews appeared in April and May, 1993, respectively, by George Cothran and Peter Hegarty in the *SF Weekly*, a San Francisco tabloid, and by Robert J. Friedman in the New York weekly *The Village Voice*. Cothran and Hegarty observed:

Examples abound of the ADL's brazen invasion into the lives of people who happen to disagree with its political views. In 1983, the group disseminated a "blacklist" to Jewish campus leaders around the country that smeared scores of respected academics and Middle East peace activists as "pro-Arab sympathizers and propagandists who use their anti-Zionism as merely a guise for their deeply felt anti-Semitism."[22]

The ADL responded to the adverse publicity with an intense media disinformation campaign, claiming that it did nothing wrong in "sharing information on violence-prone groups with law enforcement officials," and that it "will not countenance violations of the law on the part of anyone connected with the agency."[23] This was met with healthy skepticism by many of those concerned. Robert J. Friedman had this to say:

> That's what the ADL says for public consumption. But morale is so low that its employees complain of sleepless nights and crying fits. And even as other Jewish groups circle the wagons around the ADL in a show of solidarity, many do so holding their noses. More than a few Jewish officials privately say that the ADL has to decide whether it is a human rights group or a secret police agency.[24]

Although the ADL claimed it was cooperating with police, apparently this was not entirely the case. On April 8, 1993, police armed with search warrants searched ADL offices in San Francisco and Los Angeles.

> San Francisco police raided the offices of the Anti-Defamation League yesterday looking for illegally obtained law enforcement information used in a nationwide political spy network.
> An affidavit by Inspector Ron Roth said the searches were necessary because ADL officials did not turn over files as they had promised in December. Roth said "ADL employees were less than truthful with regards to the employment of Roy Bullock and other matters."[25]

When ADL National Director Abraham Foxman went on a damage control mission to West Coast news media offices and Jewish organizations, he attacked critics of the ADL, calling them "anti-Semitic, undemocratic, and anti-American bastards."[26]

Many of the ADL's critics came from the liberal Jewish community, however. Michael Lerner, editor of *Tikkun*, a progressive Jewish magazine, said that the ADL's spying activities were "a tremendous shame and embarrassment for American Jews." He continued:

> The ADL is part of that sector of American Jews that believes that everybody is against us and anti-Semitism is likely to pop out at any moment at any place. They have no boundaries for their fears.[27]

The evidence that developed against the ADL was very strong. Not only did its paid agent take part in stealing police records—a serious felony—but there were numerous other infractions as well. There was active speculation that felony indictments against prominent ADL officials would be forthcoming. The *Detroit Jewish News* reported:

> The Anti-Defamation League, the major national Jewish organization committed to fighting racism and anti-Semitism, could face multiple felony charges for eavesdropping and other illegal activities carried out as part of an alleged nationwide intelligence network.[28]

The *Los Angeles Times* revealed that David Gurvitz, whom the ADL employed as a "fact-finder" in its Los Angeles office, was talking to police and the media about his role in the organization's spying operations.

> Among other things, he told San Francisco authorities the Los Angeles ADL office kept records of any Arab-American who had "anti-Israel leanings" or who wrote a letter to a newspaper expressing such sentiment.[29]

According to the *Los Angeles Times*, the ADL especially targeted Arab and Palestinian organizations for surveillance, including obtaining confidential information

> on a vast number of people, including as many as 4,500 members of one target group, the **Arab-American Anti-Discrimination Committee.**
>
> Each case of obtaining such data from a law enforcement officer could constitute a felony, San Francisco Police Inspector Ron Roth noted in an affidavit for a search warrant.[30]

The ADL's Misuse of Journalist "Shield" Laws

Over the years several organizations and individuals have filed lawsuits against the ADL. The San Francisco spy case was no exception. In April 1993 *San Francisco Examiner* reporters Opatrny and Winocur announced that

> Eighteen people—including the son of former Israeli Defense Minister Moshe Arens—planned to file a lawsuit Wednesday charging the Anti-Defamation League of B'nai B'rith with invasion of privacy. . . Yigal Arens . . . said in a telephone interview that he has seen the file the ADL kept on him in the 1980s, presumably because of his criticism of the treatment of Palestinians...
>
> "My understanding is that they consider all activity that is in some sense opposed to Israel or Israeli action to be part of their responsibility to investigate. . . . The ADL believes that anyone who is an Arab American . . . or speaks politically against Israel is at least a closet anti-Semite."[31]

The ADL's strategy in these and the many other lawsuits it has faced over the years is if it can't overwhelm the plaintiffs with its enormous resources to keep a suit from coming to trial, to claim "journalistic privilege" when faced with questioning about its activities, including the source of allegedly false information. The ADL claims to be a "news and information gathering organization," and as such it is entitled to protection under the journalist "shield" laws used to protect the working press from having to reveal its news sources.

In no sense, however, is the ADL on a par with the *New York Times* or *Time Magazine*, nor is it even remotely related to the working press. Its publications are designed to support the ideological agenda of the organization and its constituency, and not to provide "news." In addition, its publishing activities are only a part of its overall program, most of which is lobbying, public relations and fundraising, along with developing and maintaining its extensive enemies files. Yet, time after time judges have bought this argument and it exists as a legal precedent now. Here is what happened in San Francisco:

> The Anti-Defamation League won a major legal victory Wednesday [6 October 1993] when a San Francisco Superior Court judge ruled the organization does not have to open its files to a group of individuals suing it for invasion of privacy.
>   Judge Barbara J. R. Jones declared the ADL, in effect, a fact-gathering enterprise with a journalistic purpose whose First Amendment rights should be recognized, including the protection of confidential sources.[32]

Once again the ADL has avoided potentially damaging discovery proceedings that would have provided ample ammunition for both criminal prosecution and private lawsuits by the numerous individuals and organizations that claim to have been damaged by it. Robert I. Friedman comments on this in the liberal *Village Voice*:

> But the difference between the practice of journalism and the ADL's method of gathering information couldn't be more striking. Journalists place information in the public domain where they are held accountable for falsehoods, distortions, and libel. And for the most part, journalists don't share their files with domestic police agencies. The ADL has no such inhibitions. Because many of its files are not open to public scrutiny, false information collected by ideologically biased researchers cannot be corrected. Once a proud human rights group, the ADL has become the Jewish thought police.[33]

The ADL Gets Minimal Penalties For Its Spying

In addition to eavesdropping, the charges awaiting the ADL included tax violations, conspiracy and receiving confidential files from police agencies. They were not forthcoming. Why not? Consider this:

Some close observers believe that political pressure will make it impossible to prosecute the respected Jewish organization. "Mark my words, this is going to be obfuscated, obliterated. . . " said one veteran inspector. "It's going to be a classic study in how things get covered up. You don't do Jewish people in San Francisco. It's not PC. Especially when you have two U. S. Senators who are Jewish [Barbara Boxer and Dianne Feinstein] and the city's Chief of Protocol is Dick Goldman [a prominent fund-raiser in the Jewish Community.]"[34]

The inspector was prophetic. The ADL and its spy, Roy Bullock, were dropped from the criminal investigation in April, leaving only Tom Gerard, against whom prosecution would be very difficult. In December 1993, the San Francisco District Attorney reached a settlement with the ADL.

> After a yearlong investigation into charges that the Anti-Defamation League built a national intelligence network using illegal spying, [San Francisco] District Attorney Arlo Smith agreed Monday not to prosecute the organization in exchange for its payment of up to $75,000 to fight hate crime.
> The [ADL] had been accused of illegally receiving confidential data from police sources. As part of the agreement, the group pledged not to engage in improper information gathering in California. The case highlighted the Anti-Defamation League's intelligence operation and its infiltration of political and ethnic groups.[35]

The ADL and the FBI

The entire history of the ADL's relationship with government agencies, including the Federal Bureau of Investigation (FBI), has yet to be written. However, in working through a large stack of FBI documents obtained under a Freedom of Information Act (FOIA)[36] request, it becomes clear that the organization has labored hard and long to ingratiate itself with federal law enforcement authorities, ostensibly as "experts" on its own enemies.

Until the Reagan administration, the FBI kept the ADL at arm's length, although it readily accepted ADL information in the same manner that it does from a wide range of informants. Under J. Edgar Hoover, the bureau was particularly reluctant to get into any kind of cooperative arrangement with the ADL. Hoover, for example, repeatedly declined offers to address ADL banquets, realizing that his presence would be a propaganda coup for an organization he didn't entirely trust.

In a 4 January 1966 letter to Dore Schary, ADL national chairman, Hoover declined attendance at an ADL dinner for U. S. Supreme Court Justice Arthur J. Goldberg. A note written by FBI researchers was appended to the ADL request, which read:

> NOTE: Mr. Schary is a Hollywood producer who is well known to the Bureau. He has never been investigated but Bufiles reflect that he has been a member or sponsor of, contributed to or was in other

ways affiliated with a number of organizations cited as CP [Communist Party] front groups or which were designated as subversive pursuant to EO [Executive Order] 10450.[37]

Although factually correct, the FBI (in this case acting as a watchdog group itself) may have been making too much out of these "links" and "ties." One group Schary was associated with was Hollywood Writers Mobilization, a "popular front" group of Communists and non-Communists drumming up support for the United States and its new ally, the Soviet Union, in World War II. Former Communist Party member Dorothy Healey observes,

> With the Soviet Union as America's military ally, a new "popular front" was reborn on an even broader basis that in the 1930's. . . Locally organized groups like Hollywood Writers Mobilization drew support from all kinds of people, virtually across the political spectrum.[38]

Another group was American Youth for Democracy, also a popular front organization of mixed membership. As for Schary himself, he appeared before the House Committee on Un-American Activities in 1947 and stated, "I am not a Communist. I have never been a Communist. I never contemplated becoming a Communist, and I am opposed to Communists."[39]

An important point here is that while the ADL would almost certainly explain away Dore Schary's associations as being circumstantial and tangential, in its reports and publications it almost never extended such consideration to individuals who may have had a similarly tangential association with a racist, neo-Nazi, or holocaust-revisionist organization.

ADL Disinformation Campaigns

The reason for the FBI's distrust—aside from the radical background of certain ADL leaders—was the sheer opportunism evident in ADL tactics to compromise the independence of the bureau, and also in the shoddy quality of some ADL investigative reports on its enemies. An internal FBI memorandum dated 12 August 1965 from Assistant Director William Sullivan to R. W. Smith made reference to an ADL pamphlet on the Ku Klux Klan. Sullivan notes:

> It is stated on page 6 that a Klan plot to assassinate Martin Luther King early in 1965 leaked out, and the FBI and other law enforcement authorities threw a heavy guard around him. This is not true. . . . The pamphlet erroneously lists James Venable's National Knights of the Ku Klux Klan as the second most important group, having the support of 7,000 to 9,000. Originally formed by Venable to bring a number of small Klans into one organization, the National Knights of the Ku Klux Klan has not realized its goal.[40]

A year later FBI documents refer to another erroneous ADL report, this one inflating the strength of the Ku Klux Klan, which the ADL claimed was at about 29,500! The ADL also claimed in a September 1966 statement in the *New*

York Times that KKK membership had increased by 10,000 since the first of the year. According to another FBI memorandum:

> While the Klan has made organizational efforts in the North and Middle West, they have met with little success. There has been no indication that Klan membership has grown by 10,000 since the first of the year. . . . The present Klan membership is between 14,00 and 15,000 active members.[41]

Perhaps more significantly, however, the 1966 FBI memorandum contained the following, which is transparently evident to objective observers:

> The Anti-Defamation League has vested interest in discovering and exposing anti-Semitic organizations such as the Klan and other hate groups.[42]

ADL Hoaxes WCCO-TV

My own interest in the Anti-Defamation League came from an experience I had involving the organization in 1981. Prior to that I was confident that the ADL was merely a human rights organization with a special interest in anti-Semitism. I had spoken with ADL representatives on a couple of occasions regarding right-wing groups that I regarded as dangerous. They were polite, concerned and tried to be helpful.

In July 1981 I was contacted by WCCO-TV in Minneapolis, Minnesota, to assist it in producing a documentary on right-wing paramilitary groups. I responded with a number of leads and suggestions, and in October WCCO producer Jim Hayden, accompanied by cameraman Paul Henschel, arrived to interview me for their upcoming documentary, *Armies of the Right*, which was to air in several weeks. They had chosen me as the expert on the subject to provide background and commentary during their documentary.

During our visit we discussed an experience they had while interviewing the leaders of the New York City chapter of the Christian Patriot's Defense League (CPDL), a right-wing paramilitary group headquartered in Flora, Illinois. The two subjects in this part of the documentary identified themselves as "Jim Anderson" and "John Austin." Hayden related that they behaved strangely during the shot, often huddling together and whispering between themselves, and that Austin insisted on wearing a fake mustache. "They didn't seem right," Hayden said, noting that they seemed to be "acting" and trying to create the impression of the stereotypical right-wing racist. He wondered if they were legitimate. My response what that these movements are full of strange characters and that I could spend hours relating my own experiences interviewing them.

On 7 December 1981 WCCO-TV flew me to Minneapolis to attend the premier of *Armies of the Right* and to participate in a televised 90-minute town hall forum afterward. Also included were members of one of the groups covered in the documentary, along with representatives of civil rights groups and Morton Ryweck of the ADL. It was the first time I had seen the video.

During their videotaped segment, both "Jim Anderson" and "John Austin" did, indeed, fulfill the stereotype of the offensive bigoted racist. They had attended the CPDL's 1981 "Freedom Festival" where they taught a course in street combat and techniques of hand-to-hand violence called "street action." Interestingly, their course would probably fall within the definition of "paramilitary training," which was subsequently outlawed in several states as the result of a nationwide campaign by the ADL.

When I returned to Kansas City, however, I began my own investigation into the matter, contacting several other researchers and journalist friends who follow extremist politics. I learned that "Jim Anderson" was no less than James Mitchel Rosenberg, an agent for the ADL in much the same manner as Roy Bullock. Moreover, on 8 October 1981, a month before the premier of *Armies of the Right*, Rosenberg was arrested along with "John Austin," who turned out to be Kevin Reid, on a New York City rooftop. According to media accounts, which included a photograph,

> Kevin Reid . . . and James Rosenberg are handcuffed as they are taken into custody at Third Ave. near 44th St. yesterday. Police said they found the men on the roof of a building at 686 Third Ave. with two rifles. Reid, of Manhattan, and Rosenberg, of Queens, said they were posing for a photograph. They were charged with possession of an unregistered rifle and carrying a weapon in public view.[43]

In 1984 Rosenberg was identified as an ADL agent provocateur in a major court case as well.[44] During a deposition of Irwin Suall, head of the ADL's directorate of "Fact Finding," the question of Rosenberg's undercover work for the ADL came up. Suall's testimony was evasive as an attorney tried to pin down his involvement with Rosenberg, although Suall did admit to having contact with him during "the last few weeks." ADL attorney Barbara Wahl, noting that the deposition is a public record which might fall into the hands of newspapers, directed Suall to refuse to answer questions about Rosenberg and invoked the New York "Shield" law, which protects bona fide journalists from having to reveal confidential sources of information. Suall, of course, was in no sense whatever a journalist.

By the late 1980s Rosenberg had become well known among neo-Nazi and Ku Klux Klan leaders who, surprisingly, both suspected and tolerated him to a certain extent. Among his closest associates was veteran government informant Roy E. Frankhauser, former Grand Dragon of the Pennsylvania Ku Klux Klan. Patsey Sims, in her 1978 book *The Klan* also mentioned Rosenberg as an alleged ADL agent.[45] My own conversations with Rosenberg and his associates settled the issue.

So here we have the Anti-Defamation League allowing one of its long-time undercover operatives to pose as a right-wing paramilitary extremist for an unsuspecting television station attempting to produce a legitimate documentary. Moreover, when this was discovered, the ADL said nothing about it. This is but one more reason why journalists and others should be extremely wary of this organization.

FBI Skepticism About the ADL

Faced with problems like these, throughout the 1960s and most of the 1970s the FBI practiced a healthy skepticism about ADL information. It seemed clear that there was nothing the organization would like better than to have the primary U.S. law enforcement agency become its enforcement arm.

It wasn't until judge William Webster became FBI director in 1978 that the agency bowed to political pressures from the White House and the Jewish community and significantly stepped up its cooperation with the ADL, and this relationship fully blossomed during the Reagan administration when the FBI issued a memo in 1985 requiring all FBI field offices to develop formal liaison with some thirty ADL offices around the nation. This memo remained secret until it was uncovered in a 1990 FOIA request to an FBI field office in Minnesota, where it was released to a journalist by mistake. The memo was accompanied by two ADL publications and instructed each SAC (Special Agent in Charge) to "contact each [ADL] regional office to establish a liaison and line of communication."[46] One of those publications was the ADL's controversial 1984 publication, *Hate Groups in America*.[47]

Hate Groups in America

In 1980 the U.S. Commission on Civil Rights (USCCR) contracted with the Anti-Defamation League to produce a report on extreme right "hate groups" for a $20,000 fee. The ADL hardly needed the fee, but was thrilled at having the implied endorsement of a government agency for one of its reports. This did not work out so well, however.

After the report was completed, the USCCR rejected the report and declined to publish it on several grounds. A March 1982, letter from Paul Alexander, acting general counsel of the USCCR, to John Hope, III, acting staff director, gave the following reasons:

> I would like to raise several policy considerations. The ADL report does not in any way resemble a standard USCCR report. It is not a dispassionate attempt to present a balanced accounting of facts. The commission previously has had no difficulty in publishing reports containing defamatory information when it was verifiable and necessary to the report. Our Voting Rights Report is the most recent example. In that report, however, we did not find it necessary to mix epithets and emotionally laden labels with the facts. The ADL report is rank with epithets and labels that only distort the factual accountings of the activities of the KKK and similar organizations.
>
> The liberal use of hyperbolic epithets throughout the ADL draft sets a tone that probably precludes correction through simple adjectival laundering. The alleged inaccuracies and misrepresentations noted by the respondents present very serious problems. . . If [they] are at all representative, the report probably contains many

inaccuracies. It is doubtful that the report could survive a source-check as there does not appear to be sufficient data to support the allegations.[48]

Alexander further noted that the ADL report "bordered on jingoism." Although the USCCR wisely declined to lend its name to the report, the ADL published it anyway, with "epithets, emotionally laden labels" and "jingoism" intact. Like all ADL publications on the people and groups that it hates, its tone is one that encourages contempt for the civil liberties of its subjects and treats them in a dehumanizing manner—behaviors that the ADL purports to oppose. The report has now appeared in several editions and is widely circulated to journalists and police agencies.

Canadian "ADL" Loses Libel Case

It is a standard joke that if you don't like what the Anti-Defamation League says about you, you can always sue it with its huge legal staff and almost unlimited resources. Several lawsuits against the ADL for libel in the United States have failed. In Canada, however, which has stricter libel laws than the United States, false charges of anti-Semitism brought B'nai B'rith Canada and its League for Human Rights, the approximate equivalent of the ADL in the United States, a libel action that cost the organization $400,000. The case, brought by Winnipeg teacher and former Progressive Conservative candidate Luba Fedorkiw in 1987, was the largest defamation award in Canadian history.[49]

The ADL falsely accused Fedorkiw of anti-Semitism and attempted to ruin her career by claiming that she had said an opposing candidate "was controlled by Jews." This, of course, was not true. According to news accounts:

> In its verdict, the four-woman, two-man jury found the B'nai B'rith maliciously responsible for writing and circulating minutes of an internal May, 1984, meeting. Those minutes alleged that Fedorkiw was engaged in "Jew-baiting" in the months leading up to the 1984 election.[50]

When B'nai B'rith's allegations had been published, anti-fascist groups began a major harassment campaign. Fedorkiw began receiving obscene telephone calls, a swastika was painted on her campaign office and many of her political supporters withdrew. Ms. Fedorkiw said that publicity over the allegations "exposed her to scorn and caused her to withdraw from public life."[51] This, of course, is what a charge of anti-Semitism is supposed to do. This time it happened to someone who was innocent and fought back.

Southern Poverty Law Center

In February 1992, *USA Today* reported that Klanwatch, a division of Morris Dees' Southern Poverty Law Center, had identified a total of "346 white supremacy groups operating in the USA, up an alarming 27 percent from the past year." Included were 97 Ku Klux Klan and 203 alleged Neo-Nazi groups.[52] What Klanwatch apparently did is locate any mailing address it could find for these groups, including the large number of "post office box chapters" maintained by Klan and skinhead organizations. It also listed many groups whose actual affiliation is neither KKK nor neo-Nazi, and who would argue with the designation of "white supremacy." In short, Klanwatch fraudulently padded its list.

> This writer publishes an annual directory of these groups (and a companion directory of the American left), and can attest to this irresponsible inflation of figures by Klanwatch. In terms of *viable* groups, i.e., groups that are objectively significant, are actually functioning and have more than a handful of members, not post office box "groups" or two-man local chapters, the actual figure is a combined total of about 35—a far cry from 346! Unfortunately, this kind of exaggeration on the part of Dees and his organization is typical.[53]

Dees is the classic example of an apparently unprincipled opportunist waging a holy war against an unpopular foe and profiting from it, both financially and ideologically. His primary talents have always been in the area of fund-raising and promotion. According to a 1989 article on Dees' background in the *Atlanta Constitution*:

> In 1972, he raised $24 million as George McGovern's finance director, then used the campaign's donor list of 700,000 liberals for the law center. (He also recommended Richard Viguerie, the conservative direct-mail whiz, to friends in the Wallace campaign.) The law center now raises more than $5 million a year and has a $34 million endowment [in 1989]. . .
>
> The harshest critic is Millard Farmer, the Atlanta death penalty lawyer who teamed up with Mr. Dees before ending their relationship with a lawsuit. "It's a Jim and Tammy Faye Bakker operation," he says flatly. "You read his letters and you'd think he's on his last penny."[54]

The article also quoted a former employee to the effect that Morris Dees marketed social consciousness in the same detached way that he once marketed cakes. "The center is something he can sell. People want to contribute something to relieve their conscience."[55]

The Questionable Fundraising of the SPLC

In February 1994, the *Montgomery Advertiser* ran a series of articles exposing various aspects of the SPLC, including its highly questionable fundraising tactics and other dishonest practices. In 1993, the American Institute for Philanthropy ranked the Southern Poverty Law Center as the "fourth least-needy charity in the nation."[56] Among the issues it raised are:

The SPLC has reserve funds of $52 million. . . . Just what the Law
Center does with all that money is a source of concern.
    Some who have worked with Morris Dees call him a phony,
the "television evangelist" of civil rights who misleads donors. . .
    For 15 years, people throughout the country have sent mil-
lions to the [SPLC] to fight the Ku Klux Klan and other supremacists. But critics say the law center exaggerates the threat of hate
groups.[57]

The SPLC responded to the series with a number of veiled threats and
charged that it was a "hatchet job." Nevertheless, the series was widely praised
and is regarded as a model for courageous, objective reporting.

The SPLC's Disinformation Campaign

Former SPLC staffers have stated that aside from random acts of violence by a few of their members, the Ku Klux Klan and other white supremacist
organizations are far more image than substance. According to the *Montgomery
Advertiser's* series on the SPLC,

> Mr. Dees chose to focus on the Klan to raise money for the law
> center, said three former staff attorneys: Mr. [Dennis] Balske,
> Deborah Ellis, and Dennis Sweet, now a Mississippi legislator.
> Going after the Klan has brought in tens of millions of dollars from
> throughout the nation. "The market is still wide open for the prod-
> uct, which is Black pain and white guilt," said Gloria Browne, one
> of only two black attorneys to work at the Law Center.[58]

Atlanta Lawyer Millard Farmer, who had worked with the SPLC in the mid-
1970s until he parted ways with Morris Dees, said that filing lawsuits against
white supremacists is merely a money-raising tactic. He said,

> Attacking the Klan: courageous, tough, hard, useful, beneficial,
> necessary work—in 1930. . . . In the 1990s, it plays on a mentality
> unconnected with reality. There's not a politician in the country
> who won't fight the Klan now. It's a scheme. It's a joke.[59]

In the mid-1980s SPLC mailings said "Armed Klan paramilitary forces
freely roam our wooded hills from Texas to North Carolina" and that the "massive voter registration drives planned by blacks . . . will cause Klansmen to resort to the nightriding tactics of the past." Former Harvard Law School intern at
the SPLC Frederick Smith observed that Morris Dees' fund-raising letters distorted his view of the South. Smith had never been to the South and felt that "the
threat of the Klan sounded like an imposing possibility." He observed that after
he joined the SPLC staff and had talked to a number of people, "The picture I
got . . . was more complicated than the way it was portrayed by Dees."

> Going after the Klan "is kind of like shooting fish in a barrel. . . .
> The good thing about the Klan is you will find very few people out

there who are going to disagree with you on anything like the Klan or any kind of organization like that," he said.[60]

The SPLC and Oklahoma City

Not surprisingly, when two men were charged in the 19 April 1995 bombing of the Federal Building in Oklahoma City—a ghastly crime that killed 168 people—the SPLC was ready with its disinformation and fund-raising apparatus in place.

The SPLC began a massive mailing fourteen days after the Oklahoma City bombing. This was followed up two weeks later by letters stating, "We need your help now with the most generous special gift you can make to help us expand our Militia Task Force." Another SPLC mailing dated 27 April and which appeared to have been prepared before the bombing also asks for funds for its Militia Task Force. "You know, that's interesting. That was timely wasn't it. I mean, we didn't know the bomb was going to go off," Dees is quoted as saying.[61]

The SPLC's *Klanwatch Intelligence Report* of June 1995, claimed that "over 200 militia and support groups operate nationwide."[62] Three months later, in September 1995, the SPLC issued a report that identified seventy-three "militias or militia support groups nationwide, with a total of 30,000 to 40,000 members." The SPLC also claimed that about forty-five have "ties to the Ku Klux Klan."[63]

One hundred and twenty-seven "militia and support groups" just disappeared, now that the media was checking the SPLC out. Moreover, even Dees' more modest figures are way off base. Many of the "support groups" were just groups—some with only a few members—who shared some views with the militias, such as opposition to the income tax or gun control, and conducted no paramilitary activities themselves.

As for "ties to the Ku Klux Klan," there were a few cases where this was true, but it constitutes but a few percent of militia membership. Often these "ties" were nothing more substantial than the claim that Klansmen had attended militia meetings or that Klan literature was found there.

As for the impressive "30,000 to 40,000" figure, an actual count is impossible, but there is good reason to believe that actual, bona fide membership in the militias may have been as small as 10 percent to 20 percent of that at the time of the Oklahoma City bombing. Even the Anti-Defamation League claimed only 10,000 militia members! Moreover, SPLC claims of a massive increase in membership after the bombing are unsupported except by absurd claims of publicity seekers in the militias themselves, in some cases claiming wholly unsupportable figures of a million members.

In part the controversy surrounding alleged membership figures rests on what constitutes a "militia," and a "militia support group," and on what constitutes a "member." The SPLC uses these terms as broadly as possible and then some. It routinely includes every possible listing, including groups that are alleged to exist but not verified. As "support groups" the SPLC includes every listing, no matter how small or marginal, that have interests even vaguely similar to militias, and for "members" it uses rumored figures, figures estimated from meeting attendance (which include a large number of curiosity seekers, not to mention journalists, police and informants), and reports on mailing lists, which are always larger than bona fide membership lists. And, of course, the financial fortunes of the SPLC depend entirely on claims of a large and growing "threat" of one kind or another.

And as for militia complicity in the bombing itself—after two years of intensive investigation neither the FBI nor any other law enforcement agency have produced evidence that the perpetrators were members of or in any substantial way connected with any militia, anywhere, anytime. No militias were implicated by government prosecutors at Timothy McVeigh's trial. Militias had nothing to do with the Oklahoma City bombing. The perpetrators were acting entirely on their own. Finally, in December 1998, the Federal Bureau of Investigation wrapped up one of the most expensive and thorough investigations in its history. Its conclusion: There were no conspirators other than those indicted and militias had nothing to do with the Oklahoma City bombing, which was the product of three individuals acting on their own.[64] A county grand jury arrived at the same conclusion.[65]

So shameful was the SPLC's demonization of the militias for fundraising purposes that in June 1995, the *Montgomery Advertiser* published a report on the SPLC's fund-raising tactics as part of a continuing series of articles examining the organization. Entitled "Marketing The Militias," by Dan Morse, the report noted that "Morris Dees and the Southern Poverty Law Center are using the militia controversy to raise funds, but not all donors approve of their methods." The article quoted a former donor to the SPLC who learned that the organization had amassed $60,000,000 in reserve funds:

> "It's almost like jumping on whatever shameful thing has happened in the country to solicit funds," said Harvy Aronson, a Long Island man who has sent about $1,000 to the center. He quit giving last year when he found out about the millions in reserves. "My impression always was that they needed money. Some little group working out of practically a storefront," he said.[66]

The SPLC Legal Offensive

In 1987 Dees and the SPLC made national headlines with a $7 million civil judgment against United Klans of America (UKA), a major Ku Klux Klan organization, and six former and current members for the March 1981, slaying of Michael Donald, a black teenager. None of the defendants in the case were able to afford legal counsel, including the UKA, which was forced to turn over all of its assets and went out of business.[67]

This "$7 million judgment" was a major point in SPLC fund-raising campaigns. SPLC mailings made it clear that this wonderful bounty for the mother of the slain teenager wouldn't have been possible without its help, and that was a reason people should donate to the SPLC. What the mailings didn't mention was that the United Klans was nearly broke at the time of the judgment and Donald's mother received less than $52,000 with little possibility of getting any more. The SPLC, on the other hand, raised millions of dollars from its direct mail appeals featuring the case.

At issue in that trial was the liability of the entire UKA organization for the acts of a few of its members.[68] Had this legal doctrine that organizations are responsible for the acts of their members been established in the 1960s, it would have decimated the early civil rights movement, whose members were occasionally violent, and would have bankrupted groups like the National Association for the Advancement of Colored People and the Congress of Racial Equality, both of which this writer belonged to. Even the organized labor movement and the 1960s anti-war movement could have been crippled by lawsuits arising from the occasional violent acts of their members. Suppose a black activist organization was hit with a $7 million judgment because one of its members killed someone in the Watts Riots? This sounds far-fetched, but had the Dees precedent existed then, it probably would have happened.

Another Morris Dees case illustrates his tactics further. On the morning of 13 November 1988, in Portland Oregon, three skinheads—Kenneth Mieske, Kyle Brewster, and Steven Strasser—got into a fight with three Ethiopians—Mulugeta Seraw, Wondwosen Tesfaye, and Tilahun Antneh. All parties had apparently been drinking. When it was over, Mulugeta Seraw was dead. The three skinheads pleaded guilty: Mieske to murder, and Brewster and Strasser to manslaughter. All are serving long prison sentences as a result of this stupid, senseless tragedy.[69]

This was not the end of the matter, however. The SPLC and the ADL filed a $10 million lawsuit on behalf of Seraw's estate against Tom and John Metzger.[70] The suit attempted to link the Metzgers, a father-son team heading the White Aryan Resistance (WAR) organization, to the killing through the questionable doctrine of "vicarious liability." Morris Dees argued that the Metzgers, through the actions of a skinhead named Dave Mazella, were responsible for the killing by virtue of their alleged instructions to Mazella and his subsequent actions in organizing and motivating the Portland skinheads. No allegation was ever made that the Metzgers had given any kind of instructions to Mieske, Brewster or Strasser. As might be expected, the Metzgers had few assets and were forced to act as their own counsel. An account of Morris Dees' strategy is revealed in an article in *The National Law Journal*:

> When we first filed this lawsuit, we had a choice between state and federal court. We chose state court because Oregon discovery rules are quite different than federal rules. You can do trial by ambush in Oregon. You have no interrogatories, no production of evidence; you don't have to give the names of witnesses or give the other side your documents.[71]

After a long trial before a judge with one year's experience in which the highly questionable Mazella himself was the star witness, the jury returned a verdict against the Metzgers in October 1990. The Metzgers made plans to appeal the verdict, but when they attempted to pay for a transcript of the trial with donated money in order to prepare their appeal, Dees garnished the payment, thus impeding their access to the legal process. At this point Chicago civil liberties attorney Michael Null entered the case because of the principle involved and submitted a detailed appeal brief.[72] Unfortunately, because the Metzgers had failed to raise numerous objections to Dees' tactics during the trial, it was not possible to do so afterward under Oregon law and the appeal failed.

The SPLC and Perjury

Unlike the 1987 case, this one was watched considerably more closely. What is interesting is not that the Metzger's racist and neo-Nazi allies rallied to their defense, but that liberals and leftists expressed doubt about the verdict as well. The *Williamette Weekly*, an Oregon alternative tabloid weekly newspaper editorialized:

> In the wake of last week's stunning victory over California's white supremacist Tom Metzger at the hands of crusading civil rights lawyer Morris Dees, a number of courthouse observers are quietly raising questions about a little mentioned development in the trial. It is now clear that Dave Mazella, a star witness who provided Dees with the crucial link between Metzger and the racist skinheads who murdered Mulugeta Seraw. . . perjured himself on the witness stand.
>
> "If definite proof can be presented that Mazella committed perjury, it may be possible for the Court of Appeals to order a new trial," says Michael Simon, a local lawyer who monitored the case on behalf of the Oregon chapter of the American Civil Liberties Union.
>
> Such proof, in fact, does exist. Not only are there witnesses who insist that Mazella was lying on the stand, but there are also letters by Mazella himself that contradict his sworn testimony.[73]

Even the moderate leftist *In These Times* opined, "Jurors in a West Coast white-supremacy trial struck a blow for racial justice last week but may have bruised some civil liberties in the process." Writer John Shragg questioned the credibility of Mazella's testimony and pointed out:

> Dees was backed by his center's multi-million-dollar bankroll and its cadre of lawyers along with the equally impressive resources of the Anti-Defamation League of B'nai B'rith and the complete co-operation of federal, state and local authorities. The Metzgers represented themselves.[74]

If, in fact, Dees had permitted a sworn witness to perjure himself under oath, as it seems in the Metzger case, this would not be the first time this issue had been raised in his career.

The SPLC vs. Constitutional Rights

In a column appearing under the banner of the *Los Angeles Times/ Washington Post News Service*, Ray Jenkins, a writer for the *Baltimore Sun*, noted, "A wise judge once observed that great constitutional rights often are established in the cases that involve 'not very nice people.'" He also observed that while the State of Oregon lacked evidence to put Metzger on trial for murder in the case, what Morris Dees did was to

> convert the civil law, whose basic purpose is to settle disputes between individuals, into an arm of the criminal law. In legal abracadabra, the standard of proof in civil cases—usually only "preponderance of evidence"—is a good deal easier to meet than the higher standard of "guilt beyond a reasonable doubt" required in criminal prosecutions.
>
> Let's not forget, there are cases on record where civil law was tortured into criminal law to punish Communists in the 1950's, then civil rights groups, including the National Association for the Advancement of Colored People, in the 1960's.[75]

Conscientious civil libertarians, while strongly opposing the Ku Klux Klan and neo-Nazi groups, disdain unfair and underhanded methods used to attack them in the courts. Quite simply, anything that can be done to your enemies may, in time, be done to your friends. The SPLC proclivity to use civil suits—where constitutional protections are minimal and there is no right to counsel—against poor, working class, and often semi-literate Klansmen unable to afford an attorney, has been compared to shooting fish in a barrel.

The issue, of course, is a classic moral one, i.e., whether the ends justify the means used to accomplish them. Many moral philosophers would say that the means indirectly determine the ends, and that unjust means necessarily lead to unjust ends.

Morris Dees and the Joanne Little Case

In 1975 Dees and the SPLC represented Joanne Little, a 21-year old black woman who had been charged with capital murder after stabbing a jailer to death with an ice pick and escaping. Dees had read of the case in the newspapers and volunteered the services of the SPLC in her defense, complete with a massive fund-raising campaign. During the case, however, Morris Dees was ordered from the courtroom and arrested for attempting to get a witness to perjure herself. Such a charge is difficult to prove and the charges against Dees were dropped. The judge, however, refused to allow Dees back on the case. Little was eventually acquitted.[76]

There is more to the Joanne Little case. An account of the case in the *Columbia Journalism Review* noted that Dees' allies in the case included some of the most extreme elements of the Marxist-Leninist left:

> [T]he great untold story of the Joan (sic) Little trial . . . was the role of the Communist Party [CPUSA] through its National Alliance Against Racist and Political Repression [NAARPR], in controlling the entire . . . political movement surrounding the case. Angela Davis, a leading figure in both national organizations, became the most frequently quoted movement figure and constant

companion of Little . . . Party members were visible and influential on the defense committee, and the party frequently set up rallies of support around the country.[77]

The Watchdog Radical Fringe

The Center For Democratic Renewal

The Center For Democratic Renewal (CDR) has a fascinating history that reaches into the deepest recesses of the Marxist-Leninist American left.

On 3 November 1979, five members of the Communist Workers Party (CWP) died (nine more were wounded) in a shoot-out with Ku Klux Klansmen and neo-Nazis in Greensboro, North Carolina, during a "Death To The Klan" march through the streets of Greensboro sponsored by the CWP. Six months after the shoot-out, Terry Eastland, writing in *Commentary* magazine, described the CWP and its program:

> The CWP . . . is one of the small Maoist groups that have developed since the disintegration of the Students for a Democratic Society in 1969. . . . Although it had doctrinal differences with other Maoist groups, it agreed with them on the main goal, namely, the destruction of the American capitalist order by the working class.[78]

Eastland also disputed the notion that radicals of the day had "mellowed out" and cited both the People's Temple of Jonestown and the CWP as examples. He observed:

> The CWP can be faulted for another, potentially more deadly [form of racism]: manipulating blacks for its own political ends. The CWP went into a black community thinking that the poorer and less sophisticated of Greensboro's blacks might be successfully exploited in this campaign to abolish class in America: it did not appear to mind how many black lives thus might be endangered, even sacrificed. In this the CWP ironically made a kind of common cause with its avowed enemy, the Klan.[79]

Following the shoot-out, the Klansmen and neo-Nazis were tried on two separate occasions, both of which resulted in acquittal. A state jury found the defendants not guilty of murder in 1980, and a federal panel acquitted them on charges of conspiring to violate the CWP demonstrators' civil rights in 1984.[80]

Until the Greensboro incident, the private, nongovernmental anti-Klan effort was divided among a number of organizations, most of which could be considered of a "liberal-left" persuasion. These included the ADL, the American Jewish Committee (AJC), and a number of civil rights organization including the NAACP and the Congress of Racial Equality (CORE). These were all fairly effective in orchestrating community reaction to Ku Klux Klan and neo-Nazi groups.

A number of Marxist-Leninist groups—such as the Progressive Labor Party (PLP) and its affiliate, the International Committee Against Racism (INCAR), founded in 1973; and the Communist Party USA (CPUSA) and its affiliate, the National Committee Against Racist and Political Repression (NCARPR), founded in 1972—also took their place in the anti-Klan ranks. The 1970s and 1980s were filled with anti-Klan counter-demonstrations by these and similar organizations, usually greatly outnumbering the Klansmen and often responsible for most of the violence.

According to Wyn Craig Wade, author of *The Fiery Cross: The Ku Klux Klan In America*, a new mood was in the air. Wade recorded the change:

> In response to the Klan's 1979 attack on its non-violent marchers in Decatur and the arrest of Curtis Robinson (a Black man convicted of shooting two Klansmen), the SCLC [Southern Christian Leadership Conference] . . . called a conference in Norfolk, Virginia. Thirty organizations responded and, out of the conference the National Anti-Klan Network was born. Based in Atlanta, Georgia, the Network began by matching the ADL's research, monitoring and reporting on Nazi/Klan activity. Under the leadership of its coordinator, Lyn Wells, it took a strong stand against the Klan's corruption of children and assisted the NEA [National Education Association] in creating its curriculum guide.[81]

"Links and Ties" of CDR Staffers

Rev. C. T. Vivian, Chairman of the National Anti-Klan Network (NAKN), was named in a 31 March 1964 report by the Atlanta office of the Federal Bureau of Investigation as having been active in the Communist Party during the 1940s.[82] On the Executive Committee of the NAKN we find Ann Braden, a founding sponsor of the U. S. Peace Council (USPC), an affiliate of the communist-controlled World Peace Council (WPC). Ann Braden and her husband, the late Carl Braden, have long been associated with Communist front organizations. Carl, for example, was one of the leaders of the National Alliance Against Racist and Political Repression (NAARPR), co-chaired by then CPUSA leader Angela Davis.[83] Ann Braden was elected Vice-Chair of the NAARPR in May 1983.[84] In 1990 she was one of three co-chairs, along with Angela Davis and Lennox Hinds, who had served as the United Nations representative of the International Association of Democratic Lawyers (IADL), a Soviet-controlled front. Executive Director was Charlene Mitchell, a long-time member of the CPUSA.[85] Professor Harvey Klehr describes the nature of Communist front groups:

> The essence of a front organization, of course, is that its members include non-communists. The rationale is that a group made up only of devoted communists and their close allies would lack credibility and effectiveness; its motives would be suspect. By

lending their names and reputations to an organization, respectable people make the organization look respectable. [86]

Ann Braden was a participant at the 1989 Marxist Scholars Conference in Louisville, Kentucky. Her panel, to be chaired by Reverend Alan Thomson, of the National Council of American-Soviet Friendship (NCASF), was on "Progressive and Reactionary Trends in World Religions." Thomson had recently been indicted for attempting to launder $17,000 he received from the WPC to operate his Communist front group.

> In June, 1992, the Reverend Alan Thomson, NCASF executive director, pled guilty (U.S. v. Alan Thomson, U. S. District Court, Western District of New York) to evading currency regulations in 1989 by concealing a $17,000 cash subsidy that Thomson brought back from the USSR. The plea agreement ending the case included the transcript of Thomson's secretly videotaped hand over of the $17,000 to an associate, Barbara Makuch, who turned out to be an FBI operative for the past 21 years. [87]

Joseph Lowrey, another director of the CDR, was a speaker at the World Peace Council's assembly in Prague, Czechoslovakia. Executive Director of the World Peace Council is Michael Meyerson, a member of the Communist Party USA and board member of the NAARPR. [88] Also on the NAKN's board is Marilyn Clement, who is active with the New York Marxist School (NYMS) and a writer for the *Guardian*, a Marxist-Leninist weekly tabloid. We also find Martha Nathan, wife of Communist Workers Party member Michael Nathan who died in a shoot-out with Ku Klux Klansmen. [89]

Lyn Wells and the Communist Party, Marxist-Leninist

NAKN National Coordinator Lyn Wells is a former member of the Central Committee of the October League (OL), a Marxist-Leninist group which evolved into the Communist Party, Marxist-Leninist (CPML). A 1979 study of the alternative media of the far left has detailed the history of the Communist Party, Marxist-Leninist thus:

> The CPML was actually founded out of the SDS [Students for a Democratic Society] ruins. It began in late 1969 as the "October League" under the chairmanship of Michael Klonsky, immediate past national secretary of SDS and son of a long-time CPUSA organizer. In June, 1977 it held a "founding congress" at which it dropped its old name and established itself under the new one. In July, 1977 Klonsky and several associates were received and publicly welcomed in Peking by Hau Kuo-Feng and other officials of the new Chinese leadership. [90]

In 1972 Wells gave an address to an OL labor conference. Standing below photos of Marx, Engles, Lenin, Stalin and Mao Tse-Tung, she said:

It is true that building a party requires conscious work on the part of communists. A party is the organized conscious expression of the working-class struggle and cannot develop out of the struggle spontaneously. It takes years of difficult work, developing an experienced core of cadre, raising the theoretical level and deepening ties with the masses. While being close to the united front, the communist organization is at the same time separate with an independent life of its own.[91]

A casual reading of *The Call*, official publication of the CPML, or its other journal, *Class Struggle*, reveals flagrant support and justification of totalitarian Marxism-Leninist regimes.

Leonard Zeskind and the Sojourner Truth Organization

Another NAKN activist with extremist "links and ties" is Leonard Zeskind, a former organizer for the Marxist-Leninist group, the Sojourner Truth Organization (STO) during the 1970s and 1980s. On the editorial board of *Urgent Tasks: Journal of the Revolutionary Left*, published by the STO, Zeskind routinely engaged in classical Marxist-Leninist rhetoric. *Urgent Tasks* acquired its name from a pamphlet by Lenin that asserted the urgent task of party workers was:

not to serve the working class at each of its stages, but to represent the interests of the movement as a whole, to point out to this movement its ultimate aim and political tasks, and to safeguard its politics and ideological independence.[92]

In a 1980 issue of *Urgent Tasks*, Zeskind comments on events in Afghanistan and on U. S. imperialism:

The United States government, for its part, has constructed its own web of fabrications and deceptions around the Afghan events. It is using the occasion as another opportunity to galvanize the U. S. people around a war policy and to resurrect the military as a tool of U. S. imperialism. . .

By concocting a new Soviet policy of aggression, Carter has placed the revitalization of the military as the top item on the national agenda. [93]

Portrait Of A Marxist-Leninist Activist

In January 1981, Kansas City writer Bruce Rodgers did a story on radical activism for *City* magazine. He had this to say about Zeskind:

Speaking freely is something Lenny Zeskind doesn't do to people he doesn't know. Call him on the phone and he'll answer with a near hysterical, "Who is this?" Zeskind needs an answerphone to calm his nerves. Plainly, Zeskind won't talk to bourgeoisie writers representing The Establishment Press.

The STO [Sojourner Truth Organization] was brought to Kansas City by Zeskind and his wife, Elaine, around 1973. Where they imported it from would be a good guess. Chicago is where the printed arm of today's STO is published. Both Lenny and Elaine have written for *Urgent Tasks: Journal of the Revolutionary Left.*

Alternately ridiculed, condemned, feared, pitied or admired, Zeskind does exercise control over his group. They are tight-knit, distrust the press and view everyone outside their group with suspicion. They surface on occasion to distract and intimidate non-violent groups working for social change.

The STO is not well-known by political historians. In fact, a recent study (1979) tracing the development of American radical movements, *Power on the Left*, does not even acknowledge the organization.

Whatever its origins, somewhere in Kansas City Zeskind gathers a dozen fellow travelers in an apartment decorated with revolutionary banners and a picture of Sojourner Truth. Led by him, the mostly white, mostly female group study Lenin, seek justification for their beliefs, and pay homage to a former slave and 19th century champion of black and women's rights.[94]

By 1982 Zeskind apparently found the response to traditional class-struggle Marxism-Leninism disappointing, as have many other American leftists, and shifted his focus to anti-racism. He created the Institute for Research and Education on Human Rights, Inc., and began publishing *The Hammer* (with Lyn Wells on the board), before hooking up with the National Anti-Klan Network.

A 1986 article in the *Kansas City Jewish Chronicle* gave an account of a talk by Zeskind before the Jewish Community Center Women's Guild Auxiliary. According to Zeskind, the Nazi press describes him as "intense and humorless." The article said:

> And just who is he, really? Zeskind isn't saying . . . Zeskind likes to keep a low profile.
>
> No photos, he insists, because he is already the target of a number of anti-Semitic, racist groups who would love to see him, well, out of a job. He also is reticent about his background because this, too, could be used by his enemies.[95]

In spite of his radical past, Leonard Zeskind had apparently impressed somebody important with his work. In June 1998 he was a recipient of a $295,000 award from the MacArthur Foundation.[96]

Leonard Zeskind, Gerry Gable and Searchlight

It's not known when Zeskind first linked up with Gerry Gable and his publication, *Searchlight,* but in the February 1983 issue of *The Hammer,* he carried a two-thirds page advertisement for it listing a post office box for "Searchlight Distribution, USA" at a post office box next to his own.[97] In May 1988, *Searchlight* published a full-page laudatory review of Zeskind's work and publications.[98] Commencing with Zeskind's role as research director for the CDR, he began writing regularly for *Searchlight* and became its U.S. correspondent.

Searchlight, Britain's premier "anti-fascist" magazine, began publishing in its current form in 1975, with Maurice Ludmer as its editor and Gerry Gable second-in-command. Previously, Ludmer has been a reporter for *Morning Star,* the Communist Party's daily newspaper. *Searchlight's* primary constituency was, and always has been, Britain's extreme left, with whom the magazine collaborates extensively.

Maurice Ludmer was a founder and member of the steering committee of the Anti-Nazi League (ANL), and a platform speaker at its first conference on 15 July 1978. According to a 1978 series appearing in *News Line*, publication of the Workers Revolutionary Party (WRP):

> The Anti-Nazi League was launched by the Socialist Workers Party in November, 1977. It was subsequently welcomed by the International Marxist Group—in an editorial in *Socialist Challenge* of 5 May 1978, headed "Hats off to the SWP!"—and by the Communist Party.
>
> The Communist Party's daily paper, the *Morning Star*, urged party members on 16 May 1978, to join the Anti-Nazi League and participate fully in its activities.[99]

Under Ludmer's leadership, the organization staged frequent counter-demonstrations against the National Front (NF) and other right-wing groups, many of which became violent and in some cases causing many injuries, including to policemen. In a 1980 article published in the *Guardian*, Polly Toynbee observed:

> If by creating a public order problem there is hope that Chief Constables will ban the Front marches as they banned Mosley's, then he feels the counter-demonstrations are valuable. [100]

In December 1976, a British magistrate accused *Searchlight* of actually inciting racial violence. Magistrate John Milward condemned what he described as the "grave and sinister" feature of the magazine. He said:

> What purpose can there be in advertising opponents meetings except for the purpose of identifying them and creating disorder and public violence. This seems to be an attempt to stir up trouble which is to be very strongly depreciated.[101]

The comments came at the end of proceedings against Maurice Ludmer, then managing editor of *Searchlight*. Ludmer had been accused of two counts of criminal libel. Magistrate Milward declined to commit Ludmer for trial in the matter.

An important point needs to be made here: Western countries, unlike Marxist-Leninist dictatorships, have traditionally allowed wide latitude with respect to freedom of expression, including the right to hold meetings and demonstrations. Anti-fascist groups have been frustrated in their goal of ideological hegemony by governments which respect the rights of their opposition. The tactic they have used to overcome this, including in the United States, is to sponsor counter-demonstrations with the intention that they will create public disorder and cause authorities to prohibit meetings, demonstrations or marches by their adversaries for reasons of public safety.

In the United States, for example, whenever groups like the Ku Klux Klan have planned demonstrations, they are often confronted by very large, and often violent, counter-demonstrations. The public associates the violence with the Ku Klux Klan, and not the anti-racist counter-demonstrators. In some cases Klan demonstrations of less than a dozen members have been confronted by well-organized counter-demonstrations of several thousand.

Born in January 1937, Gerry Gable was a member of the Young Communist League and stood as a Communist Party candidate in the Northfield Ward of Stamford Hill, North London, on Thursday 10 May 1962.[102] He claims to have quit the CP in 1962. On 14 January 1964, Gerry Gable and Manny Carpel pleaded guilty to breaking and entering with intent to commit a felony. Gable and Carpel, along with another man, had obtained false identification and posed as utility repairmen at the home of David Irving, a British author known for his controversial books on World War II. According to the *Evening Standard*:

> One of them, David Freedman, was alleged to have told a policeman, "This man is a fascist. We got in because we wanted to get some of these books and papers of his and he knows a lot of Nazis who are top brass." Sgt. Tavener said Freedman pointed at a number of books and papers on the table in the room.
>
> Charged with breaking and entering with intent to commit a felony were Freedman, 19, electrician, of Solander Gardens, Stepney; Gerald Gable, 26, electrician, of Lynmouth Road, Stoke, Newington; and Manny Carpel, 20, unemployed, of Downs Park Road, Dalston, who appeared on remand. Gable was also charged with stealing a G.P.O. pass card.[103]

Carpel, an intimate *Searchlight* associate, was convicted of assaulting P. C. William Nield and having an "offensive weapon" in 1963.[104] Carpel and *Searchlight* secretary Michael Cohen pleaded guilty to attempting to break into W. H. Jones Ltd. printing works on 20 July 1966, with intent to commit a felony and to possessing housebreaking implements by night. The company was the printer for a right-wing magazine. Carpel was also jailed for two and a half years for arson at Lewes Criminal Court, 13 April 1981.[105]

Harry Bidney, another *Searchlight* associate, was fined in 1977 after being found guilty on eight charges of living off the earnings of prostitutes. According to the *Daily Telegraph*:

Harold Bidney, 54, company secretary of Dennett House, Bernoe Road, Bow, was fined a total of 1,600 pounds after being found guilty of eight charges concerning eight female prostitutes; that between January 1973 and October last, he knowingly lived in part on the earnings of prostitution.[106]

Interestingly, in the June 1987 of *Searchlight*, Harry Bidney's "long and honorable life fighting fascism" was glowingly described.[107]

Ray Hill, a former member of the National Front who subsequently became an employee of *Searchlight*, jumped bail on a fraud charge in Johannesburg, South Africa in 1979, two days before his scheduled hearing. He forfeited 1,500 pounds bail which had been put up by his wife. According to the *Guardian*:

The police in Johannesburg confirmed yesterday that Mr. Hill had also faced prosecution in connection with the alleged embezzlement of £20,000 from the funds of the Sons of England, a Masonic organization of which he was secretary.

Mr. Hill, a former member of the British Movement, was a housemaster at a boys' home in Johannesburg earning about 250 pounds a week. He is reportedly intending to open a night club in Britain.[108]

In 1981 *Searchlight* reporter David Roberts was convicted at Birmingham Crown Court with conspiracy to burn down an Asian restaurant.[109]

Another *Searchlight* regular is Graeme Atkinson. Like many *Searchlight* people, Atkinson grew up in a family steeped in Marxism-Leninism. His father was a member of the Communist Party during many years of Communism's purges, killings and slave labor camps in the USSR and elsewhere. The elder Atkinson finally quit the party in 1956 over the brutal repression in Hungary. Graeme became active in anti-fascism in 1962 during a wave of anti-Semitic activity in Europe. He worked closely with the "62 group" in London, many of whom were members of the Communist Party.

According to Atkinson, "Our job is to stick the Nazi label on right-wingers. We keep the issue of Nazis before the general public."[110] He also acknowledged that *Searchlight* has placed informants in all "fascist organizations," and that occasionally there had been "captured" documents. Through its supporters in the media, he says that, "We know who to talk to, to get a story out."[111]

On 23 April 1989, Lenny Zeskind spoke at a rally in Leeds, England, where he shared the platform with Martin Becher of the radical Berlin-based Anti-Fascist Action Group. According to press reports, Zeskind and Becher were "touring the country as part of a campaign mounted by *Searchlight*, the anti-fascist magazine."[112]

The rally was sponsored by the "Blair Peach 10 Anniversary Committee" along with several other radical left groups, including Anti-Fascist Action, Azania Worker, Asian Youth Movement, Camden Black Workers Group, and

Black Action. Peach was a black supporter of the Anti-Nazi League who was killed by police in 1979 and became a martyr to the cause.[113]

In May 1989, Zeskind again addressed a *Searchlight* rally where he shared the platform with *Spotlight's* Ray Hill. An article in the *Jewish Chronicle* referred to Zeskind as "one of America's leading Nazi catchers."[114]

In November 1990, Gerry Gable addressed a benefit for the Center for Democratic Renewal held in Kansas City, Missouri. Gable lamented the collapse of Communism throughout Europe, blaming that on what he said was an "increase in racial attacks against minority groups." Lenny Zeskind claimed that the average age for skinheads in the United States had dropped from 22 and 21 years old to 16 and 17 years old. He said:

> We're not concerned about these new kids committing acts of violence. We're seeing more David Dukes coming down the road at us. These people aren't just violent thugs. They're racists who have attained a level of sophistication.[115]

None of this transpired. David Duke's career is moribund and the skinhead movement, such as it is, has continued to decline. It is probably safe to say that none of them have acquired any level of sophistication. In any event, the presence of a couple thousand adolescent "skinheads" in a country of 260 million people, while lamentable, is hardly a national crisis that needs the help of Gerry Gable and Lenny Zeskind to remedy.

Leonard Zeskind, Lyn Wells and NAKN/CDR

The NAKN has been regarded with sectarian skepticism by other Marxist-Leninist groups. A November 1982 article in *Workers Vanguard*, journal of the Spartacist League (a Trotskyist sect), described it thus:

> NAKN is a loose coalition of the remnants of the pro-Peking Stalinists of Mike Klonsky/Lyn Wells disintegrating "Communist Party Marxist Leninist" with Southern black ministers headed by SCLC's Rev. C. T. Vivian, who organized in 1979 an "alternative" to the communists in the wake of outrage over Greensboro.[116]

In 1986 the NAKN changed its name to the Center For Democratic Renewal, perhaps an attempt to blur its radical roots. The masthead of its newsletter, *The Monitor*, however, continued to list Lyn Wells as executive director and Leonard Zeskind as director of research.[117] In 1987 Lynora Williams, another writer for the now-defunct Marxist-Leninist *Guardian*, took over as executive director, replacing Zeskind, who had been acting director.[118] Jean Hardisty of Political Research Associates and Randall Williams of the Southern Poverty Law Center have also been CDR board members.[119]

Zeskind's name no longer appears on CDR letterheads, but he continues to maintain the Kansas City office of the organization. In 1989 after accounts of his Marxist-Leninist background began appearing, he was quoted in an article in the *Kansas City Jewish Chronicle* as follows:

I was never the kind of Marxist-Leninist that they think of. I was somebody who thinks that socialism is a good thing. I believe a society that's fair to its citizens is important. I don't think I'm a socialist either now. At one time, I did. But that's not a defining feature of my politics now.[120]

The CDR and the Paranoid Style

In November 1989 *Atlanta Constitution* writer Alan Sverdlik wrote an article on the CDR in which he detailed the paranoid-like mentality that surrounds the organization:

> They operate in quasi-secrecy out of a basement in a southwest Atlanta office building. They won't give out the street address. They use real names and pseudonyms interchangeably and have unlisted home phone numbers.
> This bunker mentality belongs to the Center for Democratic Renewal, one of the nation's principle monitors of far-right hate groups.[121]

Sverdlik also noted that the CDR had a $300,000 annual budget and quoted ADL southern counsel Charles Wittenstein that "They have a left-wing political agenda that we don't have. . . . We don't have any working relationship with them." CDR employee Daniel Levitas is quoted as complaining that the ADL has "consistently red-baited us."[122]

The February 1991, issue of *Details* magazine contains an article on Lenny Zeskind by James Ridgeway in which former right-winger Tom Turnipseed, chairman of George Wallace's 1968 presidential campaign, now vice-chair of the CDR, is quoted as saying, "His hands kinda shake . . . [Lenny] is probably scared shitless all the time." The article also observes that "Lenny has no known fixed address" and that he has a fake address on his drivers license. Only a few top executives of the telephone company know the exact location of his telephones, and his home is protected by an alarm system that would go off if "someone should toss a firebomb through a window."[123]

> And Lenny, who likes to hunt, owns a semiautomatic Mini .14, the far right's weapon of choice. He also has a shotgun. But when his mother offered Lenny her .38 revolver, he declined. The handgun he wants is a stylish 9mm automatic, which his mom has promised to get him for his birthday.[124]

It's fairly common for extremist groups to enlist police "infiltrators" of opposing extremist groups into their ranks. These people are a source for opposition research and impress contributors who imagine they are now getting inside information. During the 1960s, for example, a number of conservative right-wing groups had former government agents on their payroll as experts. In

1990 the CDR acquired the services of former San Diego police reservist Douglas K. Seymour, who had infiltrated the Ku Klux Klan, and he was listed on the CDR letterhead as a "Special Assistant to the Chairman." In 1989 Seymour had received a $300,000 settlement from the San Diego police, claiming "emotional suffering" as the result of his two-and-a-half years of work as an infiltrator into the Ku Klux Klan. Seymour's relationship with the CDR didn't last long, however. In May 1991 he was convicted of embezzlement in La-Crosse, Wisconsin.[125] CDR's trusted source was quietly dropped from its letterhead.

Lenny Zeskind and Oklahoma City

Following the 1995 Oklahoma City bombing, Zeskind teamed with James Ridgeway, who writes on right-wing politics for various liberal and leftist serials, and produced a conspiracy theory of their very own. They said:

> There is every reason to believe that the attack was a call for revolution by the far right wing of this country, organized through the widespread militia movement and carried out by one of the leaderless terror cells created by that movement.
> It is probable that the three men being held in connection with the bombing—Timothy McVeigh, James Nichols and his brother Terry Nichols—are all members of that same militia cell.[126]

None of this proved true, of course, and one of the most intensive investigations in FBI history has failed to link these three to any militia organization in any significant way whatsoever. In addition, James Nichols is not even a defendant in the case. The article also refers to the Posse Comitatus, a radical tax protest group of mythical proportions, as a precursor to the militias.

> Kansas is an old center for the posse. During the 1980's federal law enforcement sources said that as many as one-third of all Kansas state sheriffs were either involved in, or sympathetic to, the posse. Posse doctrine holds that the highest law of the land is the county sheriff.[127]

A rather incredible charge. Checking with the Kansas Attorney General's office and the officers of the Kansas Sheriffs Association, I was informed that they did not know of a single sheriff who had been in any way "involved in or sympathetic to" the Posse Comitatus. In point of fact, Kansas sheriffs, and presumably sheriffs everywhere, tended to view posse members as "idiots" and troublemakers who were more of a nuisance than a bona fide threat. The occasional posse member who ran afoul of the law was swiftly dealt with by Kansas or other law enforcement officers.

In 1996 Zeskind was a contributor along with Chip Berlet and others to *Conspiracies: Real Grievances, Paranoia, and Mass Movements*, edited by Eric Ward and published by "Peanut Butter Publishing." The general thrust of their contributions was to attack conspiracy theories of the right while ignoring those of the left. Zeskind, in a typical overstatement, says that during the infamous Tuskegee study of syphillis 400 black men were "deliberately infected" with the disease. This was not true. They had independently contracted the disease on their own but were intentionally denied treatment in an effort to track the course of the disease.[128]

In a generally sympathetic but honestly critical review of the book, Kent Chadwick of the *Washington Free Press* observed that to be "intellectually honest" progressives need to "clearly distinguish our moral values and our political agenda." He objects to the "almost exclusive concentration on conspiracies of right-wing groups" in the compilation. He warns that this biased partisanship risks that we "cheapen our own values and become true believers, mirror images of the self-righteous we froth against on the right."[129] With Zeskind and Berlet it appears that this may have already happened.

The CDR and the Great Black Church Arson Conspiracy Hoax

In 1996 a huge media campaign commenced in the United States to publicize an alleged conspiracy by white racists, neo-Nazis and Ku Klux Klansmen to set fire to black churches throughout the South—one of the most widespread acts of intimidation against American blacks since the 1960s. The Center For Democratic Renewal was the primary organization pushing the story, which it described as the work of "a well-organized white supremacist movement." Mac Charles Jones, a CDR leader and associate of Leonard Zeskind in Kansas City, characterized it as a terrifying resurgence of white racism. CDR chair C. T. Vivian blamed the arsons on the Christian conservative movement, noting that there was only a "slippery slope" from conservative Christians and those who are really doing the burnings.[130]

However, the issue was not this simple. On 5 July 1996 *Associated Press* writer Fred Bayles noted that of the 409 church fires since 1990, two-thirds were at white churches, while of the 148 fires since 1995, more than half were also at white churches. In the fires at black churches "only random links to racism" could be found. Bayles concluded that there was "no evidence that most of the 73 black church fires since 1995 can be blamed on a conspiracy or a general climate of racial hatred."[131]

A detailed analysis of the claims by the CDR and other players in the church burning conspiracy appeared in *New Yorker* magazine. Writer Michael Kelly noted that

> There is no evidence of a massive plot by organized hate groups. The people who set racially motivated fires at black churches tend to be loners and losers and copycats acting largely on drunken impulse, and they are few in number.[132]

Michael Fumento, writing in *Commentary* magazine, reported on his own independent investigation, and concluded that the controversy was close to a "deliberate hoax." His investigation soon focused on the CDR. He noted that the CDR has a "rather more explicit" agenda than that of a "watchdog" or "anti-hate" group. This includes working "with progressive activists and organizations to build a movement to counter right-wing rhetoric and public-policy initiatives."[133] According to Fumento,

> What I found was that beginning last winter and throughout the spring, the CDR, in conjunction with the National Council of Churches (NCC), had been feeding the media a steady diet of "news" about black church burnings in the South. . . . Since 1990, the CDR . . . alleged, there had been 90 arson attacks against black churches in nine Southern states; the number had been rising every year; and each and every culprit "arrested and/or detained" was white.
>
> I established that the CDR had systematically failed to count fires set by blacks in black churches, had labeled as arson a number of fires which responsible authorities insisted were attributable to other causes, and had altogether ignored fires in white churches.[134]

What was the motive behind this CDR hoax? According to Fumento, an article in the 9 August 1996 edition of the *Wall Street Journal* revealed that the NCC had been having a hard time raising money to support its anti-racist programs. Working with seven other groups, the CDR and NCC established a special fund for burned churches and "to challenge racism throughout the country."

> By early August it had accumulated $9 million from Americans sincerely alarmed by the specter of burning black churches, and contributions were continuing to pour in at the rate of approximately $100,000 a day.[135]

Fumento also observes that the person in charge of the Burned Churches Fund is a NCC employee by the name of Don Jojas, former press secretary to the late Marxist-Leninist leader of Granada, Maurich Bishop.

Political Research Associates

According to its own literature, Political Research Associates (PRA) began in Chicago in 1981 under the name Midwest Research. In 1987, Midwest Research moved to Cambridge, Massachusetts, and effected its name change in the process. In addition to numerous reports, articles and books, PRA publishes *The Public Eye* quarterly newsletter. The two principle officers of PRA have always been Jean Hardisty, director, and John Foster "Chip" Berlet, analyst.[136]

Another PRA regular is Russ Bellant, who in 1988 wrote a PRA document purporting to show that the Reagan administration was infiltrated by Nazis. The publication, *Old Nazis, The New Right and the Reagan Administration*,[137] roundly denounced by Republican Party officials and virtually ignored in the mainstream press, was favorably reviewed in the *People's Daily World*, publication of the Communist Party USA, which quoted Berlet as follows:

> Only one-third of the report is devoted to the so-called ethnic Nazis. . . . Other chapters reveal how these fascists worked hand-in-glove with the American Security Council, the World Anti-Communist League and other fascist-like groups and how their activities overlapped with the Iran-contra affair and U.S. foreign policy in South Africa and Central America. The bottom line is that a fascist and authoritarian network, whose guiding ideology is anti-communism, has been recruited into the Republican Party."[138]

Bellant's publication was also favorably reviewed in *Searchlight*, which was not surprising since it drew on that publication for much of its information. It concluded its review with "We now know who our enemies are."[139]

Chip Berlet and the National Lawyers Guild

The Public Eye was for years a semi-official organ of the National Lawyers Guild (NLG), of which Chip Berlet is a long-standing member. A 1989 biographical sheet on Berlet distributed by PRA admits that he is a "former vice-president of the NLG and currently serves as Secretary of the NLG's Civil Liberties Committee." He also coordinates joint work between the NLG and the National Committee Against Repressive Legislation [NCARL]."[140] A 1981 issue of the publication states unequivocally that "*The Public Eye* is produced in conjunction with the National Lawyers Guild Committee Against Government Repression and Police Crimes." It also lists Chip Berlet as a managing editor.[141] What was not included in the biographical sheet is Berlet's history as a writer for *High Times*, the virtual house organ of the recreational drug industry. Berlet's articles appeared from 1976 to 1981.[142]

Professor Harvey Klehr of Emory University, in his detailed book *Far Left of Center: The American Left Today*, details the Marxist-Leninist roots of the NLG:

> The NLG is an affiliate of the Soviet-controlled International Association of Democratic Lawyers (IADL), founded in 1946. Expelled from France in 1949, the IADL is now headquartered in Brussels. Over the years it has steadfastly supported every twist and turn in Soviet foreign policy, including the invasions of Hungary, Czechoslovakia and Afghanistan.[143]

During the 1960s and 1970s the NLG experienced considerable growth with the rise of the radical student movement. Several NLG figures were active revolutionaries, including Bernardine Dohrn, the NLG student organizer in 1967 and fixture on the FBI's "most wanted list" for several years. Another was Judith Clark, now serving a long sentence for murder in the 1981 Brinks armored car robbery undertaken to fund radical leftist activities. According to Professor Gunter Lewy of the University of Massachusetts:

By the early 1970s, Old and New Left elements in the Guild had come to terms, for they shared basic goals, the most immediate of which was the victory of the Vietnamese Communists . . . Marxist-Leninist terminology, previously shunned, now was used openly in Guild proceedings and publications.[144]

Chip Berlet and Jean Hardisty and the Marxist-Leninist Guardian

On 13 January 1984 an open letter to Judge Charles Sifton entitled "Political Grand Juries Must Be Stopped!" appeared in the New York-based Marxist-Leninist tabloid, *Guardian*. The letter expressed outrage at federal grand juries who were investigating the activities of leftist revolutionaries who have "supported mass struggle against the military . . . development of an armed clandestine movement [and] broad struggle against repression."

Among its signers were Chip Berlet and Jean Hardisty—an astounding confession of their true politics and the company they keep. Other signers included convicted communist spy Morton Sobel; and William Kunstler and Arthur Kinoy, attorneys actively involved in the National Lawyers Guild and closely associated with Communist and revolutionary causes. Among the organizations represented were the Prairie Fire Organizing Committee (PFOC), John Brown Anti-Klan Committee (JBAKC), International Workers Party (IWC), League for Revolutionary Workers (LRW), May 19th Communist Organization (M19CO), National Lawyers Guild, Provisional Government of the Republic of New Afrika (PGRNA), Revolution in Africa Action Committee (RAAC), Sojourner Truth Organization (STO); Women Against Imperialism (WAI) and the Youth International Party (YIP).[145]

The PFOC, formed in 1974, was the publishing arm of the Weather Underground Organization (WUO), the terrorist derivative of Students For A Democratic Society (SDS). Its first pamphlet was *Prairie Fire: The Politics of Revolutionary Anti-Imperialism*, written by Bernardine Dohrn, Bill Ayers and Jeff Jones. According to Professor Harvey Klehr:

> It announced that "we are communist men and women" and urged its supporters to form an above-ground arm of the WUO. Chapters soon formed in several cities with perhaps a thousand members. Members of PFOC helped facilitate communication and logistics for WUO members living underground.[146]

The PFOC also published *Breakthrough*, a quarterly journal which routinely called for widespread resistance to U. S. imperialism, and ran article after article praising third-world single party Marxist-Leninist dictatorships.

Another Weather Underground front, the John Brown Anti-Klan Committee, was formed in 1978 and soon had chapters in over a dozen cities with about 300 members.[147] It quickly took its place alongside other Marxist-Leninist-based anti-Klan organizations and proceeded to stage violent confrontations with small Klan groups when they held marches or demonstrations.

The JBAKC counter-demonstrators were almost always more violent than the Klansmen they protested. In 1983, for example, the JBAKC attempted to halt a parade of seventy Klansmen in Austin, Texas. Counter-demonstrators threw rocks, injuring twelve people, including several police officers. Two members of the JBAKC—Elizabeth Ann Duke and Linda Evans—were among those involved in the openly terrorist May 19th Communist Organization.[148] In 1984 the JBAKC publication, *Death To The Klan*, published the following communiqué:

> November 7, 1983
> Tonight we bombed the U. S. Capitol building. We attacked the U.S. Government to retaliate against imperialist aggression that has sent the marines, the CIA and the army to invade sovereign nations. . .
> We are acting in solidarity with all those leading the fight against U. S. imperialism—the peoples of Granada, Lebanon, Palestine, El Salvador, and Nicaragua—who are confronting direct U.S. aggression . . .
> Our action carries a message to the U. S. imperialist ruling class: we purposely aimed out attack at the institutions of imperialist rule rather than at individual members of the ruling class and government. We did not choose to kill any of them at this time.[149]

The May 19th Communist Organization acquired its notoriety from the role of several members in the attempted holdup of a Brinks armored truck in Nyack, New York, in November 1981 that left two policemen and one security guard dead. A May 19th press release claimed that it was being persecuted because it supported armed struggle of oppressed nations like American blacks and Puerto Ricans as well as the militant struggle against white supremacy.[150] Approximately six months later on 11 July 1984, another letter, this time addressed "To All Progressive People" appeared in the Marxist-Leninist *Guardian* tabloid that included the following:

> We, the undersigned, are grand jury resisters, former grand jury resisters, people who have been targets of grand jury investigations, and people who have consistently fought for non-collaboration with the grand jury. We are united now to protest the current escalation of grand jury attacks. . .
> Criminal contempt is a "legal" mechanism to establish political internment in the United States . . . an attempt to instill a "snitch mentality" in which fear of jail overrides justice and principle.
> We urge you to join us in refusing to collaborate with the grand jury or the FBI. Now more than ever before we need a powerful resistance movement that would never give the U. S. government or its agencies any information about the national liberation struggles and progressive movements, that refuses to collaborate with the military draft, that is willing to harbor Central American refugees, that staunchly resists the U. S. War mobilization. We won't cooperate! Stop the grand jury! .[151]

Among the over one hundred signers—a virtual who's who of the extreme radical left—were Chip Berlet and Jean Hardisty. Other signers included David Gilbert, Kathy Boudin and Judith Clark, all members of the radical Weather Underground organization and all serving prison sentences for the murder of a Brinks armored truck guard in 1981. Among the numerous organizations included was the Sojourner Truth Committee

This letter is an example of the classic Marxist-Leninist approach to the crimes of Marxism-Leninism. Here we see an attempt to shift attention from what Marxist-Leninists have done to what has been done to them. By focusing on the civil liberties implications of the government's case against the Weather Underground, they seek to dodge the question of the crimes committed by them, and the historic crimes of Marxist-Leninists generally.

The *Guardian* contained a long article by Chip Berlet and Jean Hardisty in a 1981 *Guardian Special Report*. Entitled "An Anatomy of the New Right," they say:

> The paramilitary, neo-fascist and ultra-right branch [of the right-wing] has ties to both the old right and the new right, but is publicly shunned by both. This branch includes groups such as the Ku Klux Klan, the Nazis, Posse Comitatus and other armed militants.
>
> The new right, by inflaming public opinion and promoting fear, is attempting to galvanize its followers into a militant anti-Communist crusade reminiscent of the cold war.[152]

In 1983 an issue of *The Public Eye* contained a statement by Cathlyn Wilkerson, a captured fugitive from the ill-fated Weather Underground terrorist bomb factory that blew up in March 1970, killing three people, "prior to her imprisonment for Weather Underground Activities, January 15, 1981":

> Today I am going to prison to serve a three-year term. I have been identified as one who sought to attack the foundations of American justice. . . . I want to take this opportunity to extend my solidarity to the people and communist parties of Vietnam and Cuba . . . and I want to send special love and solidarity to the sisters and brothers of the Puerto Rican Movement who are P.O.W.'s in our prisons.[153]

Much of this issue of *The Public Eye* was devoted to the "New McCarthyism" surrounding the 1981 Brinks armored car robbery. In a preface to an article critical of press coverage of the event, *The Public Eye* had the following lead:

> The Brinks Robbery ushered in a new phase for the current witch hunt. As before, the press becomes a willing, almost eager, partner in circulating the most ludicrous charges regarding progressive political groups and individuals, as long as someone could be quoted alleging a connection to the Brinks robbery.[154]

One cannot but reflect on the many articles by Chip Berlet "linking and tying" individuals to various right-wing causes based on "someone being quoted alleging a connection."

Chip Berlet and Chicago Area Friends of Albania

His long-standing relationship with the NLG notwithstanding, perhaps the most outrageous Marxist-Leninist link Chip Berlet possesses is his membership in the Chicago Area Friends of Albania (CAFA). Founded in 1983, CAFA is dedicated toward individuals who "are friendly and supportive of the People's Socialist Republic of Albania."[155] In 1985 when Albanian dictator Enver Hoxa died, CAFA circulated a letter to its mailing list requesting "condolences" be sent to Hoxas' wife and other communist officials there.[156]

Albania, now going through the rigors of transformation from a one-party Marxist-Leninist dictatorship to some semblance of a democracy, was for decades the most repressive of Communist countries. Moreover, this characteristic has been so widely documented that no one could not be aware of the horrible, murderous nature of the Marxist-Leninist Albanian regime. According to Freedom House, which monitors human rights around the world:

> Albania is a traditional Marxist-Leninist dictatorship. While there are a number of elected bodies, including an assembly, the parallel government of the Communist Party (4.5 percent of the people) is decisive at all levels; elections offer only one list of candidates.
>
> Press, radio, and television are completely under government or party control, and communication with the outside world is minimal. Media are characterized by incessant propaganda, and open expression of opinion in private conversations can lead to long prison sentences. There is an explicit denial of freedom of thought for those who disagree with the government. Imprisonment for reasons of conscience is common; torture is frequently reported, and execution is invoked for many reasons.[157]

Nevertheless, on 26 June 1987, when Political Research Associates was preparing to make its move to Boston, CAFA held an open house and farewell party in Berlet's honor. A CAFA flyer requested:

> Help C.A.F.A. say goodbye and good luck to one of its long-time members, Chip Berlet. Chip and his family are moving to the Boston area, to continue their anti-fascist work there. Chip was one of our founding members, and a steadfast friend of Albania through thick and thin. Come give him a good send off.[158]

After this information was made public in 1992, Berlet was challenged concerning it. In an Internet posting under the heading of the NLG Civil Liberties Committee dated 13 August 1993 Berlet responded thus:

> I joined the Albania group at a time when I was investigating why Yugoslav agents were harassing the émigrés from Albania and

Kosovar in Chicago. One did not have to support the government
of Albania to join. I have always opposed Stalinism.[159]

Chip Berlet and U.S. Law Enforcement and Intelligence Agencies

Concern about anti-Communism represents a thread that runs through
almost everything Chip Berlet does. In 1991 Chip Berlet and Linda Lotz released a revised version of their *Reading List On Intelligence Agencies and Political Repression* for distribution by a clutch of far left groups including the
Movement Support Network (MSN), Center for Constitutional Rights (CCR),
and National Lawyers Guild Civil Liberties Committee. The list consists mainly
of works attacking United States intelligence and law enforcement agencies, and
virtually none of some 150 titles are critical of the intelligence or law enforcement activities of any Communist regime. The list notes that "This is the reading
list circulated by Phil Agee at his Speakout lectures."[160]

Who is Linda Lotz? According to a biographical note on the *Reading
List*:

> Ms. Lotz was formerly a staff organizer for the now-
> defunct Campaign for Political Rights, a Washington,
> D.C.-based coalition which organized against covert
> action abroad and political surveillance at home.[161]

The Campaign For Political Rights (CPR) was originally founded in
1977 as the Campaign To Stop Government Spying (CSGS) with the help of
Morton Halperin and the National Lawyers Guild. It changed its name in 1978.
The primary role of the organization, in addition to crippling American intelligence efforts overseas, was to undertake a disinformation campaign on behalf of
radical-left and Marxist-Leninist terrorists in the United States. According to
Scott Steven Powell:

> Under the leadership of Morton Halperin, CPR became the work-
> horse in the campaign against the CIA, FBI, and local law-
> enforcement agencies.
> For Halperin there are, it seems, "no enemies on the Left."
> One of his CPR assistants, Esther Herst, was national director for
> the National Committee Against Repressive Legislation (NCARL).
> . . . Halperin flew to London in 1977 for the defense of Philip
> Agee, who was being deported from Great Britain as a security risk
> after his continuing collaboration with Cuban intelligence.[162]

Who is Phillip Agee? Agee is a renegade Central Intelligence Agency
officer implicated in revealing the names of CIA officials in a manner leading to
their endangerment, and in at least one case, that of Richard Welch, their
death.[163] Agee was deeply involved in the anti-government *Counterspy* magazine, which made a practice of such disclosures. Referring to *Counterspy*, a
Washington Post editorial asked, "What other result than the killing did Mr.
[Timothy] Butz and his colleagues at *Counterspy* expect when they fingered Mr.

Welch?"[164] Butz, incidentally, was on the editorial staff of *The Public Eye*, along with Chip Berlet and Russ Bellant.[165]

U.S. Senator John Chaffee, a ranking member of the Select Committee on Intelligence, pointed out in the *Congressional Record*:

> At the time of the Welch assassination, *Counterspy* magazine claimed they had leaked the names of 225 alleged CIA agents. Now, five years later, Louis Wolf of *Covert Action Information Bulletin* can boast that he has helped to disclose the names of more than 2,000 American intelligence officers stationed around the world.[166]

Agee is one of Chip Berlet's heroes, and the old *Counterspy* and *Covert Action Information Bulletin* crowd include some of his close working associates. Agee gave a revealing account of his politics in an interview with a Swiss magazine in 1975:

> The CIA is plainly on the wrong side, that is, the capitalistic side. I approve [of] KGB activities, communist activities in general, when they are to the advantage of the oppressed. In fact, the KGB is not doing enough in this regard.[167]

Unlike the far right, where alliances are difficult and unstable and individuals tend not to work well together, alliances and linkages among this element of the extreme left are common and more enduring.

In the spring of 1997, a Berlet article attacking domestic counter-terrorism practices of various police departments appeared in *Overthrow*, the appropriately named organ of the far-left Youth International Party. Among those cited were the Chicago Police Department Intelligence Unit, the Texas Department of Public Safety, the Indianapolis Police Department and the Detroit Police Department.[168]

Chip Berlet and the United Front Against Fascism

On 10 August 1991 Chip Berlet was a featured speaker at a rally on "Racism, Fascism and the New Right," in Seattle, Washington, sponsored by the United Front Against Fascism. Endorsers of the event included such diverse elements as the Freedom Socialist Party (FSP), on whose premises the rally was held, and Asian Lesbians Outside Asia (ALOA).[169] The FSP was formed in 1964 when the Seattle branch of the Socialist Workers Party (SWP) broke away from the national organization. The organization has slowly shifted its emphasis from traditional Marxism-Leninism to revolutionary feminism and anti-racism.[170] Its principles include:

> The working class is international and bound by global abuse. It must liberate itself through socialism. We support revolution on all fronts and seek to transform it into world socialism, which alone can defeat capitalism.

The struggles of the oppressed minorities against racism objectively challenge the basic core of the American political system. The resistance of people of color, who suffer dual oppression, spurs all other sections of the working class to advanced political consciousness and militancy.

History has proven that only a thoroughly democratic and centralized vanguard party can lead the proletariat and its many allies to power. The FSP, a product of the living tradition of Marx, Engels, Lenin, and Trotsky, aspires to become a mass organization capable of providing direction for the coming American Revolution.[171]

The Freedom Socialist Party has branches in Australia and Canada in addition to ten branch offices in the United States. Its membership is estimated at several hundred.

Chip Berlet and the Socialist Scholars Conference

On 24, 25, 26 April 1992 the 10th annual Socialist Scholars Conference was held in New York City. Sponsors included the Marxist-Leninist *Guardian* newspaper, the New York Marxist School (NYMS), the Research Group on Socialism and Democracy (RGSD), and the Radical Philosophy Association (RPA), to name just a few. The program included panels with Angela Davis, member of the Central Committee of the Communist Party USA (CPUSA), and Carl Bloice, editor of the CPUSA's *People's Daily World.*

Chip Berlet, along with Dennis King (a 10-year veteran of the extreme left Progressive Labor Party), Linda Hunt and A. J. Weberman conducted a panel on "How to Investigate the Right," sponsored by Political Research Associates. Other panels on radical topics were conducted by the *Socialist Register* and *Monthly Review* magazines; the Workers Defense League (WDL); the U.S.-Soviet Workers Information Committee (SWIC); and *Social Text* magazine.[172]

Chip Berlet and the Brecht Forum/New York Marxist School

In the extremist underworld of New York City's Marxist subculture there exists a complex of organizations governed by an interlocking directorate consisting of the Brecht Forum/New York Marxist School/Institute for Popular Education. For all practical purposes these are one and the same. Of special interest is the Brecht Forum, named after Marxist-Leninist writer Bertolt Brecht. Regarding the role of the Communist functionary Brecht had this to say:

He who fights for Communism must be able to fight and to renounce fighting, to say the truth and not say the truth, to be helpful and unhelpful, to keep a promise and to break a promise, to go into danger and to avoid danger, to be known and to be unknown. He who fights for Communism has of all the virtues only one: that he fights for Communism.[173]

The New York Marxist School was established in 1973 by Arthur Felberbaum, a Young Socialist Alliance (YSA) activist, in collaboration with the Marxist Educational Collective (MEC).[174] On the board of directors of the BF/NYMS/IPE we find Marilyn Clement, formerly of the *Guardian* and Center For Democratic Renewal. On the advisory board we find Carl Bloice, former editor of the Communist Party USA's *People's Weekly World*.[175]

In September 1994 Chip Berlet conducted a three-lecture seminar on "The Resistable Rise of Neofascism."[176] Other recent programs by the group have included presentations by Irwin Silber, former editor of the *Guardian*, current editor of *Crossroads;* and Peter Camejo, former officer of the Socialist Workers Party;[177] and a "two-week intensive study entitled "Marxism vs. The Contract On America."[178]

Chip Berlet and the Midwest Anti-Fascist Network (MAFNET)

On 25 September 1995 the second annual "Midwest Anti-Fascist Network" held a three-day conference in Columbus, Ohio. Speakers included Chip Berlet, along with the following:

> Rita Bo Brown, former member of the nominally terrorist George Jackson Brigade (JGB). Jackson was killed in August 1970 when his brother attempted to free him from Soledad Prison by bursting in to a Marin County, CA, courtroom handing guns to three convicts and taking five hostages. In the shootout that ensued five people were killed including the judge.
>
> Signe Waller, former member of Jerry Tung's Worker's Viewpoint Organization (WPO), which evolved into the Communist Workers Party (CWP), a small, violence-prone Marxist-Leninist sect. In 1979 armed members of the CWP were killed in a shootout with Ku Klux Klansmen in Greensboro, NC. Her husband, Michael Waller, was one of five people killed.[179]

Also in attendance were representatives of Southern Poverty Law Center's Klanwatch project, Lenny Zeskind's Center For Democratic Renewal and RASH, an anti-racist skinhead organization. Seminars were held on such diverse subjects as "Doing Revolutionary Anti-Klan Work" and "What Is Fascism."

Marxism-Leninism: A Hidden Agenda?

Marxism-Leninism is not just Marxism, nor is it just "socialism" as in social democracy. It is the "Leninism" in Marxism-Leninism that makes it particularly lethal. Admittedly, many western Marxist-Leninists have been critical of one Communist regime or another, usually for ideological deviations of various kinds. Pro-Peking Marxist-Leninists, for example, are critical of the Soviet Union, and pro-Albania Marxist-Leninists tend to be critical of all others. Zeskind's article on Afghanistan, for example, was pointedly critical of Soviet foreign policy. Nevertheless, in certain critical respects Marxist-Leninists tend to share certain characteristics in common, particularly in their denigration of "bourgeois" individual rights and freedom of speech.

Marxism-Leninism, to which Zeskind and Lyn Wells both subscribed, and which characterizes a number of the individuals and organizations in this chapter, is best understand as a theory of organization, i.e., a political program for victory. Motivated by causes and concerns they feel are just, Marxist-Leninists tend to adopt the position that the end justifies the means, hence their reputation for stealth and secrecy. Individuals may differ in their personal approach, but certain themes tend to prevail among people who call themselves Marxist-Leninists. Frederick M. Watkins discusses one of Lenin's first writings on political organization:

> In one of [Lenin's] more notable early writings, *What Is To Be Done*, he laid down the specifications for a new and truly revolutionary type of political entity. . . . The functions of this well-disciplined elite would be to infiltrate and gain positions of leadership in more popular organizations, using them as "transmission belts" for the exercise of power. In this way a small nucleus of party members would be able to control the activities of a vastly larger number of outsiders, and use them for revolutionary purposes.[180]

Although Marxism-Leninism basically concerns itself with political and economic issues and the creation of a Communist society, the basic theory of organization is quite adaptable. Some right-wing leaders, such as Robert B. DePugh of the long-defunct paramilitary Minuteman organization, read Lenin extensively. So has Tom Metzger of the neo-Nazi White Aryan Resistance. Consider this from Lenin's works:

> According to its form, a strong revolutionary organization may also be described as a conspirative organization . . . and we must have utmost conspiracy for an organization of that kind. Secrecy is such a necessary condition for such an organization that all other conditions (number, and selection of members, functions, etc.) must be subordinated to it.[181]

Afterword

This review of so-called watchdog organization makes rather poignant the old adage of "who watches the watchman." Scholars, researchers, and representatives of the news media have tended to take the pronouncements of groups such as the ADL, SPLC, CDR and PRA uncritically and without researching their backgrounds. It is in the interest of accuracy and truth that they subject their sources to the same kind of critical examination as they apply to the organizations and individuals they write about.

Notes

[1] Wilcox Collection on Contemporary Political Movements, Spencer Research Library, University of Kansas, Lawrence, KS 66045.

[2] Austin J. Turn, *Political Criminality* (Beverly Hills, CA: Sage Publications, 1982), 71.

[3] Betty A. Dobratz and Stephanie L. Shanks-Meile, *White Power, White Pride!: The White Separatist Movement in the United States* (New York: Twayne Publishers, 1997), 2-3.

[4] Irving Janis, *Victims of Groupthink* (New York: Houghton Mifflin, 1972), 9.

[5] David Sapiro, *Neurotic Styles* (New York: Basic Books, 1965), 66.

[6] Orrin E. Klapp, *Collective Search For Identity* (New York: Holt, Rinehart, 1969), 274.

[7] *Canadian Jewish News*, 14 November 1991.

[8] "Harassment of Jews Rose in '93, Anti-Defamation League Reports," *New York Times*, 25 January 1994.

[9] Debra Nussbaum Cohen, "Paradox of Anti-Semitism in America: Perception vs. Reality," *Kansas City Jewish Chronicle* (8 January 1993).

[10] Ibid.

[11] Ibid.

[12] *New York Times*, 8 January 1992.

[13] J. J. Goldberg, "Tide of Anti-Semitic Acts Exposes 'Perception Gap,'" *Jewish Week*, 18 November 1988.

[14] Ibid.

[15] J. J. Goldberg, "Scaring The News," *The New Republic*, 17 May 1993.

[16] Ibid.

[17] Phillip Matler and Andrew Ross, "Former S. F. Cop Focus of Probe," *San Francisco Chronicle*, 15 January 1993.

[18] Rachel Gordon, "Supervisors Seek Probe in Spy Case, " *San Francisco Examiner*, 27 January 1993; K. Bradley Hudson, "Big Brother In San Francisco," *San Francisco Sentinel*, 4 February 1993; "San Francisco Cop Probed For Sale of Intelligence to Israel," *Israeli Foreign Affairs*, 5 February 1993; Richard C. Paddock, "San Francisco Probes Private Spy Network," *Los Angeles Times*, 26 February 1993.

[19] Dennis J. Opatrny and Scott Winokur, "Police Said To Aid Spying On Political Groups," *San Francisco Examiner*, 9 March 1993.

[20] James Zogby, "Harassment and Surveillance of Arab-Americans," *San Francisco Examiner*, 4 March 1993.

[21] Opatrny and Winokur, "A New Target In S.F. Spy Probe," *San Francisco Examiner*, 1 April 1993.

[22] George Cothran and Peter Hegarty, "Spies for Zion," *SF Weekly*, 28 April 1993.

[23] Robert J. Friedman, "The Anti-Defamation League Is Spying On You," *Village Voice*, 11 May 1993.

[24] Ibid.

[25] Ken Hoover, "Anti-Defamation League Raided by S. F. Cops," *San Francisco Examiner*, 9 April 1993.

[26] Garth Wolkoff, "ADL Chief Lashes Out At Critics, Press, D.A.," *Jewish Bulletin of Northern California*, 7 May 1993.

[27] David Tuller, "Fury At Spying By Jewish Group: Anti-Defamation League Kept Data on Friends as Well as Foes," *San Francisco Chronicle*, 10 April 1993.

[28] "ADL Could Face Felony Charges," *Detroit Jewish News*, 16 April 1993.

[29] Richard C. Paddock, "Spy: 40 Years of Undercover Work For ADL," *Los Angeles Times*, 13 April 1993.

[30] Ibid.

[31] Opatrny and Winocur, "18 Litigants Draft Suite Charging ADL Spying," *San Francisco Examiner*, 14 April 1993.

[32] Opatrny and Winkour, "Judge Rules ADL Need Not Open Its Files In Civil Suit," *San Francisco Examiner*, 7 October 1993.

[33] Friedman, op. cit.

[34] Cothran and Hegarty, op. cit.

[35] "Deal Lets Anti-Defamation League Escape Trial on Spy Charges," *St. Louis Post-Dispatch*, 17 November 1993.

[36] Freedom of Information-Privacy Act request #312724, by Laird Wilcox (1988-1995).

[37] Appended to J. Edgar Hoover, letter to Dore Schary, National Chairman, Anti-Defamation League of B'nai B'rith, 4 January 1966.

[38] Dorothy Healey, *Dorothy Healey Remembers: A Life in the American Communist Party* (New York: Oxford University Press, 1990), 87.

[39] Dore Schary, testimony before the House Committee on Un-American Activities (29 October 1947).

[40] W. C. Sullivan, "Memorandum," to R. W. Smith, "Review of Pamphlet, Report on the Ku Klux Klan, by Arnold Forster and Benjamin R. Epstein," 12 August 1965.

[41] W. C. Sullivan, "Memorandum," to F. J. Baumgardner, "Investigation of Klan Organizations, Racial Matters-Klan," 22 September 1966.

[42] Ibid.

[43] "Nabbed With Weapons," *Daily News*, 8 October 1981, n.p.

[44] Lyndon LaRouche vs. National Broadcasting Company, Civil Action 84-0136-A, U. S. District Court, Eastern District of Virginia (1984).

[45] Patsey Sims, *The Klan* (New York: Stein & Day, 1978), 334.

[46] Federal Bureau of Investigation AIRTEL, "Anti-Defamation League of B'nai B'rith (ADL), Information Concerning Civil Rights Matters," 4 February 1985.

[47] Anti-Defamation League, *Hate Groups in America: A Record of Bigotry and Violence* (New York: Anti-Defamation League, 1983).

[48] Paul Alexander, Acting General Counsel, Letter to John Hope, III, Acting Staff Director, United States Commission on Civil Rights, 8 March 1982.

[49] Mary Jane MacLennan, "Fedorkiw Wins $400,000 for Slurs," *The Winnipeg Sun*, 26 November 1987, 5.

[50] David Roberts, "B'nai B'rith Guilty of Libel, Jury Finds," *Winnipeg Free Press*, 26 November 1987.

[51] Geoffrey York, "B'nai B'rith Won't Change Despite Judgment," *Globe and Mail*, 27 November 1987.

[52] Mark Mayfield, "Hate Groups Increase—As Do Their Crimes," *USA Today*, 20 February 1992.

[53] Laird Wilcox, *Guide to the American Right: Directory and Bibliography* (Olathe, KS: Editorial Research Service, 1996); *Guide to the American Left: Directory and Bibliography* (Olathe, KS: Editorial Research Service, 1996).

[54] Drew Jubera, "A Wealth of Contradictions," *Atlanta Constitution*, 26 October 1989.

[55] Ibid.

[56] Dan Morse, op. cit.

[57] Greg Jaffe and Dan Morse, "Rising Fortunes: Morris Dees and the Southern Poverty Law Center," *Montgomery Advertiser*, November 1990.

[58] Ibid.

[59] Ibid.

[60] Ibid.

[61] Dan Morse, "Marketing The Militias," *Montgomery Advertiser*, 26 June 1995.

[62] Southern Poverty Law Center, "Over 200 Militias and Support Groups Operate Nationwide," *Klanwatch Intelligence Report* (June 1995).

[63] Dick Foster, "10 Militias at Home in Colorado," *Rocky Mountain News*, 6 September 1995.

[64] Diana Baldwin, "Some Still Hunt for John Doe 2," *Sunday Oklahoman*, 13 December 1998, A-8.

[65] Ron Jenkins, "Oklahoma Bomb Jury Rules Out Conspiracy," *Associated Press*, 30 December 1998.

[66] Dan Morse, op. cit.

[67] Gary Mitchell, "Civil Rights Leader Praises Verdict Against Klan," *The Tampa Tribune*, 14 February 1987.

[68] Robin Toner, "Experts Say Verdict on Klan May Chasten Other Racists," *New York Times*, 14 February 1987.

[69] Elinor Langer, "The American Neo-Nazi Movement Today," *The Nation*, July 16/23 1990, 98.

[70] *Berhanu v. Metzger*, A 8911-07007 (Cir. Ct., Multnomah Co., Ore.).

[71] "Finding the Forum for A Victory," *The National Law Journal*, 11 February 1991.

[72] Appeal No. CA A67833, In The Court of Appeals of the State of Oregon (1992).

[73] "Everything But the Truth: Dave Mazella's Perjury Could Be Tom Metzger's Salvation," editorial, *Williamette Weekly*, 29 October 1990.

[74] John Schrag, "Supremacy Verdict Hurts Civil Liberties," *In These Times*, 31 October - 6 November 1990, 2.

[75] Ray Jenkins, "Even a Scoundrel Is Due a Fair Trial," *Los Angeles Times/Washington Post Service*, (November 1990).

[76] Bill Stanton, *Klanwatch: Bringing the Ku Klux Klan To Justice* (New York: Penguin Books, 1991), 17-18.

[77] Mark Pinsky, *Columbia Journalism Review* (March/April 1976).

[78] Terry Eastland, "The Communists And The Klan," *Commentary* (May 1980), 65-66.

[79] Ibid.

[80] Elizabeth Wheaton, *Code Name Greenkill: The 1979 Greensboro Killings* (Athens: University of Georgia Press, 1987).

[81] Wyn Craig Wade, *The Fiery Cross: The Ku Klux Klan in America* (New York: Simon & Schuster, 1987), 391.

[82] David J. Garrow, *The FBI and Martin Luther King* (New York: Murrow, 1986), 116.

[83] Mari Jo Buhle, Paul Buhle and Dan Georgakas, *Encyclopedia of the American Left* (Urbana, IL: University of Illinois Press, 1992), 105, 183.

[84] Flyer, National Alliance Against Racist and Political Repression, n.d.

[85] *Organizer* (April-June 1990); Harvey Klehr, *Far Left Of Center: The American Radical Left Today* (New Brunswick, NJ: Transaction Books, 1988), 165.

[86] Klehr, op. cit.

[87] *Newsletter of the Historians of American Communism* (September, 1992, Vol 11, No. 3), 1.

[88] Klehr, op. cit.

[89] Wheaton, op. cit., 170.

[90] Francis M. Watson, Jr., *The Alternative Media* (Rockford, IL: Rockford College Institute, 1979), 69.

[91] Lyn Wells, *The Call* (April 1973).

[92] V. I. Lenin, *The Urgent Tasks of Our Movement*, pamphlet (n.d.).

[93] Leonard Zeskind, "The Events In Afghanistan: A State-Capitalist Viewpoint," *Urgent Tasks*, No. 8, Spring 1980.

[94] Bruce Rogers, "Radical Chic, Kansas City Style," *City* (January 1981).

[95] Elizabeth Kaplan, "Keeping Tabs On Anti-Semitism a Full-Time Job," *Kansas City Jewish Chronicle*, 28 March 1986, 2A.

[96] "29 Are Chosen for the MacArthur Foundation's Fellowships," *New York Times*, 2 June 1998.

[97] *The Hammer* (February 1983).

[98] *Searchlight* (May 1988).

[99] *News Line* (10 July to 13 July 1978).

[100] *Guardian* (25 February 1980).

[101] "Magazine Accused of Race Incitement," *Birmingham Post*, 31 December 1976.

[102] *Hackney Gazette and North London Advertiser*, 8 May 1962 and 15 May 1962.

[103] "Bogus GPO Men Tried To Grab Nazi Papers," *Evening Standard*, 18 December 1963; *Focal Point*, 30 May 1981.

[104] *Jewish Chronicle*, 26 August 1966.

[105] *Focal Point*, 30 May 1981.

[106] *Daily Telegraph*, 6 August 1977.

[107] *Searchlight*, June 1987.

[108] *The Guardian*, 18 April 1979.

[109] *Focal Point*, 30 May 1981.

[110] Graeme Atkinson, interview with Jeffrey Kaplan, 27 February 1997, Helsinki, Finland.

[111] Ibid.

[112] "Rallying Point For Harmony," *Yorkshire Evening Post*, 24 April 1989.

[113] *Searchlight*, May 1989; flyer, Blair Peach 10 Anniversary Committee, nd.

[114] "Neo-Nazism On The Rise," *Jewish Chronicle*, 5 May 1989.

[115] Steve Penn, "Attacks On Minorities Climb With Communism's Collapse," *Kansas City Star*, 22 November 1990, C-16.

[116] "Killer Klan Must Be Smashed," *Workers Vanguard*, 12 November 1982, 1, 11-12.

[117] *The Monitor*, January 1986, 2.

[118] *Southern Changes*, August 1987, 7.

[119] Ibid.

[120] Rick Hellman, "Zeskind Draws Fire From Extremist Critic," *Kansas City Jewish Chronicle*, 1 December 1989.

[121] Alan Sverdlik, "Keeping An Eye On The Hate Groups," *Atlanta Journal and Constitution*, 3 November 1989, B-2.

[122] Ibid.

[123] James Ridgeway, "Klanbuster: Penetrating the Racist Underground in America's Heartland," *Details*, February 1991.

[124] Ibid.

[125] "Former Klan Spy Found Guilty of Embezzlement," *Tribune*, 9 May 1991.

[126] James Ridgeway and Leonard Zeskind, "Revolution U.S.A.," *Village Voice*, 2 May 1995.

[127] Ibid.

[128] Eric Ward, ed., *Conspiracies: Real Grievances, Paranoia, and Mass Movements* (Washington: Peanut Butter Press, 1997).

[129] Kent Chadwick, "Conspiracies of Hate," *Washington Free Press*, (1977).

[130] Michael Fumento, "Politics and Church Burnings," *Commentary*, October 1996.

[131] Fred Bayles, Associated Press article (5 July 1996).

[132] Michael Kelly, "Playing With Fire," *New Yorker*, 15 July 1996.

[133] Michael Fumento, op. cit.

[134] Ibid.

[135] Ibid.

[136] *Unmasking The Political Right: A Ten Year Report, 1981-1991* (Cambridge: Political Research Associates, 1992).

[137] Russ Bellant, *Old Nazis, The New Right and the Reagan Administration* (Cambridge: Political Research Associates, 1988).

[138] Tim Wheeler, "The Bush Campaign—Fascists On Board," *People's Daily World*, 22 September 1988.

[139] "Reviews," *Searchlight*, May 1989, 20.

[140] Political Research Associates, Biographical Information: Chip Berlet (1989).

[141] *The Public Eye*, Volume III, Issues 1 and 2 (1981).

[142] Chip Berlet, "Where the Candidates Stand on Dope Reform," *High Times* (May 1976); "Inside The DEA," *High Times* (December/January 1976); "National Anti-Drug Coalition," *High Times* (May 1981).

[143] Harvey Klehr, op. cit., 161.

[144] Gunter Lewy, *The Cause That Failed: Communism in American Political Life* (New York: Oxford University Press, 1990), 285.

[145] *Guardian*, 11 January 1984.

[146] Harvey Klehr, op. cit., 109.

[147] *Montgomery Journal*, 10 February 1983.

[148] John George and Laird Wilcox, *Nazis, Communists, Klansmen and Others on the Fringe* (Buffalo, NY: Prometheus Books, 1992), 158.

[149] "Armed Resistance Unit Bombs US Capitol," *Death To The Klan* (Winter, 1984, No. 3).

[150] May 19th Communist Organization, Press Release (2 November 1981).

[151] *Guardian*, 11 July 1984, reprinted in *Stop The Grand Jury, John Brown Anti-Klan Committee* (November 1984).

[152] *Guardian Special Report* (Fall, 1981), reprinted by *Public Eye* magazine.

[153] *The Public Eye* (Volume IV, Issues 1 & 2, 1983), 20-21.

[154] *The Public Eye*, op. cit., 23.

[155] Chicago Area Friends of Albania, form letter signed by Sally Olson (6 June 1983).

[156] Chicago Area Friends of Albania, form letter signed by Sally Olson (12 April 1985).

[157] Raymond D. Castill, *Freedom In The World: Political Rights and Civil Liberties, 1987-1988* (New York: Freedom House, 1989).

[158] Chicago Area Friends of Albania, flyer, (26 June 1987)

[159] H2JArticle 16502...in alt.conspiracy, From: NLG Civil Liberties Committee. Date: 13 Aug 93 20:29 PDT. Subject: 4mRe: Who Is Chip Berlet?.

[160] Chip Berlet and Linda Lotz, *Reading List on Intelligence Agencies and Political Repression* (New York: National Lawyers Guild Civil Liberties Committee, 1991).

[161] Berlet and Lotz, op. cit.

[162] S. Steven Powell, *Covert Cadre: Inside the Institute For Policy Studies* (Ottawa, IL: Green Hill Publishers, 1987), 72-73.

[163] "Richard S. Welch," *Washington Post*, 29 December 1975, p. A16.

[164] Ibid.

[165] "Public Eye Staff," *The Public Eye* (Vol II, Issues 1 & 2, 1979), 3.

[166] "For The Record," *Washington Post*, 27 July 1980.

[167] Peter Studer, "Philip Agee—Turncoat CIA Agent," *Tages Anzeiger* (Zurich, Switzerland), March 1975 (undated clipping).

[168] Chip Berlet, "Secret Police Political Spying Network Revealed," *Overthrow*, Vol. 9, No. 1, (Spring 1987).

[169] Flyer, United Front Against Fascism, Seattle, WA, n.d.

[170] Mari Jo Buhle, Paul Buhle and Dan Georgakas, op. cit., 785.

[171] Freedom Socialist Party—Its Program and Principles: Where We Stand, Freedom Socialist Party, n.d.

[172] Flyer, Tenth Annual Socialist Scholars Conference, April 24, 25, 26 1992, Borough of Manhattan Community College, NY, n.d.

[173] Quoted in Irving Howe and Lewis Coser, *The American Communist Party: A Critical History (1919-1957)* (New York: Praeger, 1962), 505.

[174] Mari Jo Buhle, Paul Buhle, and Dan Georgakas, op. cit., 650.

[175] Schedule of Events, January-March 1997, Brecht Forum.

[176] Bracht Forum/New York Marxist School/Institute for Popular Education, September-October 1994 Schedule.

[177] Ibid.

[178] Brecht Forum / New York Marxist School / Institute for Popular Education, May-July 1995 Schedule.

[179] John George and Laird Wilcox, op. cit.; Elizabeth Wheaton, *Code Name Greenkill: The 1979 Greensboro Killings* (Athens, GA: University of Georgia Press, 1987).

[180] Frederick M. Watkins, *The Age of Ideology—Political Thought, 1750 to the Present* (Englewood Cliffs, NJ: Prentice-Hall, 1964), 86.

[181] V. I. Lenin, "What Is To Be Done" (1901-1902), *Selected Works* (New York: International Publishers, 1937), Vol. 2, p. 150.

Index

About the Contributors

Mattias Gardell is a researcher with the Center for Migration Studies (CEIFO) at Stockholm University. He is the author of *In the Name of Elijah Muhammad: Louis Farrakhan and the Nation of Islam* (1996) and *Gods of Blood* (forthcoming).

Massimo Introvigne is Managing Director of CESNUR, the Center for Studies on New Religions, in Torino, Italy, and the author or coauthor of thirty books in Italian (some translated into French and German) on new religious and magical movements, including the monumental *Enciclopedia delle religioni in Italia* (*Encyclopedia of Religions in Italy*, 2001).

Jeffrey Kaplan is an assistant professor of Religion at the University of Wisconsin, Oshkosh and is the author of *Encyclopedia of White Power: A Sourcebook on the Radical Racist Right* (2000); *Radical Religion in America: Millenarian Movements From the Far Right to the Children of Noah* (1997) and *Beyond The Mainstream: The Emergence Of Religious Pluralism In Finland, Estonia And Russia* (2000). He is coauthor with Leonard Weinberg of *The Emergence of an Euro-American Radical Right* (1998) and coeditor with Bron Taylor of the *Encyclopedia of Religion and Nature* (forthcoming). He has published several anthologies as well as a number of articles on the far right and other millenarian movements which have appeared in such journals as *Terrorism and Political Violence*, *Christian Century* and *Nova Religio*.

László Kürti is professor of political science and social anthropology at the University of Miskolc, Hungary, and author of two books on east-central European culture, politics and nationalism: *The Remote Borderland: Transylvania in the Hungarian Imagination*, and *Beyond Borders: Remaking Cultural Identities in the New East and Central Europe* coedited with Juliet Langman. He is currently secretary of the European Association of Social Anthropologists (EASA).

Heléne Lööw has a Ph.D. in history from Gothenburg University. From 1994 to 1997 she was at CEIFO, Stockholm University, and in 1996, she was appointed to the National Council of Crime Prevention in Stockholm, Sweden. She has published two books and numerous articles about national socialism, racism, anti-Semitism, religious and political violence, and women in the radical right. She has contibuted to journals such as the *Scandinavian Journal of History*, *Terrorism and Political Violence*, and *Journal of Scandinavian Studies in Crimi-*

nology and Crime Prevention. She has also contributed to *Modern Europe after Fascism 1943-1980,* edited by Stein Uglevk Larsen, as well as *Nation and Race. The developing Euro-American Racist Subculture* edited by Jeffrey Kaplan and Tore Björgo.

J. Gordon Melton is the director of the Institute for the Study of American Religion in Santa Barbara, California and a research specialist with the Department of Religious Studies at the University of California, Santa Barbara. He is the author more than twenty-five books, including the *Encyclopedia of American Religions* (sixth edition, 1999) and he is coeditor of the *Religions of the World: A Comprehensive Encyclopedia of Beliefs and Practices* (2002).

Timothy Miller is a professor of Religious Studies at the University of Kansas. His academic research has focused on alternative religions and communal movements. He has written, coauthored, or edited eight books, including *When Prophets Die: The Postcharismatic Fate of New Religious Movements, America's Alternative Religions, The Hippies and American Values, The Quest for Utopia in Twentieth-Century America,* and *The 60s Communes.*

Frederick J. Simonelli received his Ph.D. in history from the University of Nevada, Reno. He is currently associate professor of History and chair of the Department of History And Political Science at Mount St. Mary's College in Los Angeles. He is the author of *American Fuehrer: George Lincoln Rockwell and the American Nazi Party.*

Bron Taylor is Oshkosh Foundation Professor of Religion, and director of environmental studies at the University of Wisconsin, Oshkosh. He is the author of *Affirmative Action at Work: Law, Politics, and Ethics,* and editor of *Ecological Resistance Movements: The Global Emergence of Radical and Popular Environmentalism.* He is coediting the forthcoming *Encyclopedia of Religion and Nature* with Jeffrey Kaplan.

Laird Wilcox is coauthor with John George of *Nazis, Communists, Klansmen And Others on the Fringe,* an award-winning account of American extremist groups. He is also founder of the Wilcox Collection on Contemporary Political Movements in Spencer Research Library at the University of Kansas. The Wilcox Collection, founded in 1965, is one of the largest collections of its kind and is regularly used by researchers and scholars. Mr. Wilcox also publishes two annual guides: *The Guide To The American Right: Directory and Bibliography,* and *The Guide To The American Left: Directory and Bibliography.*